ANNUAL EDITIONS

Comparative Politics 12/13
Thirtieth Edition

T5-ANR-424

EDITOR

O. Fiona Yap
University of Kansas

O. Fiona Yap is an Associate Professor of Political Science and the Director of Undergraduate Studies at the University of Kansas. Her research work is available through journals such as the *British Journal of Political Science, Social Science Quarterly, Journal of East Asian Studies, Japanese Journal of Political Science, Korea Observer, Journal of Theoretical Politics,* and *Comparative Political Studies* as well as chapter contributions in edited volumes. Prior to assuming the editorship, she served as an Academic Advisory Board member for *Annual Editions: Comparative Politics.* She is also a reviewer for numerous journals, including *American Journal of Political Science, Journal of Politics, British Journal of Political Science, Comparative Politics, International Studies Quarterly, International Studies Perspective, Social Science Quarterly, Governance, Asian Survey, Political Research Quarterly,* and *Journal of East Asian Studies.*

ANNUAL EDITIONS: COMPARATIVE POLITICS, THIRTIETH EDITION

Annual Editions is published by the **Contemporary Learning Series** group within the McGraw-Hill Higher Education division.

1 2 3 4 5 6 7 8 9 0 QDB/QDB 1 0 9 8 7 6 5 4 3 2

ISBN 978-0-07-805116-6
MHID 0-07-805116-9
ISSN 0741-7233
ISSN 2158-3250

Managing Editor: *Larry Loeppke*
Developmental Editor II: *Jill Meloy*
Permissions Supervisor: *DeAnna Dausener*
Senior Marketing Communications Specialist: *Mary Klein*
Senior Project Manager: *Joyce Watters*
Design Coordinator: *Margarite Reynolds*
Cover Graphics: *Studio Montage, St. Louis, Missouri*
Buyer: *Susan K. Culbertson*
Media Project Manager: *Sridevi Palani*

Compositor: Laserwords Private Limited
Cover Image Credits: Ingram Publishing (inset); © Veer Incorporated (background)

Editors/Academic Advisory Board

Members of the Academic Advisory Board are instrumental in the final selection of articles for each edition of ANNUAL EDITIONS. Their review of articles for content, level, and appropriateness provides critical direction to the editors and staff. We think that you will find their careful consideration well reflected in this volume.

ANNUAL EDITIONS: Comparative Politics 12/13
30th Edition

EDITOR

O. Fiona Yap
University of Kansas

ACADEMIC ADVISORY BOARD MEMBERS

Preface

Comparative politics focuses on the empirical study of political behaviors, institutions, and rules to facilitate explanations, predictions, and theory-building. This book sets as its task the presentation of information based on systematic study of such behaviors, institutions, and rules.

To complete this task, the volume is organized to emphasize political behaviors, institutions, and rules from a comparative perspective. Current comparative politics texts make similar arguments regarding the need for such a focus and probably support it. However, few are able to depart from a presentation that is country specific.

This book makes that departure. Instead of providing information on a country basis, each unit presents information about how people and governments behave and interact politically, given the rules and institutions that are in place, across a range of countries and political systems. The point I emphasize is this: Systematic generalizations that address the questions of "why, what, and how" regarding political behaviors and institutions apply across countries and political systems. I do not dispute that country-relevant information contextualizes behavior and interactions. Rather, I consider it necessary to clarify the generalizations that provide baseline knowledge regarding "why, what, and how" of political behaviors and institutions. With this baseline in place, particularities that are observed become even more interesting or unusual.

Each unit begins with an overview that introduces students to the systematic questions of "why, what, and how" regarding political behaviors and institutions. Often, the first readings in the units introduce students to debates and discussions regarding these systematic questions in the discipline. Subsequent readings provide the empirical "flesh," drawn from the news, public press, or academic studies. They also show that the answers to the systematic questions apply across different countries. This structure—the questions in the discipline and the answers from "real world" studies—ensures that students see how the discipline connects with the real world.

This is articulated in all the units, beginning with Unit 1. For those new to comparative politics, it is probably important to consider why we are interested in comparative politics. The issues raised in this section—from the instability of transitioning societies such as Afghanistan, to the social unrest in industrialized democracies such as Great Britain and Norway, to the difficulty of combating drug wars in the contemporary world—underscores that

our interest in foreign governments and societies may no be longer as an interested spectator. Rather, in the global society or economy, poor or weak governments or institutions have direct consequences on our lives.

Unit 2 introduces comparative politics as a vigorous and important subfield in political science, and compares how other disciplines study governments and politics to showcase the significance of the comparative political science approach. To all those who see that the comparison highlights how comparative political science compares—focusing on why, how, and what—I say "Bravo!" For those who may need "meat" to chew on, Unit 2 showcases articles on the study of democratic theory to emphasize that comparative politics is more than just a survey of countries. It is a theoretically driven enterprise, with its requisite debates, tests, and counter-arguments raised and evaluated over time.

Unit 3 builds upon the discussion of democratic theory to highlight the relevance of citizen participation and address systematically why and how citizen participation is organized, and in what forms. The emphasis in Unit 3 is on the relevance of interest groups and political parties as outlets of political behavior that, if repressed or ignored, may lead people to find "less democratic ways" to participate.

Units 4 through 6 consider the institutions of government to address questions regarding the roles they play in the political process, how they affect political behaviors, and, perhaps most importantly, how their successes or failures are evaluated. Unit 4 looks at the executive, noting that accountability and responsiveness to the public is the performance bar for the position. Unit 5 looks at legislative representation and accountability and show how representation in legislatures increases citizens' satisfaction with democracy. Given the importance of representation, the subsequent articles ask how to improve participation of minorities, including women, and how electoral systems may hinder or improve that representation. Unit 6 examines the unelected policymakers—the judiciary, military, and intelligence agencies—to consider the bases of popular resentment against these unelected officials.

Unit 7 completes the volume by considering how institutional changes occur. The relationship between institutions and political behaviors is clearly reciprocal, so the question of how institutional changes occur is timely and important. The transitions in the Middle East certainly reveal that our thinking about how transitions occur need to be revisited, and the first two articles in this unit point out how we may have been misguided in our interpretations. Domestic demand and new pressures are essential for initiating institutional changes; however, it is not culture but, rather, tolerance and equality that fuel the strengthening of democracy. Equally important, the readings also note that there are ways that authoritarian governments circumvent this push for democratic accountability and responsiveness. Aspiring comparativists may take heart in that knowledge that even as these autocrats drag their feet in the process, there are no "cultures" that are beyond accountability, responsiveness, representation, and civic participation and the changes implemented inevitably opens up political and social space.

The final article brings us full circle to the first article in Unit 1: If the UN is so weak, would it not be easy to strengthen it by adding more members to the UN that represent the diversity of nations, including the emerging BRIC players? As Article 40 points out, that solution assumes that these BRICs will step up and demand for humanitarian and social solutions that are in line with the industrialized democracies. Yet, the domestic political realities in these BRICs suggest that they may be more inclined to temper demands rather than step up on institution-building. This reminds us, once more, how important it is to understand foreign political institutions and policy-processes.

There are several individuals to thank for this current volume. Thanks go to the editorial staff at McGraw-Hill, particularly Jill Meloy, Senior Developmental Editor, for her immense patience and insightful advice. I am also grateful to Larry Loeppke, Managing Editor for the *McGraw-Hill Contemporary Learning Series,* for his support. My colleagues at the University of Kansas—particularly Gary Reich, Hannah Britton, Donald Haider-Markel, and Dorothy Daley—must be acknowledged for their support, advice, and critiques that helped with the construction and completion of this volume. The responses of the advisory board members in critiquing and suggesting selections in this edition are instrumental; I am indebted to their painstaking efforts and commitment to see an improved, accessible, and academically rigorous edition. Finally, thanks to the readers, whose comments helped with the selection of readings. I hope that you will continue to help improve future editions by keeping me informed of your reactions and suggestions for change.

O. Fiona Yap
Editor

The Annual Editions Series

VOLUMES AVAILABLE

Adolescent Psychology

Aging

American Foreign Policy

American Government

Anthropology

Archaeology

Assessment and Evaluation

Business Ethics

Child Growth and Development

Comparative Politics

Criminal Justice

Developing World

Drugs, Society, and Behavior

Dying, Death, and Bereavement

Early Childhood Education

Economics

Educating Children with Exceptionalities

Education

Educational Psychology

Entrepreneurship

Environment

The Family

Gender

Geography

Global Issues

Health

Homeland Security

Human Development

Human Resources

Human Sexualities

International Business

Management

Marketing

Mass Media

Microbiology

Multicultural Education

Nursing

Nutrition

Physical Anthropology

Psychology

Race and Ethnic Relations

Social Problems

Sociology

State and Local Government

Sustainability

Technologies, Social Media, and Society

United States History, Volume 1

United States History, Volume 2

Urban Society

Violence and Terrorism

Western Civilization, Volume 1

World History, Volume 1

World History, Volume 2

World Politics

Contents

UNIT 1
Why Comparative Politics?

1. **Intensive Care for the United Nations,** Thomas G. Weiss, *Current History,* November 2010

   Sometimes, the relevance of studying the **political institutions and policies of foreign countries** is **underplayed** because there are regional and international agencies, such as the Organization of American States and the **United Nations,** that focus on such specifics. This article clarifies why this justification is dangerous: First, institutions with large memberships such as the UN are far from functional. Second, **sovereign** countries are generally reluctant to accept an **over-arching authority.** The author points out four significant problems with the UN that may require "radical" changes to achieve functionality. Notably, the solutions involve: (1) recognizing that no country is an island onto itself, i.e., **state** policies **reverberate** onto the **international** arena and vice versa; (2) **creative partnerships** that include rich and poor nations. Clearly, inattention to the politics and policies of foreign countries—even small ones—comes at a peril.   4

2. **Seeing "Islamic Terror" in Norway,** Fairness and Accuracy in Reporting (FAIR), *Global Research,* July 25, 2011

   The article complements Article 1 to point out how overlooking politics and policies leads to erroneous conclusions. It also underscores the differences between political **punditry** versus **systematic** political **study.** This will be especially apparent when comparing the pieces cited here against Article 17 of Unit 3. Perhaps what is most alarming is this: The pieces cited in this report seem to be making a trade-off between paying attention to global trends versus those in the country. Yet, is Jennifer Rubin, political blogger of the *Washington Post,* right that "there are many more jihadists than blond Norwegians out to kill Americans, and we should keep our eye on the . . . far more potent threats . . ."?   9

3. **Britain's Riots: A Society in Denial of the Burning Issues,** Finian Cunningham, *Global Research,* August 9, 2011

   If one thinks that the attack in Norway is an isolated incident unlikely to occur in other western industrialized democracies, Britain's five-day riot and looting quickly dispels that thought. The author points out that explaining the incident as one of "law and order" overlooks its causes, which lie in the **institutional failure** to address poverty, high unemployment, and huge disparities in wealth, against a background of increasing erosion of **social welfarism.** Are there discernible similarities between the Norwegian incident and that in Great Britain?   11

4. **Flawed Miracle: India's Boom Bypasses Rural Poor,** Tom Wright and Harsh Gupta, *Wall Street Journal,* April 30, 2011

   This article brings in one of the hot emerging economies, India, to compare against the older western industrialized democracies. As one of the economic powerhouses of the BRIC group, will India be able to "grow" its way out of the social and political issues that weigh on the other less successful economies? Does economic growth offer the panacea to these problems? The answer: No. Indeed, the author traces much of the deep political and social discontent to the **failure of political institutions** to treat the root causes of underdevelopment. Instead of correcting the problems, the solutions adopted have fueled other problems like **corruption.** This has deepened political and **social discontent,** which may threaten the country's continued economic and political development.   13

The concepts in bold italics are developed in the article. For further expansion, please refer to the Topic Guide.

UNIT 2
Studying Comparative Politics: Developing Theories, Culling Evidence, and Interpretation over Time

The concepts in bold italics are developed in the article. For further expansion, please refer to the Topic Guide.

UNIT 3
Political Participation: From Preferences to Policies

The concepts in bold italics are developed in the article. For further expansion, please refer to the Topic Guide.

UNIT 4
The Executive: Instituting Accountability and Responsiveness

The concepts in bold italics are developed in the article. For further expansion, please refer to the Topic Guide.

UNIT 5
The Legislature: Representation and the Effects of Electoral Systems

The concepts in bold italics are developed in the article. For further expansion, please refer to the Topic Guide.

UNIT 6
Unelected Thugs or Expert Protectors? The Judiciary, Intelligence Agencies, and the Military

The concepts in bold italics are developed in the article. For further expansion, please refer to the Topic Guide.

UNIT 7
Trends and Challenges: Institutional Change through Capitalism, Globalization, or Supra-National Government?

The concepts in bold italics are developed in the article. For further expansion, please refer to the Topic Guide.

Topic Guide

This topic guide suggests how the selections in this book relate to the subjects covered in your course. You may want to use the topics listed on these pages to search the Web more easily.

On the following pages a number of websites have been gathered specifically for this book. They are arranged to reflect the units of this Annual Editions reader. You can link to these sites by going to www.mhhe.com/cls

All the articles that relate to each topic are listed below the bold-faced term.

Citizen Participation and Mobilization

3. Britain's Riots: A Society in Denial of the Burning Issues
6. It Takes the Villages
8. What Democracy Is . . . and Is Not
9. Twenty-Five Years, Fifteen Findings
10. Why Middle East Studies Missed the Arab Spring: The Myth of Authoritarian Stability
11. Transitional Failure in Egypt and Tunisia
12. Advanced Democracies and the New Politics
15. Civil Society, Youth and Societal Mobilization in Democratic Revolutions
16. Online Activism
18. China's Cyberposse
26. When Politics is Not Just a Man's Game: Women's Representation and Political Engagement
28. Social Pressure, Surveillance, and Community Size: Evidence from Field Experiments on Voter Turnout
38. Why Democracy Needs a Level Playing Field
39. Democracy in Cyberspace: What information Technology Can and Cannot Do

Elections and Regime Types

8. What Democracy Is . . . and Is Not
9. Twenty-five Years, Fifteen Findings
10. Why Middle East Studies Missed the Arab Spring: The Myth of Authoritarian Stability
11. Transitional Failure in Egypt and Tunisia
14. What Political Institutions Does Large-Scale Democracy Require?
15. Civil Society, Youth and Societal Mobilization in Democratic Revolutions
17. Smart Dictators Don't Quash the Internet
19. In Belated Inauguration, Ivory Coast's President Urges Unity
20. Tangled Webs: Institutions
21. The General Election in Costa Rica
22. The Legislative and Presidential Elections in Indonesia
23. The Resilient Authoritarians
24. Satisfaction with Democracy: Do Institutions Matter?
26. When Politics Is Not just a Man's Game: Women's Representation and Political Engagement
27. The Impact of Electoral Reform on Women's Representation
28. Social Pressure, Surveillance, and Community Size: Evidence from Field Experiments on Voter Turnout
29. The Case for a Multi-Party U.S. Parliament?
31. Rule of Law, Russian-Style
32. Getting the military out of Pakistani politics: How Aiding the Army Undermines Democracy
33. Thailand: From violence to Reconciliation?
36. The weekend interview with Bernard Lewis
38. Why democracy needs a level playing field

The Executive or Legislature in Less-Democratic Systems

10. Why Middle East Studies Missed The Arab Spring: The Myth of Authoritarian Stability
11. Transitional Failure in Egypt and Tunisia
13. Capitalism and Democracy
15. Civil Society, Youth and Societal Mobilization in Democratic Revolutions
16. Online Activism
17. Smart Dictators Don't Quash the Internet
19. In Belated Inauguration, Ivory Coast's President Urges Unity
23. The Resilient Authoritarians
31. Rule of Law, Russian-style
32. Getting the Military Out of Pakistani Politics: How Aiding the Army Undermines Democracy
33. Thailand: From Violence to Reconciliation?
36. The Weekend Interview with Bernard Lewis
38. Why Democracy Needs a Level Playing Field
40. Not Ready for Prime Time

The Executive or Legislature in Parliamentary Systems

2. Seeing "Islamic Terror" In Norway
3. Britain's Riots: A Society in Denial of Burning Issues
4. Flawed Miracle: India's Boom Bypasses Rural Poor
14. What Political Institutions Does Large-Scale Democracy Require?
20. Tangled Webs; Institutions
24. Satisfaction With Democracy: Do Institutions Matter?
25. The Famous Dutch (In)Tolerance
27. The Impact of Electoral Reform on Women's Representation
29. The Case for A Multi-Party U.S. Parliament?
33. Thailand: From Violence to Reconciliation?
34. In Britain, Phone Hacking Sullies Famed Scotland Yard
38. Why Democracy Needs a Level Playing Field

The Executive or Legislature in Presidential Systems

6. It Takes the Villages
7. The New Cocaine Cowboys
14. What Political Institutions Does Large-Scale Democracy Require?
21. The General Election in Costa Rica, February 2010
22. The Legislative and Presidential Elections in Indonesia In 2009
23. The Resilient Authoritarians
28. Social Pressure, Surveillance, And Community Size: Evidence from Field Experiments on Voter Turnout
33. Thailand: From Violence To Reconciliation?

xv

Social Change

The Economy and Economics

Internet References

The following Internet sites have been selected to support the articles found in this reader. These sites were available at the time of publication. However, because websites often change their structure and content, the information listed may no longer be available. We invite you to visit www.mhhe.com/cls for easy access to these sites.

Annual Editions: Comparative Politics 12/13

General Sources

Central Intelligence Agency
www.cia.gov/library/publications/the-world-factbook/index.html

Use this official home page to get connections to The CIA Factbook, which provides extensive statistical and political information about every country in the world.

Human Rights Watch
www.hrw.org

The official website of Human Rights Watch describes its beginnings in 1978 as Helsinki Watch. The website tracks the extent and evolution of political and civil rights across all regions. There are detailed and extensive discussions for countries under watch regarding the level of civil and political liberties and their effects on those fighting for enfranchisement, particularly the poor, women, and children.

Research and Reference (Library of Congress)
www.loc.gov/rr

This massive research and reference site of the Library of Congress will lead you to invaluable area studies information on politics and changes across the globe. It also provides links to bibliographies for those interested in delving more deeply into a topic.

The United Nations
www.un.org/en/members/index.shtml

This United Nations webpage provides brief profiles of member countries and links to the individual countries. The country links include websites to news agencies and sources.

U.S. Department of State
www.state.gov

This site provides definitions, documents, and discussion on topics of global relevance, such as terrorism, diplomatic relations, democracy, and aid. Extensive discussion and follow-up.

U.S. Embassies, Consulates, and Diplomatic Missions
www.usembassy.gov

This website provides links to U.S. embassies and missions around the globe. Each country link, in turn, provides up-to-date information regarding issues and concerns of the country as well as U.S. efforts and presence to address them.

UNIT 1: Why Comparative Politics?

Africa News Online
http://allafrica.com

Open this site for extensive, up-to-date information on all of Africa, with reports from Africa's leading newspapers, magazines, and news agencies. Coverage is country-by-country and regional. Background documents and Internet links are among the resource pages.

BBC World News
http://news.bbc.co.uk/2/hi/africa/default.stm

This page of the British Broadcasting Corporation provides an up-to-date online resource for Africa and contains links to the news in the Middle East and other regions.

The Carnegie Endowment for International Peace
http://carnegieendowment.org

NAMI, a tri-national public-affairs organization concerned with the emerging "regional space" of Canada, the United States, and Mexico, provides links for study of trade, the environment, and institutional developments.

The Human Rights Watch
www.hrw.org/americas

The site provides one of the most extensive discussions of political and civil developments in Latin America in general, and Mexico in particular. The website also has an evolving features page, which provides indepth studies of the security and justice system to contextualize human rights conditions in the countries.

Inter-American Dialogue (IAD)
www.thedialogue.org

This is the website for IAD, a premier U.S. center for policy analysis, communication, and exchange in Western Hemisphere affairs. The 100-member organization has helped to shape the agenda of issues and choices in hemispheric relations.

UNIT 2: Studying Comparative Politics: Developing Theories, Culling Evidence, and Interpretation Over Time

Political Science blog of Professors Henry Farrell, Andrew Gelman, John Sides, Joshua Tucker, and Erik Voeten
http://themonkeycage.org/blog/category/comparative-politics

The website of these leading political scientists and scholars provides running commentaries on events around the world and the usefulness of systematic comparative politics in understanding these events.

Professor Mathew Shugart's political blog
http://fruitsandvotes.com

A leading political scientist and scholar, Professor Shugart's blog comprises the whimsical and the serious on elections, electoral systems and reforms comparatively and in domestic America. The website also contains a number of links to other sources of political science and politics.

Professor Robert Elgie's political blog
http://web.mac.com/relgie/The_Semi-presidential_One/Blog/Blog.html

A leading political scientist and scholar, Professor Elgie's blog of politics around the world adds an important theoretical perspective to ongoing political events and conditions.

Internet References

Unit 3. Political Participation: From Preferences to Policies

Freedom House
http://freedomhouse.org/template.cfm?page=1

The organization, founded in 1941, monitors political participation and civic associations across regions to champion open polities and societies. The website provides news as well as publications related to democratic opening.

The Human Rights Watch—Americas
www.hrw.org/americas

The site provides one of the most extensive discussions of political and civil developments in Latin America. The website also has an evolving features page, which provides indepth studies of the security and justice system to contextualize human rights conditions in the countries.

The Human Rights Watch–Middle East and North Africa
www.hrw.org/middle-east/n-africa

The site provides exhaustive information on developments in the countries of the Middle East and North Africa. The website also has an evolving features page, which provides indepth studies of the security and justice system to contextualize human rights conditions in the countries.

National Geographic Society
www.nationalgeographic.com

This site provides links to National Geographic's archive of maps, articles, and documents. There is a great deal of material related to political cultures around the world.

Research and Reference (Library of Congress)
www.loc.gov/rr

This massive research and reference site of the Library of Congress will lead you to invaluable area studies information on politics and changes across the globe. It also provides links to bibliographies for those interested in delving more deeply into a topic.

UNIT 4: The Executive: Instituting Accountability and Responsiveness

Asian Development Bank
www.adb.org/Countries

The website provides up-to-date information on 44 developing member countries in Asia regarding political, social, and economic policies to reduce poverty and improve the quality of life of the people.

BBC World News
www.bbc.co.uk/news/world/europe

This page of the British Broadcasting Corporation provides an up-to-date online resource for Europe and also contains links to news on the continent.

Europa: European Union
http://europa.eu/index_en.htm

This server site of the European Union will lead you to the history of the EU; descriptions of EU policies, institutions, and goals; discussion of the monetary union; and documentation of the treaties and other materials.

Inter-American Dialogue (IAD)
www.thedialogue.org

This is the website for IAD, a premier U.S. center for policy analysis, communication, and exchange in Western Hemisphere affairs. The 100-member organization has helped to shape the agenda of issues and choices in hemispheric relations.

Latin American Network Information Center, University of Texas at Austin
http://lanic.utexas.edu/la/region/government

The Latin American Network Information Center (LANIC) provides Internet-based information on Latin America and includes source-links to other websites that provide information on Latin American countries.

Russian and East European Network Information Center, University of Texas at Austin
http://reenic.utexas.edu

This is the website for information on Russia and the former Soviet Union. The site also contains links to research a topic in greater depth.

UNIT 5: The Legislature: Representation and the Effects of Electoral Systems

Asian Development Bank
www.adb.org/Countries

The website provides up-to-date information on 44 developing member countries in Asia regarding political, social, and economic policies to reduce poverty and improve the quality of life of the people.

Election Resources on the Internet
http://electionresources.org

The website provides updated electoral information on elections as they occur around the world, with brief discussions of the political systems to contextualize the information.

Inter-Parliamentary Union
www.ipu.org/wmn-e/world.htm

This website of the IPU comprises data for women representatives in national parliaments and some regional assemblies. The IPU is the international organization of Parliaments of sovereign States (Article 1 of the Statutes of the Inter-Parliamentary Union), established in 1889.

Latin American Network Information Center, University of Texas at Austin
http://lanic.utexas.edu/la/region/government

The Latin American Network Information Center (LANIC) provides Internet-based information on Latin America and includes source-links to other websites that provide information on Latin American countries.

World Bank
www.worldbank.org

News (press releases, summaries of new projects, speeches) and coverage of numerous topics regarding development, countries, and regions are provided at this site.

Internet References

UNIT 6: Unelected Thugs or Expert Protectors? The Judiciary, Intelligence Agencies, and the Military

Carnegie Endowment for International Peace
http://carnegieendowment.org

This organization's goal is to stimulate discussion and learning among both experts and the public at large on a wide range of international issues. The site provides links to the journal *Foreign Policy*, to the Moscow Center, to descriptions of various programs, and much more.

Central Intelligence Agency
www.cia.gov

Use this official home page to get to The CIA Factbook, which provides extensive statistical and political information about every country in the world.

Research and Reference (Library of Congress)
www.loc.gov/rr

This massive research and reference site of the Library of Congress will lead you to invaluable area studies information on politics and changes across the globe. It also provides links to bibliographies for those interested in delving more deeply into a topic.

Russian and East European Network Information Center, University of Texas at Austin
http://reenic.utexas.edu

This is the website for information on Russia and the former Soviet Union. The site also contains links to research a topic in greater depth.

World Wide Web Virtual Library: International Affairs Resources
www.etown.edu/vl

Surf this site and its extensive links to learn about specific countries and regions, to research international organizations, and to study such vital topics as international law, development, the international economy, and human rights.

UNIT 7: Trends and Challenges: Institutional Change through Capitalism, Globalization, or Supra-National Government?

Carnegie Endowment for International Peace
http://carnegieendowment.org

This organization's goal is to stimulate discussion and learning among both experts and the public at large on a wide range of international issues. The site provides links to the journal *Foreign Policy*, to the Moscow Center, to descriptions of various programs, and much more.

Freedom House
http://freedomhouse.org/template.cfm?page=1

The organization documents and provides access to annual reports tracking democratic and political developments in about 180 countries.

Europa: European Union
http://europa.eu/index_en.htm

This server site of the European Union will lead you to the history of the EU; descriptions of EU policies, institutions, and goals; discussion of monetary union; and documentation of treaties and other materials.

ISN International Relations and Security Network
www.isn.ethz.ch

This site, maintained by the Center for Security Studies and Conflict Research, is a clearinghouse for extensive information on international relations and security policy. Topics are listed by category (Traditional Dimensions of Security, New Dimensions of Security) and by major world regions.

NATO Integrated Data Service (NIDS)
www.nato.int/structur/nids/nids.htm

NIDS was created to bring information on security-related matters to the widest possible audience. Check out this website to review North Atlantic Treaty Organization documentation of all kinds, to read NATO Review, and to explore key issues in the field of European security.

UNIT 1
Why Comparative Politics?

Unit Selections

1. **Intensive Care for the United Nations,** Thomas G. Weiss
2. **Seeing "Islamic Terror" in Norway,** Fairness and Accuracy in Reporting (FAIR)
3. **Britain's Riots: A Society in Denial of the Burning Issues,** Finian Cunningham
4. **Flawed Miracle: India's Boom Bypasses Rural Poor,** Tom Wright and Harsh Gupta
5. **More Aid Is Not the Answer,** Jonathan Glennie
6. **It Takes the Villages,** Seth G. Jones
7. **The New Cocaine Cowboys,** Robert C. Bonner

Learning Outcomes

After reading this Unit, you will be able to:

- Distinguish between comparative politics and international politics.

- Explain why the United Nations is considered ineffective as an institution.

- Explain what it means that countries view sovereignty as "sacrosanct."

- Describe the problems identified in the countries in this unit.

- Explain if the problems described are unique to the countries. If not, what does it mean?

- Explain how the problems affect other countries.

- Explain how the United Nations or foreign aid has posed problems.

- Explain how political institutions or institutional development address or fail to address the problems.

Student Website
www.mhhe.com/cls

Internet References

Africa News Online
http://allafrica.com
BBC World News
http://news.bbc.co.uk/2/hi/africa/default.stm
The Carnegie Endowment for International Peace
http://carnegieendowment.org
The Human Rights Watch
www.hrw.org/americas
Inter-American Dialogue (IAD)
www.thedialogue.org

Why do we study foreign government institutions or the policies they make? Clearly, part of the answer is "interest." That is, we study foreign government institutions, their policymaking processes or the resultant policies because of an innate curiosity with learning what is similar or different from us. This unit points out that there is now an imperative to studying foreign governments: security, well-being, economics, and humanitarian considerations emphasize the need to gain knowledge and insights into foreign government institutions, their policymaking processes, and their policies.

Why? Globalization has brought with it many advantages from economic, social, and cultural exchange. However, it has also left us more exposed to the frailties of foreign governments and policy failures. We are no longer insulated from the ramifications of recalcitrant governments or citizens in foreign countries. Instead, issues ranging from regime stability in Afghanistan, drugwars in Mexico, and the debt crises in Greece are directly affecting our lives or livelihoods. These reverberations stress that whereas geography may previously pose a viable line of defense against weak or erratic governments, the increasing interconnectedness of countries through trade, migration, and the Internet—a process termed globalization—has rendered physical boundaries almost meaningless.

The need to understand institutions and policy-processes is all the more relevant given that we do not have successful regional or international institutions for mediating conflicts or addressing the humanitarian, welfare, or social problems that arise. The piece by Professor Weiss on the United Nations is a stark reminder that many such regional or international agencies are far from functional. Further, with information disseminated at lightning speed, we are prone to inaccurate interpretations and incorrect conclusions without a basic political and social knowledge of any country. This is clearly illustrated in the piece on the Norway, which shows how quickly political pundits jumped to the conclusion that the attack was instigated by Islamic extremists.

Why is knowing what happens and why they happen in other countries important? Consider, for instance, that the long history of aid-extension to Africa has brought few successes, in part because the aid was fueled by the clamor to "do something." And, the poor success has spurred an "anti-aid" position that almost seems ideological. What does this tell us? More so than before, there is a need to for us to be equipped to participate as a global citizen: to gain knowledge and understanding of political institutions, processes, and systems in order to contribute meaningfully and empathetically. Also, the porous financial and geographical borders of globalization mean that we come face to face with the fallout of political and social instability more often and sooner than previous eras. And, these occur across industrialized democracies such as Norway and Britain, as well as less-industrialized countries of India, Afghanistan, and in the African continent. If we think we are insulated from the problems of failed political institutions and corruption, take a look at the reports of the felony and criminal charges that the U.S. Securities and Exchange Commission has filed, and think again. Or, should we consider—in light of the economic doldrums in the United States—that the experience in Britain may be more

© Comstock/PunchStock

relevant to us than we would like to admit?

Clearly, there are humanitarian, economic, and social imperatives of learning about foreign government institutions and policy processes. And, this is not relevant only from the perspective of an aid-giver. It is also important to consider given that the porous borders of globalization may lead us to face the same political, social, or economic circumstances.

Now comes the challenge: How do we learn about foreign governments and policies? And what do we need to take away from that learning? This is no small task: The UN recognizes 192 countries; that does not include several that are not UN members.[1] The U.S. government recognizes 195 autonomous countries in the world.[2] The list easily expands beyond 250 if we include nations that are self-governing as well as those that are not. A nation is defined as "a group of people whose members share a common identity on the basis of distinguishing characteristics and claim to a territorial homeland."[3] Each of these nations or countries has long histories that may bear on the government's behaviors or the responses of their people and also influence what institutions and rules are considered and adopted. Clearly, learning about the particularities of even one country requires considerable time and effort, let alone the more than 100 formally recognized ones.

How do we accomplish this in a manner that is rewarding without that singular task dominating our lives? From the political science perspective, it means we start with some fundamentals, such as: What is comparative politics? What do we compare? How do we compare? Why do we compare?

What is comparative politics? *Comparative Politics* refers to the study of governments. That seems clear. Yet, popular dictionaries such as the Merriam-Webster's and Oxford Dictionary contain no less than five and as many as ten different ways of conceiving the word "government." They include[4]:

1. The exercise of authority over a state, district, or territory.
2. A system of ruling, controlling, or administering.
3. The executive branch of a government.
4. All the people and institutions that exercise control over the affairs of a nation or state.
5. The study of such systems, people, and institutions.

These definitions emphasize several concepts integral to comparative politics: authority, system, people and institutions, and state, district, or territory.

What do we compare? In the broadest sense, comparative politics involves the systematic comparison of authority, systems, people, and institutions across states, districts, or other territories. Its focus is on what Joseph La Palombara once called *Politics Within Nations.*[5] In other words, comparative politics focuses on the patterns of politics within a domestic territory, where political parties, interest groups, civil servants, the public, and the press interact under specified laws to influence who gets what, when, how, and why.

How do we compare? Comparative politics emphasizes careful empirical study as the way to gain knowledge about how people and governments behave and interact politically, given rules and institutions that are in place. It is important to note that other disciplines also study how people and governments behave; however, their goals or ends for such study are different. Figure 1 lists six disciplines that study governments and describes what they are, the focus, method, strengths, appeal, and weaknesses of each of these disciplines.

Figure 1: Disciplinary differences in the study of governments

Discipline	History	Sociology	Area Studies	Political Science	Economics	Journalism
What it is	Describe, interpret, or explain individual events or time-related series of events	Understand what connects the person (personal) to the group (social)	Provide country or region-specific information, particularly on language, customs, religion, or culture	Identify systematic patterns over time	Deductive reasoning from mathematical models	"Spot" analysis/description of individual events or policy
Focus	Past events	Groups, relations	City, region, country, area	Institutions, behaviors	Mathematical models	Current events, policies
Method	Akin to fitting a jigsaw—are all the pieces there? The end picture is available	Solving mystery—what group identities lead people to behave the way they do?	Akin to fitting a jigsaw—are all the pieces there? The end picture is sometimes available	Solving mystery—what do people do in order to keep/protect what they have?	Solving mystery—how do different incentives lead people to behave differently? (behaviors are known)	Uncovering information—through investigation, expert testimony, debate, inference
Strengths	Uncovers situation, information, motivations, personalities about the past	Clarify racial, ethnic, area, and women's studies (probabilistic predictions)	Rich, detailed knowledge of predispositions	Prediction, generalization (probabilistic predictions)	Prediction, generalization (probabilistic predictions)	Details (information, motivations) from spot analysis of situation, event
Appeal	Intelligence and information to enhance interpretation and accuracy	Provide connections between student and larger society	Intelligence & information to enhance interpretation and accuracy. Story-telling and puzzle-solving approach allows students to improve insights and affirm expectations.	Explains why and how institutions/processes are developed, evolved, changed	Mathematical modeling allows for study and theorizing of human behaviors	Storytelling, expose, investigation, debate spot analysis
Weaknesses	Focus on interpretation and insights, not predictions. Therefore, theories not always generalizable.	Individual motivations entirely developed from the group.	Focus on interpretation and insights, not predictions. Therefore, theories not always generalizable.	Individual events are low on totem pole of study.	Empiricism not always important.	Not theoretically driven—therefore, cannot explain change or predict (conjecture).

Why do we compare? Two reasons are particularly note-worthy: First, it provides a way to systematically consider how people and institutions across different countries, districts, or systems balance the competing goals of stability, change, security, freedom, growth, accountability, and responsiveness.[6] Thus, for the political practitioner, analyst, or scholar, comparative politics is applied to describe, clarify, and, subsequently, understand change or stability. Second, as depicted in Figure 1, we compare in order to enhance theory-building. Theory-building is predicated on examination and evaluation, testing and retesting, in order to achieve generalizability and predictive strength. The comparative method in political science is one of the means towards the end of theory-building.

Thus, comparative politics provides systematic generalizations regarding political behaviors, processes, and institutions to promote learning with greater efficiency. This understanding of why we compare in political science is important because it distinguishes political science from other disciplines. For example, the history discipline may also study governments; however, the focus of such study is directed at fact-finding and gathering to enhance interpretation and accuracy. Importantly, then, knowing a lot about a country or an area does not make one a comparative political scholar.

Each of the following units in this book introduces some of the generalizations in comparative politics. They show how even nations, institutions, or behaviors that are conventionally presented as particularistic or peculiar, are actually consistent with such generalizations. This is not to say that the particularities are not important. Rather, it emphasizes that generalizations provide baseline knowledge from which particularities are observed, described, explained, and anticipated.

From this perspective, comparative politics may interpret the articles in this introductory unit thus: While North Korea is clearly an errant government, it is not the only way by which global security and well-being is compromised. Irresponsible governments such as in Sudan also endanger wellbeing. Weak government such as that in Somali may engender problems. So, too, does institutional weakness in Mexico. That is, notwithstanding different countries and systems, there are fundamental behaviors, processes, and institutions needed to achieve the balance between stability, change, security, freedom, growth, accountability, and responsiveness. This text sets as its task the identification of those behaviors, processes, and institutions in order to map out what is needed for the balance.

Notes

1. The United Nations. http://un.org/News/Press/docs//2007/org1479.doc.htm

2. U.S. Department of State. www.state.gov/s/inr/rls/4250.htm

3. Michael Sodaro. 2007. *Comparative Politics: A Global Introduction,* 3rd edition. New York: McGraw Hill.

4. *Oxford Dictionary* http://oxforddictionaries.com/definition/government?region=us; *Merriam-Webster's Online Dictionary.* www.merriam-webster.com/dictionary/government

5. Joseph La Palombara. 1974. *Politics within Nations.* Englewood Cliffs, NJ: Prentice Hall.

6. See also G. Bingham Powell, Russell Dalton, and Kaare Strom. 2012. *Comparative Politics Today: A World View, 10th edition.* New York: Pearson Longman Publishers.

Intensive Care for the United Nations

"A gap is steadily growing between the major challenges facing the planet and the ability of international decision-making processes to deal with them . . . ."

THOMAS G. WEISS

In October 2010, the United Nations turned a venerable 65 years old. In the spirit of the Beatles song that once asked, "Will you still need me, will you still feed me, when I'm sixty-four?", now seems a good time to inquire whether the UN, a baby boomer from the post–World War II era, has aged well. Should the world body be retired—or should it be revitalized? What are the institution's prospects?

Most countries, and especially major powers like the United States, are loath to allow any overarching central authority to constrain their capacity for autonomous action. State sovereignty remains sacrosanct. Even so, the logic of globalization, interdependence, and technological advances—along with a growing number of trans-boundary crises—should increasingly raise doubts about the sanctity of sovereignty, even in Washington. It is not far-fetched to imagine that the community of nations in coming years will witness a gradual advance of intergovernmental agreements and powers, along the lines of what Europe has nurtured.

The former UN secretary-general Kofi Annan frequently speaks of "problems without passports." What he means is that many of the most intractable challenges facing humankind are transnational; they need no visas to cross borders. Such problems range from climate change, pandemics, and terrorism to unlawful migration, destabilizing financial flows, and the proliferation of weapons of mass destruction (WMD). Effectively addressing any of these threats requires policies and vigorous actions that are not unilateral, bilateral, or even multilateral—they must be global.

Yet the policy authority and the resources for tackling such problems remain vested in the 192 member states of the United Nations individually, rather than in the universal body collectively. The fundamental disjuncture between the growing number of global threats and the currently inadequate structures for international problem solving and decision making goes a long way toward explaining the world's fitful, tactical, and short-term local responses to challenges that require sustained, strategic, and longer-term global action.

For all of its shortcomings and weaknesses, the United Nations with its system of specialized agencies and programs is the closest approximation the global stage can offer to a central institutional presence. This is why the world organization urgently requires strengthening.

Indispensable but Sick

Shortly before his inauguration, US President Barack Obama announced not only that the United States was prepared to reengage with other countries (both friends and foes), but also that multilateralism in general and the UN in particular would be essential to American foreign policy under his administration. He declared straightforwardly that "the global challenges we face demand global institutions that work."

Many of Obama's first steps—which included paying America's back dues to the UN, funding programs for reproductive health, joining the Human Rights Council, moving ahead with nuclear arms reductions, and expressing support for the Comprehensive Test Ban Treaty—were steps in the right direction. But more vigorous and sustained efforts are needed.

The Group of 7 or 8, and even the Group of 20, which includes emerging powers, have their purposes. These groupings are not, however, "global institutions that work." Neither are the ad hoc "coalitions of the willing," such as were mustered for invasions of Iraq and Afghanistan, or the "league of democracies" that the policy analyst Robert Kagan favors. The world needs a universal body that can formulate global norms, make global law, and enforce global decisions. Anything less represents wishful thinking, a desire to escape the complexities of daunting global challenges.

As the Obama administration faces growing dissension regarding the morass in Afghanistan, it is worth pondering how best to fill holes in a global security order that has been an American obsession since the terrorist attacks of September 11, 2001. In this regard, Secretary of Defense Robert Gates's comments in December 2008—that "the United States cannot kill or capture its way to victory" and "is unlikely to repeat another

Iraq or Afghanistan: that is, forced regime change followed by nation building under fire"—bear remembering. The sobering experiences of occupation in Iraq and Afghanistan have highlighted the limits of US military and diplomatic power, limits akin to Washington's equally obvious and mammoth inability to go solo in addressing the recent global financial and economic crises.

What other trans-boundary problems should be included on a sensible priority list for this or any other US administration? Most informed Americans would acknowledge that when it comes to spotting, warning of, and managing international health hazards—for example, the severe acute respiratory syndrome (SARS) outbreak in 2003, avian flu more recently, and AIDS perennially—the UN-based World Health Organization is indispensable and unrivaled. Also based within the UN system are capacities for monitoring international crime and the narcotics trade, policing nuclear power and human trafficking, and undertaking numerous other important global functions.

Washington's short list for UN involvement would presumably include post-conflict rebuilding in Afghanistan and Iraq, fighting terrorism (for instance, when it comes to sharing information and monitoring money laundering), pursuing environmental sustainability, providing humanitarian aid, addressing global poverty, rescheduling debt, and fostering trade. (Interestingly all of these items were on a laundry list presented by President George W. Bush in an address to the September 2005 World Summit on the occasion of the UN's 60th anniversary.) After attacks on shipping in the Gulf of Aden and elsewhere, we should add piracy to the list.

At the same time, the diagnosis of the world body is clear: The United Nations is paralyzed. But before we prescribe a course of treatment for the UN's ailments, we must first understand the underlying causes. Essentially there are four.

What Ails It

The first is the enduring concept of the international community as a system of sovereign states, a notion dating back to the 1648 Treaties of Westphalia. The basis for membership in the United Nations, of course, reflects the theoretical equality of states. But a gap is steadily growing between the major challenges facing the planet and the ability of international decision-making processes to deal with them; this is the result of sovereignty's continuing grip. This gap characterizes NATO, the Organization for Economic Cooperation and Development, and the European Union, as well as the UN—all bodies in which states make decisions based almost exclusively on narrowly defined national interests.

Indeed, for national decision makers and so-called realist scholars of international relations, vital national interests, narrowly defined, are apparently the *only* basis on which to make commitments, or avoid them. Paradoxically, the United Nations is the last and most formidable bastion of sacrosanct state sovereignty—even as technological advances, globalization, and the proliferation of trans-boundary problems render national borders less and less salient.

Paradoxically, the United Nations is the last and most formidable bastion of sacrosanct state sovereignty.

The myopically calculated interests of major powers, particularly the United States, thus create obstacles to action by the UN. But powerful states are not the only ones impeding collective, policy making. Smaller and poorer, newer and less powerful states are just as vehemently protective of their so-called sovereignty as the major powers are.

The second cause of the UN's problems stems from the burlesque that passes for diplomacy on Manhattan's First Avenue or Geneva's Avenue de la Paix. The main drama proceeds from an artificial divide between the aging acting troupes from the industrialized north and those from the developing countries of the global south.

The Nonaligned Movement and the Group of 77 developing countries—vehicles launched in the 1950s and 1960s as a way to create diplomatic space in security and economic negotiations for countries on the margins of international politics—once featured creative voices. Now they have become prisoners of their own rhetoric. These rigid and counterproductive groups, along with the toxic atmosphere and unnecessary divisions that they create, constitute almost insurmountable barriers to diplomatic initiatives. Serious conversation becomes virtually impossible and is replaced by meaningless posturing designed to score points back home.

Examples of marquee "stars" in this charade include Venezuelan President Hugo Chávez and the former US ambassador to the UN John Bolton. In the fall of 2006, in the limelight of the General Assembly's stage, Chávez gave a performance in which he referred to George W. Bush as the devil, said "it smells of sulfur," and complained that Bush "came here talking as if he were the owner of the world." Bolton responded by calling Chávez irrelevant and warned that Venezuela would be "disruptive" if elected to the UN Security Council. The former Canadian politician and senior UN official Stephen Lewis has written that "Men and women cannot live by rhetoric alone"—but clearly UN ambassadors and officials are exceptions.

The third cause of the UN's malady is a structural one, and it arises from the overlapping jurisdictions of various UN bodies, the lack of coordination among their activities, and the absence of centralized financing for the system as a whole. All this makes turf struggles more attractive than sensible cooperation. The UN's various moving parts work at cross purposes instead of in a more integrated, mutually reinforcing, and collaborative fashion. Agencies relentlessly pursue cutthroat fundraising to finance expanding mandates, pursue mission creep, and stake out territory.

The UN's organizational chart refers to a "system," but this term falsely implies coherence and cohesion. The body in reality has more in common with a feudal society than with a modern organization. At the UN, frequent use also is made of the word "family." This folksy term is actually preferable to "system" because, like many families, the UN is dysfunctional and divided. Former senior UN staff members Brian Urquhart and Erskine Childers correctly described the world organization when they wrote in 1994 that "The orchestra pays minimum heed to its conductor."

The UN's organizational chart refers to a "system," but this falsely implies coherence and cohesion.

Sir Robert Jackson—the Australian logistics genius who moved goods to Malta and the Middle East during World War II and subsequently over-saw a number of key UN humanitarian operations—observed in a 1969 evaluation of the UN development system that "the machine as a whole has become unmanageable in the strictest sense of the word. As a result, it is becoming slower and more unwieldy, like some prehistoric monster." The lumbering dinosaur is now four decades older but is certainly not better adapted.

The fourth cause of the UN's ailments is the overwhelming weight of the organization's bureaucracy, its low productivity, and the underwhelming leadership within international secretariats. The stereotype of the UN's administration as bloated is misleading in some ways because such a portrayal ignores the efforts of many talented and dedicated individuals. However, the world body's recruitment and promotion methods are certainly part of what ails it. The UN's successes usually have more to do with serendipity and individual personalities than with recruiting the best people for the right reasons or with institutional structures designed to foster collaboration.

Staff costs account for the lion's share of the UN's budget, and much of this money is poorly spent. This situation could quickly improve if the international civil service were regarded as a potential resource and its composition, productivity, and culture were changed. But the short run holds little hope of this, as Secretary-General Ban Ki-moon's lackluster leadership will last for at least another year, and perhaps even until the middle of this decade.

As it stands now, Rube Goldberg would be hard pressed to design something exceeding in futile complexity the UN's array of agencies, each focusing on a different substantive area, with relevant UN partners often located in different cities and maintaining separate budgets, governing boards, organizational cultures, and executive heads. Challenges such as climate change, pandemics, terrorism, and WMDs require multidisciplinary perspectives, inspired leadership, and firm central direction of cross-sector efforts. The UN rarely supplies any of these.

Rube Goldberg would be hard pressed to design something exceeding in futile complexity the UN's array of agencies.

Taking the Cure

Is it possible to heal the United Nations? Can palliatives, if not cures, be found? In fact, the four sources of the institution's illness themselves suggest ways to initiate surgery that, if not radical, would certainly be more than cosmetic.

The first remedy requires building on spotty yet significant progress made to date in recasting national interests in terms of good global citizenship and enhancing international responsibilities. This prescription for the Westphalian system's ailments consists of encouraging yet more recognition of the benefits of cooperating to provide global public goods and respecting international commitments. Democratic member states of the UN, whether large or small, should theoretically find this pill relatively easy to swallow; they have a long-term, rational, and vital interest, along with a moral responsibility, in promoting multilateral cooperation.

While this statement will undoubtedly have a Pollyannaish ring to American ears, a demonstrable therapeutic benefit can be derived from "good international citizenship" (an expression coined by Gareth Evans, the former Australian foreign minister and one-time president of the International Crisis Group). This notion under-pins the conviction that there is a relationship between the provision of basic rights and wider international security. Nothing illustrates the idea better than "the responsibility to protect," or "R2P," a doctrine that defines state sovereignty not as absolute but as contingent on a modicum of respect for human rights. R2P imposes the primary responsibility for human rights on governmental authorities, but it argues that if a state is unwilling or unable to honor its responsibility—or worse, if it is itself the perpetrator of mass atrocities—then the responsibility to protect the rights of individuals shifts upward to the international community of states.

This doctrine illustrates how to move in the direction of reframing state sovereignty, a break-through in values after centuries of passive, mindless acceptance of the proposition that state sovereignty is a license to kill. Both President Obama and Susan Rice, the current US ambassador to the United Nations, have clearly expressed the need for Washington to take the lead in addressing conscience-shocking situations around the world, instead of repeating mistakes such as President Bill Clinton's lamentable decision to stay out of Rwanda during the genocide there in 1994.

The Washington-based "Enough" project, which campaigns to prevent genocide in places like Darfur, the Democratic Republic of Congo, and Zimbabwe, has referred to Africa specialist Rice, Secretary of State Hillary Clinton, National Security Adviser General James Jones, and Samantha Power, the senior director for multilateral affairs at the National Security Council, as a "dream team." An essay that Obama published in *Foreign Affairs* while a presidential candidate attracted wide attention because he asserted the importance of "military force in circumstances beyond self-defense" and specifically listed the need to "confront mass atrocities."

To date there has been no indication of American diplomatic or military teeth behind that promising early rhetoric. One has to worry, for example, how Washington and the international community will respond if a January 2011 referendum in Sudan results in the breakup of Africa's largest state, producing in all likelihood mass atrocities and massive forced displacement.

Nonetheless, the history of international diplomacy and law shows us how states have gradually accepted limits on their conduct by ratifying treaties that have constrained their margins for maneuver. Additionally, the definition of sovereignty has been altered by the spread of ideas about human rights—by what Eleanor Roosevelt presciently predicted in 1948 would be "a curious grapevine." The challenge for the Obama administration, as well as for future administrations, will be to squarely face the reality that the domestic institutions on which the United States and every society depend to provide public goods do not exist at the global level—not for genocide prevention or for any other crucial international issue.

Not to put too fine a point on it, the international order has no power to tax, conscript, regulate, or quarantine. Are these not precisely the attributes required if global problems are to be effectively addressed through international decisions?

Less Posturing, Please

The second prescription for what ails the United Nations involves redressing the north-south quagmire. Fortunately, states have on occasion forged creative partnerships across the fictitious border that supposedly divides industrialized from developing countries. Examples of wide-ranging coalitions formed across continents and ideologies include those that have negotiated treaties to ban landmines and have agreed to establish the International Criminal Court.

Unfortunately, the United States has not joined those coalitions, and in fact during the Bush administration many divides became wider. In the future, Washington should build bridges on issues such as climate change, development finance, nonproliferation, reproductive rights, and terrorism, to name a few. The Obama administration at least has this advantage: Its actions are judged against the extremely poor cooperation record of its predecessor, an administration during which expectations in both the global south and the global north became very low. When it comes to key global challenges, Washington should seek to build within international institutions larger, more legitimate "coalitions of the willing" than the skimpy, illegitimate coalitions that were cob-bled together for Iraq and Afghanistan.

The United States also can build on the Global Compact, a UN effort to bring nonstate actors, including civil society and transnational corporations, into a more intense partnership with the UN. In any case, for the future health of the world organization and world politics, both north and south must engage in less posturing and role-playing.

The third course of treatment would be to pursue the possibility, however remote, of making the UN work more coherently (as advocated in "Delivering as One," a report initiated by Annan before his departure as UN secretary-general). Outside the body itself, the mere mention of reform that might improve coordination among UN agencies causes eyes to glaze over.

But as Mark Malloch Brown (the former administrator of the UN Development Program and *chef de cabinet* for Annan) has suggested, the UN is the only institution where reform is a more popular topic around water coolers than sex.

No reform effort to date has even modestly reduced the turf battles and unproductive competition for funds that characterize the so-called UN system. But could it? Yes—if donor nations would stop talking out of both sides of their mouths and actually insist on the centralization and consolidation that they often espouse in UN forums and before parliamentary bodies. This is not an impossible thing to imagine. Nor is it impossible to imagine adopting modest alternative means of financing for the world body—such as assessing infinitesimally low taxes on financial transfers or airline tickets. Washington, however, has routinely fought such measures in the past because they would give the world organization the autonomy that it requires.

The final element of therapy would be to reinvigorate the staff of the United Nations. Reviving the notion of an autonomous international civil service, as championed by the UN's second secretary-general, Dag Hammarskjöld, is urgently needed. (In fact, Hammarskjöld's ideal goes back to what a working group of the Carnegie Endowment for International Peace during World War II called the "great experiment" of the League of Nations.) Competence and integrity should outweigh nationality, gender considerations, and cronyism, which have become the principal criteria for recruitment, retention, and promotion.

Staff reform for the United Nations would involve recruiting people with integrity and talent. There are numerous ways in which more mobile, younger staff members could be attracted, at the same time that turnover and rotation from headquarters to the field are increased, fewer permanent contracts are offered, and the world organization's career development improves. Staff expenditures account for 90 percent of the organization's budget; near the top of any to-do list should be strengthening performance and productivity by improving output and efficiency.

Obama and the UN

The United States does not dominate the world the way it once did. China and India are rising, and multipolarity has returned in the form of the G-20. Moreover, the world is not desperately longing for Washington to make good on Ambassador Rice's commitment in her confirmation hearing "to refresh and renew America's leadership in the United Nations." But if the League of Nations represented a first generation of international institutions, and the UN system is the second generation, creating a third generation should move to the top of the US foreign policy agenda.

A next generation would have world-class and independent executive leadership with more centralization and better funding. As with the EU, community-wide calculations of interest on many issues would replace those based on narrowly conceived national interests. While not a world government by any stretch of the imagination, international institutions would incorporate elements of overarching authority and enhanced mechanisms for ensuring compliance—indeed, the World Trade Organization (WTO) already has some.

Instituting the four remedies described here would amount to the establishment of a third generation of international institutions. To be sure, there are few precedents for the deliberate destruction of existing international institutions and the establishment of new ones (other than the transfer of assets from the League of Nations to the UN and from the General Agreement on Tariffs and Trade to the WTO). Moreover, initial expectations surrounding the Obama administration were as impossibly high in the international arena as they were in the domestic one. Obama's honey-moon was short, and public appetite for foreign policy initiatives is limited. Nonetheless, the US administration has exercised modest leadership—in the Middle East, on nuclear nonproliferation, on climate change, and in the aftermath of the recent financial and economic crisis.

Will the United States sit on the sidelines; try to take charge unilaterally; or will it make the UN a central component of its strategic interests? It is also worth asking whether the UN—a heavily bureaucratic institution deeply troubled by its own failings—is ready for an energetic United States.

The global financial crisis and subsequent economic slowdown have made clear the risks, problems, and costs associated with a global economy that lacks adequate international institutions with democratic decision-making ability and the power to ensure compliance with collective decisions. No less towering a commentator than Henry Kissinger wrote this about the realities of a globalizing world and the limits of a self-regulating worldwide market: "The financial collapse exposed the mirage. It made evident the absence of global institutions to cushion the shock and to reverse the trend." Trillions of dollars, euros, and pounds have been used mainly to paper over the cracks that the crisis revealed. Business as usual remains the standard operating procedure, even in the wake of the Great Recession.

But can we perhaps learn from history? In a recent book about the origins of American multilateralism, Stewart Patrick, a senior fellow at the Council on Foreign Relations, made a persuasive case that "the fundamental questions facing the 1940s generation confront us again today. As then, the United States remains by far the most powerful country in the world, but its contemporary security, political, and economic challenges are rarely amenable to unilateral action."

Charles de Gaulle famously called the United Nations *le machin,* thereby dismissing international cooperation as frivolous in comparison with the real red meat of international affairs—national interests and realpolitik. But de Gaulle conveniently ignored the fact that the decision to create "the thing" was formalized not by the UN Charter signed in June 1945, but rather by the "Declaration by the United Nations" adopted in Washington in January 1942. That is, the 26 countries that defeated fascism also viewed the establishment of a world organization as an essential extension of their wartime commitments. These were not pie-in-the-sky idealists. The UN system was viewed not as a liberal plaything but as a vital necessity for postwar order and prosperity.

Urquhart—one of the first individuals recruited by the United Nations, and undoubtedly the most respected commentator on the world organization—recalled the "remarkable generation of leaders and public servants" who led the United States during and after World War II. These pragmatic idealists, he observed, were "more concerned about the future of humanity than the outcome of the next election; and they understood that finding solutions to postwar problems was much more important than being popular with one or another part of the American electorate." Could this same farsighted political commitment rise again under the Obama administration—if not in the next two years, then at least by the end of a second term?

Critical Thinking

1. Describe how decisions are made in the United Nations.
2. Which states have power in the United Nations? How is that power exercised?
3. According to the author, why is it important for the United States to be involved in the United Nations or politics of other countries?

THOMAS G. WEISS is a professor of political science and director of the Ralph Bunche Institute for International Studies at The Graduate Center of The City University of New York. He is the author of *What's Wrong with the United Nations and How to Fix It* (Polity Press, 2009), from which this essay is adapted.

From *Current History,* November 2010, pp. 322–330. Copyright © 2010 by Current History, Inc. Reprinted by permission.

Seeing "Islamic Terror" in Norway

FAIRNESS AND ACCURACY IN REPORTING (FAIR)

Right-wing terror suspect Anders Behring Breivik reportedly killed 76 people in Norway on Friday, by all accounts driven by far-right anti-immigrant politics and fervent Islamophobia. But many early media accounts assumed that the perpetrator of the attacks was Muslim.

On news of the first round of attacks—the bombs in Oslo—**CNN**'s Tom Lister (7/22/11) didn't know who did it, but knew they were Muslims: "It could be a whole range of groups. But the point is that Al-Qaeda is not so much an organization now. It's more a spirit for these people. It's a mobilizing factor." And he speculated confidently about their motives:

> You've only got to look at the target—prime minister's office, the headquarters of the major newspaper group next door. Why would that be relevant? Because the Norwegian newspapers republished the cartoons of Prophet Mohammad that caused such offense in the Muslim world. . . . That is an issue that still rankles amongst Islamist militants the world over.

CNN terrorism analyst Paul Cruickshank (7/22/11) took to the airwaves to declare that "Norway has been in Al-Qaeda's crosshairs for quite some time." He added that the bombing "bears all the hallmarks of the Al-Qaeda terrorist organization at the moment," before adding, almost as an afterthought, that "we don't know at this point who was responsible."

On **Fox News Channel**'s **O'Reilly Factor** (7/22/11), guest host Laura Ingraham declared, "Deadly terror attacks in Norway, in what appears to be the work, once again, of Muslim extremists." Even after Norwegian authorities arrested Breivik, former Bush administration U.N. Ambassador John Bolton was in disbelief. "There is a kind of political correctness that comes up when these tragic events occur," he explained on **Fox**'s **On the Record** (7/22/11). "This kind of behavior is very un-Norwegian. The speculation that it is part of right-wing extremism, I think that has less of a foundation at this point than the concern that there's a broader political threat here."

Earlier in the day on **Fox** (7/22/11), Bolton had explained that "the odds of it coming from someone other than a native Norwegian are extremely high." While he admitted there was no evidence, Bolton concluded that "it sure looks like Islamic terrorism," adding that "there is a substantial immigrant population from the Middle East in particular in Norway."

An early **Wall Street Journal** editorial (7/22/11) dwelled on the "explanations furnished by jihadist groups to justify their periodic slaughters," before concluding that because of Norway's commitment to tolerance and freedom, "Norwegians have now been made to pay a terrible price."

Once the alleged perpetrator's identity did not conform to the **Journal**'s prejudice, the editorial was modified, but it continued to argue that Al-Qaeda was an inspiration: "Coordinated terrorist attacks are an Al-Qaeda signature. But copycats with different agendas are surely capable of duplicating its methods."

Many pundits and outlets had to scramble to justify their ideological presumptions in the wake of the unexpected suspect. **Washington Post** blogger Jennifer Rubin (7/22/11) had called the Norwegian violence "a sobering reminder for those who think it's too expensive to wage a war against jihadists," citing Thomas Joscelyn of the **Weekly Standard**'s assertion that "in all likelihood the attack was launched by part of the jihadist hydra." In a follow-up post (7/23/11), Rubin insisted that even though she was wrong, she was right, because "there are many more jihadists than blond Norwegians out to kill Americans, and we should keep our eye on the systemic and far more potent threats that stem from an ideological war with the West."

New York Times columnist Ross Douthat (7/25/11) likewise argued that we should respond to the horror in Norway by paying more attention to the alleged perpetrator's point of view:

> On the big picture, Europe's cultural conservatives are right: Mass immigration really has left the Continent more divided than enriched, Islam and liberal democracy have not yet proven natural bedfellows and the dream of a postnational, postpatriotic European Union governed by a benevolent ruling elite looks more like a folly every day . . . . Conservatives on both sides of the Atlantic have an obligation to acknowledge that Anders Behring Breivik is a distinctively right-wing kind of monster. But they also have an obligation to the realities that this monster's terrible atrocity threatens to obscure.

The **New York Times**' July 23 report explained that while early speculation about Muslim terrorists was incorrect, there was ample reason for concern that terrorists might be responsible. In 2004 and again in 2008, the No. 2 leader of Al-Qaeda, Ayman al-Zawahri, who took over after the death of Osama bin Laden, threatened Norway because of its support of the American-led NATO military operation in Afghanistan.

Of course, anyone who kills scores of civilians for political motives is a "terrorist"; the language of the **Times,** though, suggested that a "terrorist" would have to be Islamic.

The **Times** went on:

> Terrorism specialists said that even if the authorities ultimately ruled out Islamic terrorism as the cause of Friday's assaults, other kinds of groups or individuals were mimicking Al-Qaeda's brutality and multiple attacks.
>
> "If it does turn out to be someone with more political motivations, it shows these groups are learning from what they see from Al-Qaeda," said Brian Fishman, a counterterrorism researcher at the New America Foundation in Washington.

It is unclear why any of Breivik's actions would be considered connected in any way to terrorist groups like Al-Qaeda, which certainly did not invent the idea of brutal mass murder. But the **Times** was able to turn up another expert the following day who saw an Islamist inspiration for Islamophobic terrorism (7/24/11):

> Thomas Hegghammer, a terrorism specialist at the Norwegian Defense Research Establishment, said the manifesto bears an eerie resemblance to those of Osama bin Laden and other Al-Qaeda leaders, though from a Christian rather than a Muslim point of view. Like Mr. Breivik's manuscript, the major Qaeda declarations have detailed accounts of the Crusades, a pronounced sense of historical grievance and calls for apocalyptic warfare to defeat the religious and cultural enemy.
>
> "It seems to be an attempt to mirror Al-Qaeda, exactly in reverse," Mr. Hegghammer said.

To the paper's credit, the **Times**' Scott Shane wrote a strong second-day piece (7/25/11) documenting the influence of Islamophobic bloggers on Breivik's manifesto:

> His manifesto, which denounced Norwegian politicians as failing to defend the country from Islamic influence, quoted Robert Spencer, who operates the Jihad Watch website, 64 times, and cited other Western writers who shared his view that Muslim immigrants pose a grave

danger to Western culture . . . . Mr. Breivik frequently cited another blog, Atlas Shrugs, and recommended the Gates of Vienna among websites.

(Spencer was one of the anti-Muslim pundits profiled in FAIR's 2008 report, "Meet the Smearcasters: Islamophobia's Dirty Dozen.")

Shane's piece noted that the document, rather than being an Al-Qaeda "mirror," actually copied large sections of Ted Kaczynski's 1995 Unabomber manifesto, "in which the Norwegian substituted 'multiculturalists' or 'cultural Marxists' for Mr. Kaczynski's 'leftists' and made other small wording changes."

It is not new for media to jump to the conclusion that Muslims are responsible for any given terrorist attack; the same thing was widespread after the 1995 Oklahoma City bombings (**Extra!,** 7/8/95). "It has every single earmark of the Islamic car-bombers of the Middle East," syndicated columnist Georgie Anne Geyer (**Chicago Tribune,** 4/21/95) asserted. "Whatever we are doing to destroy Mideast terrorism, the chief terrorist threat against Americans, has not been working," wrote **New York Times** columnist A.M. Rosenthal (4/21/95). "Knowing that the car bomb indicates Middle Eastern terrorists at work, it's safe to assume that their goal is to promote free-floating fear," editorialized the **New York Post** (4/20/95). It is unfortunate that so many outlets have failed to learn any practical lessons from such mistakes—or question the beliefs that drive them.

Critical Thinking

1. Describe the bases of the reports in the article for speculating that the Norwegian attack is from Islam extremists.

2. According to the reports cited in the article, what is the real threat to the United States?

3. What led to the attack in Norway?

Britain's Riots: A Society in Denial of the Burning Issues

Finian Cunningham

Britain saw its third consecutive night of widespread burning of properties and looting as riot police failed to contain gangs of masked youths marauding several parts of the capital, London.

There were reports too of violence fanning out to other cities across Britain. And some commentators were even suggesting that the British Army might have to be redeployed from Northern Ireland to help restore order. Armoured police vehicles are now patrolling London streets amid calls in the media for the use of water cannons and plastic bullets.

Politicians, police chiefs and the media have reacted to the chaos by labelling it as the result of "mindless criminality" that has seemingly sprung from nowhere. 'The Rule of the Mob' declared the rightwing Daily Telegraph. 'Mob Rule' is how the more liberal Independent put it.

Home Secretary Theresa May stridently denounced "unacceptable thuggery." London Metropolitan Police Commissioner Tim Godwin vowed that culprits would be tracked down and brought before the courts. He appealed to Londoners to identify individuals caught on CCTV and amateur video footage.

Nearly 500 arrests have been made so far and police numbers in the capital have been tripled overnight to 16,000, with officers being drawn in from other parts of the country.

Although the arson attacks on commercial and residential premises do have an element of criminal spontaneity by disparate groups of youths, it is simply delusional for Britain's political leaders, police forces and the media to claim that it is all a matter of law and order.

The burning issues that need to be addressed to explain the outburst of arson, looting and rioting are endemic racism endured by Britain's black community and, more generally, the deepening poverty that is increasingly racking British society.

Conservative Prime Minister David Cameron cut short his summer holiday in Italy by flying home to London to hold a special "emergency security" meeting with other Cabinet members.

Speaking outside Downing Street today and visibly vexed by the unfolding chaos, Cameron condemned "pure and simple criminality that must be defeated." The government, he said, stands with "all law-abiding citizens."

Opposition Labour party leader Ed Milliband and the Conservative Mayor of London Boris Johnson are also making hasty returns to the capital from abroad to deal with a crisis that seems to be spiralling out of control. The British Parliament is to be recalled from its summer recess later this week so that "all parliamentarians can stand to together" to face down the sudden disorder.

The disturbances—the worst in almost 30 years—began last Saturday in the rundown north London inner-city area of Tottenham. That followed the shooting dead two days earlier of a young black man by police officers.

Mark Duggan was fatally shot by an armed police unit as he sat in his car. Police claimed that the man was threatening to use a gun. However, family and friends of the 29-year-old victim strongly denied that he was armed or involved in any criminal activity. The death is the subject of a police inquiry, but it has emerged that only two shots were fired in the incident, both by police officers.

Sinisterly, BBC news reports on the killing have invariably showed what appeared to be a family photo of Duggan taken before his death in which he is seen holding up his hand up in mock gangster style.

Angered by what they saw as a gratuitous police shooting and lack of immediate answers from authorities, the mixed black and white community in Tottenham held a vigil for the victim on Saturday. With tensions running high in the area, the peaceful rally turned into a riot against police, and several properties, including police cars, were attacked and set alight.

Since then, similar disturbances have now spread to other parts of the capital, including Peckham, Brixton, Hackney, Lewisham and Clapham. A Sony factory was reduced to a charred shell in Enfield in north London. In the outer south London district of Croydon—several miles from Tottenham—there was a huge blaze last night after a large commercial property was torched. Even the affluent, leafy borough of Ealing in west London saw upmarket boutiques and residences attacked and destroyed by fire.

The distraught owner of the razed family business in Croydon struggled to comprehend why his 150-year-old furniture shop had been targeted. Nevertheless his few words of disbelief had a ring of truth that the politicians and media commentators seem oblivious to. "There must be something deeply wrong about the [political] system," he said.

Police forces are seen to be struggling to contain the upsurge in street violence, with groups of youths appearing to go on the rampage at will, breaking into shop fronts and stealing goods. A real fear among the authorities is the spreading of disorder and violence to other cities, with reports emerging of similar disturbances in the centre of Birmingham in the British midlands, and further north in Nottingham, Liverpool and Manchester.

Inner-city deprived black communities in Britain complain of routine heavy-handed policing that is openly racist. Community leaders tell of aggressive stop-and-search methods by police that target black youths. The community leaders say that racist policing is as bad as it was during the 1980s when riots broke out in 1985 after a black woman, Cynthia Jarrett, died in a police raid on her home in Broadwater Farm, London.

In the latest spate of violence—on a much greater scale than in the 1980s—there is no suggestion that subsequent street disturbances to the initial Tottenham riots are racially motivated. The growing number of areas and youths involved in arson, rioting and looting do not appear to be driven merely out of solidarity for the young black victim of police violence last week, although that may be a factor for some. Many of the disturbances in London and elsewhere seem to be caused by white and black youths together and separately.

But there is one common factor in all of this that the politicians and media are studiously ignoring: the massive poverty, unemployment and social deprivation that are now the lot for so many of Britain's communities.

Britain's social decay has been seething over several decades, overseen by Conservative and Labour governments alike. As with other European countries and the United States, the social fabric of Britain has been torn asunder by economic policies that have deliberately widened the gap between rich and poor.

The collapse of manufacturing bases, the spawning of low-paid menial jobs, unemployment and cuts in public services and facilities have all been accompanied by systematic lowering of taxation on the rich elite. Britain's national debt, as with that of the Europe and the US, can be attributed in large part to decades of pursuing neoliberal policies of prosperity for the rich and austerity for the poor—the burden of which is felt most keenly in inner-city neighbourhoods.

David Cameron's Conservative-Liberal Coalition government has greatly magnified this debt burden on the poor with its swingeing austerity cuts since coming to office last year. Ironically, only days before the latest burnings and riots, British government spokesmen were congratulating themselves for "making the right decision" in driving through crippling economic austerity measures that have so far spared the United Kingdom from the overt fiscal woes seen elsewhere in Europe.

But as thousands of Britain's youths now lash out at symbols of authority/austerity, breaking into shops to loot clothes and other consumer goods that they wouldn't otherwise be able to afford, the social eruption may be just a sign of even greater woes to come for the Disunited Kingdom.

Critical Thinking

1. Describe what happened in Britain.
2. According to authorities (media, government, police), what are the reasons for the incident?
3. According to the author, what are the reasons for the incident?
4. Is Great Britain unique in the problems identified by the author? If not, what does it mean?

FINIAN CUNNINGHAM is a Global Research Correspondent based in Belfast, Ireland.

Flawed Miracle: India's Boom Bypasses Rural Poor

Tom Wright and Harsh Gupta

Nakrasar, India—India has its own version of America's Depression-era Works Progress Administration: a gigantic program designed to create jobs through building infrastructure in a developing nation's most-backward rural areas.

But unlike its American counterpart eight decades ago, the Indian program, its detractors assert, is keeping the poor down, rather than uplifting them.

The Mahatma Gandhi National Rural Employment Guarantee Scheme, as the $9 billion program is known, is riddled with corruption, according to senior government officials. Less than half of the projects begun since 2006—including new roads and irrigation systems—have been completed. Workers say they're frequently not paid in full or forced to pay bribes to get jobs, and aren't learning any new skills that could improve their long-term prospects and break the cycle of poverty.

In Nakrasar, a collection of villages in the dusty western state of Rajasthan, 19 unfinished projects for catching rain and raising the water table are all there is to show for a year's worth of work and $77,000 in program funds. No major roads have been built, no new homes, schools or hospitals or any infrastructure to speak of.

At one site on a recent afternoon, around 200 workers sat idly around a bone-dry pit. "What's the big benefit?" said Gopal Ram Jat, a 40-year-old farmer in a white cotton head scarf. He says he has earned enough money through the program—about $200 in a year—to buy some extra food for his family, but not much else. "No public assets were made of any significance."

Scenes like this stand in stark contrast to India's image of a global capitalist powerhouse with surging growth and a liberalized economy. When it comes to combating rural poverty, the country looks more like a throwback to the India of old: a socialist-inspired state founded on Gandhian ideals of noble peasantry, self-sufficiency and a distaste for free enterprise.

Workers in the rural employment program aren't allowed to use machines, for example, and have to dig instead with pick axes and shovels. The idea is to create as many jobs as possible for unskilled workers. But in practice, say critics, it means no one learns new skills, only basic projects get completed and the poor stay poor—dependent on government checks.

"It actually works against the long-term future of the poor because it doesn't give them any long-term solutions to poverty," says Gurcharan Das, an author who has written about India's economic development. "It's a Band-Aid solution."

Indian officials acknowledge that the program is flawed, though they say it has provided an important safety net for the 50 million households, comprising more than 200 million people, that have participated in the past year alone. Proponents of the plan, including left-leaning economists and activists, say that because the pay is often better than other rural jobs, it has given workers a bargaining tool to demand higher wages. Echoing the Gandhian ideals for which the program is named, they say workers are also better off staying in their villages, close to their families, instead of moving to the cities in search of work and winding up in slums.

"The scheme has been a big success in creating employment for rural people," Sonia Gandhi, president of the ruling Congress party, told a meeting in February of officials who administer the program. "However, there have been complaints of irregularities and corruption, too."

Niten Chandra, a senior official at the federal rural affairs ministry, says the aim was never to build major highways or other large infrastructure, but to create work and raise wages. He says that state governments, whose job it is to monitor projects and ensure audits are carried out, are at fault for failing in many cases to guard against corruption and unfinished work.

Some villages have run out of ideas for new projects. In Churu, the district capital a few miles from Nakrasar, senior officials say villagers simply dig new irrigation pits every time one is washed away in the monsoons.

The repercussions go far beyond irrigation projects. India's failure to uplift its poor and improve the economy in rural areas—where two thirds of the country's 1.2 billion people live, mostly untouched by the boom—threatens the country's growth, economists say. India has so far relied on its services industry in cities to fuel growth. But the country is running out of skilled workers and its agricultural dwellers are ill-suited to fill the gap. India's success or failure in boosting the size of its middle class will determine the long-term attractiveness of the market to foreign investors.

Yet the number of people relying on the program is expected to rise after the government earlier this year decided to tie wages to the cost of living, automatically increasing the 100-rupee maximum for a day's work to about 125 rupees in many states. That's higher in some places than the daily wage for farm labor. The result is that many more millions will likely become dependent on the government for income despite a two-decade-old push to reduce the state's role in the economy.

In Haryana, a state that borders New Delhi, workers are paid some of the highest wages anywhere under the program. But Gurdayal Singh, a 56-year-old former soldier who was recently supervising work at a water-irrigation pit, said the extra cash he earns isn't enough to pay for the private English-language schooling his children need to compete for better jobs. "It's not satisfactory," Mr. Singh said. "How will I be able to get my children a good education?"

The ruling Congress party, which swept to power in 2004, has been keen to woo the rural poor because they are a potent voting bloc. In that election, the creation of the rural employment act was among Ms. Gandhi's foremost campaign promises. When Congress was re-elected in 2009, its central platform was the lifting of the "aam aadmi," or common man, out of poverty.

Rajasthan was one of the first places to receive funding when the program started. It is among India's poorest states. Around 50% of women are illiterate. Farmers travel by camel-drawn carts between fields planted with grain. In the year ending March 31, the state received one fifth of all funds dedicated to the jobs program nationwide. And it typifies many of the program's problems.

In Karauli district, a landscape of jagged hills and thorny bushes, locals say they have taken up work under the program as a last resort.

At one site in Kaladevi sub-district, some 40 workers were recently piling up rocks to build a dam to catch rain water. Some 20 other workers on an attendance list weren't present, according to supervisors. The site had no medical kit, resting area or child-care facilities, as mandated by law.

"We work because there's high unemployment here and the land is less fertile," said Abdul Jameel Khan, a farmer who was supervising the work. But he questioned the point. "There's no meaning to it. Instead of this they should build proper roads."

Others said the ban on mechanization limits the scope of projects to gravel roads and pits to capture water. Such programs last for only a couple of years and do little to improve village life. Balveer Singh Meena, a 31-year old farmer in the village of Mohanpura in northern Karauli, ekes out a living growing wheat and chickpeas. He eats a single Indian flat-bread known as roti and vegetables for every meal. By selling what little excess food they produce, Mr. Meena and his three brothers are able to make just over $400 per year, which must stretch to pay for an extended family of eight people.

Mr. Meena's modest aim in joining the program, under which he worked 65 days in 2007, earning about $80, was to save cash to help rebuild his family's mud-and-thatch house with bricks and mortar. With rising building material costs, in part due to high inflation in rural areas, Mr. Meena says he couldn't make it happen.

He says the government should offer training in new skills which could help him get a better-paying job. And he's angered at corruption in the program, which he claims has led to village elders giving jobs to family and friends, not to all those who demand work, including himself. "The common man is not getting work easily. There is too much corruption," Mr. Meena said.

District officials confirm that graft in Karauli has been extreme. A 2009 crackdown found that a quarter of 200,000 job cards were fake, according to Niraj Kumar Pawan, a senior government bureaucrat who oversaw Karauli at the time.

A report in 2008 by the Institute of Development Studies in the state capital of Jaipur, one of a number of reports commissioned by the national government to measure the program's efficacy, found that influential villagers in the district got enrolled to work and claimed pay without turning up. Some community leaders used mechanized diggers, which aren't allowed, to finish work quickly and then claim payment for more hours than they actually worked.

These are the very problems the creators of the program sought to avoid. In the past, anti-poverty funds were routinely stolen by the bureaucrats in charge. Rajiv Gandhi, a former Indian prime minister and Ms. Gandhi's husband, who was assassinated in 1991, had estimated only 15% of money spent historically on India's poor had made it to the intended recipients.

The architects of the rural employment program tried to address this by putting village councils, headed by the local mayor, or "sarpanch", in charge of paying workers and deciding what to build. The hope was that these leaders would have a greater incentive than mid-level bureaucrats to ensure funds were spent properly since the local electorate would hold them accountable for wrongdoing. The program guaranteed up to 100 days of work a year at up to 100 rupees ($2) per day for any household that wants it.

But shortly after the program started in February 2006, workers complained that local leaders were docking pay and asking for money in return for job cards. The central government responded in 2008 by sending money directly to workers' bank accounts. But according to workers and auditors, the money takes so long to reach those accounts—up to 45 days—that workers are often forced to accept lesser cash payments from local leaders on the condition that they repay the money at the full amount.

Audits of the program in the southern state of Andhra Pradesh found that about $125 million, or about 5% of the $2.5 billion spent since 2006, has been misappropriated. Some 38,000 local officials were implicated, and almost 10,000 staff lost their jobs.

In one study of eastern Orissa state, only 60% of households said a member had done any of the work reported on their behalf. Earlier this month, the central government gave the green-light for the Central Bureau of Investigation, India's top federal criminal investigation body, to launch a probe into alleged misuse of program funds in Orissa.

In other states, audits are nonexistent or have faced a backlash. Non-governmental groups that have tried to carry out audits in Rajasthan have complained that village leaders often refuse to hand over documents about the employment program. At times, auditors say, they have faced harassment and physical intimidation.

In Nakrasar's one-room village council office, people continue to sign up for the program—many of them women whose husbands have gone to work in urban areas. Shilochandra Devi, a 37-year-old with her program work book in hand, said she could buy more spices because of the program. "And anyway, we're not doing anything else. So why not?"

Critical Thinking

1. Describe the problems in India.
2. Describe the "band-aid" solution.
3. Are the problems unique to India? What are the similarities, if any, between India, Great Britain, and Norway?

More Aid Is Not the Answer

"Most analysts on the continent do not share donor nations' optimism that a big push in aid will make a big difference in the lives of poor Africans."

JONATHAN GLENNIE

Africa needs help—of this there should be no doubt. Some African countries in the past decade saw encouragingly strong growth in gross domestic product (GDP), and this can be an important part of poverty reduction. Yet hopes that the region would be somewhat immune to the recent global financial crisis have proved unfounded, and the continent remains by the far the world's poorest.

In the past two years, not only has global demand for African commodity exports shrunk (except in China), but the region's financial architecture has turned out to be not as independent from the rest of the world as had been supposed. And while Africa receives relatively little foreign investment compared to other parts of the world, even that has fallen significantly.

So Africa does need aid. The question is, what kind of aid? The simple (and simplistic) calculation at the heart of the developed world's present attitude toward Africa is this: Sub-Saharan Africa is poor; if rich countries send it more money, it will be less poor, and people living in poverty will be better off.

The theory seems both logical and fair. More aid should mean less poverty, more schools and hospitals, fewer children dying of preventable diseases, and more roads and infrastructure to support developing economies. But, unfortunately, it is not that simple. Official aid to Africa (as distinct from private charity) has often meant more poverty, more hungry people, worse basic services for poor people, and increased damage to already precarious democratic institutions.

For African nations, along with other developing countries, the recent financial crisis and the ongoing global downturn present an opportunity to emerge from a vicious cycle of aid dependency and lack of accountability, and to move toward a virtuous circle of accountability and independence. The many options and decisions regarding aid currently on the international community's and African nations' table should be judged in this light. And they should be assessed with the understanding that what matters are not just economic consequences, but also shifts in power and accountability.

The New Aid Era

According to the World Bank, developing countries in 2010 face a financing shortfall of up to $700 billion, as a consequence of falling export receipts, remittances, and foreign investment. Aid has been the standard response to cash shortages in the past and, predictably, it is again one of the central issues under debate. Pressure has mounted both to reduce aid (as donor governments seek to balance their budgets and focus on national priorities) and to increase aid (to help poor countries that, according to the accepted wisdom, are not responsible for the global crisis yet are suffering its consequences).

As donor governments look for ways to cut expenditures on non-priority activities, some aid campaigners are shifting away from calling for a doubling of aid to Africa, instead trying to ensure that assistance at least does not tail off. But to continue to focus attention on the amount of aid provided would be both to ignore mistakes of the past and to miss opportunities that the present offers.

Aid to Africa has risen year on year since the turn of the millennium, though ambitious targets set by donors have not been reached. Official data show development aid to Africa, depending on which figures you use, either doubling or almost tripling since 2000, with predictions of more increases in years to come. As Angel Gurria, the secretary general of the Organization for Economic Cooperation and Development, has observed, "We are talking here about an increase in official development assistance of a magnitude and in a time frame that has never been attempted before in the history of the aid effort."

Underpinning the impressive numbers are influential studies published in the past few years (such as a 2005 report on the United Nations' Millennium Project, directed by the globe-trotting American economist Jeffrey Sachs, and a 2005 report by the Commission for Africa, chaired by then-Prime Minister Tony Blair of Britain) that provide the theoretical and evidentiary basis for this new era of aid. These reports buttress the aid optimism that is now the political consensus in donor countries, and they seek to turn back a tide of literature that, beginning in the 1990s, has questioned the impact of aid on poverty reduction.

But most analysts on the continent do not share donor nations' optimism that a big push in aid will make a big difference in the lives of poor Africans. It is hard to find a single African nongovernmental organization that is actively campaigning for aid increases, while many explicitly reject the idea that huge increases in assistance are the way to achieve growth and development.

In a 2005 literature review, Moses Isooba of Uganda's Community Development Resource Network found that "a majority of civil society actors in Africa see aid as a fundamental cause of Africa's deepening poverty." He went on to acknowledge that foreign assistance can make "a lasting difference in helping people to lift themselves out of poverty," but he called for a radical rethinking regarding the purpose and nature of aid giving. Charles Lwanga-Ntale of Development Research and Training, another Ugandan NGO, has observed "almost unanimous pessimism among African civil society and academia about the unworkable nature of aid, given the way in which it is structured and delivered."

According to Siapha Kamara of the Social Enterprise Development Foundation of West Africa: "Official Africa tends to be more enthusiastic about the anticipated increase in international aid than civil society . . . . The more African governments are dependent on international aid, the less ordinary citizens such as farmers, workers, teachers, or nurses have a meaningful say in politics and economic policies."

Good, Bad, Ugly

Why should so many experts in Africa question the good that aid is doing their countries? Because, while most people in rich countries consider aid to be a simple act of generosity, Africans understand it is far more complex.

To get a clearer picture of what is happening, it helps to distinguish among the various effects of foreign aid in Africa. One category is direct impacts. These are easiest to measure, and they are the ones about which we hear the most in the media—how many people have been vaccinated, how many schools have been built, and so on. Direct impacts also include less publicized and often harmful side effects such as, for example, the displacement of people by large projects like dams or mines.

A second type of impact is indirect macroeconomic consequences. Large inflows of foreign money affect prices and incentives, and the effects can be damaging to poor people if me inflows are not managed well. For example, increases in aid to Tanzania in the late 1990s led to inflation, which in turn led authorities to tighten credit, which meant private firms found it harder to expand. The syndrome that economists call Dutch Disease is a potentially serious problem for African aid recipients. When a country's exchange rate is allowed to fluctuate, large aid inflows strengthen the national currency, which makes exports less competitive and imports cheaper. As a result, people depending on export industries suffer, as do domestic producers that compete with imports.

Constituting a third and highly controversial category are the impacts of aid conditionality. Official development assistance provided by multilateral institutions and foreign governments often comes with conditions attached, and these in effect dictate policy making. These policy prescriptions have not always been helpful. For example, international demands during economic downturns for reduced deficits and increased interest rates have reflected the policies that many developed countries, with the sovereignty to make their own decisions, typically avoid.

But even more problematic than the policies promoted by donors is a fourth impact of aid—its effect on the relationship between governments and the governed. It is generally agreed that African governments' shortcomings in accountability and effectiveness over recent decades have been a major factor in the region's low growth and insignificant poverty reduction. What is less discussed, but is becoming increasingly clear, is that dependency on aid from foreign donors has undermined development of the basic institutions needed to govern and the vital link of accountability between state and citizen.

In Mali, a recent study by Isaline Bergamaschi found that, as donors' influence over policy has grown, the government's will and capacity to take the lead and manage the aid relationship has declined. "If the current political situation seems characterized by a certain degree of inertia, a lack of development strategy, weak capacities, and compliance with donors," wrote Bergamaschi, "it can only be understood as the result of the weakening of the state and donor entanglement in national institutions and politics, and several decades of aid dependence." Likewise, observers have described Ghana's federal budget as a façade, aimed at satisfying aid donors rather than serving as a genuine and thought-through spending plan.

The effect of such dependency has been to retard African civic development in fundamental and long-lasting ways. It is what Kamara was referring to when he talked about ordinary people not having a meaningful say in decisions about how their countries are run.

Optimists and Pessimists

In response to gradually building pressure around the globe for more aid, the Group of Eight industrial nations in July 2005 met in Scotland and released a communiqué promising substantially more assistance, though not all that was being demanded. On top of an agreement to forgive large amounts of debt, the G-8 members pledged $50 billion (some of it previously announced) in aid to developing nations by 2010, of which half would go to Africa.

A spokesman for Oxfam International, a leading British NGO, commented at the time that "The G-8's aid increase could save the lives of 5 million children by 2010—but 50 million children's lives will still be lost because the G-8 didn't go as far as they should have done. If the $50 billion increase had kicked in immediately, it could have lifted 300 million people out of poverty in the next five years."

This kind of claim is common on the aid campaigning circuit. Campaigners need to make clear statements about the impacts of policies. But even allowing for the fact that mega-calculations will always be more than slightly arbitrary, yet are still important to convey the magnitude of what is at stake, this statement was highly misleading. Why? Because it was made on the basis of a very lopsided analysis, which looks only at the most direct and beneficial outcomes of aid.

If one considers only the positive column on the balance sheet, ignoring all the damaging consequences of aid, it is certainly possible that, if spent well, aid money could have the kinds of benefits alluded to. Aid spent well can put children through school, build infrastructure, and save lives.

But what about all the other impacts? What about the possibly harmful effects on exchange rates and prices, with the serious consequences these might have on workers and consumers? What about the long-term consequences of consistently immature and unaccountable state institutions? Where are these impacts taken into account when we calculate millions of lives saved per billions of aid dollars spent?

At the other extreme in debates about aid to Africa are the aid pessimists. The economist Dambisa Moyo is currently the most notable of these, having attracted wide attention with her 2009 book *Dead Aid: Why Aid Is Not Working and How There Is Another Way for Africa*. Moyo's critique of aid dependency is valid. She is right about the harm done to the development of effective and accountable governance in Africa by high levels of government-to-government aid. But hers is not a serious analytical study. It is an anti-aid polemic of a sort common in the conservative media of the United States, where the only facts cited are ones that bolster a case, and where exaggeration is considered par for the course.

Rather than accepting simplistic notions—that more aid equals less poverty, or that aid only and always increases poverty—we need to look at the evidence. All the evidence. In contrast to aid optimists and aid pessimists, who selectively use evidence either to support or to dismiss aid, we need to recognize that the impacts of aid are complex. Only when we assess these effects dispassionately and systematically can we have any real expectation of making a positive and sustained impact on human rights, development, and poverty reduction in Africa.

Aid Realism

This approach can be termed aid realism. Aid realism means not getting swept away by trie ethical clamor to "do something" when a proper analysis shows that what is being done is ineffective or harmful. And it means not bowing to an ideological anti-aid position in the face of the rights and urgent needs of millions of people. It means carefully analyzing the overall impact of foreign aid in African nations—first, to see how aid in itself can be improved, and, second,

to question its importance in relation to other policies and factors that influence development and poverty reduction in the region.

Such an analysis emphatically does not lead to the conclusion that the West should leave Africa alone. African civil society, while heavily critical of foreign assistance, is not sitting on its haunches in despair, and neither should anyone else. There are many positive measures that rich countries should take right now to help Africans reduce poverty and improve human rights.

For example, far more money flows out of the continent each year than arrives there in aid, but where are the campaigns to stem illegal capital flows via tax havens? Likewise, rich countries need to overhaul rules on international property rights and foreign investment. They should act on climate change, and invest more in transferable technology. They should better regulate an arms trade that causes turmoil in Africa. They should do many things they are not doing now.

In fact, it will be almost impossible for African states to reduce their reliance on aid without the international community's adopting a range of supporting measures. If the first reason to stop campaigning for aid increases is that aid may be doing more harm than good in some countries, the second is that all the emphasis on aid is obscuring more important policies that the West should be adopting to help Africans escape poverty.

The dominance of aid in the West's thinking about Africa is one of the reasons that other, more important, actions are not taken. Rich-country leaders are not feeling enough political pressure to make the important changes. Aid is easier—never mind all the problems it brings with it—and it benefits donors.

After all, geopolitical considerations, not analyses of poverty, have governed most donor choices about aid spending. Assistance to Africa swelled during the cold war and then declined in the 1990s, when poverty on the continent was increasing sharply. Now, in the context of a global war on terrorism, donor nations—including particularly the United States—again want to use aid to influence the politics of other countries. But aid is not always good for the recipient nations' citizens and institutions.

Decades of Dependency

Dependency is the one issue that, more than any other, separates the current period from previous episodes of aid enthusiasm. Aid dependency can be measured by looking at aid as a percentage of a recipient country's GDP, and seeing how that ratio changes over time. When official development assistance started in the 1960s, it accounted for 2.3 percent of African GDP, similar to the proportion in South Asia (home to large aid recipients like India and Bangladesh).

What has happened since is instructive. While aid to South Asia has steadily declined, and now makes up around

1 percent of GDP, aid to Africa has trended the other way, skyrocketing in the 1980s and hardly falling since. It now averages around 9 percent of GDP across Africa (excluding South Africa and Nigeria), with many countries receiving much more than that.

Since the turn of the millennium, when this new era of aid began, aid increases have been directed not to countries hoping for a boost to help them out of short-term trouble, but to countries now severely dependent on aid. When we look at aid levels in the rest of the developing world, the contrast is stark. Only a handful of countries scattered elsewhere across the globe, such as Nicaragua and Haiti and the small islands of Oceania, come close to the type of aid dependence seen in Africa. Vietnam, which has seen aid rise significantly since the 1980s, still relies on it for only 4 percent or less of its GDP. Aid to poor countries in the Americas has progressively shrunk from 0.7 percent of GDP in the 1960s to under 0.3 percent today.

It is not that no other countries have ever received large amounts of aid before. The key factor is that, in Africa, very high aid receipts have now lasted for decades and have become the norm. Never has any group of countries been so dependent on foreign aid for their basic functioning, for so long. There is a big difference between receiving aid as a welcome support and needing it as a fundamental part of the national budget.

Dependence on foreign governments for financial assistance has undermined development efforts in Africa, and it will continue to do so despite the modern (and laudable) emphasis on "good governance" and "country ownership." Although aid dependency has drawn considerable comment both in Africa and among the rich nations, the fretting has had virtually no impact on donor policy. Instead, the trend continues—and it will get worse if promised aid increases actually do kick in. While the rest of the world (with some exceptions) appears to be moving on from aid, Africa is getting more and more aid-dependent.

Government-to-government aid will always have an important supporting role, a role it has played with occasional success over the years. In some countries, depending on their economic and political contexts, aid increases may be appropriate and helpful. But most countries in Africa, rather than seeking more aid, should be reducing the amount they accept. Why? Because when the whole range of aid's impacts are taken into account, it becomes clear that aid at present levels is hindering rather than helping many countries' development prospects.

Less Aid, More Help

The biggest headline from the London Group of 20 Summit in 2009 was, as usual, a huge pledge of aid (over $1 trillion, much of it double-counted) to help poor countries. And yet, for all the efforts put into "aid effectiveness," the undermining of institutions continues to be endemic in the aid relationship. A course needs to be set to reduce, rather than entrench, aid

dependency. In this regard, in response to the recent global crisis, an overhaul of the global financial system would provide a unique opportunity to undo measures that until now have prevented developing countries from maximizing their development resources.

One issue coming under increasing scrutiny, for example, is the complex global web of tax havens that serves no serious purpose for rich nations or poor, but is responsible for allowing dodgy deals, theft, and other crimes to abound. Poor African countries lose far more every year through capital flight to tax havens than they receive in aid. Plugging this leak, cracking down on corruption, and building better national financial systems could make more credit available to small and medium-sized businesses—and would also open an avenue toward reduced dependence on aid. The likelihood of such reforms has grown since the global financial crisis erupted.

Other measures that have been considered or adopted at a range of global meetings in 2009 and 2010 could have repercussions for decades to come, as the financial architecture is redrawn, and crucial issues that were previously considered off the table are suddenly on it. Reform of financial institutions such as the International Monetary Fund has been discussed for decades, but the political will to do something may finally emerge as a result of the crisis.

Aid will certainly continue to play a role in this new context, and some African countries could benefit from aid increases. Botswana is one example. It received high levels of assistance in the 1960s and 1970s (averaging 17 percent of GDP), and during that period its growth performance exceeded the growth rates of Hong Kong, Taiwan, Malaysia, and Thailand. In contrast to almost all other African countries, aid to Botswana has steadily declined over the decades. Today it receives negligible levels of assistance. Yet its economic boom has been brought to a tragic end by an AIDS pandemic that slashed life expectancy from 56 years to 35 in a decade. Botswana could use more aid again as it seeks to recover.

Other countries, however, should ideally receive less. Rwanda already funds half its government spending with aid. Rather than seeking to increase this proportion, Rwanda should set itself the goal of reducing it over time. So should other nations. Developing countries have reduced poverty when they have implemented the right policies, and when foreign governments have taken supportive measures. Aid has been at best marginal to this effort, and at worst has undermined it.

On the other hand, while government-to-government aid can have adverse effects, support for civil society and provision of global public goods, such as climate change measures and health technologies, would be a constructive use of increased aid resources. Politicians promise more aid when they do not want to make changes that are more fundamental. Now is the time for substantial reform, not for counting aid dollars.

Critical Thinking

1. Is there a "band-aid" solution in Africa? Describe what that solution is and explain how it is a "band-aid" solution.

2. Describe the types of aid to Africa.

3. Describe the problems in Africa. Are the problems unique to Africa?

4. According to the author, is withholding aid the answer? What needs to be done?

JONATHAN GLENNIE, a country representative for Christian Aid, is the author of *The Trouble with Aid: Why Less Could Mean More for Africa* (Zed Books, 2008).

It Takes the Villages

S ETH G. J ONES

I met Abdul Salam Zaeef, the Taliban ambassador to Pakistan, twice in 2009 and was quickly drawn to his unassuming demeanor and erudition. His jet-black beard and round spectacles gave him the aura of a soft-spoken professor, not a battle-hardened guerrilla fighter who had first tasted war at the age of 15. Zaeef told me about his childhood in southern Afghanistan, the Soviet invasion, his life with the Taliban, and the three years he spent in prison in Guantánamo Bay, Cuba. What was particularly striking was his contempt for the United States and what he regarded as its myopic understanding of Afghanistan. "How long has America been in Afghanistan?" Zaeef asked rhetorically. "And how much do Americans know about Afghanistan and its people? Do they understand its culture, its tribes, and its population? I am afraid they know very little."

Zaeef is largely correct. In fact, U.S. Major General Michael Flynn, deputy chief of staff for intelligence in Afghanistan, echoed this point in early 2010: "Eight years into the war in Afghanistan," Flynn wrote in a poignant unclassified paper, "the vast intelligence apparatus is unable to answer fundamental questions about the environment in which U.S. and allied forces operate and the people they seek to persuade."

Three new books provide important insights into that environment. The first is Zaeef's own *My Life with the Taliban,* which serves as a counternarrative to much of what has been written about Afghanistan since 1979. It offers a rare glimpse into the mind of a senior Taliban leader who remains sympathetic to the movement. "I pray to almighty Allah" he writes, "that I will be buried beside my heroes, brothers and friends in the Taliban cemetery."

The other two books are edited and written, respectively, by Antonio Giustozzi, a research fellow at the London School of Economics who has spent several decades working in Afghanistan. In *Decoding the New Taliban: Insights from the Afghan Field,* Giustozzi compiles essays from journalists, former government officials, aid workers, and academics to examine the nature of the insurgency. Some chapters offer refreshing new insights, especially those that deal with Helmand Province, in the country's south; Uruzgan, in the center; and the problems of eastern Afghanistan. Others, such as the chapter on Kandahar, contribute little to what has already been published. In *Empires of Mud,* Giustozzi assesses the dynamics of warlordism. The book focuses on Abdul Rashid Dostum in the north, Ismail Khan in the west, and Ahmad Shah Massoud in the Panjshir Valley.

All three books provide a nuanced micro-level view of the country. More important, they offer a chilling prognosis for those who believe that the solution to stabilizing Afghanistan will come only from the top down—by building strong central government institutions. Although creating a strong centralized state, assuming it ever happens, may help ensure long-term stability, it is not sufficient in Afghanistan. The current top-down statebuilding and counterinsurgency efforts must take place alongside bottom-up programs, such as reaching out to legitimate local leaders to enlist them in providing security and services at the village and district levels. Otherwise, the Afghan government will lose the war.

The Center Will Not Hold

Experts on state building and counterinsurgency in Afghanistan fall into two competing camps. The first believes that Afghanistan will never be stable and secure without a powerful central government capable of providing services to Afghans in all corners of the country. The other insists that Afghanistan is, and always has been, a quintessentially decentralized society, making it necessary to build local institutions to create security and stability.

Since the Bonn agreement of December 2001—which established an interim government and a commission to draft a new constitution—international efforts in Afghanistan have unfortunately focused on initiatives directed by the central government to establish security and stability. On the political front, the focus has been supporting the government of Hamid Karzai and strengthening institutions in Kabul. On the security front, the international community has built up the Afghan National Police and the Afghan National Army as bulwarks against the Taliban and other insurgent groups. Yet this effort has been unsuccessful: there are too few national security forces to protect the population, the police are legendary for their corruption and incompetence, and many rural communities do not want a strong central government presence. On the development front, the focus has been improving the central government's ability to deliver services to the population, including through such institutions as the Ministry of Rural Rehabilitation and Development. These top-down strategies reflect the conventional wisdom among many policymakers and academics, but this consensus view is misinformed.

Current international efforts to establish security and stability from the center are based on a fundamental misunderstanding of Afghanistan's culture and social structure. After all, few non-Afghan civilians ever spend time in the violent areas of eastern, southern, and western Afghanistan. And security concerns prevent far too many U.S. and NATO officials from traveling outside their bases or urban areas. Likewise, most academics cannot access rural areas central to the insurgency because these areas are deadly for Westerners. Yet the insurgency is primarily a rural one. The growing size of the international bases in Bagram, Kabul, Kandahar, and other areas is a testament to this risk aversion, which prevents foreigners from understanding rural Afghanistan and its inhabitants. This is harmful, because state building and counterinsurgency tend to be context-specific; history, culture, and social structure matter.

As Giustozzi convincingly argues, the well-intentioned proponents of the top-down model have survived for too long solely on an idealist's diet of John Locke and Immanuel Kant. "My purpose with this book," he writes in *Empires of Mud,* "is to inject a fair dose of Hobbes, Machiavelli, and Ibn Khaldun in the mix"—the latter a reference to the fourteenth-century North African historian and social commentator who developed theories of tribalism and social conflict.

Western officials seeking to stabilize Afghanistan would do well to heed his advice. They must begin by accepting that there is no optimal form of state organization and that there are not always clear-cut "best practices" for solving public administration problems. Although some tasks, such as central banking reform, are suited to technocratic tinkering by outsiders, others, such as legal reform, can be more difficult. The challenge for Washington, then, is to combine its knowledge of administrative practices with a deeper understanding of local conditions.

Beyond the State

Many Western countries are characterized by strong state institutions, in which power emanates from a central authority. But in a range of countries—including many in South Asia and Africa—the central government has historically been weak. Top-down reconstruction strategies may have been appropriate for countries such as Japan after World War II and Iraq after 2003, both of which had historically been characterized by strong centralized state institutions. But they do not work as well in countries such as Afghanistan, where power is diffuse.

David Kilcullen, who served as a senior counterinsurgency adviser to General David Petraeus in Iraq, notes in *Decoding the New Taliban* that the social structure in Pashtun areas of Afghanistan is based on what anthropologists call a "segmentary kinship system": people are divided into tribes, subtribes, clans, and other subsections based on their lineage from common male ancestors. As Zaeef argues, the identity of Afghans "lies with their tribe, their clan, their family, and their relative." It is a patently local sense of identification Tom Coghlan, a correspondent for *The Times* in London and *The Economist,* repeats this theme in his chapter of Giustozzi's book, noting that the structure of social relations in Helmand Province is premised on the qawm—a form of kinship-based solidarity that can distinguish almost any social group, from a large tribe to a small isolated village, and is used to differentiate between "us" and "them."

A tribe or subtribe in one area may be very different in its structure and political inclinations than the same tribe or subtribe in another area. In working with leaders of the Noorzai tribe in 2009 to establish local security and basic services, for example, I found significant differences in the social and cultural practices between communities in western Herat and those in southern Kandahar Province. Despite these regional variations, power tends to remain local in Pashtun areas, which is where the insurgency is largely being fought. Pashtuns may identify with their tribe, subtribe, clan, qawm, family, or village based on where they are at the time, who they are interacting with and the specific event. Pashtunwali, the Pashtun code of behavior, shapes daily life through obligations of honor, hospitality, revenge, and providing sanctuary. Jirgas and shuras—which are decision-making councils—remain instrumental at the local level, where state legal institutions are virtually nonexistent.

Martine van Bijlert, who served as a political adviser to the European Union's special representative in Afghanistan, writes that among the Pashtuns in Uruzgan, the subtribe—which can vary in size from a few hundred to thousands of people— "remains the main solidarity group, defining patterns of loyalty, conflict and obligations of patronage." She goes on to argue that subtribal affiliations have become more important since 2001 due to the absence of central government institutions. Opinion polls conducted by the Asia Foundation indicate that Afghans continue to turn to community leaders—not officials in Kabul—to solve their problems,

In the absence of strong government institutions, groups formed based on descent from a common ancestor help the Pashtuns organize economic production, preserve political order, and defend themselves against outside threats. These bonds tend to be weaker in urban areas, where central government control is stronger and where individuals may identify themselves with their city rather than their tribe. This phenomenon is clearly illustrated by the growing number of people who identify themselves as "Kabulis" because they live in Afghanistan's heterogeneous capital. (And unlike among the Pashtuns, tribal identity tends to be weaker or nonexistent among many other Afghan ethnic groups, such as the Tajiks, the Uzbeks, and the Hazaras.)

In Pashtun areas where tribal and subtribal relationships remain strong, they are not the only force governing local politics. Additional social structures have evolved over the past several decades because of war, drought, migration, sedentarization, and other factors. As a result, a range of other identities can transcend tribal structures, such as identities based on reputations earned during the anti-Soviet jihad, land ownership, or wealth acquired through licit or illicit activity (such as road taxes or the drug trade). In such an environment, outsiders—especially foreign soldiers—have a limited ability to shape local politics.

The insurgency takes advantage of this situation. It is composed of a loose amalgam of groups, such as the Taliban, allied tribes and subtribes, drug traffickers and other criminals, local powerbrokers, and state sponsors such as Iran and Pakistan. How these groups come together varies considerably from village to village. In parts of Khost Province, for example, the insurgency includes members of the Haqqani network, Zadran subtribes, timber traders, and al Qaeda operatives. In some areas of Helmand, the insurgency includes Taliban fighters, Ishaqzai tribal leaders, and poppy traffickers. A failure to understand these nuances can be fatal to counterinsurgency efforts, especially because the Taliban and other insurgent groups have developed their own local strategies for co-opting or coercing existing tribal and other local networks.

The Prince of Kabul

One of the most significant contributions of all three books is their insights into the modus operandi of the insurgency. Zaeef offers a particularly interesting discussion of the Taliban's origins and the group's effectiveness in working with locals. In 1994, state authority had collapsed, and governance was fractured among a range of warlords and local commanders. A network of mullahs in southern Afghanistan decided to take action. "The founding meeting of what became known as 'the Taliban(TM)'" Zaeef writes, "was held in the late autumn of 1994." Zaeef was present with a number of religious leaders and local commanders, including Mullah Muhammad Omar, who became the Taliban's leader. "Each man swore on the Qur'an to stand by [Mullah Omar], and to fight against corruption and the criminals."

The Taliban moved quickly, beginning in Kandahar Province. They co-opted some groups through bribery and promises of power sharing, such as Mullah Naqib's Alikozai tribe, which agreed to ally with the Taliban and hand over the city of Kandahar. When the Taliban failed to co-opt others, such as fighters loyal to Commander Saleh, who operates along the Kandahar-Kabul highway, Taliban forces defeated them on the battlefield. These negotiations and battlefield successes had a domino effect, and before long, a growing number of local groups had allied themselves with the Taliban. After establishing control in an area, Taliban leaders would set up sharia courts in which their handpicked judges adjudicated local disputes.

As Giustozzi explains in *Empires of Mud,* the Taliban continued to use this bottom-up strategy when they expanded beyond the south beginning in 1995. In western Afghanistan, for instance, the Taliban allied with the warlord Dostum in

order to defeat Ismail Khan's militia in Herat Province. In eastern Afghanistan, the Taliban co-opted a range of local Pashtun tribes, subtribes, and powerbrokers. The large Suleiman Khel tribe in Paktika asked the Taliban to take over the province's capital, Sharan, after hearing they had conquered nearby Ghazni.

Today, Taliban leaders have adopted a similar approach in fighting the Karzai government and U.S. and NATO forces. As in the 1990s, they aim to co-opt or coerce local leaders and their networks by capitalizing on grievances against the government or international forces, offering money, and conducting targeted assassinations of those they regard as anti-Taliban collaborators. To more effectively reach out to the population, the Taliban often appoint commanders who come from local subtribes or clans. They frequently reach out to tribes and other local communities that have been marginalized by those favored by the government, such as the Popalzais and the Barakzais.

Decoding the New Taliban describes this micro-level strategy in detail. Coghlan argues that in Helmand Province, Taliban officials secured the loyalty of a range of Ishaqzai leaders marginalized by Kabul, well as that of some Kakars and Hotaks. The government's appointment of Alizai leaders to many of the district governor positions, Noorzais to police chief posts, and Alikozais and others to key intelligence positions appears to have angered their Ishaqzai rivals, exacerbated the tribal fissures in the area, and facilitated the co-optation of marginalized tribes by the Taliban.

The Taliban is not the only insurgent group that effectively uses local networks to its advantage. One of the most significant is the Haqqani network, which was established by the legendary mujahideen commander and former CIA ally Jalaluddin Haqqani and now operates in eastern Afghanistan. As Thomas Ruttig explains in *Decoding the New Taliban,* one of the Haqqani network's strongest support bases is the Mezi subtribe of the Zadrans, who live along the Afghan-Pakistani border. The Haqqani network also co-opted a range of Kuchis, who are nomadic herdsmen, in Paktia and Khost and developed a close relationship with Ahmadzai subtribes across the border in Pakistan.

There is a common thread in many of these accounts: the Taliban and other insurgent groups have recognized the local nature of politics in Afghanistan and have developed a local strategy—combining ruthlessness with cunning diplomacy. The Afghan government and U.S. and NATO forces, meanwhile, have largely been missing at the local level.

All Politics Is Local

There is an urgent need to refine the international community's state-building and counterinsurgency efforts in response to the Taliban's bottom-up strategy.

One key area is security. During Afghanistan's most recent stable period, that of the Musahiban dynasty (1929–78), the Afghan rulers Nadir Shah, Zahir Shah, and Daoud Khan—who established a republic in 1973—used a combination of centralized and decentralized strategies that are worth emulating today. National forces established security in urban areas and along key roads, and local communities established security in rural areas with Kabul's blessing and aid. In Pashtun areas, locals used traditional police forces, such as arbakai, and other small village-level police forces under the control of recognized local institutions, such as Jirgas or shuras.

These were not militias, in the sense of large offensive forces under the command of warlords, which tend to be used today in the Tajik and Uzbek areas of northern and western Afghanistan. "In the King's time it was an honor to be a member of an arbakai," a tribal leader in eastern Afghanistan proudly told Ruttig. Then, the central government did not establish a permanent security presence in many rural areas, especially Pashtun ones, nor did locals generally want the government to play that role. While traveling through rural Pashtun areas over the past year, I discovered that many of these traditional policing institutions still exist, although some have been co-opted by the Taliban. If leveraged by the Afghan government, they could help trigger a revolt against the Taliban in rural areas. This would require identifying those local communities already resisting the Taliban; providing training, monitoring, and equipment to facilitate their resistance; and then trying to turn others against the Taliban.

U.S. and NATO forces must do a better job of capitalizing on popular grievances against the Taliban, who are much weaker than is generally recognized: most Afghans do not subscribe to their religious zealotry. Although Taliban leaders are influenced by the Deobandi movement—an Islamic school of thought that originated in India in 1866—their brand of Islam would not be recognizable to the Deobandi movement's founders. And despite popular misconceptions, Taliban commanders tend to be even more corrupt than Afghan government officials. As the former ABC News reporter Gretchen Peters describes in a chapter of *Decoding the New Taliban,* a significant portion of the Taliban's funding comes from taxes collected from poppy farmers, levies imposed on drug shipments, and kidnapping ransoms. Public opinion polls continue to show low levels of support for the Taliban, even compared to the Afghan government. In a January 2010 poll conducted by ABC News and other organizations, 90 percent of the Afghans polled said they supported the government, whereas only six percent claimed to support the Taliban.

The growing number of local tribes and communities resisting the insurgency is evidence of the Taliban's waning popularity. They range from the Noorzais, the Achakzais, and the Alikozais in the west and south to the Shinwaris, the Kharotis, and the Zadrans in the east. Afghan, U.S., and NATO forces have taken advantage of some of these opportunities through the Local Defense Initiative, a new program that supports village-level community police by providing training, radios, and uniforms.

U.S. forces have opted not to pay these local police, based on the belief that individuals should be motivated to work for their communities and not outsiders. Instead, the Afghan government and international organizations have provided development projects to participating communities. They have also established a quick-reaction force to assist local communities that come under attack from the Taliban and other insurgents. In southern Afghanistan, the program has been particularly successful in helping local leaders protect their populations and draw them away from the Taliban.

These local efforts can also have a positive impact on the defection of mid- and lower-level insurgents, which is more commonly called "reintegration." As Coghlan explains, most insurgents are not ideologically committed. Rather, they are motivated by tribal or subtribal friction, grievances against the Afghan government or U.S. and NATO forces, money, or coercion by insurgent leaders. Battlefield successes against the insurgency, sustainable development, and effective cooperation with local communities can significantly improve the chances of defection. As van Bijlert points out in *Decoding the New Taliban,* the local nature of power in Afghanistan makes the Taliban highly vulnerable to defection and double-dealing. I witnessed this firsthand in southern and western Afghanistan in 2009: Villages that decided to resist the Taliban gave insurgent sympathizers in their communities a stark choice—leave the area or give up. In a country where loyalty and group solidarity are fundamental to daily life, community pressure can be a powerful weapon.

Long Live the King

When I last spoke with Zaeef, he remained bewildered by the international community's lack of understanding of rural Afghanistan. Kabul, with its restaurants that cater to Western guests and its modern indoor shopping mall with escalators and glass elevators, is vastly different from the rural areas where the insurgency is being waged. He reminded me that a better understanding of Afghanistan would help establish peace. Rural communities have been protecting their villages for centuries and can do it better than the Afghan government or international forces.

In his conclusion to *Empires of Mud,* Giustozzi writes that a durable peace will likely require a careful combination of top-down institutionalization and bottom-up co-optation of local leaders. Focusing only on the former has failed to help the Afghan population, which continues to feel deeply insecure because of insurgent and criminal activity. Moreover, there has been—and will likely continue to be—an insufficient number of U.S., NATO, and Afghan national forces to protect the local population in rural areas. But that is all right, since many rural Afghans do not want a permanent central government presence in their villages; they want to police their own communities.

Some worry that empowering local leaders may help the Afghan government and the international community achieve short-term goals but will undermine stability in the long run by fragmenting authority. This is an academic debate. Afghan social and cultural realities make it impossible to neglect local leaders, since they hold much of the power today.

The old monarchy's model is useful for today's Afghanistan. It combined top-down efforts from the central government in urban areas with bottom-up efforts to engage tribes and other communities in rural areas. The central government has an important role to play. National army and police forces can be critical in crushing revolts, conducting offensive actions against militants, and helping adjudicate tribal disputes when they occur. But the local nature of power in the country makes it virtually impossible to build a strong central government capable of establishing security and delivering services in much of rural Afghanistan—at least over the next several decades. Afghans have successfully adopted this model in the past, and they can do so again today.

Critical Thinking

1. According to the author, what strategy is not working in Afghanistan? Why?
2. Describe the unit of organization in Afghanistan.
3. According to the author, what are the reasons to be hopeful that the Taliban's popularity is waning?

SETH G. JONES is a Senior Political Scientist at the RAND Corporation and the author oiln the Graveyard of Empires: Americas War in Afghanistan. In 2009, he served as a Plans Officer and Adviser to the Commanding General of U.S. Special Operations Forces in Afghanistan.

From *Foreign Affairs*, vol. 89, issue 3, May/June 2010, pp. 120–127. Copyright © 2010 by Council on Foreign Relations, Inc. Reprinted by permission of Foreign Affairs. www.ForeignAffairs.com

The New Cocaine Cowboys

How to defeat mexico's drug cartels.

ROBERT C. BONNER

The recent headlines from Mexico are disturbing: U.S. consular official gunned down in broad daylight; Rancher murdered by Mexican drug smuggler; Bomb tossed at U.S. consulate in Nuevo Laredo. This wave of violence is eerily reminiscent of the carnage that plagued Colombia 20 years ago, and it is getting Washington's attention.

Mexico is in the throes of a battle against powerful drug cartels, the outcome of which will determine who controls the country's law enforcement, judicial, and political institutions. It will decide whether the state will destroy the cartels and put an end to the culture of impunity they have created. Mexico could become a first—world country one day, but it will never achieve that status until it breaks the grip these criminal organizations have over all levels of government and strengthens its law enforcement and judicial institutions. It cannot do one without doing the other.

Destroying the drug cartels is not an impossible task. Two decades ago, Colombia was faced with a similar—and in many ways more daunting—struggle. In the early 1990s, many Colombians, including police officers, judges, presidential candidates, and journalists, were assassinated by the most powerful and fearsome drug—trafficking organizations the world has ever seen: the Cali and Medellin cartels. Yet within a decade, the Colombian government defeated them, with Washington's help. The United States played a vital role in supporting the Colombian government, and it should do the same for Mexico.

The stakes in Mexico are high. If the cartels win, these criminal enterprises will continue to operate outside the state and the rule of law, undermining Mexico's democracy. The outcome matters for the United States as well—if the drug cartels succeed, the United States will share a 2,000—mile border with a narcostate controlled by powerful transnational drug cartels that threaten the stability of Central and South America.

The Mexican Connection

Over the last two decades, Mexican drug cartels have acquired unprecedented power to corrupt and intimidate government officials and civilians. Three factors account for their rise: preexisting corruption, the inability of weak law enforcement institutions to counter them, and the demand for illegal drugs in the United States.

Drug trafficking and cross-border smuggling certainly existed in Mexico before the 1980s, but the trade was chiefly confined to marijuana and small quantities of heroin and involved a large number of small trafficking organizations. Almost no cocaine was smuggled through Mexico into the United States before 1984; the vast majority of illegal shipments came through the Bahamas or directly from Colombia to Florida on propeller planes. This changed in the mid-1980s, after the United States shut down the direct flow of cocaine into southern Florida and the Bahamas and made it increasingly difficult to smuggle large amounts of cocaine through the Caribbean. In reaction to Washington's increasingly successful interdiction strategy, the Colombian cartels forged a connection with major Mexican trafficking organizations. They dispatched a representative to Mexico, Juan Ramón Matta Ballasteros, who came to an agreement with Mexican drug-trafficking organizations in 1984. In exchange for $1,000 per kilogram of cocaine, the Mexican trafficking organizations would smuggle Colombian cocaine into the United States.

Within a few years, 80–90 percent of the cocaine being smuggled into the United States—hundreds of metric tons annually—was moving through Mexico. After the Mexican connection was forged, Colombian propeller planes—with extra fuel tanks and stripped of seats—began landing on remote airstrips in northern Mexico, carrying 600–800 kilos of cocaine per flight. The smuggling business added greatly to the overall revenues of the major Mexican trafficking organizations. As a result, powerful, more consolidated drug cartels began to emerge in Mexico, including the Gulf, Juárez, Sinaloa, and Tijuana cartels.

At first, the Mexican cartels acted primarily as transporters for the Colombian cartels and were paid in cash. But by the early 1990s, the Colombian cartels were paying them in powder cocaine, which led the Mexican trafficking organizations to create their own distribution networks in the United States and within Mexico, eventually eclipsing the Colombians' influence. Over the last two decades, these organizations have evolved into vertically integrated, multinational criminal groups. They are headquartered in Mexico, but they have distribution arms in over 200 cities throughout the United States—from Sacramento to Charlotte—and have established a presence in Guatemala and other Central American nations. Their major markets for cocaine are not just in the United States but also in Mexico itself and as far away as Europe. Although their primary business is cocaine and, more recently, methamphetamine, these groups also engage in other criminal activities, including human trafficking, kidnapping, and extortion.

In February 1985, when Enrique "Kiki" Camarena, a U.S. Drug Enforcement Administration agent, was kidnapped, tortured, and killed, the U.S. government began to grasp the full extent of the problem in Mexico. The Guadalajara cartel had murdered Camarena in an attempt to intimidate the United States. The DEA's investigation of the killing uncovered widespread corruption and complicity in drug trafficking at all levels of the Mexican government. A large portion of the Jalisco state police force, it turned out, was on the payroll of the Guadalajara cartel. Indeed, it was Jalisco state police officers who had abducted Camarena, at the behest of the Guadalajara cartel. The corruption extended beyond the state police and into the governor's office and even into the federal government, including the principal internal security agency, the Federal Directorate of Security. The investigation revealed that the comandantes of the Mexican Federal Judicial Police (MFJP), who at the time oversaw all federal police in each state, had been bought off by the drug cartels; comandante positions in the northern Mexican states were going for several million dollars each. The "bagman" was a senior official in the attorney general's office.

In 1986, the Mexican government took action against the Guadalajara cartel, arresting and imprisoning its leaders, Rafael Caro Quintero, Ernesto Fonseca Carillo, and, eventually, Miguel Félix Gallardo. The security directorate was dissolved, and ultimately there was an attempt to create a new federal police agency to replace the disgraced and corrupt MFJP. This effort at reform failed, however, and the Gulf, Juárez, Sinaloa, and Tijuana cartels remained intact.

The problem had become exponentially worse by the 1990s, as the major trafficking organizations began reaping enormous profits from the cocaine trade. Mexico's one-party political system, which was dominated by the Institutional Revolutionary Party (PRI) for 70 years, permitted these major drug cartels to increase their influence and power, This was partially due to entrenched corruption and the government's lack of accountability. But it was also the result of weak law enforcement agencies, which could not take effective action against major cartel leaders even when the political will to do so existed.

The cartels largely controlled the state and municipal police, and the federal police lacked the skills and authority to carry out effective investigations; they were also compromised by the cartels, which often paid for their housing and supplemented their incomes. In more than one instance, cartel kingpins were tipped off before the federal police could arrest them. Judicial and penal officials, too, were subject to outright bribery, as evidenced by the 2001 jailbreak of Joaquín "El Chapo" Guzman, the head of the Sinaloa cartel, who paid off several prison guards to facilitate his escape.

During the 1990s, the governments of Carlos Salinas and Ernesto Zedillo made sporadic attempts to rein in the drug cartels, but they lacked any systematic strategy or sustained effort. To his credit, Zedillo tried to dismantle the Tijuana cartel, an endeavor that involved forming a joint task force with the DEA and U.S. Customs. He also created a national drug-control center with a powerful director to serve as a counterpart to the U.S. drug czar and oversee a federal crackdown. However, not long thereafter, in 1997, evidence was uncovered that the Mexican drug czar, Jesús Gutiérrez Rebollo, was on the payroll of the Juárez cartel.

The Pain in Juarez

A major turning point came in 2000, when the PRI lost power and Vicente Fox of the National Action Party, or PAN, became president. The end of one-party rule was profoundly important for Mexico's evolution toward true democracy, and it also signaled a new era for the drug cartels. The acquiescence of the federal government could no longer be taken for granted in a democratic state in which most of the public abhorred the drug cartels and the culture of impunity.

As Shannon O'Neil pointed out in the July/August 2009 issue of this magazine, the end of one-party rule set in motion a seismic political shift that undermined the cartels' cozy relationship with the government and their ability to intimidate its officials. Indeed, things began to change, albeit slowly, under Fox: he took initial steps to clean up the customs service and attempted to reform the federal police, and he dispatched the Mexican military to Nuevo Laredo in 2005 when the Gulf cartel, through its paramilitary assassins, the Zetas, threatened to take total control of the city. Most important, there was a sharp increase in extraditions of drug traffickers to the United States. This trend has accelerated under Felipe Calderón, who became president in December 2006. Before Fox, there had been only six extraditions of Mexican citizens to the United States ever; during Fox's six-year tenure, there were 133. And since Calderón came to power, there have been 144.

The government's campaign escalated dramatically after Calderón took office. Consistent with his campaign pledges, he released a national development plan declaring that his administration's main goal was to establish the rule of law by confronting organized crime and corruption. Calderón has relied heavily on the Mexican military, one of the country's few reliable institutions, to combat the drug cartels. One of his first moves as president was to deploy 6,500 Mexican army troops to his home state of Michoacán to curb the violence caused by dueling drug cartels there. More than 45,000 soldiers are currently dedicated to enforcing Calderóne anticartel policy, many of whom are stationed in Ciudad Juárez, the site of one of the most violent confrontations between rival cartels.

Calderóne initiatives have begun to destabilize the cartels, and many cartel leaders are now on the run. In December 2009, the Mexican navy—the country's least corrupt government institution—acting on intelligence, surrounded one of the cartels' kingpins, Arturo Bertrán Leyva, and killed him and a number of his bodyguards in a shootout in Cuernavaca, south of Mexico City. More recently, units of the newly constituted Mexican Federal Police captured Teodoro García Simental, the kingpin who had taken over the Tijuana cartel after the Mexican government captured the Arellano Félix brothers, the cartel's former leaders, and crippled their criminal network. Calderón has also taken action to tighten security at Mexican ports and along the country's southern border in order to disrupt the inflow of cocaine, weapons, and drug precursor chemicals. Although much remains to be done, Mexican authorities have seized over 80 metric tons of cocaine since Calderón took office. The recent seizures of four tons of pseudoephedrine, a precursor chemical used to make methamphetamine, and nearly a ton of cocaine at the ports of Veracruz and Manzanillo are evidence of Mexico's enhanced interdiction efforts.

Even so, the number of drug-related homicides has risen in the last few years. An estimated 22,000 drug-related murders have occurred since Calderón took office, with nearly 9,000 in 2009 alone. This has led some to conclude that violence in Mexico is out of control. Others have suggested that the country is on the verge of becoming a "failed state" (or, in the words of a 2008 U.S. military report, at risk of "rapid and sudden collapse"). The former is a gross exaggeration, and the latter is simply untrue.

Ninety percent of the homicides have involved members of one drug cartel killing members of another. Most of the rest have been heavily armed cartel members murdering Mexican soldiers or police. Some innocent bystanders have been killed, but they represent a small fraction of the total. Violence in Mexico today is nothing like the carnage that plagued Colombia in the late 1980s and 1990s. Last year, Chihuahua, the state in which Juárez is located, had a homicide rate of 143 per 100,000—one of the worst in the Western Hemisphere, to be sure, yet less than one-third the rate in Medellin during the last years of Pablo Escobar and the Medellin cartel in the early 1990s. Indeed, Mexico's national homicide rate last year was ten for every 100,000 people, far lower than Brazil's (25) and Venezuela's (48). Mexico may be violent, but it is not out of control.

Nor is Mexico a failed state. Most of the drug-related homicides have occurred in just six of Mexico's 32 states, and the majority of them have been in the state of Chihuahua. The increase in the number of drug-related homicides, although unfortunate, is a sign of progress: a consequence, in part, of government actions that are destabilizing the drug cartels and denying them access to areas in which they used to operate with complete impunity. As a result, the cartels are starting to fight one another. The carnage in Juárez, for example, is largely the result of fighting between the local Juárez cartel and the Sinaloa cartel for control of the Juárez-Chihuahua corridor, one of the primary smuggling routes into the United States. (There was a similar, but worse, increase in violence in Colombia during the death throes of the cartels there.) Once these cartels are broken, public safety and security will follow, as was the case in Colombia. One need only look at Medellin today.

From Medellin to Michoacan

The situation Mexico faces today is in many ways similar to the one that Colombia confronted 20 years ago. In 1990, two enormously powerful Colombian drug cartels—in Cali and Medellin—dominated the world cocaine trade. Both cartels were made up of three to four large drug—trafficking organizations, each with its own kingpin and organizational structure. The cartels hid their cocaine labs in remote and jungle regions, where Marxist insurgents provided them cover; in exchange, rebel groups such as the Revolutionary Armed Forces of Colombia, or farc, derived much of their funding from the cartels. In urban areas, the cartels worked by bribing police, politicians, and judges. Those who could not be bribed were intimidated; the cartels threatened to kill them and their families, and often they did. The phrase in Spanish is *plata o plomo?*—"money or lead?"

Two decades ago, the challenges faced by the Colombian government, even with U.S. support, seemed insurmountable. Colombia was on the verge of failure due to the two quasi-military drug cartels, spiraling rates of political violence, criminality, and an extraordinarily high national homicide rate of 80 per 100,000—eight times Mexico's current rate. Today, neither cartel poses a threat to the Colombian state; both are gone.

There are several lessons to be drawn from Colombia's successful campaign. First, since the cartels were vertically integrated, transnational organizations, the campaign against them required the involvement of more than just one country. A multinational approach, with strong support and assistance from the United States, was necessary. The provision of U.S. technical and operational assistance to the Colombian government, in particular the Colombian National Police and the Colombian military, was crucial. Likewise, Mexico's cartels cannot be eliminated unless they are attacked from both within and outside the country.

Second, the goal must be clear. In Colombia, the objective was to dismantle and destroy the Cali and Medellin cartels—not to prevent drugs from being smuggled into the United States or to end their consumption. Indeed, there are still drug traffickers in Colombia, and cocaine is still produced there, but compared with the old cartels, the trafficking groups there today are smaller, more fragmented, and far less powerful—and, most important, they no longer pose a threat to Colombian national security. From a law enforcement perspective, the problem in Colombia today is manageable. The United States must accept that the goal in Mexico is similar: the destruction of the large Mexican cartels, nothing more and nothing less.

Third, a divide-and-conquer strategy can be effective. It worked in Colombia, and it can work in Mexico. The Colombian government wisely chose to attack one cartel at a time, rather than fighting a two—front war. The Medellin cartel was obliterated by the end of 1993, and the coup de grâce was the killing of Escobar, a key figure in the tel. The Colombian government then its forces against the Cali cartel, unraveled after the capture of the Orejuela brothers and the Urdinola brothers and the killing of Jose Bantacruz Londoño, all of which was accomplished by the end of 1996. In less than a decade, the Cali and Medellin cartels, two of the most powerful criminal organizations the world has ever seen, were destroyed. The Colombian government's more recent successes against armed insurgent groups would not have been possible had the cartels not first been defeated.

Fourth, the United States and Mexico must rely on a proven strategy, such as the "kingpin strategy," which was used to defeat the Colombian cartels. Success in Colombia hinged on identifying, locating, and capturing the kingpins and key lieutenants of the organizations that made up the Cali and Medellin cartels and then imprisoning them in secure facilities. (Some were killed resisting arrest.) The strategy required attacking every vulnerability of the trafficking organizations at every step of the process: disrupting the cartels' flows of money and weapons, their ability to acquire drugs and drug precursor chemicals, and their distribution networks, while fully exploiting their communications vulnerabilities. The goal was to weaken these criminal organizations to the point where their leaders and potential future leaders could be captured and removed.

Contrary to popular belief, not anyone can effectively run a large, multinational drug-trafficking organization. Removing the kingpin and his potential successors is the death knell for such organizations. In Colombia, the extradition to the United States of cartel leaders and potential leaders was therefore an indispensible part of the kingpin strategy. Focusing the efforts of various U.S. agencies on the same targets made the operations more effective, and using polygraph tests and other anticorruption measures to vet Colombian law enforcement officers helped ensure that the U.S. intelligence shared with Colombian counterparts was not compromised.

Fifth, law enforcement and judicial institutions must be aggressively reformed. Long-term success in Colombia required strengthening the capacity and integrity of the country's policing, prosecutorial, and judicial institutions, allowing criminals to be captured, prosecuted, and penalized. Before these reforms, Colombian judges lived in fear, and hundreds of investigative magistrates were killed when they did not succumb to bribery. With significant assistance from Washington, Mexico, like Colombia, could better protect its judges, prosecutors, and witnesses from corruption and intimidation. Moreover, the Colombian National Police worked to hire better-vetted and better-educated officers, pay them more, rotate personnel, and introduce the concept of internal-affairs investigations. Colombian laws were changed to permit prosecution for conspiracy and money laundering and to allow the use of informants and lawful wiretapping to produce evidence usable in court.

Sixth, the limits on the usefulness of the military must be understood. The Colombian military played an important part in the battle against the Cali and Medellin cartels, attacking and destroying remote cocaine labs and battling farc guerrillas and other paramilitary groups in the countryside. Yet it did not play a decisive role in the defeat of the cartels—the Colombian National Police did. Militaries are ill suited to carry out the actions necessary to ultimately bring down criminal organizations. These include investigations to support prosecutions, the recruitment of informants, and the use of electronic surveillance to gather evidence.

In Mexico today, the military is taking the lead in the war against the drug cartels. They are doing so out of sheer necessity, but it is a stopgap solution. The country desperately needs to reform and overhaul its hundreds of separate state and municipal police forces. It will be several more years before the Mexican Federal Police are strong enough to take over this war from the army. And even then, the military will likely have to assist the police in confronting heavily armed paramilitary units of the cartels.

As Washington sends money south as part of the Merida Initiative, an effort to combat crime and drug trafficking in Mexico, it must be careful not to focus too much on military assistance and neglect other, more effective forms of aid that are essential to success. In Colombia, almost all the initial U.S. aid came in the form of military equipment, giving the Colombian government the erroneous impression that the cartels could be destroyed using military force alone. The United States has made the same mistake in Mexico. Virtually all of the first $300 million of Merida funding—25 percent of the total so far—went to military equipment. Some of this equipment is useful, of course, but it is more important in the long run for the United States to concentrate its assistance on the development, training, and professionalization of Mexico's law enforcement officers. At the federal level, Mexico desperately needs to create a Mexican equivalent of the FBI, together with a real anti-corruption and internal-affairs investigative capacity that can gain credibility through publicized prosecutions. At the state level, Mexico needs new police officers who are paid well enough to make them less susceptible to bribery. The best solution may be to abolish the municipal police departments altogether and have reformed state police agencies, comprised of officers trained at a national police academy, take over policing in the cities.

Finally, extradition is vital. Trial and imprisonment in the United States was the only thing that the Colombian drug traffickers truly feared. Once weakened, several cartel kingpins surrendered to Colombian authorities rather than face extradition. Although the Cali and Medellin cartels were destroyed in less than a decade, this could have been accomplished faster if costly errors, such as the temporary abolition of extraditions, had not been made along the way. (Colombian traffickers bribed Colombian lawmakers to secure passage of the extradition ban.)

Endgame

Although the Colombian drug cartels of 20 years ago were even more powerful than the Mexican cartels of today, Colombia had some advantages that Mexico does not have. Colombia is one of the oldest continuous democracies in Latin America, whereas Mexico's democracy is still evolving. Colombia has a strong central government, whereas Mexico is a federal republic, with all the complexities and fragmentation that entails. It is far easier to reform and reorganize one national police force, as was done in Colombia, than to reform and reorganize two federal, 32 state, and over 1,500 municipal police agencies, as will be necessary in Mexico.

Still, virtually all the key lessons learned from the defeat of the Colombian cartels in the 1990s are applicable to the current battle against the Mexican cartels. Mexico's government is already reforming and professionalizing its federal police. Hiring standards and vetting have improved, and some anticorruption best practices are being adopted. And at long last, Mexico will soon have a federal police authority to parallel the U.S. Border Patrol, which will permit rapid exchanges of information between the United States and Mexico and provide better border security for both nations. The Calderón government is shoring up Mexico's own porous southern border, has plans to reform and transform its customs service, and is upgrading its information technology infrastructure, which will permit intelligence sharing through secure databases.

For its part, the United States must do more to rally its own law enforcement community around a common strategy to be sure the various Washington agencies involved play their assigned roles. Specifically, the United States should use much of the remaining Merida funding to help build the capacity of the Mexican federal and state police and develop a command-and-control center for intelligence sharing and communications. Washington should also improve its efforts to stanch the flow of weapons and cash across the United States' border into Mexico. A small binational group is needed to target, coordinate, and oversee the rapid implementation of a kingpin-style strategy. And as part of a longerterm effort, both nations, but especially the United States, should seek to reduce the domestic demand for drugs through education and treatment programs.

There are less than three years left in Calderóne presidency, and victory in the war against the drug cartels may not be achieved before his term ends. (Under the Mexican constitution, presidents are limited to a single six-year term.) There is a very real risk that the Mexican public will grow weary of the violence and turn against his strategy of defeating the cartels. Indeed, the former Mexican foreign minister Jorge Castañeda has called for the government to enter into a "tacit deal" with some or all of the drug cartels, under which the government would allow them to operate their illegal businesses with impunity in exchange for curbing public violence.

The United States knows from its own experience with organized crime that such a pact would be a serious mistake. The public will never believe in the rule of law if the government itself permits certain criminal groups to operate above it. Not only would this approach cause widespread public cynicism; it would also result in the return of large-scale graft, one of the very things that Calderón is trying to eliminate. It is the government that should enforce the peace and public safety, not organized criminal enterprises.

Victory can be achieved. Mexico's drug cartels are becoming desperate. If Mexico takes the lessons of Colombia to heart and continues to show strong leadership and firm political will, it can, with U.S. assistance, rid itself of the cartels for good.

Critical Thinking

1. According to the author, what is the threat of the drug cartels in Mexico?

2. According to the author, what must be the objective in dealing with the drug cartels? Is this objective surprising? Why is this objective important?

3. What are the institutions that must be strengthened in order to deal with the drug problem?

ROBERT C. BONNER is Senior Principal of the Sentinel HS Group. He was Administrator of the U.S. Drug Enforcement Administration from 1990 to 1993 and Commissioner of U.S. Customs and Border Protection from 2001 to 2005.

From *Foreign Affairs*, vol. 89, issue 4. July/August 2010, pp. 35–47. Copyright © 2010 by Council on Foreign Relations, Inc. Reprinted by permission of Foreign Affairs. www.ForeignAffairs.com

UNIT 2

Studying Comparative Politics: Developing Theories, Culling Evidence, and Interpretation over Time

Unit Selections

Learning Outcomes

After reading this Unit, you will be able to:

- Discuss how citizen participation affects democracy.
- How is "theory" on democratization relevant to the "real world"?
- How is capitalism and democracy related?
- What does the Middle-east revolution indicate about citizen participation?
- How does the Middle-east revolution help theory-building on democratization?
- Is democracy in the western countries in jeopardy? In what ways? In what ways not?
- What does western democracies have to offer for theory-building on democratization?

Student Website

www.mhhe.com/cls

Internet References

Political Science blog of Professors Henry Farrell, Andrew Gelman, John Sides, Joshua Tucker, and Erik Voeten
www.themonkeycage.org/comparative_politics
Professor Mathew Shugart's political blog
http://fruitsandvotes.com

U nit 2 builds upon the discussion of why we compare in Unit 1. In part, it describes how theory-building is achieved, that is, it describes the process of examination and evaluation, testing and retesting, verifying sources, and collecting credible evidence in order to achieve generalizability and predictive strength. Generalizations are essential for providing baseline knowledge from which particularities are observed, described, explained, and anticipated. To concretize what this means, this unit looks into one of the oldest theoretical debates in political science: Democratic theory. We track how leading scholars ruminate about democratic theory before looking at how additional studies—on participation, mature democracies, transitioning regimes, and the relationship between capitalism and democracy—build on some of the theoretical foundations laid out.

The first article in this unit sets the tone for distinguishing between democracy as studied in political science and conventional usage. As the authors note, democracy is a term most widely used among politicians; scholars actually "hesitate" to use it "because of the "ambiguity" of the term." Nevertheless, given its popular use, the authors admonish that users clarify what it is, and is not. Importantly, at the outset, the authors point out that democracy should be clarified in terms of its concepts, procedures, and principles.

Fast-forward twenty-five years later: One of the architects of the first article provides a review of the study of democracy. His first paragraph contains several points that are noteworthy about the process of theory-building: It is based on *cases* (that is, evidence) and the *literature* (that is, scholastic writings). This underscores the essential parts of theory-building: The generalizability of theories derives from systematic scholastic examination and evaluation through evidentiary support. The author goes on to outline fifteen interesting conclusions or considerations from twenty-five years of democratic study, including an elaboration of why he considered that "civil society might have a significant role, but it would be a short-lived one."

Two subsequent articles in the unit show us what it means to do political science research: The research is situated in the debate in the literature and based on evidentiary evaluation. In this regard, Articles 10 on Middle East studies and 11 on the transitioning states of Egypt and Tunisia are useful: Both show evidence that citizen participation is fundamental to democracy; in fact, citizen mobilization was the key to unseating the previous authoritarian governments in Tunisia and Egypt. Yet, as Article 11 notes, that same participation and mobilization may threaten the institutionalization of democratic accountability in both transitioning states. Further, there is the reminder in Article 12 on advanced democracies, which points out that increasing citizen participation allows practices and procedures to evolve and, hence, promotes stability. The articles in Unit 1 of the social trouble in the advanced industrialized democracies of Great

© McGraw-Hill Companies, Inc./Jill Braaten, photographer

Britain and Norway show us what reducing or dismissing citizen participation means: It leads to potentially dangerous forms of participation to push for change. Is this what Schmitter articulated 25 years ago and reiterated recently?

Discussion and argumentation, fact-finding; and evidentiary support are the essential elements to theory-building so that the generalizable patterns that are identified withstand scrutiny and evaluation. This is the "theoretically informed" comparative study. Indeed, it is because the theoretical fundamentals are in place that subsequent articles are able to develop from this baseline to examine particularities that are observed, described, explained, and anticipated. Thus, Articles 10 and 11 note the difficulties of transitioning to democracy, while Article 12 notes the problems faced in mature democracies. Whether in transitioning regimes or mature democracies, the articles point out that viable outlets for citizen participation are key to maintaining political stability and enhancing development. And, if we think that the debate is near exhaustion, consider the "new" angle added on whether capitalism drives democracy or if democracy leads to economic development.

We will continue to assess how democratization occurs, what it takes to consolidate democracies, and what processes will enrich emergent and mature democracies. That is, theory-building is likely to continue, as it well should. Importantly, the discussion, evaluation, and testing reveals to us the problems of letting our own biases dictate who gets to participate, and how or when. In the process, we also learn a fundamental and important lesson about participation: If we provide for citizen participation, the expanded venues provide the release of any bottled up responses that may otherwise find relief through dangerous or extremist appeals. That is a generalization and baseline that will enhance political development in any country and region.

What Democracy Is . . . and Is Not

Philippe C. Schmitter and Terry Lynn Karl

For some time, the word democracy has been circulating as a debased currency in the political marketplace. Politicians with a wide range of convictions and practices strove to appropriate the label and attach it to their actions. Scholars, conversely, hesitated to use it—without adding qualifying adjectives—because of the ambiguity that surrounds it. The distinguished American political theorist Robert Dahl even tried to introduce a new term, "polyarchy," in its stead in the (vain) hope of gaining a greater measure of conceptual precision. But for better or worse, we are "stuck" with democracy as the catchword of contemporary political discourse. It is the word that resonates in people's minds and springs from their lips as they struggle for freedom and a better way of life; it is the word whose meaning we must discern if it is to be of any use in guiding political analysis and practice.

The wave of transitions away from autocratic rule that began with Portugal's "Revolution of the Carnations" in 1974 and seems to have crested with the collapse of communist regimes across Eastern Europe in 1989 has produced a welcome convergence toward [a] common definition of democracy.[1] Everywhere there has been a silent abandonment of dubious adjectives like "popular," "guided," "bourgeois," and "formal" to modify "democracy." At the same time, a remarkable consensus has emerged concerning the minimal conditions that polities must meet in order to merit the prestigious appellation of "democratic." Moreover, a number of international organizations now monitor how well these standards are met; indeed, some countries even consider them when formulating foreign policy.[2]

What Democracy Is

Let us begin by broadly defining democracy and the generic *concepts* that distinguish it as a unique system for organizing relations between rulers and the ruled. We will then briefly review *procedures*, the rules and arrangements that are needed if democracy is to endure. Finally, we will discuss two operative *principles* that make democracy work. They are not expressly included among the generic concepts or formal procedures, but the prospect for democracy is grim if their underlying conditioning effects are not present.

One of the major themes of this essay is that democracy does not consist of a single unique set of institutions. There are many types of democracy, and their diverse practices produce a similarly varied set of effects. The specific form democracy takes is contingent upon a country's socioeconomic conditions as well as its entrenched state structures and policy practices.

Modern political democracy is a system of governance in which rulers are held accountable for their actions in the public realm by citizens, acting indirectly through the competition and cooperation of their elected representatives.[3]

A *regime or system of governance* is an ensemble of patterns that determines the methods of access to the principal public offices; the characteristics of the actors admitted to or excluded from such access; the strategies that actors may use to gain access; and the rules that are followed in the making of publicly binding decisions. To work properly, the ensemble must be institutionalized—that is to say, the various patterns must be habitually known, practiced, and accepted by most, if not all, actors. Increasingly, the preferred mechanism of institutionalization is a written body of laws undergirded by a written constitution, though many enduring political norms can have an informal, prudential, or traditional basis.[4]

For the sake of economy and comparison, these forms, characteristics, and rules are usually bundled together and given a generic label. Democratic is one; others are autocratic, authoritarian, despotic, dictatorial, tyrannical, totalitarian, absolutist, traditional, monarchic, obligarchic, plutocratic, aristocratic, and sultanistic.[5] Each of these regime forms may in turn be broken down into subtypes.

Like all regimes, democracies depend upon the presence of *rulers*, persons who occupy specialized authority roles and can give legitimate commands to others. What distinguishes democratic rulers from nondemocratic ones are the norms that condition how the former come to power and the practices that hold them accountable for their actions.

The *public realm* encompasses the making of collective norms and choices that are binding on the society and backed by state coercion. Its content can vary a great deal across democracies, depending upon preexisting distinctions between the public and the private, state and society, legitimate coercion and voluntary exchange, and collective needs and individual preferences. The liberal conception of democracy advocates circumscribing the public realm as narrowly as possible, while the socialist or social-democratic approach would extend that realm through regulation, subsidization, and, in some cases, collective ownership of property. Neither is intrinsically more democratic than the other—just *differently* democratic. This implies that measures aimed at "developing the private sector" are no more democratic than those aimed at "developing the public sector." Both, if carried to extremes, could undermine the practice of democracy, the former by destroying the basis for satisfying collective needs and exercising legitimate authority; the latter by destroying the basis for satisfying individual preferences and controlling illegitimate government actions. Differences of opinion over the optimal mix of the two provide much of the substantive content of political conflict within established democracies.

Citizens are the most distinctive element in democracies. All regimes have rulers and a public realm, but only to the extent that they are democratic do they have citizens. Historically, severe restrictions on citizenship were imposed in most emerging or partial democracies according to criteria of age, gender, class, race, literacy, property ownership, tax-paying status, and so on. Only a small part of the total population was eligible to vote or run for office. Only restricted social categories were allowed to form, join, or support political associations. After protracted struggle—in some cases involving violent domestic upheaval or international war—most of these restrictions were lifted. Today, the criteria for inclusion are fairly standard. All native-born adults are eligible, although somewhat higher age limits may still be imposed upon candidates for certain offices. Unlike the early American and European democracies of the nineteenth century, none of the recent democracies in southern Europe, Latin America, Asia, or Eastern Europe has even attempted to impose formal restrictions on the franchise or eligibility to office. When it comes to informal restrictions on the effective exercise of citizenship rights, however, the story can be quite different. This explains the central importance (discussed below) of procedures.

Competition has not always been considered an essential defining condition of democracy. "Classic" democracies presumed decision making based on direct participation leading to consensus. The assembled citizenry was expected to agree on a common course of action after listening to the alternatives and weighing their respective merits and demerits. A tradition of hostility to "faction," and "particular interests" persists in democratic thought, but at least since *The Federalist Papers* it has become widely accepted that competition among factions is a necessary evil in democracies that operate on a more-than-local scale. Since, as James Madison argued, "the latent causes of faction are sown into the nature of man," and the possible remedies for "the mischief of faction" are worse than the disease, the best course is to recognize them and to attempt to control their effects.[6] Yet while democrats may agree on the inevitability of factions, they tend to disagree about the best forms and rules for governing factional competition. Indeed, differences over the preferred modes and boundaries of competition contribute most to distinguishing one subtype of democracy from another.

The most popular definition of democracy equates it with regular *elections*, fairly conducted and honestly counted. Some even consider the mere fact of elections—even ones from which specific parties or candidates are excluded, or in which substantial portions of the population cannot freely participate—as a sufficient condition for the existence of democracy. This fallacy has been called "electoralism" or "the faith that merely holding elections will channel political action into peaceful contests among elites and accord public legitimacy to the winners"—no matter how they are conducted or what else constrains those who win them.[7] However central to democracy, elections occur intermittently and only allow citizens to choose between the highly aggregated alternatives offered by political parties, which can, especially in the early stages of a democratic transition, proliferate in a bewildering variety. During the intervals between elections, citizens can seek to influence public policy through a wide variety of other intermediaries: interest associations, social movements, locality groupings, clientelistic arrangements, and so forth. *Modern democracy, in other words, offers a variety of competitive processes and channels for the expression of interests and values—associational as well as partisan, functional as well as territorial, collective as well as individual. All are integral to its practice.*

However central to democracy, elections occur intermittently and only allow citizens to choose between the highly aggregated alternatives offered by political parties . . .

Another commonly accepted image of democracy identifies it with *majority rule*. Any governing body that makes decisions by combining the votes of more than half of those eligible and present is said to be democratic, whether that majority emerges within an electorate, a parliament, a committee, a city council, or a party caucus. For exceptional purposes (e.g., amending the constitution or expelling a member), "qualified majorities" of more than 50 percent may be required, but few would deny that democracy must involve some means of aggregating the equal preferences of individuals.

A problem arises, however, when *numbers* meet *intensities*. What happens when a properly assembled majority (especially a stable, self-perpetuating one) regularly makes decisions that harm some minority (especially a threatened cultural or ethnic group)? In these circumstances, successful democracies tend to qualify the central principle of majority rule in order to protect minority rights. Such qualifications can take the form of constitutional provisions that place certain matters beyond the reach of majorities (bills of rights); requirements for concurrent majorities in several different constituencies (confederalism); guarantees securing the autonomy of local or regional governments against the demands of the central authority (federalism); grand coalition governments that incorporate all parties (consociationalism); or the negotiation of social pacts between major social groups like business and labor (neocorporatism). The most common and effective way of protecting minorities, however, lies in the everyday operation of interest associations and social movements. These reflect (some would say, amplify) the different intensities of preference that exist in the population and bring them to bear on democratically elected decision makers. Another way of putting this intrinsic tension between numbers and intensities would be to say that "in modern democracies, votes may be counted, but influences alone are weighted."

Cooperation has always been a central feature of democracy. Actors must voluntarily make collective decisions binding on the polity as a whole. They must cooperate in order to compete. They must be capable of acting collectively through parties, associations, and movements in order to select candidates, articulate preferences, petition authorities, and influence policies.

But democracy's freedoms should also encourage citizens to deliberate among themselves, to discover their common needs, and to resolve their differences without relying on some supreme central authority. Classical democracy emphasized these qualities, and they are by no means extinct, despite repeated efforts by contemporary theorists to stress the analogy with behavior in the economic marketplace and to reduce all of democracy's operations to competitive interest maximization. Alexis de Tocqueville best described the importance of independent groups for democracy in his *Democracy in America*, a work which remains a major source of inspiration for all those who persist in viewing democracy as something more than a struggle for election and re-election among competing candidates.[8]

In contemporary political discourse, this phenomenon of cooperation and deliberation via autonomous group activity goes under the rubric of "civil society." The diverse units of social identity and interest, by remaining independent of the state (and perhaps even of parties), not only can restrain the arbitrary actions of rulers, but can also contribute to forming better citizens who are more aware of the preferences of others, more self-confident in their actions, and more civic-minded in their willingness to sacrifice for the common good. At its best, civil society provides an intermediate layer of governance between the individual and the state that is capable of resolving conflicts and controlling the behavior of members without public coercion. Rather than overloading decision makers with increased demands and making the system ungovernable,[9] a viable civil society can mitigate conflicts and improve the quality of citizenship—without relying exclusively on the privatism of the marketplace.

Representatives—whether directly or indirectly elected—do most of the real work in modern democracies. Most are professional politicians who orient their careers around the desire to fill key offices. It is doubtful that any democracy could survive without such people. The central question, therefore, is not whether or not there will be a political elite or even a professional political class, but how these representatives are chosen and then held accountable for their actions.

As noted above, there are many channels of representation in modern democracy. The electoral one, based on territorial constituencies, is the most visible and public. It culminates in a parliament or a presidency that is periodically accountable to the citizenry as a whole. Yet the sheer growth of government (in large part as a byproduct of popular demand) has increased the number, variety, and power of agencies charged with making public decisions and not subject to elections. Around these agencies there has developed a vast apparatus of specialized representation based largely on functional interests, not territorial constituencies. These interest associations, and not political parties, have become the primary expression of civil society in most stable democracies, supplemented by the more sporadic interventions of social movements.

The new and fragile democracies that have sprung up since 1974 must live in "compressed time." They will not resemble the European democracies of the nineteenth and early twentieth centuries, and they cannot expect to acquire the multiple channels of representation in gradual historical progression as did most of their predecessors. A bewildering array of parties, interests, and movements will all simultaneously seek political influence in them, creating challenges to the polity that did not exist in earlier processes of democratization.

Procedures That Make Democracy Possible

The defining components of democracy are necessarily abstract, and may give rise to a considerable variety of institutions and subtypes of democracy. For democracy to thrive, however, specific procedural norms must be followed and civic rights must be respected. Any polity that fails to impose such restrictions upon itself, that fails to follow the "rule of law" with regard to its own procedures, should not be considered democratic. These procedures alone do not define democracy, but their presence is indispensable to its persistence. In essence, they are necessary but not sufficient conditions for its existence.

Robert Dahl has offered the most generally accepted listing of what he terms the "procedural minimal" conditions that must be present for modern political democracy (or as he puts it, "polyarchy") to exist:

1. Control over government decisions about policy is constitutionally vested in elected officials.
2. Elected officials are chosen in frequent and fairly conducted elections in which coercion is comparatively uncommon.
3. Practically all adults have the right to vote in the election of officials.
4. Practically all adults have the right to run for elective offices.
5. Citizens have a right to express themselves without the danger of severe punishment on political matters broadly defined. . . .
6. Citizens have a right to seek out alternative sources of information. Moreover, alternative sources of information exist and are protected by law.
7. . . . Citizens also have the right to form relatively independent associations or organizations, including independent political parties and interest groups.[10]

These seven conditions seem to capture the essence of procedural democracy for many theorists, but we propose to add two others. The first might be thought of as a further refinement of item (1), while the second might be called an implicit prior condition to all seven of the above.

1. Popularly elected officials must be able to exercise their constitutional powers without being subjected to overriding (albeit informal) opposition from unelected officials. Democracy is in jeopardy if military officers, entrenched civil servants, or state managers retain the capacity to act independently of elected civilians or even veto decisions made by the people's representatives. Without this additional caveat, the militarized polities of contemporary Central America, where civilian control over the military does not exist, might be classified by many scholars as democracies, just as they have been (with the exception of Sandinista Nicaragua) by U.S. policy makers. The caveat thus guards against what we earlier called "electoralism"—the tendency to focus on the holding of elections while ignoring other political realities.

2. The polity must be self-governing; it must be able to act independently of constraints imposed by some other overarching political system. Dahl and other contemporary democratic theorists probably took this condition for granted since they referred to formally sovereign nation-states. However, with the development of blocs, alliances, spheres of influence, and a variety of "neocolonial" arrangements, the question of autonomy has been a salient one. Is a system really democratic if its elected officials are unable to make binding decisions without the approval of actors outside their territorial domain? This is significant even if the outsiders are relatively free to alter or even end the encompassing arrangement (as in Puerto Rico), but it becomes especially critical if neither condition obtains (as in the Baltic states).

Principles That Make Democracy Feasible

Lists of component processes and procedural norms help us to specify what democracy is, but they do not tell us much about how it actually functions. The simplest answer is "by the consent of the people"; the more complex one is "by the contingent consent of politicians acting under conditions of bounded uncertainty."

In a democracy, representatives must at least informally agree that those who win greater electoral support or influence over policy will not use their temporary superiority to bar the losers from taking office or exerting influence in the future, and that in exchange for this opportunity to keep competing for power and place, momentary losers will respect the winners' right to make binding decisions. Citizens are expected to obey the decisions ensuing from such a process of competition, provided its outcome remains contingent upon their collective preferences as expressed through fair and regular elections or open and repeated negotiations.

The challenge is not so much to find a set of goals that command widespread consensus as to find a set of rules that embody contingent consent. The precise shape of this "democratic bargain," to use Dahl's expression,[11] can vary a good deal from society to society. It depends on social cleavages and such subjective factors as mutual trust, the standard of fairness, and the willingness to compromise. It may even be compatible with a great deal of dissensus on substantive policy issues.

All democracies involve a degree of uncertainty about who will be elected and what policies they will pursue. Even in those polities where one party persists in winning elections or one policy is consistently implemented, the possibility of change through independent collective action still exists, as in Italy, Japan, and the Scandinavian social democracies. If it does not, the system is not democratic, as in Mexico, Senegal, or Indonesia.

But the uncertainty embedded in the core of all democracies is bounded. Not just any actor can get into the competition and raise any issue he or she pleases—there are previously established rules that must be respected. Not just any policy can be adopted—there are conditions that must be met. Democracy institutionalizes "normal," limited political uncertainty. These boundaries vary from country to country. Constitutional guarantees of property, privacy, expression, and other rights are a part of this, but the most effective boundaries are generated by competition among interest groups and cooperation within civil society. Whatever the rhetoric (and some polities appear to offer their citizens more dramatic alternatives than others), once the rules of contingent consent have been agreed upon, the actual variation is likely to stay within a predictable and generally accepted range.

This emphasis on operative guidelines contrasts with a highly persistent, but misleading theme in recent literature on democracy—namely, the emphasis upon "civic culture." The principles we have suggested here rest on rules of prudence, not on deeply ingrained habits of tolerance, moderation, mutual respect, fair play, readiness to compromise, or trust in public authorities. Waiting for such habits to sink deep and lasting roots implies a very slow process of regime consolidation—one that takes generations—and it would probably condemn most contemporary experiences *ex hypothesi* to failure. Our assertion is that contingent consent and bounded uncertainty can emerge from the interaction between antagonistic and mutually suspicious actors and that the far more benevolent and ingrained norms of a civic culture are better thought of as a *product* and not a producer of democracy.

How Democracies Differ

Several concepts have been deliberately excluded from our generic definition of democracy, despite the fact that they have been frequently associated with it in both everyday practice and scholarly work. They are, nevertheless, especially important when it comes to distinguishing subtypes of democracy. Since no single set of actual institutions, practices, or values embodies democracy, polities moving away from authoritarian rule can mix different components to produce different democracies. It is important to recognize that these do not define points along a single continuum of improving performance, but a matrix of potential combinations that are *differently* democratic.

1. *Consensus*: All citizens may not agree on the substantive goals of political action or on the role of the state (although if they did, it would certainly make governing democracies much easier).

2. *Participation*: All citizens may not take an active and equal part in politics, although it must be legally possible for them to do so.

3. *Access*: Rulers may not weigh equally the preferences of all who come before them, although citizenship implies that individuals and groups should have an equal opportunity to express their preferences if they choose to do so.

4. *Responsiveness*: Rulers may not always follow the course of action preferred by the citizenry. But when they deviate from such a policy, say on grounds of "reason of state" or "overriding national interest," they must ultimately be held accountable for their actions through regular and fair processes.

5. *Majority rule*: Positions may not be allocated or rules may not be decided solely on the basis of assembling the most votes, although deviations from this principle usually must be explicitly defended and previously approved.

6. *Parliamentary sovereignty*: The legislature may not be the only body that can make rules or even the one with final authority in deciding which laws are binding, although where executive, judicial, or other public bodies make that ultimate choice, they too must be accountable for their actions.

7. *Party government*: Rulers may not be nominated, promoted, and disciplined in their activities by well-organized and programmatically coherent political parties, although where they are not, it may prove more difficult to form an effective government.

8. *Pluralism*: The political process may not be based on a multiplicity of overlapping, voluntaristic, and autonomous private groups. However, where there are monopolies of representation, hierarchies of association, and obligatory memberships, it is likely that the interests involved will be more closely linked to the state and the separation between the public and private spheres of action will be much less distinct.

9. *Federalism*: The territorial division of authority may not involve multiple levels and local autonomies, least of all ones enshrined in a constitutional document, although some dispersal of power across territorial and/or functional units is characteristic of all democracies.

10. *Presidentialism*: The chief executive officer may not be a single person and he or she may not be directly elected by the citizenry as a whole, although some concentration of authority is present in all democracies, even if

it is exercised collectively and only held indirectly accountable to the electorate.

11. *Checks and Balances*: It is not necessary that the different branches of government be systematically pitted against one another, although governments by assembly, by executive concentrations, by judicial command, or even by dictatorial fiat (as in time of war) must be ultimately accountable to the citizenry as a whole.

While each of the above has been named as an essential component of democracy, they should instead be seen either as indicators of this or that type of democracy, or else as useful standards for evaluating the performance of particular regimes. To include them as part of the generic definition of democracy itself would be to mistake the American polity for the universal model of democratic governance. Indeed, the parliamentary, consociational, unitary, corporatist, and concentrated arrangements of continental Europe may have some unique virtues for guiding polities through the uncertain transition from autocratic to democratic rule.[12]

What Democracy Is Not

We have attempted to convey the general meaning of modern democracy without identifying it with some particular set of rules and institutions or restricting it to some specific culture or level of development. We have also argued that it cannot be reduced to the regular holding of elections or equated with a particular notion of the role of the state, but we have not said much more about what democracy is not or about what democracy may not be capable of producing.

There is an understandable temptation to load too many expectations on this concept and to imagine that by attaining democracy, a society will have resolved all of its political, social, economic, administrative, and cultural problems. Unfortunately, "all good things do not necessarily go together."

First, democracies are not necessarily more efficient economically than other forms of government. Their rates of aggregate growth, savings, and investment may be no better than those of nondemocracies. This is especially likely during the transition, when propertied groups and administrative elites may respond to real or imagined threats to the "rights" they enjoyed under authoritarian rule by initiating capital flight, disinvestment, or sabotage. In time, depending upon the type of democracy, benevolent long-term effects upon income distribution, aggregate demand, education, productivity, and creativity may eventually combine to improve economic and social performance, but it is certainly too much to expect that these improvements will occur immediately—much less that they will be defining characteristics of democratization.

Second, democracies are not necessarily more efficient administratively. Their capacity to make decisions may even be slower than that of the regimes they replace, if only because more actors must be consulted. The costs of getting things done may be higher, if only because "payoffs" have to be made to a wider and more resourceful set of clients (although one should never underestimate the degree of corruption to be found within autocracies). Popular satisfaction with the new democratic government's performance may not even seem greater, if only because necessary compromises often please no one completely, and because the losers are free to complain.

Third, democracies are not likely to appear more orderly, consensual, stable, or governable than the autocracies they replace. This is partly a byproduct of democratic freedom of expression, but it is also a reflection of the likelihood of continuing disagreement over new rules and institutions. These products of imposition or compromise are often initially quite ambiguous in nature and uncertain in effect until actors have learned how to use them. What is more, they come in the aftermath of serious struggles motivated by high ideals. Groups and individuals with recently acquired autonomy will test certain rules, protest against the actions of certain institutions, and insist on renegotiating their part of the bargain. Thus the presence of antisystem parties should be neither surprising nor seen as a failure of democratic consolidation. What counts is whether such parties are willing, however reluctantly, to play by the general rules of bounded uncertainty and contingent consent.

Governability is a challenge for all regimes, not just democratic ones. Given the political exhaustion and loss of legitimacy that have befallen autocracies from sultanistic Paraguay to totalitarian Albania, it may seem that only democracies can now be expected to govern effectively and legitimately. Experience has shown, however, that democracies too can lose the ability to govern. Mass publics can become disenchanted with their performance. Even more threatening is the temptation for leaders to fiddle with procedures and ultimately undermine the principles of contingent consent and bounded uncertainty. Perhaps the most critical moment comes once the politicians begin to settle into the more predictable roles and relations of a consolidated democracy. Many will find their expectations frustrated; some will discover that the new rules of competition put them at a disadvantage; a few may even feel that their vital interests are threatened by popular majorities.

Finally, democracies will have more open societies and polities than the autocracies they replace, but not necessarily more open economies. Many of today's most successful and well-established democracies have historically resorted to protectionism and closed borders, and have relied extensively upon public institutions to promote economic development. While the long-term compatibility between democracy and capitalism does not seem to be in doubt, despite their continuous tension, it is not clear whether the promotion of such liberal economic goals as the right of individuals to own property and retain profits, the clearing function of markets, the private settlement of disputes, the freedom to produce without government regulation, or the privatization of state-owned enterprises necessarily furthers the consolidation of democracy. After all, democracies do need to levy taxes and regulate certain transactions, especially where private monopolies and oligopolies exist. Citizens or their representatives may decide that it is desirable to protect the rights of collectivities from encroachment by individuals, especially propertied ones, and they may choose to set aside certain forms of property for public or cooperative ownership. In short, notions of economic liberty that are currently put forward in neoliberal economic models are not synonymous with political freedom—and may even impede it.

Democratization will not necessarily bring in its wake economic growth, social peace, administrative efficiency, political harmony, free markets, or "the end of ideology." Least of all will it bring about "the end of history." No doubt some of these qualities could make the consolidation of democracy easier, but they are neither prerequisites for it nor immediate products of it. Instead, what we should be hoping for is the emergence of political institutions that can peacefully compete to form governments and influence public policy, that can channel social and economic conflicts through regular procedures, and that have sufficient linkages to civil society to represent their constituencies and commit them to collective courses of action. Some types of democracies, especially in developing countries, have been unable to fulfill this promise, perhaps due to the circumstances of their transition from authoritarian rule.[13] The democratic wager is that such a regime, once established, will not only persist by reproducing itself within its initial confining conditions, but will eventually expand beyond them.[14] Unlike authoritarian regimes, democracies have the capacity to modify their rules and institutions consensually in response to changing circumstances. They may not immediately produce all the goods mentioned above, but they stand a better chance of eventually doing so than do autocracies.

Notes

1. For a comparative analysis of the recent regime changes in southern Europe and Latin America, see Guillermo O'Donnell, Philippe C. Schmitter, and Laurence Whitehead, eds., *Transitions from Authoritarian Rule*, 4 vols. (Baltimore: Johns Hopkins University Press, 1986). For another compilation that adopts a more structural approach see Larry Diamond, Juan Linz, and Seymour Martin Lipset, eds., *Democracy in Developing Countries*, vols. 2, 3, and 4 (Boulder, Colo.: Lynne Rienner, 1989).

2. Numerous attempts have been made to codify and quantify the existence of democracy across political systems. The best known is probably Freedom House's *Freedom in the World: Political Rights and Civil Liberties*, published since 1973 by Greenwood Press and since 1988 by University Press of America. Also see Charles Humana, *World Human Rights Guide* (New York: Facts on File, 1986).

3. The definition most commonly used by American social scientists is that of Joseph Schumpeter: "that institutional arrangement for arriving at political decisions in which individuals acquire the power to decide by means of a competitive struggle for the people's vote." *Capitalism, Socialism, and Democracy* (London: George Allen and Unwin, 1943), 269. We accept certain aspects of the classical procedural approach to modern democracy, but differ primarily in our emphasis on the accountability of rulers to citizens and the relevance of mechanisms of competition other than elections.

4. Not only do some countries practice a stable form of democracy without a formal constitution (e.g., Great Britain and Israel), but even more countries have constitutions and legal codes that offer no guarantee of reliable practice. On paper, Stalin's 1936 constitution for the USSR was a virtual model of democratic rights and entitlements.

5. For the most valiant attempt to make some sense out of this thicket of distinctions, see Juan Linz, "Totalitarian and Authoritarian Regimes" in *Handbook of Political Science*, eds. Fred I. Greenstein and Nelson W. Polsby (Reading Mass.: Addison Wesley, 1975), 175–411.

6. "Publius" (Alexander Hamilton, John Jay, and James Madison), *The Federalist Papers* (New York: Anchor Books, 1961). The quote is from Number 10.

7. See Terry Karl, "Imposing Consent? Electoralism versus Democratization in El Salvador," in *Elections and Democratization in Latin America, 1980–1985*, eds. Paul Drake and Eduardo Silva (San Diego: Center for Iberian and Latin American Studies, Center for US/Mexican Studies, University of California, San Diego, 1986), 9–36.

8. Alexis de Tocqueville, *Democracy in America*, 2 vols. (New York: Vintage Books, 1945).

9. This fear of overloaded government and the imminent collapse of democracy is well reflected in the work of Samuel P. Huntington during the 1970s. See especially Michel Crozier, Samuel P. Huntington, and Joji Watanuki, *The Crisis of Democracy* (New York: New York University Press, 1975). For Huntington's (revised) thoughts about the prospects for democracy, see his "Will More Countries Become Democratic?," *Political Science Quarterly* 99 (Summer 1984): 193–218.

10. Robert Dahl, *Dilemmas of Pluralist Democracy* (New Haven: Yale University Press, 1982), 11.

11. Robert Dahl, *After the Revolution: Authority in a Good Society* (New Haven: Yale University Press, 1970).

12. See Juan Linz, "The Perils of Presidentialism," *Journal of Democracy* 1 (Winter 1990): 51–69, and the "ensuing" discussion was published prior to first (winter/fall, 1990) by Donald Horowitz, Seymour Martin Lipset, and Juan Linz in *Journal of Democracy* 1 (Fall 1990): 73–91.

13. Terry Lynn Karl, "Dilemmas of Democratization in Latin America" *Comparative Politics* 23 (October 1990): 1–23.

14. Otto Kirchheimer, "Confining Conditions and Revolutionary Breakthroughs," *American Political Science Review* 59 (1965): 964–974.

Critical Thinking

1. List the conditions that Robert Dahl identifies as "minimal" for democracy.
2. What does it mean that "no single set of actual institutions, practices, or values embodies democracy"?
3. What do the authors say democracy "is not"?

PHILIPPE C. SCHMITTER is professor of political science and director of the Center for European Studies at Stanford University. **TERRY LYNN KARL** is associate professor of political science and director of the Center for Latin American Studies at the same institution. The original, longer version of this essay was written at the request of the United States Agency for International Development, which is not responsible for its content.

Twenty-Five Years, Fifteen Findings

Philippe C. Schmitter

When Guillermo O'Donnell and I were writing *Transitions from Authoritarian Rule: Tentative Conclusion about Uncertain Democracies* a quarter of a century ago, we had few cases and almost no literature upon which to draw.[1] Mostly we ransacked the monographs of colleagues who were taking part in the same Woodrow Wilson Center project as we were. We also reached back to the classics of political thought. I personally drew much inspiration from the work of Niccolò Machiavelli who, I discovered, had grappled some time ago with regime change in the opposite direction—that is, from "republican" to "princely" rule.

Neither of us imagined that the fledgling efforts we were then observing in Southern Europe and Latin America would soon be followed by more than fifty other regime transformations all around the world. These "divine surprises," especially the ones in Central and Eastern Europe and the former Soviet Union, brought not only much scientific opportunity and personal normative satisfaction, but also a major intellectual risk. To what extent could the assumptions, concepts, hypotheses, and "tentative conclusions" that we had derived from the early cases be stretched to fit a much larger and highly varied set of countries? The stretching that we were considering seemed even more problematic in light of how opposed our ideas were to most prevailing theories about "really existing democracies."[2]

We insisted, for example, on a clear distinction between liberalization and democratization. We refused to accept the notion that democracy requires some fixed set of economic or cultural prerequisites. We emphasized the key role of elite interaction and strategic choice during the transition and in most cases ascribed limited importance to mass mobilization from below. We pointed to the demobilizing effect of the electoral process and said that while civil society might have a significant role, it would be a short-lived one. We noted how most transitions began from within the previous autocratic regime, whose collapse or self-transformation by no means guaranteed the eventual success of democracy. Finally, and perhaps most subversively, we argued that it was possible (if not always probable) that one could bring about democracy *without* having any democrats on hand. In other words, the favorable cultural and normative traits or "civic culture" that comparative survey research had detected and found essential to all stable democracies was better conceived as a *product* of democracy rather than its producer.

As a comparativist, I welcomed the challenge of "stretching" our original work and applying it to such different cases. I found it gratifying to observe how often, how far away, and even how controversially these "cross-regional" comparisons were attempted, and I am convinced that they contributed to a fuller understanding of democratization. What I found much less gratifying was the tendency of critics and other readers to apply our book to topics that were manifestly not within its purview. It had been no accident that Guillermo and I had given the book a title stressing transitions *away from* authoritarianism rather than *to* democracy, yet many treated our tome as if it purported to contain a magic formula for success or even lessons in how to consolidate democracy.

Not only did we refuse to presume a *telos* that would lead to such a felicitous result, we were obsessed with the likelihood of regression to autocracy. Admittedly, we were concerned all along with the implications that different transitional situations might have for democracy's ability to emerge and persist, but we wrote nothing about what such an outcome might look like. Guillermo and I have since written a good deal on this topic, but nothing in our original joint effort allows one to assume that voluntaristic, structurally underdetermined action would continue to dominate the politics of new democracies once they passed through the highly uncertain transition period, or that strategic machinations among elites would continue to count for more than mass mobilization and popular participation.

Much has happened over the last two decades, including a burgeoning of democratization studies, from which I have learned much. The editors of the *Journal of Democracy* have asked me to share this retrospective wisdom with their readers:

1. Democratization has proven far easier to accomplish in the contemporary historical context than I had at first thought it would be. Back in the late 1970s, I estimated that in Latin America since 1900 roughly two of every three efforts to democratize had failed, with an obvious (and usually violent) relapse into autocracy ensuing within three to five years. I wince when I come across the accusation that, in choosing to compare South European and Latin American cases, Guillermo and I had been "cherry picking" the easy cases, with crippling implications for our tentative conclusions about supposedly harder cases elsewhere. Nothing could have been further from my mind, especially since I had been researching the highly tumultuous and uncertain transition that had been going on in Portugal since 1974. It is certainly not our fault that none of the countries in Southern Europe or Latin America has as yet suffered a manifest or sudden regression to autocracy, although several spent a long time in transition (Brazil), some have had close calls (Paraguay, Peru), and a few have developed symptoms of gradual deterioration (Bolivia, Ecuador, Nicaragua).

The lack of authoritarian regressions is all the more astonishing when one considers that many of the factors said to be vital (or at least helpful) to the consolidation of liberal democracy have been missing in many if not most of these cases. Rates of employment and economic growth have not always been higher under democracy as opposed to autocracy; social equality and income distribution have not always improved significantly; trust in rulers has often deteriorated; critical measures of "civic culture" have declined—and yet basic democratic institutions have remained in place.

It must be kept in mind, finally, that the distinction between "easy" and "hard" cases of transition can only apply to those cases in which, for whatever reasons, an actual transition to democracy is attempted, as signaled by the holding of free and fair "founding elections" complete with contending parties and an uncertain outcome. Cases in which some elite from the old autocracy keeps control of the process—typically allowing some degree of liberalization as a tactic to fend off democratization— do not count. This means that one must exclude all the Central Asian cases when considering transitions in the post-Soviet world, and that only Turkey and, more recently, Lebanon need be counted by "transitologists" who study the Middle East and North Africa.

2. Democratization may have been easier than I had anticipated, but it has also been less consequential. Considering the consequences of previous efforts at democratization, scholars and activists alike expected that such a transformation would bring about much more significant changes in power relations, property rights, policy entitlements, economic equality, and social status than those that have in fact occurred so far. This is not to claim that "nothing changed." In the realm of respect for human rights, more decent treatment of citizens by authorities, and a sense of greater personal freedom, significant changes have occurred and citizens appreciate them (even if the changes are often rapidly "discounted"). But in terms of those factors that are most likely to influence the longer-term distribution of power and influence within the polity, recent democratizations have accomplished much less than did those in the past. In some cases—most of which are found in Central and Eastern Europe and the former USSR—those running the new democracies have close ties to (or may even be) the very people who ran the old autocracies. Try to imagine France or the young United States after their respective revolutions with officials from the time of monarchy peacefully back in power under the new modes and orders of the early republic!

Admittedly, with respect to the recent cases, the time frame for evaluating such consequences is foreshortened, and the typical mode of transition has hardly been revolutionary. In what Terry Karl and I have called "pacted" or "imposed" transitions, there is every reason to expect less consequential changes. Under such circumstances, major and irreversible shifts in the distribution of resources that can be converted into power and influence are more or less ruled out. Only after these transitional arrangements have ended, whether by mutual agreement or by one party pulling out, can one expect the sheer persistence of democracy to produce some of these changes through normal political competition. One could say that new democracies buy time to consolidate; only then do redistributive consequences begin to appear in response to competitive pressures.

3. Democratization has been easier than anticipated precisely because it has been less consequential than anticipated. During the uncertainty of the initial transitions, no one could have known this—I certainly did not. The Portuguese case suggested the contrary. Only later was I to learn how exceptional it had been, and how ephemeral had been its consequences. Spain and later several Latin American cases showed that the socially dominant and economically privileged had much less to fear from democratization than they might at first have thought. After things in Portugal settled down, and later after the USSR collapsed, it became clear that political freedoms and partisan competition under democratic conditions would not have to lead to either majority tyranny or minority radicalization. Rotation in power would not have to produce wild fluctuations in either policies or the distribution of benefits. My hunch is that the learning of these lessons sealed democracy's irreversibility in these countries. Those who had once backed autocracy began to realize that their interests would be better protected under democracy than they had been under authoritarianism—and without the added costs that the latter might bring in terms of violent repression, international opprobrium, and the like.

4. Really existing democracy has been disappointing to both its intended beneficiaries and to us academics. In countries that have democratized since 1974, disenchantment with both the practices and products of democracy is widespread. Analysts vie to find the most deprecating adjective to place in front of the word "democracy": defective, electoral, partial, pseudo, low-intensity, sham, ersatz, and, of course, delegative. This effort has contributed to the general impression—reflected in opinion polls—that most of the regime changes over the past 25 years have resulted in poor-quality regimes unworthy of the struggles and sacrifices that it cost to bring them about.

The first thing to note here is that such disenchantment is hardly restricted to new democracies. In the established ones as well, analogous "morbidity symptoms" are rife. Almost everywhere, voter turnout has declined, as have union membership, the prestige of politicians, the perceived importance of parliaments, the strength of party identification, the stability of electoral preferences, and the levels of trust in most public institutions. Conversely, there has been a rise in litigiousness, corruption charges (and convictions), and populist antiparty candidacies. While it would be an exaggeration to call this a full-scale "crisis" of democratic legitimacy, the striking ubiquity of these symptoms suggests (but does not prove) that there may be something more generically deficient in democracy's institutions and practices. Communism's collapse and democracy's spread have not brought about an "end of history" rooted in democracy's insuperability. Far from enjoying smooth sailing, today's really existing democracies face storms of criticism from many directions.

5. Really existing democracy may be especially disappointing where it has been recently attained, but the impact of this disaffection does not seem to threaten it. No matter how many citizens disapprove of their elected leaders and shun politics as unsavory, there is virtually no sign of mass desire for any form of government other than democracy, and few signs of growing support for avowedly undemocratic parties or politicians. Those agents who in the past frequently used force or fraud to bring about the breakdown of democracy are astonishingly absent. Economic and social crises that once would have been enough to trigger regime change now only shake up electoral politics or spur somewhat irregular depositions of elected officials and their replacement by others.

According to comparative survey research, satisfaction with present rulers and trust in existing institutions are both abysmal (with a certain amount of nostalgia for the autocratic "strong hand" not unknown either), but none of this does much if anything to make authoritarian regression more likely. Even in countries that have done fairly well in objective economic terms (Brazil, Chile, Hungary, and Poland), subjective assessments give democracy low performance grades without anyone expecting that this is going to mean autocracy's return. For a while in Latin America, the prospect of *autogolpes* ("self-coups" by means of which elected rulers extended their powers and perpetuated themselves in office by decree) seemed a plausible threat, but these gambits failed fairly quickly. My hunch is that this is a product of what I call the "second law of political dynamics"—namely, that no regime is ever displaced or replaced unless and until an alternative to it already exists. With no credible and appealing alternative form of rule in the offing, really existing democracy—however unbeloved—remains "the only game in town."

Moreover, it is at least debatable whether this should be considered a sign of democracy's intrinsic inferiority. Democratic theorists (but not theorists of democratization) have tended to assume that democratic stability hinges on the flourishing of a "civic culture" replete with ample intergroup tolerance, trust in institutions, and readiness to compromise. What we seem to be observing in new democracies today is a political culture that is less "civic" than "cynical." I have a hunch and a hope about this. My hunch is that this may not be as corrosive or dangerous a situation as was once presumed. My hope is that if ruling elites can be tricked into playing the competitive-politics game (even in defective form) for fifteen or twenty years, then the next crisis will most likely be resolved by a shift to a different subtype of democracy rather than to a nondemocratic regime. Disenchantment with democracy, in other words, could lead not to autocracy, but to different and perhaps even better forms of democracy.

6. Democratization may have been different in "post-totalitarian" versus "post-authoritarian" settings, but not in the way that specialists predicted. Twenty years ago, it seemed reasonable to assume that democratizing the postcommunist states would be much harder than democratizing those states where some form of autocracy other than communism had held sway. The former states, after all, would need not merely political reform but also massive economic, social, and even cultural or mental transformations to undo decades of comprehensive and ideologically reinforced collectivism. This assumption was widespread, and it has been proven wrong. On the contrary, in Central and Eastern Europe and even in several of the more western republics of the former Soviet Union, the transition away from autocracy and the consolidation of democracy have proven to be easier—not to mention faster and more thorough—than they were in either Latin America or Southern Europe. Most of the horrors and dilemmas predicted for postcommunism have not happened. One could even argue that having to make so many changes at once was an advantage. It gave the new rulers an enlarged policy space in which they could negotiate with powerful holdover elites and reach compromises—not the least of which was an exchange of the claim to rule for the right to make money. Explosions of ethnic violence were mostly confined to what had once been Yugoslavia, where Soviet-style totalitarian rule and political culture had long been in decline. In the cases where nondemocratic regimes did install themselves immediately (the five Central Asian republics) or after a short competitive interlude (Belarus and Russia), transitions did not fail—rather, they were never even seriously attempted as ex-communists calling themselves nationalists and social democrats seized control, won noncompetitive elections, and used preexisting organizational advantages to keep themselves in power.

7. Pacts negotiated between old-regime elites and opposition groups do seem to have made a difference in the short to medium run, but their longer-term effect is more dubious. Along with transitions simply "imposed" by ruling elites, "pacted" transitions have since 1974 out-numbered the historically most common forms of democratic transition, which are revolution and reform. Hence it is worth pointing out a problem that pacted and imposed transitions share: Both have a tendency to "lock in" existing privileges and make redistributive reforms harder. What is particularly noxious for the future of democracy about such pacts is that they tempt elites to extend their agreements beyond the period of early uncertainty and reinforce a pattern of collusion between political parties that generates corruption and citizen disillusionment. Venezuela, long a classic case of pacted transition, illustrates these toxic dynamics.

8. Political parties matter, even if they usually play an insignificant role in bringing about the transition, but they have made less of a contribution to democratic stability than expected. No democratization process can afford to do without parties, especially once elections are convoked. For better or worse, parties seem to be indispensable in structuring competition for representation within territorially defined constituencies. For "founding elections" to have their effect, the full range of potential parties must be allowed to take part and to choose their candidates without exclusions. Depending on the rules adopted, later elections will see the number of parties shrink, but the effect of these initial contests (Guillermo and I called them "civic orgies") will persist. In earlier waves of democratization, revolutions from below tended to produce a single dominant party that governed for a substantial period and played a key role in crafting the new rules of the regime. More recently, pacted and imposed transitions have become much more common and produced different short-term outcomes. Pacts tends to spawn collusive two-party systems; an imposed transition usually leads to a far more fragmented party landscape—at least among those political forces that opposed the former autocracy. The unexpected outcome is that, when it comes to preventing authoritarian regression and consolidating democracy, both modes seem to work. This is so, puzzlingly, even though the new parties are often very weak, with few regular supporters, little fundraising ability, and scant public trust or esteem. New democracies in both Latin America and Eastern Europe have seen record-breaking levels of volatility from one election to another, as well as high rates of party birth and death. Citizens show strong political interest and fairly clear preferences, but have trouble translating these into stable partisan identifications. Since 1974, the winning parties in "founding elections" have only rarely been able to gain a second consecutive term. Turnover in power has become the rule. In other words, many a new democracy has "shocked the experts" by consolidating as a regime without having first consolidated its party system.

9. Civil society has figured prominently and favorably in the literature on democratic transition and consolidation, but it may be a mixed blessing. Its robust presence has been regarded as vital to the success of both processes. In "classic" reform transitions, the self-organization of excluded or marginalized groups and their threatening (but nonviolent) expressions of discontent spur ruling elites' concessions. Once transition occurs, the willingness of these organizations to play by the new rules supposedly ensures regime stability. Civil society did play a major role in the Philippines, South Korea, Peru, and Czechoslovakia, and later in the Georgian and Ukrainian "color revolutions," albeit more as a force for transition than for consolidation. Most cases of transition since 1974 have been close to the "pacted" or "imposed" sort, in which civil society's role is less clear. Civil society could not choose the nature or timing of change; at best, civil society played an indirect part by bringing old-regime soft-liners and moderate oppositionists to the table, or by convincing rulers that repression would cost too much. Once transitions began, civil society mobilized to push rulers beyond the comfort zone of mere liberalization and highly restrictive elections.

But civil society can also play an ambiguous or even malign role. In Yugoslavia, the mobilization of civil society (or societies) along mutually hostile ethnic lines helped to fuel protracted violence. Something similar occurred when the USSR began to break up and the Baltic and Caucasus regions witnessed various civil societies gearing up to assert nationalist claims, sometimes through force. There are certainly circumstances in which civil society mobilization can make it harder rather than easier to agree on new rules and stick by them.

10. Parliamentarism, decentralizaztion (federalism), and checks and balances (horizontal accountability) were thought to be magic ingredients of successful consolidation, but many countries have opted for different institutions and have done just as well. If I have learned one thing about institutions during the last 25 years, it is that there is no magic formula—nothing works everywhere. Latin American polities have not done so badly during this time with presidentialism,[3] and I see no evidence that either corruption or ethnic conflict is significantly greater in the region's more centralized states. Central and Eastern Europe have not done so badly with either parliamentarism or semi-presidentialism, and federalism ended with the disintegration of federal states in Czechoslovakia, Yugoslavia, and the USSR. The EU demanded more regional autonomy and horizontal-accountability from prospective members, but it is hard to tell just what difference this made apart from the more general (and definitely favorable) impact of EU membership itself. Where overweening presidentialism and centralism plus a lack of checks and balances have been associated with failures to democratize (Armenia, Belarus, Central Asia, and Russia), the problem has not been this or that institution so much as too many holdover ex-communist elites with too much power. These allegedly democracy-unfriendly institutions are symptoms, not causes. Thus it seems safest to conclude that the choice of institutions can make a difference (and is related to the mode of transition—or its absence), but that it does not make the same difference in all cases.

11. Of all the economic and cultural prerequisites or preconditions of democracy, the one that must command the most urgent attention is the need for prior agreement on national identity and borders. The notion that democratization is intrinsically dangerous because it will inflame ethnolinguistic tensions is widespread, and is sometimes cited as a reason why democratization should not be tried. It is certainly the case that democratic mechanisms cannot be used to discover who is a member of the *demos,* and only rarely will they be useful in determining contested borders. In our book, Guillermo and I did not pay attention to this. In the Southern Europe and Latin America of the 1970s, questions of borders and identities were (with few exceptions such as that of the Basques in Spain) not prominent. Later, to my surprise, ethnically based mobilizations became a major feature in the politics of several highly centralized Andean countries. These mobilizations have made politics more tumultuous, to be sure, but they have yet to threaten really existing democracy itself. It was in Central and Eastern Europe and the former USSR that "nationhood" issues became most salient. In all but the worst cases, however, ethnolinguistic disputes have neither stopped democracy from moving toward consolidation nor prevented borders from being agreed upon. Tensions persist, no doubt, but it appears that democracy can, if practiced long enough, prove a powerful force for producing a national *demos,* even if it is one that contains multiple identity groups with relative autonomy inside their respective internal borders.

12. Despite the neoliberal enthusiasm for privatization and globalization, democratization continues to rely on a political unit with a capacity for exercising legitimate public coercion and implementing collective decisions within a distinct territory—that is, a state. Although it is an exaggeration to claim that without a state there can be no democracy, citizens are likely to demand some reasonably coherent, resourceful, and permanent administrative apparatus to protect them and satisfy their demands. All regimes in the contemporary world—democratic or autocratic, legitimate or illegitimate—require some degree of "stateness" in order to survive (and autocratic or illegitimate ones require considerably more of it). What is especially problematic for new democracies in the short term is the likelihood that the transition will bring a steep perceived decline in stateness. Some newly enfranchised citizens will confuse regime change with freedom not to pay taxes or obey laws. And since crime and corruption are typically underreported in autocracies, things will seem worse than they are when democracy and its free flow of information arrive. Nearly all new democracies pass through such an uncomfortable period, and most recover (as a rule, crime and corruption are lower in consolidated democracies than in all types of autocracy). What then becomes key is not stateness itself, but its ideal nature and reach. These questions become the stuff of normal democratic political competition.

13. Liberalization may still precede democratization in most cases, but is less and less a determinant of democratization's outcome. Guillermo and I stressed the role of a revived civil society as the link between liberalization and subsequent democratization. Even in postcommunist cases, this sequence largely obtained. By the time of transition, most of the communist regimes had taken a step back from totalitarianism as communist parties found their grip slipping and citizens increasingly demanded and received a degree of respect for individual rights. Czechoslovakia, Romania, and certain ex-Soviet republics seem to have been exceptions, with transition experiences that differed accordingly. What has called the link between liberalization and democratization into question is the spectacle of Middle Eastern and North African autocrats who toy with liberalization, then switch it off with no ill effects. Why Arab-Islamic civil societies have proven so docile remains a bit of a mystery to me. It could be due either to the presence of suppressed religious or ethnic cleavages that liberalization makes dangerously threatening to incumbent rulers, or to the fragile and state-dependent nature of the region's middle classes.

14. Democratization requires not just amateur citizens but also professional politicians. There is a persistent myth that elected officials are just normal people who lend themselves temporarily to public service. Amateurs may lead the struggle against autocracy and occupy top posts early in a transition, but they will soon give way to political professionals. Politicians today need ample party and personal resources to win elections, require specialized knowledge in order to hold technocrats accountable, and must surround themselves with experts in polling and the like in order to stay in office. The rise of a professional political class may be unavoidable, but it is also one of the gravest sources of citizen disenchantment with really existing democracy. The social and cultural gap between citizens and those who claim to represent them is a serious problem, as is the politicians' growing dependence on funds raised from sources (such as higher taxes or shady private contributors) that arouse citizen resentment or suspicion.

15. The international context has become an increasingly significant determinant of both the timing and the mode of transition, as well as its outcome. Guillermo and I asserted the predominance of domestic factors as one of our "tentative conclusions." With regard to the cases from Southern Europe and Latin America that we were studying, I would stick by that claim. By contrast, those cases that occurred later in the Eastern bloc would have been unimaginable without a prior change in the hegemonic pretensions of the Soviet Union, and would not have gone as far and as fast as they did without the incentives offered by EU membership. Moreover, once the postcommunist transitions began (Poland was the first), a strong process of diffusion and imitation set in among them.

As a variable, the international context is notoriously difficult to pin down. It is almost by definition omnipresent, since complete political isolation is so hard to achieve in today's world. Yet the causal impact is often indirect, working in opaque and unintended ways through ostensibly national agents. It varies greatly according to the size, resource base, regional context, geostrategic location, and alliance structure of the country involved. Two of its aspects, however, we did not anticipate. The first is the formation of a vast number and variety of non- or quasi-governmental organizations devoted to promoting democracy and human rights across national borders; the second is the EU's assumption of a responsibility to assist nearby fledgling democracies materially and through incentives tied to the prospect of membership.

A whole new world "beneath and beyond the nation-state" opened up and literally enveloped transitional polities, first in Central and Eastern Europe and later in Asia and Africa. Private associations, movements, foundations, consultancies, and party internationals provided ideas, contacts, and minor financial support. National governments and regional or global organizations provided far more money and, in the EU's case, even a whole new form of external intervention—namely, "political conditionality." What made EU conditionality so compelling was the linking of possible membership in the "European club" to compliance with the *acquis communautaire* (which is EU-speak for the entire set of EU rules and decisions compiled since 1958) as well as to the assimilation of a newer set of political norms, the so-called Copenhagen Criteria, which had been devised explicitly to condition the behavior of candidate states. A toned-down version of conditionality now applies to all EU trade agreements made with the so-called ACP (Africa-Caribbean-Pacific) countries, and is supposed to guide the EU's "Neighbourhood" and "Mediterranean" policies regarding the areas to Europe's immediate east and south, respectively. Other regional organizations such as the Organization of American States, the (British) Commonwealth, and even the African Union have taken steps down a similar path by adopting formal agreements that commit their members to responding collectively in the event of "unconstitutional" regime changes.

Since really existing democracy is a perpetually unfinished product, democratization will always be on the research agenda of political scientists. And since nothing seems to work well everywhere, they will have plenty of explaining to do.

Notes

1. Guillermo O'Donnell and Philippe C. Schmitter, *Transitions from Authoritarian Rule: Tentative Conclusions about Uncertain Democracies* (Baltimore: John Hopkins University

Press, 1986). This is the fourth volume of the collection *Transitions from Authoritarian Rule,* which was coedited by O'Donnell, Schmitter, and Laurence Whitehead.

2. A "really existing democracy" in my view must: a) call itself democratic; b) be recognized as such by other self-proclaimed democracies; and c) be classified as democratic by most political scientists applying standard procedural criteria.

3. The revival of "delegative democracy" or "hyperpresidentialism" in Latin America with the recent spate of regimes imitating that of Hugo Chávez in Venezuela does not seem (to me) to be the result of failed transitions, but rather a reaction to practices of consolidated democracies that were excessively collusive (Venezuela) or that were insensitive to the demands of excluded ethnic groups (Bolivia and Ecuador). Only in the case of Nicaragua can it be said to be the product of a protracted (and corrupted) transition.

Critical Thinking

1. What does it mean when the author says, "Really existing democracy has been disappointing"?

2. Why do political parties matter? If political parties matter, what does it mean about participation?

3. What does it mean that "civil society . . . may be a mixed blessing"?

PHILIPPE C. SCHMITTER is professor emeritus at the European University Institute in Florence, Italy. In 2009, he received the Johan Skytte Prize from the University of Uppsala for his work in comparative political science and the study of democratization, as well as the Mattei Dogan Prize for lifetime achievement from the International Political Science Association.

Why Middle East Studies Missed the Arab Spring: The Myth of Authoritarian Stability

F. GREGORY GAUSE III

The vast majority of academic specialists on the Arab world were as surprised as everyone else by the upheavals that toppled two Arab leaders last winter and that now threaten several others. It was clear that Arab regimes were deeply unpopular and faced serious demographic, economic, and political problems. Yet many academics focused on explaining what they saw as the most interesting and anomalous aspect of Arab politics: the persistence of undemocratic rulers.

Until this year, the Arab world boasted a long list of such leaders. Muammar al-Qaddafi took charge of Libya in 1969; the Assad family has ruled Syria since 1970; Ali Abdullah Saleh became president of North Yemen (later united with South Yemen) in 1978; Hosni Mubarak took charge of Egypt in 1981; and Zine el-Abidine Ben Ali ascended to Tunisia's presidency in 1987. The monarchies enjoyed even longer pedigrees, with the Hashemites running Jordan since its creation in 1920, the al-Saud family ruling a unified Saudi Arabia since 1932, and the Alaouite dynasty in Morocco first coming to power in the seventeenth century.

These regimes survived over a period of decades in which democratic waves rolled through East Asia, eastern Europe, Latin America, and sub-Saharan Africa. Even the Arab countries' neighbors in the Muslim Middle East (Iran and Turkey) experienced enormous political change in that period, with a revolution and three subsequent decades of political struggle in Iran and a quasi-Islamist party building a more open and democratic system in secular Turkey.

For many Middle East specialists, this remarkable record of regime stability in the face of numerous challenges demanded their attention and an explanation. I am one of those specialists. In the pages of this magazine in 2005 ("Can Democracy Stop Terrorism?" September/

October 2005), I argued that the United States should not encourage democracy in the Arab world because Washington's authoritarian Arab allies represented stable bets for the future. On that count, I was spectacularly wrong. I also predicted that democratic Arab governments would prove much less likely to cooperate with U.S. foreign policy goals in the region. This remains an open question. Although most of my colleagues expressed more support for U.S. efforts to encourage Arab political reform, I was hardly alone in my skepticism about the prospect of full-fledged democratic change in the face of these seemingly unshakable authoritarian regimes.

Understanding what we missed and what we overestimated in our explanations of the stability of Arab authoritarianism—and understanding why we did so—is of more than just academic significance. Regional analysts must determine what changed in the forces that underpinned four decades of Arab regime stability and what new elements emerged to spark the current revolts. Doing so will allow U.S. policymakers to approach the Arab revolts more effectively by providing them insight into the factors that will drive postrevolutionary politics in the Arab world.

Arab States and Their Militaries

The first task is to establish what academia knew and did not know. To begin with, it is important to recognize that few, if any, political scientists working on the Middle East explained the peculiar stability of Arab regimes in cultural terms–a sign of progress over the scholarship of earlier eras. The literature on how Arab dictators endured did not include old saws about how Islam is inimical to democracy or how Arab culture remains too patriarchal and traditional to support democratic change. We recognized how popular the concept of democracy was in the Arab world and that when given real electoral choices, Arabs turned out to vote in large numbers. We also understood that Arabs did not passively accept authoritarian rule. From Algeria to Saudi Arabia, Arab autocrats were able to stay in power over the past 40 years only by brutally suppressing popular attempts to unseat them, whether motivated by political repression or food prices. Arab citizens certainly demonstrated the desire and ability to mobilize against their governments. But those governments, before 2011, were extremely successful in co-opting and containing them.

As a result, academics directed their attention toward explaining the mechanisms that Arab states had developed to weather popular dissent. Although different scholars focused on different aspects of this question, from domestic institutions to government strategies, most attributed the stability of Arab dictatorships to two common factors: the military-security complex and state control over the economy. In each of these areas, we in the academic community made assumptions that, as valid as they might have been in the past, turned out to be wrong in 2011.

Most scholars assumed that no daylight existed between the ruling regimes and their military and security services. That assumption was not unreasonable. Many Arab presidents served in uniform before they took office, including Ben Ali and Mubarak. In the wake of the Arab military coups of the 1950s and 1960s, Arab leaders created institutions to exercise political control over their armies and, in some cases, established rival military forces to balance the army's weight. Arab armies helped ruling regimes win their civil wars and put down uprisings. As a result, most Middle East experts came to assume that Arab armies and security services would never break with their rulers.

This assumption obviously proved incorrect. Scholars did not predict or appreciate the variable ways in which Arab armies would react to the massive, peaceful protests this year. This oversight occurred because, as a group, Middle East experts had largely lost interest in studying the role of the military in Arab politics. Although this topic once represented a central feature of U.S. scholarship on the Middle East—when the Arab military coups of the 1950s and 1960s occupied the academics of that era—the remarkable stability of the Arab regimes since then led us to assume that the issue was no longer important. Yet a preliminary review of the unfolding revolts suggests that two factors drive how Arab militaries react to public unrest: the social composition of both the regime and its military and the level of institutionalization and professionalism in the army itself.

The countries in which the military, as an institution, sided with the protesters, Egypt and Tunisia, are two of the most homogeneous societies in the Arab world. Both

are overwhelmingly Sunni. (The Coptic Christian minority in Egypt plays an important social role there but has little political clout.) Both the Egyptian and the Tunisian armies are relatively professional, with neither serving as the personal instrument of the ruler. Army leaders in both nations realized that their institutions could play an important role under new regimes and thus were willing to risk ushering out the old guard.

In Arab countries featuring less institutionalized forces, where the security services are led by and serve as the personal instruments of the ruler and his family, those forces have split or dissolved in the face of popular protests. In both Libya and Yemen, units led by the rulers' families have supported the regimes, while other units have defected to the opposition, stayed on the sidelines, or just gone home.

In divided societies, where the regime represents an ethnic, sectarian, or regional minority and has built an officer corps dominated by that overrepresented minority, the armies have thus far backed their regimes. The Sunni-led security forces in Bahrain, a Shiite-majority country, stood their ground against demonstrators to preserve the Sunni monarchy. The Jordanian army remains loyal to the monarchy despite unrest among the country's Palestinian majority. Saudi Arabia's National Guard, heavily recruited from central and western Arabian tribes, is standing by the central Arabian al-Saud dynasty. In each country, the logic is simple: if the regime falls and the majority takes over, the army leadership will likely be replaced as well.

The Syrian army's reaction to the crisis facing the Assad regime will offer an important test of this hypothesis. Members of the Assad family command important army units, and Alawites and members of other minority groups staff a good portion of the officer corps in the Sunni-majority country. If minority solidarity with the regime endures, Assad is likely to retain power. Yet if disaffected officers begin to see the army as an instrument of the Assad family itself, they could bring down the regime. Either way, once the dust settles, Middle East scholars will need to reexamine their assumptions about the relationship between Arab states and their militaries-perhaps the key element in determining regime survival in a crisis.

The Reform Factor

State control over the economy in the Middle East was another pillar of regime stability identified by academics. Scholars posited that Arab states with oil reserves and revenues deployed this wealth to control the economy, building patronage networks, providing social services, and directing the development of dependent private sectors. Through these funds, Arab rulers connected the interests of important constituencies to their survival and placated the rest of their citizens with handouts in times of crisis. Indeed, since the current uprisings began, only Libya among the major oil exporters (Algeria, Iraq, Kuwait, Libya, Qatar, Saudi Arabia, and the United Arab Emirates) has faced a serious challenge. Buoyed by high oil prices, the other oil exporters have been able to head off potential opposition by distributing resources through increased state salaries, higher subsidies for consumer goods, new state jobs, and direct handouts to citizens. Qaddafi's example establishes that oil money must be allocated properly, rather than wasted on pet projects and harebrained schemes, for it to protect a regime. The recent Arab revolts, then, would seem to validate this part of the academic paradigm on regime stability.

Yet this year's revolts have called the economic foundations of the regime stability argument into question when it comes to non-oil-producing states. Although Arab petrostates have relied on their oil revenues to avoid economic reform, changes in the world economy and the liberalizing requirements of foreign aid donors have over the past two decades forced non-oil-producing states to modernize their economies. A number of Arab regimes, including in Egypt, Jordan, Morocco, and Tunisia, have privatized state enterprises, encouraged foreign investment, created incentives to kick-start the private sector, and cut subsidies and state expenditures that previously consumed government budgets. Such Washington consensus-style economic reforms exacerbated inequalities and made life more difficult for the poor, but they also opened up new opportunities for local entrepreneurs and allowed the upper classes to enjoy greater consumer choice through liberalized trade regimes. Some Middle East specialists thought that economic liberalization could establish new bases of support for Arab authoritarians and encourage the economic growth necessary to grapple with the challenges of growing populations (as economic reforms in Turkey have led to greater support for the ruling Justice and Development Party there). Meanwhile, Western governments pushed the idea that economic reform represented a step toward political reform.

But these economic reforms backfired on those governments that embraced them most fully: Cairo and Tunis. Although both Egypt and Tunisia had achieved decent economic growth rates and received praise from the International Monetary Fund as recently as 2010, politically driven privatizations did not enhance the stability of their regimes. Instead, they created a new class of superwealthy entrepreneurs, including members of the presidents' families in both countries, which became the targets of popular ire. And the academics' assumption that these beneficiaries of economic reform would support the authoritarian regimes proved chimerical. The state-bred tycoons either fled or were unable to stop events and landed in postrevolutionary prison. The upper-middle class did not demonstrate in favor of Ben Ali or Mubarak. In fact, some members became revolutionary leaders themselves.

It is supremely ironic that the face of the Egyptian revolt was Wael Ghonim, the Egyptian Google executive. He is exactly the kind of person who was poised to succeed in the Egypt of Mubarak–bilingual, educated at the American University of Cairo, and at home in the global business world. Yet he risked his future and life to organize the "We are all Khaled Said" Facebook page, in memory of a man beaten to death by Egyptian police, which helped mobilize Egyptians against the regime. For him and many others in similar economic circumstances, political freedom outweighed monetary opportunity.

Seeing what happened in Cairo and Tunis, other Arab leaders rushed to placate their citizens by raising state salaries, canceling planned subsidy cuts, and increasing the number of state jobs. In Saudi Arabia, for example, in February and March, King Abdullah announced new spending plans of more than $100 billion. The Saudis have the oil money to fulfill such pledges. In non-oil-producing states, such as Jordan, which halted its march down the road of economic reform once the trouble began, governments may not have the money to maintain the old social contract, whereby the state provided basic economic security in exchange for loyalty. Newly liberated Egypt and Tunisia are also confronting their inherited economic woes. Empowered electorates will demand a redistribution of wealth that the governments do not have and a renegotiation of the old social contract that the governments cannot fund.

Many Middle East scholars recognized that the neoliberal economic programs were causing political problems for Arab governments, but few foresaw their regime-shaking consequences. Academics overestimated both the ameliorating effect of the economic growth introduced by the reforms and the political clout of those who were benefiting from such policies. As a result, they underestimated the popular revulsion to the corruption and crony privatization that accompanied the reforms.

Oil wealth remains a fairly reliable tool for ensuring regime stability, at least when oil prices are high. Yet focused on how Arab regimes achieved stability through oil riches, Middle East scholars missed the destabilizing effects of poorly implemented liberal economic policies in the Arab world.

A New Kind of Pan-Arabism

Another factor missed by Middle East specialists had less to do with state policies and institutions than with cross-border Arab identity. It is not a coincidence that major political upheavals arose across the Arab world simultaneously. Arab activists and intellectuals carefully followed the protests of Iran's 2009 Green Movement, but no Arabs took to the streets in emulation of their Iranian neighbors. Yet in 2011, a month after a fruit vendor in Tunisia set himself on fire, the Arab world was engulfed in revolts. If any doubts remain that Arabs retain a sense of common political identity despite living in 20 different states, the events of this year should put them to rest.

Such strong pan-Arab sentiments should not have surprised the academic community. Much of the work on Arab politics in previous generations had focused on Arab nationalism and pan-Arabism, the ability of Arab leaders to mobilize political support across state borders based on the idea that all Arabs share a common political identity and fate. Yet many of us assumed that the cross-border appeal of Arab identity had waned in recent years, especially following the Arab defeat in the 1967 war with Israel. Egypt and Jordan had signed treaties with Israel, and the Palestinians and Syria had engaged in direct negotiations with Israel, breaking a cardinal taboo of pan-Arabism. U.S.-led wars against Iraq in 1990-91 and beginning in 2003 excited opposition in the Arab world but did not destabilize the governments that cooperated with the U.S. military plans—a sign of waning pan-Arabism as much as government immunity to popular sentiment. It seemed that Arab states had become strong enough (with some exceptions, such as Lebanon and post-Saddam Hussein Iraq) to fend off ideological pressures from across their borders. Most Middle East scholars believed that pan-Arabism had gone dormant.

They thus missed the communal wave of 2011. Although the events of this year demonstrate the continued importance of Arab identity, pan-Arabism has taken a very different form than it did a half century ago under the leadership of Egyptian President Gamal Abdel Nasser. Then, Nasser, a charismatic leader with a powerful government, promoted popular ideas and drove events in other countries, using the new technology of his day, the transistor radio, to call on Arabs to oppose their own governments and follow him. Now, the very leaderless quality of the popular mobilizations in Egypt and Tunisia seems to have made them sources of inspiration across the Arab world.

In recent decades, Arab leaders, most notably Saddam during the Gulf War, have attempted to embrace Nasser's mantle and spark popular Arab movements. Even the Iranian leader Ayatollah Ruhollah Khomeini-a Persian, not an Arab-appealed to Islam to mobilize Arabs behind his banner. All these attempts failed. When the people of Tunisia and then Egypt overthrew their corrupt dictators,

however, other Arabs found they could identify with them. The fact that these revolts succeeded gave hope (in some cases, such as in Bahrain, false hope) to other Arabs that they could do the same. The common enemy of the 2011 Arab revolts is not colonialism, U.S. power, or Israel, but Arabs' own rulers.

Academics will need to assess the restored importance of Arab identity to understand the future of Middle East politics. Unlike its predecessor, the new pan-Arabism does not appear to challenge the regional map. Arabs are not demonstrating to dissolve their states into one Arab entity; their agendas are almost exclusively domestic. But the Arab revolts have shown that what happens in one Arab state can affect others in unanticipated and powerful ways. As a result, scholars and policymakers can no longer approach countries on a case-by-case basis. The United States will have a hard time supporting democracy in one Arab country, such as Egypt, while standing by as other allies, such as Bahrain, crush peaceful democratic protests.

In addition, the new pan–Arabism will eventually bring the issue of Arab–Israeli peace back to the fore. Although none of the 2011 Arab revolts occurred in the name of the Palestinians, democratic Arab regimes will have to reflect popular opinion on Israel, which remains extremely low. Arab public opinion on the United States is influenced by Arabs' views on the Israeli-Palestinian conflict as much as by U.S. actions in other Arab countries. As a result, the United States will need to reactivate Israeli-Palestinian peace talks to anticipate the demands of Arab publics across the Middle East.

Back to the Drawing Board

Academic specialists on Arab politics, such as myself, have quite a bit of rethinking to do. That is both intellectually exciting and frightening. Explaining the stability of Arab authoritarians was an important analytic task, but it led some of us to underestimate the forces for change that were bubbling below, and at times above, the surface of Arab politics. It is impossible for social scientists to make precise predictions about the Arab world, and this should not be a goal. But academics must reexamine their assumptions on a number of issues, including the military's role in Arab politics, the effects of economic change on political stability, and the salience of a cross-border Arab identity, to get a sense of how Arab politics will now unfold.

As paradigms fall and theories are shredded by events on the ground, it is useful to recall that the Arab revolts resulted not from policy decisions taken in Washington or any other foreign capital but from indigenous economic, political, and social factors whose dynamics were extremely hard to forecast. In the wake of such unexpected upheavals, both academics and policymakers should approach the Arab world with humility about their ability to shape its future. That is best left to Arabs themselves.

Critical Thinking

1. What are the reasons that most failed to anticipate the Arab Spring?

2. Explain what the failure to anticipate the Arab Spring means for theory-building.

3. What explanations are rejected for explaining the failure of democracy in the Middle-East?

4. According to the author, what were the oversights that undermined predictions of the Arab Spring?

F. Gregory Gause III is Professor of Political Science at the University of Vermont.

From *Foreign Affairs*, vol. 90, issue 4. July/August 2011, pp. 81–90. Copyright © 2011 by Council on Foreign Relations, Inc. Reprinted by permission of Foreign Affairs. www.ForeignAffairs.com

Transitional Failure in Egypt and Tunisia

MARINA OTTAWAY

Egypt and Tunisia have entered a dangerous phase of their transitions. The interim governments have little legitimacy—they were set up as caretakers to organize quick elections. But elections are being postponed in both countries, the transition is stretching on and disillusioned crowds are taking to the streets again. Popular pressure, necessary to maintain the momentum of reform, risks degenerating into the rule of the street.

Countries in transition face contradictory imperatives: they need to move fast to elect legitimate governments that can implement real reforms, but they need time to achieve some consensus about the fundamental principles that should underpin the new political system and to enact laws to regulate elections and the formation of political parties. Finding a balance is a difficult task. The experience of Tunisia and Egypt provides important lessons.

Both countries opted originally for rapid movement toward elections, with Tunisia choosing July 14 as the election date and Egypt's Supreme Council of the Armed Forces (SCAF) pledging to complete the election process in six months. With such a short timetable, the limited legitimacy of the interim governments did not appear to be too serious a problem because they were not expected to do more than organize elections.

But the timetable slipped, partly for technical reasons—a lot needs to be done to hold credible elections in countries that had none in the past—and partly for political ones—the new parties emerging from the uprising begged for more time to organize. Elections were moved from July 14 to October 23 in Tunisia; in Egypt, the government has just announced that it has nominated a judge to form an election commission that will start work on September 14, with voting to take place about two months later.

The delay is putting new pressure on the transitional governments. Governance cannot be in abeyance forever. Decisions need to be made, measures enacted. People are tired of waiting; they want to see change; they want officials of the old regime to be brought to justice; they demand economic improvement. And they are sending a clear message by taking to the streets again. This is initiating a vicious circle. Governments have less legitimacy than ever, yet they are expected to act. And they are feeling directly under attack, which is beginning to prompt an authoritarian response.

Egypt in particular is teetering between authoritarianism and the diktats of the street. Under pressure, the SCAF and government are reverting to positions reminiscent of the Mubarak government—trying to ban protests, stipulating which organizations can receive outside funding and, most dangerously, floating the idea that the new constitution must make the military the guarantor of Egyptian democracy. The latter is an oxymoron modeled on the Turkish constitution of 1960 that created a legacy from which Turkey is still trying to extricate itself painfully today.

But the protesters' demands are equally dangerous. They want selected ministers to be fired now and those responsible for the deaths of protesters in February to be brought to justice immediately. What Egypt needs, however, is not ad hoc decisions taken to pacify protesters. It needs a legitimate government set up on the basis of clear criteria and a transitional justice mechanism that avoids revenge and witch hunts but deals with accusations against officials of the old regime on the basis of law and political consensus. Instead, it is getting a hastily decided cabinet reshuffle already rejected by protesters and the sudden dismissal of hundreds of high-ranking police officers, a move that smacks of political expediency rather than due process.

The lesson of Tunisia and Egypt for countries likely to enter transition soon is that it is impossible—as well as unadvisable—to organize elections in a few months.

Too much needs to happen first—constitutional amendments, new laws, new parties and some consensus on principles. But a slower process requires a clear roadmap and timetable, with benchmarks and deadlines, not a vague process left to the whims of governments with scant legitimacy and of impatient crowds. Such a process should ideally be agreed upon early on.

Tunisia and Egypt did not do so and are paying the price now in the form of increasingly chaotic situations. The two governments must at least announce a roadmap and timetable to cover the period between now and the elections, negotiating with political parties and protesters an understanding of what must be done in the next few months and what will have to wait until after elections. They cannot allow the street to dictate in an arbitrary fashion what the government must do, but they cannot expect that people will forever accept the equally arbitrary decisions taken by interim governments.

Critical Thinking

1. What are the lessons for theory-building on democratization from the Arab spring?
2. What is the role of protest in democratization?
3. Explain how the Arab Spring shows that civil society is a mixed blessing for democratization.

Advanced Democracies and the New Politics

RUSSELL J. DALTON, SUSAN E. SCARROW, AND BRUCE E. CAIN

Over the past quarter-century in advanced industrial democracies, citizens, public interest groups, and political elites have shown decreasing confidence in the institutions and processes of representative government. In most of these nations, electoral turnout and party membership have declined, and citizens are increasingly skeptical of politicians and political institutions.[1]

Along with these trends often go louder demands to expand citizen and interest-group access to politics, and to restructure democratic decision-making processes. Fewer people may be voting, but more are signing petitions, joining lobby groups, and engaging in unconventional forms of political action.[2] Referenda and ballot initiatives are growing in popularity; there is growing interest in processes of deliberative or consultative democracy;[3] and there are regular calls for more reliance on citizen advisory committees for policy formation and administration—especially at the local level, where direct involvement is most feasible. Contemporary democracies are facing popular pressures to grant more access, increase the transparency of governance, and make government more accountable.

Amplifying these trends, a chorus of political experts has been calling for democracies to reform and adapt. Mark Warren writes, "Democracy, once again in favor, is in need of conceptual renewal. While the traditional concerns of democratic theory with state-centered institutions remain importantly crucial and ethically central, they are increasingly subject to the limitations we should expect when nineteenth-century concepts meet twenty-first century realities."[4] U.S. political analyst Dick Morris similarly observes, "The fundamental paradigm that dominates our politics is the shift from representative to direct democracy. Voters want to run the show directly and are impatient with all forms of intermediaries between their opinions and public policy."[5] As Ralf Dahrendorf recently summarized the mood of the times, "Representative government is no longer as compelling a proposition as it once was. Instead, a search for new institutional forms to express conflicts of interest has begun."[6]

Many government officials have echoed these sentiments, and the OECD has examined how its member states could reform their governments to create new connections to their publics.[7] Its report testifies:

> New forms of representation and public participation are emerging in all of our countries. These developments have expanded the avenues for citizens to participate more fully in public policy making, within the overall framework of representative democracy in which parliaments continue to play a central role. Citizens are increasingly demanding more transparency and accountability from their governments, and want greater public participation in shaping policies that affect their lives. Educated and well-informed citizens expect governments to take their views and knowledge into account when making decisions on their behalf. Engaging citizens in policy making allows governments to respond to these expectations and, at the same time, design better policies and improve their implementation.[8]

If the pressures for political reform are having real effects, these should show up in changes to the institutional structures of democratic politics. The most avid proponents of such reforms conclude that we may be experiencing the most fundamental democratic transformation since the beginnings of mass democracy in the early twentieth century. Yet cycles of reform are a recurring theme in democratic history, and pressures for change in one direction often wane as new problems and possibilities come to the fore. What is the general track record for democratic institutional reforms in the advanced industrial democracies over the latter half of the twentieth century? And what are the implications of this record for the future of democracy?

Three Modes of Democracy

In a sense, there is nothing new about the call to inject "more democracy" into the institutions of representative government. The history of modern democracies is punctuated by repeated waves of debate about the nature of the democratic process, some of which have produced major institutional reforms. In the early twentieth century, for example, the populist movement in the United States prompted extensive electoral and governing-process reforms, as well as the introduction of new forms of direct democracy.[9] Parallel institutional changes occurred in Europe. By the end of this democratic-reform period in the late 1920s, most Western democracies had become much more "democratic" in the sense of providing citizens with access to the political process and making governments more accountable.

A new wave of democratic rhetoric and debate emerged in the last third of the twentieth century. The stimulus for this first appeared mainly among university students and young professionals contesting the boundaries of conventional representative democracy. Although their dramatic protests subsequently waned, they stimulated new challenges that affect advanced industrial democracies to this day. Citizen interest groups and other public lobbying organizations, which have proliferated since the 1960s, press for more access to government; expanding mass media delve more deeply into the workings of government; and people demand more from government while trusting it less.

The institutional impact of the reform wave of the late twentieth century can be understood in terms of three different modes of democratic politics. One aims at improving the process of *representative democracy* in which citizens elect elites. Much like the populism of the early twentieth century, reforms of this mode seek to improve electoral processes. Second, there are calls for new types of *direct democracy* that bypass (or complement) the processes of representative democracy. A third mode seeks to expand the means of political participation through a new style of *advocacy democracy,* in which citizens participate in policy deliberation and formation—either directly or through surrogates, such as public interest groups—although the final decisions are still made by elites.

1) Representative democracy. A major example of reform in representative democracy can be seen in changes to processes of electing the U.S. president. In a 30-year span, these elections underwent a dramatic transformation, in which citizen influence grew via the spread of state-level primary elections as a means of nominating candidates. In 1968, the Democratic Party had just 17 presidential primaries while the Republicans had only 16; in 2000 there were Democratic primaries in 40 states and Republican primaries in 43. As well, both parties—first the Democrats, then the Republicans—instituted reforms intended to ensure that convention delegates are more representative of the public at large, such as rules on the representation of women. Meanwhile, legislators introduced and expanded public funding for presidential elections in an effort to limit the influence of money and so promote citizen equality. If the 1948 Republican and Democratic candidates, Thomas E. Dewey and Harry S. Truman, were brought back to observe the modern presidential election process, they would hardly recognize the system as the same that nominated them. More recently, reformers have championed such causes as term limits and campaign-finance reform as remedies for restricting the influence of special interests. In Europe, populist electoral reform has been relatively restrained by institutionalized systems of party government, but even so, there are parallels to what has occurred in the United States in many Euro-

pean countries. On a limited basis, for example, some European political parties have experimented with, or even adopted, closed primaries to select parliamentary candidates.[10]

In recent decades, changes in both attitudes and formal rules have brought about a greater general reliance on mechanisms of direct democracy within the advanced industrial democracies.

Generally, the mechanisms of representative democracy have maintained, and in places slightly increased, citizen access and influence. It is true that, compared with four decades ago, electoral turnout is generally down by about 10 percent in the established democracies.[11] This partially signifies a decrease in political access (or in citizens' use of elections as a means of political access). But at the same time, the "amount of electing" is up to an equal or greater extent. There has been a pattern of reform increasing the number of electoral choices available to voters by changing appointed positions into elected ones.[12] In Europe, citizens now elect members of Parliament for the European Union; regionalization has increased the number of elected subnational governments; directly elected mayors and directly elected local officials are becoming more common; and suffrage now includes younger voters, aged 18 to 20. Moreover, the number of political parties has increased, while parties have largely become more accountable—and the decisions of party elites more transparent—to their supporters. With the general expansion in electoral choices, citizens are traveling to the polls more often and making more electoral decisions.

2) Direct democracy. Initiatives and referenda are the most common means of direct democracy. These allow citizens to decide government policy without relying on the mediating influence of representation. Ballot initiatives in particular allow nongovernmental actors to control the framing of issues and even the timing of policy debates, further empowering the citizens and groups that take up this mode of action. In recent decades, changes in both attitudes and formal rules have brought about a greater general reliance on mechanisms of direct democracy within the advanced industrial democracies. The Initiative and Referendum Institute calculates, for example, that there were 118 statewide referenda in the United States during the 1950s but 378 such referenda during the 1990s. And a number of other nations have amended laws and constitutions to provide greater opportunities for direct democracy at the national and local levels.[13] Britain had its first national referendum in 1975; Sweden introduced the referendum in a constitutional reform of 1980; and Finland adopted the referendum in 1987. In these and other cases, the referendum won new legitimacy as a basis for national decision making, a norm that runs strongly counter to the ethos of representative democracy. There has also been mounting interest in expanding direct democracy through the innovation of new institutional forms, such as methods of deliberative democracy and citizen juries to advise policy makers.[14]

How fundamental are these changes? On the one hand, the political impact of a given referendum is limited, since only a single policy is being decided, so the channels of direct democracy normally provide less access than do the traditional channels of representative democracy. On the other hand, the increasing use of referenda has influenced political discourse—and the principles of political legitimacy in particular—beyond the policy at stake in any single referendum. With Britain's first referendum on European Community membership in 1975, for instance, parliamentary sovereignty was now no longer absolute, and the concept of popular sovereignty was concomitantly legitimized. Accordingly, the legitimacy of subsequent decisions on devolution required additional referenda, and today contentious issues, such as acceptance of the euro, are pervasively considered as matters that "the public should decide." So even though recourse to direct democracy remains relatively limited in Britain, the expansion of this mode of access represents a significant institutional change—and one that we see occurring across most advanced industrial democracies.

3) Advocacy democracy. In this third mode, citizens or public interest groups interact directly with governments and even participate directly in the policy-formation process, although actual decisions remain in the official hands. One might consider this as a form of traditional lobbying, but it is not. Advocacy democracy involves neither traditional interest groups nor standard channels of informal interest-group persuasion. Rather, it empowers individual citizens, citizen groups, or nongovernmental organizations to participate in advisory hearings; attend open government meetings ("government in the sunshine"); consult ombudsmen to redress grievances; demand information from government agencies; and challenge government actions through the courts.

Evidence for the growth of advocacy democracy is less direct and more difficult to quantify than is evidence for other kinds of institutional change. But the overall expansion of advocacy democracy is undeniable. Administrative reforms, decentralization, the growing political influence of courts, and other factors have created new opportunities for access and influence. During the latter 1960s in the United States, "maximum feasible participation" became a watchword for the social-service reforms of President Lyndon Johnson's "Great Society" programs. Following this model, citizen consultations and public hearings have since been embedded in an extensive range of legislation, giving citizens new points of access to policy formation and administration. Congressional hearings and state-government meetings have become public events, and legislation such as the 1972 Federal Advisory Committee Act even extended open-meeting requirements to advisory committees. While only a handful of nations had freedom-of-information laws in 1970, such laws are now almost universal in OECD countries. And there has been a general diffusion of the ombudsman model across advanced industrial democracies.[15] "Sunshine" provisions reflect a fundamental shift in understanding as to the role that elected representatives should play-one which would make Edmund Burke turn in his grave, and which we might characterize as a move away from the *trustee* toward the *delegate* model.

Reforms in this category also include new legal rights augmenting the influence of individuals and citizen groups. A pattern of judicialization in the policy process throughout most Western democracies, for instance, has enabled citizen groups to launch class-action suits on behalf of the environment, women's rights, or other public interests.[16] Now virtually every public interest can be translated into a rights-based appeal, which provides new avenues for action through the courts. Moreover, especially in European democracies, where direct citizen action was initially quite rare, the expansion of public interest groups, *Bürgerinitiativen,* and other kinds of citizen groups has substantially enlarged the public's repertoire for political action. It is worth noting that "unconventional" forms of political action, such as protests and demonstrations, have also grown substantially over this time span.

Citizens and the Democratic State

If the institutional structure of democracy is changing, how does this affect the democratic process? The answer is far from simple and not always positive, for democratic gains in some areas can be offset by losses in others, as when increased access produces new problems of democratic governability. In the following pages, we limit our attention to how these institutional changes affect the relationship between citizens and the state.

Robert A. Dahl's writings are a touchstone in this matter.[17] Like many democratic theorists, Dahl tends to equate democracy with the institutions and processes of representative democracy, paying much less attention to other forms of citizen participation that may actually represent more important means of citizen influence over political elites. Thus, while we draw from Dahl's *On Democracy* to define the essential criteria for a democratic process, we broaden the framework to include not only representative democracy but direct democracy and advocacy democracy also. Dahl suggests five criteria for a genuinely democratic system:[18]

1. **Inclusion:** With minimal exceptions, all permanent adult residents must have full rights of citizenship.

2. **Political equality:** When decisions about policy are made, every citizen must have an equal and effective opportunity to participate.

3. **Enlightened understanding:** Within reasonable limits, citizens must have equal and effective opportunities to learn about relevant policy alternatives and their likely consequences.

4. **Control of the agenda:** Citizens must have the opportunity to decide which matters are placed on the public agenda, and how.

5. **Effective participation:** Before a policy is adopted, all the citizens must have equal and effective opportunities for making their views known to other citizens.

Robert A. Dahl's Democratic Criteria

Democratic Criteria	Representative Democracy	Direct Democracy	Advocacy Democracy
Inclusion	**Universal suffrage provides inclusion**	**Universal suffrage provides inclusion**	Equal citizen access *(Problems of access to nonelectoral arenas)*
Political Equality	**One person, one vote with high turnout maximizes equality** *(Problems of low turnout, inequality due to campaign finance issues, etc.)*	**One person, one vote with high turnout maximizes equality** *(Problems of equality with low turnout)*	Equal opportunity *(Problems of very unequal use)*
Enlightened Understanding	*(Problems of information access, voter decision processes)*	*(Problems of greater information and higher decision-making costs)*	**Increased public access to information** *(Problems of even greater information and decision-making demands on citizens)*
Control of the Agenda	*(Problems of control of campaign debate, selecting candidates, etc.)* **Control through responsible parties**	**Citizen initiation provides control of agenda** *(Problems of influence by interest groups)*	**Citizens and groups control the locus and focus of activity**
Effective Participation	*(Principal-agent problems: fair elections, responsible party government, etc.)*	**Direct policy impact ensures effective participation**	**Direct access avoids mediated participation**

Note. Criteria that are well addressed are presented in **bold**, criteria that are at issue are presented in *italics* in the shaded cells.

The first column of the Table lists Dahl's five democratic criteria. The second column summarizes the prevailing view on how well representative democracy fulfills these criteria. For example, advanced industrial democracies have met the *inclusion* criterion by expanding the franchise to all adult citizens (by way of a long and at times painful series of reforms). General success in this regard is illustrated by the bold highlighting of "universal suffrage" in the first cell of this column.

Nearly all advanced industrial democracies now meet the *political equality* criterion by having enacted the principle of "one person, one vote" for elections, which we have highlighted in the second cell. In most nations today, a majority of citizens participate in voting, while labor unions, political parties, and other organizations mobilize participation to achieve high levels of engagement. Indeed, that noted democrat, the late Mayor Richard Daley of Chicago, used to say that electoral politics was the only instrument through which a working-class citizen could ever exercise equal influence with the socially advantaged. At the same time, certain problems of equality remain, as contemporary debates about campaign financing and voter registration illustrate, and full equality in political practice is probably unattainable. We note these problems in the shaded area of the second cell. Nevertheless, overall the principle of

equality is now a consensual value for the electoral processes of representative democracy.

At first glance, it may seem that expanding the number of elections amounts to extending these principles. But increasing the number of times that voters go to the polls and the number of items on ballots actually tends to depress turnout. And when voter turnout is less than 50 percent, as it tends to be in, say, EU parliamentary elections—or less than 25 percent, as it tends to be in local mayoral or school-board elections in the United States—then one must question whether the gap between "equality of access" and "equality of usage" has become so wide that it undermines the basic principle of *political equality*. Moreover, second-order elections tend to mobilize a smaller and more ideological electorate than the public at large, and so more second-order elections tend to mean more distortions in the representativeness of the electoral process.

The tension between Dahl's democratic criteria and democratic practice becomes even more obvious when we turn to the criterion of *enlightened understanding*. Although we are fairly sanguine about voters' abilities to make informed choices when it comes to high-visibility (for instance, presidential or parliamentary) elections, we are less so when it comes to lower-visibility elections. How does a typical resident of Houston,

Texas, make enlightened choices regarding the dozens of judgeship candidates whose names appeared on the November 2002 ballot, to say nothing of other local office seekers and referenda? In such second- and third-order elections, the means of information that voters can use in first-order elections may be insufficient or even altogether lacking. So the expansion of the electoral marketplace may empower the public in a sense, but in another sense may make it hard for voters to exercise meaningful political judgment.

Another criterion is citizen *control of the political agenda.* Recent reforms in representative democracy have gone some way toward broadening access to the political agenda. Increasing the number of elected offices gives citizens more input and presumably more avenues for raising issues, while reforming political finance to equalize campaign access and party support has made for greater openness in political deliberations. More problematic, though, is performance on the *effectiveness of participation* criterion. Do citizens get what they vote for? Often, this principal-agent problem is solved through the mechanism of party government: Voters select a party, and the party ensures the compliance of individual members of parliament and the translation of electoral mandates into policy outcomes.[19] But the impact of recent reforms on the *effectiveness of participation* is complex. On the one hand, more openness and choice in elections should enable people to express their political preferences more extensively and in more policy areas. On the other hand, as the number of office-holders proliferates, it may become more difficult for voters to assign responsibility for policy outcomes. Fragmented decision making, divided government, and the sheer profusion of elected officials may diminish the political responsiveness of each actor.

How much better do the mechanisms of direct democracy fare when measured against Dahl's five criteria (see column 3 of the Table)? Because referenda and initiatives are effectively mass elections, they seek to ensure inclusion and political equality in much the same way as representative elections do. Most referenda and initiatives use universal suffrage to ensure inclusion and the "one person, one vote" rule to ensure political equality. However, whereas turnout in direct-democracy elections is often lower than in comparable elections for public officials, the question of democratic inclusion becomes more complicated than a simple assessment of equal access. For instance, when Proposition 98—which favored altering the California state constitution to mandate that a specific part of the state budget be directed to primary and secondary education—appeared on the 1996 general election ballot, barely half of all voting-age Californians turned out, and only 51 percent voted for the proposition. But as a consequence, the state's constitution was altered, reshaping state spending and public financing in California. Such votes raise questions about the fairness of elections in which a minority of registered voters can make crucial decisions affecting the public welfare. Equality of opportunity clearly does not mean equality of participation.

Moreover, referenda and initiatives place even greater demands for information and understanding on voters. Many of the heuristics that they can use in party elections or candidate elections are less effective in referenda, and the issues

themselves are often more complex than what citizens are typically called upon to consider in electing office-holders. For instance, did the average voter have enough information to make enlightened choices in Italy's multi-referendum ballot of 1997? This ballot asked voters to make choices concerning television-ownership rules, television-broadcasting policy, the hours during which stores could remain open, the commercial activities which municipalities could pursue, labor-union reform proposals, regulations for administrative elections, and residency rules for mafia members. In referenda, voters can still rely on group heuristics and other cues that they use in electing public officials,[20] but obviously the proliferation of policy choices and especially the introduction of less-salient local issues raise questions about the overall effectiveness of such cue-taking.

The real strengths of direct democracy are highlighted by Dahl's fourth and fifth criteria. Referenda and initiatives shift the focus of agenda-setting from elites toward the public, or at least toward public interest groups. Indeed, processes of direct democracy can bring into the political arena issues that elites tend not to want to address: for example, tax reform or term limits in the United States, abortion-law reform in Italy, or the terms of EU membership in Europe generally. Even when referenda fail to reach the ballot or fail to win a majority, they can nevertheless prompt elites to be more sensitive to public interests. By definition, moreover, direct democracy should solve the problem of effective participation that exists with all methods of representative democracy. Direct democracy is unmediated, and so it ensures that participation is effective. Voters make policy choices with their ballot—to enact a new law, to repeal an existing law, or to reform a constitution. Even in instances where the mechanisms of direct democracy require an elite response in passing a law or a revoting in a later election, the link to policy action is more direct than is the case with the channels of representative democracy. Accordingly, direct democracy seems to fulfill Dahl's democratic criteria of agenda control and effective participation.

But direct democracy raises questions in these areas as well. Interest groups may find it easier to manipulate processes of direct democracy than those of representative democracy.[21] The discretion to place a policy initiative on the ballot can be appealing to interest groups, which then have unmediated access to voters during the subsequent referendum campaign. In addition, decisions made by way of direct democracy are less susceptible to bargaining or the checks and balances that occur within the normal legislative process. Some recent referenda in California may illustrate this style of direct democracy: Wealthy backers pay a consulting firm to collect signatures so as to get a proposal on the ballot, and then bankroll a campaign to support their desired legislation. This is not grassroots democracy at work; it is the representation of wealthy interests by other means.

The expansion of direct democracy has the potential to complement traditional forms of representative democracy. It can expand the democratic process by allowing citizens and public interest groups new access to politics, and new control over political agendas and policy outcomes. But direct democracy also raises new questions about equality of actual influence, if not formal access, and the ability of the public to make fair and reasoned judgments about issues. Perhaps the most important question about direct democracy is not whether it is expanding, but *how* it is expanding: Are there ways to increase access and influence without sacrificing inclusion and equality? We return to this question below.

Formal Access and Actual Use

The final column in our Table considers how new forms of advocacy democracy fulfill Dahl's democratic criteria. These new forms of action provide citizens with significant access to politics, but it is also clear that this access is very unevenly used. Nearly everyone can vote, and most do. But very few citizens file lawsuits, file papers under a freedom-of-information act, attend environmental-impact review hearings, or attend local planning meetings. There is no clear equivalent to "one person, one vote" for advocacy democracy. Accordingly, it raises the question of how to address Dahl's criteria of inclusion, political equality, and enlightened understanding.

"Equality of access" is not adequate if "equality of usage" is grossly uneven. For instance, when Europeans were asked in the 1989 European Election Survey whether they voted in the election immediately preceding the survey, differences in participation according to levels of education were very slight (see the Figure, Social-Status Inequality in Participation). A full 73 percent of those in the "low education" category said they had voted in the previous EU parliamentary election (even though it is a second-order election), and an identical percentage of those in the "high education" category claimed to have voted. Differences in campaign activity according to educational levels are somewhat greater, but still modest in overall terms.

A distinctly larger inequality gap emerges when it comes to participation through forms of direct or advocacy democracy. For instance, only 13 percent of those in the "low education" category had participated in a citizen action group, while nearly three times the percentage of those in the "high education" category had participated. Similarly, there are large inequalities when it comes to such activities as signing a petition or participating in a lawful demonstration.

With respect to the criterion of *enlightened understanding,* advocacy democracy has mixed results. On the one hand, it can enhance citizen understanding and make for greater inclusion. Citizens and public interest groups can increase the amount of information that they have about government activities, especially by taking advantage of freedom-of-information laws, attending administrative hearings, and participating in government policy making. And with the assistance of the press in disseminating this information, citizens and public interest groups can better influence political outcomes. By ensuring that the public receives information in a timely fashion, advocacy democracy allows citizens to make informed judgments and hold governments more accountable. And by eliminating the filtering that governments would otherwise apply, advocacy democracy can help citizens to get more accurate pictures of the influences affecting policy decisions, with fewer cover-ups and self-serving distortions. On the other hand, advocacy democracy makes greater cognitive and resource demands on citizens, and thus may generate some of the same inequalities in participation noted above. It requires much more of the citizen to participate in a public hearing or to petition an official than it does simply to cast a vote. The most insightful evidence on this point comes from Jane Mansbridge's study of collective decision making in New England town meetings.[22] She finds that many participants were unprepared or overwhelmed by the deliberative decision-making processes.

Advocacy democracy fares better when it comes to the remaining two criteria. It gives citizens greater control of the political agenda, in part by increasing their opportunity to press their interests outside of the institutionalized time and format constraints of fixed election cycles. By means of advocacy democracy, citizens can often choose when and where to challenge a government directive or pressure policy makers. Similarly, even though advocacy democracy typically leaves final political decisions in the hands of elites, it nevertheless provides direct access to government. Property owners can participate in a local planning hearing; a public interest group can petition government for information on past policies; and dissatisfied citizens can attend a school board session. Such unmediated participation brings citizens into the decision-making process-which ultimately might not be as effective as the efforts of a skilled representative, but greater direct involvement in the democratic process should improve its accountability and transparency (see the bold entries in these last two cells of the Table).

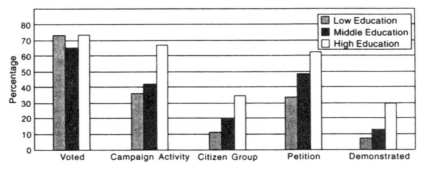

Social-Status Inequality in Participation

Source: Eurobarometers 31 and 31A conducted in connection with the 1989 European Parliament election. Results combine the 12 nations weighted to represent the total EU population.

All in all, advocacy democracy increases the potential for citizen access in important ways. It can give citizens and public interest groups new influence over the agenda-setting process, and it can give them unmediated involvement in the policy-formation process. These are significant extensions of democratic participation. At the same time, advocacy democracy may exacerbate political inequality on account of inequalities in usage. New access points created through advisory panels, consultative hearings, and other institutional reforms empower some citizens to become more involved. But other citizens, relatively lacking in the skills or resources to compete in these new domains, may be left behind. In other words, advocacy democracy may in some ways respond to the strength of the claimants, rather than to the strength of their claims. It can even alter the locus of political expertise. While advocacy democracy values know-how and expertise in the citizenry, it devalues those same characteristics among policy makers.

Environmental policy provides a good illustration of this problem. Here, citizens and public interest groups have gained new rights and new access to the policy process. But these are disproportionately used by relatively affluent and skilled citizens, who are already participating in conventional forms of representative democracy, while the poor, the unskilled, and the otherwise disadvantaged tend to get left behind. So while environmentalism is an example of citizen empowerment, it is also a source of increasing inequality.

No form of democratic action is ideal, each having its advantages and limitations. As democratic practice shifts from a predominant reliance on representation toward a mixed repertoire—including greater use of direct and advocacy democracy—a new balance must be struck among democratic goals. It is possible that new institutional arrangements will maximize the benefits of these new modes while limiting their disadvantages—as, for example, the institutions of representative democracy depend on parties and interest groups. But thus far, the advanced industrialized democracies have not fully recognized the problems generated by the new mixed repertoire of democratic action, and so have yet to find institutional or structural means of addressing them. Democratic reforms create opportunities, but they also create challenges. Our goal should be to ensure that progress on some democratic criteria is not unduly sacrificed for progress on others.

Notes

1. Martin P. Wattenberg, *Where Have All the Voters Gone?* (Cambridge: Harvard University Press, 2002); Susan E. Scarrow, "From Social Integration to Electoral Contestation," in Russell J. Dalton and Martin P. Wattenberg, eds., *Parties Without Partisans: Political Change in Advanced Industrial Democracies* (New York: Oxford University Press, 2000); Russell J. Dalton, *Democratic Challenges, Democratic Choices: The Decline in Political Support in Advanced Industrial Democracies* (Oxford: Oxford University Press, 2004); Susan J. Pharr and Robert D. Putnam, eds., *Disaffected Democracies: What's Troubling the Trilateral Countries?* (Princeton: Princeton University Press, 2000).

2. Russell J. Dalton, *Citizen Politics: Public Opinion and Political Parties in Advanced Industrial Democracies* (New York: Chatham House, 2002), ch. 4; Ronald Inglehart, *Modernization and Postmodernization: Cultural, Economic, and Political Change in 43 Societies* (Princeton: Princeton University Press, 1997); Sidney Verba, Kay Schlozman, and Henry Brady, *Voice and Equality: Civic Volunteerism in American Politics* (Cambridge: Harvard University Press, 1995), 72.

3. James S. Fishkin, *The Voice of the People: Public Opinion and Democracy* (New Haven: Yale University Press, 1995); John Elster, *Deliberative Democracy* (New York: Cambridge University Press, 1998).

4. Mark Warren, *Democracy and Association* (Princeton: Princeton University Press, 2001), 226.

5. Dick Morris, *The New Prince: Machiavelli Updated for the Twenty-First Century* (New York: Renaissance Books, 2000).

6. Ralf Dahrendorf, "Afterword," in Susan J. Pharr and Robert D. Putnam, eds., *Disaffected Democracies: What's Troubling the Trilateral Countries?* 311.

7. OECD, *Government of the Future: Getting from Here to There* (Paris: Organization for Economic Co-operation and Development, 2000).

8. OECD, *Citizens as Partners: OECD Handbook on Information, Consultation and Public Participation in Policy-Making* (Paris: Organization of Economic Cooperation and Development, 2001), 9.

9. Lawrence Goodwyn, *Democratic Promise: The Populist Movement in America* (New York: Oxford University Press, 1976).

10. Susan E. Scarrow, Paul Webb, and David M. Farrell, "From Social Integration to Electoral Contestation," in Russell J. Dalton and Martin P. Wattenberg, eds., *Parties without Partisans: Political Change in Advanced Industrial Democracies;* Jonathan Hopkin, "Bringing the Members Back in: Democratizing Candidate Selection in Britain and Spain," *Party Politics* 7 (May 2001): 343–61.

11. Martin P. Wattenberg, *Where Have All the Voters Gone?*

12. Russell J. Dalton and Mark Gray, "Expanding the Electoral Marketplace," in Bruce E. Cain, Russell J. Dalton, and Susan E. Scarrow, eds., *Democracy Transformed? Expanding Political Opportunities in Advanced Industrial Democracies* (Oxford: Oxford University Press, 2003).

13. Susan E. Scarrow, "Direct Democracy and Institutional Design: A Comparative Investigation," in *Comparative Political Studies* 34 (August 2001): 651–65; also see David Butler and Austin Ranney, eds., *Referenda Around the World* (Washington, D.C.: American Enterprise Institute, 1994); Michael Gallagher and Pier Vincenzo Uleri, eds., *The Referendum Experience in Europe* (Basingstoke: Macmillan, 1996).

14. James S. Fishkin, *The Voice of the People: Public Opinion and Democracy;* Forest David Matthews, *Politics for People: Finding a Responsive Voice,* 2nd ed. (Urbana: University of Illinois Press, 1999).

15. Roy Gregory and Philip Giddings, eds., *Righting Wrongs: The Ombudsman in Six Continents* (Amsterdam: IOS Press, 2000); see also Christopher Ansell and Jane Gingrich, "Reforming the Administrative State," in Bruce E. Cain, Russell J. Dalton, and

Susan E. Scarrow, eds., *Democracy Transformed? Expanding Political Opportunities in Advanced Industrial Democracies.*

16. Alec Stone Sweet, *Governing with Judges: Constitutional Politics in Europe* (New York: Oxford University Press, 2000).

17. Robert A Dahl, *Polyarchy: Participation and Opposition* (New Haven: Yale University Press, 1971); *Democracy and Its Critics* (New Haven: Yale University Press, 1991); *On Democracy* (New Haven: Yale University Press, 1998).

18. Robert A. Dahl, *On Democracy,* 37–38.

19. Hans-Dieter Klingemann et al., *Parties, Policies, and Democracy* (Boulder: Westview, 1994).

20. Arthur Lupia, "Shortcuts versus Encyclopedias," *American Political Science Review* 88 (March 1994): 63–76.

21. Elisabeth Gerber, *The Populist Paradox: Interest Group Influence and the Promise of Direct Legislation* (Princeton: Princeton University Press, 1999); see also David S. Broder, *Democracy Derailed: Initiative Campaigns and the Power of Money.*

22. Jane Mansbridge, *Beyond Adversary Democracy* (New York: Basic Books, 1980).

Critical Thinking

1. What are some important trends in mature democracies?

2. If "no form of democratic action is ideal," what are the problems with the forms described?

3. What are the five democratic criteria discussed? Which is most achievable? Which is hardest?

RUSSELL J. DALTON is director of the Center for the Study of Democracy at the University of California, Irvine. **SUSAN E. SCARROW** is associate professor of political science at the University of Houston. **BRUCE E. CAIN** is Robson Professor of Political Science at the University of California, Berkeley, and director of the Institute of Governmental Studies. This essay is adapted from their edited volume, *Democracy Transformed? Expanding Political Opportunities in Advanced Industrial Democracies* (2003).

Capitalism and Democracy*

GABRIEL A. ALMOND

Joseph Schumpeter, a great economist and social scientist of the last generation, whose career was almost equally divided between Central European and American universities, and who lived close to the crises of the 1930s and '40s, published a book in 1942 under the title, *Capitalism, Socialism, and Democracy*. The book has had great influence, and can be read today with profit. It was written in the aftergloom of the great depression, during the early triumphs of Fascism and Nazism in 1940 and 1941, when the future of capitalism, socialism, and democracy all were in doubt. Schumpeter projected a future of declining capitalism, and rising socialism. He thought that democracy under socialism might be no more impaired and problematic than it was under capitalism.

He wrote a concluding chapter in the second edition which appeared in 1946, and which took into account the political-economic situation at the end of the war, with the Soviet Union then astride a devastated Europe. In this last chapter he argues that we should not identify the future of socialism with that of the Soviet Union, that what we had observed and were observing in the first three decades of Soviet existence was not a necessary expression of socialism. There was a lot of Czarist Russia in the mix. If Schumpeter were writing today, I don't believe he would argue that socialism has a brighter future than capitalism. The relationship between the two has turned out to be a good deal more complex and intertwined than Schumpeter anticipated. But I am sure that he would still urge us to separate the future of socialism from that of Soviet and Eastern European Communism.

Unlike Schumpeter I do not include Socialism in my title, since its future as a distinct ideology and program of action is unclear at best. Western Marxism and the moderate socialist movements seem to have settled for social democratic solutions, for adaptations of both capitalism and democracy producing acceptable mixes of market competition, political pluralism, participation, and welfare. I deal with these modifications of capitalism, as a consequence of the impact of democracy on capitalism in the last half century.

At the time that Adam Smith wrote *The Wealth of Nations*, the world of government, politics and the state that he knew—pre-Reform Act England, the French government of Louis XV and XVI—was riddled with special privileges, monopolies, interferences with trade. With my tongue only half way in my check

I believe the discipline of economics may have been traumatized by this condition of political life at its birth. Typically, economists speak of the state and government instrumentally, as a kind of secondary service mechanism.

I do not believe that politics can be treated in this purely instrumental and reductive way without losing our analytic grip on the social and historical process. The economy and the polity are the main problem solving mechanisms of human society. They each have their distinctive means, and they each have their "goods" or ends. They necessarily interact with each other, and transform each other in the process. Democracy in particular generates goals and programs. You cannot give people the suffrage, and let them form organizations, run for office, and the like, without their developing all kinds of ideas as to how to improve things. And sometimes some of these ideas are adopted, implemented and are productive, and improve our lives, although many economists are reluctant to concede this much to the state.

My lecture deals with this interaction of politics and economics in the Western World in the course of the last couple of centuries, in the era during which capitalism and democracy emerged as the dominant problem solving institutions of modern civilization. I am going to discuss some of the theoretical and empirical literature dealing with the themes of the positive and negative interaction between capitalism and democracy. There are those who say that capitalism supports democracy, and those who say that capitalism subverts democracy. And there are those who say that democracy subverts capitalism, and those who say that it supports it.

The relation between capitalism and democracy dominates the political theory of the last two centuries. All the logically possible points of view are represented in a rich literature. It is this ambivalence and dialectic, this tension between the two major problem solving sectors of modern society—the political and the economic—that is the topic of my lecture.

Capitalism Supports Democracy

Let me begin with the argument that capitalism is positively linked with democracy, shares its values and culture, and facilitates its development. This case has been made in historical, logical, and statistical terms.

*Lecture presented at Seminar on the Market, sponsored by the Ford Foundation and the Research Institute on International Change of Columbia University, Moscow, October 29–November 2.

Albert Hirschman in his *Rival Views of Market Society* (1986) examines the values, manners and morals of capitalism, and their effects on the larger society and culture as these have been described by the philosophers of the 17th, 18th, and 19th centuries. He shows how the interpretation of the impact of capitalism has changed from the enlightenment view of Montesquieu, Condorcet, Adam Smith and others, who stressed the *douceur* of commerce, its "gentling," civilizing effect on behavior and interpersonal relations, to that of the 19th and 20th century conservative and radical writers who described the culture of capitalism as crassly materialistic, destructively competitive, corrosive of morality, and hence self-destructive. This sharp almost 180-degree shift in point of view among political theorists is partly explained by the transformation from the commerce and small-scale industry of early capitalism, to the smoke blackened industrial districts, the demonic and exploitive entrepreneurs, and exploited laboring classes of the second half of the nineteenth century. Unfortunately for our purposes, Hirschman doesn't deal explicitly with the capitalism–democracy connection, but rather with culture and with manners. His argument, however, implies an early positive connection and a later negative one.

Joseph Schumpeter in *Capitalism, Socialism, and Democracy* (1942) states flatly, "History clearly confirms . . . [that] . . . modern democracy rose along with capitalism, and in causal connection with it . . . modern democracy is a product of the capitalist process." He has a whole chapter entitled "The Civilization of Capitalism," democracy being a part of that civilization. Schumpeter also makes the point that democracy was historically supportive of capitalism. He states, ". . . the bourgeoisie reshaped, and from its own point of view rationalized, the social and political structure that preceded its ascendancy . . ." (that is to say, feudalism). "The democratic method was the political tool of that reconstruction." According to Schumpeter capitalism and democracy were mutually causal historically, mutually supportive parts of a rising modern civilization, although as we shall show below, he also recognized their antagonisms.

Barrington Moore's historical investigation (1966) with its long title, *The Social Origins of Dictatorship and Democracy; Lord and Peasant in the Making of the Modern World*, argues that there have been three historical routes to industrial modernization. The first of these followed by Britain, France, and the United States, involved the subordination and transformation of the agricultural sector by the rising commercial bourgeoisie, producing the democratic capitalism of the 19th and 20th centuries. The second route followed by Germany and Japan, where the landed aristocracy was able to contain and dominate the rising commercial classes, produced an authoritarian and fascist version of industrial modernization, a system of capitalism encased in a feudal authoritarian framework, dominated by a military aristocracy, and an authoritarian monarchy. The third route, followed in Russia where the commercial bourgeoisie was too weak to give content and direction to the modernizing process, took the form of a revolutionary process drawing on the frustration and resources of the peasantry, and created a mobilized authoritarian Communist regime along with a state-controlled industrialized economy. Successful capitalism dominating and transforming the rural agricultural sector, according

to Barrington Moore, is the creator and sustainer of the emerging democracies of the nineteenth century.

Robert A. Dahl, the leading American democratic theorist, in the new edition of his book (1990) *After the Revolution? Authority in a Good Society*, has included a new chapter entitled "Democracy and Markets." In the opening paragraph of that chapter, he says:

> It is an historical fact that modern democratic institutions . . . have existed only in countries with predominantly privately owned, market-oriented economies, or capitalism if you prefer that name. It is also a fact that all "socialist" countries with predominantly state-owned centrally directed economic orders—command economies—have not enjoyed democratic governments, but have in fact been ruled by authoritarian dictatorships. It is also an historical fact that some "capitalist" countries have also been, and are, ruled by authoritarian dictatorships.
>
> To put it more formally, it looks to be the case that market-oriented economies are necessary (in the logical sense) to democratic institutions, though they are certainly not sufficient. And it looks to be the case that state-owned centrally directed economic orders are strictly associated with authoritarian regimes, though authoritarianism definitely does not require them. We have something very much like an historical experiment, so it would appear, that leaves these conclusions in no great doubt. (Dahl 1990)

Peter Berger in his book *The Capitalist Revolution* (1986) presents four propositions on the relation between capitalism and democracy:

> Capitalism is a necessary but not sufficient condition of democracy under modern conditions.
>
> If a capitalist economy is subjected to increasing degrees of state control, a point (not precisely specifiable at this time) will be reached at which democratic governance becomes impossible.
>
> If a socialist economy is opened up to increasing degrees of market forces, a point (not precisely specifiable at this time) will be reached at which democratic governance becomes a possibility.
>
> If capitalist development is successful in generating economic growth from which a sizable proportion of the population benefits, pressures toward democracy are likely to appear.

This positive relationship between capitalism and democracy has also been sustained by statistical studies. The "Social Mobilization" theorists of the 1950s and 1960s which included Daniel Lerner (1958), Karl Deutsch (1961), S. M. Lipset (1959) among others, demonstrated a strong statistical association between GNP per capita and democratic political institutions. This is more than simple statistical association. There is a logic in the relation between level of economic development and democratic institutions. Level of economic development has been shown to be associated with education and literacy, exposure to mass media, and democratic psychological propensities such as subjective efficacy, participatory aspirations and skills. In a major investigation of the social psychology of industrialization and modernization, a research team led by the sociologist Alex Inkeles (1974) interviewed several thousand workers in the modern industrial and the traditional economic sectors of six countries of differing culture. Inkeles found empathetic, efficacious, participatory and activist propensities much more frequently among the modern industrial workers, and to a much lesser extent in the traditional sector in each one of these countries regardless of cultural differences.

The historical, the logical, and the statistical evidence for this positive relation between capitalism and democracy is quite persuasive.

Capitalism Subverts Democracy

But the opposite case is also made, that capitalism subverts or undermines democracy. Already in John Stuart Mill (1848) we encounter a view of existing systems of private property as unjust, and of the free market as destructively competitive—aesthetically and morally repugnant. The case he was making was a normative rather than a political one. He wanted a less competitive society, ultimately socialist, which would still respect individuality. He advocated limitations on the inheritance of property and the improvement of the property system so that everyone shared in its benefits, the limitation of population growth, and the improvement of the quality of the labor force through the provision of high quality education for all by the state. On the eve of the emergence of the modern democratic capitalist order John Staurt Mill wanted to control the excesses of both the market economy and the majoritarian polity, by the education of consumers and producers, citizens and politicians, in the interest of producing morally improved free market and democratic orders. But in contrast to Marx, he did not thoroughly discount the possibilities of improving the capitalist and democratic order.

Marx argued that as long as capitalism and private property existed there could be no genuine democracy, that democracy under capitalism was bourgeois democracy, which is to say not democracy at all. While it would be in the interest of the working classes to enter a coalition with the bourgeoisie in supporting this form of democracy in order to eliminate feudalism, this would be a tactical maneuver. Capitalist democracy could only result in the increasing exploitation of the working classes. Only the elimination of capitalism and private property could result in the emancipation of the working classes and the attainment of true democracy. Once socialism was attained the basic political problems of humanity would have been solved through the elimination of classes. Under socialism there would be no distinctive democratic organization, no need for institutions to resolve conflicts, since there would be no conflicts. There is not much democratic or political theory to be found in Marx's writings. The basic reality is the mode of economic production and the consequent class structure from which other institutions follow.

For the followers of Marx up to the present day there continues to be a negative tension between capitalism, however

reformed, and democracy. But the integral Marxist and Leninist rejection of the possibility of an autonomous, bourgeois democratic state has been left behind for most Western Marxists. In the thinking of Poulantzas, Offe, Bobbio, Habermas and others, the bourgeois democratic state is now viewed as a class struggle state, rather than an unambiguously bourgeois state. The working class has access to it; it can struggle for its interests, and can attain partial benefits from it. The state is now viewed as autonomous, or as relatively autonomous, and it can be reformed in a progressive direction by working class and other popular movements. The bourgeois democratic state can be moved in the direction of a socialist state by political action short of violence and institutional destruction.

Schumpeter (1942) appreciated the tension between capitalism and democracy. While he saw a causal connection between competition in the economic and the political order, he points out ". . . that there are some deviations from the principle of democracy which link up with the presence of organized capitalist interests. . . . [T]he statement is true both from the standpoint of the classical and from the standpoint of our own theory of democracy. From the first standpoint, the result reads that the means at the disposal of private interests are often used in order to thwart the will of the people. From the second standpoint, the result reads that those private means are often used in order to interfere with the working of the mechanism of competitive leadership." He refers to some countries and situations in which ". . . political life all but resolved itself into a struggle of pressure groups and in many cases practices that failed to conform to the spirit of the democratic method." But he rejects the notion that there cannot be political democracy in a capitalist society. For Schumpeter full democracy in the sense of the informed participation of all adults in the selection of political leaders and consequently the making of public policy, was an impossibility because of the number and complexity of the issues confronting modern electorates. The democracy which was realistically possible was one in which people could choose among competing leaders, and consequently exercise some direction over political decisions. This kind of democracy was possible in a capitalist society, though some of its propensities impaired its performance. Writing in the early years of World War II, when the future of democracy and of capitalism were uncertain, he leaves unresolved the questions of ". . . Whether or not democracy is one of those products of capitalism which are to die out with it . . ." or ". . . how well or ill capitalist society qualifies for the task of working the democratic method it evolved."

Non-Marxist political theorists have contributed to this questioning of the reconcilability of capitalism and democracy. Robert A. Dahl, who makes the point that capitalism historically has been a necessary precondition of democracy, views contemporary democracy in the United States as seriously compromised, impaired by the inequality in resources among the citizens. But Dahl stresses the variety in distributive patterns, and in politico-economic relations among contemporary democracies. "The category of capitalist democracies" he writes, "includes an extraordinary variety . . . from nineteenth century, laissez faire, early industrial systems to twentieth century, highly regulated, social welfare, late or postindustrial systems. Even late twentieth century 'welfare state' orders vary all the way from the Scandinavian systems, which are redistributive, heavily taxed, comprehensive in their social security, and neocorporatist in their collective bargaining arrangements to the faintly redistributive, moderately taxed, limited social security, weak collective bargaining systems of the United States and Japan" (1989).

In *Democracy and Its Critics* (1989) Dahl argues that the normative growth of democracy to what he calls its "third transformation" (the first being the direct city-state democracy of classic times, and the second, the indirect, representative inegalitarian democracy of the contemporary world) will require democratization of the economic order. In other words, modern corporate capitalism needs to be transformed. Since government control and/or ownership of the economy would be destructive of the pluralism which is an essential requirement of democracy, his preferred solution to the problem of the mega-corporation is employee control of corporate industry. An economy so organized, according to Dahl, would improve the distribution of political resources without at the same time destroying the pluralism which democratic competition requires. To those who question the realism of Dahl's solution to the problem of inequality, he replies that history is full of surprises.

Charles E. Lindblom in his book, *Politics and Markets* (1977), concludes his comparative analysis of the political economy of modern capitalism and socialism, with an essentially pessimistic conclusion about contemporary market-oriented democracy. He says

> We therefore come back to the corporation. It is possible that the rise of the corporation has offset or more than offset the decline of class as an instrument of indoctrination. . . . That it creates a new core of wealth and power for a newly constructed upper class, as well as an overpowering loud voice, is also reasonably clear. The executive of the large corporation is, on many counts, the contemporary counterpart to the landed gentry of an earlier era, his voice amplified by the technology of mass communication. . . . [T]he major institutional barrier to fuller democracy may therefore be the autonomy of the private corporation.

Lindblom concludes, "The large private corporation fits oddly into democratic theory and vision. Indeed it does not fit."

There is then a widely shared agreement, from the Marxists and neo-Marxists, to Schumpeter, Dahl, Lindblom, and other liberal political theorists, that modern capitalism with the dominance of the large corporation, produces a defective or an impaired form of democracy.

Democracy Subverts Capitalism

If we change our perspective now and look at the way democracy is said to affect capitalism, one of the dominant traditions of economics from Adam Smith until the present day stresses the importance for productivity and welfare of an economy that is relatively free of intervention by the state. In this doctrine of minimal government there is still a place for a framework of rules and services essential to the productive and efficient performance of the economy. In part the government has to protect the market from itself. Left to their own devices, according to

Smith, businessmen were prone to corner the market in order to exact the highest possible price. And according to Smith businessmen were prone to bribe public officials in order to gain special privileges, and legal monopolies. For Smith good capitalism was competitive capitalism, and good government provided just those goods and services which the market needed to flourish, could not itself provide, or would not provide. A good government according to Adam Smith was a minimal government, providing for the national defense, and domestic order. Particularly important for the economy were the rules pertaining to commercial life such as the regulation of weights and measures, setting and enforcing building standards, providing for the protection of persons and property, and the like.

For Milton Friedman (1961, 1981), the leading contemporary advocate of the free market and free government, and of the interdependence of the two, the principal threat to the survival of capitalism and democracy is the assumption of the responsibility for welfare on the part of the modern democratic state. He lays down a set of functions appropriate to government in the positive interplay between economy and polity, and then enumerates many of the ways in which the modern welfare, regulatory state has deviated from these criteria.

A good Friedmanesque, democratic government would be one ". . . which maintained law and order, defended property rights, served as a means whereby we could modify property rights and other rules of the economic game, adjudicated disputes about the interpretation of the rules, enforced contracts, promoted competition, provided a monetary framework, engaged in activities to counter technical monopolies and to overcome neighborhood effects widely regarded as sufficiently important to justify government intervention, and which supplemented private charity and the private family in protecting the irresponsible, whether madman or child. . . ." Against this list of proper activities for a free government, Friedman pinpointed more than a dozen activities of contemporary democratic governments which might better be performed through the private sector, or not at all. These included setting and maintaining price supports, tariffs, import and export quotas and controls, rents, interest rates, wage rates, and the like, regulating industries and banking, radio and television, licensing professions and occupations, providing social security and medical care programs, providing public housing, national parks, guaranteeing mortgages, and much else.

Friedman concludes that this steady encroachment on the private sector has been slowly but surely converting our free government and market system into a collective monster, compromising both freedom and productivity in the outcome. The tax and expenditure revolts and regulatory rebellions of the 1980s have temporarily stemmed this trend, but the threat continues. "It is the internal threat coming from men of good intentions and good will who wish to reform us. Impatient with the slowness of persuasion and example to achieve the great social changes they envision, they are anxious to use the power of the state to achieve their ends, and confident of their own ability to do so." The threat to political and economic freedom, according to Milton Friedman and others who argue the same position, arises out of democratic politics. It may only be defeated by political action.

In the last decades a school, or rather several schools, of economists and political scientists have turned the theoretical models of economics to use in analyzing political processes. Variously called public choice theorists, rational choice theorists, or positive political theorists, and employing such models as market exchange and bargaining, rational self interest, game theory, and the like, these theorists have produced a substantial literature throwing new and often controversial light on democratic political phenomena such as elections, decisions of political party leaders, interest group behavior, legislative and committee decisions, bureaucratic, and judicial behavior, lobbying activity, and substantive public policy areas such as constitutional arrangements, health and environment policy, regulatory policy, national security and foreign policy, and the like. Hardly a field of politics and public policy has been left untouched by this inventive and productive group of scholars.

The institutions and names with which this movement is associated in the United States include Virginia State University, the University of Virginia, the George Mason University, the University of Rochester, the University of Chicago, the California Institute of Technology, the Carnegie Mellon University, among others. And the most prominent names are those of the leaders of the two principal schools: James Buchanan, the Nobel Laureate leader of the Virginia "Public Choice" school, and William Riker, the leader of the Rochester "Positive Theory" school. Other prominent scholars associated with this work are Gary Becker of the University of Chicago, Kenneth Shepsle and Morris Fiorina of Harvard, John Ferejohn of Stanford, Charles Plott of the California Institute of Technology, and many others.

One writer summarizing the ideological bent of much of this work, but by no means all of it (William Mitchell of the University of Washington), describes it as fiscally conservative, sharing a conviction that the ". . . private economy is far more robust, efficient, and perhaps, equitable than other economies, and much more successful than political processes in efficiently allocating resources. . . ." Much of what has been produced ". . . by James Buchanan and the leaders of this school can best be described as contributions to a theory of the failure of political processes." These failures of political performance are said to be inherent properties of the democratic political process. "Inequity, inefficiency, and coercion are the most general results of democratic policy formation." In a democracy the demand for publicly provided services seems to be insatiable. It ultimately turns into a special interest, "rent seeking" society. Their remedies take the form of proposed constitutional limits on spending power and checks and balances to limit legislative majorities.

One of the most visible products of this pessimistic economic analysis of democratic politics is the book by Mancur Olson, *The Rise and Decline of Nations* (1982). He makes a strong argument for the negative democracy–capitalism connection. His thesis is that the behavior of individuals and firms in stable societies inevitably leads to the formation of dense networks of collusive, cartelistic, and lobbying organizations that make economies less efficient and dynamic and polities less governable. "The longer a society goes without an upheaval, the more powerful such organizations become and the more they slow

down economic expansion. Societies in which these narrow interest groups have been destroyed, by war or revolution, for example, enjoy the greatest gains in growth." His prize cases are Britain on the one hand and Germany and Japan on the other.

> The logic of the argument implies that countries that have had democratic freedom of organization without upheaval or invasion the longest will suffer the most from growth-repressing organizations and combinations. This helps explain why Great Britain, the major nation with the longest immunity from dictatorship, invasion, and revolution, has had in this century a lower rate of growth than other large, developed democracies. Britain has precisely the powerful network of special interest organization that the argument developed here would lead us to expect in a country with its record of military security and democratic stability. The number and power of its trade unions need no description. The venerability and power of its professional associations is also striking. . . . In short, with age British society has acquired so many strong organizations and collusions that it suffers from an institutional sclerosis that slows its adaptation to changing circumstances and technologies. (Olson 1982)

By contrast, post-World War II Germany and Japan started organizationally from scratch. The organizations that led them to defeat were all dissolved, and under the occupation inclusive organizations like the general trade union movement and general organizations of the industrial and commercial community were first formed. These inclusive organizations had more regard for the general national interest and exercised some discipline on the narrower interest organizations. And both countries in the post-war decades experienced "miracles" of economic growth under democratic conditions.

The Olson theory of the subversion of capitalism through the propensities of democratic societies to foster special interest groups has not gone without challenge. There can be little question that there is logic in his argument. But empirical research testing this pressure group hypothesis thus far has produced mixed findings. Olson has hopes that a public educated to the harmful consequences of special interests to economic growth, full employment, coherent government, equal opportunity, and social mobility will resist special interest behavior, and enact legislation imposing anti-trust, and anti-monopoly controls to mitigate and contain these threats. It is somewhat of an irony that the solution to this special interest disease of democracy, according to Olson, is a democratic state with sufficient regulatory authority to control the growth of special interest organizations.

Democracy Fosters Capitalism

My fourth theme, democracy as fostering and sustaining capitalism, is not as straightforward as the first three. Historically there can be little doubt that as the suffrage was extended in the last century, and as mass political parties developed, democratic development impinged significantly on capitalist institutions and practices. Since successful capitalism requires risk-taking entrepreneurs with access to investment capital, the democratic propensity for redistributive and regulative policy tends to reduce the incentives and the resources available for risk-taking and creativity. Thus it can be argued that propensities inevitably resulting from democratic politics, as Friedman, Olson and many others argue, tend to reduce productivity, and hence welfare.

But precisely the opposite argument can be made on the basis of the historical experience of literally all of the advanced capitalist democracies in existence. All of them without exception are now welfare states with some form and degree of social insurance, health and welfare nets, and regulatory frameworks designed to mitigate the harmful impacts and shortfalls of capitalism. Indeed, the welfare state is accepted all across the political spectrum. Controversy takes place around the edges. One might make the argument that had capitalism not been modified in this welfare direction, it is doubtful that it would have survived.

This history of the interplay between democracy and capitalism is clearly laid out in a major study involving European and American scholars, entitled *The Development of Welfare States in Western Europe and America* (Flora and Heidenheimer 1981). The book lays out the relationship between the development and spread of capitalist industry, democratization in the sense of an expanding suffrage and the emergence of trade unions and left-wing political parties, and the gradual introduction of the institutions and practices of the welfare state. The early adoption of the institutions of the welfare state in Bismarck Germany, Sweden, and Great Britain were all associated with the rise of trade unions and socialist parties in those countries. The decisions made by the upper and middle class leaders and political movements to introduce welfare measures such as accident, old age, and unemployment insurance, were strategic decisions. They were increasingly confronted by trade union movements with the capacity of bringing industrial production to a halt, and by political parties with growing parliamentary representation favoring fundamental modifications in, or the abolition of capitalism. As the calculations of the upper and middle class leaders led them to conclude that the costs of suppression exceeded the costs of concession, the various parts of the welfare state began to be put in place—accident, sickness, unemployment insurance, old age insurance, and the like. The problem of maintaining the loyalty of the working classes through two world wars resulted in additional concessions to working class demands: the filling out of the social security system, free public education to higher levels, family allowances, housing benefits, and the like.

Social conditions, historical factors, political processes and decisions produced different versions of the welfare state. In the United States, manhood suffrage came quite early, the later bargaining process emphasized free land and free education to the secondary level, an equality of opportunity version of the welfare state. The Disraeli bargain in Britain resulted in relatively early manhood suffrage and the full attainment of parliamentary government, while the Lloyd George bargain on the eve of World War I brought the beginnings of a welfare system to Britain. The Bismarck bargain in Germany produced an early welfare state, a postponement of electoral equality and parliamentary government. While there were all of these differences in historical encounters with democratization and "welfarization," the important outcome was that little more than a century after the process began all of the advanced capitalist democracies had similar versions of the welfare state, smaller in scale in the case of the United States and Japan, more substantial in Britain and the continental European countries.

We can consequently make out a strong case for the argument that democracy has been supportive of capitalism in this strategic sense. Without this welfare adaptation it is doubtful that capitalism would have survived, or rather, its survival, "unwelfarized," would have required a substantial repressive apparatus. The choice then would seem to have been between democratic welfare capitalism, and repressive undemocratic capitalism. I am inclined to believe that capitalism as such thrives more with the democratic welfare adaptation than with the repressive one. It is in that sense that we can argue that there is a clear positive impact of democracy on capitalism.

We have to recognize, in conclusion, that democracy and capitalism are both positively and negatively related, that they both support and subvert each other. My colleague, Moses Abramovitz, described this dialectic more surely than most in his presidential address to the American Economic Association in 1980, on the eve of the "Reagan Revolution." Noting the decline in productivity in the American economy during the latter 1960s and '70s, and recognizing that this decline might in part be attributable to the "tax, transfer, and regulatory" tendencies of the welfare state, he observes,

> The rationale supporting the development of our mixed economy sees it as a pragmatic compromise between the competing virtues and defects of decentralized market capitalism and encompassing socialism. Its goal is to obtain a measure of distributive justice, security, and social guidance of economic life without losing too much of the allocative efficiency and dynamism of private enterprise and market organization. And it is a pragmatic compromise in another sense. It seeks to retain for most people that measure of personal protection from the state which private property and a private job market confer, while obtaining for the disadvantaged minority of people through the state that measure of support without which their lack of property or personal endowment would amount to a denial of individual freedom and capacity to function as full members of the community. (Abramovitz 1981)

Democratic welfare capitalism produces that reconciliation of opposing and complementary elements which makes possible the survival, even enhancement of both of these sets of institutions. It is not a static accommodation, but rather one which fluctuates over time, with capitalism being compromised by the tax-transfer-regulatory action of the state at one point, and then correcting in the direction of the reduction of the intervention of the state at another point, and with a learning process over time that may reduce the amplitude of the curves.

The case for this resolution of the capitalism-democracy quandary is made quite movingly by Jacob Viner who is quoted in the concluding paragraph of Abramovitz's paper, "... If ... I nevertheless conclude that I believe that the welfare state, like old Siwash, is really worth fighting for and even dying for as compared to any rival system, it is because, despite its imperfection in theory and practice, in the aggregate it provides more promise of preserving and enlarging human freedoms, temporal prosperity, the extinction of mass misery, and the dignity of man and his moral improvement than any other social system which has previously prevailed, which prevails elsewhere today or which outside Utopia, the mind of man has been able to provide a blueprint for" (Abramovitz 1981).

References

Abramovitz, Moses. 1981. "Welfare Quandaries and Productivity Concerns." *American Economic Review*, March.

Berger, Peter. 1986. *The Capitalist Revolution.* New York: Basic Books.

Dahl, Robert A. 1989. *Democracy and Its Critics.* New Haven: Yale University Press.

_____. 1990. *After the Revolution: Authority in a Good Society.* New Haven: Yale University Press.

Deutsch, Karl. 1961. "Social Mobilization and Political Development." *American Political Science Review*, 55 (Sept.).

Flora, Peter, and Arnold Heidenheimer. 1981. *The Development of Welfare States in Western Europe and America.* New Brunswick, NJ: Transaction Press.

Friedman, Milton. 1981. *Capitalism and Freedom.* Chicago: University of Chicago Press.

Hirschman, Albert. 1986. *Rival Views of Market Society.* New York: Viking.

Inkeles, Alex, and David Smith. 1974. *Becoming Modern: Individual Change in Six Developing Countries.* Cambridge, MA: Harvard University Press.

Lerner, Daniel. 1958. *The Passing of Traditional Society.* New York: Free Press.

Lindblom, Charles E. 1977. *Politics and Markets.* New York: Basic Books.

Lipset, Seymour M. 1959. "Some Social Requisites of Democracy." *American Political Science Review*, 53 (September).

Mill, John Stuart. 1848, 1965. *Principles of Political Economy,* 2 vols. Toronto: University of Toronto Press.

Mitchell, William. 1988. "Virginia, Rochester, and Bloomington: Twenty-Five Years of Public Choice and Political Science." *Public Choice*, 56: 101–119.

Moore, Barrington. 1966. *The Social Origins of Dictatorship and Democracy.* New York: Beacon Press.

Olson, Mancur. 1982. *The Rise and Decline of Nations.* New Haven: Yale University Press.

Schumpeter, Joseph. 1946. *Capitalism, Socialism, and Democracy.* New York: Harper.

Critical Thinking

1. Does capitalism lead to institutional change such as democracy?

2. Does capitalism subvert democracy?

3. According to the author, what is the direction of effect between capitalism and democracy?

GABRIEL A. ALMOND, professor of political science emeritus at Stanford University, is a former president of the American Political Science Association.

UNIT 3

Political Participation: From Preferences to Policies

Unit Selections

Learning Outcomes

After reading this Unit, you will be able to:

- Discuss how citizen participation affects democracy.

- Describe how the evidence in this unit supports or contradicts democratization theory.

- Distinguish between social, cultural, and political activism.

- Explain how citizen behavior and attitudes affect democracy or democratization.

- Explain how participation may challenge government.

- Explain how participation may support government.

- Clarify the importance of providing venues of participation.

- Explain the effects of modern technology on participation, activism, and democratization.

Student Website
www.mhhe.com/cls

Internet References

Freedom House
   http://freedomhouse.org/template.cfm?page=1
The Human Rights Watch–Americas
   www.hrw.org/americas
The Human Rights Watch–Middle East and North Africa
   www.hrw.org/middle-east/n-africa
National Geographic Society
   www.nationalgeographic.com
Research and Reference (Library of Congress)
   www.loc.gov/rr

Unit 3 builds upon one of the baseline fundamentals of democratic theory in Unit 2: It considers systematically why and how citizen participation is organized and what forms it takes. The unit begins with Robert Dahl's article, "What Political Institutions Does Large-Scale Democracy Require?", which points out two obvious advantages to organizing citizens. First, it improves efficiency and effectiveness of participation. In particular, aggregating the interests or preferences of citizens is invaluable as the size of the citizenry increases and as more people are dispersed over larger geographic areas. Second, organized citizen groups provide the counterbalance to coercive governments who may not be willing to tolerate or accommodate interests that depart from the government's goals. As the author points out, "the degree of coercion" required to suppress larger associations is generally considered objectionable. Consequently, groups are able to exist and express themselves where individual citizens may not be able.

The article on youth movements in the three post-communist countries of Serbia, Georgia, and Ukraine certainly supports the latter view. In particular, it describes how fear of the authorities hinders organizing and mobilizing. Likewise, the article on online activism in China describes how cyberprotestors, notwithstanding their anonymity, restrain themselves to areas where the law is clearly established and often do not directly challenge state authority. Yet, notably, these movements have grown in the face of possible government clampdown, in part because their large numbers provide anonymity and some insulation against adverse government repression, in part because such activism has led to a redefinition of civic associations and how they mobilize to improve political conditions and civil rights.

Importantly, participation or zeal alone does not change the status quo. Thus, the article on the youth movements in the post-communist countries describes rigorous training and organization of the youths to undercut the fear of the authorities and to present cogent, coherent challenges. Likewise, the article on online activism describes much of the Internet activity involves user-interaction that provides the grounds for changing citizens' behaviors and attitudes. These articles point out that while mass protests and demonstrations are useful, sole reliance on such mass demonstrations does not generally achieve the desired objectives. Instead, the articles show that success is based on regularized or even institutionalized funding and organization to raise awareness and support and defuse challenges to their agenda.

Also noteworthy, while attention on these new forms of civic associations has focused on their challenge of less-responsive or less-accountable governments, they may be used to buttress

© Thinkstock/Getty Images

the government. As Article 17 on "Smart Dictators Do Not Quash the Internet" points out, even as citizens have sought to use the anonymity of the Internet to galvanize and mobilize, governments–particularly unaccountable ones–have adapted technology to monitor the internet and social networking. Thus China filters the Internet, Russia uses online propaganda, and other governments have launched cyber attacks to undermine political bloggers and activism.

And, there is also a need to be wary of the citizen mobilization unleashed by the Internet. We are apt to look kindly on the Internet and social-networking given the recent political transitions in the Middle East; yet, as Article 18 on "Cyberposse" points out, the Internet may lead to citizen vigilantism and campaigns of "harassment, mass intimidation, and public revenge." As Units 1 and 2 point out, citizen participation and mobilization are important, and the failure to provide for that participation potentially leads to perilous forms of involvement to push for change. And, as article 11 in Unit 2 suggests, there is also the possibility that successful mobilization may breed impatience, and impatience is antithetical to institution-building.

Perhaps it is useful to remind citizens and policymakers alike that even as demands are building for change, there remain venues for expressing demands or dissent. Indeed, perhaps the only reasonable way to ensure that all forms of social and civic organizations do not enjoy undue influence is not to restrict them but, rather, to pluralize them. Citizen participation is fundamental to political development and social stability; this unit emphasizes that providing venues for that participation so that it does not boil over is essential to continued development and stability.

What Political Institutions Does Large-Scale Democracy Require?

ROBERT A. DAHL

What does it mean to say that a country is governed democratically? Here, we will focus on the political institutions of *democracy on a large scale*, that is, the political institutions necessary for a *democratic country*. We are not concerned here, then, with what democracy in a very small group might require, as in a committee. We also need to keep in mind that every actual democracy has always fallen short of democratic criteria. Finally, we should be aware that in ordinary language, we use the word *democracy* to refer both to a goal or ideal and to an actuality that is only a partial attainment of the goal. For the time being, therefore, I'll count on the reader to make the necessary distinctions when I use the words *democracy, democratically, democratic government, democratic country*, and so on.[1]

How Can We Know?

How can we reasonably determine what political institutions are necessary for large-scale democracy? We might examine the history of countries that have changed their political institutions in response, at least in part, to demands for broader popular inclusion and effective participation in government and political life. Although in earlier times those who sought to gain inclusion and participation were not necessarily inspired by democratic ideas, from about the eighteenth century onward they tended to justify their demands by appealing to democratic and republican ideas. What political institutions did they seek, and what were actually adopted in these countries?

Alternatively, we could examine countries where the government is generally referred to as democratic by most of the people in that country, by many persons in other countries, and by scholars, journalists, and the like. In other words, in ordinary speech and scholarly discussion the country is called a democracy.

Third, we could reflect on a specific country or group of countries, or perhaps even a hypothetical country, in order to imagine, as realistically as possible, what political institutions would be required in order to achieve democratic goals to a

> ### What Political Institutions Does Large-Scale Democracy Require?
>
> Large-scale democracy requires:
>
> 1. Elected officials
> 2. Free, fair, and frequent elections
> 3. Freedom of expression
> 4. Alternative sources of information
> 5. Associational autonomy
> 6. Inclusive citizenship

Figure 1

substantial degree. We would undertake a mental experiment, so to speak, in which we would reflect carefully on human experiences, tendencies, possibilities, and limitations and design a set of political institutions that would be necessary for large-scale democracy to exist and yet feasible and attainable within the limits of human capacities.

Fortunately, all three methods converge on the same set of democratic political institutions. These, then, are minimal requirements for a democratic country (Figure 1).

The Political Institutions of Modern Representative Democracy

Briefly, the political institutions of modern representative democratic government are

- *Elected officials.* Control over government decisions about policy is constitutionally vested in officials elected by citizens. Thus modern, large-scale democratic governments are *representative*.
- *Free, fair and frequent elections.* Elected officials are chosen in frequent and fairly conducted elections in which coercion is comparatively uncommon.

- *Freedom of expression.* Citizens have a right to express themselves without danger of severe punishment on political matters broadly defined, including criticism of officials, the government, the regime, the socioeconomic order, and the prevailing ideology.

- *Access to alternative sources of information.* Citizens have a right to seek out alternative and independent sources of information from other citizens, experts, newspapers, magazines, books, telecommunications, and the like. Moreover, alternative sources of information actually exist that are not under the control of the government or any other single political group attempting to influence public political beliefs and attitudes, and these alternative sources are effectively protected by law.

- *Associational autonomy.* To achieve their various rights, including those required for the effective operation of democratic political institutions, citizens also have a right to form relatively independent associations or organizations, including independent political parties and interest groups.

- *Inclusive citizenship.* No adult permanently residing in the country and subject to its laws can be denied the rights that are available to others and are necessary to the five political institutions just listed. These include the right to vote in the election of officials in free and fair elections; to run for elective office; to free expression; to form and participate in independent political organizations; to have access to independent sources of information; and rights to other liberties and opportunities that may be necessary to the effective operation of the political institutions of large-scale democracy.

The Political Institutions in Perspective

Ordinarily these institutions do not arrive in a country all at once; the last two are distinctly latecomers. Until the twentieth century, universal suffrage was denied in both the theory and practice of democratic and republican government. More than any other single feature, universal suffrage distinguishes modern representative democracy from earlier forms of democracy.

The time of arrival and the sequence in which the institutions have been introduced have varied tremendously. In countries where the full set of democratic institutions arrived earliest and have endured to the present day, the "older" democracies, elements of a common pattern emerge. Elections to a legislature arrived early on—in Britain as early as the thirteenth century, in the United States during its colonial period in the seventeenth and eighteenth centuries. The practice of electing higher lawmaking officials was followed by a gradual expansion of the rights of citizens to express themselves on political matters and to seek out and exchange information. The right to form associations with explicit political goals tended to follow

still later. Political "factions" and partisan organization were generally viewed as dangerous, divisive, subversive of political order and stability, and injurious to the public good. Yet because political associations could not be suppressed without a degree of coercion that an increasingly large and influential number of citizens regarded as intolerable, they were often able to exist as more or less clandestine associations until they emerged from the shadows into the full light of day. In the legislative bodies, what once were "factions" became political parties. The "ins" who served in the government of the day were opposed by the "outs," or what in Britain came to be officially styled His (or Her) Majesty's Loyal Opposition. In eighteenth-century Britain, the faction supporting the monarch and the opposing faction supported by much of the gentry in the "country" were gradually transformed into Tories and Whigs. During that same century in Sweden, partisan adversaries in Parliament somewhat facetiously called themselves the Hats and the Caps.[2]

During the final years of the eighteenth century in the newly formed republic of the United States, Thomas Jefferson, the vice president, and James Madison, leader of the House of Representatives, organized their followers in Congress to oppose the policies of the Federalist president, John Adams, and his secretary of the treasury, Alexander Hamilton. To succeed in their opposition, they soon realized that they would have to do more than oppose the Federalists in the Congress and the cabinet: they would need to remove their opponents from office. To do that, they had to win national elections, and to win national elections they had to organize their followers throughout the country. In less than a decade, Jefferson, Madison, and others sympathetic with their views created a political party that was organized all the way down to the smallest voting precincts, districts, and municipalities, an organization that would reinforce the loyalty of their followers between and during election campaigns and make sure they came to the polls. Their Republican Party (soon renamed Democratic Republican and, a generation later, Democratic) became the first popularly based *electoral* party in the world. As a result, one of the most fundamental and distinctive political institutions of modern democracy, the political party, had burst beyond its confines in parliaments and legislatures in order to organize the citizens themselves and mobilize party supporters in national elections.

By the time the young French aristocrat Alexis de Tocqueville visited the United States in the 1830s, the first five democratic political institutions described above had already arrived in America. The institutions seemed to him so deeply planted and pervasive that he had no hesitation in referring to the United States as a democracy. In that country, he said, the people were sovereign, "society governs itself for itself," and the power of the majority was unlimited.[3] He was astounded by the multiplicity of associations into which Americans organized themselves, for every purpose, it seemed. And towering among these associations were the two major political parties. In the United States, it appeared to Tocqueville, democracy was about as complete as one could imagine it ever becoming.

During the century that followed, all five of the basic democratic institutions Tocqueville observed during his visit to America were consolidated in more than a dozen other countries. Many observers in Europe and the United States concluded that any country that aspired to be civilized and progressive would necessarily have to adopt a democratic form of government.

Yet everywhere, the sixth fundamental institution—inclusive citizenship—was missing. Although Tocqueville affirmed that "the state of Maryland, which had been founded by men of rank, was the first to proclaim universal suffrage," like almost all other men (and many women) of his time he tacitly assumed that "universal" did not include women.[4] Nor, indeed, some men. Maryland's "universal suffrage," it so happened, also excluded most African Americans. Elsewhere, in countries that were otherwise more or less democratic, as in America, a full half of all adults were completely excluded from national political life simply because they were women; in addition, large numbers of men were denied suffrage because they could not meet literacy or property requirements, an exclusion supported by many people who considered themselves advocates of democratic or republican government. Although New Zealand extended suffrage to women in national elections in 1893 and Australia in 1902, in countries otherwise democratic, women did not gain suffrage in national elections until about 1920; in Belgium, France, and Switzerland, countries that most people would have called highly democratic, women could not vote until after World War II.

Because it is difficult for many today to grasp what "democracy" meant to our predecessors, let me reemphasize the difference: in all democracies and republics throughout twenty-five centuries, the rights to engage fully in political life were restricted to a minority of adults. "Democratic" government was government by males only—and not all of them. It was not until the twentieth century that in both theory and practice democracy came to require that the rights to engage fully in political life must be extended, with very few if any exceptions, to the entire population of adults permanently residing in a country.

Taken in their entirety, then, these six political institutions constitute not only a new type of political system but a new kind of popular government, a type of "democracy" that had never existed throughout the twenty-five centuries of experience since the inauguration of "democracy" in Athens and a "republic" in Rome. Because the institutions of modern representative democratic government, taken in their entirety, are historically unique, it is convenient to give them their own name. This modern type of large-scale democratic government is sometimes called *polyarchal* democracy.

Although other factors were often at work, the six political institutions of polyarchal democracy came about, in part at least, in response to demands for inclusion and participation in political life. In countries that are widely referred to as democracies today, all six exist. Yet you might well ask: Are some of these institutions no more than past products of historical struggles? Are they no longer necessary for democratic government? And if they are still necessary today, why?[5]

The Factor of Size

Before answering these questions, I need to call attention to an important qualification. We are considering institutions necessary for the government of a democratic country. Why "country"? *Because all the institutions necessary for a democratic country would not always be required for a unit much smaller than a country.*

Consider a democratically governed committee, or a club, or a very small town. Although equality in voting would seem to be necessary, small units like these might manage without many elected officials: perhaps a moderator to preside over meetings, a secretary-treasurer to keep minutes and accounts. The participants themselves could decide just about everything directly during their meetings, leaving details to the secretary-treasurer. Governments of small organizations would not have to be full-fledged *representative* governments in which citizens elect representatives charged with enacting laws and policies. Yet these governments could be democratic, perhaps highly democratic. So, too, even though they lacked political parties or other independent political associations, they might be highly democratic. In fact, we might concur with the classical democratic and republican view that in small associations, organized "factions" are not only unnecessary but downright harmful. Instead of conflicts exacerbated by factionalism, caucuses, political parties, and so on, we might prefer unity, consensus, agreement achieved by discussion and mutual respect.

The political institutions strictly required for democratic government depend, then, on the size of the unit. The six institutions listed above developed because they are necessary for governing *countries*, not smaller units. Polyarchal democracy is democratic government on the large scale of the nation-state or country.

To return to our questions: Are the political institutions of polyarchal democracy actually necessary for democracy on the large scale of a country? If so, why? To answer these twin questions, let us recall what a democratic process requires (Figure 2).

Why (and When) Does Democracy Require Elected Representatives?

As the focus of democratic government shifted to large-scale units like nations or countries, the question arose: How can citizens *participate effectively* when the number of citizens becomes too numerous or too widely dispersed geographically (or both, as in the case of a country) for them to participate conveniently in making laws by assembling in one place? And how can they make sure that matters with which they are most concerned are adequately considered by officials—that is, how can citizens *control the agenda of* government decisions?

How best to meet these democratic requirements in a political unit as large as a country is, of course, enormously difficult, indeed to some extent unachievable. Yet just as with

Why the Institutions Are Necessary In a unit as large as a country, these political institutions of polyarchal democracy. . .	. . . are necessary to satisfy the following democratic criteria:
1. Elected representatives. . .	Effective participation Control of the agenda
2. Free, fair and frequent elections. . .	Voting equality Control of the agenda
3. Freedom of expression. . .	Effective participation Enlightened understanding Control of the agenda
4. Alternative information. . .	Effective participation Enlightened understanding Control of the agenda
5. Associational autonomy. . .	Effective participation Enlightened understanding Control of the agenda
6. Inclusive citizenship. . .	Full inclusion

Figure 2

the other highly demanding democratic criteria, this, too, can serve as a standard for evaluating alternative possibilities and solutions. Clearly the requirements could not be met if the top officials of the government could set the agenda and adopt policies independently of the wishes of citizens. The only feasible solution, though it is highly imperfect, is for citizens to elect their top officials and hold them more or less accountable through elections by dismissing them, so to speak, in subsequent elections.

To us that solution seems obvious. But what may appear self-evident to us was not at all obvious to our predecessors.

Until fairly recently the possibility that citizens could, by means of elections, choose and reject representatives with the authority to make laws remained largely foreign to both the theory and practice of democracy. The election of representatives mainly developed during the Middle Ages, when monarchs realized that in order to impose taxes, raise armies, and make laws, they needed to win the consent of the nobility, the higher clergy, and a few not-so-common commoners in the larger towns and cities.

Until the eighteenth century, then, the standard view was that democratic or republican government meant rule by the people, and if the people were to rule, they had to assemble in one place and vote on decrees, laws, or policies. Democracy would have to be town meeting democracy; representative democracy was a contradiction in terms. By implication, whether explicit or implicit, a republic or a democracy could actually exist only in a small unit, like a town or city. Writers who held this view, such as Montesquieu and Jean-Jacques Rousseau, were perfectly aware of the disadvantages of a small state, particularly when it confronted the military superiority of a much larger state, and were therefore extremely pessimistic about the future prospects for genuine democracy.

Yet the standard view was swiftly overpowered and swept aside by the onrushing force of the national state. Rousseau himself clearly understood that for a government of a country as large as Poland (for which he proposed a constitution), representation would be necessary. And shortly thereafter, the standard view was driven off the stage of history by the arrival of democracy in America.

As late as 1787, when the Constitutional Convention met in Philadelphia to design a constitution appropriate for a large country with an ever-increasing population, the delegates were acutely aware of the historical tradition. Could a republic possibly exist on the huge scale the United States had already attained, not to mention the even grander scale the delegates foresaw?[6] Yet no one questioned that if a republic were to exist in America, it would have to take the form of a *representative* republic. Because of the lengthy experience with representation in colonial and state legislatures and in the Continental Congress, the feasibility of representative government was practically beyond debate.

By the middle of the nineteenth century, the traditional view was ignored, forgotten, or, if remembered at all, treated as irrelevant. "It is evident," John Stuart Mill wrote in 1861

that the only government which can fully satisfy all the exigencies of the social state is one in which the whole people participate; that any participation, even in the smallest public function, is useful; that the participation should everywhere be as great as the general degree of improvement of the community will allow; and that nothing less can be ultimately desirable than the admission of all to share in the sovereign power of the state. But since all cannot, in a community exceeding a single small town, participate personally in any but some very minor portions of the public business, it follows that the ideal type of a perfect government must be representative.[7]

Why Does Democracy Require Free, Fair, and Frequent Elections?

As we have seen, if we accept the desirability of political equality, then every citizen must have an *equal and effective opportunity to vote, and all votes must be counted as equal.* If equality in voting is to be implemented, then clearly, elections must be free and fair. To be free means that citizens can go to the polls without fear of reprisal; and if they are to be fair, then all votes must be counted as equal. Yet free and fair elections are not enough. Imagine electing representatives for a term of, say, twenty years! If citizens are to retain *final control over the agenda*, then elections must also be frequent.

How best to implement free and fair elections is not obvious. In the late nineteenth century, the secret ballot began to replace a public show of hands. Although open voting still has a few defenders, secrecy has become the general standard; a country in which it is widely violated would be judged as lacking free and fair elections. But debate continues as to the kind of voting system that best meets standards of fairness. Is a system of proportional representation (PR), like that employed in most democratic countries, fairer than the first-past-the-post system used in Great Britain and the United States? Reasonable arguments can be made for both. In discussions about different voting systems, however, the need for a fair system is assumed; how best to achieve fairness and other reasonable objectives is simply a technical question.

How frequent should elections be? Judging from twentieth-century practices in democratic countries, a rough answer might be that annual elections for legislative representatives would be a bit too frequent and anything more than five years would be too long. Obviously, however, democrats can reasonably disagree about the specific interval and how it might vary with different offices and different traditional practices. The point is that without frequent elections, citizens would lose a substantial degree of control over their elected officials.

Why Does Democracy Require Free Expression?

To begin with, freedom of expression is required in order for citizens to *participate* effectively in political life. How can citizens make their views known and persuade their fellow citizens and representatives to adopt them unless they can express themselves freely about all matters bearing on the conduct of the government? And if they are to take the views of others into account,

they must be able to hear what others have to say. Free expression means not just that you have a right to be heard. It also means that you have a right to hear what others have to say.

To acquire an *enlightened understanding* of possible government actions and policies also requires freedom of expression. To acquire civic competence, citizens need opportunities to express their own views; learn from one another; engage in discussion and deliberation; read, hear, and question experts, political candidates, and persons whose judgments they trust; and learn in other ways that depend on freedom of expression.

Finally, without freedom of expression, citizens would soon lose their capacity to influence *the agenda* of government decisions. Silent citizens may be perfect subjects for an authoritarian ruler; they would be a disaster for a democracy.

Why Does Democracy Require the Availability of Alternative and Independent Sources of Information?

Like freedom of expression, the availability of alternative and relatively independent sources of information is required by several of the basic democratic criteria. Consider the need for *enlightened understanding*. How can citizens acquire the information they need in order to understand the issue if the government controls all the important sources of information? Or, for that matter, if any single group enjoys a monopoly in providing information? Citizens must have access, then, to alternative sources of information that are not under the control of the government or dominated by any other group or point of view.

Or think about *effective participation* and influencing the *public agenda*. How could citizens participate effectively in political life if all the information they could acquire were provided by a single source, say the government, or, for that matter, a single party, faction, or interest?

Why Does Democracy Require Independent Associations?

It took a radical turnabout in ways of thinking to accept the need for political associations—interest groups, lobbying organizations, political parties. Yet if a large republic requires that representatives be elected, then how are elections to be contested? Forming an organization, such as a political party, gives a group an obvious electoral advantage. And if one group seeks to gain that advantage, will not others who disagree with their policies? And why should political activity cease between elections? Legislators can be influenced; causes can be advanced, policies promoted, appointments sought. So, unlike a small city or town, the large scale of democracy in a country makes political associations both necessary and desirable. In any case, how can they be prevented without impairing the fundamental right of citizens to participate effectively in governing? In a large republic, then, they are not only necessary and desirable but inevitable. Independent associations are also a source of *civic education and enlightenment.* They provide citizens not only with information but also with opportunities for discussion, deliberation, and the acquisition of political skills.

Why Does Democracy Require Inclusive Citizenship?

We can view the political institutions summarized in Figure 1 in several ways. For a country that lacks one or more of the institutions, and is to that extent not yet sufficiently democratized, knowledge of the basic political institutions can help us to design a strategy for making a full *transition* to modern representative democracy. For a country that has only recently made the transition, that knowledge can help inform us about the crucial institutions that need to be *strengthened, deepened, and consolidated*. Because they are all necessary for modern representative democracy (polyarchal democracy), we can also view them as establishing a *minimum level for democratization*.

Those of us who live in the older democracies, where the transition to democracy occurred some generations ago and the political institutions listed in Figure 1 are by now solidly established, face a different and equally difficult challenge. For even if the institutions are necessary to democratization, they are definitely not *sufficient* for achieving fully the democratic criteria listed in Figure 1. Are we not then at liberty, and indeed obligated, to appraise our democratic institutions against these criteria? It seems obvious to me, as to many others, that judged against democratic criteria, our existing political institutions display many shortcomings.

Consequently, just as we need strategies for bringing about a transition to democracy in nondemocratic countries and for consolidating democratic institutions in newly democratized countries, so in the older democratic countries, we need to consider whether and how to move beyond our existing level of democracy.

Let me put it this way. In many countries, the task is to achieve democratization up to the level of polyarchal democracy. But the challenge to citizens in the older democracies is to discover how they might achieve a level of democratization *beyond* polyarchal democracy.

Notes

1. Political *arrangements* sound as if they might be rather provisional, which they could well be in a country that has just moved away from nondemocratic rule. We tend to think of *practices* as more habitual and therefore more durable. We usually think of *institutions* as having settled in for the long haul, passed on from one generation to the next. As a country moves from a nondemocratic to a democratic government, the early democratic *arrangements* gradually become *practices*,

which in due time turn into settled *institutions*. Helpful though these distinction may be, however, for our purposes it will be more convenient if we put them aside and settle for *institutions*.

2. "The Hats assumed their name for being like the dashing fellows in the tricorne of the day. . . . The Caps were nicknamed because of the charge that they were like timid old ladies in nightcaps." Franklin D. Scott, *Sweden: The Nation's History* (Minneapolis: University of Minnesota Press, 1977), 243.

3. Alexis de Tocqueville, *Democracy in America*, vol. 1 (New York: Schocken Books, 1961), 51.

4. Tocqueville, *Democracy in America*, 50.

5. Polyarchy is derived from Greek words meaning "many" and "rule," thus "rule by the many," as distinguished from rule by the one, or monarchy, and rule by the few, oligarchy or aristocracy. Although the term had been rarely used, a colleague and I introduced it in 1953 as a handy way of referring to a modern representative democracy with universal suffrage. Hereafter I shall use it in that sense. More precisely, a polyarchal democracy is a political system with the six democratic institutions listed above. Polyarchal democracy, then, is different from representative democracy with restricted suffrage, as in the nineteenth century. It is also different from older democracies and republics that not only had a restricted suffrage but lacked many of the other crucial characteristics of polyarchal democracy, such as political parties, rights to form political organizations to influence or oppose the existing government, organized interest groups, and so on. It is different, too, from the democratic practices in units so small that members can assemble directly and make (or recommend) policies or laws.

6. A few delegates daringly forecast that the United States might ultimately have as many as one hundred million inhabitants. This number was reached in 1915.

7. John Stuart Mill, *Considerations on Representative Government* [1861] (New York: Liberal Arts Press, 1958), 55.

Critical Thinking

1. What political institutions are essential for democracy?

2. What does it mean for citizens to "participate effectively"?

3. How do citizens control the government? Explain: Is this effective?

4. Give some examples of "alternative and independent sources of information." Why are they important for democracy?

ROBERT A. DAHL is Sterling Professor Emeritus of Political Science, Yale University. He has published many books on democratic theory and practice, including *A Preface to Democratic Theory* (1956) and *Democracy and Its Critics* (1989). This article was adapted from his recent book, *On Democracy,* Yale University Press.

Civil Society, Youth and Societal Mobilization in Democratic Revolutions

Taras Kuzio

In the pre-revolutionary era, young people had dominated the civil societies of many post-communist states, including countries which experienced democratic revolutions in Serbia (2000), Georgia (2003), Ukraine (2004) and Kyrgyzstan (2005). Most members of post-communist civil society NGOs were under 35 and it was they who provided huge numbers of activists and volunteers. One Orange Revolution activist recalled how: "this was a real extreme, underground, creative youth movement. People sat in offices all day not for money or because they were forced to, but because simply this was the place to be cool" (Ukrayinska Pravda, January 26, 2006). Similarly, in Serbia a "sophisticated market campaign" of posters, badges and tee shirts led to a "political youth cult". Identifying with *Otpor* (Resistance) became "cool" and "*Otpor* made it fashionable to be against Milosevic", one *Otpor* activist said (Collin, 2001, p. 208).

Young people have played a central role in all democratic revolutions going back to the Philippines people's power protests in the mid-1980s to Nepal in 2006. Democratic revolutions in Serbia (2000), Georgia (2003), and Ukraine (2004), the three countries under investigation in this article, would not have taken place without the energy of young people. Youth NGOs in Serbia, Georgia and Ukraine were crucial in three inter-related areas. First, they assisted in the mobilization of protestors. Second, they provided logistical support to the protests. Third, they were often the first wave of protestors (McFaul, 2005, p. 13; *Pora, 2005;* Demes and Forbrig, 2006; Kaskiv, 2005a,b; Kuzio, 2005a,b; Way, 2005).

In Ukraine, those in the age group up to 30 years old were three times more likely to join the Orange Revolution than other age categories (Stepanenko, 2005, p. 21). The two key social groups that made the Orange Revolution a success were youth and private businessmen (Reznik, 2005). Young people participate in revolutions because they have less to lose. Few have mortgages, families or careers to be concerned about losing if they joined the opposition, youth NGOs or the revolution. As their supporters grew, young people became less afraid of attending meetings and rallies as higher educational institutions could not expel all of them.

Young women played an important role in breaking down distrust between law enforcement and the revolutionaries.

Otpor organized young women to march ahead of men as the police would be far less likely to attack them and, if they did, the ensuing footage of blood-stained girls would work to the advantage of the opposition. In Kyiv, teenage girls led the way in giving flowers to *spetsnaz* (police task forces) *Berkut* policemen posted in the cold weather outside the presidential administration. Their fraternization with the *Berkut* reduced chances of the non-violent protests becoming violent, which they had three years earlier in March 2001.

For many young people the theft of their vote in a crucial election was not simply election fraud but the theft of their future, which still lay ahead. Dmytro Potekhin, head of Ukraine's *Znayu* (I Know)! youth NGO, said, "this was a case in which something very personal was being stolen from us—our right to vote" (Slivka, 2004). In Serbia and Ukraine this sense of anger was made more urgent because Milosevic and Kuchma were both seen as criminals. Annual opinion polls by the Ukrainian Academy of Sciences from 1994 to 2005 found that "organized crime, mafia" was perceived by Ukrainians as the most influential group in Ukrainian society (Panina, 2005). The imposition of a successor who had a criminal past therefore came as a double affront. A young volunteer who ferried protestors to Kyiv for free asked, "How could they dare try to impose such a bandit on us? We will never accept it" (Daily Telegraph, November 28, 2004). Young Ukrainians especially refused to accept election fraud that led to the imposition of a "criminal" candidate as the successor to Kuchma.

The strategies deployed by Serbia's *Otpor,* Georgia's *Kmara* (Enough) and Ukraine's *Pora* (It's Time) were strikingly similar. They targeted urban youth who traditionally had been politically apathetic. Politics had to be made to be "cool". Young people were targeted because they made good volunteers and came into contact with a greater number of people each day than the older generation. The majority of the volunteers in *Otpor, Kmara* and *Pora* were students. *Otpor* was established by 15 Belgrade University students in 1998 who were, "Sick of the endless compromises, defeats and endemic apathy . . ." (Collin, 2001, p. 175). Students made up over 95 percent of members of *Pora* established in *Pora* cells in 20 universities throughout Ukraine. In Serbia, *Otpor* grew out of the Student Union of Serbia (SUS) and became a mass movement during the 2000 elections.

The article provides a five-point framework to understand the different aspects of the revolutionary process that took place in the three case studies covered in this article (Serbia, Georgia, Ukraine). Competitive authoritarian regimes are most vulnerable during a specific time, like election cycles, and regime change in Serbia, Georgia and Ukraine took place during *electoral revolutions*. *Organization* of young people in *Otpor, Kmara* and *Pora* was an important second condition in preparing to confront election fraud. Youth NGOs were able to overcome divisions and quarrels that plagued older generations and assisted in the creation of unified democratic opposition blocs. The third section deals with the importance of pre-revolutionary *training*. In the three countries discussed, the democratic revolutions were preceded by acute socio-economic and political crises when the opposition had failed in their attempts at removing the incumbents from power. The fourth section surveys the *strategies* employed by youth NGOs during the elections and democratic revolutions. This includes such strategies as an adroit use of humour and the provision of carnival-music festival atmospheres. The fifth section covers the *authorities' response* that targeted youth NGOs with repression and counter-propaganda.

Electoral Revolutions

Serbia differed from Georgia and Ukraine in that Milosevic could not, after being indicted for war crimes in Kosovo and Bosnia, convince the West that he would hold free and fair elections. In Georgia and Ukraine both leaders still sought to keep channels open to the West, particularly to the US. Both countries multi-vector foreign policies sought to balance relations with a hegemonic Russia by good relations with the US and NATO, with whom both countries participated in the Partnership for Peace program. Shevardnadze was also concerned at maintaining his reputation and integrity as the Soviet Foreign Minister under Mikhail Gorbachev who had refused to sanction military interventions in central Europe. In 2003, Kuchma sent the third largest military contingent to support US-led coalition forces in Iraq (the largest non-NATO member contingent) during the low ebb in Ukraine's relations with the West. Only a year earlier the US had accused Kuchma of authorizing the sale of "Kolchuga" military radars to Iraq in summer 2000.

Ukraine has a long-standing and respected election monitoring NGO staffed by young people, the Committee of Voters of Ukraine (http://cvu.org.ua). The assistance of the Committee of Voters (KVU) is invaluable for OSCE long-term observers who spend two months in Ukraine's regions prior to election day. The KVU has played an important role in organizing election monitoring and liaison with local OSCE observers and with the OSCE and Council of Europe headquarters in Kyiv. In Serbia, the Center for Free Elections and Democracy NGO played a similar role to the KVU.

The KVU have also assisted in coordinating election monitoring with the European Network of Election Monitoring Organizations (ENEMO). In the 2004 elections ENEMO sent 700–1000 monitors in rounds two and three (http://enemo.org.ua). ENEMO attends many elections in post-communist states from which their monitors are drawn. In this sense they are able to

counter the views of the CIS Election Observation Mission (CIS EOM) established to give an alternative viewpoint to that of the OSCE.

Ukraine's youth election-monitoring groups organized two coalitions. The New Choice coalition brought together many well-known youth and election monitoring NGOs and was supported by the Europe XXI Foundation (http://europexxi.org.ua). New Choice grew out of the Civic Monitoring Committee that was active in the 2002 elections, and was one of the first examples of re-energized young activism. The Freedom of Choice coalition brought together 300 NGOs active in civil society and election monitoring (http://coalition.org.ua) and published a news website (http://hotline.net.ua). The Freedom of Choice coalition included the "yellow" wing of *Pora*.

Youth election-monitoring groups were involved in a wide range of activities in an attempt to counter violations and get out the youth vote. Youth groups launched legal cases against the common practice of state officials campaigning on the job for Yanukovych. Kherson oblast governor, Serhiy Dovhan, was forced to defend his agitation to vote for Yanukovych but was soon removed after the case became widely publicized.

In both Serbia and Ukraine, youth divided their tactics in two ways. "Get out the vote" campaigns were organized by one set of NGOs, following a pattern set in the 1998 Slovak elections. This type of NGO activity is not unusual in mature democracies and often targets those sectors of society most disinclined to vote, such as young people and uneducated voters.

A second tactic, closely related to the get out the vote campaigns, was to undertake "black operations" against corrupt officials who were suspected of being organizers of fraud in the upcoming elections. Both wings of this youth NGO strategy ("white" and "black operations") prepared to defend voters democratic choice through post-election protests. This made Serbia, Georgia and Ukraine different to Slovakia. In Slovakia the "get out the vote" campaign dominated NGOs' activity as the authorities were not expected to resort to election fraud and would accept the election result.

In Ukraine, "white operations" were led by the youth election-monitoring group *Znayu!* (I know) that provided positive information on the elections, educated election monitors, and attempted to block election fraud (http://znayu.org.ua). *Chysta Ukrayina* (Clean Ukraine) and student groups also took part in the "get out the vote" campaign (http://chysto.com and http://studenty.org.ua). "Get out the vote" and information strategies complimented "black operations" by *Pora* to publicize corruption by election officials who were suspected of attempting to take bribes in return for falsifying the election results.

Organization

Serbia and Georgia produced united *Otpor* and *Kmara* NGOs whereas *Pora* in Ukraine was comprised of a "yellow" and "black" wing, named after the colour of their symbols. Both wings of *Pora* were established in spring 2004, although only "black" *Pora* had laid the groundwork in 2002–2003. *Otpor* was led by people born in the 1970s but the bulk of its rank and file members were born in the 1980s. *Otpor*, therefore, incorporated both the 1970s and 1980s generations or what constituted in Ukraine two wings of *Pora*. The former, the 1970s generation, remembered the Josip Broz Tito era while the latter only remembered war and economic collapse during the Slobodan Milosevic regime. In Georgia, veterans of earlier protests based at the Liberty Institute NGO functioned as *Kmara's* mother organization. As in Serbia, younger activists were brought into civil society activity by veterans involved in earlier civil society campaigns that had failed to meet their objectives.

Kmara and "black" *Pora* both had symbols similar to *Otpor's;* and *Kmara's* clenched fist was an exact replica of *Otpor's*. In Ukraine, *Pora* decided against using a clenched fist as this was believed to be too provocative. Instead, a clock was used showing how it was time for Kuchma to leave the office. Indeed, "black" *Pora* focused on the need to remove "Kuchmizm" from Ukraine.

Otpor, Kmara and "black" *Pora* had horizontal, leaderless structures working autonomously in decentralized networks with no leaders. "Yellow" *Pora* was different. Vladyslav Kaskiv was the leader of "yellow" *Pora* and the Freedom of Choice coalition. Both wings of *Pora* and *Otpor* stressed underground, guerrilla style organization, a strategy that harped back to World War II Serbian partisans and Ukrainian nationalist guerrillas. In Georgia, such tactics could not be used as Georgia did not have a historical tradition of nationalist partisans. *Kmara* succeeded in exaggerating the size of their NGO's members by astute use of propaganda and street actions (Kandelaki, 2005).

Kmara and "black" *Pora* copied *Otpor's* tactics which were, in turn, taken from Western theories of non-violent resistance. The Belgrade-based Center for Non-violent Resistance provided non-violent training to Belarus's *Zubr* (Bison), *Kmara* and "black" *Pora*. "Yellow" *Pora* trained and operated independently of these three NGOs. Serbia's *Otpor* circulated Serbian-language versions of Gene Sharp's classic text on non-violent resistance, which has since been translated into Georgian, Belarusian and Ukrainian (Sharp, 1973; Ackerman and Duval, 2000; Karatnycky and Ackerman, 2005, http://aeinstein.org, http://nonviolent-conflict.org).

Robert Helvey, a retired US Army colonel worked closely with Sharp and assisted in training *Otpor* through the help of the US-based International Republican Institute. Advice centered on analyzing the sources of power within Serbian society, winning support within the government, the psychological effect of fear and methods of overcoming it, psychological methods to improve public views of *Otpor,* crisis management and how to avoid unnecessary risks. Sharp's work proved so influential that *Otpor* praised it as, "an astoundingly effective blueprint for confronting a brutal regime" (Whither the Bulldozer, August 2001).

In Ukraine two wings of Pora were a product of generational differences and different tactics. "Black" *Pora* incorporated Western traditions of non-violent resistance diffused through *Otpor, Zubr* and *Kmara*. "Yellow" *Pora* sought to find more specifically Ukrainian approaches to creating a youth NGO. At the same time, both *Poras* understood the need for non-violent strategies following the violent March 2001 riots in Kyiv. Mykhailo Svystovych, a founder of "black" *Pora* and the

http://maidan.org.ua website, was present during the 2001 riots and learnt lessons from them:

> And, only after two weeks did it become clear that a portion of people were frightened by potential repression and another part by hooligan actions. That was when we recalled *Otpor* and its successful non-violent movement. And in April 2001 the first *Otpor* members arrived in Ukraine (Ukrayinska Pravda, March 9, 2006).

The riots were provoked by extreme right nationalist provocateurs, working together with the Security Service of Ukraine (SBU). The public fall out led to the collapse of public support for the anti-Kuchma protests (Lutsenko, 2005). The authorities sentenced twenty members of UNA (Ukrainian National Assembly) providing them with ammunition to attack the opposition as "extremists". Throughout the 2004 elections the authorities staged numerous provocations in an attempt at inciting a violent counter-attack in what Russian political technologists working for the Yanukovych campaign described as "directed chaos" (Kuzio, 2005c). The opposition refused to rise to the bait and the Orange Revolution ended without violence (Kuzio, in press).

"Yellow" *Pora* was led by "professional radicals" of earlier campaigns going back to Ukraine's drive for independence and student hunger strike in 1990–1991 (Zerkalo Nedeli, December 11–17, 2004). Based in Kyiv, it was also closer to the Yushchenko election camp and his Our Ukraine bloc. The Freedom of Choice coalition had planned to establish Wave of Freedom as a "get out the vote" NGO, drawing inspiration from Slovakia's Campaign Ok 98. Pavol Demes, German Marshal Fund director in Slovakia and an activist from the 1998 Slovak elections, had close ties to "yellow" *Pora*. The planned Wave of Freedom NGO was renamed as *Pora*, copying the already launched "black" *Pora* and thereby creating confusion with the existence of two *Pora* organizations (http://kuchmizm.info, http://pora.org.ua). The "get out the vote" message was taken over by the *Znayu* NGO.

"Black" *Pora* was led by western Ukrainian students who had played a role in the anti-Kuchma protests of 2000–2001. They were younger, more active and better organized in Ukraine's regions. In 2001 the youth NGO *Za Pravdu* (For Truth) united different youth groups under the umbrella of the opposition Committee of National Salvation, the political body that had grown out of the Ukraine Without Kuchma! protests. Two smaller NGOs, *Opir Molodi* (Youth Resistance) and *Sprotyv* (Resistance) were spin offs of the *Za Pravdu* (For Truth) NGO.

Pora was organized in 2002–2003 from these hard-core activists spread over different youth NGOs. They also participated in supporting the democratic opposition in the 2002 parliamentary elections and the 2002–2003 Arise Ukraine! protests. In 2001–2002 they established links with Serbia's *Otpor* that then trained the "black" wing of *Pora*. Mykhailo Svistovych, editor of the http://maidan.org.ua website that had also grown out of the Ukraine Without Kuchma movement, provided key links to *Otpor* and became one of "black" *Pora's* founders.

Both *Otpor* and "black" *Pora* worked independently of the Vojislav Kostunica and Yushchenko campaigns. "Yellow" *Pora* was again different, working closely with the Yushchenko campaign in the 2004 elections and never attempted to prove its impartiality to the extent that *Otpor* and "black" *Pora* undertook to. "Yellow" *Pora* established an election bloc with the pro-Yushchenko Reform and Orders Party to contest the 2006 parliamentary elections. "Black" *Pora* refused to re-form as a political party. Both *Otpor's* and "yellow" *Pora's* attempts at entering the Serbian and Ukrainian parliaments failed.

In 2002–2003, Dutch, British and Polish foundations provided assistance for training seminars in 23 oblasts organized and coordinated by http://maidan.org.ua. *Otpor, Kmara* and *Zubr* (Bison) activists assisted the training seminars. "Black" *Pora's* main financial support came from domestic sources and West European foundations. This made "black" *Pora* very different to *Otpor* which could not rely on domestic sources for funding as the Serbian middle classes had been decimated by war, economic mismanagement and international economic blockade (Gordy, 1999; Krnjevic-Miskovic, 2001, p. 103; Thompson and Kuntz, 2004). *Otpor* received a large injection of US funds after Milosevic was indicted at the Hague for Kosovo crimes in 1999 and NATO's bombing campaign. The US did not provide funds for *Otpor's* partner in Ukraine, "black" *Pora,* while *Kmara* obtained its funds from the Soros Foundation, rather than from the US government (Fairbanks, 2004, p. 115).

"Yellow" *Pora* had greater access to domestic and international funds. Vladyslav Kaskiv, leader of "yellow" *Pora,* denied receiving funding from abroad (2000, January 21, 2005). However, they were able to tap into Western funds sent to the Freedom of Choice Coalition, a bloc of NGOs created to combat election fraud. Freedom House helped train the Coalition's election monitors at a Crimean camp in August 2004. Freedom of Choice volunteers often doubled as "yellow" *Pora* activists.

"Black" *Pora's* first activity was in March 2004 when it posted leaflets throughout Ukraine calling upon Ukrainians to remove "Kuchmizm" from Ukraine. One month later a second group, "yellow" *Pora,* emerged as a component of the Freedom of Choice Coalition. "Yellow" *Pora* underwent baptism by fire in the April 2004 mayoral election in the Trans-Carpathian town of Mukachevo. Although Yushchenko's candidate won the election the authorities declared their candidate victorious. They then dispatched organized crime enforcers ("skinheads") to intimidate and beat up officials and destroy evidence of election fraud.

Both wings of *Pora* played a crucial role in providing a dedicated, hard-core group of young activists who erected a tent city in Kyiv immediately after round two of the election on November 21, 2004. These hard-core *Pora* activists, together with other youth NGOs, helped mobilize millions of Ukrainians in Kyiv and the provinces to participate in the Orange Revolution. The same was true of *Otpor* in Serbia.

Training

During preceding political crises the opposition's attempts in Serbia, Georgia and Ukraine at removing incumbents from power invariably had failed leading to introspection within opposition movements as to the need to change tactics. After

numerous failed attempts by the Serbian opposition in the 1990s, the Serbs were beginning to lose faith in their ability to change the country's leadership. *Otpor* played a central role in revitalizing this apathy and feeling of lack of efficacy by, "shaking people out of their slumber" (Ilić, 2001). In Georgia, *Kmara* also faced the task of combating widespread political apathy among Georgians living in the provinces and among young people (Kandelaki, 2005).

Learning from past failures is taken on board in a greater way by the more impatient younger generation. *Otpor, Kmara* and *Pora* set examples to the older generation by uniting a broad range of political views within youth NGOs. Their elders continued to fail to unite into opposition blocs during parliamentary elections and failed to field a single candidate in presidential elections. The authorities divide and rule the opposition, eroding some parties while co-opting others with lucrative government or diplomatic positions.

Youth NGOs are usually the first to clamor for opposition parties to unite in the face of a common threat, either of Milosevic winning another election after being indicted for crimes in Kosovo and Bosnia or of Kuchma installing his successor, Yanukovch. In Georgia and Kyrgyzstan democratic revolutions took place during parliamentary elections where voter's protests were initially brought on by election fraud that then spiraled into demands for Eduard Shevardnadze and Askar Akayev to leave office. Opposition parties and *Kmara* had initially intended to use the example of 2003 parliamentary elections to mobilize in preparation for the 2005 presidential elections when Shevardnadze was to step down after two terms in office. The use of blatant election fraud, especially in Ajaria, Shevardnadze's refusal to compromise and public anger all combined to lead to the earlier than expected Rose Revolution. In all four cases there was a widespread feeling that the incumbent and the regime he had put in place needed to be changed.

Serbian democratic opposition leaders had failed to mount a serious challenge to Milosevic throughout the 1990s. Various democratic coalitions had been formed during elections and protests but none of them could match the breadth of the Democratic Opposition of Serbia (DOS) 18-party coalition established in the 2000 election, the successor to the Alliance for Change and Together coalitions. The only democratic party outside DOS was Vuk Draskovich's Serbian Renewal Movement. The failure of the 1996–1997 protests in Serbia galvanized Belgrade's students to create *Otpor* in 1998 (Collin, 2001, p. 175).

In Ukraine the opposition united in the second round around Yushchenko's candidacy with the Communists the only party refusing to join. *Otpor* played a greater role than *Pora* in pressurising the opposition to unite in crucial elections. Until spring 2000, Serbia's political opposition had proven itself unable to offer a serious alternative and a threat to the Milosevic regime (Ilić, 2001). Youth NGOs aligned with united opposition alliances proved unstoppable in Serbia, Georgia and Ukraine.

The creation of a united opposition was not the only required factor for a successful democratic revolution. There was also a need for a deep preceding crisis during which youth NGOs and parties could train, receive outside support and learn from their mistakes. Serbia experienced thirteen years of rule by Milosevic during which he had destroyed the most liberal of communist regimes, Yugoslavia, where standards of living had been relatively high for a communist state. By the 2000 elections many Serbs had reached the conclusion that they had enough of Milosevic, who had destroyed their own country and lost nationalistic wars in Slovenia, Croatia, Bosnia and Kosovo.

Georgia was similar to Serbia in being a post-war country. Shevardnadze had come to power in a *coup d'état* after President Zviad Gamsakhurdia had launched disastrous wars to withdraw autonomous status from Abkhazia and South Ossetia that he had then lost to Russian-backed separatists. Shevardnadze had presided over a stagnating and corrupt failed state and proved unable to re-take two territories beyond central control. In a third—Ajariad—the local elites were permitted, like Donetsk in Ukraine, to act as though it was their personal fiefdom provided they did not threaten to secede (King, 2001; Miller, 2004; Fairbanks, 2004).

There would have not been an Orange Revolution in Ukraine without the preceding Kuchmagate crisis, when a tape was released in parliament allegedly showing President Kuchma having authorized violence against opposition journalist Heorhiy Gongadze. The Kuchmagate crisis and subsequent protests did not lead to Kuchma's downfall. Nevertheless, they severely undermined the legitimacy of the ruling elites, discredited Kuchma, and created a hard core group of activists ready to participate in the 2002 and 2004 elections. Most importantly, they awakened the traditionally apathetic young people from their political lethargy.

"Black" *Pora* activists defined the anti-Kuchma protests as Ukraine's "1905", because they failed to unseat Kuchma, while Ukraine's "1917" (Orange Revolution) successfully prevented Kuchma's chosen successor, Yanukovych, from coming to power. The 2000 movement "Ukraine without Kuchma", during which young people created their own NGOs that evolved into *Pora*, was the "first rehearsal". The follow up Arise Ukraine! protests, "showed leadership ability to magnetize and guide large numbers of people". These two rehearsals, Interior Minister Yuriy Lutsenko believes, "made the Maidan possible" (Zerkalo Nedeli, December 11–17, 2004).

Protests in Ukraine after November 2000 elections had a profound effect on young people who, like the generation before them, dreamt and worked towards living in a "normal" European country. During the anti-Kuchma protests a revolution did not take place, but a profound change did take place in people's hearts and minds, a young activist, Volodymyr Chemerys, argued. This was especially among young people. Accusations against Kuchma meant he could no longer "stand above the political process" and claim to be the nation's leader. Ukrainians withdrew their support from Kuchma whose ratings plummeted and trust in state institutions reached an all-time low. "Internally Ukraine is already without Kuchma", Chemerys concluded. A revolutionary situation failed to materialize in 2002 during the Arise Ukraine! protests and only arose in 2004 during the Orange Revolution (Ukrayinska Pravda, December 13, 2002).

Since the 1980s a new post-communist generation has grown up in Serbia, Georgia and Ukraine which is less affected by, and

tolerant of, communist and Soviet political culture. In Serbia the left was destroyed under Milosevic when he transformed the Socialist Party into an extreme nationalist party. In Serbia, Georgia and Ukraine the young post-communist generation emerged as a civil society force first in Serbia after the 1996 protests and then in Georgia and Ukraine during the 2000–2004 elections.

"Generation Orange" was a new phenomenon for Ukraine. "Kuchma never feared my generation. However, he forgot that we would have children and these children never knew the KGB", Andre Kurkov said (Gruda, 2004). "Generation Orange" has traveled abroad to work, for holidays or on scholarships, and has access to a globalized world through satellite television and the internet. "Generation Orange" knew there were alternatives to a Ukraine ruled by Kuchma's anointed successor, Yanukovych.

Strategies
Globalization and Modern Communication

Young people use modern communications to a greater extent than other generations and modern communications are often introduced into households by its younger members. These "e-revolutionaries" drew on the latest technology and communications to circumvent the authorities. The "info-age revolution" meant that a *coup d'état* without violence" was possible (Durden-Smith, 2005).

In Serbia the internet took off during the 1999 NATO bombardment. But, by the 2000 elections and revolution the internet was still a low-used medium. The bombing of Kosovo did lead to a massive surge in cell phones as parents bought them for their children. Cell phones were useful in ensuring rapid communication between different areas of the country and NGOs. They were used for mass messages. During the elections the texts would be mass mailed and the recipients would be asked to send them on further.

Cell phones also played a useful role as camera phones. Evidence of fraud was collected by students in Ukraine who filmed professors illegally ordering them how to vote. This film was made available to download from the internet and used as evidence in court prosecutions during which the authorities were accused of rigging the election results.

Georgia and Ukraine proved to be different to Serbia where the internet played a less important role (Prytula, 2006). The internet had sufficiently developed in Georgia and Ukraine to ensure that this medium played an important role in their revolutions. Ukraine has been described as the world's first "internet revolution". The internet opened up possibilities for private chat rooms to discuss tactics and strategy, e-mail, bloggers, and hosting NGO websites.

Modern technology was also used in promoting reports by independent television stations, such as Rustavi-2 in Georgia and Channel 5 and Era in Ukraine (http://rustavi2.com.ge, http://5tv.com.ua, http://eratv.com.ua). Large television screens provided 24-hour news and commentary by Channel 5 during the Orange Revolution. US scholars and policy makers could be interviewed in the Voice of America office in Washington and then be broadcast live on Channel 5 and on the Maidan.

Humor and Ridicule

Fear of instability, civil war and extremism were potent weapons in damping political activism and atomizing the Serbian and Ukrainian populations (Collin, 2001, pp. 191–192). Humor and ridicule were crucial in undermining fear of the authorities with young people playing a central role in promoting them. Ridicule and humor broke down fear of the authorities which had played an important role in de-mobilizing the middle aged and older generations and creating widespread apathy. Older Serbs, Georgians and Ukrainians felt they could do nothing to change their situations.

Fear had also been ingrained from the Soviet era in Ukraine because of a past history of periodic cycles of repression, a factor especially prevalent in Ukraine leading to the common refrain *"Moya khata z krayu"* (literally "My house is on the outskirts" but meaning "I'm staying out"). *Otpor* activists, "hoped to resuscitate Serbia with demonstrations of individual courage. The idea was to deprive the regime of the fear that had become its greatest weapon and thereby withdraw the consent of Serbia's governed" (Whither the Bulldozer, August 2001).

Otpor was one of the first to ridicule the Serbian authorities. Such ridicule could draw on the most unlikeliest of influences, such as the British 1970s comedy series, Monty Python's Flying Circus. Monty Python was useful in providing "silly, provocative humor" (Markovic, 2005). Monty Python provided, "allegorical, absurdist performance art", one *Otpor* activist recalled (Collin, 2001, p. 177).

In Georgia, the humorous message propagated by *Kmara* also poked fun of the regime. In one street action, similar to those by *Otpor* and *Pora* in Serbia and Ukraine, *Kmara* displayed large banners on streets where passers by could take photos of themselves flushing Shevardnadze and his government down the toilet. Other street actions included mock funerals when the government presented its new economic program. Such actions, "produced a group of young people with an extremely high degree of motivation, courage and 'quality activism'", capable of mobilizing broad swathes of Georgian society (Kandelaki, 2005).

The most elaborate campaign that drew upon humor was in Ukraine and the choice of official candidate—Yanukovych—made the use of humor easy and enjoyable (Chornuhuza, 2005; Yanuykdotyi. Politicheskiye anekdotyi). With young NGOs and the opposition dominating the internet, this forum became a major location for a wide range of humor and ridicule against the authorities. Internet websites, "savaged Yanukovych with high road criticism and low road ridicule, inflicting a political death of a thousand cuts" (Kyj, 2006, p. 79).

That Yanukovych was intellectually challenged could be readily seen by his inability to speak either literary Russian or Ukrainian. His official CV submitted to the Central Election Commission was signed by "Proffessor" at a fictitious Western scholarly institution. "Proffessor Yanukovych" became the butt of jokes throughout the 2004 elections and Orange Revolution.

Yanukovych's intellectual challenge led to the emergence of an entire sub-culture within youth NGOs and websites directed against him.

Yanukovch's intellectual challenge was also ridiculed because of his frequent use of criminal slang and his illiteracy. A 13-series internet film ('Operation ProFFessor') was produced consisting of excerpts of popular Soviet comedies with voices performed by impersonators of well known politicians dubbed over the characters. The series was a massive hit.

Yanukovych collapsed after being hit by an egg on a visit to Ivano-Frankivsk after the attempted poisoning of Yushchenko. The incident, filmed by independent Channel 5 Television, became a smash hit, downloadable from numerous websites and re-played ridiculing the "tough man Yanukovych". Yanukovych had been primed before traveling to Ivano-Frankivsk that he was to be hit by a blank bullet in an attempt at portraying Yushchenko's supporters as "terrorists", a precursor to similar accusations against youth NGOs the following month. Immediately after Yanukovych was struck by an egg the authorities' political machine went into high gear blaming the "terrorist" attack on Yushchenko's "nationalist" supporters.

Dmytro Romaniuk, the student who threw the egg before the blank could be fired, was a typical product of the gradual politicization of young people during the 2004 elections. Romaniuk was disinterested in politics until he threw the egg that made him an instant celebrity. At the last minute he had decided to purchase two eggs because he was angry at how the local authorities were pretending that Yanukovych had great support in his home town in Western Ukraine. After the egg incident he was arrested and accused of "terrorism", steps that made him an instant local and national celebrity. He joined the Student Brotherhood who elected him to be its deputy head. "With many friends I took part in the Orange Revolution in the Khreshchatyk", Romaniuk recalled (Ukrayina Moloda, December 23, 2004).

A traveling "Political Theatre" mocked Yanukovych over his presumed fear of eggs using a traveling artificial egg. *Pora* released chickens outside the Cabinet of Ministers building in Kyiv where Yanukovych had his offices. Websites appeared that included a rapidly growing number of egg jokes. There were many series of egg cartoons "Merry Eggs" (*Veseli Yaytsa*) in which two funny eggs sang songs and joked. "Boorish Egg" and "Jolly Eggs" games and cartoons were developed on-line (http://eggs.net.ua, http://ham.com.ua).

Yanukovych's criminal past also provided a great deal of ammunition for humor. On weekends *Pora* members dressed in prison uniform and campaigned for Yanukovych on Kyiv's main thoroughfare. Passers by were told that "prisoners" had been let out for the weekend to campaign for one of their own (Yanukovych). If there was a Yanukovych election stand the *Pora* members would stand next to it and chant "Yanukovych!, Yanukovych!". Yanukovych was depicted in numerous cartoons as a former *"zek"* (prisoner) or "bandit", accusations made easier by his origins in Donetsk, a region with the highest rate of criminality in Ukraine. A play on his name, "Yanucharii" (Janissaries), was made popular through posters and cartoons.

A cartoon printed in the mass circulation Silski Visti (December 23, 2004), a newspaper sympathetic to the Socialist Party, included two prison guards talking to each other outside an empty prison cell. One asked the other, "Where are the brothers (reference to criminal brotherhoods)?" His fellow officer replied, "Don't worry. They will soon return as they have just gone to campaign for their own . . ." (that is Yanukovych).

Music and Carnivals

Traditional music, concerts and carnivals have been used by nationalist and regional groups throughout Europe to raise national consciousness and politically mobilize voters. Regions in the Celtic fringe—Wales, Ireland, Scotland, Cornwall and Brittany—have revived traditional music festivals to raise national awareness. Such festivals have played an important role in re-connecting to young people, traditionally the most integrated generation in the globalized English-speaking world (Gemie, 2005).

Democratic revolutions in Serbia, Georgia and Ukraine took place in late autumn or winter. Young people are more hardy to cold weather and more capable of living in tent camps or roughing it on sofas or floors. Assisting them in staying for long periods of time and roughing the accommodation was an adroit use of music and carnival atmosphere. The most well known youth bands played for free for weeks to large crowds.

In Serbia the music scene was confused as the nationalist authorities had attempted to influence young people through their promotion of turbo-folk, a mix of patriotic folk and modern rave music (Gordy, 1999). *Otpor* had to be more adroit in its use of patriotic motives in music as nationalism had been monopolized and discredited by the Milosevic regime. Nevertheless, "healthy" nationalism, as one *Otpor* activist described it, did play a role inside the NGO (Collin, 2001, p. 200). Instead, they mocked the post-Tito Socialist-nationalist regime with dark humor and playing on totalitarian motifs. The inspiration for this Serbian opposition music was New Slovenian Art and bands such as Labiach, a play on the German name for Ljubljana. Yugoslav rock from the 1980s touched on nostalgia for an era which was peaceful, prosperous and the state took care of its citizens.

Politics and music were deliberately mixed together. The Millennium concert was preceded by a four minute film on recent Serbian and Yugoslav history. After the film the 10,000 strong crowds were advised to go home as there was nothing to celebrate with a concert (Collin, 2001, p. 177). The "*Vremie je*" (Its Time) rock concert tour with the independent B2-92 radio station featured the best Yugoslav bands in 25 cities throughout Serbia and reaching 150,000 young people (Collin, 2001, p. 208).

In Georgia, young artists, poets and musicians toured the country supporting change and calling on students in regional universities to join the Rose Revolution. In Ukraine the opposition could draw on patriotic music as the authorities could be readily portrayed as disinterested in national interests and the rights of citizens. Ukraine's Orange Revolution was a symbiosis of "political meeting and rock festival" (Klid, 2006, p. 2). Ukraine's best known and modern bands played for Yushchenko while traditional bands and singers from Russia played for Yanukovych.

The hymn of the Orange Revolution was written by the hitherto unknown Ivano-Frankivsk hip hop band *Grandzioly*. Their song "We are many, we cannot be defeated" became a rallying cry in the Orange Revolution and was downloaded 1.5 million times from the internet. The elite Kyiv Mohyla Academy, the location of Yushchenko's press center, coined the slogan. The "spirit of the opposition lives in the yards" of the Academy and "its students make up *Pora's* avant guard", one "yellow" *Pora* activist recalled (Polyukhovych, 2004). *Otpor's* slogans were typically more forthright: *Gotov Je* (He's Finished), "Kill Yourself Slobodan and Save Serbia" and "To The Hague, to the Hague, get Slobodan to the Hague".

Another *Pora* activist remembered, "From 2000 we studied the experience of non-violent revolution in different countries—and one of these factors contributing to these changes was carnival" (Ukrayinska Pravda, November 22, 2005). Young people creatively thought up ways to distribute information. Vendors selling music CDs would provide free copies of other CDs with windows media player files showing "How the authorities are undertaking free elections".

Okean Yelzy, one of Ukraine's most popular bands, was typical of the apolitical Ukrainians who became politicized during the elections and Orange Revolution. *Okean Yelzy* singer Sviatoslav Vakarchuk was made an adviser to President Yushchenko. *Okean Yelzy* played on the Maidan throughout the Orange Revolution and one of their new songs gave hope to the protestors that "spring" was very close at hand. "Spring" was a euphemism for the victory of Yushchenko. As in Serbia, Ukrainian well known sports personalities, such as Vitali and Vladimir Klichko brother boxers, who were icons for young people, often appeared on the Maidan. During the 2006 elections the Klichkos headed the *Pora*-Reforms and Order election bloc.

Orange Revolution music, which was continually played on the Maidan either by live bands or through music CDs, also touched upon Ukraine's national identity and the choice they were making at that moment in history. As with the name of Yushchenko's bloc, Our Ukraine, many songs mobilized Ukrainians to demand the return of what was understood as their stolen country. This is "Our Ukraine" which had been taken over by a small group of usurpers; it was time for the country to be returned to its rightful owners, Ukraine's citizens. These usurpers were depicted as a de *facto* foreign occupation army supported by Russia.

Orange Revolution songs also demanded that Ukrainians did not contemplate passivity as the stakes were too high. Some songs, such as *Okean Yelzy's* song "*Vstavay!*" (Arise!) openly called for an uprising. Although written before the elections, it became popular during the Orange Revolution. Songs such as "*Ukrayina*" by the well known band *Mandry* called upon Ukrainians to look at their ancestors who were looking down upon them at this critical time. The option of staying passive was morally wrong as too many Ukrainian intellectuals had already suffered and died in the former USSR. The insinuation was that with the election of Yanukovych their Ukraine, from a nationally conscious point of view, would be irrevocably lost. Other Orange Revolution music called upon Ukrainians to rush to Kyiv to defend this "sacred" city from a Yanukovych victory.

Everybody should travel to Kyiv as soon as they could by any means possible.

Music also played a role in humor. During the separatist congress held on December 2, 2004 after round two, Ludmilla Yanukovych, the wife of a presidential hopeful, accused the organizers of the Yushchenko tent city of distributing oranges injected with narcotics to force protestors to stay there. She also claimed that *valenki* (fur knee length boots) had been sent free of charge by the US, a hint that the CIA was behind the Orange Revolution. Satirical songs immediately appeared that poured ridicule on these claims by inter-lacing her comments with other words. The tent city began to hang up *valenki* with "MADE IN USA" scrawled on them.

Authorities' Response

During the 2003 Georgian and 2004 Ukrainian elections the authorities came to increasingly fear *Otpor, Kmara* and *Pora,* even though their numbers and influence were often exaggerated. Ukrainian authorities feared the diffusion of Serbian and Georgian revolutionary know-how. During the 2004 elections, Aleksandar Marich, a founder of *Otpor,* was detained at Kyiv's Borispol airport and deported. Marich had a multi-entry visa and had spent most of the previous two months in Ukraine, but official fear of *Otpor* bringing the "Serbian-Georgian scenario" into Ukraine led to his deportation from Ukraine.

Democratic diffusion through Western assistance was understood by the Serbian, Georgian and Ukrainian authorities as "subversion". One week before the October 2004 crackdown on Ukrainian youth NGOs, the pro-presidential camp had called upon the National Security and Defense Council to take tougher action against opposition plans to undertake mass civil disobedience (Ukrayinska Pravda, October 7, 2004). Valeriy Pustovoitenko, head of the coordinating council of political parties supporting Yanukovych, warned that, "certain forces are preparing for disturbances on election night in all of Ukraine's regions" (Ukrayinska Pravda, October 13, 2004).

The reason for the rising tension was that the Ukrainian authorities' repeated claim that they were organizing free and fair elections was at odds with reality. Ukrainian youth NGOs were alerted to the authorities' plans for election fraud after the April 2004 mayoral elections in Mukachevo. These elections were the first occasion when one wing of *Pora* had taken an active role. The presidential election campaign was not conducted in a free and fair manner.

After Yushchenko was poisoned in September 2004, the opposition camp reached the conclusion that the authorities would never let them win. As in Mukachevo, the opposition could win the election but the authorities would declare their own candidate to be elected. It was therefore rational for the opposition and civil society to prepare to defend their vote and counter election fraud in a non-violent manner. Youth NGOs played a central role in these preparations, as did training assistance from Otpor and *Kmara.*

Opposition and civic groups attempted to ensure as few violations as possible on election day, given the proclivity of law enforcement bodies and election officials to support the authorities. Yushchenko's campaign also issued a statement that the authorities were losing control of the situation and were not confident of Yanukovych's victory, making them nervous and thereby rely to an even greater extent on election fraud. Presidential adviser Mikhail Pogrebynsky admitted, "We have a situation whereby the bigger part of the authorities' team does not believe in their success". He added that there was a widespread, "feeling that the authorities will lose" (glavred.info, October 6, 2004).

During Ukraine's 2004 presidential election the authorities became increasingly nervous about the increased activity of youth NGOs monitoring the election. This culminated in an onslaught against youth NGOs in October 2004 that included a large number of intimidation tactics and targeted violence. As in Serbia, these tactics failed and backfired, only serving to attract larger numbers of members.

Different youth NGOs had complained that the SBU (*Sluzhba Bezpeky Ukrainy* or Security Service of Ukraine) had questioned their members regarding opposition's preparation for an alleged coup. President Kuchma had repeatedly warned throughout the 2004 elections that the authorities would not tolerate a "Georgian-style" revolution. Both wings of *Pora* were especially targeted because the authorities labeled them "extremists" and "terrorists", as *Otpor* had been in Serbia. Both *Pora* and *Otpor* were denounced as "fascist" and "terrorist" structures beholden to American paymasters. The Serb authorities introduced new anti-terrorist legislation to counter *Otpor* which they described as "hooligans, terrorists and paramilitaries" (Collin, 2001, p. 179). Such charges failed to find fertile ground in Serbia but had considerable resonance in Russophone Eastern Ukraine. This was a component of the anti-Yushchenko campaign that depicted him as an American stooge and "nationalist extremist".

Otpor and *Pora* were perceived as radical by the Serbian and Ukrainian authorities because their young members were not cowed by fear. Ukrainian authorities remained fixated on the possibility that the 2004 election would trigger a repeat of the Serbian and Georgian revolutions in Ukraine, which they believed were instigated by the US. To counter *Pora's* success, the authorities created an anti-*Pora* organization, *Dosyt'* (Enough) which proved to be a flop (http://maidan.org.ua, November 10, 2004, Ukrayinska Pravda, November 12, 2004).

During a search of *Pora's* Kyiv office, witnessed by opposition parliamentary deputies, the police found nothing incriminating except anti-Yanukovych leaflets. But during a second search, with only the police present, a bomb was allegedly found. The Prosecutor General then launched a criminal case accusing *Pora* leaders of "terrorism" and "destabilization of the situation in the country". *Pora* was accused of being an illegal "military formation—a terrorist group" (Ukrayinska Pravda, October 16, 2004). The Prosecutor General's office attempted to link the alleged bomb to the August 2004 terrorist act in a Kyiv market which it had originally blamed on political parties allied to Our Ukraine.

A widespread media campaign linked *Pora* to Our Ukraine, and thus its presidential candidate Yushchenko, whom the authorities were desperate to portray as an "extremist" in media outlets that specialized in blackening the opposition (http://temnik.com.ua, October 18 and 19, 2004).

Such tactics were part of an overall strategy advised by Russian political technologists on how to destabilize Ukraine and pit the "pro-Russian" Yanukovych against the "nationalist" Yushchenko. It was more difficult for the Serbian authorities to describe Kostunica as an "extremist" as he held moderate nationalist views and had eschewed politics until the 2000 elections. In Georgia the authorities never resorted to the same extreme measures as in Ukraine in trying to discredit opposition parties. The Georgian elections were dominated by competition between two Georgian and Ajarian parties of power, on the one hand, and the opposition.

"Yellow" *Pora* issued a rebuttal to charges of "terrorism" in which they described themselves as the "vanguard of peaceful opposition". They called upon all of their activists and Ukrainian citizens to "legally, peacefully, and in a non-violent manner defend constitutional rights and freedoms in Ukraine" (http://pora.org.ua, October 18, 2004). This statement reflected a desire, as in Serbia and Georgia, to use non-violent tactics.

What most perturbed the authorities was that Yushchenko had overwhelming support among the educated younger generation, those most likely to be mobilized and active in civil society. In Serbia and Ukraine the authorities usually paid people, including students, to attend rallies on behalf of their candidates, a step that often backfired. On September 29, 2004 Ukrainian students paid to join a Kyiv rally responded "Yes!" to a call from Yanukovych's campaign activists when asked if they desired "Free and Fair Elections". But when asked "And you will vote for Yanukovych?" they replied "No!" on live television. The organizers abruptly ended the rally.

Student Wave organized a mass student rally on October 16, 2004 in Kyiv that brought 30,000 students from across Ukraine in support of Yushchenko. The rally began with a free concert in central Kyiv featuring Ukraine's two best known rock bands. As with all student rallies, it was intended to mobilize students behind demands for a free and fair election and provide concrete advice to students on how to resist pressure and intimidation from the authorities. According to the organizers, "The authorities are not happy of the level of support of the people's candidate, Viktor Yushchenko, among students" (http://yuschenko. com.ua, October 12, 2004).

The training and functions of Ukrainian police *spetsnaz* units were televised with the intention of instilling fear against undertaking election protests. Kuchma had warned against revolution and street protests during a deliberately timed visit to a Crimean BARS *spetsnaz* unit in August 2004. The unit had belonged to one of the best National Guard units until it was dismantled and transferred to the Interior Ministry in 2000. During the Orange Revolution the Crimean BARS unit guarded the presidential administration, leading to rumors that Russian *spetsnaz* units were in Kyiv. Oleksandr Milenin, Deputy Minister of Interior and head of Kyiv's police, leaked the existence of a new "ninja" police unit "trained in special measures" (Financial Times, October 19, 2004). Milenin also claimed that "new means" had "been approved by the health ministry" and were available to suppress protests, making him confident that "There won't be any revolution here" in Ukraine.

Ultimately, these threats to use force failed as Kuchma could not rely on the military, SBU or parts of the Interior Ministry who defected in the Orange Revolution to Yushchenko (Kuzio, in press). The use of non-violent tactics by both wings of Ukrainian *Pora, Otpor* in Serbia and *Kmara* in Georgia proved better at undermining the security forces than the violent tactics used by some elements of the opposition in Kyiv in March 2001.

Another related aspect of the authorities' response in both Serbia and Ukraine was an unprecedented rise in anti-Americanism (UKRAINE, 2004; Kuzio, 2004a). This aspect of the authorities' response proved to be less pronounced in Georgia, although Shevardnadze and other senior Georgian officials did denounce George Soros's funding of the Liberty Institute NGO. The Georgian Young Lawyers Association, Open Society-Georgia Foundation and International Society for Fair Elections and Democracy were also important NGOs. But, the main target of official attacks was on alleged links between *Kmara* and the Russian intelligence services. Shevardnadze had narrowly missed two assassination attempts that were assumed to have been organized by Russia and two separatist regions were under *de facto* Russian control. This made the Georgian authorities more nervous of Russia than the USA.

In Serbia the inflaming of anti-Americanism was not surprising as NATO had bombed Serbia in 1999 to force it to halt its ethnic cleansing of Kosovo. Anti-Americanism was a staple of Milosevic's xenophobic view of the outside world, pitting "little Serbia" against the US, NATO and the West. *Otpor* was routinely denounced as an "agent of American imperialism" (Ilić, 2001).

In Ukraine, anti-Americanism was a new and contradictory phenomenon associated with Kuchma's second term in office after he re-oriented Ukraine to Russia in the wake of the Kuchmagate crisis. Anti-Americanism was promoted at the same time as Ukraine outlined a desire for NATO membership (2002), had sent a large military contingent to Iraq (2003) and changed its military doctrine to include a desire for NATO and EU membership (2004). This was during the same period when anti-Americanism was used as part of an election strategy to blacken Yushchenko (Kuzio, 2004b).

The aspect of the anti-American campaign that concerns this study is the attempts to link domestic NGOs to Western (especially the US) governments. This alleged link reflected the deeply ingrained Soviet political culture evident in the pro-Kuchma centrist camp and Communists. In the former USSR, Soviet propaganda regularly denounced domestic dissidents as allegedly possessing links to Western intelligence. Such links were brought out in Russia in December 2005 when it linked Russian NGOs to British intelligence. The new Russian law on NGOs is imbued with this Soviet era culture that attempts to portray NGOs as imported, unnatural, un-Russian implants. Similar legislation and regime propaganda is evident in Belarus.

In Georgia and Ukraine the alleged American connection was made through direct US and Western support to civil society and NGOs, as well as through training assistance provided by Serbian *Otpor* activists. *Otpor* had been instrumental in assisting in the establishment of the Belarusian youth *Zubr* NGO in February 2001 with the aim of it taking a leading role in that year's September presidential elections. In Ukraine, *Otpor* activists had begun to train Ukrainian young NGO activists in 2002–2003. Following the Rose Revolution of November 2003, Georgian *Kmara* activists also became active in training Ukrainians. During the Orange Revolution, Georgian and Belarusian flags were conspicuously the largest of all foreign flags.

Conclusion

This article has shown how in Serbia, Georgia and Ukraine there were striking similarities in how young people played a decisive role in their democratic revolutions. The five factors that this article focused on to provide a cross-country comparative study are electoral revolutions, organization, training, strategies and the authorities response. All three revolutions in Serbia, Georgia and Ukraine followed similar paths of eschewing violence and upholding non-violent tactics, the ideas for which drew upon earlier successful examples of people power and Western theories. These three case studies in turn, drew upon the diffusion of ideas and strategies employed earlier in other post-communist states (Bunce and Wolchik, in this issue). Non-violent tactics adopted by youth NGOs, together with the presence of large numbers of people on the streets, proved to be crucial in undermining the competitive regimes in Serbia, Georgia and Ukraine. These strategies also dissuaded the regimes from using violence to suppress protests.

Hale and D'Anieri in this issue devoted to democratic revolutions focus upon elites and, particularly, splits in ruling elites as leading to regime fragmentation. There is little doubt that in Serbia, Georgia and Ukraine, divisions within the ruling elites worked towards a democratic revolution. Elites brought with them resources (finances, media outlets, institutions, international ties) that were crucial to the success of the opposition. Oligarchs are typically untrustworthy allies of the executive in elections and crises.

A focus on elites should not lead to an ignoring of the election and revolutionary process from the bottom up where young people play a central role. In Serbia, Georgia and Ukraine the new post-communist young generation and civil society NGOs played a disproportionate role in overcoming widespread fear and apathy and in mobilizing millions of people to participate in the democratic revolutions. Their selfless actions provided an example to older generations that empowered them with the view that "We have the power to change things". Young people also proved instrumental in setting aside their personal differences and successfully pushing political parties to unite into opposition coalitions.

Since these three democratic revolutions have taken place, followed by Kyrgyzstan in 2005, authoritarian elites in the CIS have understood the importance of youth and civil society to democratic change (Herd, 2005). In Russia and Belarus the introduction of legislation to control NGOs has been introduced since the success of these four democratic revolutions. Anti-Western youth NGOs in Russia and Belarus have also been launched by the regimes to counter local manifestations of *Otpor, Khmara* and *Pora.*

Websites

www.5tv.com.ua
www.aeinstein.org
www.dif.org.ua
www.eggs.net.ua
www.eratv.com.ua
www.glavred.info
www.ham.com.ua
www.helsinki.org.yu
www.kuchmizm.info.org
www.maidan.org.ua
www.nonviolent-conflict.org
www.pora.org.ua
www.pravda.com.ua
www.rustavi2.com.ge
www.temnik.com.ua
www.yuschenko.com.ua
www.zn.kiev.ua

References

Ackerman, P., Duval, J., 2000. *A Force More Powerful. A Century of Nonviolent Conflict.* Palgrave, New York.

Chornuhuza, O. (Ed.), 2005. *Tak! Ukrayintsi Peremahayut Smiyuchys.* VUS, Kyiv.

Collin, M., 2001. *This is Serbia. Rock 'N' Roll Radio and Belgrade's Underground Resistance.* Serpents Tail, London.

Demes, P., Forbrig, J., 2006. Pora— "Its Time" for Democracy in Ukraine. In: Aslund, A., McFaul, M. (Eds.), *Revolution in Orange.* Carnegie Endowment, Washington, DC, pp. 85–102.

Durden-Smith, J., October 3, 2005. *No more people power.* The New Statesman.

Fairbanks, C.H., 2004. Georgia's rose revolution. *Journal of Democracy* 15 (2), 110–124.

Gemie, S., 2005. Roots, rock, Breizh: music and the politics of nationhood in contemporary Brittany. *Nations and Nationalism* 11 (1), 103–120.

Gordy, E.D., 1999. *The Cult of Power in Serbia. Nationalism and the Destruction of Alternatives.* Penn State University, University Park.

Gruda, A., December 5, 2004. *Generation orange.* La Presse.

Herd, G.P., 2005. Colorful revolutions and the CIS. "Manufactured" versus "managed" democracy? *Problems of Post Communism* 52 (2), 3–18.

Ilić, V., 2001. *Otpor—in or beyond Politics,* Helsinki Committee for Human Rights in Serbia. www.helsinki.org.yu/files_contents .php?lang=en&;idpub=54.

Kandelaki, G., 2005. *Rose Revolution: A Participant's Story.* US Institute of Peace.

Karatnycky, A., Ackerman, P., 2005. *How Freedom is Won. From Civic Resistance to Durable Democracy.* Freedom House, New York.

Kaskiv, V., January 21, 2005a. *Interview.* 2000 Newspaper.

Kaskiv, V., 2005b. *A case study of the civic campaign PORA and the Orange Revolution in Ukraine.* Kyiv, Pora. http://pora.org .ua/eng/content/view/2985/325/.

King, C., 2001. Potemkin democracy. Four myths about post-Soviet Georgia. T*he National Interest,* 93–104.

Klid, B., March 23–26, 2006. Rock, pop and politics in the 2004 Ukrainian presidential elections and Orange Revolution. Association for the Study of Nationalities. Convention paper.

Krnjevic-Miskovic, D. de, 2001. Serbia's prudent revolution. *Journal of Democracy* 12 (3), 96–110.

Kuzio, T., October 8, 2004a. Large scale anti-American campaign planned in Ukraine. Jamestown Foundation, *Eurasian Daily Monitor* 1 (102).

Kuzio, T., September 30, 2004b. Ukrainian officials increasingly denounce opposition as "extremists" and "terrorists". Jamestown Foundation, *Eurasian Daily Monitor* 1 (96).

Kuzio, T., 2005a. Ukraine's Orange Revolution. The opposition's road to success. *Journal of Democracy* 16 (2), 117–130.

Kuzio, T., 2005b. Kuchma to Yushchenko: Ukraine's 2004 elections and "Orange Revolution". *Problems of Post-Communism* 52 (2), 29–44.

Kuzio, T., 2005c. Russian policy to Ukraine during elections. *Demokratizatsiya* 13 (4), 491–517.

Kuzio, T. *"Directed chaos" and non-violence in Ukraine's Orange Revolution.* Swedish National Defense College, Stockholm, in press.

Kyj, M.J., 2006. Internet use in Ukraine's Orange Revolution. *Business Horizons* 49 (1), 71–80.

Lutsenko, Y., February 10, 2005. Minister of Interior, Interview, Washington, DC.

Markovic, I., March 5, 2005. Otpor activist, Interview, Washington, DC.

McFaul, M., 2005. Transitions from postcommunism. *Journal of Democracy* 16 (3), 5–19.

Miller, E.A., 2004. Smelling the roses. Eduard Shevardnadze's end and Georgia's future. *Problems of Post-Communism* 51 (2), 12–21.

Panina, N., 2005. *Ukrainian Society 1994–2005: Sociological Monitoring.* Institute of Sociology, National Academy of Sciences. Available at www.dif.org.ua/publics/doc.php?action=11/us5.

Polyukhovych, Y., November 11, 2004. Interview with Kyiv Coordinator of Pora. Kyiv Post.

Pora, February 2005. Ukraine's Orange Revolution. A Chronicle in PORA Newsletters. Pora, Kyiv.

Prytula, O., 2006. The Ukrainian media rebellion. In: Aslund, A., McFaul, M. (Eds.), *Revolution in Orange.* Carnegie Endowment, Washington, DC, pp. 103–124.

Reznik, O., 2005. Sotsialno-Politychni Peredumovy Fenomenon Pomaranchevoii Revolutsii. *Politychnyi Portret* 33, 5–14.

Sharp, G., 1973. *The Politics of Nonviolent Action.* Porter Sargent Publishers, Boston.

Slivka, A., January 1, 2004. *Orange alert.* The New York Times Magazine.

Stepanenko, V., 2005. Chy povernetsia dzyn u pliashku? Osoblyvosti natsionalnoii hromadianskoii aktyvnosti. *Politychnyi Portret* 33, 15–27.

Thompson, M.R., Kuntz, P., 2004. Stolen elections: the case of the Serbian October. *Journal of Democracy* 15 (4), 159–172.

UKRAINE: *Anti-Americanism an election tool for Kuchma,* January 8, 2004. Oxford Analytica.

Way, L., 2005. Kuchma's failed authoritarianism. *Journal of Democracy* 16 (2), 131–145.

Whither the Bulldozer? Nonviolent Revolution and the Transition to Democracy in Serbia, United States Institute of Peace Special Report, August 6, 2001.

Critical Thinking

1. What roles do young people play in democratic revolutions?

2. Describe the strategies to target youths in Serbia, Georgia, and Ukraine.

3. What methods are employed to mobilize youths in the democratic revolutions?

Online Activism

GUOBIN YANG

Online activism is an integral part of the broader landscape of citizen activism in contemporary China. It assumes a variety of forms, from cultural and social activism to cyber-nationalism and online petitions and protests. Technological development and social transformation provide the basic structural conditions. A fledgling civil society of online communities and offline civic associations, the logic of social production in the internet economy, and the creativity of Chinese internet users combine to sustain online activism under conditions of growing political control of the internet in China.

Online activism is a new form of popular contention in China. In some cases, the Internet serves to mobilize street protest. More often, protest takes place online. The most common forms include online petitions, the hosting of campaign websites, and large-scale verbal protests. The most radical is perhaps the hacking of websites. These forms of contention may be found in blogs, Internet bulletin boards, online communities, and podcast and YouTube-type websites.

Online activism first appeared in China in the late 1990s. Over the years, despite tight political control of the Internet, it has become more frequent and influential. Why?

It is useful to begin by differentiating among four types of online activism: cultural, social, political, and nationalistic. Cultural activism expresses concern over values, morality, lifestyles, and identities. When in 2003 Internet users (or "netizens") debated a provocative blog that a young woman who called herself Muzimei posted about her sex life, they were engaged in cultural activism. Social activism focuses on such problems as corruption, environmental degradation, and the rights of disadvantaged groups. In an influential 2003 case, the death of a migrant in Guangzhou City provoked widespread cyberprotests that resulted in the cancellation of an outdated regulation on urban vagrancy. An influential 2007 case exposed the criminal abduction of teenagers into slave labor on illegally operated industrial kilns in Shanxi Province.

Although cultural and social activism are also political in important ways, I single out specifically political activism as a distinct type in order to stress its oppositional nature. Online political activism focuses on human rights, political reform, and other issues that touch directly on how China is governed, by whom, and on what basis. Charter 08, the recent online petition calling for democratic reform, is a leading example of such activism.[1] Finally, there is online nationalism, which stands out by virtue of its frequency, scale, and impact. Nationalistic protest in cyberspace often involves large-scale online mobilizations and the use of radical tactics such as "hacktivism." In some cases, street demonstrations may also be involved.

Technological developments and social changes have combined to make online activism more widespread and prominent. China received its first Internet connection in 1994. By December 2008, the number using the Internet had reached 298 million, or about a quarter of all Chinese. The underside of China's economic development, including the socioeconomic polarization, pollution, corruption, and rights violations that have gone with it, provides the grievances that motivate activists, both online and offline.

Yet online activism in China also depends on several specific conditions. The first is the existence of a fledgling civil society of grassroots civic groups, nongovernmental organizations (NGOs), and—most important of all—online communities. Civil society groups flourished in the 1980s, but then suffered a setback with the repression of student protests in 1989. Since the mid-1990s, however, they have revived, expanded, and taken on new features such as relative administrative and financial autonomy from state agencies. Officially registered civic organizations numbered 360,000 at the end of 2006; estimates put the actual number at about three million.[2] As in other countries, Chinese civil society groups actively use the Internet in order to share information, educate the public, organize events, and mobilize friends and followers. A survey of 129 such organizations that I conducted in 2003 found that 106 of them (or 82 percent) were connected to the Internet and 69 (65 percent) had their own websites.[3] The growing connectivity of these civic groups facilitates their activities.

Online communities, an important new form of civic association, are where the action is. They encompass numerous types, and many are predominantly spaces for play and socializing. Anonymity can make senseless verbal attacks easier, but it also allows netizens to express themselves more freely than usual.[4] Yet Chinese online communities have diverse functions. Play is mingled with politics. Online debates and protests about social and political issues abound. Besides general-interest communities, there are numerous special-interest online communities, such as websites run by Chinese Catholics and Protestants, gay-oriented websites, scholarly communities of neoleftist or liberal intellectuals, and sites dedicated to various charitable and poverty-alleviation efforts. There are also many sites and blogs devoted to exposing social ills and fighting for citizens' rights as consumers or as workers who deserve protection from discrimination in the workplace.

One reason why contentious activities thrive in online communities is that controversy is good for business—disagreement raises interest, and with it, site traffic. Within limits, websites encourage users to participate in contentious interactions. Some sites strategically promote and guide controversial discussions in order to generate traffic. Behind this business strategy of promoting user participation is the logic of nonproprietary social production in today's Internet economy.[5] Internet consumers are Internet-content producers too. When they post on message boards, write blogs, upload videos, or protest online, they contribute directly to the Internet economy.

Chinese Internet users are active and prolific content producers. A January 2008 nationwide survey shows that about 66 percent of China's 210 million Internet users have contributed content to one or more sites. More than 35 percent indicated that in the past six months they had either posted or responded to messages in online forums. About 32 percent had uploaded pictures, while 18 percent had uploaded films, television programs, or other video materials.[6]

A third important condition is the creativity of Chinese netizens. Generally speaking, netizens try to stay within legal bounds and refrain from directly challenging state power. As skilled observers of Chinese politics, they understand which issues allow more leeway for discussion, and when. To a certain extent, the four types of online activism reflect netizens' strategic responses to the political opportunities for pursuing different issues. If the cultural, social, and nationalist varieties of activism online are more widespread than political activism, that is partly because the former types enjoy more political legitimacy. As in street protests, cyberprotests directly challenging the state are much more constrained than those that can be based either on existing laws or else on claims about justice and morality that do not touch directly on questions of state authority.[7]

Even so, keyword filtering, site blocking, and other means of watching and controlling what people do online pose constant challenges for Internet-based activists. In response, Chinese netizens have developed ingenious methods of dealing with Internet control. Some people run multiple blogs or use overseas servers to host their sites. Others use chatrooms for "secret meetings." Many know how to use the versatility of the Chinese language to create characters that easily beat the best filtering technologies.[8] Consequently, as political control of the Internet becomes more sophisticated, so do forms of resistance. Chinese netizens' creativity renders government control of the Internet only partly effective.

Does online activism matter? It has undoubtedly induced changes in the behavior of the state by undermining information control and creating social pressure for more government transparency. As a new source of public opinion and citizen mobilization, it has often led to policy changes. Perhaps more important, online activism is directly linked to changes in citizens' attitudes and behavior toward power. On 13 January 2008, the popular *Southern Metropolis News* carried a story bearing the subtitle "Don't Even Think About Deceiving Netizens." Referring to the many cases of online activism in 2007, the story argued that in the Internet age netizens will no longer let themselves be deceived by anyone, because "suppression and deception will only strengthen netizens' desire to express themselves."[9] These changes in citizens' political attitudes and behavior are not sufficient for democratization, but at the same time they are essential aspects of any process leading to it.

Notes

1. See Perry Link, trans. "China's Charter 08," *New York Review of Books,* 15 January 2009. See also *Journal of Democracy* 20 (April 2009): 179–82.

2. Gao Bingzhong and Yuan Ruijun, "Introduction: Stepping into Civil Society," in Beijing University Civil Society Research Center, *Zhongguo gongmin shehui fazhan lanpi shu* (Blue book of civil society development in China) (Beijing: Beijing University Press, 2008).

3. Guobin Yang, "How Do Chinese Civic Associations Respond to the Internet? Findings from a Survey," *China Quarterly* 189 (March 2007): 122–43.

4. In recent years, Chinese mass media have often condemned "Internet verbal violence," although such condemnations are often meant to provide the pretext for calls to tighten Internet control.

5. Yochai Benkler, *The Wealth of Networks: How Social Production Transforms Markets and Freedom* (New Haven: Yale University Press, 2006).

6. China Internet Network Information Center, "Survey Report on Internet Development in China," January 2008; available at www.cnnic.net.cn/en/index/index.htm.

7. Ching Kwan Lee, *Against the Law: Labor Protests in China's Rustbelt and Sunbelt* (Berkeley: University of California Press, 2007); Kevin J. O'Brien and Lianjiang Li, *Rightful Resistance in Rural China* (Cambridge: Cambridge University Press, 2006); Elizabeth J. Perry, "Chinese Conceptions of 'Rights': From Mencius to Mao—and Now," *Perspectives on Politics* 6 (March 2008): 37–50.

8. A hilarious example is discussed in Michael Wines, "A Dirty Pun Tweaks China's Online Censors," *New York Times,* 12 March 2009; available at www.nytimes.com/2009/03/12/world/asia/12beast.html.

9. Hu Chuanji, "Wangluo gongmin de jueqi: shui du bie xiang meng wangmin" (The rise of Internet citizens: Don't even think about deceiving netizens), *Nanfang dushi bao* (Southern Metropolis News), 13 January 2008.

Critical Thinking

1. What is online political activism? What aspects does it cover?

2. What is online cultural activism? What is online social activism?

3. What qualities facilitate online activism?

4. Is citizen participation necessary for democratiztion? Is it sufficient? Explain.

GUOBIN YANG is an associate professor in the Department of Asian and Middle Eastern Cultures at Barnard College, Columbia University. He is the author of *The Power of the Internet in China: Citizen Activism Online* (2009).

Smart Dictators Don't Quash the Internet

Mubarak had no idea how to counter the power of social media; China, Russia and Iran know better.

Evgeny Morozov

The tragic death of Khaled Said–the 28-year-old who in June 2010 was dragged from an Internet cafe in Alexandria and beaten by the Egyptian police–was the event that galvanized young Egyptians, pushing them to share their grievances on Facebook. A group called "We Are All Khaled Said" quickly reached hundreds of thousands of members and played an instrumental role in promoting the protests that eventually swept Hosni Mubarak from power.

The Egyptian experience suggests that social media can greatly accelerate the death of already dying authoritarian regimes. But while it's important to acknowledge the role that the Internet played in the Egyptian uprising, we shouldn't lose sight of the fact that the protesters were blessed with a government that didn't know a tweet from a poke–as illustrated most of all, perhaps, by its desperate (and belated) gambit in temporarily shutting off the country's access to the outside world. The lethal blow that the Internet has helped to deliver to the Mubarak regime is likely to push fellow tyrants to catch up on the latest developments in Silicon Valley and learn the ropes of online propaganda.

Take the Khaled Said incident. Although the two police officers suspected of beating up Mr. Said were eventually arrested, the Egyptian government ignored the anger of their netizens for far too long. That anger subsided, but it never went away; the turn of events in Tunisia helped to reinvigorate it.

Compare Egypt's experience to a similar case in China, where in 2009 Li Qiaoming, a 24-year-old peasant detained for illegal logging, was soon reported dead. The police told Mr. Li's parents, implausibly, that he had hit his head on a wall while playing a game of hide-and-seek with fellow inmates. The incident quickly generated almost 100,000 comments on just one popular Chinese blogging site, and the authorities reacted quickly.

Instead of trying to suppress online conversation, they reached out to the outraged netizens, inviting them to apply to become members of a commission to investigate the circumstances of Mr. Li's death. The resulting commission wasn't really allowed to investigate anything, of course, but by then the social unrest was quelled.

In retrospect, it's shocking how few pre-emptive steps Mr. Mubarak's regime had taken to control the Internet. There were no China-style attempts at Internet filtering; no Kremlin-style online propaganda chiefs or government-paid bloggers; virtually no cyber-attacks on the websites of bloggers and activist organizations. Mr. Mubarak's only foray into the world of Internet control was to beat up and jail bloggers–a tactic that only helped to publicize their cause.

It's not surprising, then, that officials were caught off-guard by the protests, which were mostly planned and discussed publicly online. Only after the online movement had gained an impressive offline momentum in Tahrir Square did Mr. Mubarak's associates choose to switch off the Internet for a few days, further revealing their incompetence. It's not that the Egyptian regime lost the online battle. They simply never entered it to begin with. It wasn't the Internet that destroyed Mr. Mubarak–it was Mr. Mubarak's ignorance of the Internet that destroyed Mr. Mubarak.

Other authoritarian regimes are taking cues from the events in Egypt, toughening their Internet controls. The Syrian government lifted a ban on Facebook and YouTube–nominally as a "concession" to opposition groups–but this was almost certainly done in order to more easily monitor public dissent. During the ban, Syrian dissidents could always get access to Facebook by using various tools for circumventing censorship and concealing their identities. This made Facebook slow and cumbersome to use, but it provided an extra degree of protection from the prying eyes of the Syrian police. Now that the ban has been lifted, the general population will flock to Facebook and expose themselves to the attention of the authorities.

In Sudan, Oman Al-Bashir has promised to extend electricity to the remote corners of the country so that his supporters can go online and defend him on Facebook. Meanwhile, the country's police officials have been distributing false information about protests via social media sites and text messaging in order to lure and then arrest anyone who shows up at the advertised venues.

Following this week's protests in Bahrain, Twitter was flooded with pro-government propaganda in a poorly veiled attempt to make it a less credible source of information about the protests. As for the authorities in Iran, they have learned their lesson from the 2009 uprising and have developed the most comprehensive Internet control strategy in the Middle East, setting up dedicated units of "cyber-police" and experimenting with advanced Internet surveillance techniques that may even allow them to detect dissidents who are using anti-censorship tools.

The most urgent Internet question facing many dictators today is what to do about American social networking sites like Facebook. Many are bound to follow the lead of Russia and China, which have championed homegrown competitors. An online group calling for the overthrow of the Russian government wouldn't survive for long on Vkontakte, Russia's alternative to Facebook.

Russian social networking sites already dominate the online landscape in most of the former Soviet republics, and it's highly unlikely they would side with pro-democracy protesters. In December 2010, as anti-government protests were brewing in Belarus after its contested presidential election, an online group supporting one of the candidates mysteriously disappeared from Vkontakte, depriving opposition groups of an important tool for mobilizing sympathizers.

In Vietnam, the government has banned Facebook and started its own site with the forbidding name of goonline.vn, hoping to make it the most popular state-run social networking site in the country.

Judging by the relative success of Moscow and Beijing in taming the democratic potential of the Web, it seems dictators learn fast and are perfectly capable of mastering the Internet. It's only by anticipating their response that those of us who care about democracy in the West can make their tough methods less effective. After all, these regimes have turned mostly to Western companies and consultants for advice about the technology of repression.

Triumphalism about recent events in the Middle East is premature. The contest is still in its early stages, and the new age of Internet-driven democratization will endure only if we learn to counter the sophisticated measures now being developed to quash it.

Critical Thinking

1. How does social networking promote democratization?

2. Describe the controls that government may use on internet and social networks.

3. Explain why smart dictators don't squash the internet. What does squashing the internet do?

Evgeny Morozov, a visiting scholar at Stanford University, is the author of *The Net Delusion: The Dark Side of Internet Freedom.*

From *The Wall Street Journal,* February 19, 2011, pp. C3. Copyright © 2011 by Dow Jones & Company, Inc. Reprinted with permission.

China's Cyberposse

Tom Downey

The short video made its way around China's Web in early 2006, passed on through file sharing and recommended in chat rooms. It opens with a middle-aged Asian woman dressed in a leopard-print blouse, knee-length black skirt, stockings and silver stilettos standing next to a riverbank. She smiles, holding a small brown and white kitten in her hands. She gently places the cat on the tiled pavement and proceeds to stomp it to death with the sharp point of her high heel.

"This is not a human," wrote BrokenGlasses, a user on Mop, a Chinese online forum. "I have no interest in spreading this video nor can I remain silent. I just hope justice can be done." That first post elicited thousands of responses. "Find her and kick her to death like she did to the kitten," one user wrote. Then the inquiries started to become more practical: "Is there a front-facing photo so we can see her more clearly?" The human-flesh search had begun.

Human-flesh search engines—*renrou sousuo yinqing*—have become a Chinese phenomenon: they are a form of online vigilante justice in which Internet users hunt down and punish people who have attracted their wrath. The goal is to get the targets of a search fired from their jobs, shamed in front of their neighbors, run out of town. It's crowd-sourced detective work, pursued online—with offline results.

There is no portal specially designed for human-flesh searching; the practice takes place in Chinese Internet forums like Mop, where the term most likely originated. Searches are powered by users called *wang min,* Internet citizens, or Netizens. The word "Netizen" exists in English, but you hear its equivalent used much more frequently in China, perhaps because the public space of the Internet is one of the few places where people can in fact act like citizens. A Netizen called Beacon Bridge No Return found the first clue in the kitten-killer case. "There was credit information before the crush scene reading 'www.crushworld.net,' " that user wrote. Netizens traced the e-mail address associated with the site to a server in Hangzhou, a couple of hours from Shanghai.

A follow-up post asked about the video's location: "Are users from Hangzhou familiar with this place?" Locals reported that nothing in their city resembled the backdrop in the video. But Netizens kept sifting through the clues, confident they could track down one person in a nation of more than a billion. They were right.

The traditional media picked up the story, and people all across China saw the kitten killer's photo on television and in newspapers. "I know this woman," wrote I'm Not Desert Angel four days after the search began. "She's not in Hangzhou. She lives in the small town I live in here in northeastern China. God, she's a nurse! That's all I can say."

Only six days after the first Mop post about the video, the kitten killer's home was revealed as the town of Luobei in Heilongjiang Province, in the far northeast, and her name—Wang Jiao—was made public, as were her phone number and her employer. Wang Jiao and the cameraman who filmed her were dismissed from what the Chinese call iron rice bowls, government jobs that usually last to retirement and pay a pension until death.

"Wang Jiao was affected a lot," a Luobei resident known online as Longjiangbaby told me by e-mail. "She left town and went somewhere else. Li Yuejun, the cameraman, used to be core staff of the local press. He left Luobei, too." The kitten-killer case didn't just provide revenge; it helped turn the human-flesh search engine into a national phenomenon.

At the Beijing headquarters of Mop, Ben Du, the site's head of interactive communities, told me that the Chinese term for human-flesh search engine has been around since 2001, when it was used to describe a search that was human-powered rather than computer-driven. Mop had a forum called human-flesh search engine, where users could pose questions about entertainment trivia that other users would answer: a type of crowd-sourcing. The kitten-killer case and subsequent hunts changed all that. Some Netizens, including Du, argue that the term continues to mean a cooperative, crowd-sourced investigation. "It's just Netizens helping each other and sharing information," he told me. But the Chinese public's primary understanding of the term is no longer so benign. The popular meaning is now not just a search *by* humans but also a search *for* humans, initially performed online but intended to cause real-world consequences. Searches have been directed against all kinds of people, including cheating spouses, corrupt government officials, amateur pornography makers, Chinese citizens who are perceived as unpatriotic, journalists who urge a moderate stance on Tibet and rich people who try to game the Chinese system. Human-flesh searches highlight what people are willing to fight for: the political issues, polarizing events and contested moral standards that are the fault lines of contemporary China.

Versions of the human-flesh search have taken place in other countries. In the United States in 2006, one online search singled out a woman who found a cellphone in a New York City taxi and started to use it as her own, rebuffing requests from the phone's rightful owner to return it. In South Korea in 2005, Internet users identified and shamed a young woman who was caught on video refusing to clean up after her dog on a Seoul subway car. But China is the only place in the world with a nearly universal recognition (among Internet users) of the concept. I met a film director in China who was about to release a feature film based on a human-flesh-search story and a mystery writer who had just published a novel titled "Human-Flesh Search."

The prevailing narrative in the West about the Chinese Internet is the story of censorship—Google's threatened withdrawal from China being only the latest episode. But the reality is that in China, as in the United States, most Internet users are far more interested in finding jobs, dates and porn than in engaging in political discourse. "For our generation, the post-'80s generation, I don't feel like censorship is a critical issue on the Internet," Jin Liwen, a Chinese technology analyst who lives in America, told me. While there are some specific, highly sensitive areas where the Chinese government tries to control all information—most important, any political activity that could challenge the authority of the Communist Party—the Western media's focus on censorship can lead to the misconception that the Chinese government utterly dominates online life. The vast majority of what people do on the Internet in China, including most human-flesh-search activity, is ignored by censors and unfettered by government regulation. There are many aspects of life on and off the Internet that the government is unwilling, unable or maybe just uninterested in trying to control.

The focus on censorship also obscures the fact that the Web is not just about free speech. As some human-flesh searches show, an uncontrolled Internet can be menacing as well as liberating.

On a windy night in late December 2007, a man was headed back to work when he saw someone passed out in the small garden near the entryway to his Beijing office building. The man, who would allow only his last name, Wei, to be published, called over to the security guard for help. A woman standing next to the guard started weeping. Wei was confused.

Wei and the guard entered the yard, but the woman, Jiang Hong, was afraid to follow. As they approached the person, Wei told me, he realized it was the body of someone who fell from the building. Then he understood why Jiang wouldn't come any closer: the body was that of her sister, Jiang Yan, who jumped from her apartment's 24th-floor balcony while Hong was in the bathroom. Two days earlier, Yan, who was 31, had tried to commit suicide with sleeping pills—she was separated from her husband, Wang Fei, who was dating another woman—but her sister and her husband had rushed her to the hospital. Now she had succeeded, hitting the ground so hard that her impact left a shallow crater still evident when I visited the site with Wei a year and a half later.

Hong soon discovered that her sister kept a private diary online in the two months leading up to her death and wanted it to be made public after she killed herself. When Hong called her sister's friends to tell them that Yan had died, she also told them that they could find out why by looking at her blog, now unlocked for public viewing. The online diary, "Migratory Bird Going North," was more than just a reflection on her adulterous husband and a record of her despair; it was Yan's countdown to suicide, prompted by the discovery that her husband was cheating on her. The first entry reads: "Two months from now is the day I leave . . . for a place no one knows me, that is new to me. There I won't need phone, computer or Internet. No one can find me."

A person who read Yan's blog decided to repost it, 46 short entries in all, on a popular Chinese online bulletin board called Tianya. Hong posted a reply, expressing sadness over her sister's death and detailing the ways she thought Yan had helped her husband: supporting him through school, paying for his designer clothes and helping him land a good job. Now, she wrote, Wang wouldn't even sign his wife's death certificate until he could come to an agreement with her family about how much he needed to pay them in damages.

Yan's diaries, coupled with her sister's account of Wang's behavior, attracted many angry Tianya users and shot to the top of the list of the most popular threads on the board. One early comment by an anonymous user, referring to Wang and his mistress, reads, "We should take revenge on that couple and drown them in our sputa." Calls for justice, for vengeance and for a human-flesh search began to spread, not only against Wang but also against his girlfriend. "Those in Beijing, please share with others the scandal of these two," a Netizen wrote. "Make it impossible for them to stay in this city."

The search crossed over to other Web sites, then to the mainstream media—so far a crucial multiplier in every major human-flesh search—and Wang Fei became one of China's most infamous and reviled husbands. Most of Wang's private information was revealed: cellphone number, student ID, work contacts, even his brother's license-plate number. One site posted an interactive map charting the locations of everything from Wang's house to his mistress's family's laundry business. "Pay attention when you walk on the street," wrote Hypocritical Human. "If you ever meet these two, tear their skin off."

Wang is still in hiding and was unwilling to meet me, but his lawyer, Zhang Yanfeng, told me not long ago: "The human-flesh search has unimaginable power. First it was a lot of phone calls every day. Then people painted red characters on his parents' front door, which said things like, 'You caused your wife's suicide, so you should pay.' "

Wang and his mistress, Dong Fang, both worked for the multinational advertising agency Saatchi & Saatchi. Soon after Netizens revealed this, Saatchi & Saatchi issued a statement reporting that Wang Fei and Dong Fang had voluntarily resigned. Wang's lawyer says Saatchi pushed the couple out. "All the media have the wrong report," he says. "[Wang Fei] never quit. He told me that the company fired him." (Representatives for Saatchi & Saatchi Beijing refused to comment.) Netizens were happy with this outcome but remained vigilant. One Mop user wrote, "To all employers: Never offer Wang Fei or Dong Fang jobs, otherwise Moppers will human-flesh-search you."

What was peculiar about the human-flesh search against Wang was that it involved almost no searching. His name was revealed in the earliest online-forum posts, and his private information was disclosed shortly after. This wasn't cooperative detective work; it was public harassment, mass intimidation and populist revenge. Wang actually sought redress in Chinese court and was rewarded very minor damages from an Internet-service provider and a Netizen who Wang claimed had besmirched his reputation. Recently passed tort-law reform may encourage more such lawsuits, but damages awarded thus far in China have been so minor that it's hard to imagine lawsuits having much impact on the human-flesh search.

For a westerner, what is most striking is how different Chinese Internet culture is from our own. News sites and individual blogs aren't nearly as influential in China, and social networking hasn't really taken off. What remain most vital are the largely anonymous online forums, where human-flesh searches begin. These forums have evolved into public spaces that are much more participatory, dynamic, populist and perhaps even democratic than anything on the English-language Internet. In the 1980s in the United States, before widespread use of the Internet, B.B.S. stood for bulletin-board system, a collection of posts and replies accessed by dial-up or hard-wired users. Though B.B.S.'s of this original form were popular in China in the early '90s, before the Web arrived, Chinese now use "B.B.S." to describe any kind of online forum. Chinese go to B.B.S.'s to find broad-based communities and exchange information about everything from politics to romance.

Jin Liwen, the technology analyst, came of age in China just as Internet access was becoming available and wrote her thesis at M.I.T. on Chinese B.B.S.'s. "In the United States, traditional media are still playing the key role in setting the agenda for the public," Jin told me. "But in China, you will see that a lot of hot topics, hot news or events actually originate from online discussions." One factor driving B.B.S. traffic is the dearth of good information in the mainstream media. Print publications and television networks are under state control and cannot cover many controversial issues. B.B.S.'s are where the juicy stories break, spreading through the mainstream media if they get big enough.

"Chinese users just use these online forums for everything," Jin says. "They look for solutions, they want to have discussions with others and they go there for entertainment. It's a very sticky platform." Jin cited a 2007 survey conducted by iResearch showing that nearly 45 percent of Chinese B.B.S. users spend between three and eight hours a day on them and that more than 15 percent spend more than eight hours. While less than a third of China's population is on the Web, this B.B.S. activity is not as peripheral to Chinese society as it may seem. Internet users tend to be from larger, richer cities and provinces or from the elite, educated class of more remote regions and thus wield influence far greater than their numbers suggest.

I found the intensity of the Wang Fei search difficult to understand. Wang Fei and Jiang Yan were separated and heading toward divorce, and what he did cannot be uncommon. How had the structure of the B.B.S. allowed mass opinion to be so effectively rallied against this one man? I tracked down Wang Lixue, a woman who goes by the online handle Chali and moderates a subforum on Baidu.com (China's largest search engine, with its own B.B.S.) that is devoted entirely to discussions about Jiang Yan. Chali was careful to distance herself from the human-flesh search that found Wang Fei and Dong Fang. "That kind of thing won't solve any problems," she told me.

"It's not good for either side." But she didn't exactly apologize. "Everyone was so angry, so irrational," Chali says. "It was a sensitive period. So I understand the people who did the human-flesh search. If a person doesn't do anything wrong, they won't be human-flesh-searched."

Chali was moved by the powerful feeling that Wang shouldn't be allowed to escape censure for his role in his wife's suicide. "I want to know what is going to happen if I get married and have a similar experience," Chali says. "I want to know if the law or something could protect me and give me some kind of security." It struck me as an unusual wish—that the law could guard her from heartbreak. Chali wasn't only angry about Jiang Yan's suicide; she also wanted to improve things for herself and others. "The goal is to commemorate Jiang Yan and to have an objective discussion about adultery, to talk about what you want in your marriage, to find new opinions and have a better life," Chali says. Her forum was the opposite of the vengeful populism found on some B.B.S.'s. The frenzy of the occasional human-flesh search attracts many Netizens to B.B.S.'s, but the bigger day-to-day draw, as in Chali's case, is the desire for a community in which people can work out the problems they face in a country where life is changing more quickly than anyone could ever have imagined.

The plum garden Seafood Restaurant stands on a six-lane road that cuts through Shenzhen, a fishing village turned factory boomtown. It has a subterranean dining room with hundreds of orange-covered seats, an open kitchen to one side and a warren of small private rooms to the other. Late on a Friday night in October 2008, a security camera captured a scene that was soon replayed all over the Chinese Internet and sparked a human-flesh search against a government official.

In the video clip, an older man crosses the background with a little girl. Later the girl runs back through the frame and returns with her father, mother and brother. The subtitles tell us that the old man had tried to force the girl into the men's room, presumably to molest her, and that her father is trying to find the man who did that. Then the girl's father appears in front of the camera, arguing with that man.

There is no sound on the video, so you have to rely on the Chinese subtitles, which seem to have been posted with the video. According to those subtitles, the older man tells the father of the girl: "I did it, so what? How much money do you want? Name your price." He gestures violently and continues: "Do you know who I am? I am from the Ministry of Transportation in Beijing. I have the same level as the mayor of your city. So what if I grabbed the neck of a small child? If you dare challenge me, just wait and see how I will deal with you." He moves to leave but is blocked by restaurant employees and the girl's father. The group exits frame left.

The video was first posted on a Web site called Netease, whose slogan is "The Internet can gather power from the people." The eighth Netizen comment reads: "Have you seen how proud he was? He's a dead man now." Later someone chimed in, "Another official riding roughshod over the people!" The human-flesh search began. Users quickly matched a public photo of a local party official to the older man in the video and identified him as Lin Jiaxiang from the Shenzhen Maritime Administration. "Kill him," wrote a user named Xunleixing. "Otherwise China will be destroyed by people of this kind."

While Netizens saw this as a struggle between an arrogant official and a victimized family of common people, the staff members at Plum Garden, when I spoke to them, had a different take. First, they weren't sure that Lin had been trying to molest the girl. Perhaps, they thought, he was just drunk. The floor director, Zhang Cai Yao, told me, "Maybe the government official just patted the girl on the head and tried to say, 'Thank you, you're a nice girl.'" Zhang saw the struggle between Lin and the family as a kind of conflict she witnessed all too often. "It was a fight between rich people and officials," she says. "The official said something irritating to her parents, who are very rich."

Police said they did not have sufficient evidence to prosecute Lin, but that didn't stop the government from firing him. It was the same kind of summary dismissal as in the kitten-killer case—Lin drew attention to himself, and so it was time to go. The government had the technology and the power to make a story like this one disappear, yet it didn't stand up to the Netizens. That is perhaps because this search took aim at a provincial-level official; there have been no publicized human-flesh searches against central-government officials in Beijing or their offspring, even though many of them are considered corrupt.

Rebecca MacKinnon, a visiting fellow at Princeton University's Center for Information Technology Policy, argues that China's central government may actually be happy about searches that focus on localized corruption. "The idea that you manage the local bureaucracy by sicking the masses on them is actually not a democratic tradition but a Maoist tradition," she told me. During the Cultural Revolution, Mao encouraged citizens to rise up against local officials who were bourgeois or corrupt, and human-flesh searches have been tagged by some as Red Guard 2.0. It's easy to denounce the tyranny of the online masses when you live in a country that has strong rule of law and institutions that address public corruption, but in China the human-flesh search engine is one of the only ways that ordinary citizens can try to go after corrupt local officials. Cases like the Lin Jiaxiang search, as imperfect as their outcomes may be, are examples of the human-flesh search as a potential mechanism for checking government excess.

The human-flesh search engine can also serve as a safety valve in a society with ever mounting pressures on the government. "You can't stop the anger, can't make everyone shut up, can't stop the Internet, so you try and channel it as best you can. You try and manage it, kind of like a waterworks hydroelectric project," MacKinnon explained. "It's a great way to divert the *qi,* the anger, to places where it's the least damaging to the central government's legitimacy."

The chinese government has proved particularly adept at harnessing, managing and, when necessary, containing the nationalist passions of its citizens, especially those people the Chinese call *fen qing,* or angry youth. Instead of wondering, in the run-up to the 2008 Beijing Olympics, why the world was so upset about China's handling of Tibet, popular sentiment in China was channeled against dissenting individuals, painted as traitors. One young Chinese woman, Grace Wang, became the target of a human-flesh search after she tried to mediate between pro-Tibet and pro-China protesters at Duke University, where she is an undergraduate. Wang told me that her mother's home in China was vandalized by human-flesh searchers. Wang's mother was not harmed—popular uprisings are usually kept under tight control by the government when they threaten to erupt into real violence—but Wang told me she is afraid to return to China. Certain national events, like the Tibet activism before the 2008 Olympics or the large-scale loss of life from the Sichuan earthquake, often produce a flurry of human-flesh searches. Recent searches seem to be more political—taking aim at things like government corruption or a supposedly unpatriotic citizenry—and less focused on the kind of private transgressions that inspired earlier searches.

After the earthquake, in May 2008, users on the B.B.S. of Douban, a Web site devoted to books, movies and music, discussed the government's response to the earthquake. A woman who went by the handle Diebao argued that the government was using the earthquake to rally nationalist sentiment, and that, she wrote, was an exploitation of the tragedy. Netizens challenged Diebao's arguments, saying that it was only right for China to speak in one voice after such a catastrophe. These were heady days, and the people who disagreed with Diebao weren't content to leave it at that. In Guangzhou, the capital of Guangdong, Feng Junhua, a 25-year-old man who on the Internet goes by the handle Hval, was getting worried. Feng spent a lot of time on Douban, and, he told me later, he saw where the disagreement with Diebao was going—the righteous massing against the dissenter. He e-mailed Diebao, who

lived in Sichuan Province, to warn her of the danger and urge her to stop fighting with the other Netizens. "I found out that the other people were going to threaten her with the human-flesh search engine," he told me. "She wrote back to me, saying she wanted to talk them out of it."

The group started to dig through everything Diebao had written on the Internet, desperate to find more reasons to attack her. They found what they were looking for, a stream-of-consciousness blog entry Diebao posted right after the earthquake hit: "I felt really excited when the earthquake hit. I know this experience might happen once in a lifetime. When I watched the news at my aunt's place, I found out that it caused five people to die. I feel so good, but that's not enough. I think more people should die." Diebao wrote this right after the earthquake struck her city, possibly while she was still in shock and before she knew the extent of the damage.

The group tried to use this post to initiate a human-flesh search against Diebao. At first it didn't succeed—no one responded to the calls for a search. (There are hundreds, maybe thousands of attempts each week for all kinds of human-flesh searches, the vast majority of which do not amount to much.) Finally they figured out a way to make their post "sparkle," as they say in Chinese, titling it, "She Said the Quake Was Not Strong Enough" and writing, of Diebao: "We cannot bear that an adult in such hard times didn't feel ashamed for not being able to help but instead was saying nonsense, with little respect for other people's lives. She should not be called a human. We think we have to give her a lesson. We hereby call for a human-flesh search on her!"

This time it took hold. A user named Little Dumpling joined the pile-on, writing: "Earthquake, someone is calling you. Please move your epicenter right below [Diebao's] computer desk." Juana0906 asked: "How could she be so coldblooded? Her statement did greater harm to the victims than the earthquake." Then from Expecting Bull Market, the obligatory refrain in almost every human-flesh search, "Is she a human?"

Feng, the user who tried to warn Diebao of the impending search, became angry that so many people were going after Diebao. "I cannot stand seeing the strong beating the weak," he told me. "I thought I should protect the right of free speech. She can say anything she wants. I think that she just didn't think before she spoke." But the searchers managed to rally users against Diebao. "Her school read a lot of aggressive comments on the Internet and got pressure from Netizens asking them to kick out this girl," Feng told me. Shortly after the human-flesh search began, Diebao was expelled from her university. "The school announced that it was for her own safety, to protect her," Feng says.

Feng decided to get revenge on the human-flesh searchers. He and a few other users started a human-flesh search of their own, patiently matching back the anonymous ID's of the people who organized against Diebao to similar-sounding names on school bulletin boards, auction sites and help-wanted ads. Eventually he assembled a list of the real identities of Diebao's persecutors. "When we got the information, we had to think about what we should do with it," Feng says. "Should we use it to attack the group?"

Feng stopped and thought about what he was about to do. "When we tried to fight evil, we found ourselves becoming evil," he says. He abandoned the human-flesh search and destroyed all the information he had uncovered.

Critical Thinking

1. How does social networking hurt democratization?
2. What does internet vigilantism mean?
3. What is the internet mainly used for?

UNIT 4

The Executive: Instituting Accountability and Responsiveness

Unit Selections

Learning Outcomes

After reading this Unit, you will be able to:

- Explain the advantages and problems of an executive.
- Clarify the need for limitations on the executive.
- Explain how term limits on the executive are useful and not useful.
- Explain how elections may and may not support democratic development.
- Describe how institutional strengths foster democratic development.
- Describe how an executive is strong.
- Clarify if controls on executives only need to occur in some countries.

Student Website

www.mhhe.com/cls

Internet References

Asian Development Bank
www.adb.org/Countries
BBC World News
www.bbc.co.uk/news/world/asia_pacific
Europa: European Union
http://europa.eu/index_en.htm
Inter-American Dialogue (IAD)
www.thedialogue.org
Latin American Network Information Center, University of Texas at Austin
http://lanic.utexas.edu/la/region/government
Russian and East European Network Information Center, University of Texas at Austin
http://reenic.utexas.edu

The previous units focused on the study of comparative politics, particularly in relation to democratic theory and the effect of citizen participation on political development. The next three units consider the complement to democratic development: government. In particular, we consider the different institutions of government, how they balance democratic responsiveness and accountability with effective policymaking, and how their performance as institutions and in policymaking may run up against political development. The institutions are the executive, the legislature, and the unelected officers of the judiciary and the military. Unit 4 addresses the systematic questions (why, what, and how) regarding executives and their performance in democratic development.

We begin with the question, "Why executives?" The explanation may be found in political theories of government, articulated by venerated theorists such as John Locke, John Stuart Mill, Jean-Jacques Rousseau, and the framers of the U.S. Constitution: to achieve efficient and efficacious policy-making. Even if a community is small enough to allow everyone to partake in policy-making and implementation, it is inefficient to do so. Think about a community the size of a country and it becomes clear that it is prohibitive to have everyone partake in policy-making. Thus, citizens choose a representative government to make those policies on their behalf.

The paradox is that the more diverse the society, the larger and more diverse the representative government becomes. That, in turn, progressively works against efficient policymaking. This is why we need executives in political systems: executives remove that potential spiral into inefficiency by bringing the "power," "tyranny," and "arbitrariness" of a single decisionmaker into policy-making without the objectionable aspects of those qualities.1 Or, to put it kindly, they rise above the fray of legislative bickering or indecision to ensure that policies are formulated, approved, and implemented.

Yet, the hazards of leaving power in the hands on one are considerable. Thus, the first article in this unit describes the extended fight that President Laurent Gbago gave to president-elect Alassane Outtara of the Ivory Coast because of the former's refusal to honor the election outcome. It took the concerted efforts of the French and UN military, and scanctions by the European Union, the United States, and regional governments to undermine Gbago's hold of the office.

Nor are these hazards limited to transitioning countries or emerging democracies. Italy, for instance, has its share of problems in Prime Minister Silvio Berlusconi. Few will be blamed for focusing on Berlusconi's encounters with corruption and sex scandals that have dogged his tenure. But, the real problems are the economic and institutional weaknesses that have led to his continuation in office. And, if Berlusconi has his way, he is on-route to further dilute the institutional strengths of the judiciary and the media. Clearly, regularly elected executives may dominate politics and policymaking because the other institutions that act as "checks" on the executive are weak.

So, how do we ensure that (1) that there are checks on the executive and (2) that the checks work? The next two articles point the way. Institutionally, be it Costa Rica or Indonesia, the

© Steve Allen/Brand X Pictures

same structural checks on the executive apply, that is, elections that are free and fair, legislators that are committed to representation of the citizens rather than winning reelections, and term limits. Term limits, in particular, capture the last line of defense against the tyranny of the single policymaker.

Is there a need for this last line of defense? Consider that there is a lot of attention—and, hence, reward—paid to an executive's ability to deliver policy performance, specifically, economic performance. Thus, the performances of the political leaders in China and Putin are considered excellent by the measure of economic performance. In fact, according to the article on the resilient autocrats in China and Russia, much of the ability of the political elites in China and of Putin to remain popular lies in their ability to deliver on economic performance. Indeed, the author suggests that for China, economic performance, tinged with small improvements in social and civil rights, has maintained political stability in the country. Importantly, the Chinese model appears to be emulated by countries such as Russia, Vietnam, and Cuba.

Thus, in China and Russia, there is adherence to the "letter" of democratic development but not its spirit. Clearly, policy performance alone is not enough as a marker of executive performance. Instead, the readings suggest that it is political leaders have to demonstrate responsiveness and accountability. The hope is that, notwithstanding the efficient policymaking and implementation, executives embrace and promote "social diversity" rather than choke it if they are responsive and accountable.3 And, most importantly, executives need to move beyond cronyism, corruption, moral manipulation, and divisive policies.

This is why term limits may be useful and why the relaxation of term–limits on the executive represents a cause for concern. It is a particularly troubling political development if a sitting executive reaps the rewards of such changes. Yet, as events in Russia show, executives such as Putin do not need to be reelected to office in order to ensure that his or her legacy continues.

101

In Belated Inauguration, Ivory Coast's President Urges Unity

ADAM NOSSITER

Dakar, Senegal—Alassane Ouattara was formally inaugurated Saturday as Ivory Coast's president in a ceremony in the West African nation's capital, Yamoussoukro, nearly six weeks after his predecessor was forcibly removed from office with the help of French and United Nations military strikes.

Mr. Ouattara called for reconciliation and peace in a country that was once one of Africa's richest but that has been devastated by years of unrest, political division and civil war.

"The time has arrived for Ivorians to come together," Mr. Ouattara, a former economist and banker, said in a speech that did not deviate from his habitually austere manner. "Dear brothers and sisters, let's celebrate peace. Like the great people we are, we are going to reunite. Yes, we are going to come together. Let us learn to live together again."

The country is still reeling from a four-month armed standoff that killed as many as 3,000 people, according to officials and human rights groups, and that sent tens of thousands of refugees fleeing violence into neighboring lands. About 160,000 are still in exile in Liberia, according to the International Rescue Committee.

Sanctions imposed by the European Union, the United States and regional governments had crippled the economy as President Laurent Gbagbo, who decisively lost the presidential election in November, refused to give up office.

Life is slowly returning to a semblance of normalcy. Banks have reopened, the nation's vital cocoa exports have resumed and civil servants have returned to their desks with two months' back pay.

Mr. Ouattara must govern under the burden of multiple handicaps. The country is still split between his supporters and those of Mr. Gbagbo, who received 46 percent of the vote in the election; whole villages and cocoa farms in the west remain devastated; and Mr. Ouattara was installed largely by foreign forces.

Months of African diplomacy proved ineffectual in dislodging Mr. Gbagbo, and Mr. Ouattara's fighters played a secondary role. Ultimately, it was the French missile attacks against Mr. Gbagbo's heavy-weapons installations that led to his defeat.

France's central role was recognized at the ceremony in Yamoussoukro when its president, Nicolas Sarkozy, in the audience, was the first head of state to be saluted by Mr. Ouattara, and received sustained applause. Yet much of the population, especially Mr. Gbagbo's supporters, resent the former colonial master and consider Mr. Ouattara as France's man.

About 20 heads of state attended the ceremony, including African leaders who have clung to office for decades and are themselves beneficiaries of disputed or fraudulent elections. The event took place in Yamoussoukro, the native village of Ivory Coast's founding president, Félix Houphouët-Boigny, and its official capital, although Abidjan is the main commercial city and center of government.

Mr. Gbagbo remains under house arrest in the northern town of Korhogo, where he has been interrogated by Ouattara officials with a view to possible prosecution, and about 200 members of his government are also to be questioned, according to officials.

Mr. Gbagbo's wife, Simone, a powerful influence in his government, has been interrogated in a separate location.

Mr. Ouattara has promised a South African-style "dialogue, truth and reconciliation" commission to look into the conflict, and he has asked the International Criminal Court to investigate crimes committed "since Nov. 28," the date of the election whose result Mr. Gbagbo refused to acknowledge.

Mr. Ouattara's call for the investigation to include "all of Ivorian territory" reiterates his position that any atrocities committed by forces that eventually declared their loyalty to him, including a massacre in which hundreds died in Duékoué in the west, should also be punished. Nonetheless, according to Human Rights Watch, "the majority of abuses during the first three months were by forces under Gbagbo's control" and "probably amounted to crimes against humanity."

Indeed, the civilian population in Abidjan was repeatedly attacked, over the course of months, by uniformed men directly under Mr. Gbagbo's control, in what appeared to be deliberate state policy. The killings of Gbagbo supporters that took place at the end of the conflict were carried out by ragtag forces that only belatedly swung to Mr. Ouattara.

Mr. Ouattara, a former prime minister and deputy managing director of the International Monetary Fund, faces the immense task of rebuilding a country damaged by civil war, 10 years of what is widely acknowledged as the corrupt leadership of Mr. Gbagbo and fierce ethnic divisions. The new government filed suit in Swiss courts this month against Mr. Gbagbo and his entourage to recover tens of millions of dollars in assets.

It was less than three weeks ago that the last pro-Gbagbo mercenaries were finally rooted out of Abidjan, fleeing across the lagoons to the west and killing dozens as they went. United Nations investigators later discovered a mass grave containing some 68 bodies in the neighborhood where the Gbagbo forces had been entrenched.

Critical Thinking

1. What support did Alassane Outtara have?
2. Who were Gbago's supporters?
3. What are the lessons of the Ivory Coast for democratization advocates?

Tangled Webs; Institutions

THE ECONOMIST

Anyone looking for entertaining television in Italy at the end of the day would do well to flick past the Milan football derby and "Italy's Next Top Model" and pick a political talk show instead. These combative, insult-laden programmes are hard to watch and harder to turn off. "Opponents are presented not so much as wrong but as losers or, better, sexually inadequate losers," wrote Tim Parks in the New Yorker recently.

Americans might shrug at this, but in Italy things are different–and not just because there is more sex. In America conservatives may rage against Supreme Court rulings like Roe v Wade, but only a far-flung fringe questions the right of the court to make such decisions. In Italy that fringe is in government.

The lines that run between political parties, the civil service, the media, business and the judiciary are more like ribbons that can be bent to any shape under slight pressure. Italy lacks referees who can intervene when this process goes too far, argues Ferdinando Giugliano of Oxford University. Institutions are further weakened by the conflicts of interest that pop up everywhere. The prime minister's ownership of the country's largest television network is merely the biggest of them.

Back in the 1990s it seemed to some that Italy was on the threshold of an institutional transformation. Membership of the euro would prevent Italy from devaluing its currency whenever exports became uncompetitive, forcing the country to undertake reforms to boost productivity. The breaking up of the Christian Democrats' monopoly on power achieved by the "clean hands" corruption trials would allow Italy to become a more normal democracy in which power alternates between two main parties, providing strong government.

This has not happened. The problems of the Italian economy are still substantially the same as they were 15 years ago, though the government's direct involvement in industry has diminished. Italy has not developed a two-party system: the left is made up of squabbling coalitions of interests that can sometimes be glued together for the sake of winning power but then tend to disintegrate. People of Freedom (PdL), the main party on the right, governs in coalition with another with which it disagrees on fundamental issues, such as how much regional devolution there should be. Moreover, part of the PdL is not so much a party as a group of Berlusconi fans and ex-employees. Giulio Tremonti, the finance minister, was Mr Berlusconi's tax lawyer; Mara Carfagna, the minister for equal opportunities, used to jiggle in a bikini on one of his television channels.

The parties' credibility has also been damaged by frequent tinkering with the rules for electing deputies and senators in Rome. After the clean hands trials Italy pursued piecemeal electoral reform, which did produce strong governments with more stable majorities. But a Berlusconi-led government in 2005 brought in a closed-list system, in the hope that it would make the left even more fragmented than it was already. That did not happen, but it increased the control of party managers and broke the direct link between voters and constituents.

Keeping the political circus going is also strikingly expensive. Parties receive generous subsidies to fund their election expenses: according to the Court of Auditors, between 1994 and 2008 they received EUR 2.2 billion ($3.1 billion) from general taxation to cover their election expenses, but only EUR 579m of this expenditure could be verified. A cynical reading of this would suggest Italy's political parties made a profit of EUR 1.67 billion at taxpayers' expense over this period.

Conflicts of interest affect journalism and business too. The largest shareholder of the company that owns the country's most famous newspaper, *Corriere della Sera,* is Mediobanca, an octopus-like investment bank which holds large stakes in many of Italy's biggest companies. The paper's reporters are independent, but that does not stop Italians indulging in dietrologia, the study of whose interest lies behind the stories. Italy's second-biggest newspaper, *La Repubblica*, is owned by Carlo De Benedetti, a veteran industrialist, and managed by his son, Rodolfo. Fiat (whose controlling shareholder, the Agnelli family, has a small shareholding in *The Economist*) owns *La Stampa* and also has a large holding in Corriere. Silvio Berlusconi's brother owns *Il Giornale*, and the prime minister provided the capital to start another friendly newspaper, *Il Foglio*. But it is hard to argue that newspaper proprietors in Italy are vastly more powerful than elsewhere, and there are enough voices to ensure competition.

The same cannot be said of television, which is where most Italians get their news. Mr Berlusconi owns the biggest commercial broadcaster, but his government also has influence over appointments at RAI, the public broadcaster. That twin grip gives him formidable power over how his government is seen on television. Freedom House, an American NGO, reckons that in his 2001-06 government Mr Berlusconi had control over 90% of the broadcast media. That assessment has yet to be updated, but not a lot has changed.

Even without the country's dominant media owner in the Chigi Palace, RAI would be rife with political influence. Seven out of nine members of the body that supervises the broadcaster are elected by parliamentary committee. They spend their time haggling over the share of airtime allocated to their political parties instead of allowing RAI's journalists to keep balance.

Board Games

Italian capitalism differs from other varieties in three respects: the use of cross-shareholdings, whereby company A owns shares in company B and vice versa; cascading ownership structures, which allow holders of a relatively small number of shares in a large company to control it via a series of shell companies; and shallow equity markets, which are partly a result of the other two oddities.

In theory the rules for the governance of publicly listed companies are exemplary. In practice they do not deliver the goods: witness Pirelli's value-destroying shopping spree ten years ago which lost it more than EUR 3 billion ($4.1 billion) on its stake in Telecom Italia, at the instigation of a shareholder who owned just 8% of its equity. Minority shareholders can expect to be frozen out unless they make pacts with other shareholders. One such pact, led by Capitalia and UniCredit, two large banks, governs the ownership of Mediobanca, which has proved expert at using small stakes in companies to get its way. The government still owns large stakes in big public companies like Eni, an oil and gas company that is 30% owned by the Ministry of Economy and Finance, and Enel, which generates and distributes electricity and is 31% owned by the same ministry.

One result is that retail investors stay away. Combined with the widespread family ownership of medium-sized companies (which restricts the number of listed firms), this means Italian capitalism does a poor job of connecting the country's ample private savings with companies in need of capital. Two recent changes—a European directive known as Record Date and an edict from Italy's stockmarket regulator giving independent directors a veto over some manoeuvres—may help the minnows. But like other aspects of Italian life, corporate culture has a way of remaining essentially unchanged no matter what the law may say.

Justice Deferred

To understand how these conflicts block change, consider the government's current proposal to reform the judiciary. Italy's courts follow the principle that appeals should be allowed at each stage of the process so as to minimise the chance of an injustice. This praiseworthy ambition produces nightmarish results. A study by the European Council found that in 2005 it took an average of 1,210 days for a contractual dispute to be resolved in Italy, compared with 229 in Britain and 331 in France. Turin's courts have managed to cut the delays by giving priority to older cases and publishing the rate at which judges clear them. Unfortunately these innovations have not been copied elsewhere, so the foot-dragging continues.

Hence the government's reform proposal. It mixes some things that might help a bit—such as separating the career paths of prosecutors and judges—with some things that would be disastrous, such as making it possible to bring civil lawsuits against magistrates and judges and giving elected politicians a say in which cases should be prioritised. But this reform ought to go nowhere anyway because of the conflicts of interest that come with it. On the government's side the prime minister has been engaged in a fight with "communist" prosecutors since he entered office, and now dedicates a day a week to doing battle with them. There is no way that his government can propose a disinterested reform. As for the magistrates, some of them seem to be politically motivated. Antonio di Pietro, one of the principal judges in the clean hands trials, now has his own political party. But judges, even if they have fought political corruption, should not become elected politicians. So reforming the courts is impossible because everybody's motives are questionable.

"Italy would be relatively normal if it were not for all the little Berlusconis," says James Walston, a political scientist at the American University of Rome. Conflicts of interest and blurred boundaries between institutions seem to be the norm, and powers are amalgamated rather than separated. But all these tangles seem modest by comparison with the prime minister's own. One reason for his remarkable success may be sympathy from people who see something of themselves in him."

Like other aspects of Italian life, corporate culture has a way of remaining essentially unchanged no matter what the law may say"

Critical Thinking

1. What are the institutions that may pose a constraint on the executive?

2. Describe how political parties may pose a constraint on the executive.

3. What is the judicial reform proposed in Italy? Explain how the reform is good but still a conflict of interest.

The General Election in Costa Rica, February 2010

Bruce M. Wilson and Juan Carlos Rodríguez-Cordero

On 7 February 2010, almost 2 million Costa Ricans (69% of the registered electorate) voted in the country's general election, the fifteenth consecutive general election to be held since the end of the short but bloody civil war of 1948. Laura Chinchilla was elected as Costa Rica's first woman president but her *Partido Liberación Nacional* (National Liberation Party, PLN) fell short of a parliamentary majority and so will have to sustain agreements with other parties in the legislature in order to pursue its policy agenda.

1. Electoral System

General elections take place once every four years on the first Sunday in February. Voters are presented with a ballot paper for the offices of the president and two vice presidents; a separate ballot is used for to elect all 57 deputies (*diputados*), the members of the single-chamber national legislative assembly. Simultaneously, the 495 representatives for the 81 municipal governments are also elected on a separate third ballot (*Regidores Municipales*, *Propietarios* and *Suplentes*, regular representatives and alternates). Neither deputies nor the president can seek immediate reelection: the former must sit out a four-year term, while presidents can seek a second stint only after sitting out two full terms. (From, 1969 until 2003, presidents could only serve a single term; a ruling by the Constitutional Chamber of the Supreme Court in 2003 removed the prohibition and returned to the original constitutional provision that allowed reelection after eight years out of office.)

For presidential elections, the country is treated as a single constituency where the candidate with the largest vote share is declared winner so long as he or she received more than the 40% threshold. If no candidate receives more than 40% of the vote, a second round is held one month later between the two leading candidates. In the post-Civil War period, only one presidential election has required a second round: in 2002, Abel Pacheco de la Espriella fell approximately one percentage point short of the threshold and went on to win the run-off (Wilson, 2003 and Lehoucq and Rodríguez-Cordero, 2004).

For legislative elections, Costa Rica uses a closed-list, proportional representation (PR) electoral system. The country's seven geographic provinces serve as seven multi-member districts, with the total number of representatives for each district allocated in proportion to its population (as measured by the most recent census but with updates based on population estimates by the *Instituto Nacional de Estadística y Censos* (National Institute for Statistics and Census, INEC)). The distribution of seats for the 2010 elections is the same as those used in the last two elections and is based on the 2000 census. In this particular version of PR, the quotient is calculated by dividing the number of votes cast in a district by the number of seats allocated to that district. If no party has enough remaining votes to secure a seat through the quotient, a sub-quotient (50% of the quotient) is used. Any seats remaining once the sub-quotient has been exhausted go to the party with the largest remainder. By way of an illustrative example, San José, the most populous province, was allocated 20 of the 57 seats. A total of 690,336 votes was cast in the 2010 Legislative Assembly election (90,000 more than in the 2006 election), which produced a quotient of 34,517 votes per seat (almost 4000 votes more per seat than in 2006) and a sub-quotient of 17,258.

2. Electoral Administration

Elections are staged under the auspices of the *Tribunal Supremo de Elecciones* (TSE, Supreme Tribunal of Elections). The TSE, a constitutionally mandated quasi-fourth branch of government, controls all aspects of electoral administration and is composed of three full-time Magistrates (*Magistrados Propietarios*) who are appointed by the Supreme Court to renewable six-year terms. Supreme Court Magistrates, for their part, are elected to eight-year terms by a supermajority vote of the Legislative Assembly, which helps enhance the political independence of the TSE. Twelve months before the general election, two "supplemental magistrates" (*Magistrados Suplentes*) are added to the Tribunal's three sitting members. Their term ends six months after the election.

While Section 6 of Constitutional Article 102 is commonly interpreted as transferring total control of the police forces to the TSE during elections, this formerly important power has now become largely symbolic. Nevertheless, the TSE does function as an election court and must examine any Legislative Assembly bill related to elections before it can be passed into law. The *Registro Civil* (Civil Registry), under the authority of TSE, is also charged with registration of births, marriages, and deaths, with creating the electoral roll, and with ballot design (a lottery being used to allocate individual candidates' positions on the ballot). The TSE also regulates the election campaign: it licenses polling companies and sets the rules concerning when polls can be conducted; it enforces the *tregua navideña* (a two week Christmas truce, when all campaigning is put on hold); and it maintains scrutiny over parties' election funding and expenditure. The 2010 saw one significant example of this role of judicial oversight. A *recurso de amparo electoral* (a writ of protection) case was filed with the TSE during the election campaign. Its ruling served as a reminder to church leaders that they should not interfere in the elections by openly endorsing candidates regarded as more likely to uphold church doctrine. In the case (Sentence 3281-E1-2010) the TSE admonished a Catholic bishop for "telling his parishioners for whom to vote"), a contradiction of Constitutional Article 28 (Vizcaíno, 2010b).

The TSE's election monitoring system is sophisticated and comprehensive. There are over 6000 polling rooms housed in almost 2000 polling stations (*centros de votación*), generally schools but also old people's homes, jails, and indigenous areas, with the goal of facilitating the as high a turnout as possible. Each polling station is staffed by representatives of political parties (*miembros de mesa*) who are trained by the TSE to keep the balloting process fair. As well as the Costa Rican monitors, over 100 international observers fan out across the country visiting polling stations to monitor the process. In 2010, the international observers reported the process as being fair with no evidence of corruption or malpractice. One reason why electoral fraud is so rare is that there is a total ban on absentee balloting. In order to cast a vote, electors must be physically present in their TSE-assigned polling station, have their original *cédula de identidad* (a virtually tamper-proof, TSE-issued photo identification card). The practice of voters dipping their index finger into indelible ink once they had voted was discontinued for the 2006 elections. (And the prohibition on absentee voting will be lifted for the forthcoming referendum on same-sex civil unions, scheduled for December 2010).

Finally, perhaps the most popular measure taken during the 2010 election was a minor reform of the Electoral Code to repeal the application of the "Ley Seca" (literally, Dry Law) during national elections. This widely unpopular law, designed to prevent political disturbances during the election period, banned the sale and distribution of any alcoholic beverages from the day before the election until the day afterwards. In spite of its repeal, no political disturbances were reported (Vizcaíno, 2010a).

3. Parties and Candidates

For forty years after the 1948 civil war, Costa Rican politics was dominated by the left-of-centre PLN and its opponents, a collection of more conservative anti-PLN parties which contested presidential elections together in a coalition before eventually becoming a single party, *Partido Unidad Social Cristiana* (United Social Christian Party, PUSC), in 1982. The supremacy of these parties came under challenge in the late 1990s and the weakening of their supremacy was confirmed in the 2002 elections. The 2006 and 2010 elections appear to have cemented the new multiparty character of Costa Rican politics. While the PLN remains strong, its policy positions have shifted to the right. Meanwhile, the PUSC collapsed in the 2006 election and was electorally dislodged by a new leftist party, *Partido Acción Ciudadana* (Civic Action Party, PAC) and an increasingly competitive libertarian party, *Movimiento Libertario* (Libertarian Movement, ML). A few other parties exist and can win some representation, but they tend to be small.

The complete ban on incumbents seeking reelection is an unusual feature of Costa Rican politics. It means that informal election campaigns tend to start immediately after the inauguration of the president, with rising party leaders trying to position themselves as their party's next presidential candidate. Although Laura Chinchilla, a former Vice President under outgoing President Oscar Arias, was the first woman to lead a major political party in Costa Rica and was standing to be its first female president, gender was not a major issue during the campaign. A much more central concern was the possibility of *continuismo*: that Chinchilla would provide a front behind which the outgoing president Arias could retain control. The PAC pushed this idea through TV advertisements depicting Chinchilla as a puppet controlled by actors portraying President Oscar Arias and his brother, Rodrigo (YouTube, 2010).

Chinchilla attempted to stay above this fray and to present herself as the logical choice, the only person qualified to be president, using the slogan "Laura: firme y honesta" (Laura: firm and honest). Her campaign was very cautious and largely error-free, and, according to Costa Rican political analysts, she was the clear winner in the TV debates, coming across as the most "presidential" candidate.

Ultimately, after a contentious primary between the party's founder, Ottón Solís, and his former vice presidential running mate, Epsy Campbell, the *Partido Acción Ciudadana* (Civic Action Party, PAC) did not pose a major challenge to the PLN slate. Towards the end of the campaign, the PAC formed an electoral pact with *Alianza Patriótica* candidate Rolando Araya Monge, a disaffected former PLN presidential hopeful. This helped to shore up support from the PAC's disaffected left-leaning sympathisers but, according to Jorge Vargas Cuellell, one of Costa Rica's leading political scientists, "in the final analysis, the move was largely ineffectual" (Vargas Cuellell, 2010).

Otto Guevara headed the *Movimiento Libertario* (Libertarian Movement, ML) ticket for the third successive presidential election. The party began as an ideological libertarian force but currently campaigns as a right-of-centre party with the slogans "*cambio ya*" (Change Now) and "*mano dura*" (Strong Hand). The first appeals to voters' disaffection with the old parties and with "politics as usual," while the second tapped into a growing–and well-founded–perception that crime and personal insecurity is becoming a major problem. National polls in the final months of the election campaign suggested that ML might succeed in its bid to force a second round of presidential voting but, as in the 2006 election, the polls fluctuated wildly and did not accurately foretell the final outcome.

Each of the three major parties (PLN, PAC, and ML) had clear objectives in the election. For the PLN, as the largest party, the goal was to win in the first round by clearing the 40% threshold; for the PAC and the ML, the goal was to take second place in the first round and then win the head-to-head contest with the PLN in a second round. Meanwhile, the formerly powerful PUSC effectively abandoned the presidential race when, in the months leading up to the election, its candidate, former president Rafael Ángel Calderón, received a five-year jail sentence for corruption. Calderón was replaced on the ticket by Luis Fishman, a divisive figure in the party.

4. Results

A growing concern over the last few general elections has been the decline in participation. Historically, turnout was relatively high, averaging over 80%, but from 1998 it began to slip and by 2006 had fallen to 65%. The increase to 69% in the 2010 election therefore provided some relief, but regional variation in abstention rates remains a concern. Turnout is generally lower in the less populated rural districts, falling to 60% in Puntarenas compared to 74% in the more populous district of Cartago (TSE, 2010a,b,c).

PLN candidate Laura Chinchilla won 47% of the presidential vote, which gave her an outright victory in the presidential election and eliminated the need for a second round. Her coattails, though, were not enough to give her party a majority share of the seats in the Legislative Assembly. The PLN's vote share in the Assembly election was ten points lower than Chinchilla's presidential showing, and that proved insufficient to win the 29 seats necessary to control a majority of the seats. Indeed, the PLN's 23 seats is two less than in the party had in the 2006 Assembly elections. The election has cemented the realignment of Costa Rica's party system with the PUSC, formerly one of the two dominant parties, reduced to the status of a minor player. The PUSC's vote share has collapsed over the last three elections: having won 39% of the vote in the Legislative Assembly elections of 2002, it

Table 1 Results of the Presidential and Legislative Assembly Elections in Costa Rica, 7 February 2010.

Political Party	Candidate	Presidential Votes %	Assembly Votes %	Assembly Seats (2006)
Liberación Nacional	Laura Chinchilla Miranda	46.9	37.3	23(25)
Acción Ciudadana	Ottón Solís Fallas	25.1	17.6	11(17)
Movimiento Libertario	Otto Guevara Guth	20.9	14.5	9(6)
Unidad Social Cristiana	Luis Fishman Zonzinski	3.9	8.2	6(5)
Accesibilidad Sin Exclusión	Óscar López Arias	1.9	9.0	4(1)
Restauración Nacional		–	1.6	1(1)
Frente Amplio	Eugenio Trejos Benavides	0.4	3.6	1(1)
Renovación Costarricense	Mayra González León	0.7	3.9	1(0)
Others[a]		0.2	4.3	1(1)
Total		100.0	100.0	57(57)

– Restauración Nacional did not contest the Presidential election.

Source: TSE, (2010b,c).

[a] *Alianza Patriótica* won an Assembly seat in 2010 and is included in 'Others.'

received just 8% in both the 2006 and 2010 elections. The party's 6 seats together with the PLN's 23 would create a majority voting bloc, but weak party discipline and policy differences between the parties would make it a very fragile working majority. For these reasons, Laura Chinchilla had to negotiate a major agreement with Otto Guevara of the Libertarian Party on the upcoming legislative agenda. And, immediately after the inauguration of the new Legislative Assembly in May 2010, the PLN began a dialogue with the PAC concerning the legislative agenda to try to cobble together working majorities for specific policies (Table 1).

Even if parties agree to work together in the Assembly, the notoriously low levels of party discipline in Costa Rica–especially as the internal party presidential candidate elections heat up–will inevitably make policymaking difficult. The fragmentation of the party system in the Legislative Assembly will further exacerbate the new President's problems in pushing her agenda through. A notable advance by a hitherto minor party was made by the *Partido Accesibilidad Sin Exclusión,* PASE (Party Accessibility without Exclusion), which increased its representation in the Assembly from one deputy after the 2006 elections to four deputies in 2010. The party, led by Óscar López, a visual impaired former deputy, does not really sit on the traditional left-right spectrum and is therefore likely to be a difficult party to deal with in the Assembly. Compounding the problems of governability are the legislature's rules which strengthen the role of the smaller parties in the congressional policymaking process. For example, any group of ten deputies can send a bill to the Constitutional Chamber of the Supreme Court for a review of its constitutionality. Thus, the smaller parties can (and frequently do) harness the assertive constitutional court to block, delay, or modify policy as it passes through the congress (Wilson, 2010).

References

Lehoucq and F., Rodríguez-Cordero, J.C., 2004 Modificando el mayoritarismo? Los orígenes del umbral electoral del 40 por ciento.

Revista Parlamentaria, 12 2 (2004), pp. 239–262.

TSE (Tribunal Supremo de Elecciones), 2010a. Plan general de elecciones, Available at www.tse.go.cr/pdf/varios/2010_plan_general.pdf.

TSE (Tribunal Supremo de Elecciones), 2010b. Declaratoria de elección de Diputados a la Asamblea Legislativa, No. 1820-E11-2010. Available at// www.tse.go.cr/pdf/declaratorias/2010/diputados2010.pdf.

TSE (Tribunal Supremo de Elecciones), 2010c. Declaratoria de elección de Presidente y Vicepresidentes de la República, No. 1310-E11-2010. Available at //www.tse.go.cr/pdf/declaratorias/2010/presidente2010.pdf.

Vargas Cuellell, J., 2010. Personal correspondence with the author, 7 June.

Vizcaíno, I.2010a. Costa Rica elige a su primera presidenta. La Nación, 8 February, Available at wvw.nacion.com/ln_ee/2010/febrero/08/pais2252302.html.

Vizcaíno, I.2010b. Vizcaíno, TSE condena a obispo por influir en voto de fieles. La Nación, 7 May, Available at //www.nacion.com/2010-05-07/ElPais/FotoVideoDestacado/ElPais2363229.aspx.

Wilson, B.M. 2003. The elections in Costa Rica, February and April 2002. Electoral Studies, 22 (3), pp. 509–516.

Wilson, B.M. 2010. Enforcing rights and Exercising an Accountability function: Costa Rica's constitutional court, G. Helmke, J. Ríos-Figueroa, Editors , Courts in Latin America, Cambridge University Press, Cambridge.

YouTube, 2010. Marionetas 1: La Conferencia de Laura Chinchilla, Available at www.youtube.com/watch?v=7l8x2f-T9oQ.

Critical Thinking

1. Describe the constraints on the executive in Costa Rica.

2. Are elections a good indicator of democracy? Why or why not?

3. Describe how term limits help and hurt democratic development.

The Legislative and Presidential Elections in Indonesia in 2009

ANDREAS UFEN

1. Background: Electoral Democracy with Cartel Parties

Indonesia is a politically stable electoral democracy with Freedom House scores at two for political rights and three for civil liberties (on a seven-point scale with one as the highest rating). According to these ratings, the country is the most democratic in Southeast Asia. The human rights situation has improved markedly since the downfall of President Suharto and the authoritarian New Order administration in 1998. Violent conflicts in Poso and the Moluccas have been settled, and the peace agreement with the guerrilla movement in Aceh has been successful as well. Civilian control over the military has been expanded. Elections to parliament, to the presidency, and since 2005 the so-called *pilkada* (direct elections for governors, district chiefs and mayors), have so far been conducted mostly successfully. In line with this, the latest legislative and presidential elections, on 9 April and 8 July 2009 respectively, were mostly peaceful and considered by observers to be "free and fair".

Parties and parliaments are now at the center of political power, thereby signifying one of the most profound changes in comparison with Suharto's New Order (1966–1998). Yet Indonesia's democracy remains elitist. Politicians in provincial and district parliaments are often unfamiliar with the concept of a legitimate and organized parliamentary opposition. Corruption, collusion and nepotism, all typical characteristics of the New Order, have been re-established in new forms. Voters' links to social milieus and political parties continue to weaken.

2. Political Parties

It is difficult to place Indonesian parties on a left-right spectrum. The most prominent cleavage in the Indonesian party system is that between secularist and Islamic/Islamist parties.[1] After the 1999 elections, three of the five largest parties were Islamic (PPP/Partai Persatuan Pembanguan, United Development Party; PAN/Partai Amanat Nasional, National Mandate Party; PKB/Partai Kebangkitan Bangsa, National Awakening Party) and two were predominantly secularist (PDI-P/Partai Demokrasi Indonesia—Perjuangan, Indonesian Democratic Party—Struggle; Golkar/Partai Golongan Karya, Party of Functional Groups). The traditionalist PKB and the modernist PAN are linked to the Muslim mass organizations Nahdatul Ulama and Muham-madiyah respectively. The PKB is particularly strong in rural regions, while PAN mostly represents the urban middle class. The PPP consists of traditionalist as well as modernist Muslims. The PDI-P has many non-Muslims and non-orthodox Muslims among its members and voters and is to a large extent defined by the legacy of the first nationalist and charismatic Indonesian president Sukarno. It styles itself a party for the "little people" and decidedly opposes the Islamization of politics. Golkar, once the ruling party in Indonesia, which is broadly secularist while retaining a strong orthodox Islamic wing, has redefined itself and at least partly distanced itself from the New Order.

In 2004, the PD (Partai Demokrat, Democratic Party) and the PKS (Partai Keadilan Sejahtera, Prosperous Justice Party) joined the ranks of the established parties. PD, founded in 2001 and preponderantly secular, is committed to serving the former general and current president Susilo Bambang Yudhoyono. PKS is an Islamist cadre party, supported by academics and students. It received 7.3% of the votes in the 2004 elections, mostly from young, devout Muslims searching a credible alternative to the other, allegedly corrupt parties.

In 2009, two other small personalist parties entered parliament. In 2006, Hanura (Partai Hati Nurani Rakyat, People's Conscience Party) was founded by retired generals led by Wiranto, formerly commander of the armed forces, minister of defence and coordinating minister for political and security affairs. Wiranto, who was indicted for crimes against humanity committed in East Timor in 1999, had won 22% of the votes in the first ballot of the presidential election in 2004. Hanura was highly visible during the 2009 campaign due to its extensive financial means and the prominence of its leader. This was also true of the nationalist Gerindra (Partai Gerakan Indonesia Raya, Greater Indonesian Movement Party), another new party under the direction of a retired general, in this case Prabowo Subianto. As Suharto's son-in-law, Prabowo had risen quickly through military ranks prior to 1998. He has never been convicted of alleged human rights violations in East Timor or during the last months of the New Order era. He is also chairman of the Indonesian Farmer's Association (HKTI), providing him with a large potential constituency of support.

3. Institutional Context[2]

Indonesia has a presidential system with a bicameral parliament. The First Chamber, the House of Representatives (DPR, Dewan

Perwakilan Rakyat), currently consists of 560 members elected via a multi-member plurality system in 77 multi-member constituencies (ranging in size from three to ten seats). The less important Second Chamber, the People's Congress (MPR, Majelis Permusyawaratan Rakyat), consists of the DPR members and an additional 132 parliamentarians. The latter are elected through plurality votes in multi-member constituencies at the provincial level and must not belong to a party. These 132 delegates simultaneously form the Regional Chamber (DPD, Dewan Perwakilan Daerah), which only has consultative powers. Since 2004, the president and vice president have been elected directly, and as of 2005 direct elections have also included mayors, district chiefs and governors.[3]

Based on a December 2008 decision by the constitutional court, only candidates winning a plurality of votes in their constituency will become members of parliament. Thus, the law on parliamentary elections has been significantly changed since 1999. Previously, a small circle of party leaders in Jakarta was able to select candidates for closed lists. In 2004, the system changed to one in which voters could choose either a party or a candidate. However, that candidate was required to win by large margins and only two candidates were allocated a seat on this basis. This meant that, de facto, the closed list system was still in place. The constitutional court decision signified the transition to open lists, although voters retain their right to vote for parties rather than single candidates.

Changing the law has weakened the power of the central party leaderships in Jakarta and given locally-rooted party elites a better chance of success. This strengthening of local elites bears considerable risks. In multi-member constituencies candidates from the same party compete with each other, thus potentially increasing factionalism at the local level. More broadly, this kind of decentralization may result in deinstitutionalization. Yet such pessimistic prognoses are contradicted by Indonesia's experience so far with direct local elections: most elected candidates have proved to be competent and have not been involved in corruption scandals. Parliamentarians are now encouraged to represent voters' interests more effectively.

Because parties or party coalitions can only nominate presidential candidates if they receive 25% of the votes or 20% of seats in the preceding polls, the new rules allow a maximum of three or four pairs of candidates to take part in elections.[4] The financing of election campaigns has also been reformed. Sponsors must be identified by name in the event that the donation exceeds 1 billion rupiah (approx. US$100,000) for individuals or 5 billion rupiah for organizations.

4. Legislative Elections

On 9 April Indonesians had the opportunity to cast no fewer than four votes: for the 560 seats in the DPR, for the members of the Regional Chamber (DPD), for the 33 provincial parliaments, and for about 500 district and municipal parliaments. The first of these, the most important, was contested by 38 parties (up from 24 in the 2004 elections). In order to participate, parties were required to have a certain number of branches in Indonesia's sub-districts, districts, cities, and provinces.[5] This regulation prevents parties that represent merely the interests of a single region or ethnic group from gaining power. A new threshold stipulated that only parties with at least 2.5% of the vote could gain parliamentary representation.

Given the vast size of Indonesia, voter registration and the distribution of more than 700 million ballot papers to 528,000 polling stations presented an enormous logistical challenge. There were more than 11,000 candidates for the 560 seats in the DPR. More than 340,000 candidates ran for the Regional Chamber as well as for the provincial, district and municipal parliaments. The drafting of complete and accurate voter registers was particularly difficult. Millions of voters did not receive ballots, and some areas had to rerun their elections. The national human rights organization Komnas HAM even estimated that between 25% and 40% of the voters were unable to exercise their electoral rights due to the irregularities. Official statistics recorded more than 171 million eligible voters. The election commission, KPU (Komisi Pemilihan Umum), came under heavy criticism (Sukma, 2009),[6] and PDI-P, Gerindra and Hanura were among the parties that disputed the election results.

The election campaign began officially on 12 July 2008 and ran until 5 April 2009, but party candidates were allowed to hold public talks no sooner than 16 March 2009. By and large, campaigning was characterized by a lack of policy substance and a focus instead on personalities. For the most part, the campaign was at least conducted peacefully; only in provinces with special autonomy status, such as Aceh and Papua, did violence occur. In the former, three politicians from the Partai Aceh were murdered, and there were also kidnappings, shootings and bomb attacks. In Papua, two nights before polling day, three motorcycle-taxi drivers were stabbed and a girl killed in an explosion at a fuel depot. The following day, on the eve of polling, a police station in Jayapura was attacked by a hundred people armed with bows and arrows. One person was killed by the police.

Turnout on election day was 71%, with 121.6 m voters casting a ballot (although 14% of votes cast were invalid). The official election results confirmed the predictions of various polls. With 20.8% of the votes, well up on its 2004 performance and more than six percentage points clear of its nearest rival, the PD emerged as the definite winner (Table 1). Golkar and PDI-P lost a lot of ground compared with 2004, as did the PPP, the PKB and the smaller Islamic parties. In 2004 Golkar had still been the strongest faction in the DPR with 21.6% of the votes and 128 mandates, but its vote share fell by more than seven percentage points. The PDI-P took only 14%, down four points from 2004 and miles adrift of its 1999 showing when it was the strongest party with almost 34%. Both PDI-P and Golkar look to have lost votes to Gerindra and Hanura. Meanwhile, the halving of PKB's vote share may have been caused by internal party conflict between the group around Chairman Muhaimin Iskandar and the wing that instead supports his uncle Abdurrahman Wahid (Indonesian president from 1999 to 2001). Finally, the PKS gained some votes, but far fewer than it expected.

Generally, the party system has been dominated by secular parties, and this remained the case after the 2009 elections, with secular parties taking up 392 seats in the DPR compared to 168 seats for Islamic and Islamist parties. Indonesia's political parties have distinct geographical strongholds. The PDI-P's support is based in Bangka Beli-tung, Central Java, West Kalimantan, Central Kalimantan and North Sulawesi, where it received between 20% and 25% of votes in this year's election, and, especially, in Bali, where it received about 40%. Golkar performed best in Riau, South Sumatra, South Sulawesi, and North Sulawesi (between 20% and 25%), in Gorontalo (30%) and in West Papua (32%). The PD was exceptionally strong in Aceh (41%) and the capital Jakarta (35%). However, the regional distribution of votes is today more balanced than in 1999, when, for example, the PDI-P received nearly 80% in Bali and Golkar polled between 50% and 67% in the (then) four provinces of Sulawesi.

5. Presidential Election

The PD victory further strengthened the position of the incumbent president, Susilo, whose popularity ratings had already been

Table 1 Results of Elections to the Indonesian House of Representatives (DPR), 1999–2009.

Party[a]	1999		2004		2009	
	Votes (%)	Seats	Votes(%)	Seats	Votes(%)	Seats
PD	–	–	7.5	57	20.8	148
	22.5	120	21.6	128	14.4	106
PDI-P	33.8	153	18.5	109	14.0	94
PKS[b]	1.4	7	7.3	45	7.9	57
PAN	7.1	34	6.4	52	6.0	45
PPP	10.7	58	8.2	58	5.3	38
PKB	12.6	51	10.6	52	4.9	28
Gerindra	–	–	–	–	4.5	26
Hanura	–	–	–	–	3.8	18
Others	11.9	77[c]	19.9	49	18.4	0
Total	100	500	100	550	100	560

[a] Party names are set out in full in the text of the note.

[b] Known as the PK in 1999.

[c] The military were automatically awarded 38 seats in 1999. Source: Sukma (2009, 319).

boosted by positive economic trends. The opinion research institute Lembaga Survei Indonesia conducted a survey which found that satisfaction with Susilo was strongly correlated with the perceived success of his economic policies and the popularity of the PD (Mujani and Liddle, 2009). According to this survey, the PD would have won 16% of the votes in an election at the end of 2006. This number fell to 9% in mid-2008 but then increased sharply to 24% in February 2009. Susilo's popularity rating also fluctuated considerably: it fell from 67% to 45% and rose again to 70% over the same period. The decline in popularity was a consequence of a cut to fuel and kerosene subsidies. Yet economic conditions improved during the second half of 2008, and various policy measures also won widespread approval, such as compensation payments for the poor hit by the 29% increase in oil prices in May 2008. Furthermore, 80% of the people surveyed evaluated Susilo's fight against corruption, pledged on first assuming office, either "positively" or "very positively".

During the weeks following the legislative elections, parties discussed potential coalitions and candidate pairs for the presidential election on July 8. One day after the parliamentary election the PDI-P announced plans to form a coalition with Gerindra and Hanura, much to the disappointment of pro-democratic activists within the party. PD and Golkar debated a renewed coalition for a while, yet the latter ultimately decided to terminate the partnership. Golkar's decision not to run Jusuf Kalla again as vice-presidential candidate next to Susilo, but instead have him run for the presidential office itself, caused some controversy within the party. The faction surrounding former party chairman Akbar Tanjung argued that Kalla had no realistic chance of winning the presidency.

Three pairs were finally decided on. Susilo ran with Boe-diono, governor of the central bank and a surprising choice for most people since he is not a member of a party and was considered to be an economic expert without entrepreneurial interests. They were supported by PD, PKS, PAN, PPP, PKB and 18 parties without seats, although the four Islamic parties were dismayed with the selection of Boediono. Megawati Sukarnoputri, daughter of Indonesia's first president Sukarno, chairwoman of the PDI-P and Susilo's

predecessor, paired up with Gerindra's Prabowo. They were supported by PDI-P, Gerindra, and seven parties without seats. Finally, Jusuf Kalla, nominated by Golkar and Hanura, ran for office with Wiranto as his choice for vice president.

The presidential election campaign began on 2 June and ran until 4 July. Again, few substantial policy differences came to the fore. The televised debates between 18 June and 2 July were lacklustre and tedious. From the start, Megawati—whose performance as president between 2001 and 2004 was not generally highly rated—and Jusuf Kalla were perceived as weak figures, whereas Susilo, with the advantage of incumbency, could thrive on his performance as president. It came as no surprise, then, when election day saw Susilo and Boediono achieve a comfortable majority with 73.9 m votes (61%), followed by Megawati and Prabowo (32.5 m votes, 27%) and Jusuf Kalla and Wiranto (15.1 m votes, 12%).

In the following weeks, elites across parties made considerable efforts at reconciliation. In early October, Taufik Kiemas, Megawati's husband, was elected speaker of the Second Chamber, and the PDI-P signalled its intention not to act as permanent opposition to the government. When Aburizal Bakrie won the Golkar chairmanship around the same time, it became apparent that the party would support the new president.[7] Finally, the United Indonesia Cabinet II, announced on 21 October, was made up of six parties, and the tradition of "rainbow coalitions" with no real opposition was prolonged.

6. Impact on Party Politics

The introduction of direct presidential elections has led to the presidentialization of parties, which now often serve as mere vehicles for presidential candidates. A case in point is Susilo Bambang Yudhoyono's PD. The presidentialization and personalization of politics is the result of institutional changes (the introduction of presidentialism, the *pilkada,* and the open list) as well as the increased commercialization of party politics (Mietzner, 2008) and the growing impact of the mass media. The latter is reflected in the large sums that parties now spend on television spots. Most parties rely on spin doctors and pollsters to manage public relations and to organize election campaigns. With extensive financial support, it is today possible in Indonesia to establish a party apparatus within a short period of time and to set up a successful professional campaign, especially if it is geared towards a single candidate. This certainly applies to the PD, which took a surprising 7.5% of the votes in its first election in 2004 and has now become the largest party, less than a decade after its founding. And two still newer parties, Gerindra and Hanura, both obtained almost as many votes as the Islamic parties by means of enormous funds and despite lacking a clear policy profile.

The meteoric rise of these new parties is also a consequence of generally weakening loyalties towards parties. With party choice is much less securely anchored in voters' social backgrounds (Ufen, 2008), electoral volatility remains relatively high (Lembaga Survei Indonesia, 2008). The *pilkada* and the open list system (and, albeit to a lesser extent, the establishment of the Regional Chamber), as well as the administrative decentralization that began in 2001, have all contributed to the localization of politics over the past few years. Until the 2009 elections, central party leaderships in Jakarta were able to maintain a sense of party discipline due to the lack of intra-party democracy, the centralization of party finances, and the so-called recall mechanism in the DPR (which allows a party's leadership to expel insubordinate parliamentarians). Although internal party conflicts had always generated splinter parties and thus fragmented the party system, Indonesia's parties were not like the kind of loosely organized patronage apparatuses—with politicians frequently shifting between them—seen in nearby states such as the Philippines. The introduction of open lists has already made local identities more prominent, as was evident during the 2009 electoral campaign. Candidates from the same party now compete against each other and are more independent of their party's headquarters in Jakarta. The national parliament now includes delegates who are firmly based in their constituency. The long-term effects of this are unclear: on the one hand, open lists could lead to the factionalization of parties; on the other, it could increase the pressure on national party elites to democratize their decision processes.

Notes

1. A party is defined here as Islamist if it supports more or less openly the far-reaching implementation of *shari'a* (including the penal code) and the establishment of an Islamic state. On this reading, the PPP and the PKS (q.v.) are Islamist parties. On the parties and party system, see Sherlock (2009) and Johnson Tan (2009).

2. For a more detailed description, see Sherlock (2009) and Mietzner (2009).

3. In Indonesia, candidates always campaign in pairs for a particular office—whether president, governor, district chief or mayor—and its deputy. In many cases, candidates that have paired up come from different religious milieus and regions.

4. Indonesia's Constitutional Court ruled that independent candidates would not be allowed to run.

5. An additional six parties were allowed to compete in Aceh province due to special autonomy rights.

6. One focus of this criticism was the KPU's failure to provide timely and clear rules on campaign finance: "There was effectively no real transparency and accountability regarding campaign funds in this year's legislative elections," (Indonesia Corruption Watch, 2009).

7. "Kalla Minta Golkar Tetap Kontrol Pemerintah", *Kompas* 8 October 2009.

References

Indonesia Corruption Watch, 2009. Purchasing Power. In: Inside Indonesia. http://insideindonesia.org/content/view/1222/47/ (accessed 05.09.09).

Johnson Tan, P., 2009. Reining in the reign of the parties: party and party system institutionalization in Indonesia. www.mcgill.ca/files/cdas/Tan.Indonesia.pdf (accessed 05.09.09).

Lembaga Survei Indonesia, 2008. Kecenderungan Swing Voter Menjelang Pemilu Legislatif 2009. In: Trend Opini Publik November. www.lsi.or.id (accessed 05.04.09).

Mietzner, M., 2008. Soldiers, parties and bureaucrats: illicit fundraising in contemporary Indonesia. South East Asia Research 16 (2), 225–254.

Mietzner, M., 2009. Indonesia's 2009 Elections: Populism, Dynasties and the Consolidation of the Party System. Lowy Institute for International Policy, Sydney.

Mujani, S., Liddle, R.W., 2009. Parties and Candidates in the Run-up to the 2009 Indonesian National Elections. Lembaga Survei Indonesia, Jakarta.

Sherlock, S., 2009. Indonesia's 2009 elections: the new electoral system and the competing parties, CDI policy papers on political governance, 2009/01. www.cdi.anu.edu.au/_research/2008-09/D_P/2009_03_RES_PPS6_INDON_Sherlock/2009_04_PPS6_INDON_Sherlock.pdf (accessed 05.04.09).

Sukma, R., 2009. Indonesian politics in 2009: defective elections, resilient democracy. Bulletin of Indonesian Economic Studies 45 (3), 317–336.

Ufen, A., 2008. From aliran to dealignment: political parties in post-Suharto Indonesia. South East Asia Research 16 (1), 5–41.

Critical Thinking

1. What indicators show that Indonesia is succeeding as a democracy?

2. How does decentralization of political parties occur?

3. Describe the constraints on the executive in Indonesia.

The Resilient Authoritarians

"China and Russia, along with a number of other countries, demonstrate that capitalism can exist without Western-style democracy, at least for a period of time."

MARTIN DIMITROV

When the Berlin Wall fell, political scientists were wildly optimistic about the global spread of democracy. In the 1990s a number of authoritarian regimes did democratize. But others, such as China and Cuba, have proved remarkably resilient, and Russia has backtracked significantly on democracy. Of these countries, China is the most important. Weathering countless predictions of its imminent collapse, the regime in Beijing has thus far defied assumptions about the global triumph of democracy. How can we explain this resilience? As a model for development, does China's progress toward free market capitalism in the absence of democracy present a viable alternative to Western liberalism?

The received wisdom on China is that the regime has preserved popular support by promoting capitalism to deliver rapid economic growth. Yet, while it is true that growth matters, it is only part of the story. In addition to economic growth, the Chinese Communist Party has relied on two other pillars to maintain popular acceptance of one-party rule. One is nationalism: China is a great power and has recently started to act like one, cultivating friends abroad and standing up to Japan and the United States. The other pillar is an expansion of civil and political rights. Chinese citizens today have rights they have never enjoyed in the past, and when these rights are violated, the citizenry can make use of various options for defending them. In short, the recipe for the stamina of the Chinese regime contains three ingredients: capitalism, nationalism, and legal rights.

Notably absent from this list are the institutions typically associated with democracy—strong civil society, competitive elections, and the separation of powers. Nevertheless, opinion polls conducted by Westerners and Chinese alike indicate that the regime enjoys widespread popular support. This raises the possibility that we are witnessing the emergence of an alternative model to that of Western-style democracy, not an example of insufficient or delayed political development.

Indeed, a number of countries appear to be mirroring China's experience. Consider Vladimir Putin's Russia. Thanks to high oil and gas prices, the Russian economy is booming. Like China, Russia has invested in promoting nationalism and in acting more assertively in international affairs. President Putin, moreover, has stressed the primacy of law and has attempted to strengthen the court system, particularly the commercial (arbitrazh) courts. Yet Russia is not a democracy. Its elections are "managed," its media are not free, and its civil society groups face restrictions on their activities. Putin's popularity is sky high nevertheless. Russians seem to like what they are getting from their government, even if it falls short of Western democracy.

Meanwhile, countries as different as Vietnam and Venezuela can also be loosely classified in the same group as China and Russia. While it is impossible to know how much longer the regimes in Beijing and these other countries will endure, their experience, at least so far, seems to challenge the widely held assumption that capitalism, the rule of law, and democracy always go hand in hand.

China's Market Reforms

Had it not initiated economic reforms, China would probably have followed the fate of the Eastern European communist regimes that collapsed at the end of the 1980s. Instead, Deng Xiaoping, the architect of the Chinese economic miracle, 30 years ago launched the policy of "reform and openness," which eventually catapulted the People's Republic to its current status as an economic powerhouse. Three decades ago China was poor; 82 percent of its population lived in the countryside, and the average per capita income was about $165 (measured in 2000 US dollars). Today 43 percent of Chinese live in cities, and average incomes have increased eleven-fold. To put it simply, everybody—rich and poor alike—has benefited from China's growth. No other country in the world has been able to pull off such a feat in so short a time.

How has China been able to achieve its spectacular growth? Deng favored gradual reform, focusing first on agricultural de-collectivization, the reinvigoration of markets, and the legalization of private entrepreneurial activity. It was much later that the regime turned to more sensitive tasks, such as the privatization of inefficient state-owned enterprises, the clearing of staggering loads of bad loans plaguing Chinese banks, and the introduction of some competition in government monopoly sectors, such as telecommunications and insurance services. Meanwhile, foreign direct investment and foreign trade have been instrumental in ensuring China's continuous growth during the reform period. Cumulatively, the country has absorbed over $700 billion in foreign investment over the past 30 years. This has fueled China's export-oriented services, which in turn have allowed the nation to amass the largest foreign currency reserves in the world, currently valued at $1.4 trillion.

The process begun in 1978—aiming to create a capitalist free market economy in a country run by a communist party—has been uneven, but it is now complete. Private property is protected to a significant extent, both by the Chinese constitution and by a series of laws governing property and contracts. The stock exchanges in Shanghai and Shenzhen are booming. Commercial disputes are resolved not by dispatching thugs, but by appealing to highly trained judges. Each year, China's courts handle over a million commercial cases. This is a marked departure from the 1980s, when property rights were far less secure and private entrepreneurs had limited legal recourse to make sure contracts were enforced. Capitalists, once branded "counterrevolutionaries" and "poisonous weeds," are now celebrated in the press, and private entrepreneurs are encouraged to join the Chinese Communist Party—underscoring how definitive the break with the planned economy has been.

China's growth, averaging about 10 percent a year over the past three decades, has lifted hundreds of millions of Chinese out of poverty. Yet, while both peasants and urbanites have seen absolute improvements in their incomes, some have benefited much more than others. China entered its reform period as a highly equal society. Thirty years later, it has reached levels of income inequality that place it on a par with the United States, the most unequal advanced industrial society in the world. This is a direct result of China's reform strategy, which privileged the development of coastal provinces and scrapped generous social service provisions for urban workers, such as subsidized housing and free health care.

Inequality breeds discontent, and significant levels of discontent can lead to regime instability. Justly concerned, President Hu Jintao has advanced the concept of "scientific development," which aims to diffuse social discontent by targeting funds for the unemployed, migrants, and residents of China's poor hinterland provinces. The task of achieving balanced development while maintaining high levels of growth is gargantuan, but the current leaders appear to understand that the stability of their regime will depend on how well they handle this challenge.

Rights and Accountability

During the Mao years, the Chinese regime ruled through coercion. During the reform period, the Communist Party has been mindful of the need to extend certain rights and liberties to the people. After all, this makes it easier to rule, because individuals are more likely to comply with government policies if they feel they have a say.

Thus, the reform period has witnessed a remarkable emergence of civil and political rights. Chinese citizens can elect local officials at the village level and in some urban neighborhoods. They can also create nongovernmental organizations (NGOs) and other social groups that can have an impact on policy making. For example, green NGOs such as Friends of Nature and Global Village have undertaken important campaigns to educate both the public and government officials about the need to protect the environment. The Chinese today are freer to follow their religious beliefs, even though some important restrictions remain. They have access to a press that is relatively free to report on topics that were taboo in the past, such as official corruption and malfeasance. Finally, while the internet is controlled and certain websites are often blocked, many Chinese use proxy servers and other methods to circumvent official firewalls and obtain the information they want.

Not only do individuals in Chinese society have rights, they also have means at their disposal through which they can defend these rights. Since the late 1980s citizens have been permitted to sue government officials for abuse of discretion, and they win such suits more and more often. Other available avenues for defending rights include complaints to upper-level leaders, mobilization of the press, and petitions. While problems in exercising these options persist, the Chinese today have more meaningful rights than they have ever had in the past.

In Western democracies, the typical method for establishing political accountability is elections. As mentioned, competitive elections do exist in China, but only at the lowest levels of the political system. However, another mechanism is available for establishing a certain degree of accountability: mass protests. In 2005, for instance, 87,000 mass protests occurred in China, representing a tenfold increase over the number of protests 10 years earlier. While some interpret these protests as an indicator of regime weakness, in fact the central government tolerates them because they increase its legitimacy. The protests typically are directed against abuses of power committed by local government officials. The central government is seen as an ally of the protesters—as long as it punishes corrupt lower-level officials. From time to time, the central government even punishes top leaders who are involved in corruption scandals. When ordinary citizens suffer because of bureaucratic malfeasance, the central government will make a show of stepping in and taking action.

The Power of Nationalism

Another way the Chinese government is responsive to public needs is by tolerating the expression of nationalist sentiment among the people. Modern-day Chinese nationalism is not a reaction to the possibility of external attack. It is driven rather by a victimization narrative ("China's century of national humiliation" from the mid-1800s to 1949) and a desire to restore China to its former glory. In the early 1990s, regime-sponsored think tanks stoked nationalist passions by writing about the Japanese atrocities committed in China in the 1930s and 1940s, about Taiwanese moves toward independence, and about American hegemony. Blockbuster publications such as *China Can Say No* appeared with government encouragement, strongly criticizing America and Japan. And individuals were allowed to engage in organized anti-Japanese or anti-American protests. From the government's perspective, this was a win-win strategy: The people had an oudet for venting frustration, yet they were not protesting against the regime.

In the current decade there has been some contention among China specialists about the regime's ability to control mass nationalism. Some argue that the government is fostering and manipulating nationalist sentiment. Others contend that, from the mid-1990s onward, the regime has been reacting to mass nationalism rather than proactively encouraging it. There is evidence that the government initiated and steered the rise of anti-Japanese rhetoric by sponsoring research on the Nanjing massacre, creating the Beijing War of Resistance Museum, and sensitizing the Chinese public to the publication of nationalistic Japanese textbooks. Even so, China-based scholars seem to agree that the most recent round of extensive anti-Japanese protests in 2005 was not organized by the regime, and that the government saw it more as a nuisance than as something that was desirable. The palpable potential that anti-Japanese agitation might turn into anti-government protests led the regime to move quickly to check the demonstrations.

The Chinese experience invites mention of two potential pitfalls with the instrumental use of nationalism. First, nationalist activity not controlled by the regime can backfire and turn into anti-regime protests and thus undermine government legitimacy rather than bolster it. Second, while externally oriented nationalism can be the glue that keeps people together and ensures greater regime support, it can easily degenerate into anti-minority nationalism. In China, most people are Han Chinese, but about 100 million are representatives of non-Han minorities such as Uighurs and Tibetans. The government has made efforts to avoid the anti-minority nationalism that proved so destructive in Yugoslavia in the 1990s. So far, China seems to have been successful at integrating minorities and incorporating all ethnic groups into the notion of a great nation potentially threatened by two external powers: Japan and the United States.

Undemocratic but Responsive

What is distinctive about the Chinese experience over the past three decades? Primarily, it is China's successful transformation from a poor developing country into a country with middle levels of wealth—a transformation made possible by the aggressive pursuit of free market capitalism (though the United States has yet to formally recognize China as a market economy). The unusual thing about this development trajectory is that a communist party was responsible for initiating and steering forward these pro-market reforms. It is also unusual that the reforms show no signs of ushering in Western-style liberal democracy.

What China has instead of liberal democracy, at least for the time being, is a leadership that is responsive to the public. This responsiveness is manifested in the accommodation of limited civil and political rights and the encouragement or toleration of nationalist sentiment. The leadership has also become more accountable to the public. In China, protests, corruption probes, and village elections provide a certain degree of accountability without democracy.

China's experience shows that capitalism, the rule of law, and democracy do not always coexist. While democracy has undeniable advantages for promoting accountability, non-democratic regimes can also establish some limited accountability to the public and can respond to the needs of the people. Traditionally, it has been assumed that all nondemocratic regimes rule through coercion, rather than by relying on quasi-voluntary compliance. This is not the case in China.

A growing body of evidence emerging from both Western and Chinese scholarship suggests that the Chinese regime is legitimate in the eyes of the public. Scholars distinguish between specific and diffuse regime support. Specific support has to do with how happy individuals are with concrete government policies, such as taxation. Diffuse support has to do with citizens' overall satisfaction with their existing system of governance. Current research indicates that, while the Chinese are dissatisfied with specific actions of government officials, there is widespread diffuse support for the regime. In other words, the Chinese leadership enjoys significant levels of legitimacy despite the absence of democracy.

Does this suggest the emergence of a Chinese development model that others might decide to emulate? Perhaps so. China's experience is attractive to two groups of countries whose ruling elites do not wish to establish Western-style liberal democracies. The first group consists of countries whose rapid economic growth rates are based on natural resource extraction, such as Russia, the Central Asian states, and Venezuela. The second group is made up of non-democracies that are resource-poor, such as Vietnam and Cuba. States belonging to both of these groups are united by their commitment to maintaining growth and establishing some institutions for popular voice and official accountability stopping short, however, of democracy.

The Case of Russia

Russia in the 1990s was a democracy, albeit a flawed one. It had elections, which international observers at the time certified as free and fair. With the benefit of hindsight, we now know these observers were often looking the other way. In the 1996 presidential race in particular, election observers tolerated fraud that allowed the reelection of Boris Yeltsin. The international community was committed to preventing Gennady Zyuganov (a reformed communist) from capturing the presidency of what had been the world's second most powerful country, even if that meant pouring significant resources into the reelection of the deeply unpopular (yet anticommunist) Yeltsin. Electoral manipulations aside, Yeltsin's Russia had the other trappings of Western-style democracy—a functioning parliament, a multi-party system, a free press, and a large civil society.

Although it was democratic, Yeltsin's Russia had neither a free market economy nor the rule of law. Yeltsin did unleash a massive privatization program, but it was very poorly implemented. Corrupt privatization schemes helped enrich a small group of individuals, collectively known as the "oligarchs," who were able to grab the most appetizing morsels of Russia's vastly profitable extractive industries. By the end of the 1990s, ordinary Russians found themselves poorer and less happy than they had been under communism. Private property existed, but the state was too weak to protect it. Criminal gangs and mafia groups provided "security services," but citizens could not feel secure about their property in Yeltsin's Russia. The feeble central government was unable to collect taxes in the provinces and could not ensure that its laws were enforced across Russia's vast territorial expanse. Lawlessness and despair reigned across the country.

When Putin was appointed prime minister in March 1999, he found a state in shambles. Russia was weak both domestically and internationally. The Yeltsin years had been marked by persistent budget deficits and an erosion of the standard of living. A few robber barons had become wealthy, but Russia had no rule of law. Internationally, Russia had been reduced to a second-rate player, an "Upper Volta with nuclear weapons," to quote Margaret Thatcher.

Putin set out to transform Russia into a modern capitalist economy with the rule of law. He strengthened tax collection, clarified inconsistencies between federal and regional laws, and simplified procedures for doing business. He asserted Moscow's influence vis-à-vis the regions and ensured that the state operated more effectively than under his predecessor. Even before the sharp increase in global oil prices in 2002, Putin's measures were having an impact and the Russian economy had started to grow rapidly. Foreign investors gained confidence and, on a per capita basis, foreign investment pouring into Russia surpassed that going into China.

Unfortunately, while Putin promoted capitalism and the rule of law, he limited democracy. Electoral manipulation increased by comparison with the Yeltsin era, independent media outlets began to disappear, opposition parties were emasculated, restrictions were imposed on civil society groups, and journalists were intimidated and sometimes killed. Today, Russia's democratic institutions are largely gone. And yet, Putin's approval rating is very high: For much of his presidency, it has hovered between 70 percent and 80 percent. Russians are enjoying increased standards of living thanks to the oil bonanza and greater predictability in everyday life as a result of the strengthening of courts and other law enforcement institutions. Putin's tough handling of the oligarchs, most of whom now live in exile, won broad approval as well.

Also bolstering Putin's popularity is his promotion of the "Russian idea," which is about reviving traditional Russian values and restoring the country to its former status as a great power. Like China, Putin's Russia is nationalistic and antiWestern. Also like China, Russia has assumed a more assertive position in international affairs. Russia wants to be seen as a world power, even if that can be accomplished only by defying the United States. Russians who feel nostalgic for the Soviet era are enamored with Putin's idea of resurrecting the former greatness of the Russian nation.

How much longer is Russia likely to endure as a non-democratic state? This is anybody's guess, though the initial forecasts for this spring's presidential elections are far from optimistic. It is important to emphasize that, unlike in China, economic growth in Russia is linked to the high prices of natural resources.

Mirroring the Model

Several resource-rich former Soviet republics fit in the same category of resilient authoritarian states: Azerbaijan, Kazakhstan, Turkmenistan, and, to a certain extent, Uzbekistan. In Latin America, Venezuela also seems to be following a trajectory similar to that of Russia. Natural resource wealth has been used to keep the people happy and has allowed the president, Hugo Chavez, to gradually scale back democratic institutions. It is now well known, however, that countries with an abundance of natural resources often experience the so-called resource curse, essentially delaying the diversification of their economies while encouraging corruption and in the long run slowing down economic growth. Ultimately, this can have disastrous consequences for political stability. Indeed, countries rich in natural resources may turn out to be far less stable than resource-poor countries in which high growth is based on productive activity.

Vietnam, a resource-poor country, mirrors most closely China's reform experience. Like China, it is ruled by a communist party, yet it has a market economy and steadily expanding rights and liberties. Vietnam's economic reforms started about a decade later than China's, and have been more fitful. Nevertheless, Vietnam has enjoyed an average growth rate of about 7 percent since the initiation of dot moi (renovation) two decades ago. Surprisingly, political reform in Vietnam has progressed further than in China. Vietnam's National Assembly is directly elected (and in a somewhat competitive fashion), and it has the power to subject the government to no-confidence votes. Like China, Vietnam has emphasized legal reform and anti-corruption efforts. Also as in China, the Vietnamese regime gains some legitimacy by catering to nationalist sentiment among the citizenry. In the case of Vietnam, the targets of these sentiments are the United States and China.

Another country that seems to be drawing lessons from China is Cuba. Since 2006, when the ailing Fidel Castro handed over power to his brother Raul, the Cuban Communist Party has taken resolute steps toward economic reform. The government has encouraged both private entrepreneurial activity and foreign investment. Some of the most important investment projects on the island have been spearheaded by the European Union, China, and Venezuela. The initial results are impressive: In 2006, Cuba's GDP grew by 11 percent; the forecast for 2007 was 7 percent.

Cuba has combined economic growth with a limited political opening. The number of political prisoners has declined, for instance, and there seems to be more tolerance of dissidents. In addition to improvements in civil and political rights, the legitimacy of the Cuban regime is based on potent anti-American nationalism. While in China, Russia, and Vietnam the external threat is largely manufactured, in the case of Cuba the US trade embargo strongly reinforces the credibility of the American threat. Cuba demonstrates that nationalism can be a powerful glue for holding a country together even under unfavorable economic conditions, such as those prevalent during Cuba's periodo especial in the 1990s, when the economy was in shambles following the collapse of the Soviet Union.

Will these regimes prove resilient for much longer? This, too, is currently unclear. What is evident is that democracy and capitalism need not coexist. Non-democratic societies can develop political accountability and respond to popular needs, even if their institutions are less effective than those provided by liberal democracies.

The End of History?

There have been two historical models of democratization. In one of them, countries have had to pursue democracy, capitalism, and the rule of law simultaneously. This was the model followed by Russia in the 1990s. As we know, Yeltsin did usher in a certain degree of democracy, but capitalism and the rule of law were not established while he was in office. Simultaneous transitions to democracy and capitalism present significant difficulties for most regimes and are therefore hard to complete successfully. The other model is exemplified by the historical evolution of England, where the rise of capitalism and the rule of law preceded the establishment of democracy.

The question is whether the experience of China represents a different model altogether—a kind of resilient authoritarianism— or whether it is best understood as a country in which democratization is delayed until capitalism and the rule of law have been firmly established. In other words, is the Chinese model a passing phase within Western-style democratic development or a stable alternative to it?

It is too early to tell. Nearly two decades ago, Francis Fukuyama proclaimed the end of history, by which he meant that capitalism and democracy would triumph around the globe. Yet China and Russia, along with a number of other countries, demonstrate that capitalism can exist without Western-style democracy, at least for a period of time. Citizens may be content with a government that is able to foster economic growth, secure property rights, and demonstrate some accountability to the public absent liberal Western institutions.

It is possible that China and the other resilient authoritarian regimes will liberalize politically. Should this occur, these countries may arrive at consolidated democracy relatively quickly, because they already have capitalism and some semblance of the rule of law in place. But a second possibility is the further development of the current system without the emergence of liberal democracy. To be sure, there are pitfalls along the way—economic downturns, unequal development, rampant nationalism. All of these can lead to regime instability. However, if the governments handle these challenges effectively, and if the current institutions of accountability persist and are developed further, then China and other countries that follow a similar trajectory could become established as a new developmental category in opposition to the standard model which assumes that democracy, capitalism, and the rule of law have to be intertwined.

Critical Thinking

1. What is meant by the Chinese and Russian governments' "resilence"?
2. What are the explanations for the Chinese government's resilience?
3. What are the explanations for Putin's resilience?
4. Explain how the governments in Russia and China are "accountable" and "responsive."

MARTIN DIMITROV is an assistant professor at Dartmouth College. He is author of *Piracy and the State: The Politics of Intellectual Property in China* (Cambridge University Press, 2008).

From *Current History*, January 2008, pp. 24–30. Copyright © 2008 by Current History, Inc. Reprinted by permission.

UNIT 5

The Legislature: Representation and the Effects of Electoral Systems

Unit Selections

Learning Outcomes

After reading this Unit, you will be able to:

- Distinguish between proportional and majoritarian legislatures.

- Explain: What are important tasks of the legislature?

- Identify and describe different electoral systems.

- Describe how political participation may be increased.

- Explain why divided government poses a problem to governance.

- Explain how a parliamentary system circumvents the divided government problem.

- Explain the importance of diversity in representation.

- Clarify the importance of legislative elections in parliamentary versus presidential systems.

- Identify and discuss some of the differences between parliamentary and presidential systems.

Student Website

www.mhhe.com/cls

Internet References

Asian Development Bank
www.adb.org/Countries
Election Resources on the Internet
http://electionresources.org
Inter-Parliamentary Union
www.ipu.org/wmn-e/world.htm
Latin American Network Information Center, University of Texas at Austin
http://lanic.utexas.edu/la/region/government
World Bank
www.worldbank.org

$\mathbf{U}$nit 5 focuses on legislatures' role in the political process: how they balance democratic responsiveness and accountability with effective policymaking, and how their performance as institutions and in policymaking may run up against political development. To that effect, we systematically address the questions of "why, what, and how" regarding the legislature.

The question—"Why do we need legislatures?"—coincides with the previous unit regarding the executive: legislatures demonstrate and capture representation of their constituents in government and serve to check against the excesses of executives. That is, whereas the executive imposes the "discipline" of a single policymaker in lawmaking, the legislature aims at representing the range of citizens' responses and needs in policy and legislation making while balancing the tyranny of the single executive decisionmaker. Ideally, the legislature may be a small replica of the citizenry in all its diversity.

One of the most important tasks of legislators is to represent. This essential role is described in all the articles in this unit. How important is it that the legislature performs as a representative institution? The first article points out that representation by legislators helps explain citizens' satisfaction with democracy and politics. Now, the first three units in this book have highlighted the consequences of citizens' discontent: political and social challenge and unrest. Clearly, if representation aids in political and social stability, then we need to ensure that the legislature performs this role.

Yet, even though this role is probably embraced by all legislators, realizing it is often not so easy. Thus, the articles on women representatives point out that under-representation of minorities tends to be the norm, because countries often embrace electoral systems that privilege the majority. Why? Part of the problem may be the electoral system. The articles on women in legislatures note that most countries embrace the single-member district electoral system. In the single-member district, candidates with the most votes often win the seat as legislative representative. In practice, single-member district electoral systems also skew, rather than ensure, representativeness.

Professor Norris article describes how this occurs: Single-member district electoral systems may not achieve representation because of several factors, including the high costs of campaigning that deters new candidates, the benefits of incumbency that penalizes new candidates, the advantage of political families that daunts minorities and newcomers, and electoral rules that favor candidates with the largest popular appeal, generally the majority group. Electoral systems such as the single-member district lead to overrepresentation of the majority and underrepresentation of minorities. In these cases, a change from an electoral system of first-past-the-post, or single-member districts, to proportional or at-large systems may remove any financial or majority advantage to balance representation. Unfortunately, however, such systems lead to candidates that remain beholden to the party, which is not always a good thing for representation. What is clear is that electoral systems, including quota systems that mandate minority representation, must be considered as the first of a series of processes to facilitate representation.

Further, representation must be measured by more than physical symbol. To truly represent a constituency, a legislator must achieve successful policymaking. That is, the legislator's support or opposition to policies should reflect a considered representation of the range of citizens' wishes. It is important to note that legislators do not have to initiate policies in order to support or oppose them. What legislatures must do to demonstrate representation in policymaking is to pass or decline legislation, which entails the essential tasks of discussing, examining, and debating the policies introduced. At the various points of discussing, examining, and debating the proposed legislation, the individual legislator gets to perform her or his role of representing his or her constituency's responses and needs. Thus, in principle, the aggregation of all legislators' input ensures that proposed legislation captures or is amended in the end product to contain the diversity of citizens' responses and needs, or it is rejected.

Importantly, with increased representation, the legislature strengthens as an institution to guard against the excesses of the executive. Institutionally, the executive is structured in one of three ways: as president in a presidential system; as prime minister and cabinet in a parliamentary system; as president and prime minister in a presidential-parliamentary hybrid system. In a presidential system, the executive—the president—is independently elected to office from the legislature. In a parliamentary system, the executive—generally a reference to the prime minster, but more accurately applied to the entire cabinet—is chosen by the elected legislature or parliament. In parliamentary systems, there is no independent election for the executive. In a presidential-parliamentary hybrid system, also known as the semi-presidential system or mixed system, the president is elected independently, while the prime minister and cabinet are chosen by the legislature. The mixed system is becoming the political system of choice in emerging democracies: at last count in 2002, there were 25 nations with mixed systems, up from only three in 1946.[1] Why is that? Michael Sodaro suggests that it is because the mixed systems maximize efficiency in policymaking but provides some guard against executive authority.[2] Clearly, the representational and institutional roles of the legislature remain at the fore in emergent democracies.

Many of the potential barriers to representation from electoral systems may be relatively easy to remedy. For instance, transparent campaign finance laws have helped address the disadvantages faced by minority or women candidates. Electronic voting has undermined the strength of party discipline and emphasized individual representation in legislators. This brings us full circle to the importance of citizens' participation, particularly at the polls. Lack of participation at the polls, regardless of emergent or mature democracies, undermine the political process and its development. One remedy to address the erosion of polling participation is via social pressure and surveillance. Does this mean that big brother is really watching? Maybe so. The ends may not justify the means, but the readings here emphasize that increasing the representativeness of legislature is not merely a political principle but a means to ensuring political stability.

Notes

1. See José Antonio Cheibub and Svitlana Chernykh. 2008. "Constitutions and Democratic Performance in Semi-Presidential Democracy." *Japanese Journal of Political Science* vol. 9 no 3: 269-303.

2. See Michael Sodaro, *Comparative Politics: A Global Introduction* (*3rd edition*). New York: McGraw-Hill (2007).

Satisfaction with Democracy: Do Institutions Matter?

KEES AARTS AND JACQUES THOMASSEN

1. Introduction: Elections as Instruments of Democracy

Elections are instruments of democracy; they are instrumental in linking the preferences of citizens to the behavior of policymakers (Powell, 2000). What exactly 'linking the preferences of citizens to the behavior of policy makers' is supposed to mean, is the subject of normative theories of political representation and representative democracy. Political representation, as much as democracy, is an essentially contested concept (Connolly, 1974) and its meaning and implications differ from one normative view on political representation to the other.

A main point of difference between theories of political representation is the function of elections. Whereas in majoritarian theories the function of selecting a government and government *accountability* is emphasized, consensual theories emphasize the selection of a *representative* legislature. This difference is reflected in the choice of political institutions, in particular electoral systems, which can be ordered according to the degree of proportionality or representativeness and to the degree of accountability they tend to produce.

But in the end the performance of electoral systems cannot be assessed by only examining their mechanics. These mechanics have to be perceived and evaluated by the voters. It is still an open question to what extent different political institutions also produce different voters' perceptions of accountability and representativeness. And what effects does this have for their satisfaction with democracy? These are the general questions addressed here. Using data from the Comparative Study of Electoral Systems (CSES), we are now able to examine the micro-macro link of electoral institutions, voters' perceptions and voters' evaluations of democracy.

In the next section, we elaborate the accountability representativeness distinction. This discussion results in a set of more specific research questions. After a description of the data used for the analysis, and the operationalization of the key concepts, we will answer our research questions.

2. Which Instruments for What Kind of Democracy?

This is not the place to review the extensive literature on theories and models of political representation (but see Andeweg and Thomassen, 2005; Birch, 1971; Manin, 1997; Pitkin, 1967; Powell, 2000; Przeworski et al., 1999; Thomassen, 1994). Instead, we focus on the distinction between majoritarian and consensus models of democracy (Lijphart, 1999). The major difference between the majoritarian and proportional vision is their view on the essence of democratic government and consequently the function of elections. Both visions agree that the very essence of democracy is government by the people, be it directly or indirectly. But the two visions disagree with regard to the question who should do the governing and to whose interests the government should be responsive when the people are in disagreement and have divergent preferences.

According to the majoritarian view the answer to this question is: the majority of the people. In the consensual view the answer should be: as many people as possible (Lijphart, 1999, pp. 1–2). As a consequence these two visions attribute different functions to elections.

In the majoritarian view the single most important function of an election is the selection of a government.

It requires that the voters have a clear choice between two competing (groups of) parties. The concentration of power in the hands of an elected majority government brings the government under tight control of the majority of the electorate. Within the majoritarian view two different theoretical perspectives on the precise function of elections can be distinguished. The first one is known as the government *mandate* perspective, the second one as the government *accountability* perspective. These perspectives assume different mechanisms by which the electoral majority can control the government. Government mandate theory can be characterized as saying that the policy preferences of a knowable and coherent majority of voters determine the winner of an election and that winner takes its turn at running the government on the policy line it had promised before the election (McDonald and Budge, 2005, p. 20). More precisely, according to this theoretical perspective elections can function as an instrument of democracy when the following requirements are met:

1. Voters can choose between at least two (groups of) parties with different policy proposals.
2. Voters do vote according to their policy preferences, i.e. they choose the party that represents their policy preferences best.
3. The party or coalition of parties winning the elections takes over the government.

This is basically the mechanism assumed by the Responsible Party Model (American Political Science Association, 1950; Klingemann et al., 1994; Schattschneider, 1942; Thomassen, 1994). If all conditions are met, the winning party can be said to have a policy mandate from a majority of the electorate (Powell, 2000, p. 8).

However, this model of political representation has been criticized for a number of reasons. First, it is very demanding, in particular with regard to what is required of the voters. Secondly, a single vote can hardly provide a policy mandate for a multiple package of issue-dimensions. Therefore, this model is often claimed to be totally unrealistic and unfeasible (Riker, 1982; Thomassen, 1994). Finally, the claim that in a majoritarian political system the winning party has won a policy mandate from a majority of the electorate more often than not is an illusion. In the United Kingdom for instance, the prototype of a majoritarian system, the party winning a majority of seats in the House of Commons almost never represents a majority of the electorate. Paradoxically, a majoritarian system at the legislative and executive level usually is enforced by a pluritarian rather than a majoritarian electoral system. As a consequence, majoritarian systems perform poorly in representing the median voter compared to consensual systems of democracy with a proportional electoral system (Powell, 2000; McDonald and Budge, 2005).

Therefore, in this article we focus on a perhaps more feasible model, the accountability model, which is based on Schumpeter's idea of a competitive democracy. According to this view "modern political democracy is a system of governance in which rulers are held accountable for their actions in the public realm by citizens". In this model elections are an accountability mechanism, where the sanctions are to extend or not to extend the government's tenure (Schumpeter, 1976 [1942], Chapter 22; Powell, 2000; Przeworski et al., 1999).

The major difference with the policy mandate model is that voters make their vote choice on the basis of their evaluation of the performance of the incumbent government. If they are satisfied with that performance they will vote for the party or parties in government, if they are dissatisfied, they will 'kick the rascals out'. Or as Walter Lipmann wrote more than fifty years ago: "To support the Ins when things are going well; to support the Outs when they seem to be going badly, this . . . is the essence of popular government" (cf. Powell, 2000, p. 10). This model of accountability is far less demanding of the voters because all they need to know is which party, or coalition of parties, is in power and which one in the opposition. Their information about the content of government policy can be limited. Being satisfied or dissatisfied with the government, its policies or the outcomes thereof, is all it takes. In the minimal definition of Riker: "The essence of the liberal interpretation of voting is the notion that voting permits the rejection of candidates or officials who have offended so many voters that they cannot win an election".

An essential requirement of this model of accountability at the system level is the *clarity of responsibiüty*. Accountability is by definition close to impossible if it is not perfectly clear who, i.e. which political party or coalition of parties, is responsible for government policy. But not only the incumbent but also the possible alternative future government must be identifiable. A second requirement is that the voters' sanction of the party or parties in power is effective, i.e. that they really can kick the rascals out without the risk that they (or some of them) will return to power after having lost the elections. This mechanism can only work in a majoritarian system where two (blocks of) parties compete for a majority of the votes and the winner automatically takes (over) government responsibility. Of course, once again it might be argued that in practice this latter mechanism can only be enforced by a pluritarian rather than a majoritarian electoral system, but this does not necessarily effect the clarity of government responsibility (Powell, 2000; Przeworski et al., 1999). The effects of the clarity of responsibility on the perceptions of the voters are what we are interested in here.

In consensus models of democracies, or proportional systems, the major function of elections is to elect the members of parliament who together should be as representative as possible of the electorate as a whole. The criterion for the democratic quality of the system is how representative parliament really is. There is no coercive relationship between the election outcome and the formation of the government. As a multi party system is one of the characteristics of a consensus model of democracy, a coalition of several parties will be needed to form a majority government. Coalitions will usually be broad, making it inevitable that at least some parties will return in government after the elections even if at the elections voters clearly demonstrate their dissatisfaction with the outgoing government. Therefore, usually there is an overlap between the new and the old coalition, blurring the clarity of responsibility and making the sanction of elections as an instrument of accountability into a rather blunt weapon.

Just as in the case of a majoritarian system, we can distinguish between voters basing their vote on retrospective or prospective judgments. However, for our purposes this distinction is not really relevant. In both cases the single most important criterion of the democratic quality of the system is the representativeness of parliament.

Between them, the two models of democracy fulfill the two most important functions which elections in a representative democracy have according to mainstream normative democratic theory. First, elections should allow voters to determine the political color of their government, making government accountable to the judgment of the people. Second, elections should produce a legislature that is representative of the division of political opinion amongst the electorate. However, it may be obvious that there is a certain tension between these two functions. Electoral systems and more generally democratic systems cannot optimally serve both functions at the same time. Majoritarian models of democracy are supposed to optimize the *accountability function,* consensus models of democracy the *representation function.*

The key question then is which model serves democracy best. This, however, is hard to say because the two visions on representative democracy represent two different normative views on democracy and incorporate different electoral institutions which are supposed to serve different purposes or at least different aspects of democracy. As Powell (2000, p. 7) argues: "empirical predictions about the nature of the citizen-policymaker relationship will focus on dissimilar dependent variables and not really be alternative theories about achieving the same goal".

One way out of this dilemma is to transform these dependent variables into independent variables, and make a comparative assessment of the extent to which majoritarian and consensual systems of government are instrumental for democracy, defined at a higher level of abstraction. This is the approach taken in several major pieces of previous research. Powell for instance starts from the normative assumption that democratic policy makers should do what their citizens want them to do. The role of elections then is to link the preferences of citizens to the behavior of their policy makers (Powell, 2000, p. 251). His empirical findings prove that if this is taken as the main function of democratic elections "the proportional[1] vision and its designs enjoyed a clear advantage over their majoritarian counterparts in using elections as instruments of democracy" (Powell, 2000, p. 254)

In a similar vein Lijphart in his *Patterns of Democracy* (Lijphart, 1999) tries to assess whether the distinction between majoritarian and consensus democracy makes a difference for how well democracy works. By comparing majoritarian and consensus democracies on a number of performance indicators he comes to the conclusion that consensus democracies perform better in almost every respect. They score better on the best-known indexes of democracy, women are better represented in parliament, consensus democracies are more egalitarian, turnout is higher, citizens in consensus democracies are significantly more satisfied with democratic performance in their countries than citizens of majoritarian democracies.

Part of Lijphart's argument is based on people's *satisfaction with democracy.* Referring to earlier work of Klingemann (1999), he comes to the conclusion that citizens in consensus democracies are significantly more satisfied with democratic performance in their countries than citizens of majoritarian democracies. The difference is approximately 17 percentage points.[2]

3. Research Questions

In this article we take these latter findings as a point of departure. The problem with these findings is that we still do not know how to explain the relationship between an institutional characteristic (type of democracy) and a characteristic at the micro level (satisfaction with the functioning of democracy). In this paper we will try to assess to what extent this relationship can be interpreted by introducing people's perception of the accountability and representativeness of the political system in their country. The global design of our approach is depicted in Figure 1.

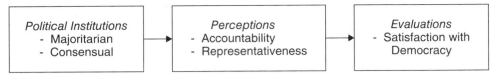

Figure 1   Research Design.

		Perception of Political Representation	
		Low	High
Perception of	Low	Low Satisfaction	Intermediate
Political			
Accountability	High	Intermediate	High Satisfaction

Figure 2   Analytical Scheme.

The Comparative Study of Electoral System's second module makes it possible for the first time to unravel the relationship between these three sets of variables. It contains questions on people's *perception* of both the *accountabiiity* and the *representativeness* of their political system in addition to a question on how satisfied people are with the functioning of democracy in their country.

We will use these questions to explain the relationship found in previous studies between models of democracy and satisfaction with democracy. We will develop our analysis in three consecutive steps. We will start by exploring the relationships at the micro level, i.e. the relationships between people's perceptions of the accountability and representativeness of the political system and their satisfaction with the functioning of democracy in their country. In this analysis our main analytic instrument will be based on the following scheme (Figure 2). Entries refer to satisfaction with democracy.

If we assume that both the perception of accountability and of representation have an effect on satisfaction with democracy, we can expect the highest satisfaction with democracy among people who are satisfied with both functions and the lowest level among people who are dissatisfied with both. But the most interesting question refers to the off-diagonal cells. Whereas the lower right cell depicts the interaction effect of perceived representation and perceived accountability, the off-diagonal cells summarize the main effects of these perceptions on satisfaction with democracy. By comparing these two cells

(or stated differently: by estimating the main effects) we will be able to assess to what extent people give different weights to the two functions in their assessment of the quality of democracy in their country.

Secondly, we will analyze the relationship between the type of political system (majoritarian versus consensual) and people's assessment of their political system: are the differences between these two types reflected in people's perceptions of accountability and representativeness, i.e. are people in majoritarian systems more satisfied with the accountability of the system, whereas people in consensus democracies are more satisfied with the representativeness of the system? And are people in consensus systems indeed more satisfied with democracy than people in countries with a majoritarian system?

And if so—and this is the third step in our analysis—can this relationship be explained by introducing people's perceptions of accountability and representativeness as intervening variables?

It would however be naive to suggest that differences in satisfaction are caused exclusively or even predominantly by institutional differences. The CSES data set includes both advanced industrial democracies and newly established democracies. In a new democracy it is difficult for people to distinguish between the performance of the incumbent government and the (new) democratic regime. Only gradually will people learn to make a distinction between the performance of the incumbent government and the performance of the regime and not to blame the regime for a poor performance of the incumbent government. Therefore, we can expect that people who are dissatisfied with government policy will be inclined to extend their dissatisfaction to the system of government, at least more so than in established democracies. If we take into consideration that the (economic) performance of many of the newly established democracies is poor, we should expect that the satisfaction with democracy in these countries, whatever their institutional arrangements, is low. Therefore, we shall take the distinction between old and new democracies into account as well.

4. Data and Operationalization of Main Concepts

4.1. Data

We make use of the final release of CSES module 2.[3] This release has been compiled from 41 election studies for 40 different elections in 38 countries, between 2001 and 2006. Two studies of the 2002 German Bundestag elections have been included in the release; we will only use one of these two studies, namely the telephone survey. Two Portuguese elections, of 2002 and 2005, have been included and we will use both since the election is the primary unit of analysis in the CSES framework. Finally, four election studies had to be omitted from the analyses because they lack at least one essential variable. These are Korea (2004), the Netherlands (2002), Norway (2001) and Taiwan (2004). The 2001 Taiwan study has been included. Most of our analyses thus employ data from 36 elections in 35 countries.

4.2. Variables at the Micro Level

Satisfaction with democracy. This concept was measured in CSES, module 2, in the same way as in many previous studies, by simply asking:

> Q8. 'On the whole, are you very satisfied, fairly satisfied, not satisfied, or not at all satisfied with the way democracy works in {country}?'

Perception of accountability. In the CSES module several questions trying to measure the perception of accountability were asked. The most relevant one for our purposes is:

> Q10. 'Some people say that no matter who people vote for, it won't make a difference to what happens. Others say that who people vote for can make a difference to what happens. Using the scale on this card, (where ONE means that voting won't make a difference to what happens and FIVE means that voting can make a difference) where would you place yourself?'[4]

Perception of representativeness. As in the case of accountability, several CSES questions measure (aspects of) people's perception of the representativeness of the political system. The following question on how well people think voters' views are represented in elections serves our purposes best.

> Q15. 'Thinking about how elections in {country} work in practice, how well do elections ensure that the views of voters are represented by MPs: very well, quite well, not very well, or not well at all?'

4.3. Variables at the Macro Level
4.3.1. Constitutional Design and Electoral System

In Powell's (2000) view, accountability and representativeness are institutional characteristics of elections. The extent to which an election can be seen as 'accountable' depends on the answers to two questions: can a voter identify the alternative future governments before the election, and does the election produce a majority for one of the identified possible future governments? Powell validates his measures of accountability and effective representation by comparing them with the constitutional design of the country: is it primarily a proportional, a majoritarian, or a mixed design? Pure proportional design is characterized by a proportional electoral rule and facilitation of opposition influence in parliamentary committees. Pure majoritarian design is characterized by single member electoral districts and government domination of parliamentary committees. Mixed designs include multimember districts and/or weak committees with shared chairs. Constitutional design appears to be a very good predictor of the macro-level measures of accountability and, to a lesser extent, of effective representation.

Applying Powell's macro-level measures of accountability and effective representation in our analysis poses some serious problems. First, many of the election studies in CSES module 2 have been conducted in relatively new democracies, in which the institutions of accountability and representation are hardly solidified yet. In these new democracies, institutions can relatively easily be changed. Secondly, we already noted that in Powell's definition accountability and representation are characteristics of elections. These measures provide reliable information about a country's institutions only when several and preferably many elections are observed per country. When, in contrast, a single election per country is observed (as is usually the case in CSES), the observed accountability and representation will be subject to serious (non-systematic) measurement error.[5]

Since Powell's macro-level measures of accountability and effective representation cannot be used in this paper, we decided to use a simpler, but effective characterization of countries by their electoral system instead.

In our analyses, we will designate the systems with a majoritarian electoral system as the category of reference. Majoritarian systems are characterized by a 'winner takes all' assignment of seats per district. Proportional systems are characterized by the assignment of seats per district on the basis of proportionality in multi-member districts. Proportional systems include, besides the list-proportional systems, also the mixed-member proportional systems (Germany, New Zealand). Mixed electoral systems include parallel systems (Tapan, Mexico, Thailand) and mixed-member majoritarian systems with partial compensation (Hungary, Italy) (cf. Shugart and Wattenberg, 2003).

4.3.2. Old and New Democracies

We argued that citizens will only gradually learn to distinguish between the performance of the incumbent government and the performance of the democratic regime. In our analyses we will therefore introduce a rough control for the age of the democratic systems. We distinguish between old, established democracies and new, recent democracies.

Most of our cases can easily be classified according to this scheme. Many are classified as old democracies with at least several decades of free and fair elections and other civil liberties. Spain and Portugal, which both regained democracy only in the 1970s, are therefore regarded as 'old' democracies. Other cases are among the newer democracies established after the breakdown of the Soviet empire, after a period of dictatorship (Philippines) or after a period of military rule (Brazil). Mexico—for many decades dominated by one single party—was until 2000 rated lower than '2' on the Freedom House index,[6] meaning that it was 'partly free' at the best. The same applies to Taiwan until the late 1990s ('partly free' according to the Freedom House index), when the newly formed Democratic Progressive Party and the Chinese New Party gradually increased their impact on Taiwan politics. For these reasons, we have classified Mexico and Taiwan under the 'new democracies' as well. Finally, Hong Kong, which did not have free elections before 1984 and was returned to China in 1997, can be regarded as a class on its own, but is classified here as a new democracy. In our analyses, we will treat the old democracies as the reference category.

The classification of our 35 political systems on the two macro-level variables, electoral system and age of democracy, is depicted in Table 1. Obviously, as this table shows, the two variables are not independent of each other:

- There is only a single case with majoritarian electoral system which is also a new democracy (Kyrgyzstan).

- Almost all cases with a mixed institutional design are new democracies (the exceptions being Japan 2004 and Italy 2006).

- All Asian cases in the analysis are instances of mixed institutional design.[7]

The problem encountered here is of course familiar to all comparativists in political science: it is attractive to portray a research problem as a multilevel problem, but the data hardly ever show enough macro-level variation to actually treat the problem with multilevel methods. At the macro level, it is generally not feasible to disentangle the impact of different system characteristics because of interdependencies. Instead, we should restrict the model specification to the most crucial variables and/or restrict the empirical domain to those observations for which the model can be expected to make sense (Achen, 2002).

Given the interdependence of our macro-indicators, the two indicators will not be used in a single analysis, as it will be unclear to which extent effects can reliably be attributed to one of them. Instead, we will present analyses which include one macro-indicator at a time, and focus in more detail on the status of the elections included.

5. Methods

Consider again the research design depicted in Figure 1. The dependent variable, satisfaction with democracy, is an ordinal measure. As a consequence, neither linear regression (which assumes interval measurement) nor multinomial logit or probit regression (which assume nominal measurement) are appropriate methods of analysis. Instead, we will apply an ordered regression model (Greene, 2000, Chapter 19; Long, 1997, Chapter 5). Ordered regression models have been developed for analyzing ordered response variables as an extension of the simple logit and probit models. The ordinal dependent variable (in our case: satisfaction with democracy) is regarded as a latent variable; we only have observations on the four categories of the indicator variable. It is assumed that the value of the indicator variable depends on the value of the latent variable: when latent satisfaction with democracy is very high, our survey indicator will be 'very satisfied'. The question is, at which point of the latent metric scale the category 'very satisfied' transforms into the category 'satisfied' (and similarly for the other bordering categories). This point is called the cutting point. When the survey indicator has four values, three cutting points must be estimated. An important

Table 1 Electoral system and age of democracy

| Age | Electoral system | | |
	Proportional	**Mixed**	**Majoritarian**
Old	Belgium 2003	Japan 2004	Australia 2004
	Denmark 2001	Italy 2006	Britain 2005
	Finland 2003		Canada 2004
	Germany 2002		France 2002
	Iceland 2003		United States 2004
	Ireland 2002		
	Israel 2003		
	New Zealand 2002		
	Portugal 2002		
	Portugal 2005		
	Spain 2004		
	Sweden 2002		
	Switzerland 2003		
New	Brazil 2002	Albania 2005	Kyrgyzstan 2005
	Bulgaria 2001	Czech Republic 2002	
	Chile 2005	Hong Kong 2004	
	Peru 2006	Hungary 2002	
	Poland 2001	Mexico 2003	
	Romania 2004	Philippines 2003	
	Slovenia 2004	Russia 2004	
		Taiwan 2001	

assumption is that the effect of explanatory variables (the regression coefficient) is constrained to be equal over the categories of the dependent variable (proportional odds model). Both logit- and probit-models are available for ML ordered regression estimation; we selected the logit model.

We present graphs showing the distributions of the three micro-level variables per election.

In the first step of our analyses, perceptions of accountability and representativeness serve as explanatory variables. The analytical scheme in Figure 2 summarizes our expectations. The most interesting question involves the comparison of the two off-diagonal cells in this figure, which refer to the effects of a combination of low accountability and high representativeness, and high accountability and low representativeness. In our simple 2 × 2 table, this comparison amounts to a comparison of main effects while including their interaction.[8]

In the second step we look at the effect of the macro variables, type of electoral system and age of democracy, on the three micro variables. In this step we will again use ordered logit regression. Finally, we investigate the combined effect of micro- and macro-explanations of satisfaction with democracy.

6. Results

6.1. Perceptions of Satisfaction with Democracy, Accountability and Representation

Figures 3–5 show the distribution of the three key variables in this paper. Figure 3 shows the distribution of the main dependent variable, satisfaction with democracy, in the 36 elections in our analysis. The elections are ordered according to the percentage of respondents who are fairly or very satisfied with the way democracy works in their country. On top are the elections in which people display high levels of satisfaction with democracy—elections in Denmark, Ireland, Australia, the United States and other countries. At the bottom of the figure satisfaction with democracy is relatively low—for example, in Bulgaria, Brazil, Mexico and Peru.

Figure 3 shows that there is considerable variation across elections in different countries with regard to the extent that voters are satisfied with democracy in their country. Citizens of countries at the top of the figure are overwhelmingly satisfied with democracy; citizens of countries at the bottom are predominantly dissatisfied. Most of the cases in the figure show a majority of fairly and very satisfied citizens. In

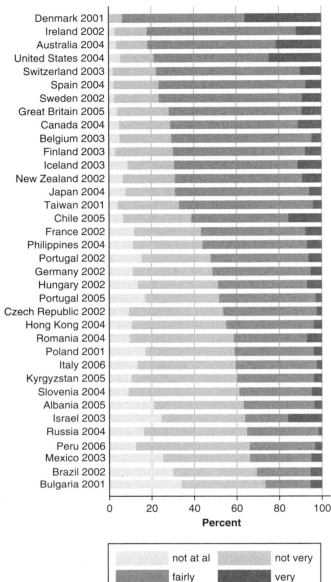

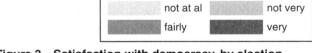

Figure 3   Satisfaction with democracy, by election.

Source: CSES Module 2, June 2007

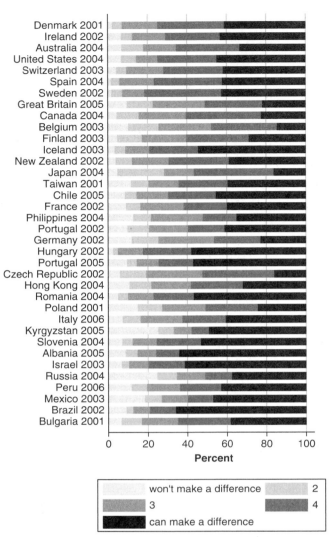

Figure 4   Perceptions of accountability, by election.

Source: CSES Module 2, June 2007

the German election of 2002, a very small majority is satisfied; in the case of Hungary and in the eight cases shown below Hungary in Figure 3, dissatisfied citizens form a majority.

Figure 4 shows the distribution of the micro-indicator for accountability, the response to the question 'does it make a difference whom one votes for?' The order of the elections in this figure and in the following is taken from Figure 3. On top are cases characterized by a largely satisfied electorate; at the bottom are cases with many dissatisfied citizens.

The larger the categories at the right of each bar in Figure 4, the more people believe that voting does make a difference. Obviously, at the level of elections the extent to which people believe that voting does make a difference does not correspond neatly with satisfaction with democracy. If we focus on categories 4 and 5 of this indicator, it appears that the Hungarians show the highest perceived accountability, followed by the Swedes, Israelis, Icelanders and Brazilians. The lowest perceived accountability is found in Germany, Belgium, Poland and Great Britain. Only in Germany and Belgium the respondents in these two highest categories of perceived accountability form a (large) minority.

Finally, Figure 5 depicts the distribution of the indicator for representation, the answer to the question 'how well do elections ensure that the views of voters are represented by MPs?', ordered according to satisfaction with democracy. Again, the correspondence of perceived representation with the satisfaction with democracy is not so clear at all at the level of elections. The cases with the highest degrees of perceived representation are Denmark, the United States, Spain, Ireland, and Belgium. The lowest degree of perceived representation is found in Japan, followed by Slovenia, the Czech Republic, Brazil, and (surprisingly) Germany. Other countries in which a majority finds itself not very well, or not well at all represented, are Albania, Portugal, Britain, Canada, Chile, Israel, Kyrgyzstan, Mexico, Peru, Finland, and Poland.

This overview of distributions of the three micro-level variables (satisfaction with democracy, perceived accountability, and perceived representation) shows that their variation between cases is considerable, and that at the same time the electionlevel relationships do not seem to be especially strong. But whether the micro-level variables are interrelated can of course only be determined by a micro-level analysis, to which we turn now.

6.2. Satisfaction with Democracy and Perceptions of Accountability and Representation

The first research question to be addressed involves the link between perceptions of accountability and representation on the one hand, and satisfaction with democracy on the other hand. Referring to the research design in Figure 1, this link connects individual perceptions with individual evaluations, and can thus be examined at the level of individual respondents.

Table 2 summarizes the results from an ordered logit regression of satisfaction with democracy on the two perception variables and their interaction, without further controls. Since the two perception variables have been recoded as dummies, their effects can simply be compared.

As expected, the largest effect on satisfaction with democracy is found when both perceived accountability and representation are high (the interaction effect is positive). While this should not come as a surprise, the interesting comparison involves the main effects of the two perception variables. Clearly, the effect of perceived representation is much more important than that of perceived accountability. This means that satisfaction with democracy is generally higher in the upper right cell of Figure 2 than in the lower left cell.[9]

For the pool of all elections in the data set, the question whether people feel represented by their members of parliament is much more important for their satisfaction with democracy than whether they think it makes a difference who they vote for.

The quality of representation is the central criterion for consensus models of democracy. The line of thought summarized in the first sections of this paper, suggests

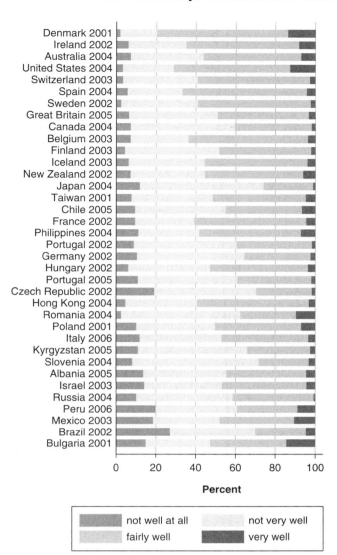

Figure 5   Perceptions of representation, by election
Source: CSES Module 2, June 2007

that a high perceived quality of representation is a direct consequence of the institutions of consensus democracy, such as a proportional electoral system. The same reasoning holds for perceived accountability and the institutions of majoritarian democracy. To further investigate the importance of democratic institutions, we thus need to analyze to what extent perceptions can be attributed to institutional context—the left part of the research design depicted in Figure 1. The next step thus involves the introduction of institutional, macro-level variables.

6.3. The Effect of Macro-Level Characteristics

We have already argued that not only institutional design, but also the age of the democracy should be taken into account when the effect of institutional characteristics on

Table 2 Evaluations and Perceptions of Democracy at the Micro Level

	Satisfaction with Democracy
Perceived accountability	1.20 (0.02)
Perceived representation	2.00 (0.03)
Accountability * representation	2.33 (0.02)
n = 46,834	Pseudo R^2 = 0.09
Cutting point 1	−0.53 (0.02)
Cutting point 2	1.36 (0.02)
Cutting point 3	4.17 (0.03)

Entries are coefficients, cutting points, and associated standard errors from an ordered logistic regression (proportional odds model); the dependent variable is the four-category 'satisfaction with democracy' measure.

people's satisfaction with democracy is analyzed. In the CSES dataset it is unfortunately not possible to include both these macro-variables in a single analysis, since they show too much overlap. We therefore first present analyses of the impact of institutional design, followed by the impact of the age of democracy.

Table 3 shows the results of three ordered logistic regressions, one for each of the three micro-variables (perceived accountability, perceived representation, and satisfaction with democracy. According to the existing theory, a majoritarian electoral system would be associated with a higher level of perceived accountability—majoritarian systems optimize the accountability function of democracy. Similarly, proportional systems would optimize the representation function of democracy. In our analyses, majoritarian design serves as the category of reference. Thus we expect a negative coefficient for the effect of proportional design on perceived accountability (compared with majoritarian systems, proportionality should lead to lower perceived accountability). And similarly, we expect a positive coefficient for the effect of proportional

design on perceived representation. We do not have clear expectations for the effects of mixed institutional design.

However, the results of the analyses in Table 3 hardly offer any support for these expectations. A proportional electoral system is positively, not negatively related with perceived accountability. And there is hardly any relationship between proportional systems and perceived representation. The relationships described in Table 3 are clearly at odds with the theories outlined earlier in this paper.

But that is not all. The third column in Table 3 shows the unmediated effects of institutional design on satisfaction with democracy. Not citizens of proportional systems or mixed systems, but those living in majoritarian systems show the highest level of satisfaction with democracy. Clearly, if the relationships between electoral system, perceived accountability, perceived representation and satisfaction with democracy conform to theoretical expectations, the results reported in Table 3 must be distorted by omitted variables bias. We suggested that one potential source of such bias is the age of the democracy.

Table 3 Constitutional Design

	Perceived Accountability	Perceived Representation	Satisfaction with Democracy
Proportional	0.30 (0.02)	−0.05 (0.02)	−0.41 (0.02)
Mixed	0.09 (0.03)	−0.23 (0.02)	−0.82 (0.03)
n	46834	46834	46834
Pseudo R^2	0.00	0.00	0.01
Cutting point 1	−2.12 (0.02)	−2.27 (0.02)	−2.54 (0.03)
Cutting point 2	−1.36 (0.02)	−0.04 (0.02)	−0.73 (0.02)
Cutting point 3	−0.44 (0.02)	2.86 (0.03)	1.96 (0.03)
Cutting point 4	0.58 (0.02)	—	—

Entries are coefficients, cutting points, and associated standard errors from ordered logistic regressions (proportional odds model); dependent variables are the five-category 'perceived accountability' measure and the four-category 'perceived representation' and 'satisfaction with democracy' measures. Reference category of 'constitutional design' is the majoritarian design; see Table 1.

Table 4 therefore summarizes the impact of the age of the democracy on the same three micro-variables.

Whether a democracy is old or new, has little impact on its perceived accountability—actually, perceived accountability is slightly higher in new democracies. But perceived representation is clearly lower in new democracies than in the older ones. And, as we expected beforehand, satisfaction with democracy is lower as well in the new democracies.

The age of the democracy thus makes a difference for the perceptions and evaluations of democracy. But the age of the democracy is also strongly related to institutional design (see Table 1), which complicates the interpretation of its effects. For example, all but one of the majoritarian cases in our analyses are old democracies. Rather than including age of democracy as a control variable, we therefore performed our analyses of the impact of institutional design on the three micro-variables separately for the old democra-cies only.[10] Since Japan and Italy are the only cases of mixed systems among the older democracies, we have also omitted Japan and Italy from the analyses. Thus, Table 5 reports analyses of the same model as in Table 3, but only for eighteen older democracies with a proportional or majoritarian electoral design.

When only old democracies with either a majoritarian or a proportional design are included, we find that citizens in democracies with a proportional electoral system have more positive perceptions of the accountability of elections. This finding again contradicts our theoretical expectations. Table 5 also reports the absence of impact of proportional design on the satisfaction with democracy. This finding contradicts the expectation as well, and contrasts with the (weak) findings of Anderson and Guillory (1997) and Lijphart (1999, pp. 278–9) that citizens in consensus democracies are more satisfied with democracy. We do not find such a relationship. Thus, proportionality seems to go together with positive perceptions of the accountability of democracy, is practically unrelated to representativeness, and is associated with relatively low evaluations of democracy.

Our final analysis combines the micro- and macro-level explanations of satisfaction with democracy. We confine ourselves again to observations in old, majoritarian or proportional democracies. Table 6 reports the regression results. We find again that proportional electoral systems are associated with lower levels of satisfaction with democracy. Furthermore, both perceived accountability and perceived representation do positively affect satisfaction. Their combined effect leads to the highest levels of satisfaction.

We are now also in a position to answer the question to what extent the relationship between type of democracy and satisfaction with democracy can be interpreted by people's perceptions of accountability and perception (cf. Figure 1). The answer is that this interpretation leads to findings opposite to our theoretical expectations. The direct relationship between proportional design and satisfaction with democracy is negative rather than positive (Table 5), and the introduction of the intervening variables perceived accountability and perceived representation does not make any difference in this respect—the negative result is basically replicated.

7. Conclusion and Discussion

How do the voters in different political systems perceive accountability and representativeness, and what effects does this have for their satisfaction with democracy? Political systems are often divided into majoritarian and consensus types, and accountability and representativeness have a quite different importance in these two types. Whereas the consensus type of democracy is believed to maximize the representation function, the majoritarian type enhances

Table 4   Age of Democracy

	Perceived Accountability	Perceived Representation	Satisfaction with Democracy
New democracy	0.12 (0.02)	−0.41 (0.02)	−1.00 (0.02)
n	46834	46834	46834
Pseudo R^2	0.00	0.00	0.03
Cutting point 1	−2.27 (0.02)	−2.37 (0.02)	−2.58 (0.02)
Cutting point 2	−1.51 (0.01)	−0.11 (0.01)	−0.71 (0.01)
Cutting point 3	−0.60 (0.01)	2.79 (0.02)	2.06 (0.02)
Cutting point 4	0.42 (0.01)	—	—

Entries are coefficients, cutting points, and associated standard errors from ordered logistic regressions (proportional odds model); dependent variables are the five-category 'perceived accountability' measure and the four-category 'perceived representation' and 'satisfaction with democracy' measures. Reference category of 'age of democracy' is 'old'; see Table 1.

Table 5 The Effect of Electoral System, Excluding New Democracies and Mixed Systems

	Perceived accountability	Perceived representation	Satisfaction with democracy
Proportional	0.27 (0.03)	−0.00 (0.03)	−0.32 (0.03)
n	25327	25327	25327
Pseudo R^2	0.00	0.00	0.00
Cutting point 1	− 2.43 (0.03)	−2.57 (0.03)	−2.76 (0.03)
Cutting point 2	−1.52 (0.02)	−0.19 (0.02)	−1.03 (0.03)
Cutting point 3	− 0.48 (0.02)	3.00 (0.04)	1.79 (0.03)
Cutting point 4	0.70 (0.02)	—	—

Entries are coefficients, cutting points, and associated standard errors from ordered logistic regressions (proportional odds model); dependent variables are the five-category 'perceived accountability' measure and the four-category 'perceived representation' and 'satisfaction with democracy' measures. Reference category of 'constitutional design' is the majoritarian design; see Table 1.

Table 6 Evaluations, Perceptions and Constitutional Design (excluding new democracies and mixed design)

	Satisfaction with Democracy
Proportional design	−0.37 (0.03)
Perceived accountability	1.29 (0.03)
Perceived representation	2.17 (0.04)
Accountability * representation	2.61 (0.03)
n = 25,327	Pseudo R2 = 0.11
Cutting point 1	−1.10 (0.04)
Cutting point 2	0.75 (0.03)
Cutting point 3	3.82 (0.04)

Entries are coefficients, cutting points, and associated standard errors from an ordered logistic regression (proportional odds model); the dependent variable is the four-category 'satisfaction with democracy' measure.

the accountability function. Satisfaction with democracy is thought to be greater in consensus type democracies, because the representation function supposedly keeps the voters of opposition parties relatively satisfied.

CSES Module 2 provides the first internationally comparative data needed to put these expectations to a test. We have operationalized the accountability and representation functions at the micro-level by two indicators from the CSES survey. The type of democracy was operationalized in terms of a majoritarian, proportional or mixed electoral system. Our findings, based on a total of 36 elections in 35 countries during the years 2001–2006, show that people's satisfaction with their democracy primarily depends on their perception of the representation function, and to a lesser degree on the accountability function. Surprisingly in view of our theoretical expectations, the accountability perception is enhanced

by a proportional-type institutional design, whereas the representation function is not. Our evaluative measure of satisfaction with democracy is also negatively affected by a proportional electoral system. It appears that at the macro-level satisfaction with democracy is primarily affected by the age of the democracy one lives in.

It is of course hardly surprising that people who are relatively satisfied with the representation and accountability functions of their democracy also express satisfaction with democracy in general. It is surprising, however, that citizens of proportional-type political systems think that the accountability function is performed better than do citizens in majoritarian systems. Does this finding imply that political scientists have been mistaken about the nature of accountability in electoral politics?

We have already (in footnote 5) pointed out that our measure of perceived accountability is less than perfect. One possible interpretation of our results could therefore be that our respondents have simply given a different interpretation to the question what difference it makes whom one votes for. They may primarily have thought about the policy range of the political parties, and this is probably wider in proportional than in majoritarian systems. Whether this alternative interpretation of the CSES survey question has occurred, is something we do not know. Obviously, future work in this area should aim at improved measurements.

References

Achen, C., 2002. Toward a new political methodology: Microfoundations and ART. Annual Review of Political Science 5, 423–450.

Anderson, C.J., Guillory, C.A., 1997. Political institutions and satisfaction with democracy: a cross-national analysis of consensus and majoritarian systems. American Political Science Review 91 (1), 66–82.

American Political Science Association, 1950. Toward a More Responsible Two-Party System. Rinehart & Co., New York.

Andeweg, R.B., Thomassen, J.J.A., 2005. Modes of political representation. Legislative Studies Quarterly 30 (4), 507–528.

Birch, A., 1971. Political Representation. Pall Mall Press and Macmillan, London.

Connolly, W.E., 1974. The Terms of Political Discourse. Princeton University Press, Princeton.

Fukuyama, F., 1992. The End of History and the Last Man. Penguin, Harmondsworth.

Greene, W.H., 2000. Econometric Analysis, fourth ed. Prentice Hall, Upper Saddle River, NJ.

Klingemann, H.-D., Hofferbert, R.I., Budge, I., 1994. Parties, Policies, and Democracy. Westview Press, Boulder.

Klingemann, H.D., 1999. Mapping political support in the 1990s: a global analysis. In: Norris, P. (Ed.), Critical Citizens: Global Support for Democratic Government. Oxford University Press, Oxford, pp. 31–57.

Lijphart, A., 1999. Patterns of Democracy. Government Forms and Performance in Thirty-Six Countries. Yale University Press, New Haven.

Long, J.S., 1997. Regression Models for Categorical and Limited Dependent Variables. Sage, Thousand Oaks.

Manin, B., 1997. The Principles of Representative Government. Cambridge University Press, Cambridge.

McDonald, M., Budge, I., 2005. Elections, Parties, Democracies. Conferring the Median Mandate. Oxford University Press, Oxford.

Pitkin, H., 1967. The Concept of Political Representation. University of California Press, Berkeley.

Powell, G.B., 2000. Elections as Instruments of Democracy. Majoritarian and Proportional Visions. Yale University Press, New Haven.

Przeworski, A., Stokes, S.C., Manin, B. (Eds.), 1999. Democracy, Accountability, and Representation. Cambridge University Press, Cambridge.

Riker, W.H., 1982. Liberalism versus Populism: A Confrontation between the Theory of Democracy and the Theory of Social Choice. W.H. Freeman, San Francisco.

Samuels, D., 2004. Presidentialism and accountability for the economy in comparative perspective. American Political Science Review 98, 425–436.

Schattschneider, E.E., 1942. Party Government. Farrar and Rinehart, New York.

Schumpeter, J.A., 1976. Capitalism, Socialism and Democracy, fifth ed. Allen and Unwin, London [1942].

Shugart, M.S., Wattenberg, M.P., 2003. Mixed-Member Electoral Systems: The Best of Both Worlds? Oxford University Press, Oxford.

Thomassen, J.J.A., 1994. Empirical research into political representation: failing democracy or failing models. In: Jennings, M.K., Mann, T.E. (Eds.), Elections at Home and Abroad; Essays in Honor of Warren Miller. University of Michigan Press, Ann Arbor, pp. 237–265.

Notes

1. Powell consistently uses 'proportional system' as a synonym for what Lijphart calls a 'consensus model of democracy'. As the former term often is used in the more limited meaning of a proportional electoral system we prefer to use Lijphart's terminology even though later on we will operationalize the distinction between a majoritarian and a consensus model of democracy in terms of their respective electoral systems.

2. Lijphart also refers to Anderson and Guillory (1997) who found that in all countries respondents who voted for the winning party or parties were more likely to be satisfied with democracy than respondents who had voted for the losing party or parties. They also found that in consensus democracies the differences between winners and losers were significantly smaller than in majoritarian democracies (Lijphart, 1999, pp. 286–7).

3. Data and documentation can be downloaded from www.cses.org.

4. The validity of this question as an indicator of the perception of accountability is disputable. What we really want to measure is the clarity of government responsibility and the possibility of voters to sanction government parties they are dissatisfied with. A majoritarian system like the British is almost perfect on both variables, but if the two main parties have learned their lessons from Downsian theory the voters will be faced with a choice between Tweedledee and Tweedledum. What this implies for people's answers to the question whether it makes a difference which party people vote for, we simply don't know. Still, this question is the best indicator for the perception of accountability available in the CSES questionnaire.

5. Samuels (2004) has questioned the issue of government accountability (for the economy) in presidential systems. Depending on whether elections for the legislature are concurrent or nonconcurrent with presidential elections (i.e., the president is, or is not elected at the same time as the legislature), government accountability will be high (concurrent) or low (nonconcurrent). In our data, only the French election in 2002 was a nonconcurrent presidential contest. We decided to categorize the French 2002 election as a majoritarian case (in agreement with Powell (2000)), even though it was not strictly

a (majoritarian) election for the assembly. The other elections in presidential systems in our data were either legislative elections only (Mexico, Taiwan) or concurrent legislative/presidential elections (Brazil, Philippines, United States).

6. Refer to: www.freedomhouse.org (accessed September 24, 2007).

7. This is a relevant observation because it has been claimed that Asian democracy should be regarded as a class of its own, with a strong emphasis on group harmony and consensus and a correspondingly lower esteem for individual liberty (see Fukuyama, 1992, pp. 235–44).

8. For interpretation purposes, we collapsed categories in both explanatory variables to create two dummy variables. For perceived accountability ('Does it make a difference whom one votes for?'), categories 1 through 3 (negative answers), and 4 and 5 (positive answers) have been combined. For perceived representation ('how well do elections ensure that the views of voters are represented by MPs'), categories 'not very well' and 'not very well at all', and 'quite well' and 'very well' have been combined. Negative answers have value '0'.

9. These results are generally robust when the analysis is conducted separately for each election. In only a few cases are the effects of perceived accountability and perceived representation on satisfaction with democracy about equally strong (Brazil, Spain and Israel).

10. There are no cases of majoritarian design among the newer democracies (see Table 1), which makes an analysis of the impact of constitutional design awkward.

Critical Thinking

1. Define accountability and representation
2. What systems generate greater accountability? What systems generate better representation?
3. What does it mean that voters are more satisfied with democracy in representative systems?

Acknowledgments—Earlier versions of this paper were presented at the International Conference on Elections and Democratic Governance, organized by the Institute of Political Science, Academia Sinica, Taipei, April 10 11, 2005; the 20th IPSA World Congress, Fukuoka, July 9 13, 2006; and the Annual Meetings of the American Political Science Association, Washington, DC, August 31 September 4, 2005 and Philadelphia, PA, August 30 September 3, 2006. The authors gratefully acknowledge comments and suggestions by the discussants at these meetings.

The Famous Dutch (In)Tolerance

"Variations of Geert Wilders's xenophobic message are shared by the majority of the political parties represented in the Dutch parliament."

JAN ERK

The Dutch have long enjoyed a reputation for tolerance, and they are indeed a tolerant people: They are tolerant of the anti-immigrant sentiment that has engulfed their country's politics over the past decade. Part of the political partnership running the Netherlands today is a party whose agenda includes ethnic registration, a tax on Muslim headscarves, repatriation of Dutch criminals of immigrant origin, a blanket ban on the construction of mosques, and outlawing the Koran.

To a large extent, this situation is a side effect of the fact that anti-Muslim discourse has encountered growing acceptance in recent years. Such discourse has allowed anti-immigrant sentiment—in the Dutch case, sentiment against the people of Moroccan and Turkish derivation who constitute a majority of the country's immigrants—to become palatable to mainstream sensibilities.

In fact, the far-right Party of Freedom (PVV) could never have gained inclusion in the political coalition governing the nation had it continued using the race-based rhetoric associated with xenophobic parties of the past. Instead, the PVV employs anti-Islam rhetoric. The words do not carry the same anti-immigrant overtones as race-based rhetoric, but they have the same effect.

In June 2010, national elections resulted in a major electoral success for the upstart PVV, which had been formed only four years before by Geert Wilders. Afterwards the PVV became a coalition partner of the Christian Democrat Appeal (CDA, a Christian Democrat party) and the People's Party for Freedom and Democracy (VVD, a right-liberal party). Leaders of the three parties unveiled a new coalition program on September 30, a cabinet was put together in the following weeks (though the PVV gained no ministerial portfolio), and the government was sworn in on October 14.

Not long before this, Wilders had tried to take his party's message to the United States, joining in the opposition to the planned construction of a Muslim community center near the former site of the World Trade Center in New York City, but he failed to attract much media interest in North America. Wilders managed to create more interest in Australia, where in an interview he called Islam a "retarded and violent" religion.

The PVV's membership in the governing coalition will likely help Wilders increase his international profile beyond Europe, where he is already well known. But how did his party, in a country renowned for its progressive politics, become a governing partner?

The Anti-Islam Norm

A simple but misleading narrative seems to dominate media reporting on the rise of the xeno-phobic right in the Netherlands. According to this narrative, a single party led by the colorful populist Wilders broke ranks with The Hague–based Dutch political establishment and stood up to the left-liberal media, thereby shaking the country's progressive foundations. This picture is clear and compelling. It is very kind to the Dutch political establishment. It is also incorrect.

Wilders's peroxide blond hair, his offensive outbursts, and his clownish antics comport with the image that the media have painted for him, that of the outsider. But in fact, variations of Geert Wilders's xenophobic message are shared by the majority of the political parties represented in the Dutch parliament. Put simply, Wilders is a product of the Dutch political system and his message is not confined to the fringes of the political spectrum. His message is disguised in anti-Islam language, which makes it more palatable than is naked xenophobia to mainstream sensibilities.

Although no member of the PVV holds a ministerial portfolio, the party's influence over the formation of the cabinet last year was recently exposed when it became clear that certain posts—including that of the minister of integration—had had to be vetted by Wilders.

Moreover, the governing coalition's program includes a number of priorities that defined the PVV's 2010 electoral campaign. The government proposes to ban the face-covering Islamic burqa. Residence without a permit is to be made a criminal act, and arranging family unification for immigrants will become harder. The governing coalition plans to halve the number of people allowed to immigrate to the Netherlands from so-called non-Western countries, and to require those who are allowed in to participate in stricter and more expensive integration courses.

Some of the PVV's anti-Islam positions are concealed in ambiguous wording. One example is the rather bizarre goal of cutting unemployment and social security benefits to those "whose clothing is not suitable for finding work"—which potentially could become a means for denying benefits to Muslims who wear traditional garb.

To be sure, not all components of the government's program necessarily represent realistic proposals. For example, this author has never seen anyone in the Netherlands wearing a burqa, so the ban against it is more a coded message to supporters than a piece of public policy. Yet this only accentuates the fact that the coalition program, while highlighting symbolic issues, has failed to address many pressing problems in the economic realm. The government has made a few selective cuts in public spending, but it has proposed no structural reform of the economy, no reform of the housing market, and no relaxation of the country's rigid labor market.

Meanwhile, immigration has become the top political issue in a country that—compared to other nations across the Western world—does not have a very large immigrant population. The four biggest immigrant communities in the Netherlands are Turks, Moroccans, Antilleans, and Surinamese; together they total just under 1 million people, in a country of 17 million. Yet these Dutch citizens now find themselves living under a coalition government that has adopted specific policies targeting them.

Margin to the Middle

This picture of Dutch politics probably clashes with the impression of the Netherlands that most foreign visitors to Amsterdam take home with them. The Netherlands is of course bigger than the old city center of the capital, and the rest of the country has always been more socially conservative than its biggest city, which among its tourist attractions offers (sanitized) vice.

In any case, Dutch people's tolerance of soft drugs, pornography, and prostitution is not the same as social permissiveness. The Dutch word that refers to the decriminalized provision of vice, *gedogen,* merely suggests that those who infringe against collective morality will be tolerated and granted tacit immunity from prosecution. Such tolerance implies no endorsement, and this is nothing new.

What is new is the acceptance of a far-right xenophobic party as a bona fide governing partner. Parties with similar agendas have appeared on the Dutch landscape in the past. These, however, not only were politically marginalized—they were pursued by magistrates for promoting discrimination.

For example, the far-right Dutch People's Union entered the parliament in 1977, but immediately became a target of prosecutors, and was banned the following year (although a complicated legal process followed). The Center Party (CP) was another such party, entering parliament in 1982. Internal splits spawned offshoots such as the Center Democrats (CD), the Center Party '86 (CP'86), the New National Party (NNP), and the Dutch Bloc. CP'86 was banned in 1996 and was dissolved by magistrates the following year for advocating discrimination and endangering public order. The same year the veteran leader of the CD (who had started his career in the CP) was found guilty of inciting racial hatred.

It is important to recall that these far-right outfits operated on the margins of Dutch mainstream politics. Yet now the two largest center-right parties in the parliament maintain a political partnership with Wilders—and they do so even though, coincident with the formation of the coalition government, Wilders was the subject of a court case that involved inciting racial hatred against Muslims. (Prosecutors themselves, who had brought the case to court partly because they had come under criticism from antiracism activists for doing too little regarding Wilders, declared their opinion that he was not guilty.)

The PVV's status as the third-largest party in the parliament might not appear to justify all the attention it has received—but the Dutch electoral system is based on the principle of proportional representation, and it lacks the nationwide vote threshold that is a feature of most other proportional systems. In Germany, for example, political parties must gain at least 5 percent of the nationwide vote to gain seats based on their proportion of the votes cast.

The absence of such a threshold in the Netherlands means that the Dutch parliament is composed of a multitude of parties ranging from the Party for Animals, with 2 seats, to the right-liberal VVD, with 31. In this context, the PVV's 24 seats give Wilders major clout within the ruling partnership. By themselves, the CDA with its 21 seats and the VVD with its 31 seats would have fallen short of a governing majority in the 150-seat parliament. With the PVV included, a parliamentary majority was achieved.

Word Games

So what explains the acceptance of the xeno-phobic PVV in mainstream Dutch politics? First, Wilders's position on Islam is shared by the majority of Dutch parties in the parliament—there is nothing preposterous or marginal about his message in the contemporary Netherlands. Wilders's immoderate language and attention-seeking antics might annoy some of his political partners, but his party's message is not alien to mainstream Dutch politics.

Second, while the xenophobic far-right parties of the past explicitly targeted immigrants, which created problems for them, Wilders's PVV has found a way around this by targeting a religion, Islam, instead of immigrants themselves. Voters need not feel they are targeting their Muslim immigrant compatriots; they are just manning the barricades to protect Western freedoms from onslaught by an intolerant, backward, Eastern culture. Of course, anti-Islam language need not in every national context equal anti-immigrant xenophobia—but the majority of Dutch immigrants are Muslims, and the connection is obvious.

The Dutch media, and Wilders himself for that matter, prefer as a descriptive prefix for his party the term "anti-Islam" (and not "anti-Muslim"). "Anti-Islam" suggests that the PVV opposes the values and teachings of the religion at an abstract, ideological level. The term attempts to obscure the fact that, in the Netherlands, the targets of anti-Islam sentiment are bound to be individual followers of Islam—that is, Dutch Muslims. The difference between "anti-Islam" and "anti-Muslim" might at first glance seem minor and semantic, but this choice in labeling has played a key role in bringing anti-immigrant sentiment into the mainstream, acceptably cloaked.

The Dutch public was already receptive to such a message. A 2005 survey by Pew Global Attitudes found that 51 percent of respondents in the Netherlands held an unfavorable opinion of Muslims living in their country—a number much higher than in other Western nations. (In the United States the number was 22 percent; in Britain it was 14 percent.)

Among younger Dutch people, the anti-Islam current is particularly pronounced. The 2009 International Civic and Citizenship Education Study, which reported on attitudes among secondary-school pupils in 39 countries, found that Dutch students (and Dutch-speaking Flemings in Belgium) held the most negative views regarding immigrants. Dutch students tended more than others to oppose the idea of granting equal rights to immigrants.

Meanwhile, labor market statistics show tendencies indicating immigrant marginalization. The analyst Peter Kee's findings on native-immigrant wage differentials (published in *Oxford Economic Papers*) reveal structural discrimination: The average nonimmigrant Dutch worker earns 35 percent more than the average Antillean-Dutch, 41 percent more than Surinamese-Dutch, 54 percent more than Turkish-Dutch, and 44 percent more than Moroccan-Dutch.

The pervasiveness of anti-Muslim sentiment goes a long way toward explaining how political parties, to varying degrees, have adopted into their programs anti-Islam views, the somewhat more intellectually acceptable sibling of anti-Muslim sentiment. But it is not clear what a Dutch political party can expect to achieve by adopting such a position. Unless Muslims somehow convert *en masse* to Christianity, demonizing Islam can only increase Muslim isolation from Dutch society while intensifying Muslims' solidarity. Worse, it could fan Islamic fundamentalism.

Unless Muslims somehow convert en masse to Christianity, demonizing Islam can only increase Muslim isolation and solidarity.

Political discussions about Islam in the Netherlands tend to lump all Muslims into one category. There are no secular or religious Muslims; no left or right; no radicals or moderates; no working class or middle class; no Shiites or Sunnis; no Turks, no Arabs, no Albanians, no Indonesians, no Iranians—just Muslims. One immediate outcome of lumping all Muslims together has been to achieve precisely that: Muslims in the Netherlands have become more unified.

Secular, liberal Muslims, especially among the Turkish-Dutch, have been pushed toward finding common cause with their conservative coreligionists. Different ethnic communities

have been brought closer together. An example is the Moroccan-Dutch and Turkish-Dutch, who had remained separate from one another since their arrival in the Netherlands. Today they are accepting the one-size-fits-all Islamic label.

It should have been self-evident that painting an entire religion as oppressive and its followers as backward could only exacerbate the ghettoization of Dutch Muslims. Then again, measures announced by the coalition government to facilitate the integration of immigrants were perhaps designed as disincentives for Muslims to remain in the Netherlands. Such measures, however, are unlikely even to bring about that outcome.

Measures to facilitate the integration of immigrants were perhaps designed as disincentives for Muslims to remain in the Netherlands.

The segments of Moroccan-Dutch and Turkish-Dutch populations that have not already inte-grated into Dutch culture and language will likely continue to live, mentally and physically, in ethnic ghettos. The well-integrated and aspirational segments of these two communities, on the other hand, are more likely than those in the ghetto to feel increasingly unwanted. If younger, educated, and better-integrated individuals start leaving the country, the Netherlands will be left with those who lack that option, thereby ensuring the perpetuation of a marginalized and disenchanted minority.

On January 10, 2010, leading figures of the Turkish-Dutch community published an open letter in the daily *Volkskrant* on precisely this issue, voicing their concerns about the increasing isolation of the young. As the educated start showing tendencies to leave, discrimination is making the remainder particularly susceptible to radical Islam.

It's Murder

Wilders did not create the anti-Islam sentiment that now pervades the ranks of the majority of the political parties and their voters—including some on the left. That trail was blazed by other, mainstream Dutch politicians before him. In fact, Wilders's success marks the culmination of a pattern evident since the late 1990s.

The first mainstream politician to court the anti-immigrant vote was a senior member of the VVD, Frits Bolkestein. The author Ian Buruma, in his 2006 book *Murder in Amsterdam: The Death of Theo van Gogh and the Limits of Tolerance*, recounts that Bolkestein told him: "One must never underestimate the degree of hatred that Dutch feel for Moroccan and Turkish immigrants. My political success is based on the fact that I was prepared to listen to such people."

Bolkestein was later appointed a commissioner of the European Union. In that post, he was able to take his anti-Islam crusade to the European level, warning against the Islamization of Europe and celebrating what he believed was a Christian,

European victory against Muslim Turks in Vienna in 1683. (Bolkestein perhaps did not know that the Ottoman army then besieging Vienna included Hungarians under the prince of Transylvania, Imre Thököly; the Moldovan army under Prince George Dusak; and Romanian and Bulgarian units, as well as a number of smaller Christian contingents. His historically creative narrative in any case fit the mood of the times.)

While Bolkestein was reminiscing about medieval battles, dour mainstream politics in the Netherlands was shaken by the appearance of a flamboyant and charismatic character who challenged the very foundations of the Dutch political establishment. Pim Fortuyn suddenly emerged in the early 2000s with a style and message that contrasted markedly with the cliquish political culture of The Hague. His main message entailed criticism of Islam and calls for tighter restrictions on immigration. But Fortuyn was more than a one-dimensional, anti-immigrant politician; he held a broadly libertarian collection of views on all aspects of politics.

Fortuyn was murdered by an animal-rights activist in 2002. This, the first political murder in the history of the Kingdom of the Netherlands, produced a nationwide shock wave. Collective disbelief and outrage reached a new high with the murder of Theo van Gogh, a contrarian author/actor/director and equal-opportunity offender whose controversial missives had targeted both Jews and Muslims. He was stabbed to death by a Moroccan-Dutch man in 2004. A note left by the murderer warned Ayaan Hirsi Ali, van Gogh's high-profile collaborator and a former Labor politician who had by then joined the VVD, that she was next in line.

Hirsi Ali, an enterprising young female Dutch politician of Somali origin, played perhaps the key role, due to her Muslim origins, in bringing anti-Islam xenophobia into the mainstream. Hirsi Ali and her carefully crafted personal story eased the lingering discomfort some felt about the targeting of Muslim immigrants: If this Muslim immigrant woman of color herself warns us about the dangers of Islam and its practitioners, it surely cannot be xenophobia; this is instead a clash between (our) democratic freedoms and (their) backward and oppressive religion.

Ruthless, Incompetent

The ranks of the VVD included another such enterprising politician, Rita Verdonk, who had raised her profile in national politics by becoming a vocal proponent of the anti-Islam viewpoint. Verdonk, who had to compete for media attention with other VVD members like Bolkestein, Hirsi Ali, and Wilders (who used to be a VVD member), managed the astonishing feat of becoming—despite being an anti-immigrant politician—the minister of immigration and integration. This allowed her to peddle her message to a bigger audience.

One of Verdonk's suggestions, as part of her 2006 proposal for a "national code of conduct," was to outlaw on the streets the use of languages other than Dutch. Also that year she managed to add her name to the "Hall of Shame" of the international monitoring group Human Rights Watch, when she tried to deport homosexual Iranian asylum seekers back to Iran.

Verdonk's anti-immigrant campaign was not an unadulterated success. In a 2006 poll, her parliamentary colleagues voted her the nation's worst politician, one who somehow managed to combine ruthlessness and incompetence. Nonetheless, her anti-Islam message resonated well with the public.

In the 2006 election she received the highest number of preference votes, surpassing VVD party leader Mark Rutte. Verdonk then tried to unseat Rutte from the party leadership. Failing to achieve that goal, she established her own party, Proud of the Netherlands, in 2008. Verdonk's popularity has not matched her ambitions, however, and her party has failed to enter parliament.

In the meantime, Rutte has shown that he can continue disseminating anti-Muslim ideas in the VVD without Verdonk and Wilders. In a 2008 interview, Rutte stated that Islam has nothing valuable to bring to the Netherlands—other than couscous. If we assume Rutte is aware that the Koran does not include recipes involving semolina granules, we can reason that his comment was not meant to attack Islam as a religion, ideology, or culture, as he might claim, but instead to attack the Muslim citizens of the Netherlands.

As Islamophobia took hold in the political mainstream, Muslim Dutch fled other parties and ended up bolstering the performance of the Dutch Labor Party in 2007 local elections. This, however, was not a welcome development as far as the Labor leader Wouter Bos was concerned. Following the election, Bos in an interview expressed unease about having immigrant representatives among municipal councilors because he viewed Muslim political culture as incompatible with Dutch values. Trying to distance his party from its growing Muslim support, Bos declared that the election results did not mean that Labor had become the party of immigrants.

Bos's message was taken up as well by the leader of the Labor party in the Amsterdam municipal council, Hannah Belliot. In an interview she sent a message to immigrants: "At home you can say whatever you want. . . . But as an economic migrant you must work, make as little use of welfare as possible, and keep quiet."

The chair of the Labor Party organization, Lilianne Ploumen, offered further support for Bos. In language that would have been unthinkable a few years before, Ploumen led calls to do away with what she saw as the failed model of tolerance. In a position paper for the Labor Party in 2008 Ploumen stated that "the criticism of cultures and religions should not be held back due to concerns about tolerance. . . . Government strategy should bring our values into confrontation with people who think otherwise." The Labor Party chair then told "newcomers to avoid self-designated victimization."

To the left of the Labor Party sits the Dutch Socialist Party (SP), which itself has not been impervious to the growing anti-immigrant mood in the Netherlands. The SP did not join the anti-Islam currents right away, but following the Bulgarian and Romanian accession to the European Union in 2007—a time when the Dutch working class was worried about a potential influx of migrants from Eastern Europe—the Socialists flirted with anti-immigrant sentiment by opposing the free movement of labor within the EU. (To be fair, some of the SP's positions can be traced to the early 1980s, when the party opposed immigration as a capitalist ploy to break working-class solidarity and bring down pay.)

Few Dissenters

Widespread Dutch acceptance of an anti-Muslim message is a little surprising in a country that not so long ago was an unwitting accessory in the massacre of around 8,000 Bosnian Muslim men and boys. In the summer of 1995, Dutch troops transferred control of the United Nations safe haven of Srebrenica to a Bosnian Serb militia besieging the town. Dutch troops then helped the Serbs separate fightingage males from the others. Women and children were moved to a nearby town, while over the following days the militia organized the systematic execution of the males. The incident was Europe's worst mass killing since World War II. The fact that the Bosnian Serb militia claimed it was protecting Christendom against Islam shows the sinister potential of such language.

Some of Wilders's ideas would be comical, on account of their bizarre reasoning and internal inconsistency, were the political stakes of his message lower. Wilders claims to stand for freedom of expression, but he wants to ban the Koran. He believes Islam and its holy book have no place in Europe—or in Western civilization—because the Koran is a fascist work identical to *Mein Kampf.* Maybe Wilders himself has not read these two books and cannot remember which region of the world spawned fascism, but of course it is not the veracity of his claims that matters. The PVV, as a far-right party seeking to expand its appeal, must make sure to disown the heritage of European fascism.

During a December 2010 official visit to Israel, Wilders called for that country to annex and settle the West Bank. He of course is not the only far-right European politician to court Israel. Filip de Winter of the Belgian party Vlaams Belang and Heinz-Christian Strache of Austria's Freedom Party have also taken their anti-Islam message there. Their professed pro-Israel views do not please all Israelis, however. Following Wilders's visit, the daily *Haaretz* portrayed these European visitors as extremists "who after trading in their Jewish demon-enemy for the Muslim criminal-immigrant model are singing in unison that Samaria is Jewish ground."

Indeed, the far right's frequent invocations of the need to defend Judeo-Christian Europe against Islam, its declarations of support for Israel, and its habit of associating Islam with fascism are tools for severing the visible links between the far right of today and that of yesterday. This helps make such parties appear more acceptable as political partners (and potentially helps restrict international criticism).

The far right's declarations of support for Israel and its habit of associating Islam with fascism are tools for severing the visible links between the far right of today and that of yesterday.

One would have expected Wilders's ideas to be scrutinized and criticized by mainstream Dutch politicians, but the majority seems either to be on the same wavelength or simply to tolerate his views. One important exception is a small minority within the CDA. The first sign of party dissent regarding partnership with the PVV was the resignation of the deputy coalition negotiator, who also quit his parliamentary seat.

More CDA unease was exposed when the new coalition program was presented to the party congress for approval. During this process, it became clear that the deputy negotiator was not the only Christian Democrat with reservations about joining forces with the far right. While there was no sign of large-scale, open dissent, 32 percent of CDA members—including some senior members—voted against the coalition agreement (while the VVD supported the agreement unanimously).

A particularly interesting split exists now within the liberal political family: While the VVD assumed the lead in bringing about the new political partnership with Wilders, the left-liberal Democrats 66 party (D66) has not shied away from voicing its dislike of Wilders and its disapproval of the governing partnership. Preceding the announcement of the new coalition program, a couple of VVD members switched allegiance to their left-liberal siblings.

While the right-liberal VVD and the left-liberal D66 share roots in the continental European liberal heritage and see eye to eye on many issues such as support for a liberal market economy, a small state, and individual rights and freedoms, it is on the issue of Islamophobia that these two liberal parties have adopted opposite positions. Meanwhile, D66's lone ally in combating anti-Muslim sentiment has been the Green-Left party, which has moved from being a single-issue environmentalist party to one that leans toward left-liberal positions on other issues.

Questioning Loyalty

Of course, no guarantee exists that the partnership among the CDA, the VVD, and Wilders's PVV will be a smooth one, or that it will last. The early days of the governing coalition were shaken by revelations that six PVV members of parliament had concealed their criminal records—including violent, sexual, and financial offenses ranging from improper relations with subordinates in the military to head-butting critics to abusing the social insurance system. These have taken some credibility away from the PVV's strong law-and-order message.

Anti-Islam sentiment might be the lowest common denominator among these parties, but in a time of economic difficulties, the parties over the coming months will have to negotiate a complex political minefield. An early example of this has been a hapless effort by Prime Minister Rutte to contain criticism of the appointment of a minis-ter of dual Dutch-Swedish citizenship to the new cabinet. Opposition to dual citizenship has been a longstanding PVV position; Wilders had objected to the inclusion of Turkish-Dutch and Moroccan-Dutch members of parliament in the previous cabinet, stating that "even if [the Moroccan-born junior minister of social affairs] had a blond mop and a Swedish passport, I would still want to see him go."

A March 2007 parliamentary motion by the PVV that questioned the loyalty of ministers with dual citizenship was supported by the right-liberal VVD. But following the swearing-in of the new cabinet in October 2010, the media reported on the dual citizenship of the new junior health minister. Rutte's response was that the Swedish citizenship of the minister was not a problem; however, it would have been different had the minister held Turkish citizenship.

The fact that Wilders himself has Indonesian immigrant roots and that he dyes his hair blond might be interesting avenues for studying the underlying psychological reasons for his xenophobic proclivities, but that is beyond the scope of this essay. What the preceding discussion shows is how changes in political discourse can make traditional xenophobia appear to be a bona fide point of view about clashing civilizations, cultures, and values.

Wilders is not the populist voice of the disen-franchised, questioning the elitist political establishment. He is part of the mainstream politics of the Netherlands, a mainstream in which the majority of the parties use the same anti-Islam language that he uses. And no matter how they try to obscure the reality, the inevitable targets of anti-Islam sentiment are individual Muslim immigrants. The message is not in fact anti-Islam. It is anti-Muslim.

Critical Thinking

1. Describe "tyranny ofthe majority."
2. Describe how anti-immigration views are mainstreamed in the Netherlands.
3. Explain the basis of PVV's influence in policymaking.

JAN ERK is an associate professor of comparative politics at the University of Leiden. He is the author of *Explaining Federalism: State, Society, and Congruence in Austria, Belgium, Canada, Germany, and Switzerland (Routledge, 2008).*

When Politics Is Not Just a Man's Game: Women's Representation and Political Engagement

JEFFREY A. KARP AND SUSAN A. BANDUCCI

1. Introduction

Past research has shown that both institutional and cultural factors are related to women's representation (e.g. Matland, 1998; Rule, 1987). However, less is known about what effects, if any, such representation has on political engagement and attitudes about the political process. Although women appear to be less interested and less engaged in politics than men, some have suggested that the presence of women as candidates and office holders can help to stimulate political engagement among women. Studies within the U.S. context have found that the presence of female candidates and representatives appears to increase women's political knowledge (Verba et al., 1997), political interest and engagement (Atkeson, 2003; Hansen, 1997), and political discussion (Campbell and Wolbrecht, 2006). In this paper, we use a cross-national approach to investigate how the election of women in national legislatures influences the political engagement and efficacy of women using data from the Comparative Study of Electoral Systems (CSES).

2. Women in the Political Arena

A number of studies have found that women are generally less interested (Jennings and Niemi, 1981; Verba et al., 1995) and less knowledgeable than men about politics (Delli Carpini and Keeter, 1996). While these studies have been focused on the U.S., similar differences also have been found elsewhere (Christy, 1987; Inglehart, 1981; Inglehart and Norris, 2003). Differential resources and lower levels of psychological involvement in politics helps to explain some of the sex differences in political activity, but there is no clear answer as to why women are less interested in politics than men. The gap between men and women in political interest remains even after controlling for socialization, resource and institutional explanations (Burns et al., 2001). In order to explain the remaining gap, some scholars have focused their attention on aspects of the political context that reflect the paucity of women in office and their subsequent invisibility in the political realm.

The presence of women either as candidates or as policymakers is thought to influence the levels of women's engagement in at least two important ways. First, women's policy issues are more likely to reach the campaign agenda when women candidates and more woman friendly policies may be passed in legislatures where women hold a higher proportion of seats (for example, see Childs and Withey, 2004). Elections have the potential to cue gender relevance when women's issues are debated in a campaign or when women run for political office (Banducci and Karp, 2000; Sapiro and Conover, 1997). There is also a link between female candidacies and social issues; while men and women are likely to employ similar campaign strategies, women are more likely to campaign on social issues (Dabelko and Herrnson, 1997).

Second, women as candidates or in positions of power may serve as a powerful symbolic cue that 'politics is not just a man's game'. Burns et al. suggest that when women live in an environment where women seek and hold public office they are more likely to know and care about politics (Burns et al., 2001, p. 383). Campbell and Wolbrecht (2006) find that the visibility of women politicians in the news inspires political engagement among adolescent girls. Similarly, Atkeson (2003) finds that women are more likely to discuss politics and have higher levels of efficacy when women ran for state-wide office in competitive races. Women are also more likely to be aware of female candidates and are more likely to be interested in the campaign when women compete (Burns et al., 2001). They estimate that the presence of even a single female contesting or occupying a state-wide public office is enough to close the gender gap in political interest and political knowledge by more than half; moreover if women were represented equally in politics, the disparity in political engagement would be wiped out (Burns et al., 2001, pp. 354–355). Other studies provide further evidence that the presence of women makes a difference. Hansen (1997) finds that the presence of a female Senate candidate on the ballot is associated with an increase in a women's attempt to persuade others to vote.

Other studies, however, have failed to find any substantive impact. Dolan (2006) examines the increased presence of women candidates in the United States over a 14-year period and finds little support that their symbolic presence translates into an increase in political attitudes and behaviours. Koch (1997) also fails to find any impact of candidate sex on political interest. The contradictory results from the studies of women candidates may result from their focus on electoral campaigns. While there may be a 'novelty factor', such effects may fade as more women run for political office. In addition, many female candidates in the U.S. are running as challengers in low visibility elections with little chance of winning given the nature of the incumbency advantage. Research on losers shows they are more likely to be dissatisfied with the political system and that repeated losses may result in lower turnout and trust (Anderson et al., 2005, pp. 68 69). This suggests that any positive impact associated with women's initial presence as candidates may be offset by dissatisfaction when women see female candidates losing.

While the evidence is mixed regarding the impact of women seeking office, there may be a mobilization effect that follows from women holding positions of political power. The presence of female candidates suggests that women can compete for political power but the presence of women in elected bodies suggests that they play a role in decision making and are able to influence policy outcomes. In this way, women may come to see representative institutions as more responsive. Past studies provide evidence for this effect. Women feel better about government when more women are included in positions of power (Mansbridge, 1999). When women are better represented on municipal legislative bodies, women are likely to be more trusting of [local] government (Ulbig, 2005). They are also likely to feel better about their representatives in Congress when they are women (Lawless, 2004).

3. Women's Descriptive Representation

The evidence discussed above on elected women is consistent with a growing amount of evidence that descriptive representation enhances political support and engagement among minority groups. While most of the research in this area is based on the U.S. it shows that having a representative of 'one's own' can increase participation (Barreto et al., 2004; Gay, 2001; Tate, 1991), reduce alienation (Pantoja and Segura, 2003), increase political efficacy (Banducci et al., 2004, 2005) and trust in government (Howell and Fagan, 1988).[1] The creation of majority minority districts in the United States and special arrangements used elsewhere are designed to facilitate minority representation (see Lijphart, 1986). A number of countries employ similar rules to help guarantee that women also gain representation. Some countries, for example, set aside a certain number of reserved seats that are only open to women (Norris, 2004). Other countries employ legislative quotas that require all parties to nominate a certain percentage of women. Parties may also set their own quotas that aim to increase the proportion of women among party candidates. In recent years more than a hundred countries have adopted legislative quotas for the selection of female candidates to political office (Krook, 2006). In June 2000 France became the first country in the world to require by law an equal number of male and female candidates for most elections (Bird, 2005). While these laws guarantee women candidates, they do not necessarily guarantee female representation. Following the implementation of the parity law in France, the proportion of elected women rose by only 1.4% to 12.3% largely because the female nominees were concentrated in unwinnable constituencies (Norris, 2004, p. 196). The use of such measures to advance the representation of women clearly follows from the *expectation* that women's representation makes a difference.

There is clear evidence that PR enhances the representation of women in national legislatures (Rule, 1994; see also Lijphart, 1999). However, mechanisms such as party quotas are shown to be more influential at increasing women's representation than proportional representation (Caul, 2001). Furthermore, the representation of women is more dependent on the responsiveness of parties to pressure to nominate women (both to appeal to voters and satisfy intra-party demands). Clearly more female candidates are a necessary precondition to higher levels of women's representation in parliaments (see Darcy et al., 1994, on this point). In new democracies, political parties play a particularly important role in helping women become candidates as women are more likely to lack the political resources necessary to reach a critical mass that would allow them to reach beyond just token representation (Matland, 1998).

The representation of women and minorities may not only provide a powerful symbolic impact that politics is a woman's game as well as a man's; it also has policy consequences. Favourable policies toward women could also prove to be influential in shaping political attitudes and behaviour. Comparative studies have focused on the influence of elected women officials, as a politically underrepresented group, on policy outcomes (Bratton and Ray, 2002; O'Regan, 2000; Schwindt-Bayer and Mishler, 2005). The objective of these studies has been to determine if there is indeed a connection between the proportion of female policy-makers and policies dealing with women's issues in various countries. Female legislators, be it through their presence in legislative bodies (Studlar and McAllister, 2002) or through the effect they have on increasing the importance given to gender equality and social welfare policy (Lovenduski and Norris,

2003) may be more effectively representing the interests of women in the electorate.

All of this suggests that women should be responsive to the context of women's representation as the political system is more responsive to them. Therefore, the election of more women to national office should have a positive influence on political attitudes and behaviour. While there have been a number of studies that have investigated the influence of women in politics on engagement, few, if any, have looked at this from a cross national perspective. In their study of gender and political participation, Burns et al. (2001, p. 349) suggest the need for a cross national approach.[2] We take this approach by examining how women's representation influences political attitudes and behaviour across a diverse range of countries that vary in terms of the number of women elected to national office.

4. Data

We rely on data from the Comparative Study of Electoral Systems (CSES) as the basis for our empirical analysis. The project involves the collaboration of national election study teams who administered a common module of questions in surveys coinciding with a national election. Module 2, administered between 2001–2006 includes a battery of questions on various forms of political participation, that include political discussion, working on a campaign, contacting politicians, voting, and political protest. The module also includes questions that ask citizens to evaluate the political process; whether leaders represent views, voters views represented well, and satisfaction with democracy. The full release of CSES Module 2 contains responses from over 50,000 respondents across 41 election studies. Of these we use data from 35 countries.[3] Eight of these countries, Belgium, Brazil, France, Korea, Mexico, Peru, the Philippines and Taiwan, employed legislative gender quotas or reserved seats in parliament at the time of the survey (IDEA).[4] All but five of the countries have electoral systems that are based on proportional representation. These systems often employ party lists that are known to facilitate women's representation. As Figure 1 reveals, the representation of women varies considerably across the CSES sample. On average, 22 percent of the members of parliament in the lower house are women. The sample includes five Nordic countries which have among the highest proportion of women represented in national parliaments in the world. Women comprise over 35 percent of the lower house in Sweden, Norway, Finland, and Denmark. In contrast, 10 countries have 15 percent or

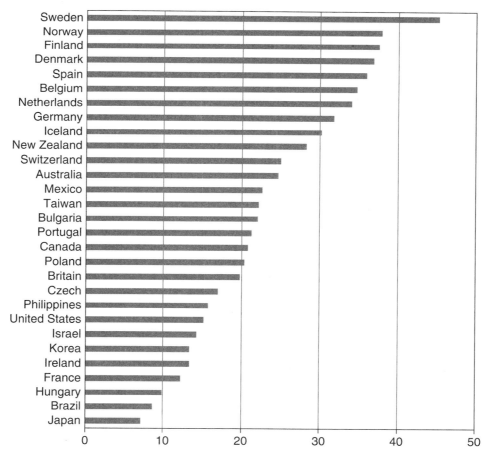

Figure 1   Women's representation in national parliaments (lower house).

Source: Inter–Parliamentary Union.

fewer women in parliament. Japan, Albania, and Brazil have the lowest levels of women in parliament. Women in established democracies are better represented than those in newer democracies; on average 26 percent of the lower house are women in established democracies compared to 17 percent in newer democracies.

Previous research leads us to expect that men are likely to be more politically engaged and more satisfied with the political process than women. Table 1 provides a summary of responses to a series of items that measure political engagement across the entire CSES sample.[5] Three items ask about long term political involvement (see Table 1). 'Over the past five years have you done any of the following things [contact, write, protest] to express your views about something the government should or should not be doing?' On average less than a fifth report having participated in any activity though this varies widely across countries.[6] In the United States, for example, 35 percent report having worked with other people who share a similar concern, while only four percent report doing so in Japan. The CSES also asked two questions about campaign involvement. Just over 20 percent of the respondents across the CSES sample report having tried to persuade others to support a particular candidate or party. As with indicators of past activity, fewer women report having done engaged in campaign related activities than men. Fewer than 15 percent report having demonstrated their support for a candidate or party by putting up a poster or attending a meeting. Similarly, fewer women report having demonstrated their support for a party or candidate by attending a meeting or putting up a poster.

Sex differences are also evident in political attitudes. The CSES includes several questions designed to measure attitudes about the democratic process. Among these is a question asking citizens whether they approve or disapprove of the way democracy works in their country. The measure frequently appears on Eurobarometer and World Values surveys and is intended to measure support for the political system (Karp et al, 2003; Norris, 1999). Table 2 summarizes responses from those who reported being either very or fairly satisfied with the way democracy works. Not only are women less likely to be engaged in the political process they are also somewhat less satisfied than men. Another question that is unique to the CSES is an item asking if elections reflect the views of citizens. We report those who responded very well or quite well. On this item there does not appear to be a difference between men and women. The CSES also asks

Table 1   Political Engagement by Sex of Respondent (%)

	Men	Women	Difference
(Have you) contacted a politician or government official either in person, or in writing, or some other way?	14.6	10.9	−3.7
(Have you) worked together with people who shared the same concern?	20.1	15.8	−4.3
(Have you) taken part in a protest, march or demonstration?	10.6	8.7	−1.9
(Did you) talk to other people to persuade them to vote for a particular party or candidate?	23.0	17.8	−5.2
(Did you) show your support for a particular party or candidate by, for example, attending a meeting, putting up a poster, or in some other way?	13.1	9.8	−3.3

Table 2   Political Attitudes by Sex of Respondent (%)

	Men	Women	Difference
On the whole, are you very satisfied, fairly satisfied, not very satisfied, or not at all satisfied with the way democracy works in [country]?	56.3	53.9	−2.4
Thinking about how elections in [country] work in practice, how well do elections ensure that the views of voters are represented by Majority Parties?	45.4	44.9	−0.5
Would you say that any of the parties in [country] represents your views reasonably well?	57.6	53.0	−4.6
Regardless of how you feel about the parties, would you say that any of the individual party leaders / presidential candidates at the last election represents your views reasonably well?	51.2	47.4	−3.8

specifically about whether citizens believe that parties and leaders represent their views.[7] Like the other items, women on average are somewhat less likely to believe that parties or leaders represent them particularly well.

The results in Tables 1 and 2 suggest that sex differentiation exists but it is unclear from these figures how responses vary across countries. It is quite possible that sizeable differences may exist in a few countries and not exist in others. To investigate this further, we examine the nature and size of sex differences in political engagement and attitudes for each of the 35 countries in the sample. We construct an indicator of engagement which takes on a value of 1 if the respondent reported taking part in any of the three prior activities listed in Table 1. Campaign activity takes on a value of 1 if the respondent reported having tried to persuade others to vote in a certain way or demonstrating support for a party or a candidate by attending a meeting or putting up a poster. As suggested earlier, these differences may result from socio-structural factors such as differences in educational attainment or labour force involvement. To control for these factors, we estimate country specific models that include education, which ranges from no education (1) to a university degree (8), age, marital status, and whether children are present in the household. We also control for whether the respondent is employed either part or full time as participation in the labour force has been found to have a positive effect on women's political activity (Welch, 1977). Given that our dependent variables are either ordinal or dichotomous, we use logit models to estimate the parameters.

Table 3 reports the estimated coefficients for respondent sex once controlling for socio-economic variables in the political engagement models.[8]. Significant sex differences are evident in 24 of the 35 countries. In all but one case, women are less likely to be engaged then men. To ease the interpretation of the logit coefficient we also provide estimates of the impact of being female (when significant) on the probability of moving from no involvement to at least one activity holding all other variables constant at their mean values. Although there are significant sex differences in many countries, the size of the differences are not substantial. The largest difference is in Albania where women are eight percent less likely than men to have engaged in at least one past activity. Similar differences are evident in France, Switzerland, the Czech Republic, the Philippines and Israel. New Zealand is the only case where women are more active than men with an estimated difference of three percent. Sex differentiation in campaign involvement is also evident in many of the same countries. The size of the differences is somewhat greater. For example, in Germany, women are nine percent less likely than men to engage in one campaign activity. No significant differences on either measure are evident in seven countries, including the Untied States, where the gender gap has been a source of concern and generated a considerable amount of scholarship.

Table 4 summarizes the results using the same model specification across the items measuring political attitudes. Fewer sex differences exist on satisfaction with democracy and assessments about elections than the items that measure attitudes toward parties and leaders. Moreover, the sex differences on assessments about elections are more inconsistent. Men give more positive assessments about elections in just three of six cases where there are significant differences. In Australia, New Zealand and France, women are more likely than men to believe that elections reflect their interests. These differences are also fairly substantial. In about half the sample, there is significant sex differentiation on attitudes about parties and leaders. In the United States, women are more likely than men to believe that leaders (who are men) reflect their views. In New Zealand, where the last two Prime Ministers have been women, men are still significantly more likely than women to respond that there is a party leader that represents their views.

5. Pooled Analysis

The descriptive representation thesis assumes that the sex differences observed above should be reduced when more women are represented in higher office. There are several explanations for why the visible presence of women in a national legislature may engage more women in the political process. Those who place an emphasis on the importance of descriptive representation claim that greater representation is not just symbolic but it also leads to policy consequences. As discussed above, there are comparative studies that find women's representation to be important in influencing the agenda in parliaments as well as policy outcomes (see Bratton and Ray, 2002; O'Regan, 2000; Schwindt-Bayer and Mishler, 2005). The positive policy outcomes for women may foster a greater sense of efficacy and this engagement. The symbolic mobilization explanation suggests that the presence of women sends a cue that politics is an appropriate activity for women.

We hypothesize that sex differences in political engagement will be minimized when more women are elected to national office. To test this hypothesis, we use the proportion of women in the lower house of parliament (as given in Figure 1). Our primary variable of interest is the cross-level interaction between the proportion of women in parliament and sex of the respondent. Several other contextual variables are included in the model as controls. We control for whether a country is a new or established democracy as political development is known to influence political engagement (Karp and Banducci, 2007) and assessments about the political process (Farrell and McAllister, 2006). Seven countries held presidential elections at the same time as legislative elections. Because concurrent presidential elections may serve to further mobilize the electorate, we have controlled for this factor. Fourteen countries in the sample are classified as new democracies.[9] Given the multilevel structure of the data, most

Table 3 Sex Differences in Political Engagement by Country

	Logit Coefficients					
	Engage			Campaign		
	Coef.		Prob.	Coef.		Prob.
Albania	−0.66	...	0.08	−0.91	...	0.15
Australia	0.12			−0.13		
Belgium	−0.41	...	0.04	−0.43	...	0.04
Brazil	−0.08			−0.14	.	
Britain	−0.17			−0.58	...	0.06
Bulgaria	−0.56	...	0.03	−0.82	...	0.03
Canada	−0.17	.	0.03	−0.55	...	0.03
Chile	−0.32	..	0.03	−0.16		
Czech	−0.59	...	0.05	−0.55	...	0.08
Denmark	−0.18	..	0.02	−0.40	...	0.05
Finland	−0.24	.	0.02	0.06		
France	−0.58	...	0.07	−0.39	...	0.06
Germany	−0.31		0.04	−0.50	...	0.09
Hungary	−0.17			−0.10		
Iceland	−0.31	...	0.04	−0.10		
Ireland	−0.05			−0.18		
Israel	−0.52	...	0.05	−0.52	...	0.08
Italy	−0.63	...	0.02	−0.59	...	0.04
Japan	−0.51	...	0.01	−0.07		
Korea	−0.38			−0.33	..	0.04
Mexico	−0.26	..	0.02	−0.21		
Netherlands	−0.31	..	0.03	−0.33	..	0.03
New Zealand	0.28	..	0.03	−0.09		
Norway	−0.22	..	0.03	−0.47	...	0.05
Peru	−0.36	...	0.03	−0.11		
Philippines	−0.43	...	0.05	−0.43	...	0.07
Poland	−0.95	...	0.03	−0.33	.	0.01
Portugal	−0.43	..	0.02	−0.05		
Romania	−0.18			−0.22		
Slovenia	−0.28			−0.73	...	0.04
Spain	−0.17			−0.23		
Sweden	−0.07			−0.03		
Switzerland	−0.39	...	0.05	−0.52		
Taiwan	−0.62	...	0.03	−0.25	...	0.02
United States	−0.02			0.05		

Variables included in the model but not shown: education, age, child in household, married, and employed. Note: Political persuasion missing in New Zealand.
***$p < 0.01$; **$p < 0.05$ *$p < 0.10$.

conventional methods of estimation will underestimate standard errors leading to a higher probability of rejection of a null hypothesis. Therefore, we proceed by estimating models using robust standard errors clustered by country. The procedure does not affect the coefficients, but it does estimate more consistent standard errors even when some of the assumptions about variance are violated. This means we can assume cases are independent across countries but not within.

Table 5 reports the results from our models of political engagement. The main effects of being female are significant and in the expected direction. These results are consistent with earlier research that found women were less engaged in politics even after controlling for socio-economic status. Education is also positive and significant. However, we find little evidence that descriptive representation matters in terms of political engagement. The coefficient for the main effects of women in

Table 4 Sex Differences in Political Attitudes by Country

	Logit Coefficients											
	Satisfaction			Elections			Party			Leader		
	Coef.		Prob.	Coef.		Prob.	Coef.		Prob.	Coef.		Prob.
Albania	0.25	.	0.06	0.05			−0.32	..	0.08	−0.25	.	0.06
Australia	0.18			0.33	...	0.08	−0.01			−0.06		
Belgium	−0.18	..	0.04	−0.25	...	0.06	N.A.			N.A.		
Brazil	−0.48	...	0.10	−0.02			−0.24	...	0.06	−0.18	..	0.04
Britain	−0.13			−0.02			−0.13			−0.12		
Bulgaria	−0.17			−0.12			−0.26	...	0.06	−0.03		
Canada	0.06			0.07			−0.50	...		−0.49	...	0.11
Chile	0.29	..	0.07	0.14			−0.09			0.11		
Czech	0.17			−0.13			0.00			−0.04		
Denmark	−0.17			0.07			−0.08			−0.06		
Finland	0.00			−0.07			−0.05			0.00		
France	−0.08			0.32	..	0.08	−0.29	..	0.07	−0.28	..	0.07
Germany	0.03			0.01			−0.18	.	0.04	0.06		
Hungary	−0.05			−0.06			0.07			−0.05		
Iceland	−0.01			−0.05			−0.19	.	0.04	−0.12		
Ireland	0.21	..	0.03	−0.18	..	0.04	−0.36	...	0.08	−0.27	...	0.06
Israel	−0.27	..	0.06	0.05			−0.14			−0.18		
Italy	−0.07			−0.18			−0.20	.	0.04	−0.09		
Japan	−0.16			−0.01			0.05			−0.24	..	0.06
Korea	−0.27	..	0.04	N.A.			−0.20			−0.26	.	0.04
Mexico	0.08			0.17			−0.06			0.14		
Netherlands	0.01			0.13			−0.20	.	0.04	N.A.		
New Zealand	0.05			0.35	...	0.09	−0.14			−0.19	.	0.04
Norway	0.09			N.A.			−0.33	...	0.05	−0.18	.	0.04
Peru	−0.24	..	0.05	−0.06			−0.13			−0.09		
Philippines	−0.17			0.06			−0.18			−0.31	..	0.06
Poland	−0.34	...	0.08	−0.12			−0.43	...	0.10	−0.55	...	0.12
Portugal	−0.26	...	0.07	−0.38	...	0.08	−0.11			−0.01		
Romania	−0.09			0.15			−0.11			−0.03		
Slovenia	−0.39	...	0.09	−0.16			−0.54	...	0.09	−0.65	...	0.12
Spain	−0.03			−0.09			−0.05			−0.14		
Sweden	−0.05			−0.17			−0.12			−0.14		
Switzerland	−0.06			−0.01			−0.66	...	0.11	−0.49	...	0.12
Taiwan	0.06			−0.16			−0.41	...	0.09	−0.31	...	0.07
United States	0.10			0.05			0.01			0.33	..	0.06

Variables included in the model but not shown: education, age, child in household, married, and employed.

$p < 0.01$; $p < 0.05$ $p < 0.10$.

parliament is not significant, indicating that citizens in countries where more women are represented in parliament are no more engaged than those where women are poorly represented. Moreover, the interaction term is not significant indicating that the gap between men and women does not vary by women's representation.

While descriptive representation does not appear to have an influence on political engagement, the results in Table 6 provide evidence that descriptive representation is associated with more positive political attitudes. In two of the four models, the proportion of women in parliament is positive and significant. Citizens in countries with greater female representation are more likely to be satisfied with the way democracy works and more likely to believe that elections reflect the views of voters.[10] The size of the effect is substantial. All other things being equal, moving from the fewest women in parliament to the most has the effect of increasing the probability of positive assessments

Table 5 Effects of Women's Representation on Political Engagement

	Logit Coefficients					
	Engage			Campaign		
	Coef.		Std. Err.	Coef.		Std. Err.
Female	−0.33	...	(0.10)	−0.34	...	(0.12)
Education	0.19	...	(0.03)	0.16	...	(0.03)
Age	0.00		(0.00)	0.00		(0.00)
Child in household	0.08	.	(0.05)	−0.01		(0.07)
Married	0.01		(0.04)	0.04		(0.06)
Employed	0.15	...	(0.06)	0.05		(0.06)
New democracy	−0.44	.	(0.26)	−0.23		(0.25)
Concurrent presidential election	0.56	..	(0.28)	0.72	...	(0.26)
Women in parliament	0.01		(0.01)	−0.01		(0.01)
Women in parliament × female	0.00		(0.00)	0.00		(0.00)
Constant 1	2.23		(0.42)	1.64		(0.39)
Constant 2	3.36		(0.43)	3.15		(0.40)
Constant 3	4.90		(0.44)			
Pseudo R^2	0.03			0.03		
Countries	35			34		
n	53,891			52,635		

Robust standard errors are in parentheses (clustered by country).

***$p < 0.01$; **$p < 0.05$; *$p < 0.10$.

about elections by close to 20 percent (from 0.38 to 0.57). These effects, however, are not conditional on the sex of the respondent. The interaction term fails to attain statistical significance in any of the models indicating that both men and women are likely to have more positive attitudes when more women are elected to parliament. Significant sex differentiation is only evident in the leadership model, indicating that women are less likely to feel that a leader reflects their views.

6. Discussion

The lack of women in political office has been the subject of much scholarly research. Advocates of increased women's representation cite many reasons for increasing descriptive representation. These reasons include more favourable policy outcomes and increased legitimacy of democratic institutions. As has been suggested in the literature on women's candidacies and representation in the U.S., the visibility of women in politics has important symbolic mobilization effects increasing the engagement of a group that has previously suffered a deficit in political activity. This increase in engagement also serves to bolster the legitimacy of democratic institutions. The comparative research presented here offers two important qualifications regarding the links between women's representation and women's political engagement: sex differentiation while statistically significant across most countries tends to be small and the positive effect of women's descriptive representation on attitudes about the political process is not confined to female citizens.

Regarding the first qualification, the scholarship on sex differentiation in political behaviourhas emphasized statistically significant differences between men and women on various measures of political engagement and attitudes. Although we find significant differences in a number of countries, the size of the gap is often modest. Our initial analysis examines sex differences in engagement across countries that remain after controlling for the usual social and structural explanations. We find that a negative and significant deficit for women is fairly consistent across countries with a few notable exceptions. The United States stands out as a counter example. While the representation of women is comparatively low, there are no significant differences between men and women in political engagement or attitudes except in one case where the gap is reversed. Furthermore, there are either negative or insignificant sex differences on assessments about whether leaders reflect the

Table 6 Effects of Women's Representation on Political Attitudes

	Logit Coefficients							
	Satisfaction		Elections		Party		Leader	
	Coef.	Std. Err.	Coef.	Std. Err.	Coef.	Std. Err.	Coef.	Std. Err.
Female	−0.07	(0.09)	0.04	(0.06)	−0.17 .	(0.10)	−0.19 ..	(0.09)
Education	0.08 ...	(0.02)	0.07 ...	(0.02)	0.09 ...	(0.02)	0.06 ..	(0.03)
Age	0.00	(0.00)	0.00	(0.00)	0.01 ..	(0.01)	0.01 ...	(0.00)
Child in household	−0.09 .	(0.05)	0.00	(0.04)	−0.13 ...	(0.05)	−0.23 ..	(0.09)
Married	0.06	(0.04)	0.05 .	(0.03)	0.20 ...	(0.04)	0.16 ...	(0.05)
Employed	0.07 .	(0.04)	−0.05	(0.04)	−0.08 .	(0.05)	0.06	(0.06)
New democracy	−1.01 ...	(0.25)	−0.41 ..	(0.19)	−0.90 ...	(0.21)	−0.49 ..	(0.23)
Concurrent presidential election	0.25	(0.25)	0.14	(0.24)	−0.11	(0.21)	0.43 .	(0.25)
Women in parliament	0.02 .	(0.01)	0.02 .	(0.01)	0.01	(0.01)	−0.01	(0.02)
Women in parliament × female	0.00	(0.00)	0.00	(0.00)	0.00	(0.00)	0.00	(0.00)
Constant 1	0.25	(0.42)	0.83	(0.36)	0.06	(0.34)	−0.06	(0.41)
Pseudo R^2	0.06		0.02		0.06		0.01	
Countries	35		33		34		35	
n	53,836		49,993		51,295		54,366	

Robust standard errors are in parentheses (clustered by country).

$^{...}p < 0.01$; $^{..}p < 0.05$; $^{.}p < 0.10$.

views of voters even when females hold leadership positions in parties that eventually lead the government such as in New Zealand and Germany.

Second, the research on women's candidacies and representation posits a link between lower levels of engagement among women to the lack of women in politics. Some have suggested that sex differences in political engagement can be reduced or even reversed when more women gain political representation. We were unable to find any evidence to support this hypothesis. Sex differences are apparent in countries with both high and low levels of women in parliament. Cross-level interaction terms between sex and women's representation were also insignificant indicating that the sex differences are not dependent on the context of representation. These findings are analogous to Lawless (2004) who failed to find any evidence that the presence of women in Congress interacted with the sex of the respondent to influence political engagement, efficacy or trust. The inability to find any differential effect for women raises questions about the importance of symbolic representation for women. While a number of studies have found that descriptive representation matters for minorities, the same cannot be said for women. One possible explanation for the differences in findings between minorities and women is that gender does not usually represent a significant political cleavage, even though in contemporary politics women tend to be left leaning (Jelen et al., 1994).

While our analysis does not find any evidence that women are more likely than men to be mobilized by women's representation, we do find that the number of women in parliament is associated with more positive evaluations of the quality of the democratic process. Scholars that examine the link women's political engagement to a gendered political context suggest that the mechanism at work is either a role model or gender cue effect whereby the presence of women indicates that political activity is acceptable for women. This mechanism implies that the effect of the number of women will affect women only. However, we find that the effect of the number of women in parliament is significant for men and women, suggesting that the mechanism by which women's representation influences evaluations is one of more favourable policy outcomes benefiting both men and women.

Notes

1. In one exception to the U.S. focus, Fennema and Tillie (1999) find that increased representation of ethnic minorities on municipal councils and voter turnout are linked. However, they also find that ethnic minorities (with the exception of Turks)

have lower rates of participation and trust than the majority population.

2. They undertook a preliminary analysis of Eurobarometer data to investigate whether there was an association between the proportion of women in a nation's parliament and women's psychological engagement in politics. Bivariate correlations revealed no significant differences.

3. Multiple datasets from Germany, Portugal and Taiwan were deposited with the CSES. We use the Portugal (2002), the Taiwan (2001) and the Germany (telephone). Election studies from Russia (2004), Kyrgyzstan (2005) and Taiwan (2004) are not included in the analysis because they were presidential rather than parliamentary elections. The French 2002 study is included in the analysis because the survey was administered between presidential and parliamentary elections.

4. Portugal adopted quotas for women in 2006.

5. Data are weighted by the sampling weight when provided by the collaborators.

6. We assume that those who gave no response did not engage in the activity.

7. Response categories are limited to yes or no.

8. Child in the household is missing in Australia and Chile and marital status is missing in Chile. These variables when missing have been set to the mean for the pooled sample

9. These countries are Albania, Brazil, Bulgaria, Chile, the Czech Republic, Hungary, Korea, Mexico, the Philippines, Poland, Peru, Romania, Slovenia and Taiwan.

10. Assessments of government performance have a substantial impacton satisfaction with democracy indicating that the measure is not necessarily tapping diffuse attitudes toward the system. Nevertheless, the exclusion of this variable from the model does not affect the results.

References

Anderson, C.J., Blais, A., Bowler, S., Donovan, T., Listhaug, O., 2005. Losers' Consent: Elections and Democratic Legitimacy. Oxford University Press, Oxford.

Atkeson, L.R., 2003. Not all cues are created equal: the conditional impact of female candidates on political engagement. *Journal of Politics* 65, 1040–1061.

Banducci, S.A., Karp, J.A., 2000. Gender, leadership and choice in multiparty systems. *Political Research Quarterly* 53, 815–848.

Banducci, S.A., Donovan, T., Karp, J.A., 2004. Minority representation, empowerment, and participation. *Journal of Politics* 66, 534–556.

Banducci, S.A., Donovan, T., Karp, J.A., 2005. Effects of minority representation on political attitudes and participation. In: Segura, G.M., Bowler, S. (Eds.), *Diversity in Democracy: Minority Representation in the United States*. University of Virginia Press, Charlottesville, pp. 193–215.

Barreto, M.A., Segura, G.M., Woods, N.D., 2004. The Mobilizing effect of majority-minority districts on Latino turnout. *American Political Science Review* 98, 65–75.

Bird, K., 2005. Lessons from France: would quotas and a new electoral system improve women's representation in Canada? In: Miller, H. (Ed.), *Steps Toward Making Every Vote Count: Electoral System Reform in Canada and its Provinces*. Broadview Press, Ontario.

Bratton, K., Ray, L., 2002. Descriptive representation, policy outcomes and municipal day-care coverage in Norway. *American Journal of Political Science* 46, 428–437.

Burns, N., Schlozman, K.L., Verba, S., 2001. *The Private Roots of Public Action: Gender, Equality, and Political Participation*. Harvard University Press, Cambridge, MA.

Campbell, D.E., Wolbrecht, C., 2006. See Jane run: women politicians as role models for adolescents. *Journal of Politics* 68, 233–247.

Caul, M., 2001. Political parties and the adoption of candidate gender quotas: a cross-national analysis. *Journal of Politics* 63, 1214–1229.

Childs, S., Withey, J., 2004. Women representatives acting for women: sex and the signing of early day motions in the 1997 British parliament. *Political Studies* 52, 552–564.

Christy, C., 1987. *Sex Difference in Political Participation: Process of Change in Fourteen Nations*. Praeger, New York.

Dabelko, K.C., Herrnson, P.S., 1997. Women's and men's campaigns for the U.S. House of Representatives. *Political Research Quarterly* 50, 121–135.

Darcy, R., Welsh, S., Clark, J., 1994. *Women, Elections and Representation*. University of Nebraska Press, Lincoln.

Delli Carpini, M.X., Keeter, S., 1996. *What Americans Know about Politics and Why it Matters*. Yale University Press, New Haven.

Dolan, K., 2006. Symbolic mobilization? the impact of candidate sex in American elections. *American Politics Research* 34, 687–704.

Farrell, D.M., McAllister, I., 2006. Voter satisfaction and electoral systems: does preferential voting in candidate-centred systems make a difference? *European Journal of Political Research* 45, 723–749.

Fennema, M., Tillie, J., 1999. Political participation and political trust in Amsterdam: civic communities and ethnic networks. *Journal of Ethnic and Migration Studies* 24, 703–726.

Gay, C., 2001. The effect of black congressional representation on political participation. *American Political Science Review* 95 (3), 589–602.

Hansen, S.B., 1997. Talking about politics: gender and contextual effects in political proselytizing. *Journal of Politics* 59, 73–103.

Howell, S.E., Fagan, D., 1988. Race and trust in government: testing the political reality model. *Public Opinion Quarterly* 52, 343–350.

Inglehart, M.L., 1981. Political interest in West European women: a historical and empirical political analysis. *Comparative Political Studies* 14, 299—326.

Inglehart, R., Norris, P., 2003. *Rising tide: gender equality and cultural change around the world*. Cambridge University Press, Cambridge.

Jelen, T.D., Thomas, S., Wilcox, C., 1994. The gender gap in comparative perspective. gender differences in abstract ideology and concrete issues in Western Europe. *European Journal of Political Research* 25, 171—186.

Jennings, M.K., Niemi, R., 1981. *Generations and Politics: A Panel Study of Young Adults and Their Parents*. Princeton University Press, Princeton.

Karp, J.A., Banducci, S.A., Bowler, S., 2003. To know it is to love it? Satisfaction with democracy in the European Union. *Comparative Political Studies* 36, 271–292.

Karp, J.A., Banducci, S.A., 2007. Political mobilization and political participation in new and old democracies. *Party Politics* 13, 217–234.

Koch, J., 1997. Candidate gender and women's psychological engagement in politics. *American Politics Research* 25, 118–133.

Krook, M.L., 2006. Reforming representation: the diffusion of candidate gender quotas worldwide. *Politics & Gender* 2, 303—327.

Lawless, J.L., 2004. Politics of presence? Congresswomen and symbolic representation. Political Research Quarterl 57, 81–99.

Lijphart, A., 1986. Proportionality by non-PR methods: ethnicrepresentation in Belgium, Cyprus, Lebanon, New Zealand, West Germany, and Zimbabwe. In: Grofman, B., Lijphart, A. (Eds.), *Electoral Laws and their Political Consequences*. Agathon Press, New York.

Lijphart, A., 1999. *Patterns of Democracy: Government Forms and Performance in Thirty-Six Countries*. Yale University Press, New Haven.

Lovenduski, J., Norris, P., 2003. Westminster women: the politics of presence. *Political Studies* 51, 84–102.

Mansbridge, J., 1999. Should blacks represent blacks and women represent women? A contingent 'yes'. *Journal of Politics* 61, 628–657.

Matland, R., 1998. Women's representation in national legislatures: developed and developing countries, 1945–1990. *Legislative Studies Quarterly* 23, 109—125.

Norris, P., 1999. Introduction: the growth of critical citizens? In: Norris, P. (Ed.), *Critical Citizens*. Oxford University Press, Oxford.

Norris, P., 2004. *Electoral Engineering: Voting Rules and Political Behavior*. Cambridge University Press, New York.

O'Regan, V., 2000. *Gender Matters: Female Policymakers' Influence in Industrialized Nations*. Praeger, Westport, CT.

Pantoja, A.D., Segura, G.M., 2003. Does ethnicity matter? descriptive representation in legislatures and political alienation among Latinos. *Social Science Quarterly* 84, 441–460.

Rule, W., 1994. Women's underrepresentation and electoral systems. PS: *Political Science and Politics* 27, 689–692.

Rule, W., 1987. Electoral systems, contextual factors and women's opportunity for election to parliament in twenty-three democracies. *The Western Political Quarterly* 40, 477–498.

Sapiro, V., Conover, P., 1997. The variable gender basis of electoral politics: gender and context in the 1992 US election. *British Journal of Political Science* 27, 497–523.

Schwindt-Bayer, L.A., Mishler, W., 2005. An integrated model of women's representation. *Journal of Politics* 67, 407–428.

Studlar, D.T., McAllister, I., 2002. Does a critical mass exist? a comparative analysis of women's legislative representation since 1950. *European Journal of Political Research* 41, 233–253.

Tate, K., 1991. Black political participation in the 1984 and 1988 presidential elections. *American Political Science Review* 85, 1159—1176.

Ulbig, S.G. 2005. *Political Realities and Political Trust: Descriptive Representation in Municipal Government*. Paper presented at the 2005 Annual Meeting of the Southwestern Political Science Association.

Verba, S., Schlozman, K.L., Brady, H., 1995. *Voice and Equality: Civic Volunteerism in American Politics*. Harvard University Press, Cambridge, MA.

Verba, S., Burns, N., Schlozman, K.L., 1997. Knowing and caring about politics: gender and political engagement. *Journal of Politics* 59, 1051–1072.

Welch, S., 1977. Women as political animals? A test of some explanations for male-female political participation differences. *American Journal of Political Science* 2, 711–730.

Critical Thinking

1. Explain why it is important to increase participation.

2. How does women's representation increase participation?

3. What is the effect of women representatives on policies?

Acknowledgments—An earlier version of this paper was presented at the Conference on Contextual Effects in Electoral Research, European University Institute, Florence, Italy. November 30–December 1, 2006. We would like to thank conference participants for helpful comments.

The Impact of Electoral Reform on Women's Representation

PIPPA NORRIS

Inclusive Democracy

Recent decades have witnessed growing demands for the inclusion and empowerment of women and minorities in elected office. Feminist theorists suggest that the presence of women leaders facilitates the articulation of different perspectives on political issues, where elected representatives are not just 'standing as' women but also 'acting for' women as a group (Phillips, 1995, 1993; Mansbridge, 1999). An accumulating body of evidence in North America, Scandinavia and Western Europe suggests that, while not transforming parliaments, women legislators do raise distinctive concerns and issue priorities (Duerst-Lahti and Kelly, 1995; Karvonnen and Selle, 1995; Dolan, 1997; Swers, 1993, 2001; Tremblay, 1993; Reingold, 2000; Tremblay and Pelletier, 2000; Carroll, 2001). If so, then the under-representation of women in parliament may have important consequences for the public policy agenda and for the articulation of women's interests, as well as for the legitimacy of democratic bodies. Inclusiveness is widely regarded as one of the key values of democratic polities, so that all major social cleavages have a voice in the policy-making process, whether the politically relevant groups are defined by gender, ethnicity, region, socioeconomic status, age, or education. The inclusion of women is one—but only one dimension—of social diversity.

The broad normative claim underlying these arguments is that legislatures should be more like the societies they serve, reflecting the politically relevant electoral cleavages. In this way, elected bodies meet the criteria of 'descriptive' representation, as Hanna Pitkin (1967) termed this notion. While these claims are widely recognized and acknowledged today, controversy remains about the most effective and appropriate ways to achieve these goals, as well as the priority which should be given to geographic, class, ethnic, and gender representation, where claims may conflict.

By these criteria, most parliaments worldwide fail to reflect the proportion of women in the electorate. This pattern persists, even in established democracies, despite trends in the home, family, school, and work-force transforming women and men's lives during the post-war era, as well as the growth of the more multicultural societies (Inglehart and Norris, 2003). NGOs, parties, and international agencies have often expressed the need for equal opportunities for all citizens in appointed and elected positions in public life. Governments have signed official National Action Plans and international conventions designed to establish conditions of gender equality in the public sphere, exemplified by the 1979 Convention on the Elimination of All Forms of Discrimination against Women (CEDAW) favoring the principle of equal opportunities in public life, ratified by 163 nations. The *1995 UN Beijing Platform for Action* expressed commitment to the empowerment of women based on the conviction that: *'Women's empowerment and their full participation on the basis of equality in all spheres of society, including participation in the decision-making process and access to power, are fundamental for the achievement of equality, development and peace.'* The UN Platform for Action (1995) explicitly aims for a 50-50 gender balance in all areas of society, and its analysis places full participation in decision-making in the foremost role.

In practice, however, multiple barriers continue to restrict the advancement of women in elected office. According to estimates by the United Nations Development Program (2002), women represent less than one-tenth of the world's cabinet ministers and one-fifth of all sub-ministerial positions. Out of 193 nations worldwide, only nine women are at the pinnacle of power as elected heads of State or Government. Despite some redoubtable and well-known world leaders, only 39 states have *ever* elected a woman President or Prime Minister. The Inter-Parliamentary Union (2005) estimates that 6,722 women currently sit in both houses of parliament worldwide, representing 15.3% of all members. This is a rise from 9% in 1937 yet if growth is maintained at this level (0.37% per annum), a simple linear projection predicts that women parliamentarians will achieve parity with men at the turn of the 22nd century.

Regional variations highlight the sharp contrasts in the position of women in elected office. Women parliamentarians do best in the Nordic nations, constituting 40% of MPs in the lower house. In Sweden, for example, women are half of all Cabinet Ministers and 149 female members sit in the Riksdag (43%), quadrupling from 10% in 1950. Women political leaders have also moved ahead in the other Nordic countries (Bergqvist *et al.*, 1999). In other global regions the proportion of women members of parliament is usually lower, including in the Americas (19%), Europe excluding the Nordic states (17%), Asia (15%), Sub-Saharan Africa (16%), and the Pacific (11%). Despite some recent reforms in Morocco, Bahrain and Iraq, the

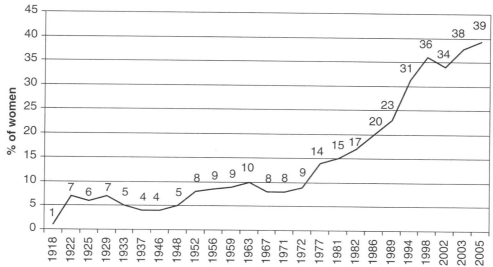

Figure 1   The growth in the proportion of women members in the Tweede Kamer, 1918–2005.

Source: Constructed from tables in Chapter 5 of Monique Leijenaar (2004).

worst record remains in Arab states, where women are 9% of elected representatives. Women continue to be barred by law from standing for parliament in Qatar, Saudi Arabia, Oman, and the United Arab Emirates. The level of human development and the length of democratic experience may be important for achieving gender equality in parliaments, but these are neither necessary nor sufficient factors; in Rwanda, Mexico, Lithuania, and the Czech Republic, for example, women politicians are more successful than in the United States and Japan, two of the most affluent democracies in the world.

In the light of these global patterns, the contemporary record of the Netherlands is impressive, as one of the countries that has led the world in the representation of women in parliament. The Inter-Parliamentary Union (2005) ranks the Netherlands sixth highest worldwide in the proportion of women in parliament, beaten only by the Scandinavian nations with a long tradition of gender equality in political leadership, as well as more recently by Rwanda. Nor is this a temporary phenomenon; the Netherlands has consistently been ranked fifth or sixth in this world league table for at least two decades. The proportion of women in the Tweede Kamer was fairly low from 1922 until 1972, and it then grew steadily in successive elections (with the exception of a slight dip in 2002), rising to 59 women in the lower house in 2005 or 39.3% (see Figure 1) (for details, see Leijenaar, 2004). This figure is high when compared against the global picture, and it is almost double the EU average (22.7%).

Gender is not the only criteria for the inclusiveness of representative bodies, by any means. The class and educational background of elected members have long been a matter of concern in many established democracies, with the under-representation of manual workers, and in recent years the issue of including more ethnic minority representatives has arisen in importance. In this regard, compared with size of the foreign-born population, ethnic minorities are represented almost proportionally in the Tweede Kamer. An analysis of the biographies of current members of the House of Representatives, classified by place

of birth, indicates that 13 out of 150 members were born overseas (8.7%)[1]. This compares with a foreign-born population in the Netherlands estimated by the OECD (2005) to include 1.7 million people or 10.6% of the total population.

Given this record, if the Netherlands introduces some single-member districts, the challenge would be how to maintain and preserve gender diversity in elected office. Three main policy options are open for consideration by parliament including the basic *type of electoral system* that is selected, the introduction of a *statutory gender quota* regulating the candidate selection process used by all parties, and the use of *reserved seats* for women in the legislature. Another alternative is that political parties can employ *voluntary gender quotas* in their candidate selection processes. What are the pros and cons of these options?

The Impact of Electoral Systems

As discussed earlier in this volume, electoral reform involves multiple alternatives ranging from more modest amendments to the current Dutch system of nationwide PR to outright revision. What would be the consequences of reform for the representation of women?

A series of studies since the mid-1980s have confirmed that more women have usually been elected to parliament under party list proportional representation (PR) than under majoritarian electoral systems (Norris, 1985; Matland, 1998; Reynolds, 1999; Kenworthy and Malami, 1999; Siaroff, 2000; Moser, 2001). This pattern holds both within established democracies and also across a broader range of developing societies worldwide. Within proportional electoral systems, the mean district magnitude has commonly been found to be a particularly important factor, with more women usually elected from systems using large multimember constituencies.

The comparison in Table 1, without any controls, illustrates how women are far more successful under PR list systems. The results demonstrate that today around the globe roughly twice as many women get elected to national parliaments under PR

Table 1 Women's Representation by Type of Electoral System, 2005

	% of Women in the Lower House of Parliament, 2000	Number of Nations
All majoritarian	10.5	72
Alternative vote	8.5	4
Block vote	7.4	10
Second Ballot	12.0	20
First-past-the-post	11.4	35
Single non-transferable vote	3.1	3
All combined	13.6	36
Combined independent	12.6	27
Combined dependent	16.8	9
All proportional	19.6	67
Single transferable vote	11.3	2
Party list	19.9	64
Total	14.3	175

Note: The percentage of women in the lower house of national parliaments 2005, 175 nations worldwide. Note that six nations did not hold any elections. For the classification of electoral systems see Norris (2004).

Source: Data on the proportion of women in the lower house of parliament calculated from Inter-Parliamentary Union (2005).

(19.6%) than under majoritarian electoral systems (10.5%). 'Combined' or 'mixed' electoral systems fall between these poles (13.6%). As a simple rule, therefore, *women proved almost twice as likely to be elected under proportional as under majoritarian electoral systems.* In 'combined' electoral systems, women candidates enjoy greater success in the more proportional 'combined-dependent' electoral systems (16.8%) rather than in the 'combined-independent' systems (12.6%).

The comparative evidence has been confirmed in multiple studies but nevertheless the cross-national pattern could be attributed to many other factors associated with PR, however, for example the type of colonial heritage, political culture, the party system, or the level of democratic development of the countries that chose this type of electoral system. Another way to examine the evidence is to consider within country comparisons of simultaneous contests in 'combined' electoral systems where the results for women and men are analyzed by the type of ballot. Here the impact of the electoral system is also confirmed, although the gender differences are usually weaker. As shown in Table 2, in five countries using combined systems, slightly more women were usually elected from the PR party lists than from the single-member districts. It should be emphasized that this contrast is most evident in Italy and Germany; in the former, for example, women are 8.8% of those elected through the SMDs but they are 18.6% of the members of the Chamber of Deputies elected via the party lists in multimember districts.

Comparisons can also be drawn with how many women are elected where the electoral system has changed within a particular country, such as New Zealand (NZ). The proportion of women in the NZ parliament grew from 16.5% in 1990 to 21.2% in 1993, immediately after the switch from the SMD plurality to the MMP system, before jumping to 29% in 1996, since when the proportion has largely stabilized (Human Rights Commission, 2004). Nevertheless

Table 2 The Proportion of Women MPs in Mixed Electoral Systems in Five Nations

	Single Member Districts		Multi Member Districts	
	N Women	% Women	N Women	% Women
Lithuania 2004	13/71	18.3	16/70	22.8
New Zealand 2002	19/62	30.6	16/51	31.3
Italy 2005	43/475	8.8	30/161	18.6
Monaco 2003	3/16	18.8	2/8	25.0
Germany 1998	76/328	23.2	130/341	38.1

Sources: Lithuania, http://www.vrk.lt/2004/seimas/rezultatai/rez_isrinkti_e_20_1.htm;Italy, http://english.camera.it/;New Zealand, http://www.ps.parliament.govt.nz/mps.htm;Monaco, http://assembly.coe.int;Germany, http://www.bundeswahlleiter.de/wahlen/download/abc2002e.pdf.

it remains difficult to establish that this development was directly attributable to electoral reform *per se,* given many other simultaneous changes in the political system, coupled with the observation in Table 2 that almost the same proportions of women have been elected to the New Zealand parliament from the SMDs and the party lists in the multimember districts (Table 3).

Despite the general cross-national patterns, considerable variations in the representation of women were also clear within each major electoral family, as shown by the distribution shown in Figure 2. More women were elected in certain majoritarian electoral systems, such as in Australia and Canada, than in some other highly proportional party list systems, as exemplified by Israel. Although there is a strong and consistent association, by itself the basic type of electoral system is neither a necessary nor a sufficient condition to guarantee women's representation.

These variations within families of electoral systems could be attributed to many intervening conditions, including:

- Average district magnitude (the mean number of candidates per district);
- Levels of proportionality;
- The use of statutory and voluntary gender quotas;
- Party ideologies (with parties on the left found to be generally more sympathetic towards gender equality); and
- The type of party organization.

Table 3 Statutory Gender Quotas in Use Worldwide

Country	Date of law	Gender quota %	Legislative body	Electoral system	List open or closed	% women MPs before law (i)	% women MPs after law (ii)	Change (i)-(ii.)
France	1999	50	Lower	Majoritarian	—	11	12	+1
Costa Rica	1997	40	Unicameral	Proportional	Closed	14	19	+5
Belgium	1994	33	Lower	Proportional	Open	13	23	+5
Bosnia & Herzegovina	2001	33	Lower	Proportional	Open		14.3	
Argentina	1991	30	Lower	Proportional	Closed	6	27	+21
Peru	1997	30	Unicameral	Proportional	Open	11	13	+7
Venezuela	1993	30	Lower	Combined	Closed	6	13	+7
Panama	1997	30	Unicameral	Combined	Closed	3	10	+2
Venezuela	1993	30	Senate	Combined	Closed	3	9	+2
Bolivia	1997	30	Lower	Combined	Closed	11	12	+1
Mexico	1996	30	Senate	Combined	Closed	15	16	+1
Bolivia	1997	30	Senate	Combined	Closed	4	4	0
Brazil	1997	30	Lower	Proportional	Open	7	6	−1
Mexico	1996	30	Lower	Combined	Closed	17	16	−1
Indonesia	2003	30	Lower	Proportional	Closed	9	N/a	N/a
Macedonia	2001	30	Lower	Combined	Closed		17.5	
Serbia	2002	30	Lower	Proportional	Open	7.5	N/a	N/a
Dominican Rep	1997	25	Lower	Proportional	Closed	12	16	+4
Ecuador	1997	20	Unicameral	Combined	Open	4	15	+11
Paraguay	1996	20	Senate	Proportional	Closed	11	13	+7
Paraguay	1996	20	Lower	Proportional	Closed	3	3	0
Korea, North	—	20	Lower	Majoritarian	—		20.1	
Philippines	1995	20	Lower	Combined	Closed		17.3	
Armenia	1999	5	Lower	Combined	Closed		3.1	
Nepal	1990	5	Lower	Majoritarian	—		5.9	
Iraq[a]	2005	25	Lower	Proportional	Closed		31.5	
Average		*30*				*10*	*14*	*+4*

Note: *Statutory gender quotas* for the lower house of national parliaments are defined as legal regulations specifying that each party must include a minimum proportion of women in their candidate lists. Change is estimated based on the percentage of women MPs in the parliamentary election held immediately before and after implementation of the gender quota law.
[a]The Iraqi Transitional National Assembly.
Sources: Htun (2001); Htun and Jones (2002); International IDEA.

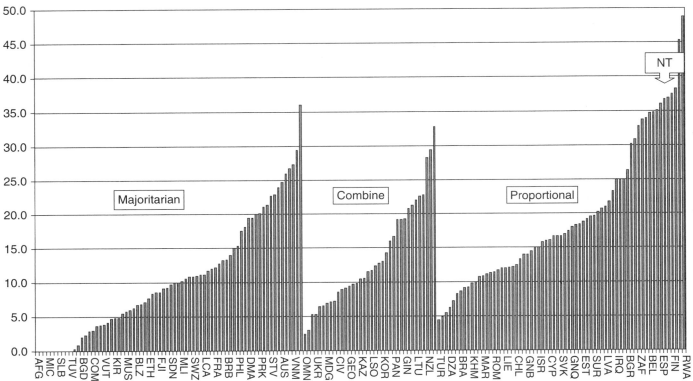

Figure 2   Countries classified by electoral systems and ranked by the percentage of women in the lower house of parliament, 2005.

Source: Inter-parliamentary Union (2005).

To understand the reasons for the outcome, it helps to distinguish the different stages in the candidate selection process, using the model illustrated schematically in Figure 3. The type of electoral system, and the use of statutory quotas or reserved seats, regulates the context of the candidate selection process used within each party. The 'demand' of party selectors and the 'supply' of candidates interact to generate the pool of parliamentary candidates. In the final stage, demand by the electorate (for parties or candidates) determines the composition of parliament.

Given this process, we can theorize that women usually benefit from PR for three possible reasons: party vote maximizing strategies; patterns of incumbency turnover; and the implementation of positive action strategies.

Vote-Maximizing Strategies

Under proportional systems, each party presents the public with their collective list of candidates for each multimember district. As such, parties have an electoral incentive to maximize their collective appeal in such lists by including candidates representing all the major social cleavages in the electorate, for example, by including both middle class professionals and blue-collar workers, rural farmers and urban shopkeepers,

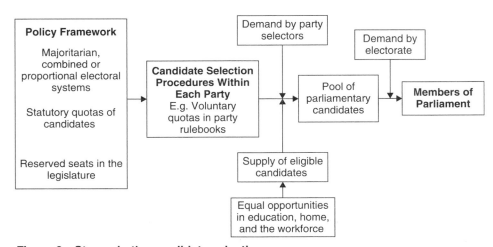

Figure 3   Stages in the candidate selection process.

Catholics, Protestants and Muslims, as well as women and men. Multimember districts encourage collective party accountability for the complete list of candidates. The larger the district, the longer the candidate list, and the easier it is for the party to juggle all forms of social considerations to create a 'balanced' ticket. The smaller the list of candidates, the more difficult it is to include all groups. Where parties have to nominate a slate of candidates for a multimember district, the exclusion of any major social sector, including women or minorities, could signal discrimination, and could therefore risk an electoral penalty at the ballot box. By contrast in first-past-the-post systems, parliamentary candidates are selected to run within each single member district. Where the selection process is in the hands of the local constituency party, this creates minimal incentive for each particular constituency to pick a ticket that is 'balanced' at the district or national level. Local party members often want a representative who will maximize their chances of winning in that constituency, irrespective of the broader consequences for the party or parliament (Norris and Lovenduski, 1995). The selection of the default option (i.e., a candidate reflecting the traditional characteristics and qualifications of previous parliamentarians) may be expected to predominate in many cases, as the rational vote-maximizing strategy designed to minimize electoral risks. Where parliaments remain disproportionately male, a risk-averse strategy increases the probability that in SMDs, selectorates will probably select another man.

Incumbency Turnover

Moreover rates of incumbency turnover play a role. One major barrier to women and minority candidates lies through the strength of incumbency, with elected officials returned over successive contests, due to the personal vote advantages of familiarity, name recognition, and media attention, as well as greater financial and organizational resources that accompany legislative office (Somit *et al.*, 1994). In many contests the key challenge facing women and minorities is not just becoming a candidate, but contesting a winnable seat in single-member districts, or being ranked near the top of the party list of candidates in PR systems. Matland and Studlar's (2004) comparison of election to the lower house of the national parliament in 25 established democracies from 1979 to 1994 found that on average about two-thirds of all incumbents were returned from one general election to the next, including 66% in PR electoral systems and 70% in majoritarian elections. This difference is modest but it could generate slightly more opportunities for challengers, including 'outgroups' in the pipeline for elected office. In Britain, for example, it was Labour's landslide in 1997, coupled with the use of positive action placing women in target seats, which doubled the number of women in the UK House of Commons. As incumbents, Labour women MPs were re-elected in the 2001 British general election, despite the fact that the original positive action strategy was discontinued. In the United States, Carroll and Jenkins (2001) established that from 1998 to 2000 women increased their numbers in states with term limitations more than elsewhere, although this effect was reversed in states like California where women representatives have already made much progress. In general, 85% of incumbent congressional representatives have been returned in successive US election from the late 1970s to the mid-1990s, reducing the opportunities for new candidates (Caress 1999).

Implementation of Positive Action Strategies

Party list PR also facilitates the implementation of positive action strategies used for women and minorities. Candidate quotas can also be used under majoritarian electoral systems as well, as shown by the British Labour party, but it can be harder to implement quotas within single member districts than within party lists. Reserved seats can also be used within majoritarian electoral systems, for example in New Zealand for Maoris prior to reform, but reserved seats have been less commonly employed in most established democracies. For all these reasons, PR systems are more likely to produce more women in parliament than majoritarian electoral systems. In terms of the options being debated for the Dutch electoral system, the introduction of an open list system would probably have minimal impact upon gender equality. The adoption of a combined-dependent system with SMDs, such as that used in Germany, would probably reduce the proportion of women in the Tweede Kamer, as would the de Graaf proposal of a combined-dependent system with SNTV, for all the reasons already discussed.

Statutory Quotas

If the Netherlands opts for an electoral system with some single member districts, then what else could be done to promote women's opportunities in parliament? One option would be for parliament to introduce statutory quotas specifying that women or minorities must constitute a specified minimal proportional of parliamentary candidates within each party. *Statutory* quotas are implemented by law and they would apply to all parties contesting an election. This strategy should be distinguished from *voluntary* quotas, which are decided by each party and implemented by the internal party regulations and rule books. Quotas can be specified for women and men, and for other relevant forms of ethnic identity, such as nationality, language, religion, and for indigenous groups. Statutory gender quota laws have been applied to European and Latin American elections (see Table 4), as well as for appointments to public bodies and consultative committees, for example in Finland and Norway (Peters *et al.,* 1999; Caul, 2001; Dahlerup, 2005).

As shown by the last column in Table 4, monitoring short-term change in the election immediately before and after passage of the law, in some countries, and in some elections, the introduction of statutory gender quotas appears to have worked far more effectively than in other cases. Hence the substantial rise in women in parliament found in Argentina, and the modest growth in Peru and Belgium, but minimal progress evident in France, Mexico, or Brazil. Why is this? The effective implementation of statutory gender quotas depends upon multiple factors, including most importantly:

- How the statutory mechanisms are put into practice;
- The level of the gender quota specified by law;

Table 4   Reserved Seats for Women Used in the Lower House of Parliaments Worldwide

	Election	Total Number of MPs in the Lower House	Number of Seats Reserved for Women	% Of seats Reserved for Women	Appointed or Elected
Uganda	2001	292	56	19.1	Indirectly elected
Pakistan	2002	357	60	16.8	Elected
Tanzania	2000	295	48	16.2	Appointed
Zimbabwe	2000	274	37	13.5	Appointed
Djibouti	2003	65	7	10.7	Elected
Bangladesh	2001	300	30	10.0	Appointed
Sudan	2000	360	35	9.7	Elected
Morocco	2002	325	30	9.2	Elected
Botswana	1999	44	2	4.5	Appointed
Lesotho	1998	80	3	3.8	Appointed
Taiwan	1996	334	Varies	Varies	Elected
Afghanistan	2005	249	68	27	Elected

Note: Reserved seats for women in the lower house of the national parliament are defined as those that by law can only be filled by women, either by appointment or election. It should also be noted that in Nepal three seats are reserved for women in the upper house, according to the 1990 constitution.

Sources: The Electoral Institute of Southern Africa (EISA), www.eisa.org.za; *Elections Around the World*, www.electionworld.org; International IDEA, www.IDEA.int.

- Whether the rules for party lists regulate the rank order of women and men candidates;
- Whether party lists are open or closed;
- The mean district magnitude;
- Good faith compliance by parties; and also
- The penalties associated with any failure to comply with the law.

Positive action policies alter the balance of incentives for the party selectorate. Where these laws are implemented, then selectors need to weigh the potential penalties and benefits if they do or do not comply. Selectors may still prefer the default option of nominating a male candidate under certain circumstances, for example if the laws are designed as symbolic window-dressing more than as *de facto* regulations; if the regulation specify that a certain proportion of women have to be selected for party lists but they fail to specify their rank order so that female candidates cluster in unwinnable positions at the bottom of the list; or if any sanctions for non-compliance are weak or nonexistent. There may also be lagged effects, as parties adapt gradually to the new regulatory environment and as incumbents retire. As in many attempts to alter incentive structures, the devil lies in the practical details and superficially similar legislative policies may turn out to have different consequences in different nations.

Reserved Seats

An alternative policy option for the Dutch parliament would be the introduction of some reserved seats that would be only open to contestation by women candidates. This policy has been adopted to boost women's representation in local government in India, as well as to represent Maoris in New Zealand. Reserved seats have also been used in some developing nations in Africa and South Asia, particularly those with a Muslim culture, including for the lower house in Morocco, Afghanistan, Bangladesh, Pakistan, Botswana, Taiwan, Lesotho, and Tanzania (see Table 4) (Reynolds, 2005).

One advantage of this mechanism is that it guarantees a minimum number of women in elected office, without the uncertainty that arises from the implementation of statutory quotas. Critics argue, however, that the use of reserved seats may be a way to appease, and ultimately sideline, women. Being elected through this route does not necessarily mean that women would be given independent decision-making power or equal status as elected members. Where women members are appointed to reserved seats by the president or chief executive, they lack an independent electoral or organizational base, and this may reinforce control of parliament by the majority party (Tinker, 2004). Nevertheless against these arguments, where women standing for reserved seats face free and fair contested elections then they have an independent electoral base.

Voluntary Gender Quotas

An alternative policy concerns the use of voluntary gender quotas within specific parties. In this regard, while party leaders can take the initiative, this is not a matter which parliament could implement through electoral law. Rules, constitutions, and internal regulations determined within each party are distinct from electoral statutes enforceable by the courts. Parties in the Netherlands have used affirmative action strategies for women although, with the exception of Labour and Green Left, most have been reluctant to adopt quotas (Leijenaar, 2004).

Voluntary gender quotas are widely used by many parties in Scandinavia, Western Europe, and Latin America, and Communist parties in Central and Eastern Europe employed them in the past (Caul, 2001; Dahlerup, 2005).

International IDEA's *Global Database of Quotas for Women* (2005) estimates that 181 parties in 58 countries use gender quotas for electoral candidates for national parliaments. The effects of these measures can be analyzed by focusing on their use within the European Union. By 2000, among 76 relevant European parties (with at least 10 members in the lower house), almost half (35 parties) used gender quotas, and 24 of these have achieved levels of female representation in the lower house of parliament of over 24%. Among the European parties using gender quotas, on average one-third (33%) of their elected representatives were women. By contrast, in the European parties without gender quotas, only 18% of their members of parliament were women.

Nevertheless it might be misleading to assume any simple 'cause' and 'effect' at work here, since parties more sympathetic towards women in public office may also be more likely to implement gender quotas. European parties of the left commonly introduced voluntary gender quotas during the 1980s, including Social Democratic, Labour, Communist, Socialist and Greens parties, before the practice eventually often spread to other parties.

Moreover, the 'before' and 'after' test suggests that the effects of voluntary gender quotas within parties vary substantially, exemplified by the outcome in Scandinavia, Germany, and Britain. In general there are fewer guarantees that voluntary positive action strategies will work, compared with the legal policies of statutory quotas or reserved seats. At the same time, letting parties decide whether to implement gender quotas gives them greater control over these matters and preserves their autonomy as voluntary associations in civil society.

Conclusions and Summary

International agencies, governments, parties and groups concerned with increasing the representation of women and minorities have advocated a range of initiatives designed to break through the barriers in elected office. The evidence presented in this study provides further confirmation that the basic type of electoral system influences the inclusiveness of elected bodies. Women are generally more successful in being nominated and elected under proportional electoral systems than under combined or majoritarian systems. Under PR, especially systems with a large district magnitude, parties have considerable incentive to create a balanced list of candidates, to avoid any electoral penalties from the appearance of discrimination against any particular group. This electoral incentive is absent among local selectors with single member districts in majoritarian elections, where each local party can choose an individual candidate without any collective responsibility for balancing the social profile of the parliamentary party at national level.

The general conclusion is that reforms, in the Netherlands, that amend the nationwide system of proportional representation need to consider their impact upon gender equality. In particular, the introduction of a combined dependent system with some SMDs will probably serve to reduce the proportion of women in the Tweede Kamer. The adoption of a combined dependent system with SNTV (the De Graaf proposal) would probably also reduce the proportion of women in the Tweede Kamer, although probably to a lesser extent than the adoption of a combined dependent system with SMDs. What matters for women's representation with the De Graaf proposal would be the mean size of the district magnitude used for the SNTV seats. Other reforms that are under debate in the Netherlands include the use of open lists, which would probably have little, if any, systematic effect upon women's election.

To compensate for any anticipated reduction in the proportion of women in parliament, reformers should also consider implementing other compensatory policies that have proved effective for maintaining social diversity in elected office. Parliament should consider the use of statutory quotas regulating the candidate selection processes in all parties or the use of reserved seats in the legislature, while parties should consider the implementation of voluntary quotas with higher levels in party rulebooks.

References

Bergqvist, C., Borchorst, A., Christensen, A., Ramstedt-Silén, V., Raaum, N.C. and Styrkársdóttir, A. (eds.) (1999) *Equal Democracies? Gender and Politics in the Nordic Countries,* Olso: Scandinavian University Press.

Caress, A.N. (1999) 'The influence of term limits on the electoral success of women', *Women & Politics* 20(3): 45–63.

Carroll, S.J. and Jenkins, K. (2001) 'Unrealized opportunity? Term limits and the representation of women in state legislatures', *Women & Politics* 23(4): 1–30.

Carroll, S.J. (ed.) (2001) *The Impact of Women in Public Office,* Indiana: University of Indiana Press.

Caul, M. (2001) 'Political parties and the adoption of candidate gender quotas: a cross- national analysis', *The Journal of Politics* 63(4): 1214–1229.

Council of Europe (2000) 'Positive Action in the Field of Equality Between Women and Men', Final report of the Group of Specialists on Positive Action in the field of equality between women and men (EG-S-PA).

Dahlerup, D. (ed.) (2005) *Women, Quotas and Politics,* New York: Routledge.

Dolan, J. (1997) 'Support for women's interests in the 103rd Congress: the distinct impact of congressional women', *Women & Politics* 18(4): 81–94.

Duerst-Lahti, G. and Kelly, R.M. (eds.) (1995) *Gender, Power, Leadership and Governance,* University of Michigan Press.

Human Rights Commission (2004) *New Zealand Census of Women's Participation,* Wellington, New Zealand.

Htun, M. (2001) 'Electoral rules, parties, and the election of women in Latin America' Paper for the Annual Meeting ofthe American Political Science Association, San Francisco, 30 August 2001.

Htun, M. and Jones, M. (2002) 'Engendering the Right to Participate in Decision-making: Electoral Quotas and Women's Leadership in Latin America' in N. Craske and M. Molyneux (eds.) *Gender and the Politics of Rights and Democracy in Latin America,* London: Palgrave.

Inglehart, R. and Norris, P. (2003) *Rising Tide: Gender Equality and Cultural Change*, New York: Cambridge University Press.

International IDEA *Global Database of Quotas for Women*, Available at www.idea.int.

International, IDEA (2005) *Global Database of Quotas for Women*, http://www.idea.int/quota/index.cfm.

Inter-Parliamentary Union (2005) *Women in National Parliaments*, Available at www.ipu.org 30 June 2005.

Inter-Parliamentary Union (2005) *Women in Parliament Database*, Available at www.ipu.org.

Karvonnen, L. and Selle, P. (1995) *Women in Nordic Politics*, Aldershot: Dartmouth.

Kenworthy, L. and Malami, M. (1999) 'Gender inequality in political representation: a worldwide comparative analysis', *Social Forces* 78(1): 235–269.

Latner, M. and McGann, A.J. (2004) 'Geographical representation under proportional representation: the cases of Israel and the Netherlands', Paper at Scholarship Repository, University of California; http://repositories.cdlib.org/csd/04–09.

Leijenaar, M. (2004) *Political Empowerment of Women: The Netherlands and Other Countries*, Leiden: Martinus Nijhoff Publishers.

Lovenduski, J. and Norris, P. (1993) *Gender and Party Politics*, London: Sage.

Mansbridge, J. (1999) 'Should blacks represent blacks and women represent women? A contingent 'yes'', *Journal of Politics* 61(3): 628–657.

Matland, R. (1998) 'Women's representation in national legislatures: developed and developing countries', *Legislative Studies Quarterly* 23(1): 109–125.

Matland, R. and Studlar, D. (2004) 'Determinants of legislative turnover: a cross-national analysis', *British Journal of Political Science* 34: 87–108.

Moser, R.G. (2001) 'The effects of electoral systems on women's representation in post-communist states', *Electoral Studies* 20(3): 353–369.

Norris, P. (1985) 'Women in European legislative elites', *West European Politics* 8(4): 90–101.

Norris, P. (1998) *Passages to Power*, Cambridge: Cambridge University Press.

Norris, P. (2004) *Electoral Engineering*, Cambridge: Cambridge University Press.

Norris, P. and Lovenduski, J. (1995) *Political Recruitment: Gender, Race and Class in the British Parliament*, Cambridge: Cambridge University Press.

OECD (2005) *Trends in International Migration*, Paris: SOPEMI, OECD: http://stats.oecd.org.

Peters, A., Seidman, R. and Seidman, A. (1999) *Women, Quotas, and Constitutions: A Comparative Study of Affirmative Action for Women under American, German and European Community and International Law*, The Hague: Kluwer Law International.

Phillips, A. (ed) (1998) *Feminism and Politics*, Oxford: Oxford University Press.

Phillips, A. (1995) *The Politics of Presence*, Oxford: Clarendon Press.

Pitkin, H. (1967) *The Concept of Representation*, Berkeley: University of California Press.

Reingold, B. (2000) *Representing Women: Sex, Gender, and Legislative Behavior in Arizona and California*, Chapel Hill: University of North Carolina Press.

Reynolds, A. (1999) 'Women in the legislatures and executives of the world: knocking at the highest glass ceiling', *World Politics* 51(4): 547–572.

Reynolds, A. (2005) 'Reserved seats in national legislatures.', *Legislative Studies Quarterly* 30(2): 301–310.

Russell, M. (2001) 'The Women's Representation Bill: making it happen', The Constitution Unit Report, University College, London.

Siaroff, A. (2000) 'Women's representation in legislatures and cabinets in industrial democracies', *International Political Science Review* 21(2): 197–215.

Somit, A., Wildenmann, R., Boll, B. and Rommele, A. (eds). (1994) *The Victorious Incumbent: A Threat to Democracy?*, Aldershot: Dartmouth.

Swers, M. (1998) 'Are women more likely to vote for women's issue bills than their male colleagues?' *Legislative Studies Quarterly* 23(3): 435–448.

Swers, M. (2001) 'Understanding the policy impact of electing women: Evidence from research on congress and state legislatures', *PS: Political Science and Society* 34(2): 217–220.

Tinker, I. (2004) 'Quotas for women in elected legislatures: do they really empower women?' *Womens Studies International Forum* 27(5–6): 531–546.

Tremblay, M. and Pelletier, R. (2000) 'More feminists or more women? Descriptive and substantive representations of women in the 1997 Canadian federal elections', *International Political Science Review* 21(4): 381–405.

Tremblay, M. (1998) 'Do female MPs substantively represent women?' *Canadian Journal of Political Science* 31(3): 435–465.

United Nations (1995) *The Beijing Declaration 1995*, Section 13. Available at www.unifem.undp.org/beijing +5.

United Nations Development Programme (2002) *Human Development Report 2002*, New York: Oxford University Press.

Note

1. It should be noted that this may underestimate numbers as it does not classify any second-generation ethnic minority representatives, for example if one or both of their parents was born in Turkey, Suriname or Morocco. See http://www.houseofrepresentatives.nl/members_of_parliament/mps/index.jsp

Critical Thinking

1. Explain why minority representation falls short of its ratio in the population.

2. Describe alternative electoral systems to majoritarian elections.

3. Which electoral systems are barriers to electing women? Why?

Social Pressure, Surveillance and Community Size: Evidence from Field Experiments on Voter Turnout

Costas Panagopoulos

Citizens participate in elections, at least partly, because they perceive voting as a social norm (Blais, 2000; Riker and Ordeshook, 1968). Norms induce compliance because individuals prefer to avoid enforcement mechanisms—including social sanctions—that can be activated by uncooperative behavior (Shachar and Nalebuff, 1999; Knack, 1992). The desire to avoid social sanctions can be powerful enough to fuel even costly, prosocial citizen action like voting (Cialdini and Goldstein, 2004; Posner and Rasmusen, 1999; Kropf and Knack, 2003). Public visibility, or surveillance, increases the likelihood of norm-compliant behavior and applies social pressure that impels individuals to act (Tadelis, 2007).

Evidence that voters are responsive to social pressure is mounting (Schram and van Winden, 1991; Gerber et al., 2008, 2010; Panagopoulos, 2010; Davenport, 2010; Mann, 2010; Panagopoulos, forthcoming). A pioneering field experiment conducted by Gerber et al. (2008) demonstrated that social pressure stimulated turnout. Subjects who were reminded that voting is a public (and therefore verifiable) act and who were shown their own as well as their neighbors' recent voting histories were significantly more likely to vote relative to a control group that was not exposed to the treatment (Gerber et al., 2008). The findings of several field experimental interventions designed to extend Gerber et al. (2008) and to test the impact of social pressure on turnout have yielded evidence that is consistent with initial study (Gerber et al., 2010; Panagopoulos, 2010; Davenport, 2010; Mann, 2010; Abrajano and Panagopoulos, forthcoming). In fact, not only does social pressure appear to promote voting in a single election, but there are also indications the mobilizing effects of social pressure can persist in subsequent elections (Davenport et al., 2010).

Some scholars have linked social pressure to community size, advancing the notion that pressure to conform to social norms is heightened in smaller, less populous communities in which citizens interact frequently and where monitoring behavior is less onerous. These arguments are consistent with more general claims about the role of contextual factors in shaping practices and behavior (Anderson, 2009; Huckfeldt and Sprague, 1995; Mutz and Mondak, 2006) and about the relationship between community size and prosocial activity like civic involvement. Olson (1965) argued that individual incentives to contribute to collective action decline with group size and that it is therefore easier to generate collective action in smaller rather than larger groups. With respect to civic engagement more specifically, Dahl and Tufte (1973) argue that smaller communities indirectly stimulate participation by creating more opportunities for involvement. While some observers would argue that the basic conceptualization of boundary-based communities may be anachronistic (Wellman, 1979, 2002), and despite some evidence to the contrary (Fischer, 1976), numerous studies provide empirical support for the claim that citizens are more involved in smaller communities (Kasarda and Janowitz, 1974; Nie et al., 1969; Verba and Nie, 1972; Oliver, 2000). Controlling for both individual and city-level characteristics, Oliver (2000) finds that citizens residing in smaller cities are much more likely to vote in local elections, contact officials and attend community and organizational meetings relative to residents of larger metropolitan areas. Oliver (2000) attributes the higher rates of civic involvement in smaller cities partly to differences in social relations and psychological orientation between residents of larger and smaller places. The author argues residents of larger cities are less likely to be mobilized for political activity by neighbors and are less interested in local affairs (Oliver, 2000: 361). Oliver (2000: 362) concludes, "[c]ity boundaries define communities, and smaller places are civically richer".

In a recent contribution, Funk (forthcoming) also links community size to rates of electoral participation, but her theoretical explanation for this relationship focuses on social pressure as the active ingredient. Thus, while there is generally greater consensus about the general tendency to find higher levels of civic involvement in smaller communities, there is considerable disagreement about the underlying causal mechanisms that link community size to levels of civic engagement. Funk exploits a natural experiment in Switzerland to measure the relevance of social incentives in voting decisions. Starting in 1976, federal Swiss law was changed to permit the nation's 26 cantons (major districts) to introduce optional postal voting, a policy some (but not all) cantons began to implement as early as the 1980s and into the 1990s.[1] By reducing considerably the costs associated with voting, the expectation was that the reform would elevate voting rates (Downs, 1957). But the author argues the introduction of postal voting may also exert perverse effects and that different-sized communities may react differently to the introduction of postal voting. While postal voting reduces voting costs, it also removes the social pressure to vote, an effect that is especially acute in smaller communities that foster natural environments where members, "know each other better and gossip about who fulfills civic duties and who does not",(Funk, forthcoming). In short, the prospects for public surveillance of voting behavior are enhanced in less populous locales. Funk claims the social benefits of voting are high in such communities, hypothesizing that social incentives create a negative relationship between turnout and community size. In smaller communities, removing social pressure through postal voting creates an opportunity for citizens to "cheat" and refrain from voting. Since voting becomes a "blind" process in postal voting where community members cannot tell who has voted and who has not, citizens have fewer incentives to vote despite lower voting costs.

Examining quadrennial, canton-level turnout rates in national parliamentary elections between 1971 and 2003, Funk finds the introduction of optional postal voting increased aggregate cantonal turnout in parliamentary elections by 2.3 percentage points on average, but the effect is not statistically significant. However, the author finds considerable heterogeneity in the impact of the voting reform by the proportion of cantonal residents living in small communities, as hypothesized. The introduction of postal voting significantly boosted turnout (by 6.5% points on average) in cantons in which no residents reside in small communities of less than 1000 inhabitants; by contrast, turnout *dropped* (by 7 percentage points on average) in cantons in which the highest share (36%) of citizens live such small communities (Funk, forthcoming).[2]

These results lead the author to conclude that the introduction of optional postal voting transformed the social incentives associated with voting, most likely in the external benefits of norm-adherence. She argues that pure pollvoting systems in which compliance with voting norms can be readily observed and even monitored applies social pressure to vote, and that this enforcement mechanism is especially acute in small communities. With the option of postal voting, a voter who votes by mail and a non-voter are observationally equivalent, however, thereby removing social pressure to vote. Funk's study emphatically suggests community size moderates the degree of social pressure to comply with prosocial norms.

An alternative perspective on community size—with crucial implications for our expectations about its relationship to social pressure—is offered by Fowler (2005). The author argues that even large (highly-populated) communities can exhibit "small world" properties (Fowler, 2005). Individuals living in highly-populated environments often connect themselves to one another through a very small number of intermediaries. Even as some scholars find considerable variation within larger places in the degree to which individuals are part of localized communities (work-places, homes, civic associations) (Wellman, 1979, 2002), Fowler (2005) argues social networks can be quite small and well-developed, even in large communities. Thus, the prospects for surveillance of citizens' activities by other members in their personal networks may not necessarily be diminished by the fact that one's social network exists within a larger, overall community. In other words, what may matter most in terms of social influence is not the size of the community at large, but rather citizens' connections to members in their personal networks. In this regard, citizens' "sense of community", defined in Anderson (2009) as a feeling that members have of belonging, that members matter to one another and to the group, and a shared faith that members' needs will be met through their commitment together, can be as strong in larger locales as in smaller communities and can result in comparable levels of reluctance to violate social norms. One implication of this line of reasoning is that social pressure to conform to social voting norms can be potent even in large communities, suggesting community size does not necessarily alter social incentives to vote.

The discussion above suggests competing hypotheses about how community size may moderate degrees of social pressure to comply with prosocial norms. While some argue levels of interaction and the ability to monitor behavior are more pronounced in smaller communities, leading to greater social pressure (Funk, forthcoming), others suggests individuals' social networks can exert similar effects even in large communities (Fowler, 2005). To examine whether social pressure effects are heterogeneous across levels of community size, I re-examine data from the Gerber et al. (2008) social pressure field experiment discussed above to test for an interaction with community size.[3] Given the interventions in this experiment were designed explicitly to test the impact of social pressure on voter turnout, it is an ideal source of data with which to investigate community size interactions.

This article proceeds as follows. In the following section, I describe the data used in the analyses that follow. I then present the main empirical results and conclude by discussing the findings and their implications.

1. Data and Methodology

Prior to the August 2006 primary election in Michigan, Gerber et al. (2008) conducted a randomized field experiment in which households were assigned to a control group or to one of 4 treatment groups (of about 20,000 households each) assigned to receive postcard mailings that varied the level of social pressure to vote in the primary election.[4] Priming citizens' civic duty to vote was common to all of the treatments. The first message served primarily as a baseline for comparison to other treatments and simply emphasized civic duty and reminded citizens to vote. The second treatment added a mild form of social pressure by informing recipients they were bring observed and that their voting behavior would monitored by means of official public records (termed the "Hawthorne" treatment by the authors). A third treatment was designed to ratchet up social pressure by adding a listing ofthe recent voting record of each registered member in the household ("Self" treatment) and pledging to mail an updated chart following the August 2006 primary. The fourth treatment amplified social pressure even further by listing not only the household members' recent voting history but also the voting records of subjects' neighbors and indicated, as with the "self" treatment, that a follow-up mailing with updated voting history would be sent (Gerber et al., 2008).

The authors found that the basic appeal to civic duty raised turnout by 1.8% points, and the Hawthorne treatment by 2.5% points, relative to the control group. Turnout rates climbed dramatically, however, with the introduction of more intense social pressure. Showing households their own voting records revealed a 4.9 percentage-point gain in turnout, while adding neighbors' voting records boosted the turnout rate 8.1% points over the control group (Gerber et al., 2008).

Since this field experiment was conducted statewide in Michigan, there is considerable heterogeneity in the size of the communities in which subjects reside. I exploit this variation to examine the effect of community size on the impact of social pressure to vote. If arguments advanced by Funk as described above are accurate, we should observe the effects of the treatments designed to exert social pressure to be stronger in smaller (less populous) communities compared to larger setting. By contrast, if Fowler (2005) claims

that social pressure to comply with social norms can be applied as potently by the social networks of individuals residing in small as in large communities, we should find little evidence of heterogeneity in treatment effects. To explore this question, I gathered population data to correspond with subjects' residential communities and analyzed these data to investigate the possibility that community size mediated the impact of the experimental treatments.

2. Results

Subjects included in the Gerber et al. (2008) field experiment resided in geographic locales that varied considerably in terms of population. The size of the local communities ranged from 160 residents in Melvin, Michigan, to 197,800 in Grand Rapids, Michigan.[5] Overall, the mean population for cities included in the study was 25,673. Below I incorporate community size (population) in the analysis of the experimental results to investigate whether this feature conditions the impact of the treatments. The results of the main analyses are presented in Table 1. In Column 1, I replicate the original analysis to confirm the results are consistent with the estimates reported in Gerber et al. (2008; Table 3, column c). I follow the estimation procedures advanced by the authors, using linear regression to regress individual turnout on a series of dummy variables marking each of the four treatments as well as prior voting covariates[6]; themodelsalso include fixed effects for the geographic clusters (blocks) within which randomization occurred. Robust cluster standard errors account

Table 1 OLS Regression Estimates of the Effects of Four Mail Treatments Testing Social Pressure on Voter Turnout (With and Without Population I nteractions).

	Model specifications	
	(1)	**(2)**
Civic duty treatment	.018[*] (.002)	.018[*] (.003)
Hawthorne treatment	.025[*] (.002)	.026[*] (.003)
Self treatment	.048[*] (.002)	.047[*] (.003)
Neighbors treatment	.081[*] (.002)	.080[*] (.003)
Population (in hundreds of thousands)		−.014 (.032)
Civic duty × population		−.004 (.007)
Hawthorne × population		.001 (.007)
Self × population		.004 (.007)
Neighbors × population		.006 (.007)
No of individuals	344,084	342,615
Covariates[a]	Yes	Yes
Block level fixed effects	Yes	Yes

[*] $p < .001$, one-tailed; Robust cluster standard errors in parentheses. Blocks refer to clusters of neighboring voters within which random assignment occurred. Robust cluster standard errors account for the clustering of individuals within household, which was the unit of random assignment. Population (community size) estimates were obtained from the 2000 U.S. Census and range from 160 to 197,800 residents.

[a] Covariates are dummy variables for voting in general elections in November 2002 and 2000, primary elections in August 2004, 2002, and 2000.

for the clustering of individuals within households, which was the unit of randomization[7]. The estimates presented in Column 2 embellish the model to incorporate population size (in hundreds of thousands of residents) and interaction terms for the experimental treatments and population. The inclusion of the interactions leaves the estimates of the direct effects of the treatments essentially unchanged; more crucially, the results reveal no significant interactions between any of the four treatments and the population of the cities in which subjects reside. This evidence suggests social pressure operates similarly on subjects, regardless of the sizes of their residential communities.

To illustrate this point more clearly, Table 2 presents estimates of the treatment effects separately for smaller (fewer than 2,000 residents) and larger (more than 50,000 inhabitants) geographic communities. Overall, the magnitudes of the treatment effects are quite similar despite the dramatically different sizes of the populations in these select communities.[8] As expected, given the coefficients and corresponding standard errors for the interaction terms reported in Table 1 (column 2), the estimated effects of each of the four treatments do not differ significantly at conventional ($p < .05$) levels across the two subsamples. These findings reinforce the notion that the impact of social pressure is not conditional on community size.

3. Conclusion and Discussion

The analyses described above suggest community size does not moderate social pressure, at least as it relates to motivating citizens to vote. Consistent with the notion that even citizens living in highly-populated areas can be part of social networks that impose social constraints on them to comply with civic norms (Fowler, 2005), social pressure appears to operate homogeneously regardless of community size. Taken together with previous studies (Fowler, 2005; Panagopoulos, 2010), the findings I report suggest, at the very least, that the ways in which community size structures social incentives to promote (or not) compliance with civic norms remain open questions. It is conceivable that citizens, in fact, engage more regularly in civic activities in smaller, compared to larger, communities (Oliver, 2000; Funk, forthcoming), but such patterns may not be attributable to variation in the structure of social incentives. Community size may influence civic engagement and even compliance with social norms, but perhaps not because social pressure is greater in smaller communities. Ruling out some possibilities for the underlying causal mechanisms at play is a theoretically meaningful exercise that would enable scholars to hone in on more plausible explanations.

More generally, the results of this study have important implications for our understanding of how social contexts influence prosocial behavior. To be sure, my interpretation of the findings reported in this article does not stand in contradiction to the notion that contextual factors powerfully shape practices and behavior but rather that there is still much to learn about the complexities of contextual effects. Subsequent research that exploits the availability of more detailed and specific information about individuals' social networks may yield more nuanced observations. Nevertheless, the evidence I present sheds light on our understanding of how social incentives interact with environmental factors to impact citizens. Even as social features like population size appear to be related to levels of citizen engagement or other prosocial activity, causal explanations about the mechanisms that generate these relationships remain elusive.

Table 2 OLS Regression Estimates of the Effects of Four Mail Treatments Testing Social Pressure on Voter Turnout by Community Size (Population).

	Community size (population)	
	Under 2,000	**Over 50,000**
Civic duty treatment	.018** (.008)	.022*** (.007)
Hawthorne treatment	.012* (.008)	.020*** (.007)
Self treatment	.046*** (.008)	.053*** (.008)
Neighbors treatment	.071*** (.008)	.084*** (.008)
N of individuals	47,849	54,910
Covariates[a]	Yes	Yes
Block level fixed effects	Yes	Yes

*** $p < .001$, ** $p < .05$, * $p < .10$, one-tailed; Robust cluster standard errors in parentheses.

Blocks refer to clusters of neighboring voters within which random assignment occurred. Robust cluster standard errors account for the clustering of individuals within household, which was the unit of random assignment.

[a] Covariates are dummy variables for voting in general elections in November 2002 and 2000, primary elections in August 2004, 2002, and 2000.

References

Anderson, M.R., 2009. Beyond membership: a sense of community and political behavior. Political Behavior 31 (March), 603–627.

Abrajano, M., Costas, P. Does Language Matter? The Impact of Spanish Versus English-Language GOTV Efforts on Latino Turnout. American Politics Research, forthcoming.

Blais, A., 2000. To Vote or Not to Vote: The Merits and Limits of Rational Choice Theory. University of Pittsburgh Press, Pittsburgh.

Cialdini, R., Goldstein, N., 2004. Social influence: compliance and conformity. Annual Review of Psychology 55 (February), 592–621.

Dahl, R., Tufte, E., 1973. Size and Democracy. Stanford University Press, Palo Alto.

Davenport, T., Gerber, A., Green, D., Larimer, C., Mann, C., Panagopoulos, C., 2010. The enduring effects of social pressure: tracking campaign experiments over a series ofelections. Political Behavior 32 (3), 423–430.

Davenport, T.C., 2010. Public accountability and political participation: effects of a face-to-face feedback intervention on voter turnout of public housing residents. Political Behavior 32 (3), 337–368.

Downs, A., 1957. An Economic Theory of Democracy. Harper and Row, New York.

Fischer, C., 1976. The city and political psychology. American Political Science Review 69 (September), 559–571.

Fowler, J.H., 2005. Turnout in a small world. In: Zuckerman, Alan (Ed.), Social Logic of Politics. Temple University Press, Philadelphia, pp. 269–287.

Funk, Patricia. Social incentives and voter turnout: evidence from the Swiss mail ballot system. Journal of the European Economic Association, forthcoming.

Gerber, A.S., Green, D.P., Larimer, C.W., 2008. Social pressure and voter turnout: evidence from a large-scale field experiment. American Political Science Review 102 (1), 33–48.

Gerber, A.S., Green, D.P., Larimer, C.W., 2010. An experiment testing the relative effectiveness of encouraging voter participation by inducing feelings of pride or shame. Political Behavior 32 (3), 409–422.

Huckfeldt, R., Sprague, J., 1995. Citizens, Politics, and Social Communication: Information and Influence in an Election Campaign. Cambridge University Press, New York.

Kasarda, J., Janowitz, M., 1974. Community attachment in mass society. American Sociological Review 39 (August), 328–339.

Knack, S., 1992. Civic norms, social sanctions, and voter turnout. Rationality and Society, 133–156.

Kropf, M., Knack, S., 2003. Viewers like you: community norms and contributions to public broadcasting. Political Research Quarterly 56 (2), 187–195.

Mann, C.B., 2010. Is there backlash to social pressure? A large-scale field experiment on voter mobilization. Political Behavior 32 (3), 387–407.

Mutz, D.C., Mondak, J.J., 2006. The workplace as a context for cross-cutting political discourse. Journal of Politics 68, 140–155.

Nie, N., Powell Jr., G.B., Prewitt, K., 1969. Social structure and political participation: developmental relationships. American Political Science Review 63 (June), 361 –378.

Oliver, E., 2000. City size and civic involvement in metropolitan America. American Political Science Review 94 (2), 361–373.

Olson, M., 1965. The Logic of Collective Action. Harvard University Press, Cambridge.

Panagopoulos, C., 2010. Affect, social pressure and prosocial motivation: field experimental evidence of the mobilizing effects of pride, shame and publicizing voting behavior. Political Behavior 32 (3), 369–386.

Panagopoulos, C. Thank You for Voting: Gratitude Expression and Voter Mobilization. Journal of Politics, forthcoming.

Posner, R., Rasmusen, E., 1999. Creating and enforcing norms, with special reference to sanctions. International Review of Law and Economics 19 (September), 66–84.

Riker, W.H., Ordeshook, P.C., 1968. A theory of the calculus of voting. American Political Science Review 62 (1), 25–42.

Schram, A., van Winden, F., 1991. Why people vote: free riding and the production and consumption of social pressure. Journal of Economic Psychology 12 (December), 575–620.

Shachar, R., Nalebuff, B., 1999. Follow the leader: theory and evidence on political participation. American Economic Review 89 (3), 525–547.

Tadelis, S., 2007. The Power of Shame and the Rationality of Trust. http://ssrn.com/abstract=1006169 Available at SSRN.

Verba, S., Nie, N., 1972. Participation in America. University of Chicago Press, Chicago.

Wellman, B., 1979. The community question. American Journal of Sociology 84, 1201–1231.

Wellman, B., 2002. Little boxes, glocalization, and networked individualism. In: Tanabe, M., van den Besselaar, P., Ishida, T. (Eds.), Digital Cities II: Computational and Sociological Approaches. Springer-Verlag, Berlin, pp. 10–25.

Notes

1. Federal Swiss law was further revised in 1994 to require all 26 cantons to offer postal voting, but no time limit was specified for cantons to implement the change. See Funk (forthcoming) for details about when cantons implemented optional postal voting.

2. Findings reported in Panagopoulos (2010) suggest similarly that an experimental treatment that pledged to publicize the names of voters was somewhat more effective in stimulating turnout in smaller town (Monticello, Iowa) compared to a larger (Holland, Michigan) community, but evidence attributing this difference to community size is inconclusive.

3. I am grateful to these authors for sharing their experimental data with me for this analysis.

4. See Gerber et al. (2008) for additional details about the experimental protocols.

5. All population data reported are based on 2000 U.S. Census estimates. Grand Rapids is the second-largest city in Michigan, but the experimental sample did not include any subjects residing in Detroit, Michigan's largest city. Residency data was unavailable for 1469 subjects, who were excluded from the analysis.

6. For simplicity, estimates for all models reported in Tables 1 and 2 include covariates as indicated. The exclusion of covariates

alters estimates only trivially, but details are available upon request.

7. See Gerber et al. (2008) for details about the estimation procedures.

8. The cut-points reported in Table 2 are illustrative, but the findings are substantively similar across a wide range of alternative cut-points. Details available upon request.

Critical Thinking

1. Explain why high turnout is desirable.
2. Explain why small communities may have higher voter turnout.
3. Explain why voter turnout is not affected by community size.

The Case for a Multi-Party U.S. Parliament?

American Politics in Comparative Perspective.

This article supports the inclusion of American political institutions within the study of comparative politics. This is a brief on behalf of a multi-party parliamentary system for the United States that can be read as a "what if" experiment in institutional transplantation. It underscores the basic insight that institutions are not neutral but have consequences for the political process itself and encourages American students to think more broadly about the possibilities of reforming the American political system.

CHRISTOPHER S. ALLEN

Introduction

Americans revere the constitution but at the same time also sharply and frequently criticize the government. (Dionne 1991) Yet since the constitution is responsible for the current form of the American government, why not change the constitution to produce better government? After all, the founders of the United States did create the amendment process and we have seen 27 of them in 220 years.

Several recent events prompt a critical look at this reverence for the constitution: unusual developments regarding the institution of the Presidency, including the Clinton impeachment spectacle of 1998–1999; the historic and bizarre 2000 Presidential election that required a Supreme Court decision to resolve; the apparent mandate for fundamental change that President Bush inferred from this exceedingly narrow election; and the increasingly numerous constitutional questions concerning Presidential powers and the conduct of the "war on terror." In the early 21st century, American politics confronted at least three other seemingly intractable problems: significant erosion in political accountability; out of control costs of running for public office; and shamefully low voter turnout. More seriously, none of these four problems is of recent origin, as all four have eroded the functioning of the American government for a period of between 25 and 50 years! The core features of these four problems are:

- Confusion of the roles of head of state and head of government, of which the impeachment issue—from Watergate through Clinton's impeachment and beyond—is merely symptomatic of a much larger problem.
- Eroding political accountability, taking the form of either long periods of divided government, dating back to the "Do Nothing" 80th congress elected in 1946, to the recent "gerrymandering industry" producing a

dearth of competitive elections. The result is millions of "wasted votes" and an inability for voters to assign credit or blame for legislative action.

- Costly and perennial campaigns for all offices producing "the best politicians that money can buy." This problem had its origins with the breakdown of the party caucus system and the growth of primary elections in the 1960s; and
- The world's lowest voter turnout among all of the leading OECD countries, a phenomenon that began in the 1960s and has steadily intensified.

When various American scholars acknowledge these shortcomings, however, there is the occasional, offhand comparison to parliamentary systems which have avoided many of these pathologies. The unstated message is that we don't—or perhaps should never, ever want to—have that here.

Why not? What exactly is the problem with a parliamentary system? In the US, durable trust in government, sense of efficacy, and approval ratings for branches in government have all declined in recent decades. Such phenomena contribute to declining voter turnout and highlight what is arguably a more significant trend toward a crisis in confidence among Americans concerning their governing institutions. So why is institutional redesign off the table?

This article examines these four institutional blockages of the American majoritarian/Presidential system and suggests certain features of parliamentary or consensus systems might overcome these persistent shortcomings of American politics.

Less normatively, the article is framed by three concepts central to understanding and shaping public policy in advanced industrialized states with democratic constitutional structures.

First, is the issue of comparability and 'American Exceptionalism' (Lipset 1996). The article's goal is to initiate a long-delayed dialogue on comparative constitutional structures with scholars of American politics. Second, the article hopes to participate in the active discussion among comparativists on the respective strengths and weaknesses of majoritarian and consensus systems. (Birchfield and Crepaz 1998) Third, scandals surrounding money and politics in a number of democratic states (Barker 1994) should prompt a comparison of parties and party systems and the context within which they function.

This article does not underestimate the quite significant problems associated with "institutional transplantation" (Jacoby 2000) from one country to another. The more modest and realistic goal is to engage American and Comparative scholars in a fruitful debate about political institutions and constitutional design that (finally) includes American politics in a Comparative orbit.

This article is organized in 5 sections that address: 1) the cumbersome tool of impeachment; 2) eroding political accountability due to divided government and safe seats; 3) the costly, never-ending campaign process; 4) the continued deterioration of voter turnout; and 5) the quite formidable obstacles that initiating a parliamentary remedy to these problems would clearly face.

1. Impeachment: Head of State vs Head of Government

The tool of impeachment is merely a symptom of a larger problem. Its more fundamental flaw is that it highlights the constitutional confusion between the two functions of the US presidency: head of state and head of government.

Americanists have delved deeply into the minutiae of the impeachment process during the past thirty years but comparativists would ask a different question. How would other democracies handle similar crises affecting their political leaders? More than two years transpired from the Watergate break-in to Nixon's resignation (1972–74), the Iran-Contra scandal (1986–87) produced no impeachment hearings; and an entire year (1998–99) transpired from the onset of the Clinton-Lewinsky saga to the completion of the impeachment process. Finally, the revelations from 2005–2007 concerning the Bush Administration's clandestine spying on American citizens by the National Security Agency have once again caused some Democrats to mention preliminary impeachment inquiries. Comparativists and citizens of other democratic polities find this astounding, since in a parliamentary system a fundamental challenge to the executive would take the form of a vote of no confidence, (Lijphart 1994) and the issue would be politically resolved within weeks. The executive would either survive and continue or resign.

The portrayal of the Clinton impeachment and trial is characterized as historic. For only the second time in American politics, an American president has been impeached in the House and put on trial in the Senate. Yet, the idea of using impeachment has been much less rare, having been raised three times in the past thirty years; and has only a very slim possibility of being seriously considered in the early 21st century. Basically, impeachment is an extremely blunt tool that has not "worked" at all. It is either not brought to fruition (Watergate), not used when it should have been (Iran-Contra), or completely trivialized (Clinton-Lewinsky) when another path was clearly needed. But impeachment itself isn't the real problem; a larger constitutional design flaw is.

The United States has a constitutional structure based on a separation of powers, while most parliamentary systems have a "fusion" of powers in that the Prime Minister is also the leader of the major party in parliament. However, within the American executive itself, there is a "fusion" of functions, which is the exact opposite of Parliamentary regimes.

The US is the only developed democracy where head of state and head of government are fused in one person. The President is the Head of State and, effectively, the Head of Government. In Parliamentary systems these two functions are performed by two different people. (Linz 1993) Thus impeachment of one person removes two functions in one and likely explained the dichotomy of popular desire for Clinton's retention on the one hand, but also for some form of political censure on the other.

Beyond the impeachment issue, when American presidents undertake some action as head of government for which they are criticized, they then become invariably more remote and inaccessible. For example, Presidents Johnson (Vietnam), Nixon (Watergate), Reagan (Iran/Contra), Clinton (the Lewinsky Affair) and G.W. Bush (Iraq) all reduced their appearances at press conferences as criticism of their policies mounted. In short, when criticized for actions taken in their head of government capacity, they all retreated to the Rose Garden or other "safe" locations and sometimes created the impression that criticizing the President—now wearing the head of state hat (or perhaps, crown)—was somehow unpatriotic. This was especially the case with George W. Bush, who in the post 9/11 and Iraq war periods, has tried to emphasize the commander in chief aspect of the presidency rather than his role as steward of the economy and domestic politics.

Toward a Politically Accountable Prime Minister and a Ceremonial President

A parliamentary system with a separate head of state and head of government would produce two "executive" offices instead of just one. It's odd that the US is so fearful of centralized power yet allows the executive to perform functions that no other leader of an OECD country (France excepted) performs alone. The US Vice President serves many of the functions of heads of state in other countries. But the United States has a comparatively odd way of dividing executive constitutional functions. One office, the Presidency, does everything while the other, the Vice Presidency, does virtually nothing and simply waits until the president can no longer serve (although Vice President Cheney sees this role differently). An American parliamentary system would redefine these 2 offices so that one person (the head of state) would serve as a national symbol and preside over ceremonial functions. The second person (the head of government) would function much like a prime minister does in a parliamentary system, namely as the head of government who could be criticized, censured and held accountable for specific political actions without creating a constitutional crisis.

Thus were it necessary to censure or otherwise take action against the head of government (i.e. prime minister), the solution would be a relatively quick vote of no confidence that would solve the problem and move on and let the country address its political business. (Huber 1996) And unlike impeachment which is the political equivalent of the death penalty, a vote of no confidence does not preclude a politician's making a comeback and returning to lead a party or coalition. Impeachment and removal from office, on the other hand, is much more final.

Prime Ministers, unlike US presidents, are seen much more as active politicians and not remote inaccessible figures. In a parliament, the prime minister as the head of government is required to engage—and be criticized—in the rough-and-tumble world of daily politics. In short, the head of government must be accountable. The British prime minister, for example, is required to participate in a weekly "question time" in which often blunt and direct interrogatories are pressed by the opposition. (Rundquist 1991) There is no equivalent forum for the American president to be formally questioned as a normal part of the political process.

But could such a power be used in a cavalier fashion, perhaps removing the head of government easily after a debilitating scandal? This is unlikely in a well-designed parliamentary system because such cynicism would likely produce a backlash that would constrain partisanship. In fact, the Germans have institutionalized such constraints in the "constructive vote of no confidence" requiring any removal of the head of government to be a simultaneous election of a new one. The context of such a parliamentary system lowers the incentives to engage in the politics of destruction. The political impact of destroying any particular individual in a collective body such as a cabinet or governing party or coalition is much less significant than removing a directly elected president.

A parliamentary head of state is above the kind of criticism generated from no confidence votes and simply serves as an apolitical symbol of national pride. In nation states that have disposed of their monarchies, ceremonial presidents perform many of the same roles as constitutional monarchs such as Queen Elizabeth do, but much less expensively. In fact, many of these ceremonial roles are performed by the American vice president (attending state dinners/funerals, cutting ribbons, presiding over the Senate, etc.) The problem is that the Vice President is often a political afterthought, chosen more for ticket-balancing functions and/or for inoffensive characteristics than for any expected major political contributions. On the other hand, the type of individual usually chosen as a ceremonial president in a parliamentary system is a retired politician from the moderate wing of one of the major parties who has a high degree of stature and can serve as a figure of national unity. In effect, the office of ceremonial president is often a reward or honor for decades of distinguished national service, hardly the characteristics of most American vice presidents.

In retrospect, one might say that President Clinton was impeached not for abusing head of government functions, but for undermining the decorum and respect associated with heads of state. The separation of head of state and head of government would have a salutary effect on this specific point. Scandals destroying heads of state would have little real political significance since the head of state would not wield real political power. Similarly, scandals destroying heads of government would have significantly less impact than in the current American system. The head of government role, once separated from the head of state role, would no longer attract monolithic press and public attention or be subject to extraordinarily unrealistic behavioral expectations.

2. Political Accountability: Divided Government & "Safe Seats"

From the "do nothing" 80th Congress elected in 1946 to the 110th elected in 2006, a total of thirty-one Congresses, the United States has experienced divided government for more than two-thirds of this period. In only ten of those thirty-one Congresses has the president's party enjoyed majorities in both houses of Congress. (Fiorina 1992; Center for Voting and Democracy 2007) Some might observe this divided government phenomenon and praise the bipartisan nature of the American system. (Mayhew 1991) But to justify such a conclusion, defenders of bipartisanship would have to demonstrate high public approval of governmental performance, particularly when government was divided. Based on over four decades of declining trust in government, such an argument is increasingly hard to justify.

One explanation for the American preference for divided government is the fear of concentrated political power. (Jacobson 1990) Yet in a search for passivity, the result often turns out to be simply inefficiency.

While the fear of concentrated government power is understandable for historical and ideological reasons, many of the same people who praise divided government also express concern regarding government efficiency. (Thurber 1991) Yet divided government quite likely contributes to the very inefficiencies that voters rightfully lament. Under divided government, when all is well, each of the two parties claims responsibility for the outcome; when economic or political policies turn sour, however, each party blames the other. This condition leads to a fundamental lack of political accountability and the self-fulfilling prophesy that government is inherently inefficient.

Rather than being an accidental occurrence, divided government is much more likely to result due to the American constitutional design. For it is constitutional provisions that are at the heart of divided government; 2 year terms for Congress, 4 year terms for the Presidency, and 6 year terms for the Senate invariably produce divided government.

Were it only for these "accidental" outcomes of divided government, political accountability might be less deleterious. Exacerbating the problem, however, is the decline of parties as institutions. This has caused individuals to have weaker partisan attachments—despite the increased partisan rhetoric of many elected officials since the 1980s—and has thereby intensified the fragmentation of government. (Franklin and Hirczy de Mino 1998) Clearly, divided government is more problematic when partisan conflict between the two parties is greater as the sharper ideological conflict and the increased party line congressional

Table 1 Trust in the Federal Government 1964–2004

	None of the Time	Some of the Time	Most of the Time	Just about Always	Don't Know
1964	0	22	62	14	1
1966	2	28	48	17	4
1968	0	36	54	7	2
1970	0	44	47	6	2
1972	1	44	48	5	2
1974	1	61	34	2	2
1976	1	62	30	13	3
1978	4	64	27	2	3
1980	4	69	23	2	2
1982	3	62	31	2	3
1984	1	53	40	4	2
1986	2	57	35	3	2
1988	2	56	36	4	1
1990	2	69	25	3	1
1992	2	68	26	3	1
1994	1	74	19	2	1
1996	1	66	30	3	0
1998	1	58	36	4	1
2000	1	55	40	4	1
2002	0	44	51	5	0
2004	1	52	43	4	0

Percentage within study year.

Source: The National Election Studies (www.electionstudies.org/nesguide/toptable/tab5a_1.htm)

Question Text:

"How much of the time do you think you can trust the government in Washington to do what is right—just about always, most of the time or only some of the time?"

Source: The National Election Studies, University of Michigan, 2005

Table 2 The Persistence of Divided Government

Year	President	House	Senate	Divided/ Unified Government
1946	D – Truman	Rep	Rep	D
1948	D – Truman	Dem	Rep	D
1950	D – Truman	Rep	Rep	D
1952	R – Eisenhower	Rep	Rep	U
1954	R – Eisenhower	Dem	Dem	D
1956	R – Eisenhower	Dem	Dem	D
1958	R – Eisenhower	Dem	Dem	D
1960	D – Kennedy	Dem	Dem	U
1962	D – Kennedy	Dem	Dem	U
1964	D – Johnson	Dem	Dem	U
1966	D – Johnson	Dem	Dem	U
1968	R – Nixon	Dem	Dem	D
1970	R – Nixon	Dem	Dem	D
1972	R – Nixon	Dem	Dem	D
1974	R – Ford	Dem	Dem	D
1976	D – Carter	Dem	Dem	U
1978	D – Carter	Dem	Dem	U
1980	R – Reagan	Dem	Rep	D
1982	R – Reagan	Dem	Rep	D
1984	R – Reagan	Dem	Rep	D
1986	R – Reagan	Dem	Dem	D
1988	R – Bush	Dem	Dem	D
1990	R – Bush	Dem	Dem	D
1992	D – Clinton	Dem	Dem	U
1994	D – Clinton	Rep	Rep	D
1996	D – Clinton	Rep	Rep	D
1998	D – Clinton	Rep	Rep	D
2000	R – Bush	Rep	Dem*	D
2002	R – Bush	Rep	Rep	U
2004	R – Bush	Rep	Rep	U
2006	R – Bush	Dem	Dem	D

*After a 50-50 split (with Vice President Cheney as the tiebreaker), Senator Jeffords (I-VT) switched from the Republican Party shortly after the 2000 Election, thereby swinging the Senate to the Democrats.

voting since the mid-1990s would suggest. Under these circumstances, divided government seems to be more problematic, since two highly partisan parties within the American political system seem potentially dangerous. Persistent divided government over time will likely produce a fundamental change in the relationship between Presidents and the Congress. Presidents are unable to bargain effectively with a hostile congress—witness the 1995 government shutdown—leading the former to make appeals over the heads of Congress directly and, hence undermine the legitimacy of the legislative branch. (Kernell 1997) This argument parallels the one made in recent comparative scholarship (Linz 1993) regarding the serious problem of dual legitimacy in presidential systems.

A second component of the political accountability problem is the increasing non-competitiveness of American elections. Accounts of the 2000 Presidential election stressed its historic closeness, settled by only 540,000 popular votes (notwithstanding the Electoral College anomaly). And the narrow Republican majorities in the House and Senate apparently indicated that every congressional or senate seat could be up for grabs each election. The reality is something different. (Center for Voting and Democracy 2007) Out of 435 House seats, only 60 (13.8%)

were competitive, the outcome of most Senate races is known well in advance, and the 2000 and 2004 Presidential races were only competitive in 15 of 50 states. In the remaining 35, the state winners (Bush or Gore; or Bush or Kerry, respectively) were confident enough of the outcome to forgo television advertising in many of them. In essence, voters for candidates who did not win these hundreds of "safe seats" were effectively disenfranchised and unable to hold their representatives politically accountable.

For those who lament the irresponsibility—or perhaps irrelevance—of the two major parties, an institutional design that would force responsibility should be praised. Quite simply, those who praise divided government because it "limits the damage" or see nothing amiss when there are hundreds of safe seats are faced with a dilemma. They can not simultaneously complain about the resulting governmental inefficiency and political cynicism that ultimately follows when accountability is regularly clouded.

Political Accountability and the Fusion of Government

A number of scholars have addressed the deficiencies of divided government, but they suggest that the problem is that the electoral cycle, with its "midterm" elections, intensifies the likelihood of divided government in non-presidential election years. Such advocates propose as a solution the alteration of the electoral cycle so that all congressional elections are on four year terms, concurrent with presidential terms, likely producing a clear majority. (Cutler 1989) Yet this contains a fatal flaw. Because there is no guarantee that this proposal would alleviate the residual tension between competing branches of government, it merely sidesteps the accountability factor strongly discouraging party unity across the executive and legislative branches of government.

This suggestion could also produce the opposite effect from divided government, namely exaggerated majorities common to parliamentary regimes with majoritarian electoral systems such as the UK. The "safe seats" phenomenon would be the culprit just as in the UK. The most familiar examples of this phenomenon were the "stop-go" policies of post-World War II British governments, as each succeeding government tried to overturn the previous election. While creating governing majorities is important for political accountability, the absence of proportional representation creates a different set of problems.

Under a fusion of power system, in which the current presidency would be redefined, the resulting parliamentary system would make the head of the legislative branch the executive, thus eliminating the current separation of powers. Yet if a government should lose its majority between scheduled elections due to defection of its party members or coalition partners, the head of state then would ask the opposition to form a new government and, failing that, call for new elections. This avoids the constitutional crises that the clamor for impeachment seems to engender in the American system.

But what if coalition members try to spread the blame for poor performance to their partners? In theory, the greater the flexibility available in shifting from one governing coalition to another (with a different composition), the greater is the potential for this kind of musical cabinet chairs. The potential for such an outcome is far less than in the American system, however. A century of experience in other parliamentary regimes (Laver and Shepsle 1996) shows that members of such a party

capriciously playing games with governing are usually brought to heel at the subsequent election.

In other words, the major advantage to such a parliamentary system is that it heightens the capacity for voters and citizens to evaluate government performance. Of course, many individuals might object to the resulting concentration of power. However, if voters are to judge the accomplishments of elected officials, the latter need time to succeed or fail, and then the voters can make a judgment on their tenure. The most likely outcome would be a governing party or coalition of parties that would have to stay together to accomplish anything, thereby increasing party salience. (Richter 2002) Phrased differently, such an arrangement would likely lead to an increase in responsible government.

Many Americans might react unfavorably at the mention of the word coalition due to its supposed instability. Here we need to make the distinction between transparent and opaque coalitions. Some argue that coalition governments in parliamentary systems have the reputation of increased instability. That, of course, depends on the substance of the coalition agreement and the willingness of parties to produce a stable majority. (Strom et al. 1994) But in most parliamentary systems, these party coalitions are formed transparently before an election so the voters can evaluate and then pass judgment on the possible coalition prior to Election Day. It's not as if there are no coalitions in the US Congress. There they take the opaque form of ad-hoc groups of individual members of Congress on an issue-by-issue basis. The high information costs to American voters in understanding the substance of such layered bargains hardly are an example of political transparency.

Finally, for those concerned that the "fusion" of the executive and legislative branches—on the British majoritarian model—would upset the concept of checks and balances, a multi-party consensus parliamentary system produces them slightly differently. (Lijphart 1984) Majoritarianism concentrates power and makes "checking" difficult, while consensus democracies institutionalize the process in a different and more accountable form. A multi-party parliamentary system would also provide greater minority representation, fewer safe seats, and protection by reducing majoritarianism's excessive concentration of power. A consensus parliamentary system would also address the "tyranny of the majority" problem and allow checking and balancing by the voters in the ballot box since the multiple parties would not likely allow a single party to dominate. Consensus systems thus represent a compromise between the current U.S. system and the sharp concentration of British Westminster systems. Americans who simultaneously favor checks and balances but decry inefficient government need to clarify what they actually want their government to do.

Table 3 Comparative Coalitions

American	Parliamentary
Opaque	Transparent
Issue-by-Issue	Programmatic
Back Room	Open Discussion
Unaccountable	Election Ratifies
Unstable	Generally Stable

3. Permanent and Expensive Campaigns

The cost to run for political office in the United States dwarfs that spent in any other advanced industrialized democracy. The twin problems are time and money; more specifically a never-ending campaign "season" and the structure of political advertising that depend so heavily on TV money. (Gans 1993) In listening to the debates about "reforming" the American campaign finance system, students of other democratic electoral systems find these discussions bizarre. More than $2 billion was raised and spent (Corrado 1997) by parties, candidates and interest groups in the 1996 campaign, and for 2000 it went up to $3 billion. Finally, the Center for Responsive Politics estimated the total cost for 2004 Presidential and Congressional elections was $3.9 billion (Weiss 2004) and the preliminary estimates for the 2006 midterm elections—in which there was no presidential race—were approximately $3 billion.

The two year congressional cycle forces members of the House of Representatives to literally campaign permanently. The amount of money required to run for a Congressional seat has quadrupled since 1990. Presidential campaigns are several orders of magnitude beyond the House of Representatives or the Senate. By themselves they are more than two years long, frequently longer. Unless a presidential candidate is independently wealthy or willing and able to raise upfront $30–$50 million it is simply impossible to run seriously for this office.

Many of the problems stem from the post-Watergate "reforms" that tried to limit the amount of spending on campaigns which then produced a backlash in the form of a 1976 Supreme Court decision (Buckley vs Valeo) that undermined this reform attempt. In essence, Buckley vs Valeo held that "paid speech" (i.e. campaign spending) has an equivalent legal status as "free speech". (Grant 1998) Consequently, since then all "reform" efforts have been tepid measures that have not been able to get at the root of the problem. As long as "paid speech" retains its protected status, any changes are dead in the water.

At its essence this issue is a fissure between "citizens" and "consumers". What Buckley vs Valeo has done is to equate the citizenship function (campaigning, voting, civic education) with a market-based consumer function (buying and selling consumer goods as commodities). (Brubaker 1998) Unlike the United States, most other OECD democracies consider citizenship a public good and provide funding for parties, candidates and the electoral process as a matter of course. The Buckley vs Valeo decision conflates the concepts of citizen and consumer, the logical extension of which is there are weak limits on campaign funding and no limits on the use of a candidate's own money. We are all equal citizens, yet we are not all equal consumers. Bringing consumer metaphors into the electoral process debases the very concept of citizenship and guarantees that the American political system produces the best politicians money can buy.

Free Television Time and the Return of Political Party Dues

Any broadcaster wishing to transmit to the public is required to obtain a broadcast license because the airways have the legal status of public property. To have access to such property, the government must license these networks, cable channels, and stations to serve the public interest. In return, broadcasters are able to sell airtime to sponsors of various programs. Unfortunately for those concerned with campaign costs, candidates for public office fall into the same category as consumer goods in the eyes of the broadcasters. (Weinberg 1993) What has always seemed odd to observers of other democratic states is that there is no Quid Pro Quo requiring the provision of free public airtime for candidates when running for election.

Any serious reform of campaign finance would require a concession from all broadcasters to provide free time for all representative candidates and parties as a cost of using the public airways. Since the largest share of campaign money is TV money, this reform would solve the problem at its source. Restricting the "window" when these free debates would take place to the last two months before a general election would thus address the time dimension as well. Such practices are standard procedure in all developed parliamentary systems. Very simply, as long as "reform" efforts try to regulate the supply of campaign finance, it will fail. A much more achievable target would be the regulation of demand.

The United States could solve another money problem by borrowing a page from parliamentary systems: changing the political party contribution structure from individual voluntary contributions (almost always from the upper middle class and the wealthy) to a more broad-based dues structure common to parties in other developed democracies. This more egalitarian party dues structure would perform the additional salutary task of rebuilding parties as functioning institutions. (Allen 1999) Rather than continuing in their current status as empty shells for independently wealthy candidates, American political parties could become the kind of dynamic membership organizations they were at the turn of the 20th century when they did have a dues structure.

4. Low Voter Turnout?

The leading OECD countries have voter turnout ranging from 70% to 90% of their adult population while the US lags woefully behind.

Among the most commonly raised explanations for the US deficiency are: registration requirements, the role of television, voter discouragement, and voter contentment (although the latter two are clearly mutually exclusive). None are particularly convincing nor do they offer concrete suggestions as to how it might be overcome.

The two party system and the electoral method that produces it: the single member district, first past the post, or winner take all system with its attendant "safe seats" often escapes criticism. The rise of such new organizations as the Libertarian, and Green parties potentially could threaten the hegemony of the Democrats and Republicans. Yet the problem of a third (or fourth) party gaining a sufficient number of votes to actually win seats and challenge the two party system is formidable. The electoral arithmetic would require any third party to win some 25% of the vote on a nationwide basis—or develop a highly-concentrated regional presence—before it would actually gain more than a token number of seats. And failing to actually win seats produces a "wasted

Table 4 Voter Turnout and Type of Electoral System Major Developed Democracies–1945–2005

Country	% Voter Turnout	Type of Electoral System
Italy	91.9	PR
Belgium	84.9	PR
Netherlands	84.8	PR
Australia	84.4	Mixed Member
Denmark	83.6	PR
Sweden	83.3	PR
Germany	80.0	Mixed-PR
Israel	80.0	PR
Norway	79.2	PR
Finland	79.0	PR
Spain	76.4	PR
Ireland	74.9	SMD
UK	73.0	SMD
Japan	68.3	SMD/Mixed
France	67.3	SMD + runoff
Canada	66.9	SMD
USA – Presidential	55.1	SMD
USA – Congress (Midterm)	40.6	SMD

Source: Voter Turnout: A Global Survey (Stockholm: International IDEA, 2005)

Table 5 The Advantages of Proportional Representation

Higher Voter Turnout
No "Wasted" Votes
Few Safe, Uncontested Seats
More Parties
Greater Minority Representation
Greater Gender Diversity in Congress
Greater Ideological Clarity
Parties Rebuilt as Institutions
6% Threshold Assumed
No More Gerrymandered Redistricting

vote" syndrome among party supporters which is devastating for such a party. (Rosenstone et al. 1996) Most voters who become disillusioned with the electoral process refer to the "lesser of two evils" choices they face. In such a circumstance, declining voter turnout is not surprising.

The US is a diverse country with many regional, religious, racial, and class divisions. So why should we expect that two "catch all" parties will do a particularly good job in appealing to the interests of diverse constituencies? The solution to lower voter turnout is a greater number of choices for voters and a different electoral system.

Proportional Representation

Under electoral systems using proportional representation, the percentage of a party's vote is equivalent to the percentage of seats allocated to the party in parliament. Comparative analysis shows that those countries with proportional representation— and the multiple parties that PR systems produce—invariably have higher voter turnout. (Grofman and Lijphart 1986) In other words, PR voting systems provide a wider variety of political choices and a wider variety of political representation.

Eliminating majoritarian single member districts (SMDs) in favor of PR voting would have several immediate effects. First, it would increase the range of choices for voters, since parties would have to develop ideological and programmatic distinctions to make themselves attractive to voters. As examples in other countries have shown, it would lead to formation of several new parties representing long underserved interests.

Such a change would force rebuilding of parties as institutions, since candidates would have to run as members of parties and not as independent entrepreneurs. The so-called Progressive "reforms" at the turn of the 20th century and the 1960s introduction of primaries—plus TV advertising—plus the widespread use of referenda have all had powerful effects in undermining parties as coherent political organizations. (Dwyre et al. 1994) In trying to force market-based individual "consumer choice" in the form of high-priced candidates, the collective institutions that are political parties have been hollowed out and undermined.

There are, of course, a wide range of standard objections to PR voting systems by those favoring retention of majoritarian SMD systems.

The first of these, coalitional instability, was addressed briefly above, but it needs to be restated here. The US has unstable coalitions in the Congress right now, namely issue-by-issue ones, usually formed in the House cloakroom with the "assistance" of lobbyists. Few average voters know with certainty how "their" member of Congress will vote on a given issue. (Gibson 1995) With ideologically coherent parties, they would.

An American parliament with several parties could very effectively produce self-discipline. Clearly there would have to be a coalition government since it is unlikely that any one party would capture 50% of the seats. The practice in almost all other coalition governments in parliamentary systems is that voters prefer a predictable set of political outcomes. Such an arrangement forces parties to both define their programs clearly and transparently, once entering into a coalition, and to do everything possible to keep the coalition together during the course of the legislative term.

The second standard objection to PR is the "too many parties" issue. PR voting has been practiced in parliaments for almost 100 years in many different democratic regimes. There is a long history of practices that work well and practices that don't. (Norris 1997) Two countries are invariably chosen as bad examples of PR, namely Israel and Italy. There is an easy solution to this problem of an unwieldy number of parties, namely an electoral threshold requiring any party to receive a certain minimal percentage to gain seats in the parliament. The significant question is what should this minimal threshold be? The Swedes have a 4% threshold and have 7 parties in their parliament, the Germans have a 5% threshold and have 5 parties represented in the Bundestag.

The third standard objection to PR voting is "who's my representative?" In a society so attuned to individualism, most Americans want a representative from their district. This argument presumes that all Americans have a member of Congress that represents their views. However, a liberal democrat who lived in former House Speaker Tom Delay's district in Texas might genuinely wonder in what way he represented that liberal's interests. By the same token, conservative Republicans living in Vermont had for almost twenty years the independent socialist, Bernard Sanders as the state's lone member of Congress representing "their" interests.

Yet if American reformers are still insistent on having individual representatives (Guinier 1994) the phenomenon of "Instant Runoff Voting" (Hill 2003) where voters rank order their preferences could produce proportionality among parties yet retain individual single member districts. It also could be used in Presidential elections and avoid accusations of "spoiler" candidates such as Ralph Nader in 2000.

If there were PR voting in an American parliament, what would the threshold be? The US threshold probably should be at least 6%. The goal is to devise a figure that represents all significant interests yet does not produce instability. The "shake out" of parties would likely produce some strategic "mergers" of weak parties which, as single parties, might not attain the 6% threshold. For example, a separate Latino party and an African-American party might insure always attaining a 6% threshold by forming a so-called "rainbow" party. Similarly the Reform Party and the Libertarian Party might find it electorally safer to merge into one free market party.

There are four primary arguments in favor of PR.

The first is simplicity; the percentage of the votes equals the percentage of the seats. To accomplish this, the more individualistic US could borrow the German hybrid system of "personalized" proportional representation. This system requires citizens to cast two votes on each ballot: the first for an individual candidate; and the second for a list of national/regional candidates grouped by party affiliation. (Allen 2001) This system has the effect of personalizing list voting because voters have their own representative but also can choose among several parties. Yet allocation of seats by party in the Bundestag corresponds strongly with the party's percentage of the popular vote.

The second advantage to PR is diversity. The experience of PR voting in other countries is that it changes the makeup of the legislature by increasing both gender and racial diversity. Obviously, parties representing minority interests who find it difficult to win representation in 2 person races, will more easily be able to win seats under PR. (Rule and Zimmerman 1992) Since candidates would not have to run as individuals—or raise millions of dollars—the parties would be more easily able to include individuals on the party's list of candidates who more accurately represent the demographics of average Americans. What a multi-party list system would do would provide a greater range of interests being represented and broaden the concept of "representation" to go beyond narrow geography to include representation of such things as ideas and positions on policy issues that would be understandable to voters. Moreover, as for geographic representation on a list system, it would be in the self interest of the parties to insure that there was not only gender balance—if this is what the party wanted—on their list, but also other forms of balance including geography, ideology, and ethnicity, among others.

The third advantage is government representativeness. Not only is a consensus-based parliamentary system based on proportional representation more representative of the voting public, it also produces more representative governments. (Birchfield and Crepaz 1998) This study finds that consensus-based, PR systems also produce a high degree of "popular cabinet support," namely the percentage of voters supporting the majority party or coalition.

The fourth advantage to a PR system in the US is that it would eliminate the redistricting circus. Until recently, the decennial census occasioned the excruciating task of micro-managing the drawing of congressional districts. Yet, since the 2002 elections, Republicans in Texas and Georgia have redistricted a second time, creating even "safer" seats by manipulating district lines to their advantage. (Veith et al. 2003) Under PR however, districts would be eliminated. Candidate lists would be organized statewide, in highly populated states, or regionally in the case of smaller states like those in New England. To insure geographical representation, all parties would find it in their own self-interest that the candidate list included geographical diversity starting at the top of the list.

Getting from Here to There: From Academic Debates to Constitutional Reform?

Clearly, none of these four structural reforms will take place soon. But if reformers wanted to start, what would be the initial steps? Of the four proposals, two of them could be accomplished by simple statute: campaign reform and the electoral system. The other two would require constitutional change: head of state/government and divided government. Given the above caveats, it would be easiest to effect campaign reform (the Supreme Court willing) and to alter the electoral system.

The largest obstacles to such a radical change in the American constitutional system are cultural and structural. Culturally, the ethos of American individualism would have difficulty giving up features such as a single all-powerful executive and one's own individual member of congress, no matter how powerful the arguments raised in support of alternatives. Ideology and cultural practice change very slowly. A more serious obstacle would be the existing interests privileged by the current system. All would fight tenaciously to oppose this suggested change.

Finally, specialists in American politics may dismiss this argument as the farfetched "poaching" of a comparativist on a terrain that only Americanists can write about with knowledge and expertise. However, the durability of all four of the above-mentioned problems, stretching back anywhere from 25 to 50 years, suggests that Americanists have no monopoly of wisdom on overcoming these pathologies. More seriously, what this comparativist perceives is a fundamental failure of imagination based largely on the "N of 1" problem that all comparativists struggle to avoid. If a single observed phenomenon—in this case, the American political system—is not examined comparatively, one never knows whether prevailing practice is optimal or suboptimal. In essence, those who do not look at these issues comparatively suffer a failure of imagination because they are unable to examine the full range of electoral and constitutional options.

References

Allen, Christopher S. 1999. *Transformation of the German Political Party System: Institutional Crisis or Democratic Renewal?* New York: Berghahn Books.

———. 2001. "Proportional Representation." In *Oxford Companion to Politics of the World,* ed. J. Krieger. Oxford: Oxford University Press.

Barker, A. 1994. "The Upturned Stone: Political Scandals and their Investigation Processes in 20 Democracies." *Crime Law and Social Change* 24 (1):337–73.

Birchfield, Vicki, and Markus M. L. Crepaz. 1998. "The Impact of Constitutional Structures and Collective and Competitive Veto Points on Income Inequality in Industrialized Democracies." *European Journal of Political Research* 34 (2):175–200.

Brubaker, Stanley C. 1998. "The Limits of U.S. Campaign Spending Limits." *Public Interest* 133:33–54.

Center for Voting and Democracy. *Dubious Democracy 2007,* September 3 2007 [cited. Available from www.fairvote.org/?page=1917.

Corrado, Anthony. 1997. *Campaign Finance Reform: A Sourcebook.* Washington, D.C.: Brookings Institution.

Cutler, Lloyd. 1989. "Some Reflections About Divided Government." *Presidential Studies Quarterly* 17:485–92.

Dionne, E. J., Jr. 1991. *Why Americans Hate Politics.* New York: Simon and Schuster.

Dwyre, D., M. O'Gorman, and J. Stonecash. 1994. "Disorganized Politics and the Have-Notes: Politics and Taxes in New York and California." *Polity* 27 (1):25–48.

Fiorina, Morris. 1992. *Divided Government.* New York: Macmillan.

Franklin, Mark N., and Wolfgang P. Hirczy de Mino. 1998. "Separated Powers, Divided Government, and Turnout in U.S. Presidential Elections." *American Journal of Political Science* 42 (1):316–26.

Gans, Curtis. 1993. "Television: Political Participation's Enemy #1." *Spectrum: the Journal of State Government* 66 (2):26–31.

Gibson, Martha L. 1995. "Issues, Coalitions, and Divided Government." *Congress & the Presidency* 22 (2):155–66.

Grant, Alan. 1998. "The Politics of American Campaign Finance." *Parliamentary Affairs* 51 (2):223–40.

Grofman, Bernard, and Arend Lijphart. 1986. *Electoral Laws and Their Consequences.* New York: Agathon Press.

Guinier, Lani. 1994. *The Tyranny of the Majority: Fundamental Fairness in Representative Democracy.* New York: The Free Press.

Hill, Steven. 2003. *Fixing Elections: The Failure of America's Winner Take All Politics.* New York: Routledge.

Huber, John D. 1996. "The Vote of Confidence in Parliamentary Democracies." *American Political Science Review* 90 (2): 269–82.

Jacobson, Gary C. 1990. *The Electoral Origins of Divided Government: Competition in U.S. House Elections, 1946–1988.* Boulder, CO: Westview.

Jacoby, Wade. 2000. *Imitation and Politics: Redesigning Germany.* Ithaca: Cornell University Press.

Kernell, Samuel. 1997. *Going Public: New Strategies of Presidential Leadership.* 3rd ed. Washington, D.C.: CQ Press.

Laver, Michael, and Kenneth A. Shepsle. 1996. *Making and Breaking Governments: Cabinets and Legislatures in Parliamentary Democracies.* New York: Cambridge University Press.

Lijphart, Arend. 1984. *Democracies: Patterns of Majoritarian and Consensus Government in Twenty-One Countries.* New Haven: Yale University Press.

———. 1994. "Democracies: Forms, Performance, and Constitutional Engineering." *European Journal of Political Research* 25 (1):1–17.

Linz, Juan. 1993. "The Perils of Presidentialism." In *The Global Resurgence of Democracy,* ed. L. Diamond and M. Plattner. Baltimore: Johns Hopkins University Press.

Lipset, Seymour Martin. 1996. *American Exceptionalism: A Double-Edged Sword.* New York: Norton.

Mayhew, David. 1991. *Divided We Govern: Party Control, Lawmaking, and Investigations, 1946–1990.* New Haven: Yale University Press.

Norris, Pippa. 1997. "Choosing Electoral Systems: Proportional, Majoritarian and Mixed Systems." *International Political Science Review* 18 (3):297–312.

Richter, Michaela. 2002. "Continuity or Politikwechsel? The First Federal Red-Green Coalition." *German Politics & Society* 20 (1):1–48.

Rosenstone, Steven J., Roy L. Behr, and Edward H. Lazarus. 1996. *Third Parties in America: Citizen Response to Major Party Failure.* Princeton: Princeton University Press.

Rule, Wilma, and Joseph F. Zimmerman, eds. 1992. *United States Electoral Systems: Their Impact on Women and Minorities.* New York: Praeger.

Rundquist, Paul S. 1991. *The House of Representatives and the House of Commons: A Brief Comparison of American and British Parliamentary Practice.* Washington, DC: Congressional Research Service, Library of Congress.

Strom, Kaare, Ian Budge, and Michael J. Laver. 1994. "Constraints on Cabinet formation in Parliamentary Democracies." *American Journal of Political Science* 38 (2):303–35.

Thurber, James A. 1991. "Representation, Accountability, and Efficiency in Divided Party Control of Government." *PS* 24:653–7.

Veith, Richard, Norma Jean Veith, and Susan Fuery. 2003. "Oral Argument." In *U.S. Supreme Court.* Washington, DC.

Weinberg, Jonathan. 1993. "Broadcasting and Speech." *California Law Review* 81 (5):1101–206.

Weiss, Stephen. 2004. " '04 Elections Expected to Cost Nearly $4 Billion." In *opensecrets.org—Center for Responsive Politics:* www.opensecrets.org/pressreleases/2004/04spending.asp.

Critical Thinking

1. What is divided government?

2. What are the problems of divided government?

3. What are the advantages of a parliamentary system?

UNIT 6

Unelected Thugs or Expert Protectors? The Judiciary, Intelligence Agencies, and the Military

Unit Selections

Learning Outcomes

After reading this Unit, you will be able to:

- Discuss the powers and limits of the judiciary.

- Discuss the powers and limits of intelligence agencies.

- Discuss the powers and limits of the military.

- Describe the advantages and disadvantages of an elected judiciary.

- Explain "rule of law" and how it strengthens institution building.

- Describe measures to prevent a "runaway" judiciary, intelligence agency, or military.

Student Website
www.mhhe.com/cls

Internet References

Carnegie Endowment for International Peace
    www.carnegieendowment.org
Central Intelligence Agency
    www.cia.gov
Research and Reference (Library of Congress)
    www.loc.gov/rr
Russian and East European Network Information Center, University of Texas at Austin
    http://reenic.utexas.edu
World Wide Web Virtual Library: International Affairs Resources
    www.etown.edu/vl

Unit 6 describes the workings of the unelected branches of the government—the judiciary, intelligence agencies, and the military—to show their impact on policymaking. There is a clear ambivalence regarding these branches of government. In particular, as unelected officers, these officials are able to exert considerable influence as administrators and interpret if and how laws are carried out. Consequently, they have significant influence on the institutional effects over politics and society.

What does this influence mean in practice? Article 30, the first reading in the unit, reveals that where the executive or judiciary may be dragging its heels on policy making, ranging from counterterrorism to environmental protection, the judiciaries across a range of countries have executed clearer and more consistent policies in these areas. A look at these judicial decisions reveal that the claim that unelected officers are displacing elected ones is untenable: The judiciaries are ruling in areas where the executives and legislatures have failed to pursue clear policy options. The reality, then, is that the judiciary is expanding "policy space" to facilitate decision making rather than angling for a part as a policymaker. In doing so, the judiciary is engaging the other branches of government—the executive and the legislature—by applying the interpretation of foreign and international laws to cases, or stepping in to give voice to those unrepresented or poorly represented, such as following the Civil War in the United States. and during the rise of fascism in Europe

This is particularly relevant to countries where institutional-building has been short-changed. Consider the situation in Russia, as described in Article 31. The author notes that the judiciary fills in for government "failures" in representation. In particular, the author notes that the political elites in Russia are more than willing to manipulate and circumvent the law when it is "inconvenient," so that the fundamental principle that law should apply equally to everyone, without regard to money or influence, is brazenly flouted. Yet, even under these circumstances where the "fish rots from the head," the legal structure in Russia has opened access to Russian citizens through the justice-of-the-peace courts. In the process, this has ensured a "small measure of predictability." Also, perhaps as a result of availing legal information and substance, Russians—particularly human rights groups—are now using the European Court of Human Rights to further their claims.

Does this mean that the ambivalence is misguided? Not quite. The next three articles point to situations—in the military and covert institutions—that show that when unelected officials are not accountable, they may also behave in ways that destabilize the country. This is the case for transitioning countries such as Pakistan, that is, even where the military is considered an important ally and essential for political stability. The author of Article 32 "Getting the Military Out of Pakistani Politics" directly contradicts the long-held perception among policymakers in Washington that a strong military is key to the country's political and social development. Instead, he points out that the military looks strong given the institutional weaknesses in politics and society; paradoxically, the money that goes into keeping the military strong comes at the expense of political and social institution building that will support democratic development. Here,

© MHE USA

the experience of Thailand with the military's role is instructive: When a military has intervened politically to displace unpopular or corrupt political leaders, that role is likely "reduced and reconfigured," rather than eliminated. Indeed, one of the big questions when Thaksin's sister, Yingluck Shinawatra, won elections in August 5, 2011, is: Will the outcome be respected? That is, will the military step in to jettison Yingluck's premiership?

Importantly, too, it is not just the military or politics in transitioning countries or emergent democracies that lead to unaccountable unelected officials. Consider the case of the Scotland Yard: the famed 182-year-old intelligence agency is under intense scrutiny for the phone-hacking scandal related to News Corp. The investigation has turned up impropriety in other cases and includes bribery and corruption of police officers. As the article points out, the real question that investigators are evaluating is, Are there systematic flaws in accountability that permitted such transgressions?

Perhaps we need to consider changing these institutions to elected position. Are there clear advantages for continuing the practice of keeping branches of government unelected? In reviewing unelected officials, it is worthwhile to pay heed to the following argument on accountability:

"Horizontal accountability" (a concept developed by scholars such as Guillermo O'Donnell and Richard Sklar) refers to the capacity of governmental institutions—including such "agencies of restraint" as courts, independent electoral tribunals, anticorruption bodies, central banks, auditing agencies, and ombudsmen—to check abuses by other public agencies and branches of government. (It is distinguished from, and complements, "vertical accountability," through which public officials are held accountable by free elections, a free press, and an active civil society).[1]

Clearly, democratic progress in any country must build on both vertical and horizontal accountability. Like all other branches of government, these agencies or branches should not displace policymaking. Instead, an essential may be oversight or checks, so that the influence of these unelected officials do not exceed elected ones. When these unelected officials are countenanced with constraints, they stand as additional venues for citizen access. Then, they are not generally "runaway" policymakers; instead, they potentially fill in for government failures or oversights. At that level, perhaps the question is not whether they should have influence but, rather, why not.

Note

1. Harald Waldrauch of the Institute for Advanced Studies (Vienna), and the editors of the International Forum for Democratic Studies's Report on the Third Vienna Dialogue on Democracy on "Institutionalizing Horizontal Accountability: How Democracies Can Fight Corruption and the Abuse of Power," 6-29 June 1997, co-sponsored by the Austrian Institute for Advanced Studies (Vienna) and the National Endowment for Democracy's International Forum for Democratic Studies (Washington, D.C.). Available at www.ned.org/forum/reports/accountability/report.html

Reclaiming Democracy: The Strategic Uses of Foreign and International Law by National Courts

EYAL BENVENISTI

Not so long ago the overwhelming majority of courts in democratic countries shared a reluctance to refer to foreign and international law. Their policy was to avoid any application of foreign sources of law that would clash with the position of their domestic governments. Many jurists find recourse to foreign and international law inappropriate. But even the supporters of reference to external sources of law hold this unexplored assumption that reliance on foreign and international law inevitably comes into tension with the value of national sovereignty. Hence, the scholarly debate is framed along the lines of the well-known broader debate on "the countermajoritarian difficulty." This article questions this assumption of tension. It argues that for courts in most democratic countries—even if not for U.S. courts at present—referring to foreign and international law has become an effective instrument for empowering the domestic democratic processes by shielding them from external economic, political, and even legal pressures. Citing international law therefore actually bolsters domestic democratic processes and reclaims national sovereignty from the diverse forces of globalization. Stated differently, most national courts, seeking to maintain the vitality of their national political institutions and to safeguard their own domestic status vis-à-vis the political branches, cannot afford to ignore foreign and international law.

In recent years, courts in several democracies have begun to engage seriously in the interpretation and application of international law and to heed the constitutional jurisprudence of other national courts. Most recently, this new tendency has been demonstrated by the judicial responses to the global counterterrorism effort since the events of September 11, 2001: national courts have been challenging executive unilateralism in what could perhaps be a globally coordinated move. In this article I describe and explain this shift, arguing that the chief motivation of the national courts is not to promote global justice, for they continue to regard themselves first and foremost as national agents. Rather, the new jurisprudence is part of a reaction to the forces of globalization, which are placing increasing pressure on the different domestic branches of government to conform to global standards. This reaction seeks to expand the space for domestic deliberation, to strengthen the ability of national governments to withstand the pressure brought to bear by interest groups and powerful foreign governments, and to insulate the national courts from intergovernmental pressures. For this strategy to succeed, courts need to forge a united judicial front, which entails coordinating their policies with equally positioned courts in other countries by developing common communication tools consisting of international law and comparative constitutional law. The analysis also explains why the U.S. Supreme Court, which does not need to protect the domestic political or judicial processes from external pressure, has still not joined this collective effort. On the basis of this insight into the driving force behind reliance on foreign law, the article proposes another outlook for assessing the legitimacy of national courts' resort to foreign and international legal sources. It asserts that recourse to these sources is perfectly legitimate from a democratic theory perspective, as it aims at reclaiming democracy from the debilitating grip of globalization. . . .

[The article begins with a theoretical explanation in part I of the motivation behind this new judicial assertiveness. Part II sets forth the evidence of the phenomenon of interjudicial cooperation in three areas in which it can now be discerned: counterterrorism, the environment, and migration. Part III discusses the potential, limits, and legitimacy of this evolving practice. Part IV concludes the article. . . .]

Judicial Cooperation— the Evidence

The strategic use of foreign and international law characterizes interjudicial cooperation that seeks to review and shape government policies. This collective empowerment process is not required in other areas of judicial cooperation, such as in transnational civil litigation, where governmental interests are not implicated. This part argues that so far this phenomenon is discernible in at least three areas: the judicial review of global counterterrorism measures, the protection of the environment in developing countries, and the status of asylum seekers in destination countries. In these three areas courts apparently reacted to governmental responses to external pressures that the courts regarded as either too weak (in the contexts of counterterrorism and the environment) or too strong (against asylum seekers). The following examination of the evolution of judicial cooperation as the courts seek to counterbalance their governments in these three areas can offer only a broad and sketchy outline of the emerging jurisprudence. It aims, of course, at demonstrating the probability of the thesis, rather than analyzing the specific areas in depth. Therefore, it focuses more on the means of communication—the increased use of comparative constitutional law and the creative use of international law—than on the specific content of the norms. Further and more intensive research is necessary to explore these and possibly other areas of judicial cooperation more deeply.

Reviewing Global Counterterrorism Measures

More than six years into the coordinated global effort against Al Qaeda and its associated groups, it has become increasingly clear that the persistent attempts by the executive and legislative branches of various democracies to curtail judicial review of counterterrorism policies have mostly failed. These governments have not succeeded in convincing their courts to defer judgement and, in fact, have generated a counterreaction by the judiciary. Hesitant at first, the courts regained their confidence and are asserting novel claims that bolster their judicial authority.

In the wake of the terrorist attack of September 11, 2001, national courts faced a major challenge to their authority. Alarmed over the potentially devastating effects of global terrorism, governments sought to intensify restrictions on rights and liberties perceived as facilitating terrorist acts or impeding counterterrorism measures. They insisted on broad, exclusive discretion to shape and implement these constraints as they saw fit, based on the claim that the executive holds a relative advantage over the other branches of government in assessing and managing the risks of terrorism. The post-9/11 global counterterrorism effort effectively united national security agencies in a common cause. They began acting both directly in collaboration with one another and indirectly through a web of formal and informal international institutions. The central formal collective effort was founded on the authority of the United Nations Security Council; the rather informal efforts ranged from the activities of such institutional entities as the Proliferation Security Initiative and the Financial Action Task Force, to government-to-government exchanges, to complicity in illegal practices such as "extraordinary renditions" and "secret prisons."

Most legislatures submitted to these measures without demur. Far-reaching legislative changes, hurriedly introduced in most democracies in the weeks and months following the Al Qaeda attack, sailed through legislatures with little public debate or scrutiny. The immediate shock of 9/11 led many to view basic principles of due process, shaped by democratic societies' preference to err in favor of liberty, as entailing unacceptable risks.

This wave of acquiescence in national political leaders' claims to absolute discretion in acting to guarantee national security swept the courts as well. Traditionally, conformity of this nature in times of war and national crisis has been a hallmark of judicial practice. Suffice it to recall the decisions rendered by the British and U.S. highest courts during the two world wars and the early Cold War era, in which they deferred to the executive's discretion, on the basis of the limited authority and institutional capacity of the judiciary to assess and manage the risks of war. Thus, in the weeks following September 11, the familiar rhetoric of judicial deference was repeated by an alarmed court. The 9/11 attacks in some inexplicable way "proved" more clearly than ever the case for judicial silence.

But three years later, the House of Lords found that the tragic events yielded a wholly different lesson. The Belmarsh Detainees decision of December 2004, which pronounced parts of the British Anti-terrorism Act incompatible with European human rights standards, was described by one of the Law Lords as countering "the public fear whipped up by the governments of the United States and the United Kingdom since September 11, 2001 and their determination to bend established international law to their will and to undermine its essential structures." The transformation in judicial approach evident in this decision was not limited to the UK context. In light of the similar, if not as dramatic, changes in the ways national courts have reacted to their executive's security-related claims since 9/11, it is possible now to speak of a new phase in the way democracies are addressing the threat of terrorism: national courts are challenging executive unilateralism in what could perhaps be a globally coordinated move. The bold House of Lords decision of 2004 was not the first sign of judicial resistance. This should be attributed to the (much criticized) decision by the Supreme Court of Canada of January 11, 2002. Although the Court found that, in principle, there is no prohibition on deportation to a country that may inflict torture on the deportee, it did require the minister to submit a written explanation for deporting a person to a country that is likely to torture him or her. This procedural requirement set a high enough bar to prevent such instances of deportation. The most recent decision of the Canadian Supreme Court in a terrorism-related matter, the Charkaoui decision of February 2007, significantly surpassed its 2002 judgement: the Court declared unanimously that the procedures allowing for the deportation of noncitizens suspected of terrorist activities on the basis of confidential information, as well as the denial of a prompt hearing to foreign nationals, are incompatible with the Canadian Charter of Rights and Freedoms. This bold decision was replete with comparative references to foreign and international statutory and case law. The Court referred specifically to the British Anti-terrorism Act as an example of hearing procedures for suspected terrorists that the Canadian legislature should consider adopting.

This emerging judicial dialogue has not been confined to the British and Canadian courts. It currently includes courts in several other jurisdictions, including France, Germany, Hong Kong, India, Israel, and New Zealand, all in the context of limiting counterterrorism measures. In their decisions these courts explore the international obligations of their respective states, making reference to the texts of treaties on human rights and the laws of armed conflict, and to customary international law. They learn from each other's constitutional law doctrines. They cite each other extensively in this process of interpretation. For example, in a House of Lords decision concerning the admissibility of evidence obtained through torture by foreign officials, the Law Lords engaged in a comparative analysis of the jurisprudence of foreign courts, including those of Canada, the Netherlands, France, Germany, and the United States. Moreover, they compare statutory arrangements in different countries as a way to determine the measures that minimally impair constitutional rights. They do so, fully aware of their own role in the global effort to curb terrorism. As the Indian Supreme Court has acknowledged: "Anti-terrorism activities in the global level are mainly carried out through bilateral and multilateral co-operation among nations. It has thus become our international obligation also to pass necessary laws to fight terrorism. [I]n the light of global terrorist threats, collective global action is necessary." The Indian Court supported this statement with a reference to Lord Woolf 's assertion that "[w]here international terrorists are operating globally. . . . a collective approach to terrorism is important."

This aggregation of defiant judicial decisions from various jurisdictions paints a distinct picture of an evolving pattern in national courts. The trend stands in clear contrast to the passivity of legislatures toward the executive and to previous judicial trends. National courts are refusing just to rubber-stamp the actions of the political branches of government. They have unmistakably signaled their intention to constrain counterterrorism measures they deem excessive. As reflected in the reasoning of the decisions of many courts, they are seriously monitoring other courts' jurisprudence, and their invocation of international law demonstrates knowledge and sophistication.

As opposed to the jurisprudence on migration policies, discussed below, the decisions on counterterrorism reveal a discernible effort by the courts to engage their political branches rather than have the final say on the issues under debate. What characterizes many of the decisions on the lawfulness of the counterterrorism measures is their attempt to avoid, to the extent possible, making a determination on the substance of the specific executive action and, instead, to clarify the considerations that the executive must take into account in exercising its discretion, or to invite the legislature to weigh in on the matter or reconsider a hasty or vague authorization it had granted. While focusing on these institutional levels, the courts have the opportunity to set higher barriers for legislative authorization by invoking the state's international obligations as relevant considerations for the legislature to consider. Direct limitation on the legislature based on constitutional grounds—the ultimate judicial sanction—has been used only sparingly.

An instructive example of carefully climbing up the ladder of judicial review can be found in the U.S. Supreme Court's jurisprudence on the treatment of post-9/11 detainees in Guantanamo and elsewhere. Referral back to the executive or legislature was the first stage of the Court's involvement in this matter. The Rasuland Hamdi decisions asserted the Court's jurisdiction to review executive action with respect to unlawful combatants held on U.S. territory or territory under U.S. administration, and required the president to clarify the executive's authority to act. The second round came two years later with the Hamdan decision, which rejected the president's response to the previous judgements. In Hamdan, the majority relied on international law as the standard for assessing the legality of the military commissions established by the president to determine the status of Guantanamo detainees. In its judgement, the Court diverged from the executive's position in two important aspects: first, that common Article 3 of the 1949 Geneva Conventions applies to the conflict with Al Qaeda and, second, that the standards set by that article are not met by the commissions. The Justices continued to use the referral technique by indicating that the executive can still seek Congress's approval for derogating from those requirements, but four Justices hinted that the Court may eventually examine the constitutionality of Congress's intervention. The pending petition to the Supreme Court questioning the constitutionality of the Military Commissions Act of 200673 is the ultimate stage of review.

Whereas the U.S. Congress was not deterred from inflicting "a stinging rebuke to the Supreme Court" by stripping the courts of habeas corpus jurisdiction with respect to non-U.S. citizens determined by the executive to be enemy combatants, and immunizing the executive from judicial review based on the 1949 Geneva Conventions, other executive bodies and legislatures have demonstrated a stronger commitment to international standards as interpreted by their courts, despite the fact that if they wanted to, they could have the last word.

Environmental Protection in Developing Countries

One need not travel to India or Pakistan to realize the extent to which their environments are at risk. Indeed, it suffices to read the many court decisions rendered in those countries to get a sense of the health threats to their citizens posed by environmental degradation. The courts in several developing countries are responding to the deficient environmental laws and institutions, striving to ameliorate the situation as best they can. These courts are transforming themselves into lawmakers by opening their gates to potential petitioners with lenient standing requirements and by reading into the constitutional right to life a host of environmental obligations incumbent on the state. They even intervene proactively in the executive's sphere of discretion, establishing institutional mechanisms to assess and monitor environmental damage as a form of relief for petitioners. Judge Sabharwal of the Supreme Court of India hinted at this self-assigned role of the Indian courts, when he explained why the Supreme Court must depart from traditional common law doctrines of tort law to address contemporary environmental hazards:

> Law has to grow in order to satisfy the needs of the fast-changing society and keep abreast with the economic developments taking place in the country. Law cannot afford to remain static. The Court cannot allow judicial thinking to be constricted by reference to the law as it prevails in England or in any other foreign country. Though

the Court should be [open to enlightenment] from whatever source . . . it has to build up its own jurisprudence. It has to evolve new principles and lay down new norms which would adequately deal with the new problems which arise in a highly industrialized economy.

As this quote implies, aggressive judicial activism is not required in countries, particularly developed ones, where public awareness of environmental issues translates into effective political action and modern environmental legislation replaces ancient doctrines of tort law. Where public demand prompts legislators to enact legislation, courts can take a back seat. This factor may explain the distinction between the activism of the Indian Court in the environmental sphere, where existing legislation was viewed as "dysfunctional," and its passivity on employee rights, criticized for its narrow interpretation of statutes intended to expand those rights. This factor may also explain why courts in developed countries continue to defer to the domestic political process in the environmental context and refrain from implementing international standards. Indeed, the activist Indian Court declined to intervene in a petition against damming the Narmada River in view of the robust decision-making processes that led to the decision to do so.

In the absence of specific domestic legislation, courts in environmentally threatened jurisdictions can ground their formal authority to expand and enforce environment-related procedures and standards on two sources: their national constitutions and international law. These two sources enable communication with the courts of other nations, through cross-citing of one another's judgements; and, in fact, interjudicial communications have proved to be the hallmark of the jurisprudence of these courts, with the Indian Supreme Court leading the way. In 1994 the Pakistani Supreme Court made references to Indian cases. In 1996 Judge Rahman of the Bangladesh Appellate Division presented the Indian jurisprudence as a model for emulation. In 2000 the Sri Lanka Supreme Court referred to an Indian judgement with approval. The Indian Supreme Court itself referred to judgements of the courts of the Philippines, Colombia, and South Africa and of the European Court of Human Rights, as well as to a decision of the Inter-American Commission on Human Rights, noting with evident satisfaction that "the concept of a healthy environment as a part of the fundamental right to life, developed by our Supreme Court, is finding acceptance in various countries side by side with the right to development."

The absence of clear text relating to environmental protection in many constitutions has meant that courts must derive such protection from the basic right to life, which is anchored in all constitutions. The Supreme Court of India relied heavily on the constitutional right to life, holding that the right to enjoyment of pollution-free water and air is necessary for the full enjoyment of life. To develop the scope of this right, the Indian Court, as well as other courts, found inspiration and even authority in international law.

Recourse to international law, however, encounters tricky impediments. International environmental law is fragmented, many of the provisions being little more than hortatory declarations. The status of these norms in the domestic legal order often presents an additional obstacle to their judicial invocation. But faced with impending environmental disasters, courts in several countries have waived all doctrinal concerns and embraced whatever guidance they can derive from the diverse international documents dealing with the environment. The Supreme Court of India has taken the lead in tapping these international legal sources. Its decisions refer to the Declaration of the 1972 Stockholm Conference on the Human Environment as the "Magna-Carta of our environment" and import into domestic law concepts and principles such as "sustainable development," the "polluter pays" principle, and the "precautionary principle," all mentioned in international "soft law" instruments. The Court often does not explain the legal significance of these international documents, at times referring, for instance, to declarations such as the 1992 Rio Declaration on Environment and Development as "agreements" that were "enacted." The multiplicity of such nonbinding documents and their endorsement by a great number of governments at high-profile gatherings have been the apparent basis for the Court's reference to them as having been transformed into "Customary International Law though [their] salient feature[s] have yet to be finalised by the International Law Jurists." The Indian Court has grounded its decisions on standards set in unincorporated international agreements based on the premise that these conventions "elucidate and go to effectuate the fundamental rights guaranteed by our Constitution [and therefore] can be relied upon by Courts as facets of those fundamental rights and hence enforceable as such." Other courts in the region (in Pakistan, Sri Lanka, Nepal, and Bangladesh) have concurred in the Indian Supreme Court's jurisprudence by similarly invoking these principles in their judgements on the environment.

Clearly, these courts are fully aware of the potentially adverse economic implications of their pro-environment jurisprudence. Interjudicial cooperation must therefore be seen as a way to mitigate those adverse consequences. Given the grave environmental threat hovering over the Indian subcontinent, these national courts might just as doggedly have pushed for reform even without backing from their counterparts in neighboring nations. But lack of such cooperation might have made them much less resistant to pressure brought by domestic and foreign industry groups to whom lower environmental standards mean greater economic gain. These courts are not all-powerful in their quest to restrain the economic forces of globalization.

Coordinating the Migration into Destination Countries

Waves of asylum seekers from regions wasted by strife and poverty, especially since the early 1990s, have prompted developed countries to modify their migration policies by considerably restricting the access of refugees and limiting their rights. Such restrictions have increased the importance of the minimal obligations states owe to refugees under international law. The courts in destination countries have played an important role in shaping the policies regarding the various asylum seekers subject to *refoulement* or deportation. The migration policy adopted by one state had immediate effects in other states and many considered it essential to coordinate migration policies. The ways that national courts in destination countries have interpreted and applied international law on migration are therefore a key test of the thesis presented in this article.

As opposed to the two areas of judicial creativity discussed earlier in this part, the formulation of national migration policies has been high on the political agenda of many destination countries. The political branches expected the courts to respect domestic political processes and uphold both the results of sustained deliberation and public opinion. Defying the popular will by abiding by the demands of international law might incur more than heavy criticism. A court that "cooperated" with the strict requirements of international law would channel refugees to its country's shores if other courts "defected" by interpreting the international law concerning refugees less generously.

By and large, courts could not immediately reflect the transformation of national policies. The jurisprudence related to *refoulement* and expulsion to countries where torture could be committed against the expellee was too clear to be waived. Direct contact with individual refugees and their painful life stories, together with the judges' confidence in their ability to distinguish genuine from bogus claims, probably also moved courts to adopt a critical stance toward new executive and legislative policies. Decisions of courts in the majority of destination jurisdictions reflect this sentiment. Interjudicial cooperation is necessary in this area to enable the courts to stand up to the domestic political process without incurring the "costs" of increasing the numbers of refugees. The stakes, however, are high, and it would be ineffective, even irresponsible, for judges to rely only on the old practice of comparing decisions and engaging in intermittent exchanges. Perhaps such sentiments lay behind the establishment in 1995 of the International Association of Refugee Law Judges (IARLJ). In 2003 Dr. Hugo Storey, then a vice president of the UK Immigration Appeal Tribunal and a member of the IARLJ Council, explained the raison d'etre of the association: "[One] of IARLJ's principal objectives is the development of consistent and coherent refugee jurisprudence. Ideally a person who claims to be a refugee under the 1951 Convention should receive the same judicial assessment of his case whether he is in Germany, the USA, Japan or South Africa."

The constitution of the IARLJ reflects this ambitious program. Two of its preambular clauses describe the extent of the challenge:

Whereas the numbers of persons seeking protection outside of their countries of origin are significant and pose challenges that transcend national boundaries;

Whereas judges and quasi-judicial decision makers in all regions of the world have a special role to play in ensuring that persons seeking protection outside their country of origin find the 1951 Convention and its 1967 Protocol as well as other international and regional instruments applied fairly, consistently, and in accordance with the rule of law.

The IARLJ constitution also asserts that one of its objectives is "[t]o foster judicial independence and to facilitate the development within national legal systems of independent institutions applying judicial principles to refugee law issues." Membership in the IARLJ is open to judges or "quasi-judicial decision makers"; in August 2007, there were 332 members from fifty-two countries. The members can benefit from a Web-based database of court decisions applying the asylum law of different countries, and a members-only newsletter and forum. A leading expert in refugee law, James Hathaway, praised the association, viewing it as an alternative to the "more vigorously collaborative and formalized models" of international enforcement mechanisms in other areas of international human rights law, including international tribunals.

During the 1990s, national courts dealing with asylum seekers began citing each other's interpretation of the 1951 Convention Relating to the Status of Refugees, in particular its key provision regarding the definition of "refugee." This Convention provided a basis for coordinating a judicial position that often enabled these courts to strike down restrictive governmental policies without risking an influx of immigrants. This is not to suggest that the courts were always unanimous on each and every aspect of the elaborate qualifications of a "refugee." But what clearly emerges from several key decisions of the highest courts of the majority of destination states is the judicial effort to arrive at a contemporary meaning of the 1951 Convention that would expand the definition of "refugee" beyond the one envisioned in 1951, and to do so despite the concerns of contemporary governments. This effort is captured by the following statement of Lord Carswell:

The persecution of minorities and the migration of people seeking refuge from persecution have been unhappily enduring features, which did not end with the conclusion of the Second World War. . . . The vehicle [for balancing states' international obligations against their concerns] has been the [1951 Refugee Convention], which was the subject of agreement between states over 50 years ago, when the problems of the time inevitably differed in many respects from those prevailing today. That a means of reaching an accommodation suitable to cater for modern conditions has been achieved is a tribute to the wisdom and humanity of those who have had to construe the terms of the Convention and apply them to multifarious individual cases.

In their wisdom, the courts turned to construing the terms of the Convention collectively. This judicial dialogue can be traced to the early 1990s, when a 1993 judgement of the Canadian Supreme Court cited a 1985 decision of the United States Board of Immigration tribunal, to be cited itself later by the High Court of Australia in 1997, the New Zealand Refugee Status Authority in 1998, and the House of Lords in 1999. In the latter judgement, the Law Lords commend the New Zealand Refugee Status Authority for its "impressive judgement," which draws on "the case law and practice in Germany, The Netherlands, Sweden, Denmark, Canada, Australia and the U.S.A." In 2000 the U.S. Court of Appeals for the Ninth Circuit retreated from its prior interpretation, which these other courts had refused to follow, and endorsed the evolving common position, acknowledging that this position is also taken by the neighboring Canadian court. This ongoing interjudicial exchange has necessarily involved disagreements over particular aspects of the definition, but the dialogue has been conducted with the utmost respect and careful attention. "As evidenced by the Ninth Circuit's 2000 judgement in Hernandez-Montiel v. Immigration and Naturalization Service," such deliberation is ultimately capable of yielding general agreement.

In 2001 the House of Lords openly addressed the role of national courts in preventing "gross distortions" in the implementation of the 1951 Geneva Refugee Convention through "a uniformity of approach to the refugee problem." Lord Steyn insisted on a joint judicial effort to look beyond national peculiarities when interpreting a shared text:

> In principle therefore there can only be one true interpretation of a treaty. If there is disagreement on the meaning of the Geneva Convention, it can be resolved by the International Court of Justice (art 38 of the Geneva Convention). It has, however, never been asked to make such a ruling. The prospect of a reference to the International Court of Justice is remote. In practice it is left to national courts, faced with a material disagreement on an issue of interpretation, to resolve it. But in doing so it must search, untrammelled by notions of its national legal culture, for the true autonomous and international meaning of the treaty. And there can only be one true meaning.

But this very decision also demonstrated the limits of judicial independence, as well as the limited ability of the written word to withstand domestic political pressures. Some courts, most notably in France and Germany, have operated since the early 1990s in a political environment increasingly concerned about the influx of refugees. Restrictive policies were adopted in both countries by constitutional amendment. During the 1990s, many, if not most, refugees were fleeing countries affected by civil wars and intercommunal strife, and European courts were called upon to decide whether "persecution" in the sense of the 1951 Convention could be effected by nonstate agents. While the majority of the courts, including those of the United Kingdom, recognized that nonstate agents could be deemed "persecutors," some others, including those of Germany and France, refused to follow suit. As a result, German courts would not recognize as "refugees" asylum seekers from countries such as Afghanistan, Bosnia, Sri Lanka, and Somalia, who had suffered at the hands of nonstate actors, and French courts would similarly reject the applications of Algerians persecuted by militias, lacking evidence that the Algerian state had either encouraged or tolerated the persecution. The lesser protection afforded to such persons in these two countries prompted the House of Lords to quash the secretary of state's decision to send refugees from Somalia and Algeria to Germany and France, respectively, out of concern that they might be deported and face persecution.

The judicial "defections" by the French and German courts were based on the traditional justifications: the accordance of precedence to the peculiarities of national constitutions and laws implementing the international obligations; the narrow interpretation of the international obligations through the invocation of governmental practice rather than the jurisprudence of foreign courts; and the distinguishing of seemingly pertinent decisions of international courts. The French Constitutional Council and the German Federal Constitutional Court examined domestic legislation in light of the recently amended constitutions. The German Federal Administrative Court gave precedence to a domestic act that incorporated the international obligation to protect refugees, interpreting that act in light of the German Basic Law. The court did acknowledge that other courts had recognized the refugee status of those persecuted by nonstate agents (referring to the jurisprudence of the United States, the United Kingdom, France, Canada, and Australia). It even asserted that the interpretation of the same treaty by other courts usually carries "special weight," but not, it said, when the intention of the national legislator was as clear as it was in this case. Subsequently, the German court added that its understanding of international law reflected the understanding of most of the governments of the state parties to the 1951 Convention. In another decision handed down on the same day, the court refused to accept an "expansive" and "creative" conflicting interpretation by the European Court of Human Rights, noting that "[i]t is not the task of the courts to expand the boundaries of the member states' ability and willingness to absorb [refugees] through creative interpretation of treaties and thereby to disregard the constitutionally protected sovereignty of the national lawmaker and constitution maker." When the German Constitutional Court reviewed the constitutionality decisions of the Federal Administrative Court, it somewhat expanded the opportunities of asylum seekers who had fled persecution by nonstate agents. However, it did not refer to international law in its interpretation of the relevant provisions of the German law.

The coalition of courts determined to develop a consistent interpretation of the 1951 Convention and the opposing group of courts that insist on a different outcome are two sides of the same coin, the coin being the use of international law as a strategic tool by national courts. For courts that seek to establish a common front, a shared text is an asset they cultivate. At the same time, this story suggests that international law does not preempt courts' seeking to protect their domestic political process by deviating from an evolving standard. The German Federal Administrative Court serves as an example of a court that uses the language of international law to explain why the common standard should not apply in Germany.

As Gerald Neuman notes, a common interpretation of their status and rights may not always be beneficial to asylum seekers. Asylum seekers are likely to benefit from diversity of national policies. But in the trade-off between the common position of the governments and that of the courts, so far the latter has proved more beneficial to the refugees. . . .

Conclusion

This article has argued that the aspiration to "speak with one voice" is shared by a growing number of national courts across the globe. But, as opposed to what prevailed only a decade ago, these courts no longer wish to speak with the voice of their governments but, rather, to align their jurisprudence with that of other national courts. Comparative constitutional law and international law have proven to be the best tools for effectuating this strategy. The article explains this strategy as a reaction to the delegation of governmental authority to formal or informal international institutions and to the mounting economic pressures on governments and courts to conform to global standards. The judicial reaction, in turn, is designed to expand the domestic dialogue and bolster the national governments' ability to resist the attempts of interest groups and powerful foreign governments to influence them. Such motivation for transjurisdictional coordination is fully justified under democratic theories that conceive of the court as a facilitator of democratic deliberation.

As discussed, the coordination strategy is limited to situations in which courts observe that their government, their legislature, or they themselves have succumbed to, or are threatened by, economic or political powers that stifle the democratic process through coordinated supranational standards, be they formal (in treaties) or informal. This limitation suggests that courts might not be equally firm when only local dimensions mark a given dispute, as with those over conditions for detaining local criminals or the displacement of indigenous inhabitants due to dam construction.

It is too early to assess the success of this emerging trend. Every collective action depends on a sufficient number of contributors to the effort. Changes in the domestic rules protecting judicial independence could put a damper on the willingness of the courts in the relevant countries to take on an assertive role. In addition, governments may be pressured to submit to intergovernmental attempts to deprive courts of the authority or opportunity to act. But on the basis of the analysis in this article, it seems safe to assume that courts will not idly tolerate the erosion of their authority to review the actions of the political branches. In an era when governments are opting for alternatives to formal internal or international lawmaking, it is the national courts that are seriously resorting to comparative constitutional law and international law. This turn of events is a surprising mirror image of the state of affairs that prevailed only a decade ago.

Critical Thinking

1. Describe the three areas where there is growing convergence between international and domestic law.

2. Is this convergence between international and domestic law a sign of judicial "overstepping"? Why or why not?

3. Should a judiciary apply international law? Why or why not?

4. What does "expanded policy space" mean? How does it help or hurt institutional building?

EYAL BENVENISTI Professor of Law, Tel Aviv University. I thank Ziv Bohrer, Shai Dothan, George W. Downs, Alon Harel, Tally Kritzman, Ariel Porat, and Eran Shamir-Borer for their very helpful comments on previous versions, and Shay Gurion for excellent research assistance. This article is based partly on research conducted since September 11, 2001, on the ways that national courts cope with international terrorism, funded by the Israel Science Foundation and the Minerva Center for Human Rights at Tel Aviv University. The article was written during a sabbatical leave made possible by a Humboldt Research Award of the Alexander von Humboldt Foundation.

Rule of Law, Russian-Style

Kathryn Hendley

Almost without exception, Russia languishes near the bottom of indexes that purport to measure elements of the "rule of law" in countries around the world. Assessing the extent to which this contempt is deserved depends on how rule of law is defined. As the term has become part of the global political lexicon, its precise meaning has become increasingly opaque. Even so, the principle that law should apply in equal measure to everyone, irrespective of wealth or political clout, is generally accepted as the foundational principle of the rule of law. By this standard, Russia falls short today. What is worse, the continuing behavior of Russia's public officials, as well as deeply set attitudes among ordinary Russians, offers little promise of improvement any time soon.

Certainly Russia's history provides little evidence of commitment to a universalistic view of law. Both the czars and the Communist Party leadership routinely used law as a blunt instrument to advance their interests, enforcing it strictly against the powerless, but stretching it beyond recognition to accommodate themselves and their favorites. Laws were often written in the broadest terms possible so as to give officials maximum flexibility.

Beginning with Soviet leader Mikhail Gorbachev's endorsement of a "rule-of-law-based state" (*pravovoe gosudarstvo*) at the outset of perestroika, the Kremlin's rhetoric shifted. The leaders who have followed Gorbachev have likewise committed themselves to the goal of universalistic law. Vladimir Putin and Dmitri Medvedev, who like Gorbachev are legally trained, have both spoken repeatedly of the importance of institutionalizing a "supremacy of law" (*gospodstvo zakona*). Sadly, their policies have often failed to match their rhetoric.

Much like their predecessors, these post-Soviet leaders have proved willing to countenance the manipulation of law when it has been inconvenient to live up to the law. The Kremlin's seemingly endless campaign against oil tycoon Mikhail Khodorkovsky and his company, Yukos, is only the most notorious example. Not only does such behavior demonstrate the shallowness of Russia's commitment to the civil liberties embodied in the country's constitution and criminal procedure code, but it also reveals the Kremlin's lack of respect for the independence of the judicial branch.

The Kremlin's brazen disregard of legal niceties whenever the law threatens to cramp its style contributes to an "anything goes" legal culture in Russia. Human rights activists and journalists have been murdered with seeming impunity. Business is riddled with corruption. To some extent, of course, this is nothing new. Finding creative ways to get around (*oboiti*) the law has long been the norm in Russia. Indeed, it was a critical coping mechanism in response to the perennial shortages of the Soviet era.

In a perfect world, skirting the law would have become unnecessary with the end of state socialism and, more importantly, unacceptable. But the chaotic nature of the transition only emboldened those who sought to circumvent legal constraints. The well-known adage in Russia, "It is forbidden, but if you really want to do it, then go ahead" (*eto nel'zya, no esli ochen' khochetsya, to mozhno*), captures this sentiment perfectly. So long as those who engage in extralegal behavior stay out of the way of those more powerful, the state has turned a blind eye.

Dual Justice

Most outside observers have assumed that all of these shortcomings add up to a legal system that is dysfunctional and virtually unusable. As usual, Russia confounds expectations. Over the past two decades, with surprisingly little fanfare, the legislative base and institutional infrastructure of the Russian legal system have undergone a remarkable transformation. Citizens' access to the legal system has been enhanced through the introduction of justice-of-the-peace courts (*mirovye sudy*), which have absorbed the bulk of simple cases, freeing up other courts to devote attention to more complicated cases. Thanks to the internet, information about the substance of law and the activities of courts at all levels is increasingly transparent.

Not coincidentally, Russians' use of the courts has grown dramatically. The number of civil (non-criminal) cases has doubled over the past decade. But people's use of the courts is savvy. Russians seek help from the courts when they encounter disputes with those who are similarly situated; they shy away from the courts when they tangle with anyone more powerful.

The dual legal system that has evolved in Russia—in which the courts can be relied on to handle mundane cases, but are likely to bow to the will of the powerful in touchier cases—is a far cry from the rule-of-law-based state that was the initial goal. At the same time, it does provide a small measure of the sort of predictability that lies at the heart of the rule of law. In Russia's legal system an uneasy equilibrium is at play, one that has eluded the media and even many legal analysts. Russians have an innate sense of when to use the courts and when to avoid them.

How the Fish Rots

Even so, a more robust rule of law in Russia will require fundamental changes in attitudes and behavior on the part of both state and society. In my own research, when I have asked ordinary Russians how to fix their legal system, they often remind me of the proverb that "the fish rots from the head" (*ryba gniyot golovy*). To date, the political leadership has talked the talk, but has not walked the walk. The citizenry has grown weary of endless promises. The prescription for the Kremlin can be stated simply—the state and its bureaucrats need to obey the laws they impose on others. Ending the "anything goes" legal culture will not be easy. Solving problems by cutting corners and making side payments is deeply entrenched.

To outsiders, the anticorruption campaign announced by Medvedev when he became president may seem like a good first step toward reining in the state. But Russians have heard it all before. Those with long memories will recall that Putin likewise came to office with a pledge to break the stranglehold of corruption. To be fair, Medvedev has done more than pay lip service. He has acted to limit the discretion of local officials to demand repeated inspections of businesses (thereby giving them multiple opportunities to demand payoffs). He has ordered more oversight of the state procurement process. And he has pushed for fuller disclosure of state officials' incomes and assets.

However, the depth of the Kremlin's commitment to rooting out corruption remains to be seen. Public opinion polling suggests that Russians are unconvinced of that commitment. In a February 2009 survey conducted by the Levada Center, most (53 percent) felt that Medvedev's initiative had made no difference. Indeed, 21 percent believed corruption had worsened since his election.

Enhancing the rule of law in Russia is not entirely a matter of state action. Medvedev has famously railed against the "legal nihilism" of Russian society, but he has been slow to recognize

that society is taking its cues from its leaders in its disregard of the law. For anything to change, Russians have to shake off their traditional passivity vis-à-vis the state. Human rights groups have taken an important step in this regard through their use of the European Court of Human Rights. The Strasbourg court has been swamped by Russian claims, most of which allege a failure on the part of the state to live up to its obligations under the law.

For anything to change, Russians have to shake off their traditional passivity vis-à-vis the state.

But this is an elite strategy; ordinary Russians know little of the European court. In my research, I have been struck by the unwillingness of the ordinary Russians with whom I have spoken to take on any responsibility for the condition of the legal system. It does not seem to occur to them that they could demand more from their political leaders. The weakness of civil society in Russia does not augur well for the development of a more robust rule of law.

Critical Thinking

1. What is "rule of law"? How is "rule of law" achieved?

2. What are the consequences of not achieving "rule of law"?

3. What does "the fish rots from the head" refer to? Should society wait for the state to change? Why or why not?

4. What are "justice-of-the-peace" courts? How do they help or hurt institutional-building?

5. How does the European Court of Human Rights help or hurt the situation in Russia? How does this relate to the previous article?

KATHRYN HENDLEY is a professor of law and political science at the University of Wisconsin-Madison.

Getting the Military out of Pakistani Politics: How Aiding the Army Undermines Democracy

AQIL SHAH

The United States has a major stake in Pakistan's stability, given the country's central role in the U.S.-led effort to, in U.S. President Barack Obama's words, "disrupt, dismantle, and defeat" al Qaeda; its war-prone rivalry with India over Kashmir; and its nuclear arsenal. As a result, U.S. policy toward Pakistan has been dominated by concerns for its stability-providing the reasoning for Washington's backing of the Pakistani military's frequent interventions in domestic politics—at the expense of its democratic institutions. But as the recent eruption of protests in the Middle East against U.S.-backed tyrants has shown, authoritarian stability is not always a winning bet.

Despite U.S. efforts to promote it, stability is hardly Pakistan's distinguishing feature. Indeed, many observers fear that Pakistan could become the world's first nuclear-armed failed state. Their worry is not without reason. More than 63 years after independence, Pakistan is faced with a crumbling economy and a pernicious Taliban insurgency radiating from its Federally Administered Tribal Areas (fata), the semiautonomous seven districts and six smaller regions along its border with Afghanistan. It is still struggling to meet its population's basic needs. More than half its population faces severe poverty, which fuels resentment against the government and feeds political instability.

According to the World Bank, the Pakistani state's effectiveness has actually been in steady decline for the last two decades. In 2010, Foreign Policy even ranked Pakistan as number ten on its Failed States Index, placing it in the "critical" category with such other failed or failing states as Afghanistan, the Democratic Republic of the Congo, and Somalia. The consequences of its failure would no doubt be catastrophic, if for no other reason than al Qaeda and its affiliates could possibly get control of the country's atomic weapons. The Pakistani Taliban's dramatic incursions into Pakistan's northwestern Buner District (just 65 miles from the capital) in 2009 raised the specter of such a takeover.

Pakistan is, of course, a weak state with serious political, economic, and security challenges. But it is not on the fast track to failure, ready to be overturned by warlords, militants, or militias. It has an incredibly resilient civil society, which has proved itself capable of resisting both state and nonstate repression. Its numerous universities, assertive professional associations, vocal human rights groups, and free (if often irresponsible and hypernationalist) media sharply distinguish Pakistan from the likes of Afghanistan or Somalia. And its bureaucratic, judicial, and coercive branches still have plenty of fight left in them. The country's political parties are popular, and parliamentary democracy is the default system of government. The Pakistani military, moreover, is a highly disciplined and cohesive force and is unlikely to let the country slide into chaos or let its prized nuclear weapons fall into the hands of Islamists.

But although Pakistan's army is professional, it has no respect for the political system. It has not mattered whether the army is under the command of a reckless figure, such as General Pervez Musharraf, or a more prudent one, such as the current chief of staff, Ashfaq Parvez Kayani. As an institution, it deeply distrusts politicians and sees itself as the only force standing between stability and anarchy, intervening in politics whenever it decides that the politicians are not governing effectively. These repeated interventions have weakened Pakistan's civilian institutional capacity, undermined the growth of representative institutions, and fomented deep divisions in the country.

Pakistan is unlikely to collapse, but the imbalance of power between its civilian and military branches needs to be addressed if it is to become a normal modern state that is capable of effectively governing its territory. For its part, the United States must resist using the generals as shortcuts to stability, demonstrate patience with Pakistan's civilian authorities, and help them consolidate their hold on power.

The Capacity Dilemma

The Pakistani military's political power is a historical legacy of the country's birth. The immediate onset of conflict over Kashmir in 1947–48 with a militarily and politically stronger India made the military central to the state's survival and placed it above civilian scrutiny. Today, after four wars with India, the military filters every internal and external development through the lens of Pakistan's rivalry with India. Civilian governments, such as the current one, headed by President Asif Ali Zardari's Pakistan Peoples Party (ppp), and those headed by Nawaz Sharif's Pakistan Muslim League (pml-n), have typically operated in the military's lurking shadow.

The military has frequently co-opted Islamists to advance its domestic and regional agendas. In the late 1970s and into the 1980s, the generals, especially the U.S.-funded military dictator General Muhammad Zia-ul-Haq, used Islamism to gain political legitimacy. Zia suppressed secular political rivals, such as the ppp, by jailing and torturing opposition leaders, banning political parties, and enacting harsh Islamic laws to appease allies in Islamist parties, such as the Jamaat-e-Islami. Zia also armed Sunni sectarian groups in order to balance the country's Shiite minority, which had been emboldened by the recent Iranian Revolution. State patronage of violent extremism deepened sectarian rifts, militarized the society, and empowered radical Islamists, all of which in turn eroded the state's own writ and authority.

Flush with U.S. cash, the generals also fomented militancy in Kashmir to keep India bleeding and sponsored fundamentalism in Afghanistan to give Pakistan strategic depth against its archrival. Yet faced with U.S. President George W. Bush's famous ultimatum after 9/11 to either cut the military's ties to Afghan militants or prepare for war, Pakistani President Musharraf ostensibly jettisoned the generals' black-turbaned allies. He granted the United States access to Pakistani air bases, expanded Pakistan's intelligence cooperation, provided logistical support for the U.S. invasion of Afghanistan, and helped the United States with its primary objective—killing or capturing members of al Qaeda. The United States was content with this level of cooperation and did not press Pakistan to help stabilize Afghanistan or target the Afghan Taliban, who had fled to Pakistan in the wake of the U.S. invasion.

Yet by 2004, the Taliban threatened to undermine the Afghan regime from their stronghold in Pakistan, and the Bush administration demanded that Pakistan address the problem, "the sooner, the better" in the words of Zalmay Khalilzad, then U.S. ambassador to Kabul. Since then, the Pakistani military has targeted militant groups in several parts of fata and in the Malakand region of Khyber Pakhtunkhwa (formerly the North-West Frontier Province).

But the military has a pick-and-choose approach to counterterrorism, even though terrorism poses a grave threat to Pakistan's internal security and stability. It has targeted members of the Pakistani Taliban in South Waziristan and other administrative agencies in fata, for example, but has persistently refused to take action in North Waziristan, which is the headquarters of the Haqqani network, an al Qaeda–affiliated Afghan militant group that leads the cross-border insurgency in eastern Afghanistan. It also continues to allow top members of the former Afghan Taliban regime to operate from Pakistan's major cities, especially Quetta and Karachi. Although Lashkar-e-Taiba, a militant group that carries out attacks in India and Indian Kashmir, is formally banned in Pakistan, it continues to operate through proxies and aliases, recruiting operatives, organizing rallies, collecting funds for its "charitable" activities, and publishing proselytizing jihadist materials in plain sight of Pakistani intelligence authorities.

Although ending the insurgency in Afghanistan will require more than just eliminating militant sanctuaries in Pakistan, the Pakistani military's reluctance to target Afghan militants in North Waziristan has been a particularly sore point in its relationship with the United States. U.S. officials believe that the lawlessness of North Waziristan hampers the U.S. military effort in Afghanistan, since insurgents can easily escape to safety on the Pakistani side of the border. For its part, the Pakistani military denies sheltering the Afghan Taliban anywhere in the country and claims that it cannot expand its operations into North Waziristan because it is stretched thin by its existing deployments and is short of critical military hardware, such as attack and transport helicopters.

Several U.S. and Pakistani observers agree with this assessment. Writing on March 23, 2010, in *The New York Times,* the Brookings fellow Michael O'Hanlon argued that Pakistan "simply does not have the military capacity to make major moves against the Afghan fundamentalists." Former U.S. Secretary of State Colin Powell reportedly believes that Pakistan needs more armaments to successfully fight insurgents on its border with Afghanistan. And Maleeha Lodhi, former editor of *The News International* and former Pakistani ambassador to the United States, similarly contends that pushing the military to fight on multiple fronts is likely to strain its capacity and undermine its existing missions.

Yet even if capacity is a genuine issue, it is not the reason that counterterrorism in Pakistan has failed. It is a pretext for inaction, rhetorically implying that the military has undergone a strategic paradigm shift, seeing militancy as a threat to national security rather than as a useful tool of foreign policy. Yet there are reasons to be skeptical. First, the Pakistani military has shown that it does indeed have the tools it needs to fight terrorism in several tribal areas simultaneously

when it wants to. Besides, it already receives enough U.S. security assistance—roughly $300 million since 2002 in foreign military financing and around $1.1 billion since 2008 for increasing its counterinsurgency capabilities, to be followed by $1.2 billion more next year—to acquire the capacity it claims to so desperately need. In contrast, in 2010, U.S. aid for Pakistan's poorly paid, undertrained, and underresourced police forces, which are crucial to fighting insurgencies, totaled a paltry $66 million.

Second, it is unlikely that the Pakistani military has truly changed its calculation of the strategic value of militant groups. Before it moved into South Waziristan in October of 2009, the military cited similar shortages in resources yet was able to conduct a full and relatively successful mission there, clearing the area, capturing or killing many militants, and dismantling their bases and training camps. Indeed, the military seems to confront only those militants who threaten and attack the army itself. When the Pakistani government requested that the military go into South Waziristan, for example, it dragged its feet for months and was spurred into action only after militants carried out a deadly attack on its heavily guarded headquarters in the northern city of Rawalpindi. At the same time, it holds those groups that do not threaten it, including the Haqqani network, as reserve assets for the endgame in Afghanistan, when U.S. troops start pulling out this July and eventually leave by 2014. In fact, Pakistan's intelligence service has reportedly permitted Haqqani fighters to flee U.S. drone attacks in North Waziristan and relocate to bases in the nearby Kurram region.

Troublingly, the military's capacity alibi shifts the blame for the strength of Pakistan's violent extremists from the military—which has nurtured and legitimized the influence of radical Islamists—to civilian leaders and foreign patrons, who have supposedly neglected to provide the army with enough resources. Yet the extremists' growth and power in Pakistani society are a direct result of the military's pursuit of strategic depth against India. In fact, the military's permissive attitude toward radical Islamists has allowed them to infiltrate the lower echelons of Pakistan's security services. This worrying development was vividly demonstrated by the brutal murder of Salman Taseer, the governor of Punjab, Pakistan's largest province, by his own police guard on January 4 for opposing the blasphemy laws. Brazen terrorist attacks have battered the military itself, and suicide bombings in major Pakistani cities, including a spate of them in 2009 that claimed over 3,000 lives, have undermined citizens' confidence in the government's ability to provide them with security. Surprisingly, such attacks have not seemed to erode confidence in the military, especially after it provided quicker and more effective relief than the government after last year's devastating floods-although trust in the military should not be confused with public support for military rule.

Can Might Make Right?

With all the resources in the world, the Pakistani military alone would be insufficient to conquer terrorism. So far, wherever it has tried to deal with militants, it has alternated between attempting to subdue them with brute force and, when that does not work, cutting its losses by appeasing them with peace deals. Both approaches have further fueled militancy. For instance, the military's use of artillery and aerial strikes to "soften targets" (sometimes without sufficient warning to civilian populations) and its collective punishment of tribes (under the Frontier Crimes Regulation, the colonial-era law under which fata is still governed) have angered and alienated locals, reportedly facilitating militant recruitment. In exchange for a ceasefire, the peace agreements have ceded territory to the militants and given them the space to openly recruit, train, and arm themselves. The terms of the military's 2005 deal with Baitullah Mehsud, who was the leader of the Pakistani Taliban until his death in 2009, for example, stipulated that the military would release captured militants and vacate Mehsud's territory in return for a pledge that he would not harbor foreign fighters or attack

Pakistani security forces. The military claims to have learned its lesson and has adopted a new strategy of counterinsurgency based on winning hearts and minds. But even in its recent campaigns, such as the 2009 offensives in the Swat Valley and South Waziristan, which were relatively more successful in terms of clearing militants and taking back territory, the military favored a heavy use of force and displaced millions of citizens. Moreover, it failed to capture or kill any significant number of senior Taliban leaders.

Militant extremism can be fought effectively only through serious governance reforms that ensure the rule of law and accountability. This will require a strong democracy, a viable economy, and well-balanced civil-military relations. In fata, it will require abolishing the Frontier Crimes Regulation and integrating the region into the adjoining Khyber Pakhtunkhwa Province to end the Pakistani federal government's direct and oppressive rule, which the Pakistani Taliban have exploited to expand their influence, displace the already weakened tribal authority in the region, and establish parallel courts and policing systems in several fata agencies, including North and South Waziristan. All of this seems daunting, but there is really no other long-term alternative. And despite its many failings and weaknesses, there are reasons to be optimistic about democracy in Pakistan.

If the "third wave" of democratization in the 1970s and 1980s had any lesson, it is that democracy does not necessarily require natural-born democrats or a mythically selfless political leadership. In fact, a strong democratic system can mitigate the baser instincts of politicians. If anything, the experience of countries such as Chile, the Philippines, South Korea, and Thailand in the last few decades shows that the strength and quality of democracy may be linked to the stability of the party system. This is good news for Pakistan. It is true that Pakistan's civilian politics is dominated by a few families, namely the Bhuttos, who control the ppp, and the Sharifs, who control the pml-n. In a perverse way, however, the hold of the Bhuttos and the Sharifs on their parties may be one of the main reasons that these parties have survived the military's divide-and-rule repression and may consolidate democracy in the future.

Already, the demands of governing seem to be putting some positive pressure on Pakistan's politicians. The most recent civilian government is only three years old, yet the much-derided political elite seems to have developed a consensus that democracy is the only game in town and has enacted constitutional reforms to curb outsized presidential powers–an artifact of previous military regimes–especially the power to dismiss democratically elected parliaments and prime ministers, which past military or military-backed presidents used to neuter parliament. The government has also created new parliamentary committees to appoint Supreme Court and provincial High Court judges and the country's top election officials, delegated some administrative and financial authority to the provinces, and raised the share of the federal revenue pool that the provinces receive.

The best way to further boost Pakistan's democracy will be to habituate the military to democratic norms and raise the costs of undermining democratic governance. The current parliament has already removed some constitutional loopholes that military leaders used in the past to avoid prosecution for coups. It has also proscribed the judiciary's frequent practice of legalizing military rule. But more direct attempts at exerting civilian control have backfired, including the government's short-lived July 2008 decision to bring Pakistan's secretive Inter-Services Intelligence (isi)—which technically answers to the prime minister but in practice operates as the military's intelligence wing—under the control of the Interior Ministry. The move was reversed during a midnight phone call between an angry Army Chief Kayani and the prime minister. And now, the ongoing ethnic violence in the southern port city of Karachi and the politically charged turf battles between the ppp government and the Supreme Court over the judiciary's encroachments on executive authority—such as its sacking of top federal officials, its creation of judicial cells to monitor specific

corruption cases, and its fixing of basic commodity prices—could invite renewed military intervention.

But such setbacks are not uncommon in transitional democracies and should not prevent civilian politicians from continuing to take measured steps to establish civilian supremacy. For instance, instead of staying out of defense policy completely, the civilian government should call regular meetings of the cabinet's Defense Committee to discuss and make key national security decisions. Civilians should also try to exert more control over the Ministry of Defense, subject military expenditures to vigorous parliamentary debate, create a bipartisan parliamentary subcommittee for intelligence oversight, enact legislation to bring the isi under civilian control, and appoint a special cabinet committee to approve top military promotions and appointments.

Out-of-Balance Budgets

The other critical obstacle to democratization and stability in Pakistan is the country's weak economic performance. The civilian government inherited a cash-strapped, highly indebted economy from the Musharraf regime and had to ask the International Monetary Fund for a $7.6 billion bailout in 2008 to avoid default. Last summer's heavy floods, which displaced some 20 million people and caused considerable damage to Pakistan's civilian infrastructure, dealt a devastating blow to the prospects of economic resurgence. Perceptions of widespread government corruption and civilian authorities' apparent unwillingness to cut spending have not helped. Moreover, Pakistan has one of the lowest tax-to-gdp ratios in the world—only two percent of the population pays any taxes at all—yet the government has not been able to agree on critical tax reforms.

Pakistan must also reckon with the need to alleviate the economic hardships faced by its poor. Skyrocketing inflation of basic commodity prices, chronic power cuts, persistently high levels of unemployment, and general lawlessness are fueling public resentment of the current government. Some observers fear that the downward economic spiral could play into the hands of Islamists, but there is no automatic link between economic woes and the influence of Islamists in public life. In Pakistan, Islamist influence has been closely tied to state patronage, not popular support. Islamist parties continue to perform poorly at the polls, never garnering more than 10–12 percent of the vote, whereas the two main moderate parties—the ppp and the pml-n—typically claim about 60 percent of the vote and 70 percent of the seats in the national parliament.

Still, Pakistan's civilian government must stabilize the economy to bolster public confidence in democratic institutions. It must invest in Pakistan's long-term economic development and create opportunities for the country's rapidly growing population. It may even need a long-term, multibillion-dollar Marshall Plan to help build civilian institutional capacity, rebuild areas hit by last year's floods, invest in public-sector and infrastructure projects, and plug the energy shortages that have all but crippled the manufacturing sector, especially its top exporting textile industry. Of course, such a plan should come with proper controls to fight corruption and waste.

It is worth noting that Pakistan's economic difficulties are the result not just of bad luck and poor management, and therefore they cannot be fixed with development aid alone. They are rooted in fundamental structural problems as well: military expenditures dwarf spending on development. Pakistan has one of the world's largest out-of-school populations, yet it spends seven times as much on the military every year as on education, an investment with a higher national security payoff in the long run. Thus, the country must find a way to rationalize its military expenditures.

Some progress toward a resolution of the Kashmir conflict could induce Pakistan to scale back its military behemoth. It could also potentially reduce the attractiveness of using militancy as an instrument of foreign policy. As Steve Coll chronicled in *The New Yorker* in

2009, Musharraf and Indian Prime Minister Manmohan Singh were quite close to reaching a breakthrough accord on Kashmir in 2008, but it was aborted by the rapid erosion of Musharraf's authority in the face of domestic opposition to his dictatorial rule. The point is that only a strong, stable, and legitimate elected government will be able to mobilize the public opinion necessary to clinch a lasting peace with India. Both the ppp and the pml-n favor cooperation over confrontation in the region, and each has tried to mend fences with India, through high-level diplomacy as well as backdoor talks, only to be upbraided by the generals for compromising on national security. These parties need more room to pursue peace with India while holding the military at bay. This is something the United States can help provide, by firmly supporting democratic institutions in Pakistan even as it works with the military to fight al Qaeda.

No Means No

The Obama administration came into office in 2009 with a solid commitment to supporting Pakistan's then year-old civilian democratic government as a hedge against militancy and terrorism. The Kerry-Lugar-Berman bill, which was passed into law as the Enhanced Partnership With Pakistan Act of 2009, authorized the U.S. Congress to triple civilian development assistance to Pakistan, raising it to $7.5 billion between 2010 and 2014. The aid package was designed to signal a new era in the United States' relationship with Pakistan, shifting the focus of U.S. aid from the military to civilian democratic governance and social development. Continued military aid was also tied to a yearly certification by the U.S. secretary of state that the Pakistani military has refrained from interfering in politics and is subject to civilian control over budgetary allocations, officer promotions, and strategic planning.

Not surprisingly, the Pakistani military balked at this affront even as the civilian government welcomed the aid. Joining with opposition parties, the military publicly decried the bill as a threat to Pakistani national security and mobilized right-wing sections of the media against U.S. meddling. In response, the bill's sponsors buckled and effectively defanged the conditionality measures. Even though the text of the law is intact, the United States meekly assured the Pakistani military that the intent of the conditions was misinterpreted and that the United States would keep its nose out of the generals' business. Indeed, most contact between the two countries still occurs behind closed doors between the two militaries or between the cia and the isi. The cia's use of unmanned drones against militants in fata, which are reportedly flown out of Pakistani bases, exemplifies this lack of transparency. The secrecy of the program allows both the United States and Pakistan to escape responsibility for civilian casualties.

The climb-down on the Enhanced Partnership Act indicated that even though the U.S. Congress recognizes the folly of building exclusive alliances with the Pakistani military, it still prefers engaging with Pakistan's military over its civilian leaders. This is partly pragmatism: The military is still the most powerful institution in Pakistan. But by continuing to treat the Pakistani military as a state above the state, the United States only reinforces the military's exaggerated sense of indispensability and further weakens civilian rule.

If the United States had stood its ground, the Pakistani military would have eventually backed down. It is dependent on the United States for military aid and high-tech armaments, including upgrading its aging fleet of f-16 fighters. And although the military has leverage over Washington since it controls U.S. supply routes into landlocked Afghanistan, its bargaining position has weakened over time.

Although Washington generally remains reluctant to pressure the Pakistani military, appropriately using sticks has not necessarily meant losing the generals' cooperation in fighting terrorism. For example, the U.S. Congress warned that it would cut off U.S. aid in response to Pakistan's detention of a cia contractor, Raymond Davis, who was arrested in January for fatally shooting two Pakistanis in the eastern city of Lahore. In the end, Davis was released from jail in March—the families of the victims agreed to pardon him after receiving compensation. His release would not have been possible without military complicity.

Such political and diplomatic pressure should be used to censure the military for political incursions. In this spirit, the United States should signal to the military that cracking down on terrorism is not a license for it to destabilize or overrun the government. The U.S. military should remind its Pakistani counterpart that interference in politics will not be tolerated and could have serious repercussions, including a downgrading of military ties, the suspension of nondevelopment aid, and broader diplomatic isolation.

Although the United States is confronted with an economic recession of its own, more civilian aid for (and trade with) Pakistan would cost relatively little compared to the money that the United States spends fighting Afghan and Pakistani extremists. And the potential dividends could be enormous: U.S. civilian aid could help secure civilian rule in Pakistan for the long haul and diminish anti-Americanism as well. To reduce the danger of moral hazard, this aid should be tightly linked to Pakistan's economic performance, progress in combating corruption, and transparency and responsiveness in government.

One relatively easy way for the United States to boost economic productivity in Pakistan would be to grant Pakistan emergency duty-free access to the U.S. market for textiles. This concession would face opposition from politically powerful U.S. textile interests, but the Obama administration should pursue this legislation on at least a temporary basis because it could crucially improve the economic stability of a vital ally by increasing the revenue it gets from this important industry.

Although a settlement of the Kashmir conflict is unlikely in the short term, Washington should continue to push both sides to achieve that goal. Of course, there are no guarantees that peace would be sufficient to reduce Pakistan's military expenditures or restrict the military to its proper constitutional sphere. But it is worth the effort because the international community has a stake in ending the nuclearized Indian-Pakistani rivalry, which not only endangers global security but also has spilled into Afghanistan.

With over a hundred nuclear weapons, a war-prone rivalry with India, and the presence of some of the world's most dangerous terrorists on its soil, Pakistan is too important to be left to the devices of its generals. For too long, the United States has sacrificed democracy for order. The results have been less than ideal, especially for the people of Pakistan. Pakistan urgently needs support from the international community to help stabilize its civilian democratic institutions and bolster its economy. Only such support will ensure its stability and reliability as a U.S. partner in the region.

Critical Thinking

1. Describe the reasons for the international community's support a stronger military in Pakistan.
2. Describe the dual tactics of the Pakistan military on terrorism. What are the consequences of these tactics?
3. Describe how military spending affects the economy in Pakistan.

AQIL SHAH is a Postdoctoral Fellow at the Society of Fellows at Harvard University. He is the author of the forthcoming book *Out of Control: The Pakistan Military and Politics in Historical and Regional Perspective.*

From *Foreign Affairs*, vol. 90, Iss. 3, May/June 2011, pp. 69–82. Copyright © 2011 by Council on Foreign Relations, Inc. Reprinted by permission of Foreign Affairs. www.ForeignAffairs.com

Thailand: From Violence to Reconciliation?

Catharin Dalpino

In May 2010, when a month-long siege of Bangkok's elite Ratchaprasong district by "red-shirt" protesters ended, calm returned to Thailand's capital. But 85 people had died during the unrest, and another 1,378 had been injured. Preliminary estimates of property damage totaled more than $1.25 billion, and as many as 100,000 Bangkok workers and residents were left unemployed or bankrupt. This protracted period of violence was one of the most destructive episodes in Thailand's history. At the same time, it was just one phase in a four-year-long political conflict that has damaged the country's political system, social fabric, and image in the international community.

Red-shirted supporters of the United Front for Democracy Against Dictatorship (UDD) were challenging the legitimacy of Prime Minister Abhisit Vejjajiva's government and demanding new elections. The protesters' occupation of Ratchaprasong—a neighborhood that contains major banks, shopping malls, and the Thai Stock Exchange—came to a violent end after negotiations broke down, on May 19, between the Thai government and the UDD. The Abhisit administration, after divisions within the opposition caused the talks to falter, ordered security forces to disperse the red shirts' camps.

The UDD's response was to set fire to 39 buildings. These included the stock exchange and several branches of Bangkok Bank, which symbolized the Thai establishment; as well as the huge Central World mall, which was linked to business families that had allied themselves against, or fallen out with, the former prime minister Thaksin Shinawatra, a primary catalyst of the red-shirt movement. The UDD claimed the arson was a spontaneous reaction to the government's crackdown. The Abhisit administration considered the fires proof that the UDD leadership was made up of criminals and terrorists.

Since May, a state of emergency has remained in effect throughout much of the country, including a number of provinces in central, north, and northeast Thailand, where UDD influence is strongest. Shortly after the May 19 crackdown, the government announced a five-point reconciliation plan, and initial steps have been taken in that regard, but few believe that building political stability will be a quick or orderly process.

The relative calm across the nation today marks a striking contrast to the episodic violence of the spring. Thailand has receded from the front pages of international newspapers. Even so, the country remains suspended between crisis and normal political life, and is likely to remain so for at least several months.

Old Grievances

Understanding the complex political situation in Thailand is made more difficult by perceptions, prevalent in the international media, that it is a matter of easy opposites: yellow shirt versus red shirt, rich versus poor, urban versus rural, and authoritarian versus democratic. Each of these dichotomies contains an element of truth, but each also inaccurately stigmatizes (or lionizes) large numbers of people.

In reality, each group in Thailand's color-coded political conflict—the People's Alliance for Democracy (PAD), or yellow shirts; and the UDD, or red shirts—is a loose coalition of various interests. As the conflict has sharpened, however, attempts have been made to place the groups on an ideological spectrum. The yellow shirts are held to be more authoritarian and monarchist, while the red shirts are characterized as left-wing, even radical. (This ideological overlay has radiated outside Thailand and has created tensions in academic and think tank communities, as individual analysts are occasionally labeled pro–or anti–yellow shirt or red shirt.) As the country moves out of crisis mode, reducing the polarization in the Thai political arena and, to some extent, in Thai society will be a critical challenge.

An explanation frequently offered for the twists and turns in Thailand's political crisis over the past four years concerns the rise and fall of Thaksin. His popularity in the years immediately following the 1997 Asian financial crisis (of which Thailand was the epicenter); the attention he paid to rural areas in his campaigns; his abuses of power while in office; the Bangkok-based movement against him (led by a former business partner); his overthrow in a relatively tranquil military coup in 2006; his status as a fugitive after he left Thailand in advance of his trial on corruption charges; and his machinations in exile—all this has made Thaksin a storied, even legendary, figure. Without a doubt, he remains a rallying point among his followers, many of whom live in the rural north and northeast. However, a key question that is far from resolved is to what extent he remains a central factor in Thai politics today.

An important subtext of the political crisis is the gap between urban and rural Thais. As in most mainland Southeast Asian countries, the Thai political system is a centralized one, all the more so because Thailand was the only country in the region that was never colonized. In Myanmar (also known as Burma), Vietnam, Cambodia, and Laos, European colonization acted as a circuit breaker, eliminating or weakening the power of traditional monarchies and forging administrative structures that linked the capital to the provinces. Thailand's political and administrative structures, never having experienced colonial intervention, still bear a resemblance to Southeast Asia's ancient mandala system, in which power was concentrated in the center and center-province relations were often a one-way street.

Recent Thai constitutions have attempted to foster a degree of decentralization, but the results have not met expectations in the country's rural areas. Indeed, rural red-shirt discontent with Bangkok and the ongoing communal violence in Thailand's Muslim south can be viewed as two sides of the same coin: Both have as much to do with the center-province dynamic as they do with more specific grievances that have erupted in recent years.

However, the notion that Thaksin singlehandedly awakened a sleeping rural population, causing its members to demand their political and economic rights, is a romantic fallacy. Center-province relations and the distribution of economic benefits have, in fact, been central issues in Thai political discourse since the country's constitutional monarchy was established in 1932. In the "modernization" period of the 1930s, Bangkok bureaucrats fanned out to the provinces to promote a uniform view of the Thai nation, not always with positive results. During the cold war, provinces in border areas, particularly in the northeast, benefited from infrastructure and other development projects as the government attempted to push back the insurgent threat of the Communist Party of Thailand.

In the heady 1980s, when the Thai economy grew by double—digit rates for several years in a row, provinces that directly drew a large portion of tax revenue (often because of tourism)–Bangkok, Chiang Mai, and Phuket—agitated for the right to elect their own governors. (Out of this group, only Bangkok now has an elected governor.) In recent decades, modern communications, economic development, and the country's turn to elected parliamentary government in the late 1980s have afforded the provincial population new channels to communicate its views and needs to Bangkok. Although the Thaksin phenomenon no doubt accelerated the trajectory of rural activism in Thailand, the long view suggests that it is an inevitable process.

Money Politics

Another thread that runs through the political conflict is the rise of money politics, the most problematic outcome of Thailand's democratization process. In the late 1980s and early 1990s, greater emphasis was placed on political liberalization and the strengthening of the parliament relative to more traditional institutions of political rule, such as the military and the bureaucracy. But the country's strong economic growth of the time both helped and hindered the development of democracy.

Thailand's new commercial class, no longer content to depend on traditional power centers to protect its interests, packed the parliament. Some business people ran for election; others increased their influence by giving financial backing to political parties, which have tended to coalesce more around personalities than policies. Like their more traditional counterparts, however, the rising business interests focused their attention on Bangkok. They often approached rural constituencies with cash, which they used to buy or influence votes, but they seldom encouraged bottom-up processes that would give provincial voters a greater voice in the political process.

The political history of Thailand since the early 1990s can be written as an attempt to bring money politics to heel. Such an account would include, for instance, the 1991 military coup against the government of Prime Minister Chatichai Choonhavan; as well as the drafting and promulgation of the 1997 constitution, which introduced new measures of accountability for elected officials and gave the judicial system greater responsibility for curbing political corruption. (The 1997 constitution, though it was overturned in the 2006 coup, remains the template for constitutional reform.)

Accountability and constitutional issues have fueled much of the current political crisis, from the Thaksin family corruption trials (focused on the former prime minister and his former wife) to the dissolution by the courts of two political parties linked to Thaksin–the

Thai Rak Thai Party and its successor, the People's Power Party. And some aspect of constitutional reform will likely figure in the current reconciliation effort: For better or worse, Thailand finds it easy to change its constitution. The country has had 18 versions since 1932.

The Generals Weigh In

The role of the armed forces has also been a longstanding issue in Thai politics. The military, one of the principals in a 1932 coup against the absolute monarchy, views itself as the guardian of the modern Thai state. Various elements of the country's political system have concurred on occasion and have formed alliances with the military. However, the continuing importance of the monarchy and the bureaucracy has prevented the military from ruling directly as a class, at least to the extent that the military controls power in Myanmar. Thus, the term "military rule" does not quite describe the political role of the armed forces in Thailand for much of the twentieth century. Without doubt, however, a preponderance of power was concentrated in the military for protracted periods from the 1930s to the 1980s.

With the advent of parliamentary government, the military's political influence did not disappear, but it was reduced and reconfigured. Still willing to assert itself directly when civilian leaders appeared to stray too far into military affairs—regarding promotions and the annual budget allocation for the armed forces, for example—the military nevertheless began taking a more indirect role in politics. The military has continued to act as a power broker in civilian politics, however, and on two occasions has intervened directly, with the coups of 1991 and 2006.

In both coups, the Bangkok political classes were tacitly acquiescent to military intervention. In 1991, coalition politics had driven political corruption to unprecedented levels. The 2006 coup occurred well into a popular uprising in Bangkok against Thaksin, led by the PAD. Some factions of the military had turned against Thaksin by that time, and decided to make a move when he was out of the country at the opening of the United Nations General Assembly. Many Bangkok politicians, without denying that it injured democracy, supported that coup. One highranking opposition party official maintained that the intervention was "deplorable but necessary."

The response in Bangkok to the 1991 and 2006 coups shows that, although military rule is no longer acceptable, elements of the population are still willing to accept military intervention when the political system breaks down. However, the attempt by the leaders of the 2006 coup to hold on to power by installing as interim prime minister a former supreme commander, General Surayud Chulanont, was a mistake. Although Surayud had drawn public support because of his military record, his administration proved ineffective, particularly in contrast to that of Anand Panyarachun, a star technocrat who had served as interim prime minister following the 1991 coup and was the driving force behind the 1997 constitution. In any case, if the Bangkok political classes were willing to accept a military overthrow of the Thaksin government, they paid a price when Thaksin's supporters, forced underground, formed the UDD.

Extended Emergency

The current political crisis has underscored another critical issue in Thai civil-military relations: the management of internal security. Although the PAD and UDD during the recent years' unrest were in their own view defending democratic principles, in the fullness of time each was willing to embrace mob rule. The PAD seized the prime minister's office in August 2008, and for three days in November took over Bangkok International Airport. In March 2009 the UDD broke up a meeting of the Association of Southeast Asian Nations in the seaside resort of Pattaya, forcing diplomats to evacuate by helicopter from a hotel roof, or flee by sea. A crackdown by the Abhisit government briefly restored order in April, but by the following year the UDD had regrouped and set up its encampment in Ratchaprasong. That siege included a brief takeover of the Chulalongkorn University hospital where the supreme patriarch, the leader of Thailand's Buddhist Church, was a patient. In both 2008 and 2010, large-scale public protests metastasized into urban conflict.

Clearly, the PAD and UDD's actions have been motivated by a tangled set of political issues. But both the PAD's and UDD's leaders have operated on an assumption of impunity, taking advantage of Thailand's failure to build an effective and accountable internal security structure. There are numerous reasons for this failure, including a police force that has historically been weaker than the military; an uncertain division of labor between the police and the military; a lack of training; and an understandable reluctance on the part of soldiers and police to use force against fellow citizens.

Paradoxically, a strong democracy requires strong government, and building a more effective internal security capacity, though a sensitive issue, is imperative nevertheless. If this need is neglected, Thailand runs the risk that future protest, a right and a mainstay of liberal democracy, will escalate quickly into violence and eventually be constricted as a matter of course.

While the flames were still dying out in Ratchaprasong this spring, the government moved to place a tourniquet on the political crisis. For instance, owners of small and medium-sized businesses that were harmed by the siege were given grants and loans. But much of the administration's early attention was focused on disarming and otherwise constraining the red-shirt movement and apprehending its leaders.

Arrest warrants were issued for 800 UDD leaders and members believed to have ordered or implemented the encampment and the arson in Bangkok, as well as for others linked to secondary UDD attacks in the northeast. By mid-July, a little more than half of those under warrant had been detained. Authorities have also launched an investigation into the UDD's financial resources, and a list of major red-shirt funders has been compiled. The names of some red-shirt figures reportedly have surfaced on a list of people suspected of forming a movement to overthrow the monarchy, now being investigated by a 300-agent force under the Department of Special Investigations.

On July 6, 2010, the government's emergency decree, now in its fourth month, was renewed for three months in Bangkok and several northeastern provinces in an attempt to preempt the resumption of red-shirt protests. The decree bans gatherings of more than five people and places constraints both on internet content and on broadcast stations, particularly private stations associated with the UDD.

Some figures linked to the red-shirt movement have been detained for public comments, deemed sympathetic to the UDD, made after the crackdown in Ratchaprasong. Among these is Sombat Boongamanong, a civil society leader of the younger generation and founder of the well-regarded Mirror Foundation. But the emergency decree applies to all Thais, and signs of self-censorship are beginning to emerge as a result. For instance, a major university recently issued a circular to its faculty warning against "open involvement in political conflict." While many concede that the emergency decree may have been necessary at the height of the violence this spring, its seemingly open-ended nature has drawn expressions of concern in Thailand and abroad.

A Plan in Place

That the government is aware of the deeply rooted nature of the political crisis is evident in the reconciliation plan it put forward in late May. While promising "nationwide psychological rehabilitation," the authorities also conceded that "legitimate grievances of the rural poor such as . . . social injustice" need to be addressed. The plan establishes a number of commissions charged with considering constitutional reforms, as well as measures to close the country's gap in socioeconomic levels.

In a move designed to reassure Thais who recall the political turmoil of the early 1990s, the former prime minister Anand Panyarachun will chair the Committee on Reform Strategy, which will consider constitutional and other government reforms. Another group, the Committee on Reform Assembly, will canvass Thai civil society and establish a national assembly that will function as a channel for public input into the reconciliation and reform process. It is not clear, however, what sort of reception awaits public comment sympathetic to the red-shirt movement.

A third group created under the reconciliation plan is the Independent Fact-Finding Commission for Reconciliation. The commission is composed of lawyers and law school faculty; human rights advocates; journalists; the permanent secretary of the ministry of justice; criminologists; and a professor of psychology. It is charged with probing the underlying circumstances of the political crisis, but it will not function as a truth commission (a model used in countries with protracted internal conflict to identify human rights abusers on all sides of the conflict). Although the commission will have links to the judiciary, the task of identifying perpetrators of violence and abuse, and bringing them to justice, will remain with the courts.

Questions and Complications

Clearly, resolving a political crisis as longstanding and deeply rooted as the present one in Thailand is a daunting prospect. Within the reconciliation plan, it is not clear if short-term measures to curb red-shirt activity and longer-term efforts to address concerns that the UDD brought to light are being undertaken in proper proportion. Too much of the former and too little of the latter could create a backlash that might undo the fragile peace of the post-Ratchaprasong period. Although the government can buy some time with the emergency decree and the prime minister's discretionary power to determine when elections occur, it will be under heavy pressure in the next several months to answer, in particular, four questions.

First, should accountability stop with the red-shirt movement? Government officials have said that they wish to bring UDD leaders to account for the violence this spring, but also to win the "hearts and minds" of the red-shirt rank and file. The past four years in Thailand have seen an escalating series of protest cycles, alternating between yellow shirt and red shirt, and the perception of a one-sided pursuit of justice could be counterproductive.

Mindful of this, on July 12 the government announced that it was asking 80 leaders of the PAD to report to the police by September 6 to face charges related to the takeover of Government House and the seizure of the airport in 2008. Charges made against individuals in the group range from causing a public disturbance to inciting terrorism. The PAD has responded that the move is an attempt to make the government appear even-handed. PAD leaders claim that, in contrast to the UDD, they have never supported armed militants. Others maintain that the long lead time and the option to surrender voluntarily show partiality to the yellow shirts. A related issue concerns the treatment under the law of any government or security official who might be found guilty of abuses of power during the crackdown or the investigations of the events of this spring.

The second question is: What is the best time under the circumstances to hold elections? Elections were the crux of the red-shirt protests against the Abhisit government: The UDD believed that the parliamentary process through which Abhisit was selected as prime minister after the People's Power Party was dissolved, though legal under the constitution, was not politically legitimate. The UDD's demand throughout the 2009 and 2010 protests was that elections be held immediately.

Before negotiations fell apart in May, Abhisit had offered November 2010 as an election date, but has since retracted that. Government officials indicate informally that the likeliest date for elections is now April 2011, with the start of the campaign presumably coming early in the new year. Since Abhisit's term will end in December 2011, his maneuverability in this regard will be increasingly curtailed.

However, the commissions formed under the reconciliation plan have deadlines ranging from two to three years to submit their findings, with a requirement to submit progress reports to the government every six months. It is doubtful that the longer-term process of achieving genuine reconciliation will be complete before the next elections.

Even so, the elections will require that there be sufficient political stability for all parties to participate and for the outcome to be accepted. Without that, an electoral victory for the Puea Thai Party, the third-generation pro-Thaksin party, could re-energize the yellow-shirt protest movement, while a result that goes against Puea Thai could inflame red-shirt sympathizers. This very dilemma was illustrated in late July in Bangkok, when a by-election demonstrated support for the Democrat Party, and implicitly the Abhisit administration, but also sparked a red-shirt rally and a bombing incident.

The third question is: Will the present government be able to serve out its term under the law? The issue here is not that the UDD views the government as illegitimate. Rather, it was the attorney general's office that in July recommended that the Constitutional Court dissolve the Democrat Party, the main party in the government coalition, and ban several of its leaders—including Prime Minister Abhisit—from politics for five years.

Article 215 of the constitution, the so-called nuclear-option clause, abolishes a political party when its leaders are convicted of electoral or financial impropriety; this was the undoing of both the Thai Rak Thai Party and the People's Power Party. Leaders of the Democrat Party are confident they will be acquitted on legal merit of the charges, which focus on campaign contributions made in the middle of the past decade by a Thai cement conglomerate. However, even an acquittal could be problematic in a tense political climate. Given the fate of the two pro-Thaksin parties, red shirts may perceive acquittal as evidence of judicial partiality.

What about Thaksin?

The fourth question is: Should Thaksin be included in the reconciliation effort? Although there were reports of informal dialogue with the former prime minister as recently as this spring, since the upsurge of red-shirt activity the Abhisit administration has taken an increasingly hard line toward Thaksin, emphasizing his status as a legal fugitive. One of the most hotly debated topics regarding the protests is the extent to which Thaksin incited the red-shirt actions of 2009 and 2010, and whether direct causal connections can be proved.

On May 25, the Thai Criminal Court approved an arrest warrant for Thaksin on terrorism charges in connection with the Ratchaprasong violence, a crime that could carry the death penalty. In recent months, the government has pressed the international community for help in apprehending him, as well as in seizing assets he is believed to have banked abroad, with little result to date.

If the government is determined to decouple rural grievances from the UDD, it should also consider ways to decouple these issues from Thaksin himself. It is unclear whether that can best be done by further isolating him, or by considering the means and benefits of his return to Thailand. Nor is it certain that Thaksin would approach negotiations regarding his return in good faith, or indeed what he would be seeking if he did return. Would it be amnesty for outstanding criminal convictions and charges, the return of his assets, or even latitude to contest for power in the political arena?

With the Puea Thai Party still viable, it is unlikely that Thaksin's influence will fade from the country's politics altogether, but reconciliation must address the Thaksin factor in an effective manner. Closing this troubled chapter in Thai politicasl history may require dealing with Thaksin himself; it will in any case require a sustained effort that addresses both short-term and long-term grievances, and personalities as well as principles.

Critical Thinking

1. Explain how identifying the conflict in Thailand as one between the red- versus yellow-shirts is not useful.

2. Describe the source of political tensions in Thailand.

3. Describe the role of the military in Thailand.

CATHARIN DALPINO is a visiting fellow at the School of Advanced International Studies at Johns Hopkins University. She is a former U.S. deputy assistant secretary of state for democracy.

From *Current History,* vol. 109, iss. 728 , September, 2010, pp. 258–263. Copyright © 2010 by Current History, Inc. Reprinted by permission.

In Britain, Phone Hacking Sullies Famed Scotland Yard

ANTHONY FAIOLA

London—Immortalized in the pages of Sir Arthur Conan Doyle and Agatha Christie, Scotland Yard is a globally renowned symbol of policing, its constables the cherished guardians of Britain's upright rule of law.

But as the phone-hacking scandal here explodes, the bobbies of Scotland Yard are weathering their worst crisis in years, one that has portrayed some of the force's highest-ranking officials as bumbling Keystone Kops and painted others as woefully corrupt beat cops willing to accept bribes in excess of $160,000 to pass on juicy tidbits to the press.

As it exposes murky ties between Britain's muckraking tabloid press and police, the scandal is damaging the public's faith in the Yard—nickname of London's Metropolitan Police, once famously headquartered on a foggy street named Great Scotland Yard. At stake is the prestige of a 182-year-old force, with an independent inquiry set to probe corruption and mismanagement at all levels of the institution and threatening the jobs of top officials at a time when they are gearing up for a massive operation for the 2012 Olympic Games.

The scandal centers on allegations that Rupert Murdoch's *News of the World* tabloid for years used illegal methods for newsgathering, including passing fat envelopes of cash to officers and tapping into the private messages of thousands of British citizens, from crime victims to celebrities to members of the royal family.

After making just two arrests in 2006 and considering wrongdoing at the tabloid an isolated incident, Met officers dropped the case. Despite revelations in 2009 by the *Guardian* newspaper about far wider misdeeds at *News of the World*, officers reopened the case only under mounting pressure earlier this year. Until then, police investigators insisted to politicians, the press and the public that there was no more to the case.

In the spotlight now is what the relationship the force of more than 51,000 officers has with Britain's muckraking tabloids and whether that influenced their judgment. On Thursday, for instance, they arrested *News of the World's* former executive editor Neil Wallis, only to concede the same day that he had worked for Scotland Yard as a media consultant from October 2009 through September 2010. He was paid $38,000 a year to come in two days a month, despite public allegations at the time that the tabloid had engaged in widespread illegal activity during his tenure.

That came after current and former top Met officers were hauled before a parliamentary committee this week for what amounted to a public humiliation for some, with lawmakers openly laughing at John Yates, its assistant commissioner who was once in line for the Yard's top job. Calls for his resignation escalated this week after information emerged that he had dined with News Corp. editors while *News of the World* was still under investigation.

"We've heard some extraordinary things from the Met this week," Deputy Prime Minister Nicholas Clegg said Thursday. "Not least that a high-ranking officer felt it acceptable to be wined and dined by senior newspaper executives under investigation. The Met now has a big job on its hands winning back the public confidence that has been lost."

A Seedy World

The scandal is laying bare the seedy world of British tabloid journalism and the pivotal role corrupt police officers have long played in it. *Rebekah Brooks,* the high-powered News Corp. executive who resigned Friday in the wake of the scandal, had testified in Parliament as early as 2003 that *News of the World* had paid police officers for information. The Met, however, says that since

2000, only two officers have been investigated for taking bribes from any British publication. And both were cleared of wrongdoing.

A former *News of the World* deputy features editor, Paul McMullan, said in an interview that the paper routinely paid cops for tips, with cash dished out from a safe "in the managing editor's office."

"That was true especially with Diana," McMullan said, referring to the late Princess of Wales. "We would get calls from our police contacts telling us what airport she was landing in, and who was with her. That kind of information was worth several thousand pounds."

He recalled one story he worked on when $5,000 worth of British pounds was paid to a beat officer who had found the daughter of award-winning actor Denholm Elliott—known for roles in *Raiders of the Lost Ark* and *A Room With a View*—impoverished and living on the streets. "He called us up and told us about it, and we covered the story," he said. "He got the money, we got the story. She killed herself a few years later. I felt particularly guilty about that one."

"We Did Not Do Enough"

In addition to allegations of bribery—including reports in the *Guardian* this week that as many as five officers accepted *News of the World* payments in excess of $160,000—Scotland Yard is under the gun for mismanaging the investigation into the phone-hacking scandal.

Yates admitted this week that the initial investigation launched in 2005 had been woefully flawed. Scotland Yard declined a request to comment for this article, referring to public statements by its top officials. Early this week, Yates called the choice not to move forward with a broader investigation earlier "a poor decision." "We did not do enough," he said.

Observers say Scotland Yard is now bracing for the fallout of an independent inquiry into the scandal, including involvement of at least a handful of its own police officers. But more significantly could be findings of systematic flaws within Scotland Yard's management system that allowed the hacking investigation to fall between the cracks and corrupt officers to go unpunished.

"A few officers do things they shouldn't, they are corruptible, and that is not shocking whether it's the NYPD or the Met police," said Tim Newburn, professor of criminology at the London School of Economics. "But what we will discover from the inquiry now is how and whether this was being managed higher up the chain of command, about a failure to act. The judge will be asking some quite searching and very difficult questions."

Special correspondent Eliza Mackintosh contributed to this report.

Critical Thinking

1. Why does the phone-hacking incident in Great Britain sully the Scotland Yard?

2. What institutional failures are illustrated by the phone-hacking incident?

3. Explain how the Scotland Yard incident may be similar to concerns over the role of the military in the previous articles.

UNIT 7

Trends and Challenges: Institutional Change through Capitalism, Globalization, or Supra-National Government?

Unit Selections

Learning Outcomes

After reading this Unit, you will be able to:

- Explain why "tolerance" is at the heart of democratic institutionalization.

- Distinguish between superficial versus real support for democracy.

- Explain if Islam supports democracy.

- Explain the significance of strong support for institutional building.

- Clarify what it means that institutions are not unique to the countries identified in the articles.

- Clarify how IT is useful for political development and how it is not useful.

- Clarify how a country's level of political or social development may affect its posture.

Student Website
www.mhhe.com/cls

Internet References

Carnegie Endowment for International Peace
    www.ceip.org
Freedom House
    http://freedomhouse.org/template.cfm?page=1
ISN International Relations and Security Network
    www.isn.ethz.ch
NATO Integrated Data Service (NIDS)
    www.nato.int/structur/nids/nids.htm

Units 1 through 6 describe the systematic treatment of the political behaviors of citizens, interest groups, parties, the executive, legislature, and unelected officers in government. The discussions make clear the relevance of institutions and institution building in providing formal venues to regulate and regularize political behaviors so that they are clear-cut, comprehensible, constant, and, thus, predictable. But, if institutions affect political behaviors, it is also indisputable that political behaviors shape institutions. In this Unit, we examine the "what, how, and why" of institutional changes. In the process, we consider the extent to which political behaviors shape institutions in general, and democratization in particular.

What are institutional changes? Institutional changes refer to the creation or alteration of political organizations, conventions, or participation. They include modifications in political or legal processes, such as reported in the article on China's institutional changes. They may be radical or gradual, which is also suggested in the article. They may involve the creation of new political organizations, as indicated by the article on the EU. Or they may capture a change in values and conventions, as described in Article 35 "The True Clash of Civilizations."

How do institutional changes occur? Institutional changes are brought on by a combination of the following: domestic demand, such as by citizens, interest groups, and the government; or new pressures from globalization. Institutional changes generated by domestic demand often hinges on changes in valutes and attituides. Thus, the article by Inglehart and Norris points out that democratization in the Muslim world is supported or hampered by values over self-expression rather than on its cultural aptitude for democracy. It is not that culture is irrelevant to institutional changes. The problem lies not with the irrelevance of culture but, rather, the imprecise use of the term. In particular, the article by Inglehart and Norris concludes that the term is imprecise and hinges on stereotypes rather than on realistic information. Thus, Inglehart and Norris note that survey results show that, contrary to Huntington's assertion that "individualism, liberalism, constitutionalism, and human rights" are uniquely Western values, survey results show that in Albania, Azerbaijan, Bangladesh, Egypt, Indonesia, Iran, Morroco, and Turkey, "92 to 99 percent of the public endorsed democratic institutions—a higher proportion than in the US (89 percent)." The significance of values rather than culture is reiterated in Article 36 with historian Bernard Lewis, where he reiterates that there is nothing fundamentally incompatible between Islam and democracy. Rather, he echoes the previous authors to point out that the "treatment of women" is the main impediment to realizing democracy in Islamic societies.

Our survey of political behaviors and institutions across a wide net of countries returns full circle to this: Institutional changes occur in response to demands for better or more representative venues within which citizens and government may interact. While onlookers may fault institutions or even countries for failing to be more accountable, representative, or just, it is primarily the demands of domestic constituents—the citizens—that will usher in and support changes.

In this regard, two articles in this unit—"Authoritarianism's Last Line of Defense" and "Why Democracy Needs a level Playing

© Terry Vine/Blend Images/Getty Images

Field"—are particularly instructive. Both articles point out how the letter of representation and accountability may be fulfilled without the spirit. Thus, for instance, in "Authoritarianism's Last Line of Defense," the author describes how various democratic institutions may be manipulated so that they fail to meet the actual practice of democratic representation and accountability. Likewise, the authors of "Why Democracy Needs a Level Playing field" point out how the consistently successful ruling parties in Botswana and Tanzania fulfill the letter of free and frequent elections but not the spirit of fairness, since they enjoy resource disparities and media access over the opposition.

These two articles bring home what it means to study comparative politics: clarify behaviors and institutions to generate systematic generalizations that promote understanding. The significance of systematic study and knowledge cannot be overstated. In particular, the last two articles in this unit point out that any optimism or faith in other processes is or will be misplaced. Thus, for instance, Article 39 reminds us that even as the Internet and social-networking served well in the transitions in the Middle East, technology itself does not mobilize the citizens. Any faith that providing more information and disseminating it widely will usher in better or more representative political and social environs by galvanizing the citizens misreads and misunderstands that there is as much information on the Internet that is deliberately planted and monitored. Nor can international or regional agencies be expected to step up to the plate. Thus, even if the UN were to improve representation on its key councils to include the emergent BRICs or poor nations, it remains to be seen how well these countries will advocate for institution building, accountability, and representation when they have yet to do so in their home countries.

It is clear, then, that we, as responsible global citizens, should inform our opinions about institution building and policy choices through understanding. In the various units in this book, we surveyed democratic theory and how citizens' behavior and institutional performance relate to democratization to systematically consider the generalizable findings so that we may better understand particularities and departures. In doing so, we are better able to outline for the international community what it means to nurture and support citizen demands, without imposing our own preferences and impatience, in the interests of promoting stability and development within countries and in inter-nation relations.

The True Clash of Civilizations

Samuel Huntington was only half right. The cultural fault line that divides the West and the Muslim world is not about democracy but sex. According to a new survey, Muslims and their Western counterparts want democracy, yet they are worlds apart when it comes to attitudes toward divorce, abortion, gender equality, and gay rights—which may not bode well for democracy's future in the Middle East.

RONALD INGLEHART AND PIPPA NORRIS

Democracy promotion in Islamic countries is now one of the Bush administration's most popular talking points. "We reject the condescending notion that freedom will not grow in the Middle East," Secretary of State Colin Powell declared last December as he unveiled the White House's new Middle East Partnership Initiative to encourage political and economic reform in Arab countries. Likewise, Condoleezza Rice, President George W. Bush's national security advisor, promised last September that the United States is committed to "the march of freedom in the Muslim world."

But does the Muslim world march to the beat of a different drummer? Despite Bush's optimistic pronouncement that there is "no clash of civilizations" when it comes to "the common rights and needs of men and women," others are not so sure. Samuel Huntington's controversial 1993 thesis—that the cultural division between "Western Christianity" and "Orthodox Christianity and Islam" is the new fault line for conflict—resonates more loudly than ever since September 11. Echoing Huntington, columnist Polly Toynbee argued in the British *Guardian* last November, "What binds together a globalized force of some extremists from many continents is a united hatred of Western values that seems to them to spring from Judeo-Christianity." Meanwhile, on the other side of the Atlantic, Republican Rep. Christopher Shays of Connecticut, after sitting through hours of testimony on U.S.-Islamic relations on Capitol Hill last October, testily blurted, "Why doesn't democracy grab hold in the Middle East? What is there about the culture and the people and so on where democracy just doesn't seem to be something they strive for and work for?"

Republican Rep. Christopher Shays of Connecticut: "Why doesn't democracy grab hold in the Middle East? What is there about the culture and the people and so on where democracy just doesn't seem to be something they strive for and work for?"

Huntington's response would be that the Muslim world lacks the core political values that gave birth to representative democracy in Western civilization: separation of religious and secular authority, rule of law and social pluralism, parliamentary institutions of representative government, and protection of individual rights and civil liberties as the buffer between citizens and the power of the state. This claim seems all too plausible given the failure of electoral democracy to take root throughout the Middle East and North Africa. According to the latest Freedom House rankings, almost two thirds of the 192 countries around the world are now electoral democracies. But among the 47 countries with a Muslim majority, only one fourth are electoral democracies—and none of the core Arabic-speaking societies falls into this category.

Yet this circumstantial evidence does little to prove Huntington correct, since it reveals nothing about the underlying beliefs of Muslim publics. Indeed, there has been scant empirical evidence whether Western and Muslim societies exhibit deeply divergent values—that is, until now. The cumulative results of the two most recent waves of the World Values Survey (wvs), conducted in 1995–96 and 2000–2002, provide an extensive body of relevant evidence. Based on questionnaires

The Cultural Divide

Approval of Political and Social Values in Western and Muslim Societies

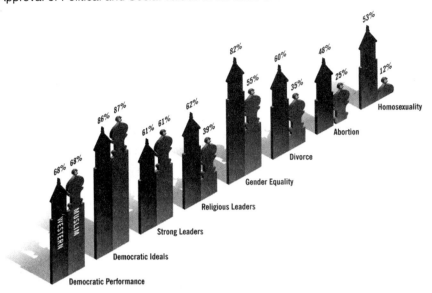

Source: World Values Survey, Pooled Sample 1995-2001; Charts (3) By Jared Schneidman for FP

The chart above draws on responses to various political and social issues in the World Values Survey. The percentages indicate the extent to which respondents agree/disagreed with or approved/disapproved of the following statements and questions:

Democratic Performance

- Democracies are indecisive and have too much quibbling. (Strongly disagree.)
- Democracies aren't good at maintaining order. (Strongly disagree.)

Democratic Ideals

- Democracy may have problems, but it's better than any other form of government. (Strongly agree.)
- Approve of having a democratic political system. (Strongly agree.)

Strong Leaders

- Approve of having experts, not government, make decisions according to what they think is best for the country. (Strongly disagree.)
- Approve of having a strong leader who does not have to bother with parliament and elections. (Strongly disagree.)

Religious Leaders

- Politicians who do not believe in God are unfit for public office. (Strongly disagree.)
- It would be better for [this country] if more people with strong religious beliefs held public office. (Strongly disagree.)

Gender Equality

- On the whole, men make better political leaders than women do. (Strongly disagree.)
- When jobs are scarce, men should have more right to a job than women. (Strongly disagree.)
- A university education is more important for a boy than for a girl. (Strongly disagree.)
- A woman has to have children in order to be fulfilled. (Strongly disagree.)
- If a woman wants to have a child as a single parent but she doesn't want to have a stable relationship with a man, do you approve or disapprove? (Strongly approve.)

Divorce

- Divorce can always be justified, never be justified, or something in between. (High level of tolerance for divorce.)

Abortion

- Abortion can always be justified, never be justified, or something in between. (High level of tolerance for abortion.)

Homosexuality

- Homosexuality can always be justified, never be justified, or something in between. (High level of tolerance for homosexuality.)

that explore values and beliefs in more than 70 countries, the WVS is an investigation of sociocultural and political change that encompasses over 80 percent of the world's population.

A comparison of the data yielded by these surveys in Muslim and non-Muslim societies around the globe confirms the first claim in Huntington's thesis: Culture does matter—indeed, it matters a lot. Historical religious traditions have left an enduring imprint on contemporary values. However, Huntington is mistaken in assuming that the core clash between the West and Islam is over political values. At this point in history, societies throughout the world (Muslim and Judeo-Christian alike) see democracy as the best form of government. Instead, the real fault line between the West and Islam, which Huntington's theory completely overlooks, concerns gender equality and sexual liberalization. In other words, the values separating the two cultures have much more to do with eros than demos. As younger generations in the West have gradually become more liberal on these issues, Muslim nations have remained the most traditional societies in the world.

. . . the real fault line between the West and Islam. . . concerns gender equality and sexual liberation. . . the values separating the two cultures have much more to do with eros than demos.

This gap in values mirrors the widening economic divide between the West and the Muslim world. Commenting on the disenfranchisement of women throughout the Middle East, the United Nations Development Programme observed last summer that "no society can achieve the desired state of well-being and human development, or compete in a globalizing world, if half its people remain marginalized and disempowered." But this "sexual clash of civilizations" taps into far deeper issues than how Muslim countries treat women. A society's commitment to gender equality and sexual liberalization proves time and again to be the most reliable indicator of how strongly that society supports principles of tolerance and egalitarianism. Thus, the people of the Muslim world overwhelmingly want democracy, but democracy may not be sustainable in their societies.

Testing Huntington

Huntington argues that "ideas of individualism, liberalism, constitutionalism, human rights, equality, liberty, the rule of law, democracy, free markets, [and] the separation of church and state" often have little resonance outside the West. Moreover, he holds that Western efforts to promote these ideas provoke a violent backlash against "human rights imperialism." To test these propositions, we categorized the countries included in the WVS according to the nine major contemporary civilizations, based largely on the historical religious legacy of each society. The survey includes 22 countries representing Western

Christianity (a West European culture that also encompasses North America, Australia, and New Zealand), 10 Central European nations (sharing a Western Christian heritage, but which also lived under Communist rule), 11 societies with a Muslim majority (Albania, Algeria, Azerbaijan, Bangladesh, Egypt, Indonesia, Iran, Jordan, Morocco, Pakistan, and Turkey), 12 traditionally Orthodox societies (such as Russia and Greece), 11 predominately Catholic Latin American countries, 4 East Asian societies shaped by Sino-Confucian values, 5 sub-Saharan Africa countries, plus Japan and India.

Despite Huntington's claim of a clash of civilizations between the West and the rest, the WVS reveals that, at this point in history, democracy has an overwhelmingly positive image throughout the world. In country after country, a clear majority of the population describes "having a democratic political system" as either "good" or "very good." These results represent a dramatic change from the 1930s and 1940s, when fascist regimes won overwhelming mass approval in many societies; and for many decades, Communist regimes had widespread support. But in the last decade, democracy became virtually the only political model with global appeal, no matter what the culture. With the exception of Pakistan, most of the Muslim countries surveyed think highly of democracy: In Albania, Egypt, Bangladesh, Azerbaijan, Indonesia, Morocco, and Turkey, 92 to 99 percent of the public endorsed democratic institutions—a higher proportion than in the United States (89 percent).

Yet, as heartening as these results may be, paying lip service to democracy does not necessarily prove that people genuinely support basic democratic norms—or that their leaders will allow them to have democratic institutions. Although constitutions of authoritarian states such as China profess to embrace democratic ideals such as freedom of religion, the rulers deny it in practice. In Iran's 2000 elections, reformist candidates captured nearly three quarters of the seats in parliament, but a theocratic elite still holds the reins of power. Certainly, it's a step in the right direction if most people in a country endorse the idea of democracy. But this sentiment needs to be complemented by deeper underlying attitudes such as interpersonal trust and tolerance of unpopular groups—and these values must ultimately be accepted by those who control the army and secret police.

The WVS reveals that, even after taking into account differences in economic and political development, support for democratic institutions is just as strong among those living in Muslim societies as in Western (or other) societies [see box, The Cultural Divide]. For instance, a solid majority of people living in Western and Muslim countries gives democracy high marks as the most efficient form of government, with 68 percent disagreeing with assertions that "democracies are indecisive" and "democracies aren't good at maintaining order." (All other cultural regions and countries, except East Asia and Japan, are far more critical.) And an equal number of respondents on both sides of the civilizational divide (61 percent) firmly reject authoritarian governance, expressing disapproval of "strong leaders" who do not "bother with parliament and elections." Muslim societies display greater support for religious authori-

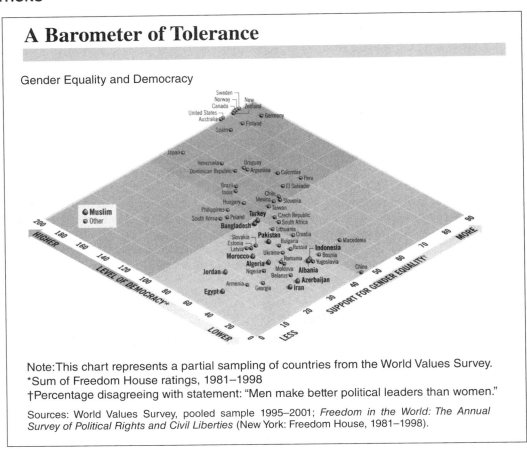

A Barometer of Tolerance

Gender Equality and Democracy

Note: This chart represents a partial sampling of countries from the World Values Survey.

*Sum of Freedom House ratings, 1981–1998

†Percentage disagreeing with statement: "Men make better political leaders than women."

Sources: World Values Survey, pooled sample 1995–2001; *Freedom in the World: The Annual Survey of Political Rights and Civil Liberties* (New York: Freedom House, 1981–1998).

ties playing an active societal role than do Western societies. Yet this preference for religious authorities is less a cultural division between the West and Islam than it is a gap between the West and many other less secular societies around the globe, especially in sub-Saharan Africa and Latin America. For instance, citizens in some Muslim societies agree overwhelmingly with the statement that "politicians who do not believe in God are unfit for public office" (88 percent in Egypt, 83 percent in Iran, and 71 percent in Bangladesh), but this statement also garners strong support in the Philippines (71 percent), Uganda (60 percent), and Venezuela (52 percent). Even in the United States, about two fifths of the public believes that atheists are unfit for public office.

However, when it comes to attitudes toward gender equality and sexual liberalization, the cultural gap between Islam and the West widens into a chasm. On the matter of equal rights and opportunities for women—measured by such questions as whether men make better political leaders than women or whether university education is more important for boys than for girls—Western and Muslim countries score 82 percent and 55 percent, respectively. Muslim societies are also distinctively less permissive toward homosexuality, abortion, and divorce.

These issues are part of a broader syndrome of tolerance, trust, political activism, and emphasis on individual autonomy that constitutes "self-expression values." The extent to which a society emphasizes these self-expression values has a surprisingly strong bearing on the emergence and survival of democratic institutions. Among all the countries included in the wvs, support for gender equality—a key indicator of tolerance and personal freedom—is closely linked with a society's level of democracy [see box, A Barometer of Tolerance].

In every stable democracy, a majority of the public disagrees with the statement that "men make better political leaders than women." None of the societies in which less than 30 percent of the public rejects this statement (such as Jordan, Nigeria, and Belarus) is a true democracy. In China, one of the world's least democratic countries, a majority of the public agrees that men make better political leaders than women, despite a party line that has long emphasized gender equality (Mao Zedong once declared, "women hold up half the sky"). In practice, Chinese women occupy few positions of real power and face widespread discrimination in the workplace. India is a borderline case. The country is a long-standing parliamentary democracy with an independent judiciary and civilian control of the armed forces, yet it is also marred by a weak rule of law, arbitrary arrests, and extra-judicial killings. The status of Indian women reflects this duality. Women's rights are guaranteed in the constitution, and Indira Gandhi led the nation for 15 years. Yet domestic violence and forced prostitution remain prevalent throughout the country, and, according to the wvs, almost 50 percent of the Indian populace believes only men should run the government.

A Widening Generation Gap

Support for Gender Equality, by Age and Type of Society

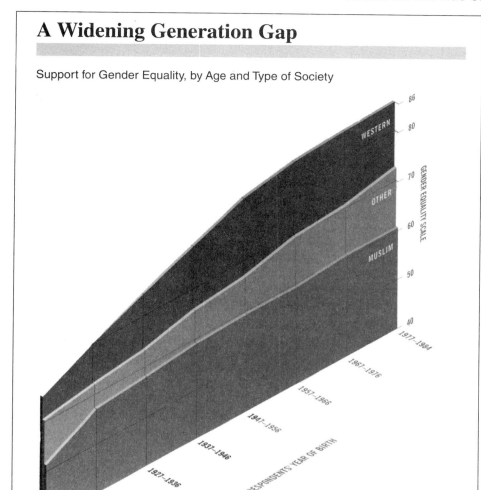

*The 100-point Gender Equality Scale is based on responses to the following five statements and questions: "If a woman wants to have a child as a single parent but she doesn't want to have a stable relationship with a man, do you approve or disapprove?"; "When jobs are scarce, men should have more right to a job than women"; "A university education is more important for a boy than a girl"; "Do you think that a woman has to have children in order to be fulfilled or is this not necessary?"; and "On the whole, men make better political leaders than women do." The scale was constructed so that if all respondents show high scores on all five items (representing strong support for gender equality), it produces a score of 100, while low scores on all five items produce a score of 0.

Source: World Values Surveys, pooled 1995–2001.

The way a society views homosexuality constitutes another good litmus test of its commitment to equality. Tolerance of well-liked groups is never a problem. But if someone wants to gauge how tolerant a nation really is, find out which group is the most disliked, and then ask whether members of that group should be allowed to hold public meetings, teach in schools, and work in government. Today, relatively few people express overt hostility toward other classes, races, or religions, but rejection of homosexuals is widespread. In response to a wvs question about whether homosexuality is justifiable, about half of the world's population say "never." But, as is the case with gender equality, this attitude is directly proportional to a country's level of democracy. Among authoritarian and quasi-democratic states, rejection of homosexuality is deeply entrenched: 99 percent in both Egypt and Bangladesh, 94 percent in Iran, 92 percent in China, and 71 percent in India. By contrast, these figures

Want to Know More?

Samuel Huntington expanded his controversial 1993 article into a book, *The Clash of Civilizations and the Remaking of World Order* (New York: Simon and Schuster, 1996). Among the authors who have disputed Huntington's claim that Islam is incompatible with democratic values are Edward Said, who decries the clash of civilizations thesis as an attempt to revive the "good vs. evil" world dichotomy prevalent during the Cold War ("**A Clash of Ignorance**," *The Nation*, October 22, 2001); John Voll and John Esposito, who argue that "The Muslim heritage. . . contains concepts that provide a foundation for contemporary Muslims to develop authentically Muslim programs of democracy" ("**Islam's Democratic Essence**," *Middle East Quarterly*, September 1994); and Ray Takeyh, who recounts the efforts of contemporary Muslim scholars to legitimize democratic concepts through the reinterpretation of Muslim texts and traditions ("**Faith-Based Initiatives**," FOREIGN POLICY, November/December 2001).

An overview of the Bush administration's **Middle East Partnership Initiative**, including the complete transcript of Secretary of State Colin Powell's speech on political and economic reform in the Arab world, can be found on the website of the U.S. Department of State. Marina Ottaway, Thomas Carothers, Amy Hawthorne, and Daniel Brumberg offer a stinging critique of those who believe that toppling the Iraqi regime could unleash a democratic tsunami in the Arab world in "**Democratic Mirage in the Middle East**" (Washington: Carnegie Endowment for International Peace, 2002).

In a poll of nearly 4,000 Arabs, James Zogby found that the issue of "civil and personal rights" earned the overall highest score when people were asked to rank their personal priorities (*What Arabs Think: Values, Beliefs and Concerns*, Washington: Zogby International, 2002). A poll available on the website of the Pew Research Center for the People and the Press ("**Among Wealthy Nations . . . U.S. Stands Alone in Its Embrace of Religion**," December 19, 2002) reveals that Americans' views on religion and faith are closer to those living in developing nations than in developed countries.

The website of the **World Values Survey** (wvs) provides considerable information on the survey, including background on methodology, key findings, and the text of the questionnaires. The second iteration of the A.T. Kearney/ Foreign Policy Magazine Globalization Index ("**Globalization's Last Hurrah?**" Foreign Policy, January/February 2002) found a strong correlation between the wvs measure of "subjective well-being" and a society's level of global integration.

For links to relevant websites, access to the FP Archive, and a comprehensive index of related Foreign Policy articles, go to www.foreignpolicy.com.

---

are much lower among respondents in stable democracies: 32 percent in the United States, 26 percent in Canada, 25 percent in Britain, and 19 percent in Germany.

Today, relatively few people express overt hostility toward other classes, races, or religions, but rejection of homosexuals is widespread. About half of the world's populations say that homosexuality is "never" justifiable.

Muslim societies are neither uniquely nor monolithically low on tolerance toward sexual orientation and gender equality. Many of the Soviet successor states rank as low as most Muslim societies. However, on the whole, Muslim countries not only lag behind the West but behind all other societies as well [see box, A Widening Generation Gap]. Perhaps more significant, the figures reveal the gap between the West and Islam is even wider among younger age groups. This pattern suggests that the younger generations in Western societies have become progressively more egalitarian than their elders, but the younger generations in Muslim societies have remained almost as traditional as their parents and grandparents, producing an expanding cultural gap.

Muslim societies are neither uniquely nor monolithically low on tolerance toward sexual orientation and gender equality. . . . However, on the whole, Muslim countries not only lag behind the West but behind all other societies as well.

Clash of Conclusions

"The peoples of the Islamic nations want and deserve the same freedoms and opportunities as people in every nation," President Bush declared in a commencement speech at West Point last summer. He's right. Any claim of a "clash of civilizations" based on fundamentally different political goals held by Western and Muslim societies represents an oversimplification of the evidence. Support for the goal of democracy is surprisingly widespread among Muslim publics, even among those living in authoritarian societies. Yet Huntington is correct when he argues that cultural differences have taken on a new importance, forming the fault lines for future conflict. Although nearly the entire world pays lip service to democracy, there is still no global consensus on the self-expression values—such as social tolerance, gender equality, freedom of speech, and interpersonal trust— that are crucial to democracy. Today, these divergent values constitute the real clash between Muslim societies and the West.

But economic development generates changed attitudes in virtually any society. In particular, modernization compels systematic, predictable changes in gender roles: Industrialization brings women into the paid work force and dramatically reduces fertility rates. Women become literate and begin to participate in representative government but still have far less power than men. Then, the postindustrial phase brings a shift toward greater gender equality as women move into higher-status economic roles in management and gain political influence within elected and appointed bodies. Thus, relatively industrialized Muslim societies such as Turkey share the same views on gender equality and sexual liberalization as other new democracies.

Even in established democracies, changes in cultural attitudes—and eventually, attitudes toward democracy—seem to be closely linked with modernization. Women did not attain the right to vote in most historically Protestant societies until about 1920, and in much of Roman Catholic Europe until after World War II. In 1945, only 3 percent of the members of parliaments around the world were women. In 1965, the figure rose to 8 percent, in 1985 to 12 percent, and in 2002 to 15 percent.

The United States cannot expect to foster democracy in the Muslim world simply by getting countries to adopt the trappings of democratic governance, such as holding elections and having a parliament. Nor is it realistic to expect that nascent democracies in the Middle East will inspire a wave of reforms reminiscent of the velvet revolutions that swept Eastern Europe in the final days of the Cold War. A real commitment to democratic reform will be measured by the willingness to commit the resources necessary to foster human development in the Muslim world. Culture has a lasting impact on how societies evolve. But culture does not have to be destiny.

Critical Thinking

1. Is it important to consider that political tolerance, rather than values, is at the heart of incompatibility between Islam and democracy? Explain why or why not.

2. According to the authors, how does economic improvement change attitudes? Is this consistent with the previous article?

3. What evidence reveals that there is "lip service" paid to support for democracy?

4. Explain how to distinguish between "lip service" support of democracy and "real" support.

Reprinted in entirety by McGraw-Hill with permission from *Foreign Policy*, March/April 2003, pp. 63–70. www.foreignpolicy.com. © 2003 Washingtonpost.Newsweek Interactive, LLC.

The Weekend Interview with Bernard Lewis: "The Tyrannies Are Doomed"

BARI WEISS

Princeton, N.J.—*What Went Wrong*? That was the explosive title of a December 2001 book by historian Bernard Lewis about the decline of the Muslim world. Already at the printer when 9/11 struck, the book rocketed the professor to widespread public attention, and its central question gripped Americans for a decade.

Now, all of a sudden, there's a new question on American minds: What Might Go Right?

To find out, I made a pilgrimage to the professor's bungalow in Princeton, N.J., where he's lived since 1974 when he joined Princeton's faculty from London's School of Oriental and African Studies.

Two months shy of his 95th birthday, Mr. Lewis has been writing history books since before World War II. By 1950, he was already a leading scholar of the Arab world, and after 9/11, the vice president and the Pentagon's top brass summoned him to Washington for his wisdom.

"I think that the tyrannies are doomed," Mr. Lewis says as we sit by the windows in his library, teeming with thousands of books in the dozen or so languages he's mastered. "The real question is what will come instead."

For Americans who have watched protesters in Tunisia, Egypt, Iran, Libya, Bahrain and now Syria stand up against their regimes, it has been difficult not to be intoxicated by this revolutionary moment. Mr. Lewis is "delighted" by the popular movements and believes that the U.S. should do all it can to bolster them. But he cautions strongly against insisting on Western-style elections in Muslim lands.

"We have a much better chance of establishing—I hesitate to use the word democracy—but some sort of open, tolerant society, if it's done within their systems, according to their traditions. Why should we expect them to adopt a Western system? And why should we expect it to work?" he asks.

Mr. Lewis brings up Germany circa 1918. "After World War I, the victorious Allies tried to impose the parliamentary system on Germany, where they had a rather different political tradition. And the result was that Hitler came to power. Hitler came to power by the manipulation of free and fair elections," recounts Mr. Lewis, who fought the Nazis in the British Army. For a more recent example, consider the 2006 electorial triumph of Hamas in Gaza.

Elections, he argues, should be the culmination–not the beginning–of a gradual political process. Thus "to lay the stress all the time on elections, parliamentary Western-style elections, is a dangerous delusion."

Not because Muslims' cultural DNA is predisposed against it—quite the contrary. "The whole Islamic tradition is very clearly against autocratic and irresponsible rule," says Mr. Lewis. "There is a very strong tradition—both historical and legal, both practical and theoretical—of limited, controlled government."

But Western-style elections have had mixed success even in the West. "Even in France, where they claim to have invented freedom, they're on their fifth republic and who knows how many more there will be before they get settled down," Mr. Lewis laughs. "I don't think we can assume that the Anglo-American system of democracy is a sort of world rule, a world ideal," he says. Instead, Muslims should be "allowed—and indeed helped and encouraged—to develop their own ways of doing things."

In other words: To figure out how to build freer, better societies, Muslims need not look across the ocean. They need only look back into their own history.

Mr. Lewis points me to a letter written by France's ambassador in Istanbul shortly before the French revolution. The French government was frustrated by how long the ambassador was taking to move ahead with some negotiations. So he pushed back: "Here, it is not like it is in France, where the king is sole master and does as he pleases. Here, the sultan has to consult."

In Middle Eastern history "consultation is the magic word. It occurs again and again in classical Islamic texts. It goes back to the time of the Prophet himself," says Mr. Lewis.

What it meant practically was that political leaders had to cut deals with various others—the leaders of the merchant guild, the craft guild, the scribes, the land owners and the like. Each guild chose its own leaders from within. "The rulers," says Mr. Lewis, "even the great Ottoman sultans, had to consult with these different groups in order to get things done."

It's not that Ottoman-era societies were models of Madisonian political wisdom. But power was shared such that rulers at the top were checked, so the Arab and Muslim communities of the vast Ottoman Empire came to include certain practices and expectations of limited government.

Americans often think of limited government in terms of "freedom," but Mr. Lewis says that word doesn't have a precise equivalent in Arabic. "Liberty, freedom, it means not being a slave . . . . Freedom was a legal term and a social term—it was not a political term. And it was not used as a metaphor for political status," he says. The closest Arabic word to our concept of liberty is "justice," or 'adl. "In the Muslim tradition, justice is the standard" of good government. (Yet judging from the crowds gathered at Syria's central Umayyad mosque last week chanting "Freedom, freedom!," the word, if not our precise meaning, has certainly caught on.)

The traditional consultation process was a main casualty of modernization, which helps explain modernization's dubious reputation in parts of the Arab and Muslim world. "Modernization . . . enormously increased the power of the state," Mr. Lewis says. "And it tended to undermine, or even destroy, those various intermediate powers which had previously limited the power of the state." This was enabled by the cunning of the Mubaraks and the Assads, paired with "modern communication, modern weapons and the modern apparatus of surveillance and repression." The result: These autocrats amassed "greater power than even the mightiest of the sultans ever had."

So can today's Middle East recover this tradition and adapt it appropriately? He reminds me that he is a historian: Predictions are not his forte. But the reluctant sage offers some thoughts.

First, Tunisia has real potential for democracy, largely because of the role of women there. "Tunisia, as far as I know, is the only Muslim country that has compulsory education for girls from the beginning right through. And in which women are to be found in all the professions," says Mr. Lewis.

"My own feeling is that the greatest defect of Islam and the main reason they fell behind the West is the treatment of women," he says. He makes the powerful point that repressive homes pave the way for repressive governments. "Think of a child that grows up in a Muslim household where the mother has no rights, where she is downtrodden and subservient. That's preparation for a life of despotism and subservience. It prepares the way for an authoritarian society," he says.

Egypt is a more complicated case, Mr. Lewis says. Already the young, liberal protesters who led the revolution in Tahrir Square are being pushed aside by the military-Muslim Brotherhood complex. Hasty elections, which could come as soon as September, might sweep the Muslim Brotherhood into power. That would be "a very dangerous situation," he warns. "We should have no illusions about the Muslim Brotherhood, who they are and what they want."

And yet Western commentators seem determined to harbor such illusions. Take their treatment of Sheikh Yusuf Qaradawi. The highly popular, charismatic cleric has said that Hitler "managed to put [the Jews] in their place" and that the Holocaust "was divine punishment for them."

Yet following a sermon Sheikh Qaradawi delivered to more than a million in Cairo following Mubarak's ouster, New York Times reporter David D. Kirkpatrick wrote that the cleric "struck themes of democracy and pluralism, long hallmarks of his writing and preaching." Mr. Kirkpatrick added: "Scholars who have studied his work say Sheik Qaradawi has long argued that Islamic law supports the idea of a pluralistic, multiparty, civil democracy."

Professor Lewis has been here before. As the Iranian revolution was beginning in the late 1970s, the name of Ayatollah Ruhollah Khomeini was starting to appear in the Western press. "I was at Princeton and I must confess I never heard of Khomeini. Who had? So I did what one normally does in this world of mine: I went to the university library and looked up Khomeini and, sure enough, it was there."

'It" was a short book called *Islamic Government*—now known as Khomeini's *Mein Kampf*—available in Persian and Arabic. Mr. Lewis checked out both copies and began reading. "It became perfectly clear who he was and what his aims were. And that all of this talk at the time about [him] being a step forward and a move toward greater freedom was absolute nonsense," recalls Mr. Lewis.

"I tried to bring this to the attention of people here. *The New York* Times wouldn't touch it. They said 'We don't think this would interest our readers.' But we got the *Washington Post* to publish an article quoting this. And they were immediately summoned by the CIA," he says. "Eventually the message got through—thanks to Khomeini."

Now, thanks to Tehran's enduring Khomeinism, the regime is unpopular and under threat. "There is strong opposition to the regime—two oppositions—the opposition within the regime and the opposition against the regime. And I think that sooner or later the regime in Iran will be overthrown and something more open, more democratic, will emerge," Mr. Lewis says. "Most Iranian patriots are against the regime. They feel it is defaming and dishonoring their country. And they're right of course."

Iranians' disdain for the ruling mullahs is the reason Mr. Lewis thinks the U.S. shouldn't take military action there. "It would give the regime a gift that they don't at present enjoy—namely Iranian patriotism," he warns.

By his lights, the correct policy is to elevate the democratic Green movement, and to distinguish the regime from the people. "When President Obama assumed office, he sent a message of greeting to the regime. That is polite and courteous," Mr. Lewis deadpans, "but it would have been much better to send a message to the people of Iran."

Let's hope the Green movement is effective. Because—and this may be hard to square with his policy prescription—Mr. Lewis doesn't think that Iran can be contained if it does go nuclear.

"During the Cold War, both the Soviet Union and the United States had nuclear weapons but both knew that the other was very unlikely to use them. Because of what was known at the time as MAD—mutually assured destruction. MAD meant that each side knew that if it used a nuclear weapon the other would retaliate and both sides would be devastated. And that's why the whole time during the Cold War, even at the worst times, there was not much danger of anyone using a nuclear weapon," says Mr. Lewis.

But the mullahs "are religious fanatics with an apocalyptic mindset. In Islam, as in Christianity and Judaism, there is an end-of-times scenario—and they think it's beginning or has already begun." So "mutually assured destruction is not a deterrent - it's an inducement."

Another key variable in the regional dynamic is Turkey, Mr. Lewis's particular expertise. He was the first Westerner granted access to the Ottoman archives in Istanbul in 1950. Recent developments there alarm him. "In Turkey, the movement is getting more and more toward re-Islamization. The government has that as its intention—and it has been taking over, very skillfully, one part after another of Turkish society. The economy, the business community, the academic community, the media. And now they're taking over the judiciary, which in the past has been the stronghold of the republican regime." Ten years from now, Mr. Lewis thinks, Turkey and Iran could switch places.

So even as he watches young Middle Eastern activists rise up against the tyrannies that have oppressed them, he keeps a wary eye on the spread of Islamic fundamentalism. It is particularly challenging because it has "no political center, no ethnic identity . . . . It's both Arab and Persian and Turkish and everything else. It is religiously defined. And it can command support among people of every nationality once they are convinced. That marks the important difference," he says.

"I think the struggle will continue until they either obtain their objective or renounce it," Mr. Lewis says. "At the moment, both seem equally improbable."

Critical Thinking

1. Explain why elections should be the culmination of the political transition to democracy.

2. What does Bernard Lewis mean that western-style democracy has failed in the West?

3. According to Bernard Lewis, does Islam support democracy? Why and why not?

Ms. Weiss is an assistant editorial features editor at the Journal.

Authoritarianism's Last Line of Defense

ANDREAS SCHEDLER

Over the past twenty years, we have seen a good amount of democratic progress across the planet. The collapse of the Soviet empire led to an impressive expansion of electoral democracy, especially in Eastern Europe and sub-Saharan Africa. At the same time, we have witnessed the startling spread of multiparty elections *without* democracy. Today the unambiguously nondemocratic regime types of the Cold War era—single-party systems, military regimes, and personal dictatorships—have almost disappeared (even as the Chinese single-party regime rules over a fifth of humanity).

The new stars in the constellation of nondemocratic governance are "electoral authoritarian" regimes, which conduct regular multiparty elections at all levels of government yet violate basic democratic standards in serious and systematic ways. Some of them are holdovers from earlier periods (such as Singapore and Egypt); some were born in transitions from single-party rule (Gabon and Cameroon); others arose after military coups (Algeria and Gambia); and still others emerged from processes of democratic erosion (Venezuela and Russia). These regimes represent the last line of authoritarian defense in a long history of struggle that has been unfolding since the invention of modern representative institutions.[1]

The system of representative government that we call "liberal democracy" rests upon a configuration of institutions that were conceived and crafted in the eighteenth century—constitutional government, individual rights and liberties, the rule of law, checks and balances, the functional and territorial division of power, representative legislatures, popular elections, civil society, and independent media. Mass political parties came later, as a product of nineteenth-century suffrage extensions. The twentieth century, while catastrophically creative in developing technologies of repression and destruction, added little to the inventory of basic democratic institutions, save for the invention of constitutional courts after World War I and the development of international human-rights law after World War II.

The ideational and factual emergence of representative institutions in the century of enlightenment and revolution did not lead to the immediate diffusion of such institutions throughout the expanding world of independent states. It did, however, trigger a long-term struggle for representative government that has been underway for more than two centuries now. This struggle has always been conducted in two stages—first the battle to establish representative institutions in form, and then the battle to render them effective in practice.

The democratic battles of the nineteenth century in Europe and the Americas largely strove to establish and empower representative institutions, to liberate them from domination by powerful elites, and to extend civil liberties and political rights beyond the propertied and educated minority. But the totalitarian regimes of terror that arose in the first half of the twentieth century swept away the democratic gains of the post—World War I period. Hitler and Stalin shut down most representative institutions; the few that they kept (criminal courts in Nazi Germany, legislatures in the Soviet Union) were fully integrated into their bureaucracies of repression and extermination.

After the eclipse of totalitarianism, the struggle for democracy resumed under changed circumstances. In the postcolonial world, democrats seeking to build effective representative institutions did not face semi-constitutional monarchies or electoral oligarchies anymore, but military regimes and single-party states. In many places they extracted limited concessions, such as the partial and contingent toleration of civil liberties, civic associations, and legislative elections. The fall of the Berlin Wall—or, rather, its artisanal destruction by a spontaneous assembly of merry quarrymen—marked yet another historical turning point in the authoritarian management of representative institutions. It triggered a broad shift from selective to comprehensive institutional concessions, and thus from selective to comprehensive institutional manipulation.

Rather than suppressing representative institutions altogether, or accepting only some of them, the new electoral authoritarian regimes of the post–Cold War era have embraced them all. They have set up the full panoply of liberal-democratic institutions—from constitutions to constitutional courts, from legislatures to agencies of accountability, from judicial systems to federal arrangements, from independent media to civic associations. Most important of all, they hold regular multiparty elections at all levels of state power. In their institutional forms, these regimes are virtually indistinguishable from liberal democracies. Yet authoritarian rulers invariably compensate for these formal concessions with substantive controls. While renouncing the suppression of representative institutions, electoral authoritarian regimes specialize in their manipulation. Operating under the primacy of repression, totalitarian systems occupied one pole on the continuum of authoritarian regimes. Operating under the primacy of institutional manipulation, electoral autocracies occupy the other.

Menus of Institutional Manipulation

All institutional creations involve some delegation of power, or at least the formal pretense of delegation. Their very existence implies that rulers put others in charge of undertaking certain tasks. Authoritarian delegation of power, however, is never meant to sanction the autonomous exercise of power by the designated agent. The institutional creatures that authoritarian regimes breed are not meant to grow and flourish in liberty. They are meant to be tame domestic animals—not merely paper tigers, but resilient workhorses. Authoritarian rulers cannot tolerate genuine institutional autonomy. They will always strive to constrain and contain their own institutional creations in order to ensure that nominally democratic bodies and procedures remain substantively authoritarian.

Authoritarian rulers may deploy a wide range of strategies to keep control over their agents, as well as their adversaries, in various institutional arenas. In electoral authoritarian regimes, elections constitute almost by definition the central arena of struggle. Accordingly, both scholars and practitioners have paid substantial attention to the diverse strategies that autocrats pursue in order to control nominally competitive electoral processes. Our conceptual coordinates and empirical maps are much less developed with respect to the manifold manipulative techniques that authoritarian rulers deploy in other institutional arenas, including the legislature and judiciary as well as the media, civil society, and subnational governments. What follows are some rough sketches of the various menus of manipulation that authoritarian rulers have at their disposal in these arenas. This "menu of menus" does not pretend to be either complete or uniform in its analytical structure, but is an initial effort to map the methods by which authoritarian rulers domesticate formally representative institutions.

The Legislature

Most authoritarian regimes establish some kind of legislative assembly. That is, they create some collective body tasked with writing the rules that the central state (backed by its coercive capacity) seeks to impose on the people. Given their relatively small size, legislatures are easy objects of authoritarian control. In order to ensure legislative subordination, rulers may pursue three broad strategies:

1. *Disempowerment.* Rulers can place formal constraints on the legislature's powers, strictly limiting what it can and cannot do;

2. *Agent control.* Even if the legislature possesses broad formal powers, authoritarian governments can transform it into a rubber stamp if they control the selection of legislators—either by directly appointing deputies or by choosing who runs for elective office. Alternatively, they can set up an irresistible incentive structure (via intimidation or cooptation) that impels deputies to cooperate with the executive;

3. *Fragmentation.* Where rulers cannot control lawmakers' behavior, they can impede coordination among them by keeping the assembly divided and encouraging the multiplication of party factions.

The Judiciary

In principle, modern judicial systems serve to adjudicate disputes between private citizens, between citizens and state authorities, and between the authorities themselves. Although no modern authoritarian regime can do without a court system, it can employ a range of methods to clip the wings of "the least dangerous branch":[2]

1. *Disempowerment.* Authoritarian rulers can place formal constraints on the powers of courts, limiting their jurisdiction to specific issue areas and denying them investigative powers (leaving them to rely on state authorities as the only source of relevant evidence). They can set up hierarchical appeals systems that centralize and homogenize judicial rulings, constraining lower-level judges by controlling the higher-level courts. They can also limit the courts' range of discretion by imposing on them dense networks of formal regulation (in other words, by bureaucratizing judicial deliberation). Finally, rulers can neutralize the effects of judicial decision making by simply "underenforcing" inconvenient rulings;

2. *Agent control.* As with the legislature, authoritarian rulers can rein in a formally powerful judiciary by controlling the judges through a mixture of appointment procedures and incentive structures: They can select politically reliable magistrates, and they can discipline them through dissuasive penalties. Authoritarian regimes are huge employment agencies for loyal servants, but they are also masters of what students of public administration call "incentive compatibility." Through mutually reinforcing sets of intrajudicial and extrajudicial incentives, they can make sure that judges find any judicial strategy other than "self-restraint" personally costly and politically self-defeating;[3]

3. *Fragmentation.* Rather than establishing a unified judiciary, authoritarian rulers can impede coordination among the courts and "contain judicial activism by engineering fragmented judicial systems" in which "exceptional courts run alongside the regular court system."[4] Special executive-dominated courts, whose jurisdictions often overlap those of regular courts, facilitate the political control of sensitive cases;

4. *Insulation.* For all their pretensions to being closed systems of rule-based dispute arbitration, judicial systems, just like all other state institutions, are embedded in their social environments. Their capacity to protect citizens "horizontally" against resourceful private actors as well as "vertically" against public authorities very much depends on the surrounding network of professional and civic associations that are willing and able to challenge powerful actors. By "incapacitating judicial support networks," authoritarian rulers can effectively preempt the emergence of judicial challenges.[5]

Elections

When authoritarian rulers convene elections, they can minimize the risk of losing by keeping them noncompetitive or, if they allow for multiparty competition, by limiting them to lower levels of government. Even if they introduce multiparty elections at all levels, thereby becoming "electroal authoritarian" regimes, they have at their disposal a broad array of manipulative tools for reducing the uncertainty that elections can bring:[6]

1. *Disempowerment.* Rulers can simply remove sensitive policy areas from the jurisdiction of an elected official's portfolio (reserved domains) or subject elected officials to veto powers by unelected actors (authoritarian tutelage);

2. *Market restrictions.* Rulers can limit the choices available to voters by excluding, subverting, or fragmenting opposition parties (supply restrictions); they can obstruct the formation of voter preferences by denying the opposition fair access to public space (demand restrictions); and they can alter the composition of the electorate through the legal or de facto disenfranchisement of citizens (voter expropriation);

3. *Preference distortions.* Rulers can prevent citizens from expressing their genuine preferences at the polls with the threat of violence (voter intimidation) or the allure of money (vote buying);

4. *Vote distortions.* Finally, once voters have expressed their will at the ballot box, the results may be seriously distorted, either through discriminatory practices (election fraud) or through discriminatory institutions put into place beforehand to incapacitate opposition parties at the polls (such as majoritarian electoral rules that deny them legislative representation).

The Media

Just as access to "alternative sources of information"[7] is an essential feature of democracy, misinformation and disinformation constitute core features of authoritarianism. To minimize citizens' exposure to competing constructions of political reality, nondemocratic rulers can place restrictions on means of communication, media content, and media consumption:

1. To restrict private control over *means of production and distribution of political information,* authoritarian regimes typically exercise state monopolies of print, broadcast, or electronic media. Claiming a full monopoly on legitimate political communication, some dictatorial states have gone even further, limiting private access to decentralized means of written communication, such as typewriters, photocopiers, computers, and the Internet. Of course, even if a regime chooses to allow nonstate media, it still has a number of ways to constrain or even eliminate those enterprises that prove troublesome—for example, by denying them operating licenses or public advertising, or by having the police, tax administration, or anticorruption bureau shut them down;

2. Authoritarian governments that leave means of communication in private hands often turn to restricting *media content.* Sometimes they use censorship regulations. At other times, they resort to more informal, indirect techniques, such as beating up journalists or subjecting outlets to harassment by the tax agency. Both legal censorship and extralegal intimidation tend to induce self-censorship;

3. To restrict the *consumption* of available information by citizens, rulers may legally prohibit or materially disable mass access to information that has been produced outside the bounds of authoritarian control (including the international media).

Civil Society

Repression and cooptation are the most obvious authoritarian strategies to keep citizens from practicing the modern "art of association." In general terms, to alleviate pressures from below, authoritarian governments can subject interest groups to state-controlled organization (hierarchy), keep citizens from acting together (disorganization), or pit civil associations against each other (division):

1. Mobilizational single-party regimes and state corporatist regimes both use hierarchical organization to prevent the emergence of autonomous civil society;

2. By contrast, demobilizing authoritarian regimes—including most electoral autocracies—aspire to confine atomized citizens in their private spheres, and then bet on the disorganization of societal forces to achieve popular acquiescence;

3. If civil society constitutes an associational realm that is autonomous with respect to the state, hierarchy and disorganization represent logically opposite modes of controlling that realm: The former establishes organization without autonomy, and the latter, autonomy without organization. For the purpose of authoritarian containment, vertical control and the disruption of horizontal communication are functionally equivalent. In between these extremes is the strategy of "divide and conquer": Through the selective dispensation of punishments and favors, rulers can sow division among existing civil society organizations. We find such intermediate situations, for instance, in the "divided structures of contestation" that help to maintain contemporary regimes in the Middle East.[8]

Local Government

Authoritarian governance seldom spells the end of local politics. To preempt the emergence of local challenges, central authorities must devise "institutional mechanisms that minimize the odds that [they] will lose control over local elites."[9] Perhaps the most prominent mechanisms are repression, bureaucratic control, accountability, and arbitration.

1. In *repressive regimes* of center-periphery relations, central authorities set up parallel bureaucracies of surveillance and physical punishment, such as the Soviet secret police under Stalin, to terrorize lower-level authorities into subservience;

2. In *bureaucratic regimes,* central authorities set up territorial layers of government in a hierarchical fashion. They control local authorities by dictating appointments from top to bottom. In such settings, each unit of subnational government is "critically constrained by the capacity of a hierarchically superior unit to appoint, remove, or dismiss [its] leading officials";[10]

3. In *accountability regimes,* authoritarian governments delegate broad authority to local actors, yet hold them accountable for severe performance failures. The criteria for such results-oriented accountability may be political (such as the maintenance of social peace) or nonpolitical (like the achievement of economic growth);[11]

4. Finally, in *arbitration regimes,* the authoritarian ruler in the capital city acts as arbiter between rival subnational factions that compete for his favors. Similar to a regional hegemon in international relations, he appears as the overpowering external actor whose intervention tips the internal balance of power within regions and localities.

Institutional Ambiguity

Students of modern authoritarianism have long been aware of the institutional bases of nondemocratic rule. Whether examining the logic of totalitarian dictatorship or of military rule, they have acknowledged the role of both military bureaucracies (including the political police) and civil bureaucracies (including single parties) as crucial instruments of dictatorial power.[12] In contrast to repressive institutions, formally representative institutions in authoritarian regimes have been given scarce attention. Observers have assumed authoritarian regimes to be realms in which formal constraints are weightless in the face of factual correlations of power and informal practices of governance.

Certainly, representative institutions make for lovely decorations in the shop windows of authoritarian regimes. Yet, in addition to their aesthetic value, such institutions are also likely to hold some instrumental value for authoritarian governments, helping them to exercise and to maintain power. Whether presiding over a premodern hierarchical state or the complex bureaucratic structures of a modern state, governments have to resolve two fundamental tasks: First, whatever the substantive goals they pursue, they must secure their ability to govern (the challenge of governance); and second, they have to secure their continuity in power (the challenge of political survival). Scholars often think of the former as a problem of "cooperation" (since subjects have to contribute labor and taxes in order to develop and maintain structures of power) and the latter as a problem of "compliance" (since subjects as well as the elite must acquiesce to the status quo in order for the rulers to stay in power).

Responding to democratizing pressures by creating and manipulating representative institutions should help authoritarian governments to ease their existential problems of governance and survival. It should help them to elicit cooperation from societal groups and individual actors, and to diminish the (actual or potential) challenges that these pose to the regime. On average, as the emerging body of comparative studies on authoritarian regimes indicates, representative institutions do seem to fulfill such regime-supporting functions.[13] Yet they inevitably, although to varying degrees, contain the seeds of subversion. Institutions are not machines. As they are run by human beings, they cannot be subject to absolute control; and if they were, they would stop serving the needs of their dictatorial creators.

This is the dilemma of authoritarian institutional concessions: Unless political institutions are granted at least a minimal range of power and autonomy, they cannot make an independent contribution to authoritarian governance and survival. But as soon as political institutions are granted some power and autonomy, they can turn against the dictator. They open up arenas of struggle and sites of resistance—public or underground, explicit or veiled, heroic or mundane, altruistic or self-interested—where multiple actors test in multiple ways the limits of the permissible.

In autocracies, then, representative institutions are arenas of control and cooptation, but also of contention. Even if authoritarian institutions work as intended, channeling, deflecting, or dispersing oppositional efforts, critics of the regime may still succeed to some extent in neutralizing these institutions or even appropriating them for their own purposes. Even if nominally democratic institutions make autocracy work and augment authoritarian rulers' *probability* of surviving in office and governing effectively, they still contain the *possibility* of eroding authoritarian stability and governance. Yet if political institutions are not simply useful but also threatening, if they have the power not just to sustain but also "the potential to undermine autocratic rule, why would any incumbent create or tolerate them?"[14]

The answer is rather straightforward: Rulers cannot have one without the other. They cannot establish institutions that will effectively secure their rule without accepting the structural risks that these involve. Such risks even extend to the repressive institutions that are designed to be the primary guardians of the authoritarian order. How many dictators have fallen victim to the paramilitary security forces that they established for their own personal protection? How many have been deposed by factions within the political parties that they had created as instruments of dominance? Even the totalitarian project of a comprehensive bureaucratization of society in the name of socialism ended up defeating itself. The all-powerful institutions of the Soviet empire "that had defined [the socialist systems] and that were, presumably, to defend them as well, ended up functioning over time to subvert both the regime and the state."[15]

The Politics of the Possible

Authoritarians certainly dream of "purging ambivalence"[16] from their institutional creations and would undoubtedly love to build regime-supportive institutions that hold no regime-subversive possibilities. Yet an authoritarian world without such inherent contradictions is the autocrat's impossible dream. Formal representative institutions may make an autocrat's life easier and longer, but they might also one day threaten their creator's very existence. As a matter of course, though, such institutions differ widely as regards the nature and magnitude of the various structural risks that they involve. In recent years, political scientists have focused much of their attention on the institution that seems to hold the greatest risk for authoritarians—multiparty elections. Responding to the expanded use of multiparty elections by authoritarian regimes, scholars have started to examine in systematic fashion "the power of elections"[17] under authoritarian governance. In faithful reflection of the ambiguous nature of authoritarian elections, the debate has experienced an intriguing bifurcation: The literature

on the political economy of dictatorship has emphasized the *regime-sustaining* value of authoritarian elections, while comparative studies of "democratization by elections" have stressed their *regime-subverting* potential. These two strands of theoretical inquiry and empirical analysis have been developing in peaceful coexistence and mutual ignorance. Although their major claims seem to be at odds with one another, they are in fact essentially compatible. That authoritarian multiparty elections are most likely to strengthen the survival capacity of the incumbent is a *probabilistic* assertion; that elections create opportunities for opposition forces to weaken or even topple the incumbent regime is a *possibilistic* assertion.[18]

Contemporary electoral autocracies have given up the longstanding battle against the establishment of representative institutions. Abandoning all pretense of ideological rivalry, they have introduced the entire set of formal institutions that we associate with liberal democracy. They have shifted their authoritarian energies from repressing formally democratic institutions to manipulating them. In response, prodemocratic opposition forces have redirected their efforts from establishing the institutional skeleton of democracy to breathing democratic life into the bones of formal representative institutions. If institutional manipulation represents the last trench of authoritarian defense, then institutional liberation—that is, the emancipation of formally democratic institutions from authoritarian controls—represents the final front in the struggle for democracy. Of course, one might say that this is only business as usual: Democracy advocates never have been simply able to take for granted the autonomy and effectiveness of representative bodies. Just as their establishment required political struggle, so does their effective functioning.

> **Contemporary electoral autocracies have given up the longstanding battle against the establishment of representative institutions. They have shifted their authoritarian energies from repressing formally democratic institutions to manipulating them.**

If setting up and running an electoral authoritarian regime involves deep ambiguities, so too does the act of opposing one. This is true for international as well as domestic opponents. Outside actors always run the risk that their efforts to undermine an authoritarian regime or push it to democratize might end up backfiring. Dictators can always blackmail international actors by threatening to harm the population that they hold hostage. Likewise, the domestic opposition must choose whether to oppose, support, or critically engage with the representative institutions maintained and manipulated by an authoritarian regime. Each option runs the risk of strengthening rather than weakening the regime, either on the spot or in the long run. Yet even if opposition forces remain aware of the *probability* that the regime will benefit from the appearance of democracy, they can draft subversive strategies and gather strength based on the realistic *possibility* that democracy could prevail.

Electoral authoritarian regimes are vulnerable. The last line of authoritarian defense—the manipulation of formally democratic institutions—is fragile. For all its difficulties, breaking through defensive lines of manipulation is easier on average than tearing down authoritarian walls of repression. Even if the odds of success seem low, the democratic opposition can reasonably embrace the politics of the possible called for by Albert O. Hirschman.[19] With realistic hope, it can engage its authoritarian adversaries in democratizing battles that it will probably lose—within a democratizing campaign that it may possibly win.

Notes

1. For a synthesis of democratic advances and setbacks since the mid-1970s, see Larry Diamond, *The Spirit of Democracy: The Struggle to Build Free Societies Throughout the World* (New York: Henry Holt, 2008), 39–87. On the rise and demise of electoral autocracies, see Andreas Schedler, ed., *Electoral Authoritarianism: The Dynamics of Unfree Competition* (Boulder, Colo.: Lynne Rienner, 2006) and Staffan I. Lindberg, ed., *Democratization by Elections: A New Mode of Transition* (Baltimore: Johns Hopkins University Press, 2009).

2. My outline of authoritarian strategies of judicial containment largely follows Tamir Moustafa and Tom Ginsburg, "Introduction: The Functions of Courts in Authoritarian Politics," in Tom Ginsburg and Tamir Moustafa, eds., *Rule by Law: The Politics of Courts in Authoritarian Regimes* (Cambridge: Cambridge University Press, 2008), 1–22, although I reframe and rename some of their analytical categories.

3. See Martin Shapiro, "Courts in Authoritarian Regimes," in Ginsburg and Moustafa, eds., *Rule by Law*, 326–35.

4. Moustafa and Ginsburg, "Introduction," 18.

5. Moustafa and Ginsburg, "Introduction," 20. See also Daniel Brinks. *The Judicial Response to Police Killings in Latin America: Inequality and the Rule of Law* (New York: Cambridge University Press, 2008).

6. See also Andreas Schedler, "Elections Without Democracy: The Menu of Manipulation," *Journal of Democracy* 13 (April 2002): 36–50, and "The Logic of Electoral Authoritarianism," in Schedler, *Electoral Authoritarianism*, 1–23.

7. Robert A. Dahl, *Polyarchy: Participation and Opposition* (New Haven: Yale University Press, 1971), 3.

8. See Ellen Lust-Okar, *Structuring Conflict in the Arab World: Incumbents, Opponents, and Institutions* (Cambridge: Cambridge University Press, 2005).

9. Pierre F. Landry, *Decentralized Authoritarianism in China: The Communist Party's Control of Local Elites in the Post-Mao Era* (New York: Cambridge University Press, 2008), 25.

10. Landry, *Decentralized Authoritarianism,* 40 and 79.

11. See Joy Langston and Alberto Díaz-Cayeros, "From Hegemony to Glory: Mexico's Governors," unpubl. ms.; Carlos Bravo, "The Science of Not Losing: Electoral Politics in Mexico during the Porfiriato," a paper presented at the Mellon Latin American History Conference, University of Chicago, 2–3 May 2008; Landry, *Decentralized Authoritarianism,* 39.

12. See, for instance, Carl J. Friedrich and Zbigniew K. Brzezinski, *Totalitarian Dictatorship and Autocracy* (New York: Praeger, 1961); Guillermo O'Donnell, *Modernization and Bureaucratic-Authoritarianism: Studies in South American Politics* (Berkeley: University of California Press, 1973); and Valerie Bunce, *Subversive Institutions: The Design and the Destruction of Socialism and the State* (Cambridge: Cambridge University Press, 1999).

13. See, for example, Jennifer Gandhi and Adam Przeworski, "Authoritarian Institutions and the Survival of Autocrats," *Comparative Political Studies* 40 (November 2007): 1279–1301; Barbara Geddes, "Why Parties and Elections in Authoritarian Regimes?" paper presented at the annual meeting of the American Political Science Association, Washington, D.C., 2005; and Beatriz Magaloni, "Credible Power-Sharing and the Longevity of Authoritarian Rule," *Comparative Political Studies* 41 (April–May 2008): 715–41.

14. Jennifer Gandhi, *Political Institutions under Dictatorship* (New York: Cambridge University Press, 2008), xvii.

15. Bunce, *Subversive Institutions,* 2.

16. Zygmunt Bauman, *Modernity and Ambivalence* (Cambridge: Polity, 1991), 24.

17. Guiseppe Di Palma, *To Craft Democracies: An Essay on Democratic Transitions* (Berkeley: University California Press, 1993), 85.

18. For an elaboration of this argument, see Schedler, "The Contingent Power."

19. Albert O. Hirschman, "In Defense of Possibilism," in Albert O. Hirschman, *Rival Views of Market Society and Other Recent Essays* (Cambridge: Harvard University Press, 1986), 171–75.

Critical Thinking

1. What does "institutional manipulation" refer to?

2. Which institutions are manipulated and how?

3. How is local government manipulated?

4. Do these manipulated institutions pave the way to democratization? If so, how?

ANDREAS SCHEDLER is professor of political science at the Centro de Investigación y Docencia Económicas (CIDE) in Mexico City. He edited the volume *Electoral Authoritarianism: The Dynamics of Unfree Competition* (2006).

From *Journal of Democracy*, vol. 21, no. 1, January 2010, pp. 69–80. Copyright © 2010 by National Endowment for Democracy and The Johns Hopkins University Press. Reprinted with permission of The Johns Hopkins University Press.

Why Democracy Needs a Level Playing Field

STEVEN LEVITSKY AND LUCAN A. WAY

Multiparty elections proliferated in the late twentieth century but often did not bring democratization. In many countries, autocrats have repeatedly thwarted opposition electoral challenges through a variety of nondemocratic measures. Among the most effective, but least analyzed, means of autocratic survival is an uneven playing field. In countries like Botswana, Georgia, Kyrgyzstan, Malaysia, Malawi, Mozambique, Senegal, Singapore, Tanzania, and Venezuela, democratic competition is undermined less by electoral fraud or repression than by unequal access to state institutions, resources, and the media.

An uneven playing field is less evident to outside observers than is electoral fraud or repression, but it can have a devastating impact on democratic competition. When the opposition is systematically denied access to finance and major media outlets, competing in elections—even clean ones—is an uphill battle. Although opposition candidates occasionally win such contests, they usually lose them. And when elections are over, resource-starved oppositions are often decimated by defection, sometimes to the point of collapse. A skewed playing field may thus enable autocratic incumbents to retain power without resorting to the kinds of blatant abuse that can threaten their international standing.

We define an uneven playing field as one in which incumbent abuse of the state generates such disparities in access to resources, media, or state institutions that opposition parties' ability to organize and compete for national office is seriously impaired.[1] These disparities rarely emerge naturally; rather, they are usually rooted in illicit or autocratic behavior, including partisan appropriation of state resources, systematic packing of state institutions and state-run media, and politicized distribution of state resources, concessions, and licenses.

Obviously, incumbent advantage exists everywhere. Incumbents in advanced democracies distribute patronage, engage in pork-barrel spending, and enjoy privileged access to media and finance. Clientelism, corruption, and other forms of particularism are pervasive in new democracies in Southeastern Europe, Latin America, and elsewhere. Yet there is a key difference between routine incumbent advantage and an uneven playing field (or what Kenneth Greene calls "hyper-incumbent advantage"[2]). Whereas patronage and corruption may affect the *quality* of democracy in Brazil, Italy, or Poland, skewed access to resources and the media in countries such as Botswana, Malaysia, and Tanzania undermines democracy itself.

To distinguish an uneven playing field from routine incumbent advantage, we set a high threshold. We consider a playing field uneven where: 1) state institutions are widely abused for partisan ends: 2) the incumbent party is systematically favored at the expense of the opposition; *and* 3) the opposition's ability to organize and compete in elections is seriously handicapped. The scope, partisan nature, and especially the impact of incumbent abuse are thus critical. Incumbents may abuse state resources in Greece, Latvia, and other democracies, but such abuse does not seriously affect the opposition's capacity to organize and compete for power.

The political playing field may be uneven in a variety of ways, but three are of particular importance: resource disparities; unequal access to the media; and unequal access to the law.

Access to Resources

Extreme resource disparities may be created in several ways. For one, incumbents may directly appropriate state resources. In Mexico in the early 1990s, the long-ruling Institutional Revolutionary Party (PRI) reportedly drew upon as much as US$1 billion in illicit state finance;[3] in Russia, tens of millions of dollars in government bonds were diverted to Boris Yeltsin's 1996 re-election campaign; and in Cameroon, the state treasury covers most of the ruling party's operating expenses. Incumbents may also make widespread partisan use of public buildings, vehicles, communications equipment, and employees—from low-level bureaucrats to security forces to teachers, doctors, and other professionals. Although such abuse is of little significance in wealthy democracies, it can have a major impact where the state apparatus is particularly large, as in Belarus, or where private-sector and other societal resources are limited, as in Malawi and Mozambique.

Incumbents may also use the state to skew access to private-sector finance. For example, they may use public credit, concessions, licensing, privatization, and other policy instruments to enrich party- or proxy-owned enterprises, as in Malaysia and Taiwan, or to corner the market on private-sector finance, as in Mexico under the PRI and in Russia under Yeltsin. They may also use state policy to punish businesses that finance the opposition. In Ghana, for example, entrepreneurs who backed opposition parties in 1992 "were blacklisted, denied government contracts and [had] their businesses openly sabotaged."[4] In Cambodia, the opposition Sam Rainsy Party (SRP) was "starved for funds by a business community told by [the government] that financing SRP was committing economic suicide."[5]

The resource disparities in these cases exceed anything seen in democratic regimes. Ruling parties in Malaysia and Taiwan built multibillion-dollar business empires. The estimated $3 billion in assets belonging to Taiwan's Kuomintang (KMT) made it the "richest party in the non-communist world"; in the mid-1990s, its $450 million annual budget exceeded that of the opposition Democratic Progressive Party (DPP) by at least 50-to-1.[6] In Mexico, the PRI reportedly spent up to twenty times more than its two major opponents combined in the 1994 legislative elections,[7] and in Russia in 1996, the Yeltsin campaign spent at least thirty times the amount permitted the opposition.[8] In some cases, including Belarus, Gabon, Malawi, Russia in the 2000s, and Senegal, opposition parties were so starved of resources that many either collapsed or were coopted by the government. As Russian opposition leader Grigory Yavlinsky complained, "How can we compete if one of the goals on a football pitch is one meter long while the other is ten meters long?"[9]

Media Access

Media access also may be skewed in several ways. In many cases, including those of Botswana, Malawi, Mozambique, Senegal, and Zambia, the state either monopolizes broadcast media or operates the only television and radio stations with a national audience. Although independent newspapers often circulate freely, in many low-income countries they reach only a small urban elite. This leaves the state-run media—almost always biased toward the ruling party—as the dominant (and in many rural areas, the only) source of news. Thus, even after Malawi's 1994 transition from dictator Hastings Kamuzu Banda to elected president Bakili Muluzi, government control of the media was such that one journalist complained, "Before it was Banda, Banda, Banda—every day. Now it is Muluzi, Muluzi, Muluzi."[10]

In other cases, private media exist but are closely linked to the governing party, via proxy ownership, bribery, or other corrupt means. In Ukraine, President Leonid Kuchma controlled television coverage through an informal network of private media entities. The head of the Presidential Administration, who also owned the popular 1 + 1 television station, issued orders to all major stations dictating how events should be covered. In Peru in the late 1990s, television owners signed "contracts" with state officials in which the former received up to $1.5 million a month in exchange for limiting coverage of opposition parties. In Malaysia, all major newspapers and television stations were controlled by allies of the governing Barisan Nasional coalition.

In such cases, elections are marked by extraordinarily unequal media access. A study of television coverage during Peru's 2000 election found that President Alberto Fujimori's share of coverage hovered close to 90 percent, and that nearly all opposition coverage was negative.[11] Similarly, in Russia's

1996 election, the head of NTV (the main private television station) served as Yeltsin's media director, major broadcasters refused to sell advertising time to the Communist opposition, and the media covered up Yeltsin's heart attack just before the second round.

Uneven Access to the Law

In many competitive authoritarian regimes, incumbents not only control the judiciary, the electoral authorities, and other nominally independent arbiters (via packing, bribery, and intimidation), they also deploy them systematically as partisan tools against opponents. Politicized control of the legal system allows incumbents to violate democratic procedure with impunity. It also ensures that major electoral, legal, and other disputes will be resolved in the ruling party's favor. In Malaysia in 1988, a packed judiciary ensured that a schism in the ruling United Malays National Organization was resolved in favor of Prime Minister Mahathir bin Mohamad, and a decade later it allowed Mahathir to imprison his main rival, Anwar Ibrahim, on dubious charges. In Belarus in 1996, the constitutional court terminated an impeachment process launched by parliamentary opponents of President Alyaksandr Lukashenka, facilitating his consolidation of autocratic rule. In Venezuela in 2003, electoral authorities invalidated signatures collected for a recall referendum against Hugo Chavez, thereby delaying the vote long enough for Chavez to rebuild public support and survive the recall election.

Why the Playing Field Matters

A skewed playing field allows incumbents to thwart opposition challenges without resorting to significant fraud or repression. This is an enormous advantage in the post–Cold War era, for it enables autocrats to retain power without sacrificing international legitimacy—effectively to have their cake and eat it too. A clear example is Botswana, which has long been considered a model democratic regime. Freedom House has classified it as Free since 1973, and its political-rights and civil-liberties scores in the 2000s were equal to or better than those of such Latin American democracies as Argentina, Brazil, and Mexico. Indeed, Botswana's elections have generally been free of fraud and intimidation, and civil liberties—though violated more frequently than often thought—have been relatively well protected.[12] Nevertheless, the ruling Botswana Democratic Party (BDP) has resoundingly won every election since independence in 1966, and it has always controlled at least 75 percent of the legislature.

This outcome is not simply a product of Botswana's robust economic growth. Rather, it is rooted in the ruling party's virtual monopoly over access to state institutions, finance, and mass media. The BDP "towers over the political scene." Whereas its privileged ties to business yield "generous donations," from the private sector, opposition parties "attract virtually no donations."[13] And whereas the BDP has routinely used state agencies and resources for partisan ends,[14] no public financing exists for opposition parties. Media access is likewise skewed. Through the late 1990s, the state owned all electronic media and the country's only daily newspaper. Although some private media emerged in the 2000s, the state-owned radio and television stations remain the dominant news source, and favor the ruling party.[15] The BDP's financial and media advantages deny opposition parties anything close to an even footing. As one newspaper editorialized before the 2004 elections, "only the [BDP] enters the race with resources to reach every voter."[16]

A similar dynamic exists in Tanzania. Outside of Zanzibar, electoral fraud and major civil-liberties violations have been relatively rare since Tanzania's 1992 transition to multiparty rule. Yet the ruling Chama Cha Mapinduzi (CCM) has overwhelmingly won every national election. In 2005, the CCM won more than 80 percent of the presidential vote and captured over 85 percent of parliament. This dominance is rooted in extreme resource and media disparities. The CCM "overwhelms the playing field."[17] The 1992 transition failed to break the ruling party's ties to the state. Consequently, the CCM either owns or makes regular partisan use of numerous public properties (including businesses, buildings, and vehicles), giving it an incalculable resource advantage. As one opposition leader put it, "In many areas, every open space is owned by the CCM. There are simply no places that we can hold meetings other than on the road side."[18] The CCM also uses its business holdings and close private-sector ties to dominate access to finance. Finally, although private radio and television stations exist, their reach is largely limited to the capital. State-owned media predominate in the rest of the country, giving the CCM "far more media exposure than opposition parties."[19] With these advantages, CCM leaders have boasted that they do not "need to cheat" in elections.[20]

Although a skewed playing field may be less visible than fraud or repression, it can be equally, if not more, damaging to democratic competition. Where oppositions lack reasonable access to resources and the media, even clean elections are markedly unfair. For example, although Mexico's 1994 presidential election was free of fraud, the PRI's resource and media advantages were so vast that Jorge Castañeda compared the race to "a soccer match where the goalposts were of different heights and breadths and where one team included 11 players plus the umpire and the other a mere six or seven players."[21] Taiwan's 1996 presidential election—though widely viewed as democratic—was marked by such extreme resource disparities that the DPP "found it nearly impossible to compete."[22] Although opposition candidates occasionally win unfair elections—Nicaragua in 1990; Zambia in 1991; Belarus, Malawi, and Ukraine in 1994; Senegal and Serbia in 2000; Kenya in 2002—the mere *possibility* of opposition victory is not sufficient for democracy. Regimes in which opposition victories are heroic exceptions rather than the norm should not be labeled democratic.

An uneven playing field also undermines the opposition's ability to organize *between* elections. Deprived of resources or access to mass media, opposition parties are often unable to maintain national organizations. Without patronage or other material inducements to offer followers, they are frequently plagued by defection, as leaders and activists jump to the ruling party in search of patronage, "pork," or a more secure political future. Indeed, unless opposition parties have unusually

strong organizations, identities, or core constituencies (Albania, Malaysia), their very survival may be threatened. Many prominent (or promising) opposition parties have thus withered away: Russia's Yabloko, Malaysia's Semangat '46, Cameroon's Social Democratic Front (SDF), and Zambia's United National Independence Party. Facing the specter of collapse, opposition parties may view joining the governing coalition as their only viable alternative. Major opposition parties in Cambodia, Cameroon, Gabon, Kenya, Malawi, Mali, Russia, Senegal, and Ukraine have succumbed to cooptation, largely in order to secure the resources necessary for political survival.

As "pragmatic" parties join the government and "principled" ones weaken, the opposition ranks may be effectively depopulated. In Cambodia, for example, the ruling party's cooptation of Funcinpec and marginalization of the more militant Sam Rainsy Party effectively eliminated serious opposition in the 2000s. In Gabon, opposition parties seriously challenged President Omar Bongo in the early 1990s, but in the decade that followed, Bongo used the state's considerable oil rents to coopt nearly all of them. By 2005, 29 of 35 registered parties had joined the governing coalition, and parties that remained in opposition did so "at the cost of losing money, and therefore supporters."[23] In Cameroon in the late 1990s, most opposition parties opted to "cooperate" with President Paul Biya's government, leaving the SDF alone in opposition, where, starved of resources, it wilted and lost prominence. In post-2002 Mali, President Amadou Touré's "consensus" strategy brought most major parties into the Presidential Bloc, leaving the country virtually without opposition. In Tanzania, no significant national opposition party has emerged in seventeen years of multiparty rule.

A brief comparison of eight so-called new democracies in southern Africa (Malawi, Mozambique, Namibia, Zambia) and Central America (El Salvador, Guatemala, Honduras, Nicaragua) illustrates the impact of an uneven playing field on political competition. Freedom House classifies all eight regimes as "electoral democracies" and has given them roughly similar political-rights and civil-liberties scores since the mid-1990s. Yet in terms of the playing field, the two sets of cases differ markedly. Whereas the Central American playing fields were reasonably level, in that private media and financing were accessible to two or more competing parties, those in southern Africa were severely tilted: State-owned media were the dominant news sources, and incumbents' abuse of state resources and massive advantage in private-sector funding generated vast resource disparities.[24]

The consequences of these disparities are striking. With the exception of transitional elections in Zambia in 1991 and Malawi in 1994, incumbents in the southern African cases have never lost. Ruling parties have been re-elected four consecutive times in Mozambique, Namibia, and Zambia and three times in Malawi. Overall, incumbents have won 15 of 17 elections and have not lost since 1994. In Central America, by contrast, incumbents usually lose. In El Salvador, Guatemala, Honduras, and Nicaragua, opposition candidates have won more than two-thirds (13 of 18) of the presidential elections held since 1989. These contrasting patterns suggest real differences in the level of democratic competition that standard measures fail to capture.

The Need for Conceptual Precision

The above discussion suggests a need to take the slope of the playing field more seriously in conceptualizing and measuring democracy. The proliferation of hybrid regimes, in particular, poses a conceptual challenge. Because most hybrid regimes hold multiparty elections, scholars seeking to differentiate them from democracies have sought to "precise" the concept of democracy by making explicit criteria that had been implicitly understood as part of its overall meaning.[25] In the 1980s and 1990s, scholars precised the Schumpeterian definition to include—or make explicit—two additional criteria: civil liberties and civilian control over the military. In our view, the concept needs to be honed further to include a reasonably level playing field. In other words, a level playing field should be treated as a *defining feature of democracy.*

Although a level playing field is implicit in most conceptualizations of democracy, standard measures of civil liberties and free elections often fail to capture key aspects of unfair competition. Abuses that tilt the playing field often are not, strictly speaking, breaches of civil liberties. Whereas closing newspapers and arresting government critics are clear violations of civil liberties, gaining de facto control of the private media via informal proxy or patronage arrangements and using state powers to secure a monopoly over private-sector finance are not. Similarly, many of the effects of a skewed playing field are felt *between* elections and are thus often missed in election evaluations. Yet when vast resource disparities weaken opposition parties, lure erstwhile opponents into the government, or deter potential challengers from entering the political arena, democratic competition is undermined in ways that do not necessarily manifest themselves on election day. Rather, incumbents effectively secure victory before the campaign ever begins.

Attention to the slope of the playing field thus highlights how regimes may be nondemocratic *even in the absence of significant fraud or civil-liberties violations.* Precising the definition of democracy to include a level playing field thus allows scholars more accurately to score cases such as Mexico and Taiwan in the mid-1990s and contemporary Botswana, Georgia, Mozambique, and Senegal, where the façade of Schumpeterian democracy belies a far less competitive reality.

Origins of an Uneven Playing Field

Uneven playing fields tend to emerge under conditions that facilitate incumbent control over key state and societal resources. Such conditions often exist in cases of incomplete transition from single-party rule. Single-party regimes tend to fuse the state and ruling party, creating a highly politicized state in which bureaucrats are also party cadres, state properties (businesses, media outlets) are also party properties, and resources from various state agencies are systematically deployed for partisan use. Transitions to multiparty rule—often

accomplished via a simple constitutional change or the calling of elections—do not necessarily alter these patterns. In countries like Cambodia, Cameroon, Gabon, Kenya, Mozambique, Serbia, Taiwan, and Tanzania in the early 1990s, the end of single-party rule did not bring an effective de-linking of state and party, and this helped incumbents to retain power in a multiparty context.

In the postcommunist world, a skewed playing field may be a legacy of incomplete transitions. Incumbents often retained dominant control over societal resources after the collapse of state socialism in 1989–91. In states that did not undergo large-scale privatization (such as Belarus and Uzbekistan), or where governments used insider privatization to establish extensive patronage ties to a new business elite (as in Russia and Serbia), incumbents often established a virtual monopoly over access to finance and the media, thereby impeding the ability of nonstate actors to emerge and challenge the government.

Another source of an uneven playing field is mineral wealth. Where petroleum or other natural-resource exports are a primary source of national revenue, and the bulk of this revenue flows through the state, governments have almost total control over societal resources. In such a context—for example, in Botswana, Gabon, and, to some extent, Venezuela—it is a huge challenge to build or sustain opposition.

Finally, an uneven playing field is often rooted in underdevelopment. In a context of widespread poverty and a weak private sector, the financial, organizational, and human resources available to opposition parties are usually quite limited. Small, economically vulnerable private sectors cannot be relied upon to finance opposition. Moreover, in the absence of a vibrant private economy, public-sector jobs, contracts, and other resources take on disproportionate importance and help governments to coopt politicians, businessmen, and activists away from the opposition. Opposition impoverishment magnifies the impact of incumbency. Even petty incumbent abuses that have no real impact in rich countries, such as the ruling party's use of public employees, buildings, or vehicles, can seriously hinder the opposition's ability to compete. In countries like Cambodia, Madagascar, Mali, and Tanzania, for example, access to 4 × 4 vehicles allows incumbents to penetrate rural areas that are largely inaccessible to opposition parties.

Underdevelopment also skews media access. In poor societies newspaper circulation is usually low, leaving television and radio as the only sources of news for much of the population. Yet weak private sectors may have difficulty sustaining national broadcasting networks. In Mali, Moldova, Mozambique, Senegal, Tanzania, Zimbabwe, and other low-income countries, only state-owned television broadcasted nationally in the 1990s and into the 2000s. Even where private media exist, they are often highly dependent on the state. Government advertising is almost invariably their major source of revenue, leaving them vulnerable to cooptation.

In a context of extreme resource scarcity and media underdevelopment, then, simply being in government can generate a significant incumbent advantage. This has an important implication: The same type of incumbent abuse can have different effects across cases, depending on the level of development. For example, incumbents use public employees and state resources for election campaigns in Malawi and Brazil, but whereas in Malawi this abuse seriously affects the opposition's ability to compete, in Brazil it does not. Likewise, government threats to withdraw advertising from private media powerfully shape media behavior in Botswana, but not in Italy or Mexico. And whereas biased public television or radio have little impact in Central Europe and South America, where private media predominate, they have a powerful impact in much of southern Africa, where they are often the only available news sources.

Overcoming an Uneven Playing Field

How can an uneven playing field be overcome? The surest way is to grow out of it. Capitalist development expands the resources available to opposition parties, creates markets capable of sustaining a pluralist media structure, and diminishes the impact of incumbent abuse. In Mexico and Taiwan, for example, economic development expanded the media market and gave rise to a more independent private sector that would become a major source of opposition finance. Thus, although the PRI and KMT continued to abuse state power during the 1990s, the impact of abuse diminished relative to earlier decades.

Short of such long-term structural developments, hyper-incumbent advantage may be overcome in several other ways. The most common is a split within the ruling elite. Where the playing field is skewed, the most viable challengers often come from within. Unlike opposition politicians, top government officials *do* have access to the state and media. When those officials defect to the opposition, their access to such resources may effectively mitigate incumbent advantage. Incumbent coalitions are especially prone to disintegration where ruling parties are weak, as in much of the former Soviet Union and Africa. In Ukraine, for example, Viktor Yushchenko, who had served as prime minister under Kuchma, was able to mount a successful presidential campaign (despite considerable incumbent abuse) with the support of leading politicians and oligarchs who, along with Yushchenko, had recently abandoned the Kuchma regime. Likewise, in Kenya in 2002, the defection of leading government officials was critical to the opposition's victory. Indeed, many of the most dramatic David-versus-Goliath-style opposition victories in recent decades (Zambia in 1991, Malawi in 1994, Senegal in 2000, Georgia in 2003) were products of massive defections of regime insiders.

Oppositions may also seek to overcome the disadvantages created by an uneven playing field by allowing themselves to be coopted and (temporarily) joining the government. Lacking access to media and finance, opposition parties and politicians have adopted this strategy in Armenia, Cambodia, Cameroon, Gabon, Kenya, Malawi, Mali, Senegal, and Serbia. Such behavior is often dismissed as opportunistic and corrupt, and opposition parties that pursue it risk being discredited. Where the playing field is skewed, however, joining the government may

be their only viable means of organizational survival. By allowing themselves to be coopted today, opposition parties may gain the resources needed to survive and compete tomorrow.

Cooperative strategies sometimes succeed: Abdoulaye Wade's Senegalese Democratic Party (PDS) joined government coalitions in 1991 and 1995, gaining access to critical patronage resources. While "pure" opposition parties languished, the PDS flourished, and Wade won the presidency in 2000. Similarly, in Kenya, opposition leader Raila Odinga aligned his National Democratic Party with the ruling Kenya African National Union (KANU) in the late 1990s and joined the government in 2001. Well-endowed with resources, Odinga rejoined the opposition in 2002 and played a central role in KANU's defeat that year.

Although these scenarios highlight how incumbents may be defeated despite an uneven playing field, neither entails an actual *leveling* of the playing field. As a result, turnover in such cases rarely brings democracy. In Belarus, Malawi, Ukraine, and Zambia in the 1990s, and in Georgia, Kenya, Madagascar, and Senegal in the 2000s, an uneven playing field persisted after transitions, and successor governments were not democratic. Democratization in such cases often requires active measures to widen access to resources and media, such as guaranteed public finance for political parties and regulations to strengthen independent media. In Mexico, for example, campaign finance and media reforms succeeded in leveling the playing field after 1996. Incumbents rarely accede to such measures, however, and equitable arrangements on paper are often not enforced in practice.

In such a context, international actors can make a difference. External assistance has at times helped opposition forces to overcome the effects of an uneven playing field.[26] In Nicaragua in 1990, for example, U.S. assistance enabled an enfeebled opposition coalition to hire staff, buy campaign vehicles, open offices across the country, and run a national campaign—all of which was critical to its stunning victory over the Sandinistas. In Serbia in 2000, Western assistance was critical to the anti-Milošević opposition's successful campaign and postelection protest movement. External assistance may also strengthen civil society organizations—such as domestic election-observer groups (OK-98 in Slovakia, Committee of Voters in Ukraine)—and support independent media outlets (Nicaragua in 1990, Cambodia in 1993, Serbia and Croatia in 2000, Ukraine in 2004). In poor countries, where a few 4 × 4 vehicles or rural radio stations can make a big difference, external efforts to level the playing field do not require large sums of money. By simply enabling opposition groups to reach voters across the country, even modest assistance can put those groups in a position to win.

An uneven playing field is an increasingly important means of sustaining authoritarian rule. Even where fraud or civil-liberties violations are widespread—as in Belarus, Cambodia, Gabon, Malaysia, Russia, and Singapore—unequal access to resources, media, and the law may be the most potent force undermining political competition. Indeed, in the contemporary era, such mechanisms may be a more effective way to "disappear" opponents than the kind of violent repression used by regimes in the past.

Notes

1. For an excellent analysis of the causes and consequences of an uneven playing field, see Kenneth F. Greene, *Why Dominant Parties Lose: Mexico's Democratization in Comparative Perspective* (New York: Cambridge University Press, 2007).

2. Greene, *Why Dominant Parties Lose.*

3. Andres Oppenheimer, *Bordering on Chaos: Guerrillas, Stockbrokers, Politicians, and Mexico's Road to Prosperity* (Boston: Little, Brown, 1996), 88.

4. Mike Oquaye, "Human Rights and the 1996 Elections," in Joseph R.A. Ayee, ed., *The 1996 General Elections and Democratic Consolidation in Ghana* (Accra: University of Ghana Department of Political Science, 1998), 109.

5. Steve Heder, "Cambodia: Hun Sen's Consolidation: Death or Beginning of Reform?" *Southeast Asian Affairs 2005* (Singapore: Institute of Southeast Asian Studies, 2005), 113–30.

6. Julian Baum, "The Money Machine," *Far Eastern Economic Review,* 11 August 2004, 62–64; Jaushieh Joseph Wu, *Taiwan's Democratization: Forces Behind the New Momentum* (Oxford: Oxford University Press, 1995), 79.

7. Oppenheimer, *Bordering on Chaos,* 110.

8. Michael McFaul, *Russia's 1996 Presidential Election: The End of Polarized Politics* (Stanford: Hoover Institution Press, 1997), 13.

9. David White, *Yabloko: Opposition in a Managed Democracy* (Surrey, U.K.: Ashgate, 2006), 205.

10. *Africa Report,* November–December 1994, 57.

11. Taylor Boas, "Television and Neopopulism in Latin America: Media Effects in Brazil and Peru," *Latin American Research Review* 40, no. 2 (2005): 36.

12. Ian Taylor, "As Good as It Gets? Botswana's 'Democratic Development,'" *Journal of Contemporary African Studies* 21 (July 2003): 215–31.

13. Taylor, "As Good as It Gets?" 218.

14. John Holm and Staffan Darnolf, "Democratizing the Administrative State in Botswana," in York W. Bradshaw and Stephen N. Ndegwa, eds. *The Uncertain Promise of Southern Africa* (Bloomington: Indiana University Press, 2000), 122.

15. Freedom House, "Freedom of the Press, 2008: Botswana"; available at www.freedomhouse.org.

16. "Botswana Elections: Free but Not Fair," *Mmegi/The Reporter,* 23 June 2004.

17. Lucan A. Way interview with Professor Stevfan Mushi, University of Dar es Salaam, Tanzania, 23 November 2007.

18. Way interview with Wilbrod Slaa, Chadema opposition party, Arusha, Tanzania, 29 November 2007.

19. Barak Hoffman and Lindsay Robinson, "Tanzania's Missing Opposition," *Journal of Democracy* 20 (October 2009): 130.

20. Hoffman and Robinson, "Tanzania's Missing Opposition," 123.

21. Jorge G. Castañeda, *The Mexican Shock: Its Meaning for the United States* (New York: New Press, 1995), 131.

22. Shelley Rigger, "The Democratic Progressive Party in 2000: Obstacles and Opportunities," *China Quarterly* 168 (December 2001): 949.

23. *Africa Confidential,* 21 January 2005, 5.

24. See Levitsky and Way, *Competitive Authoritarianism* (forthcoming, 2010), ch. 6.

25. See David Collier and Steven Levitsky, "Democracy with Adjectives: Conceptual Innovation in Comparative Research," *World Politics* 49 (April 1997): 430–51.

26. See Valerie J. Bunce and Sharon L. Wolchik, "Favorable Conditions and Electoral Revolutions," *Journal of Democracy* 17 (October 2006): 5–18.

Critical Thinking

1. How does "access to resources" create an uneven playing field?

2. How does "media access" create an uneven playing field?

3. How does "access to the law" create an uneven playing field?

4. How does an uneven playing field jeopardize democratic progress?

STEVEN LEVITSKY is professor of government at Harvard University. **LUCAN A. WAY** is assistant professor of political science at the University of Toronto. Their book *Competitive Authoritarianism: International Linkage, Organizational Power, and the Fate of Hybrid Regimes* is forthcoming from Cambridge University Press.

From *Journal of Democracy,* vol. 21, no. 1, January 2010, pp. 57–68. Copyright © 2010 by National Endowment for Democracy and The Johns Hopkins University Press. Reprinted with permission of The Johns Hopkins University Press.

Democracy in Cyberspace: What Information Technology Can and Cannot Do

IAN BREMMER

"Information technology has demolished time and distance," Walter Wriston, the former ceo of what is now Citigroup wrote in 1997. "Instead of validating Orwell's vision of Big Brother watching the citizen, [it] enables the citizen to watch Big Brother. And so the virus of freedom, for which there is no antidote, is spread by electronic networks to the four corners of the earth." Former Presidents Ronald Reagan, Bill Clinton, and George W. Bush have articulated a similar vision, and with similarly grandiose rhetoric. All have argued that the long-term survival of authoritarian states depends on their ability to control the flow of ideas and information within and across their borders. As advances in communications technology–cellular telephones, text messaging, the Internet, social networking–allow an ever-widening circle of people to easily and inexpensively share ideas and aspirations, technology will break down barriers between peoples and nations. In this view, the spread of the "freedom virus" makes it harder and costlier for autocrats to isolate their people from the rest of the world and gives ordinary citizens tools to build alternative sources of power. The democratization of communications, the theory goes, will bring about the democratization of the world.

There seems to be plenty of evidence to support these ideas. In the Philippines in 2001, protesters sent text messages to organize the demonstrations that forced President Joseph Estrada from office. In the lead-up to the 2004 presidential election in Ukraine, supporters of Viktor Yushchenko, then the leader of the opposition, used text messaging to organize the massive protests that became the Orange Revolution. In Lebanon in 2005, activists coordinated via e-mail and text messaging to bring one million demonstrators into the streets to demand that the Syrian government end nearly three decades of military presence in Lebanon by withdrawing its 14,000 troops. (Syria complied a month later, under considerable international pressure.) Over the past few years, in Colombia, Myanmar (also known as Burma), and Zimbabwe, demonstrators have used cell phones and Facebook to coordinate protests and transmit photographs and videos of government crackdowns. The flood of words and images circulated by protesters following Iran's bitterly disputed 2009 presidential election–quickly dubbed the "Twitter revolution"–seemed to reinforce the view that Tehran has more to fear from "citizen media" than from the U.S. ships patrolling the Persian Gulf.

But a closer look at these examples suggests a more complicated reality. Only in democracies—the Philippines, Ukraine, Lebanon, and Colombia—did these communications weapons accomplish an immediate objective. In Myanmar, Zimbabwe, and Iran, they managed to embarrass the government but not to remove it from power. As Wriston acknowledged, the information revolution is a long-term process, cyberspace is a complex place, and technological advances are no substitute for human wisdom. Innovations in modern communications may help erode authoritarian power over time. But for the moment, their impact on international politics is not so easy to predict.

There are many reasons why the optimistic view of the relationship among communications, information, and democracy has taken root in the United States. First, these communications tools embody twenty-first-century innovation, and Americans have long believed in the power of invention to promote peace and create prosperity. And with good reason. Admirers of Reagan argue that the United States' ability to invest in strategic missile defense sent the Soviet leadership into a crisis confidence from which it never recovered. The light bulb, the automobile, and airplane have changed the world, greater personal autonomy to many Americans. Similarly, Americans believe that the millions of people around the world who use the Internet, an American invention, will eventually adopt American political beliefs, much like many of those who wear American jeans, watch American movies, and dance to American music have. Champions of the Internet's power to promote pluralism and human rights point to bloggers in China, Russia, and the Arab world who are calling for democracy and the rule of law for their countries, sometimes in English.

But of the hundreds of millions who blog in their own languages—there are more than 75 million in China alone—the vast majority have other priorities. Many more of them focus on pop culture rather than on political philosophy, on pocketbook issues rather than political power, and on national pride rather than cosmopolitan pretensions. In other words, the tools of modern communications satisfy as wide a range of ambitions and appetites as their twentieth-century ancestors did, and many of these ambitions and appetites do not have anything to do with democracy.

Net Neutrality

A careful look at the current impact of modern communications on the political development of authoritarian states should give pause to those who hail these technologies as instruments of democratization. Techno-optimists appear to ignore the fact that these tools are value neutral; there is nothing inherently pro-democratic about them. To use them is to exercise a form of freedom, but it is not necessarily a freedom that promotes the freedom of others.

In enabling choice, the introduction of the Internet into an authoritarian country shares something fundamental with the advent of elections. Some have argued that promoting elections in one country in the Middle East will generate demand for elections elsewhere there. A free Iraq is going to help inspire others to demand what I believe is a universal right of men and women," Bush said in July 2006; elections in Iraq would prompt the citizens of Iraq's neighbors to ask why Iraqis were now free to choose their leaders whereas they were not. Similarly, some have argued that the freedom that comes with the Internet will inevitably democratize China. Once Chinese people read about the freedoms of others, the thinking goes, they will want the same for themselves. The tools of modern communications will reveal to Chinese citizens the political freedoms they do not yet have and provide the means to demand them.

But the limited history of elections the Middle East shows that people do not always vote for pluralism. Sometimes, they vote for security or absolutism, sometimes to express outrage or defend local interests. The same pattern holds true for the Internet and other forms of modern communications. These technologies provide access to information of all kinds, information that entertains the full range of human appetites—from titillation to rationalization, from hope to anger. They provide the user with an audience but do not determine what he will say. They are a megaphone, and have a multiplier effect, but they serve both those who want to speed up the crossborder flow of information and those who want to divert or manipulate it.

Cyberspace can be a very dark place. In *You Are Not a Gadget*, Jaron Lanier argues that the anonymity provided by the Internet can promote a "culture of sadism," feeding an appetite for drive-by attacks and mob justice. In China, the Internet has given voice to wounded national pride, anti-Western and anti-Japanese resentment over injuries both real and imagined, and hostility toward Tibetans, Muslim Uighurs, and other minority groups. It has also become a kind of public square for improvised violence. In an article for *The New York Times Magazine* earlier this year, Tom Downey described the "human-flesh search" phenomenon in China, "a form of online vigilante justice in which Internet users hunt down and punish people who

have attracted their wrath." The targets of these searches, a kind of "crowdsourced detective work," as Downey put it, can be corrupt officials or enemies of the state, or simply people who have made other people angry.

These problems are hardly unique to China. In Russia, skinheads have filmed murderous attacks on dark-skinned immigrants from the Caucasus and Central Asia and posted the footage online. Also in Russia—and in the United States and Europe—hate groups and militants of various kinds use the Internet to recruit new members and disseminate propaganda. Of course, beyond all this fear and loathing, many more people around the world use the Internet as a global shopping mall and a source of entertainment. The Internet makes it easier for users with political interests to find and engage with others who believe what they believe, but there is little reliable evidence that it also opens their minds to ideas and information that challenge their worldviews. The medium fuels many passions—consumerism and conspiracy theories, resentment and fanaticism—but it promotes calls for democracy only where there is already a demand for democracy. If technology has helped citizens pressure authoritarian governments in several countries, it is not because the technology created a demand for change. That demand must come from public anger at authoritarianism itself.

Stateside

Citizens are not the only ones active in cyberspace. The state is online, too, promoting its own ideas and limiting what an average user can see and do. Innovations in communications technology provide people with new sources of information and new opportunities to share ideas, but they also empower governments to manipulate the conversation and to monitor what people are saying.

The collapse of Soviet communism a generation ago taught authoritarian leaders around the world that they could not simply mandate lasting economic growth and that they would have to embrace capitalism if they hoped to create the jobs and the higher standards of living that would ensure their long-term political survival. But to embrace capitalism is to allow for dangerous new freedoms. And so in order to generate strong growth while maintaining political control, some autocrats have turned to state capitalism, a system that helps them dominate market activity through the use of national oil companies, other state-owned enterprises, privately owned but politically loyal national champions, state-run banks, and sovereign wealth funds.

Following precisely the same logic, authoritarian governments are now trying to ensure that the increasingly free flow of ideas and information through cyberspace fuels their economies without threatening their political power. In June, the Chinese government released its first formal statement on the rights and responsibilities of Internet users. The document "guarantee[d] the citizens' freedom of speech on the Internet as well as the public's right to know, to participate, to be heard, and to oversee [the government] in accordance with the law." But it also stipulated that "within Chinese territory, the Internet is under the jurisdiction of Chinese sovereignty." That caveat legitimates China's "great firewall," a system of filters and re-routers, detours and dead ends designed to keep Chinese Internet users on the stateapproved online path.

The Chinese leadership also uses more low-tech means to safeguard its interests online. The average Chinese Web surfer cannot be sure that every idea or opinion he encounters in cyberspace genuinely reflects the views of its author. The government has created the 50 Cent Party, an army of online commentators that it pays for each blog entry or message-board post promoting the Chinese Communist Party's line on sensitive subjects. This is a simple, inexpensive way for governments to disseminate and disguise official views. Authoritarian states do not use technology simply to block the free flow of unwelcome ideas. They also use it to promote ideas of their own.

Nonaligned Movement

The techno-optimists who hope that modern communications tools will democratize authoritarian states are also hoping that they will help align the interests of nondemocracies with those of democracies. But the opposite is happening. Efforts by police states to control or co-opt these tools are inevitably creating commercial conflicts that then create political conflicts between governments.

In January, Google publicly complained that private Gmail accounts had been breached in attacks originating in China— attacks that Chinese officials appeared to tolerate or even to have launched themselves. In protest, Google announced that it would no longer censor the results of users' searches in mainland China, which it had reluctantly agreed to do when it entered the Chinese market in 2006. Beijing refused to back down, and Google automatically redirected searches by Chinese users to the uncensored Hong Kong version of the site. But much to the relief of mainland users, mostly students and researchers who prefer Google's capabilities to its main domestic rival, Baidu, Chinese officials eventually announced the renewal of Google's operating license. (It is possible that they backtracked because they believed that they could control Google or use it to monitor the online activities of political dissidents.)

As Chinese technology companies begin to compete on a par with Western ones and the Chinese government uses legal and financial means to more actively promote domestic firms that see censorship as a routine cost of doing business, there will be less demand for Google's products in China. In August 2010, the state-run Xinhua News Agency and China Mobile, the country's largest cell-phone carrier, announced plans to jointly build a state-owned search–engine and media company. In response to these developments, U.S. technology companies will undoubtedly turn to U.S. lawmakers for help in creating and maintaining a level commercial playing field in China. Far from aligning American and Chinese political values and bringing the citizens of the two countries closer together, conflicts over the flow of information through cyberspace will further complicate the already troubled U.S. Chinese relationship.

Signs of strife are already visible. When Google first went public with its complaints about cyberattacks and censorship, Beijing looked past the company, which it sees as a high-tech arm of the U.S. government, and addressed its response directly to Washington. A Chinese Communist Party tabloid ran an editorial under the headline "The World Does Not Welcome the White House's Google"; it argued, "Whenever the U.S. government demands it, Google can easily become a convenient tool for promoting the U.S. government's political will and values abroad." In response, U.S. Secretary of State Hillary Clinton urged companies such as Google not to cooperate with "politically motivated censorship," further emphasizing the difference, not the convergence, of political values in the United States and China.

Revealing similar fears about the future of its political control, the United Arab Emirates and Saudi Arabia took action earlier this year against Research in Motion (RIM), the Canadian company that makes the BlackBerry, for equipping its devices with encryption technology that authorities cannot decode. Arguing that terrorists and spies could use BlackBerries to communicate within the uae without fear of being detected, Emirati officials announced in August that they would soon suspend BlackBerry service unless RIM provided state officials with some means of monitoring BlackBerry messaging. Within two days, Saudi Arabia announced a similar shutdown, although Riyadh and RIM have since reached a compromise that requires RIM to install a relay server on territory, which allows Saudi officials monitor messages sent from and within country. The UAE will probably also a deal with RIM: there are half a millon BlackBerry users in the UAE (about percent of the population), and the country wants to remain the Arab world's primary commercial and tourist hub. Yet far from promoting Western values in non-Western police states, the BlackBerry has sparked a new round of debate over the willingness of Western technology companies to protect their market shares by making concessions that help authoritarian governments spy on their citizens.

In fairness to these governments, the world's leading democracies are no less concerned about potential terrorist threats posed by unmonitored messaging. The Indian government has also threatened to ban BlackBerries unless RIM gives it access to certain data, and counterterrorism officials in the United States and Europe are considering the option as well. Via efforts to amend the Electronic Communications Privacy Act, the Obama administration has already taken steps to help the FBI gain access to "electronic communication transactional records"—recipients' addresses, logs of users' online activities, browser histories—without a court order if investigators suspect terrorism or espionage. Politicians and technology companies such as Google and RIM will be fighting these battles for years to come.

Of course, authoritarian governments, unlike democracies, also worry that individuals who are neither terrorists nor spies will use new communications tools to challenge their political legitimacy. China, Iran, Myanmar, North Korea, Saudi Arabia, and other authoritarian states cannot halt the proliferation of weapons of modern communications, but they can try to monitor and manipulate them for their own purposes. That struggle will continue as well, limiting the ability of new technologies to empower the political opposition within these countries and creating more conflicts over political values between democratic and authoritarian states.

Feedback Loops

The Internet may have changed the world, but now the world is changing the Internet. For 30 years, new communications technologies have driven globalization, the defining trend of the times. The companies that created these products made longterm plans based on the wants and needs of consumers, not governments. Their profits rose as they connected billions of customers with one another; borders became increasingly less important.

But now, the pace of technological change and the threat of terrorism are forcing policymakers to expand their definitions of national security and to rethink their definitions of "critical infrastructure." As a result, governments are turning to high-tech communications firms to help shore up emerging security vulnerabilities, and high-tech communications firms have begun to think more like defense contractors—companies whose success depends on secrecy, exclusivity, political contacts, and security clearances.

As a result, political borders, which the rise of information technology once seemed set to dissolve, are taking on a new importance: if greater openness creates new opportunities, it also creates new worries. Unable to match U.S. defense spending, China and Russia have become adept at information warfare. The Pentagon reported last August that China continues to develop its ability to steal U.S. military secrets electronically and to deny its adversaries "access to information essential to conduct combat operations." In 2007, a massive cyberattack launched from inside Russia damaged digital infrastructure in neighboring Estonia. The United States' vulnerabilities range from its nuclear power plants and electrical grids to the information systems of government agencies and major U.S. companies. Despite their political and commercial rivalries, the United States, China, Russia, India, and many other states also share a vulnerability to cyberattacks, and they have pledged to work together to build a joint cybersecurity strategy But when it comes to espionage, governments can never fully trust one another. And of course the Obama administration does not want to share technologies that would make it easier for security officials in Beijing or Moscow to track the online activities of political dissidents.

Other problems will exacerbate international tensions. Technology firms in the United States and Europe, mindful of Google's recent troubles in China, will increasingly turn to their governments for help with their own security needs. As cyberthreats become ever more sophisticated, these companies will collaborate more actively with national security agencies on developing new technologies. This will pull more technology companies into the orbit of the military-industrial complex. That, in turn, will make them even more suspect to authoritarian regimes and likelier targets for hackers and spies of all kinds. Borders are about to become much more important.

The result will be a world that has not one Internet but a set of interlinked intranets closely monitored by various governments. The Internet is not about to disappear, but the prediction that a single Internet could accommodate both the West and the evolving demands of authoritarian states was never realistic. American and European users will access the same Internet as before, but the Chinese government has already made clear its intention to declare sovereignty over an Internet of its own. Other authoritarian states have every incentive to follow its lead.

There are far too many variables at work to predict with confidence the full, longterm impact of modern tools of communications on the political development of authoritarian states. But it seems safe to expect that their effects will vary as widely as the motives of the people and the states that use them.

Critical Thinking

1. In what ways is IT useful?
2. What can IT not do?
3. What is IT generally used for?

IAN BREMMER is President of the Eurasia Group and the author of *The End of the Free Market: Who Wins the War Between States and Corporations?*

From *Foreign Affairs*, vol. 89, issue 6, November/December 2010, pp. 86–94. Copyright © 2010 by Council on Foreign Relations, Inc. Reprinted by permission of Foreign Affairs. www.ForeignAffairs.com

Not Ready for Prime Time

Why Including Emerging Powers at the Helm Would Hurt Global Governance

JORGE G. CASTAÑEDA

Few matters generate as much consensus in international affairs today as the need to rebuild the world geopolitical order. Everyone seems to agree, at least in their rhetoric, that the makeup of the United Nations Security Council is obsolete and that the G-8 no longer includes all the world's most important economies. Belgium still has more voting power in the leading financial institutions than either China or India. New actors need to be brought in. But which ones? And what will be the likely results? If there is no doubt that a retooled international order would be far more representative of the distribution of power in the world today, it is not clear whether it would be better.

The major emerging powers, Brazil, Russia, India, and China, catchily labeled the BRICS by Goldman Sachs, are the main contenders for inclusion. There are other groupings, too: the G-5, the G-20, and the P-4; the last—Brazil, Germany, India, and Japan—are the wannabes that hope to join the UN Security Council and are named after the P-5, the council's permanent members (China, France, Russia, the United Kingdom, and the United States). Up for the G-8 are Brazil, China, India, Mexico, and South Africa. The G-8 invited representatives of those five states to its 2003 summit in Evian, France, and from 2005 through 2008, this so-called G-5 attended its own special sessions on the sidelines of the G-8's.

Others states also want in. Argentina, Egypt, Indonesia, Italy, Mexico, Nigeria, Pakistan, and South Africa aspire to join the UN Security Council as permanent members, with or without a veto. But with little progress on UN reform, none of them has been accepted or rejected (although China is known to oppose admitting Japan and, to a lesser degree, India). After the G-8 accommodated the G-5, other states, generally those close to the countries hosting the summits, also started to join the proceedings on an ad hoc basis. When the global economic crisis struck in 2008, matters were institutionalized further. The finance ministers of the G-20 members had already been meeting regularly since 1999, but then the heads of state started participating. Today, the G-20 includes just about everybody who wishes to join it: the P-5 and the P-4, the G-8 and the G-5, as well as Argentina, Australia, the European Union, Indonesia,

Nigeria, Saudi Arabia, South Korea, and Turkey. Still, despite the express wishes of some—and because of the tacit resentment of others—the G-20 has not replaced the G-8. Earlier this year, the smaller, more exclusive group met at a luxury resort in Muskoka, a lake district in Canada, while the larger assembly was treated to demonstrations and tear gas in downtown Toronto.

There is some overlap in this alphabet soup. France, Russia, the United Kingdom, and the United States belong to both the P-5 and the G-8; China is in the P-5, the G-5, and the G-20; Brazil and India desperately want to join everything in sight. At the end of the day, the world's inner sanctum will be expanded to include only the few states that possess the ambition to enter it and at least one good reason for doing so—such as geographic, demographic, political, or economic heft. That means the shortlist boils down to Brazil, China, Germany, India, Japan, and South Africa.

Bric-A-Brac

The Chief rationale for inviting these states to join the world's ruling councils is self-evident: they matter more today than they did when those bodies were created. India will soon be the most populous nation on earth, just before China. In current dollars, Japan is the world's second-largest economy, with China and Germany gaining on it rapidly. Brazil combines demographic clout (it has about 200 million inhabitants) with economic power (a GDP of almost $1.6 trillion) and geographic legitimacy (Latin America must be represented), and in fact, it has already begun to play a greater role in international organizations such as the International Monetary Fund and the World Bank. Africa cannot be altogether excluded from the world's governing councils, and only South Africa can represent it effectively.

Germany and Japan are a case of their own. The two defeated powers of World War II already work closely with the permanent members of the UN Security Council (when it comes to policy having to do with Iran, for example, Germany acts together with the P-5, forming the P-6), and both belong to the Nuclear Suppliers Group, which promotes the enforcement of nuclear nonproliferation by monitoring exports of nuclear material, among other things. Germany is participating in the NATO operation in Afghanistan (as it did in the mission in Kosovo in the late 1990s); Japan supported the U.S.-led invasion and occupation of Iraq with logistical assistance on the high seas. The values and general conduct of these two highly developed democracies are indistinguishable from those of the powers already at the helm of international organizations. These states would thus provide additional clout and talent to the Security Council—the only membership at stake for them—if they joined it, but they would hardly transform it. Meanwhile, since including Germany and Japan and not others is unimaginable, for now they will have to accept the status quo: de facto participation in lieu of formal membership.

The argument for admitting Brazil, China, India, and South Africa to the helm rests on the general principle that the world's leadership councils should be broadened to include emerging powers. But unlike the case for Germany and Japan, this one raises some delicate questions. Over the past half century, a vast set of principles—the collective defense of democracy, nuclear nonproliferation, trade liberalization, international criminal justice, environmental protection, respect for human rights (including labor, religious, gender, ethnic, and indigenous peoples' rights)—have been enshrined in many international and regional treaties and agreements. Of course, this system is not without problems. A Eurocentric, Judeo-Christian tint pervades—a flaw one can acknowledge without approving of female circumcision, child soldiers and child labor, or amputation as a punishment for robbery—and the Western powers have often flagrantly and hypocritically violated those values even while demanding that other states respect them.

The United States has been an especially reluctant participant in the current world order. It has opposed the International Criminal Court, the Kyoto Protocol, and the convention to ban antipersonnel land mines, and it has undermined progress in the Doha Round of international trade negotiations by refusing to suspend its agricultural subsidies. Still, the world is a better place today thanks to the councils and commissions, the sanctions and conditions that these values have spawned—from the human rights mechanisms of the UN, the European Union, and the Organization of American States (OAS) to the International Criminal Court; from the World Trade Organization to the Nuclear Nonproliferation Treaty (NPT); from international cooperation on combating HIV/AIDS to the International Labor Organization's conventions on labor rights and the collective rights of indigenous peoples; from UN sanctions against apartheid in South Africa and the African Union's attempt to restore democracy in Zimbabwe to the OAS' condemnation of a military coup in Honduras.

Constructing this web of international norms has been slow and painful, with less overall progress and more frequent setbacks than some have wished for. Many countries of what used to be called the Third World have contributed to parts of the edifice: Mexico to disarmament and the law of the sea; Costa Rica to human rights; Chile to free trade. But now, the possible accession of Brazil, China, India, and South Africa to the inner sanctum of the world's leading institutions threatens to undermine those institutions' principles and practices.

Weak Links

Brazil, China, India, and South Africa are not just weak supporters of the notion that a strong international regime should govern human rights, democracy, nonproliferation, trade liberalization, the environment, international criminal justice, and global health. They oppose it more or less explicitly, and more or less actively—even though at one time most of them joined the struggle for these values: India wrested its independence from the United Kingdom, South Africa fought off apartheid, and Brazilian President Luiz Inácio Lula da Silva (known as Lula) opposed the military dictatorship in Brazil.

Consider these states' positions on the promotion of democracy and human rights worldwide. Brazil, India, and South Africa are representative democracies that basically respect human rights at home, but when it comes to defending democracy and human rights outside their borders, there is not much difference between them and authoritarian China. On those questions, all four states remain attached to the rallying cries of their independence or national liberation struggles: sovereignty, self-determination, nonintervention, autonomous economic development. And today, these notions often contradict the values enshrined in the international order.

It is perfectly predictable that Beijing would support the regimes perpetuating oppression and tragedy in Myanmar (also known as Burma) and Sudan. The Chinese government has never respected human rights in China or Tibet, and it has always maintained that a state's sovereignty trumps everything else, both on principle and to ward off scrutiny of its own domestic policies. Now that China wants to secure access to Myanmar's natural gas and Sudan's oil, it has used its veto in the UN Security Council to block sanctions against those states' governments.

India's stance—to say nothing of Brazil's or South Africa's—is not much better. India once promoted democracy and human rights in Myanmar, but in the mid-1990s, after seeing few results, it started to moderate its tone. In 2007, when the military junta in Myanmar cracked down more violently than usual on opposition leaders, dissenters, and monks, New Delhi issued no criticism of the repression. It refused to condemn the latest trial and conviction of the opposition leader Aung San Suu Kyi and opposed any sanctions on the regime, including those that the United States and the European Union have been enforcing since the mid-1990s. India has its reasons for responding this way—reasons that have little to do with human rights or democracy and everything to do with Myanmar's huge natural gas reserves; with getting the junta to shut down insurgent sanctuaries along India's northeastern border; and, most important, with making sure not to push the Myanmar regime into Beijing's hands. New Delhi's official support for what in 2007 it called "the undaunted resolve of the Burmese people to achieve democracy" has been more rhetorical than anything else.

India has also adopted a problematic approach toward refugees and Tamil Tiger ex-combatants in Sri Lanka. Today, a year after the civil war in Sri Lanka ended, more than 100,000 of the Tamil Tigers' supporters (and, by some accounts, as many as 290,000) remain in displaced persons camps that are virtual prisons. According to Human Rights Watch, India—together with Brazil, Cuba, and Pakistan—blocked a draft resolution by the UN Human Rights Council that would have condemned the situation; instead, it supported a statement commending the government of Mahinda Rajapaksa. New Delhi has been looking the other way, knowing full well that Sri Lanka would have bowed under pressure from India to allow displaced Sri Lankans to return home. There are perfectly logical explanations for India's stance, including the fact that India has its own social and political problems in the southern state of Tamil Nadu; the Indian politician Sonia Gandhi's husband, Rajiv, was assassinated there by a Tamil suicide bomber in 1991. New Delhi prefers to turn a blind eye toward the Sri Lankan government's violations of human rights rather than risk taking a principled stand on an issue too close to home.

One could argue, of course, that this kind of cynical pragmatism is exactly what the Western powers have practiced for decades, if not centuries. France and the United Kingdom in their former colonies, the United States in Latin America and the Middle East, even Germany in the Balkans—all readily sacrificed their noble principles on the altar of political expediency. But the purpose of creating a network of international institutions, intergovernmental covenants, and nongovernmental organizations to promote democracy and human rights was precisely to limit such great-power pragmatism, as well as to ensure that authoritarian regimes do not get away with committing abuses and that civil society everywhere is mobilized in defense of these values. India's stance does nothing more to advance these goals than does China's. In fact, given its prestige as the world's largest democracy and founder of the Non-Aligned Movement, it might be undercutting them even more when it fails to uphold them.

This last point is even truer for South Africa. No other African country enjoys such moral authority as South Africa does, thanks to Nelson Mandela's struggle against apartheid and his work on behalf of national reconciliation. But the African National Congress remains a socialist, anti-imperialist national liberation organization, and Mandela's successors at the head of the party and the country, Thabo Mbeki and Jacob Zuma, still basically endorse those values. Partly for that reason, the South African government opposed censuring the government of President Robert Mugabe in Zimbabwe even after it cracked down especially brutally on the Zimbabwean opposition following the contested elections of March 2008. Mbeki, who was then president, was unwilling to challenge his former national liberation comrade and the principal goal of not intervening in neighbors' affairs. Working through the African Union and the South African Development Community, Pretoria did help broker a power-sharing deal between the government and the opposition in Zimbabwe. But as an April 2008 editorial in *The Washington Post* argued, Mugabe managed to stay in office thanks to the support of then South African President Mbeki.

The South African government, like nearly every regime in Africa, is wary of criticizing the internal policies of other countries, even if they are undemocratic or violate human rights. Unlike other African states, however, South Africa is a thriving democracy that aspires to a regional and even an international role. So which is it going to choose: nonintervention in the domestic affairs of its neighbors in the name of the passé ethos of national liberation and the Non-Aligned Movement or the defense—rhetorical at least and preferably effective—of universal values above national sovereignty, as would befit a new member of the world's ruling councils?

Brazilian Lulabies

And which way will it be for Brazil, for whose leaders the issues of democracy and human rights were once especially dear? Like his predecessor, Lula opposed the military dictatorship that ruled Brazil between 1964 and 1985. At the time, he was an advocate of human rights, free and fair elections, and representative democracy; he often sought out foreign governments to support his cause and censure the people who were torturing members of the Brazilian opposition. But since he has been in office, he has not paid much heed to these issues. Although he has repeatedly flaunted Brazil's entry into the great-power club, he has been dismissive of the importance of democracy and human rights throughout Latin America, particularly in Cuba and Venezuela, and in places as far afield as Iran. He has reinforced the Brazilian Foreign Ministry's tendency to not meddle in Cuba's internal affairs. Earlier this year, he traveled to Havana the day after a jailed Cuban dissident died from a hunger strike. Speaking at a press conference, he practically blamed the prisoner for dying and said he disapproved of that "form of struggle." Just hours later, he posed, beaming, for a photograph with Fidel and Raúl Castro.

Lula also gave Iranian President Mahmoud Ahmadinejad a hero's welcome in Brasília and São Paulo (the latter home to a majority of Brazil's significant Jewish community) just a few months after Ahmadinejad stole his country's 2009 election and the Iranian government violently suppressed the resulting public demonstrations. Within a few months of that visit, Lula traveled to Tehran. To Venezuelan President Hugo Chávez's increasingly heavy hand, Lula has also turned a blind eye. He never questions the jailing of political opponents; crackdowns on the press, trade unions, and students; or tampering with the electoral system in Venezuela. Brazilian corporations, especially construction companies, have huge investments there, and Lula has used his friendship with Chávez and the Castro brothers to placate the left wing of his party, which is uncomfortable with his orthodox economic policies. He systematically cloaks his pragmatic—some would say cynical—approach in the robes of nonintervention, self-determination, and Third World solidarity.

Recently, Brazil seems to have changed its tune somewhat, moving slightly away from its traditional stance of nonintervention after a coup in Honduras last year. When Honduran President Manuel Zelaya was ousted from office in June 2009, Lula suddenly became a stalwart defender of Honduras' democracy. Together with allies of Zelaya, such as Raúl Castro, Chávez, and the presidents of Bolivia, Ecuador, and Nicaragua,

Lula convinced other members of the OAS, including Mexico and the United States, to suspend Honduras from the organization. Lula subsequently granted Zelaya asylum in the Brazilian embassy in Tegucigalpa, allowing him to mobilize his followers and organize against the coup's instigators from there. But since Porfirio Lobo Sosa was chosen to be Honduras' new president in free and fair elections late last year and several Latin American countries and the United States have recognized his government, Brazil's enduring support for Zelaya has increasingly come to seem intransigent and quixotic. One wonders whether Lula's position expresses the reflexive solidarity of a state that once suffered military coups itself, signals a new willingness to stand up for democratic principles, or is yet another concession to Chávez and his friends in an effort to quiet the restless and troublesome left wing of Lula's party by defending its disciple in Tegucigalpa. But this much seems clear: Brazil's first attempt to take a stance on an internal political conflict in another Latin American country did not turn out too well, and Brazil does not yet feel comfortable with leaving behind its traditional policy of nonintervention in the name of the collective defense of human rights and democracy.

It's the Bomb!

These States' ambivalence on so-called soft issues, such as human rights and democracy, tends to go hand in hand with their recalcitrance on "harder" issues, such as nuclear proliferation. With the exception of South Africa, which unilaterally gave up the nuclear weapons it had secretly built under apartheid, Brazil, China, and India have opposed the international nonproliferation regime created by the NPT in 1968. India has not deliberately helped or encouraged other countries with their nuclear ambitions. But it has never ratified the NPT, and the very fact that it went nuclear in 1974 led Pakistan, its neighbor and enemy, to do the same in 1982. Pakistan has since become one of the world's worst proliferators, thanks to the shenanigans of the rogue nuclear scientist A. Q. Khan. India cannot rightly be faulted for the actions of Pakistan, but it can be for not signing the NPT, for not doing more to assist the Nuclear Suppliers Group, and for not sanctioning states that aspire to get the bomb. It has coddled Tehran even as Tehran has seemed increasingly determined to build a nuclear weapon; it has repeatedly rejected imposing sanctions. In opposing the last batch in June of this year, Indian Prime Minister Manmohan Singh stated that Iran had every right to develop a peaceful nuclear industry and that there was scant evidence that any military intent was driving its program. He did not need to say that India is developing an important energy relationship with Iran and is seeking to build gas and oil pipelines from Iran all the way to New Delhi.

China, for its part, has an "execrable" record on proliferation, according to *The Economist* earlier this year—or rather it did until it joined the NPT in 1992 (after that, it at least nominally began to improve). The Chinese government helped Pakistan produce uranium and plutonium in the 1980s and 1990s, and it gave Pakistan the design of one of its own weapons. Beijing has not been especially constructive in trying to hinder North Korea's efforts to acquire nuclear weapons, and it has been downright unhelpful regarding Iran, systematically opposing or undermining sanctions against Tehran and threatening to use its veto on the UN Security Council if the Western powers go too far. Its recent decision to sell two new civilian nuclear power reactors to Pakistan will ratchet up the nuclear rivalry between India and Pakistan and undercut the work of the Nuclear Suppliers Group by making it easier for Islamabad to build more bombs.

Neither China nor India can be counted on to defend the nonproliferation regime. Both states seem too attached to the recent past, especially to the notion that they, huge developing nations once excluded from the atomic club, were able to challenge the nuclear monopoly held by the West and the Soviet Union thanks to the genius, discipline, and perseverance of their scientists. Not that there is anything wrong with being faithful to the past. But perhaps those states that remain faithful to the past best belong there—and not among those that will build a new international order.

Nostalgia is not the problem when it comes to Brazil. Brazil cannot be counted on when it comes to nuclear nonproliferation either, but for reasons having less to do with its past than its future. In the 1960s, it signed the Treaty of Tlatelolco, which banned nuclear weapons from Latin America, and in the 1990s, together with Argentina, it agreed to dismantle its enrichment program. When it finally ratified the NPT, in 1998, Brazil was perceived as a strong supporter of nonproliferation. But this May, eager to cozy up to Iran and wanting to be treated as a world power, it suddenly teamed up with Turkey to propose a deal that would lift sanctions on Iran if Iran took its uranium to Turkey to be enriched. Tehran nominally accepted the arrangement; the rest of the world did not. Lula and Turkish Prime Minister Recep Tayyip Erdogan claimed that the arrangement simply replicated a proposal previously put forth by the P-6 and that Obama supported their effort. Washington nonetheless called for stronger sanctions against Iran. Twelve of the UN Security Council's 15 members, including China and Russia, voted for the sanctions; only Brazil and Turkey opposed them. (Lebanon abstained.) In the end, the episode was widely seen as a clumsy scheme to get Tehran off the hook and a gambit by Lula to get the world to take Brazil more seriously. (Turkey was also deemed to be a spoiler, but at least it has real interests in the Middle East.) What Lula achieved instead was to show that Brazil is still more interested in Third World solidarity than in international leadership. Worse, now some are speculating that Brazil is laying the groundwork to resurrect its own nuclear program.

One might say that in behaving in these ways, the emerging powers of today are acting no differently from the established powers—and that this is the best proof that they have come of age. They are rising powers, and—just like the states that came before them—they act increasingly on the basis of their national interests, and those national interests are increasingly global and well defined. But unlike the existing global players, they are not subject to enough domestic or international safeguards, or checks and balances, or, mainly, pressure from civil society—all forces that could limit their power and help them define their national interests beyond the economic realm and the short term. Their discourse and conduct may seem to be as legitimate as those of the traditional powers, but they are in fact far more self-contradictory. On the one hand, the rising powers still see themselves as members of and spokespeople for the developing world, the Non-Aligned Movement, the world's poor, and so on; on the other hand, they are staking their reputations on having become major economic, military, geopolitical, and even ideological powers, all of which not only distinguishes them from the rest of the Third World but also involves subscribing to certain universal values.

To Be or Not to Be

The stance of these countries on climate change also illustrates this persistent ambivalence about what role they are ready to assume. Brazil, China, and India are among the world's top emitters of carbon dioxide (China and India are among the top five). Last December, at the Copenhagen conference on climate change, they, along with South Africa (and Sudan, which was chairing the UN's Group of 77, or G-77, a coalition of developing nations), put forward a position that they said reflected the interests and views of "the developing nations." Building on a statement they had made at the 2008 G-8 summit, they called for assigning states' responsibilities for fighting climate change according to states' capacities. They believe that reducing emissions is above all the responsibility of the developed countries. They are willing to do their share and reduce their own emissions, they say, but rich countries will have to do more, such as make deeper, legally binding emissions cuts and help the most vulnerable nations pay for the expenses of mitigating and adapting to the effects of global warming. Their case rests on a strong foundation: after all, it was over a century of the rich countries' industrial growth and unrestricted emissions that led to climate change, and the poorer countries are only now beginning to develop strongly. Placing proportional limits on the emissions of all states, the reasoning goes, would amount to stunting the economic growth of developing countries by imposing on them requirements that did not exist when the developed countries were first growing.

Perhaps, but this argument also raises the question of whom these countries are speaking for and what role they envision for themselves. Brazil's emissions are mainly the byproduct of extensive agricultural development, deforestation, and degradation; India's, like China's, come from industrialization, which both countries claim they have a right to pursue despite the pollution it causes. These are not traits common to the vast majority of the world's poor nations. On the eve of the Copenhagen summit, Jairam Ramesh, India's environment minister, described India's position clearly: "The first nonnegotiable is that India will not accept a legally binding emission cut. . . . We will not accept under any circumstances an agreement which stipulates a peaking year for India." He did say that India was prepared to "modulate [its] position in consultation with China, Brazil, and South Africa" and to "subject its mitigation actions to international review." But he added, apparently in all earnestness, that India's acceptance of such a review would depend on how much "international financing and technology" the country got.

Do the emerging powers identify more with the rich polluters whose ranks they want to join or with the poor nations, which are both potential victims of and contributors to climate change? The groups overlap (the rich nations also are victims, and the poor ones also pollute), and Brazil, China, India, and South Africa have much in common with both groups, but they cannot be part of both at once. For now, these states seem to have chosen to side with the poor countries. Partly because of that decision, the Copenhagen summit failed, and the Cancún climate summit scheduled for the end of 2010 will probably fail, too. Marina Silva, a former environment minister under Lula who is running for president against her former boss' chosen candidate, seems to have grasped the contradiction in Brazil's official position more clearly than Lula. She has made the case that Brazil should do more. "It must admit global goals of carbon dioxide emissions reduction," she said a few weeks before the Copenhagen summit last year, "and contribute to convincing other developing countries to do the same."

Some candidates for emerging power status are beginning to understand this, but just barely. Mexico, for example, had originally subscribed to the joint stance of Brazil, China, India, and South Africa on emissions caps in 2008 and 2009, but by the time of the Copenhagen summit, it realized that its $14,000 per capita income (in 2008 purchasing parity prices) placed it closer to the states of the Organization for Economic Cooperation and Development (to which it already belongs) than to those of the G-77 or the Non-Aligned Movement (to which it does not belong) and stopped signing their common documents. Similarly, during the Doha Round of trade negotiations, Mexico grasped that its myriad free-trade agreements and low levels of agricultural exports put it in the camp of the industrialized nations rather than the camp of Brazil, China, India, and South Africa. Those states presented something of a common front on behalf of, as Lula put it, "the most fragile economies," although Brazil was more interested in opening up agricultural markets and China and India were more concerned with protecting small farmers. But these are exceptions, like Turkey's attempt to join the European Union, accepting all of its conditions regarding values and institutions. None of the emerging countries, democratic or otherwise, richer or poorer, more integrated into regional groups or not, has truly undergone its political or ideological aggiornamento.

Pay to Play

The ongoing discussion about whether emerging powers should be admitted to the helm of the world geopolitical order emphasizes the economic dimension of their rise and its geopolitical consequences. Not enough attention has been paid to the fact that although these countries are already economic powerhouses, they remain political and diplomatic lightweights. At best, they are regional powers that pack a minuscule international punch; at worst, they are neophytes whose participation in international institutions may undermine progress toward a stronger international legal order. They might be growing economic actors, but they are not diplomatic ones, and so as they strive to gain greater political status without a road map, they fall back on their default option: the rhetoric and posturing of bygone days, invoking national sovereignty and nonintervention, calling for limited international jurisdiction, and defending the application of different standards to different nations.

Given this, granting emerging economic powers a greater role on the world stage would probably weaken the trend toward a stronger multilateral system and an international legal regime that upholds democracy, human rights, nuclear nonproliferation, and environmental protection. An international order that made more room for the BRICS, for Mexico and South Africa, and for other emerging powers, would be much more representative. But it would not necessarily be an order whose core values are better respected and better defended.

The world needs emerging powers to participate in financial and trade negotiations, and it would benefit immensely from hearing their voices on many regional and international issues, such as the killings in Darfur, instability in the Middle East, repression in Myanmar, or the coup in Honduras. For now, however, these states' core values are too different from the ones espoused, however partially and duplicitously, by the international community's main players and their partners to warrant the emerging powers' inclusion at the helm of the world's top organizations.

These states still lack the balancing mechanisms that have helped curb the hypocrisy of great powers: vibrant and well-organized civil societies. This lack is more obvious in some countries (China, South Africa) than in others (Brazil, India), but there is a fundamental difference between the terms of their inclusion into the inner sanctum and that of those countries that are already there (although this difference obviously applies to Russia also). Before a serious debate takes place within these countries regarding their societies' adherence to the values in question, it might not be such a good idea for them to become full-fledged world actors. Maybe they should deliberate more prudently over whether they really want to pay in order to play, and the existing powers should ponder whether they wish to invite them to play if they will not pay.

Critical Thinking

1. What countries are likely contenders for leadership roles in international institutions?

2. What are the issues that raise questions about these countries' leadership?

3. What positions on these issues are the most troubling?

4. What are the arguments in favor of admitting these emerging countries to leadership positions in international institutions?

JORGE G. CASTAÑEDA was Mexico's Foreign Minister in 2000–2003. He teaches at New York University and is a member of the Board of Directors of Human Rights Watch and a Fellow at the New America Foundation.

From *Foreign Affairs*, September/October 2010, pp. 109–122. Copyright © 2010 by Council on Foreign Relations, Inc. Reprinted by permission of Foreign Affairs. www.ForeignAffairs.com

Test-Your-Knowledge Form

We encourage you to photocopy and use this page as a tool to assess how the articles in *Annual Editions* expand on the information in your textbook. By reflecting on the articles you will gain enhanced text information. You can also access this useful form on a product's book support website at www.mhhe.com/cls.

NAME: DATE:

_____

TITLE AND NUMBER OF ARTICLE:

_____

BRIEFLY STATE THE MAIN IDEA OF THIS ARTICLE:

_____

LIST THREE IMPORTANT FACTS THAT THE AUTHOR USES TO SUPPORT THE MAIN IDEA:

_____

WHAT INFORMATION OR IDEAS DISCUSSED IN THIS ARTICLE ARE ALSO DISCUSSED IN YOUR TEXTBOOK OR OTHER READINGS THAT YOU HAVE DONE? LIST THE TEXTBOOK CHAPTERS AND PAGE NUMBERS:

_____

LIST ANY EXAMPLES OF BIAS OR FAULTY REASONING THAT YOU FOUND IN THE ARTICLE:

_____

LIST ANY NEW TERMS/CONCEPTS THAT WERE DISCUSSED IN THE ARTICLE, AND WRITE A SHORT DEFINITION:

NOTES

NOTES

NOTES

NOTES